T0323533

The Microeconomics of Wellbeing and Sustainability

The Microeconomics of Wellbeing and Sustainability

Recasting the Economic Process

Leonardo Becchetti

Luigino Bruni

Stefano Zamagni

ELSEVIER

ACADEMIC PRESS
An imprint of Elsevier

Academic Press is an imprint of Elsevier
125 London Wall, London EC2Y 5AS, United Kingdom
525 B Street, Suite 1650, San Diego, CA 92101, United States
50 Hampshire Street, 5th Floor, Cambridge, MA 02139, United States
The Boulevard, Langford Lane, Kidlington, Oxford OX5 1GB, United Kingdom

Notices

Knowledge and best practice in this field are constantly changing. As new research and experience broaden our understanding, changes in research methods, professional practices, or medical treatment may become necessary.

Practitioners and researchers must always rely on their own experience and knowledge in evaluating and using any information, methods, compounds, or experiments described herein. In using such information or methods they should be mindful of their own safety and the safety of others, including parties for whom they have a professional responsibility.

To the fullest extent of the law, neither the Publisher nor the authors, contributors, or editors, assume any liability for any injury and/or damage to persons or property as a matter of products liability, negligence or otherwise, or from any use or operation of any methods, products, instructions, or ideas contained in the material herein.

Library of Congress Cataloging-in-Publication Data
A catalog record for this book is available from the Library of Congress

British Library Cataloguing-in-Publication Data
A catalogue record for this book is available from the British Library

ISBN: 978-0-12-816027-5

For information on all Academic Press publications visit our
website at https://www.elsevier.com/books-and-journals

Publisher: Brian Romer
Acquisition Editor: Brian Romer
Editorial Project Manager: Susan Ikeda
Production Project Manager: Sujatha Thirugnana Sambandam
Cover Designer: Matthew Limbert

Typeset by TNQ Technologies

Working together
to grow libraries in
developing countries

www.elsevier.com • www.bookaid.org

Contents

Attributions   xiii
Preface   xv

1.   Economics: what it studies, with what methods,
      and how it evolved
      1.1   What is a science?   1
             1.1.1   Economics is a social science   1
      1.2   The investigative method of economic science   2
      1.3   What is an economic model?   2
      1.4   The ethical responsibility of the economist   4
      1.5   From dismal science to hopeful science?   5
      1.6   Attention to interdependencies: opportunity cost   7
      1.7   The two phases of economic analysis: positive and
             normative   9
      1.8   The theory of rational choices in the presence of constraints   11
      1.9   Microeconomics and macroeconomics   15
      1.10   Integration with other disciplines   16
      1.11   A three-dimensional approach   17
      1.12   Comparing Ptolemaics and Copernicans   19
      1.13   The schools of economic thought   20
      1.14   Colonial expansion and mercantilism   21
      1.15   France and physiocracy: François Quesnay   22
      1.16   The common elements of classical economic thought   24
             1.16.1 Economists...But not just economists   25
      1.17   The Scottish school: Adam Smith   26
             1.17.1 The invisible hand   33
      1.18   The Neapolitan school: the civil economy of Genovesi
             and Filangieri   33
      1.19   The Milan school: Verri, Beccaria, and civil competition 35
      1.20   A century of Smithean economics   38
             1.20.1 Ricardo's theory of land rent   38
             1.20.2 Malthus and population theory   40
             1.20.3 Marx and his criticism of the classical
                     economic system   41
      1.21   Neoclassical economics   42
             1.21.1 The British school   43

                                                                       v

1.21.2	The Austrian school	44
1.21.3	The Lausanne school	45
1.21.4	Pantaleoni and Pareto	45
1.21.5	20th century economics	47
	Further reading	49

2. The market

2.1	**Market: an abused term**	51
2.2	**Stylized characteristics of the market**	52
2.3	**Movements along the curves and movements of the curves**	56
2.4	**Market equilibrium**	57
2.5	**Problems relative to administratively defined non-equilibrium prices**	58
2.6	**Dynamic adjustment toward equilibrium**	64
	2.6.1　The stability of an equilibrium	64
	2.6.2　What can we observe about the behavior of markets over time?	66
2.7	**Benefits and limitations of the market**	68
	2.7.1　The benefits	69
	2.7.2　Limitations	71
2.8	**Does the market evolve spontaneously, or should targeted institutional interventions guide it?**	74
	2.8.1　The emergence of solidarity products overcomes one of the limits of the market	75
	Appendix	78
	Further analysis of supply and demand curves: the slope and elasticity of the demand curve	78
	Further reading	81

3. The theory of consumption

3.1	**The income circuit**	83
3.2	**The income circuit as a hypertext**	85
3.3	**The theory of consumption**	86
3.4	**The problem of maximizing consumer utility**	87
	3.4.1　Cardinality and ordinality of the utility function	89
	3.4.2　Indifference curves	91
	3.4.3　The marginal rate of substitution	93
	3.4.4　Choosing the optimal combination of goods	94
3.5	**Do consumer rationality and constrained maximization perhaps imply that consumers look only at price when choosing products?**	98
3.6	**How we derive individual demand curves**	100
	3.6.1　Price-consumption curves	100
	3.6.2　Income consumption curves and Engel's law	102
3.7	**Slutsky's equation**	104

3.8		**Further thoughts**	107
	3.8.1	Prices and information	107
	3.8.2	Consumer theory and anthropological models	108
	3.8.3	Intertemporal consumption	109
		Further reading	113

4.   The theory of production decisions

4.1		**The economic problem of production**	115
	4.1.1	What it means to produce in economics	115
	4.1.2	Short run and long run	116
	4.1.3	Production technology and Pareto efficiency	117
4.2		**The entrepreneur**	117
	4.2.1	The distinctive traits of entrepreneurship	117
	4.2.2	Types of companies	121
4.3		**The production function**	124
	4.3.1	The short-run production function	124
	4.3.2	The law of diminishing returns	125
	4.3.3	The variability of two inputs	126
	4.3.4	The long-run production function: returns to scale	128
	4.3.5	Diseconomies of scale	129
4.4		**Production costs**	129
	4.4.1	Types of production costs	129
	4.4.2	Short-run cost curves	131
	4.4.3	Two variable inputs: choosing the optimal combination of factors	132
	4.4.4	Long-run cost curves	134
4.5		**Economies of scale**	136
4.6		**External costs and opportunity costs**	137
		Further reading	138

5.   Perfectly competitive markets

5.1		**The problem of supply**	139
	5.1.1	The benefits of production	139
	5.1.2	Perfect competition	140
5.2		**The revenue function**	142
5.3		**Profit maximization in the short run and the supply curve of a single company**	143
5.4		**The perfectly competitive company in the long run**	144
5.5		**The supply of a good in a competitive industry**	145
5.6		**Market equilibrium in perfect competition**	148
5.7		**Social well-being in a single market**	150
5.8		**Market competition is not a competitive sport**	152
		Further reading	155

6. Non-competitive markets and elements of game theory

6.1	Markets in which companies have power over prices	157
	6.1.1 How non-competitive markets come into existence	157
	6.1.2 Technical progress	158
	6.1.3 Changes in the composition of consumption	159
6.2	Market forms and branches of economic activity	159
6.3	Monopoly	162
	6.3.1 Equilibrium in a monopoly	162
	6.3.2 Monopoly and social well-being	164
	6.3.3 Price discrimination	165
6.4	Monopolistic competition	166
	6.4.1 Equilibrium of an imperfectly competitive company	166
	6.4.2 Comparing monopolistic competition with perfect competition and monopoly	167
6.5	An oligopolistic market	168
	6.5.1 Its distinctive characteristics	168
	6.5.2 The Cournot model	169
	6.5.3 Bertrand's model	171
6.6	Incentives for collusion and cartels	172
	6.6.1 Oligopolistic collusion	172
	6.6.2 The instability of cartels	174
6.7	Contestable markets and market structure endogeneity	175
6.8	Innovations and dynamic competition: Schumpeter's approach	178
	6.8.1 Creative destruction	178
	6.8.2 Dynamic competition and the nature of profit	179
	Appendix A: an introduction to game theory (by Alessandra Smerilli)	180
	Introductory concepts	180
	Normal form games	183
	Nash equilibrium	185
	Extended form games	187
	Appendix B: trust in game theory	190
	The trust game and the paradox of trust	190
	The Genovesi version of the trust game	193
	Further reading	198

7. New theories of the firm

7.1	New lines of research in the study of the firm and markets	199
7.2	Complete contracts and competitive markets	200
7.3	Asymmetric information and opportunistic behavior	202
	7.3.1 Adverse selection	202
	7.3.2 Moral hazard	204
7.4	Managerial theories of the firm	206

	7.4.1	Baumol's model	206
	7.4.2	Capital markets and the role of takeovers	208
	7.4.3	Costs to predators and perverse effects of takeovers	209
7.5	**Optimization and "satisficing" in the enterprise: behavioral theory**		**210**
7.6	**The neo-institutionalist theory of the firm**		**212**
	7.6.1	Coase's view of the firm	212
	7.6.2	The nexus between authority and property rights	213
	7.6.3	Grossman, Hart, and Moore's theory of property rights	216
7.7	**The organizational dimension of the firm**		**218**
	7.7.1	Forms of companies and governance structures	218
	7.7.2	The holding company	220
7.8	**Alternate conceptions of the firm**		**221**
	7.8.1	The company as a commodity and shareholder value	221
	7.8.2	The problem of organizational planning	223
	7.8.3	Connective capital and company development	225
	Further reading		**226**

8. The utilitarian view of welfare economics

8.1	**What is welfare economics?**		**227**
	8.1.1	Utilitarian ethics	227
	8.1.2	The old welfare economics	229
	8.1.3	The Pareto criterion and the new welfare economics	230
8.2	**The two fundamental theorems of welfare economics**		**232**
	8.2.1	Walrasian general equilibrium	232
	8.2.2	The Edgeworth box	233
	8.2.3	The first welfare theorem: a competitive equilibrium is Pareto optimal	235
	8.2.4	The second welfare theorem: Pareto optimality and income distribution	236
8.3	**Utility-possibility frontiers and the invisible hand**		**238**
8.4	**The social welfare function and arrow's impossibility theorem**		**240**
8.5	**Market failures**		**243**
	8.5.1	Externalities	243
	8.5.2	Taxes, subsidies, and the Coase theorem	245
	8.5.3	Public goods	247
	8.5.4	Merit goods	250
8.6	**The market and distributive justice**		**251**
8.7	**Forms of public intervention and government failure**		**253**
8.8	**From the welfare state to the welfare society**		**255**
	Appendix		**258**
	Economic science and commons		258
	The We-rationality		265
	The role of civil society		266
	Conclusion		268
	Further reading		**268**

9. The theory of Homo reciprocans

9.1	Labor supply in traditional theory	271
	9.1.1 Of pyramids and hourglasses: the labor question today	274
9.2	How to select workers with a "vocation"	276
9.3	"Getting more by paying less"	279
9.4	When intrinsic motivations come into conflict with monetary incentives	282
9.5	What is a work "vocation"?	284
9.6	"Homo reciprocans"	286
	9.6.1 The principle of reciprocity	286
	9.6.2 Other approaches to reciprocity	289
	Further reading	292

10. Not just for profit: civil enterprises and values-based organizations

10.1	The non-capitalist company	295
10.2	Beyond the third sector and non-profits	297
10.3	Social firms and civil firms	299
10.4	The nature of the capitalist enterprise	303
10.5	The Paradox of the capitalist enterprise	307
10.6	From the market to the company, from the company to the market	309
10.7	For-profit and for-project firms	311
10.8	Values-based organizations (VBOs)	315
10.9	The difficult innovations of a civil enterprise	317
10.10	In praise of diversity	319
	Further reading	320

11. Corporate social responsibility

11.1	The reductionism of the traditional approach to viewing the firm	321
11.2	The definition of CSR	324
11.3	The debate among economists on corporate social responsibility	327
11.4	Can socially responsible companies overcome the challenge of economic sustainability and survival in the market?	329
	11.4.1 Consumers voting with their wallets	330
	11.4.2 Product quality signaling	331
	11.4.3 Minimizing stakeholder transaction costs	333
	11.4.4 Environmental innovation	333
	11.4.5 Increased worker productivity	334

11.5	**Is CSR sustainable? The evidence of the facts**		335
	11.5.1	What is the relationship between CSR and financial results?	337
	11.5.2	What effect does choosing social responsibility have on the stock market performance of publicly traded companies?	338
11.6	**The problem of asymmetric information in CSR: social responsibility is not an "experience good"**		340
11.7	**Next generation social firms: a particular type of socially responsible company**		341
	11.7.1	Microfinance	342
	11.7.2	Ethical banks	344
	11.7.3	Solidarity and fair trade	345
11.8	**The effects of the entrance of social market firms: CSR becomes a competitive factor**		350
11.9	**How competition changes in a global economy: the role of CSR**		355
	Further reading		358

12. Happiness, relational goods, and social progress

12.1	**The empirical verification of the a priori assumptions of "homo oeconomicus": the economics of happiness**		361
12.2	**Are the data on happiness trustworthy, and what do they really measure?**		362
12.3	**Does happiness really coincide with utility? Kahneman's approach**		365
12.4	**The stylized facts**		366
	12.4.1	Happiness and income	366
	12.4.2	The Easterlin paradox	367
	12.4.3	The problem of causality in the relationship between income and happiness	375
	12.4.4	Happiness and relational life	377
	12.4.5	Empirical results on the relationship between happiness and relational goods	378
	12.4.6	Happiness, income, and relationship: Baumol's disease and trust games	385
	12.4.7	The relationship between happiness and affectionate relationships	387
	12.4.8	Is religion a relational good?	388
	12.4.9	Happiness and work	388
	12.4.10	Happiness, inflation, and unemployment	390
	12.4.11	Happiness, health, and age	393
	12.4.12	Are we really able to explain the Easterlin paradox? Some possible explanations	395

12.5   Happiness studies results and Heisenberg's uncertainty principle   396

12.6   Remarks on happiness and economic policies   397

Further reading   400

13.   Growth and the environment in the era of globalization

13.1   The importance of the topic of growth   401

13.2   Several stylized facts on growth and poverty   407

13.3   Modeling growth   410

13.3.1   Traditional growth models   410

13.3.2   Other determinants of growth and conditional convergence: institutions and cultural and religious foundations   413

13.3.3   Regional integration as an effective means of improving the quality of institutions   415

13.3.4   Scientific knowledge and technological innovation are important: the new context created by the information revolution and communication technology and by the digital divide   416

13.3.5   The role of geography, social capital, and natural resources   419

13.4   Methodological weaknesses   420

13.5   The role of globalization in development   420

13.6   Squaring growth and the environment   424

13.7   The matrix of environmental goods   425

13.8   Revisiting the income circuit with the creation and destruction of environmental resources   427

13.9   The emissions problem and its possible solutions: classical and bottom-up approaches   431

13.10   The economic growth-environment dilemma   434

13.11   The Kuznets environmental curve   437

13.12   Toward overcoming the dilemma?   440

13.13   Some microeconomic examples   441

Further reading   443

Epilogue: from "homo oeconomicus" to "civil animal"   445

Index   451

Attributions

Chapter one is shared by the three authors

Stefano Zamagni wrote chapters 4,5, 7, 8

Leonardo Becchetti wrote chapters 2,3, 11,12,13

Luigino Bruni wrote chapter 6, 9 and 10

Alessandra Smerilli the two Appendices of chapter 6

Preface

Several reasons led us to write this textbook, which is designed for students in their early years of university economics courses, as well as for those who are curious about (or sometimes irritated by) the spread of the metaphors and language of economics in our societies and who want to understand what is being said.

The first reason is to help fill a cultural void that has been undervalued for too long. The unfortunate distinction between the natural and the social sciences, which originates in positivism, has had the effect of relegating the social sciences — and economics in particular — to the role of lesser sciences that lack solid cultural depth, or to the role of derived disciplines that thus lack their own foundation. The negative consequences of such a state of affairs are by now evident to all. It is an easily verifiable fact that today's youth live in a world saturated with economic rumors that bewilder rather than guide them, even threatening their intellectual independence. An economics textbook should thus help the student to think critically; it cannot be reduced to a mere instruction manual.

A second reason is more practical. The advanced economies are now entering a new phase of their development process, that of the so-called "integrated economy." The integrated economy emerges from the union of the best of the old and the new economies; its outcomes are difficult to foresee at the moment, but it is already bringing many innovations, particularly in the labor market. A new conception of digitalization is emerging that is no longer designed only for automation, but for collaboration as well. This requires creatively using the new information and communication technologies to manage various processes. If not used carefully these new technologies could have effects similar to antibiotics: antibiotics are quite useful, but they tend to weaken the immune system. The aspiration of this textbook is to contribute to enhancing young people's ability to make reasoned use of this new concept of computing.

The third reason requires discussion. Over the course of the last quarter century the obsolescence of economic knowledge has accelerated as never before. Those involved in teaching economics know that until recently the average life of a textbook was around fifteen years. In fact, the rate of production of new knowledge was so low as to ensure that the same text could long remain in circulation and convey knowledge with essentially unchanged incisiveness and pertinence. That is no longer the case today. New phenomena such as the globalization of markets, the financialization of the economy, the entrance of new information and communication technologies into productive activities, new regionalisms (for example, the European Union), the transition from Fordist to post-Fordist production, as well as entirely new questions to which these phenomena give rise, are such that the thought categories inherited from the economics of the past are no longer sufficient to grasp the new emerging situations, much less to propose solutions to their problems.

We offer an example to better make our point. The political economy of the classical school (from Adam Smith to J.S. Mill) was established in the era of the first Industrial Revolution, and the theoretical schema it created closely reflected the economic characteristics of that time. The subsequent emergence and triumph of neoclassical economics, spanning from the marginalist revolution of the 1870s to the end of the Keynesian revolution, proceeded in parallel with the second Industrial Revolution, and particularly with the strong internationalization of markets up to the First World War. Later, the Keynesian theoretical paradigm was the most effective response to the great 1929 crisis from either a conceptual or practical viewpoint, and more generally to the demonstrated inability of market mechanisms to self-regulate and propel the economic system along paths tending toward full employment. The list could go on. However, the situation today poses new economic problems unknown in prior eras; in trying to explain these it would be vain to seek help from theories and models designed and elaborated for different informational purposes. Consequently there is today an urgent need to encourage new economic ideas and approaches, and especially to inspire new vocations in the youth.

What specific goals should an economics study pursue that is oriented in the sense laid out above? We will point out a few that seem to us the most pertinent. The first goal is to create in students an awareness of the fact that they cannot but be drawn into economic matters either as agents or as the recipients of others' actions. Such an awareness tends to stimulate young people to understand the mechanisms and processes that govern economic relations. Indeed, we know that since the culture is oriented toward people's spontaneous creativity, it is more a *solicitation* than a causal process. Culture is not produced as one produces a commodity, even though cultural products circulate as commodities. If we want to awaken cultural forces in young people, it is not useful to utilize stimuli similar to Pavlovian conditioned reflexes; these mostly encourage stereotypical, uncreative responses.

The second goal is to encourage the reader's tendency to formulate critical — even if simple — judgments, as well as the habit of systematically investigating economic phenomena; the latter are never the result of a single cause, but rather due to the complex interactions and intersections of multiple causal factors. Among other things, this is the best antidote to a study that simply memorizes answers. It is true that culture requires specialized training as well, but culture does not consist of such training. Nor does culture consist in merely transferring information. Cultural consumption always assumes responsible participation by consumers, who must be active recipients. That entails that the text cannot be "paternalistic" — that is, it must leave to the students the hard work and the joy of discovery.

Finally, the third goal is to ensure that the study of economics contributes to the maturation process of students as citizens. By understanding the strategic nature of economic decisions and their inherently political character, young people become aware of the fact that the economic and institutional structure of the society is not a permanent and immutable datum of nature. On the contrary, it is something people created, and as such it can be changed or corrected for the better. As we know, an evolved democracy requires citizen-voters — do not forget that university students are already voters — who are able to act with intellectual independence in the chaos of information. This is why teaching economics cannot be reduced to the level of pure technicality or rote learning; we consider unacceptable approaches that are based solely on definitions, classifications, unargued propositions, or abstract examples that have no contact with reality. Faced with all this, young people have no choice but to memorize everything, but in so doing their do not intellectually grasp it. Instruction that is adequate to the stated goals must make students understand that economics is a social science, within which multiple traditions and paradigms co-exist, and that this diversity of viewpoints is a source of enrichment. Its *raison d'être* is the contribution it can make to solving the problems of people who live in societies, not in isolation as did Robinson Crusoe.

Finally, what is new in this book compared to the many valid textbooks in circulation? Its new elements all derive from the fact that, alongside the arguments developed by traditional microeconomic theory over the course of the last thirty years, the reader will find the themes of the *civil economy* paradigm laid out and discussed. First, that means that efficiency is not the only fundamental goal of economic behavior. A study from the civil economy perspective also makes room for values such as justice, fraternity, and liberty, because one cannot live by efficiency alone: seeking the conditions that make for a good life and that serve to promote public happiness is just as important as seeking the conditions that increase the efficiency of the economic system.

Second, in this book we study interpersonal relations, and not just relations between people and things. The theme of person-to-person relations is one of the central themes of the civil economy tradition of thought, a distinctly Italian tradition that dominated the scene until the end of the first half of the 18th century, when it was displaced by the political economy research program associated with Adam Smith's work. Economists do not do society a favor (other than for themselves) when they continue to ignore intersubjective relations while explaining economic facts.

Finally, the observational perspective offered by this book opens economic discourse to the category of reciprocity, which is notably absent in the approach that has dominated until now. As we will show, it is not true that the *sole* motivation that drives an economic agent is that of self-interest, and thus it is not true that the economy cannot concern itself with the notions of "gift" and "gratuitous action." This essentially says that it makes no sense to state that in order to behave rationally one must maximize an objective function of self-interest subject to constraints. *Homo oeconomicus* must have a place in economic theory, but it cannot occupy the entire space. As we will discover, *homo reciprocans* is just as rational — and in many situations even more rational — than *homo oeconomicus*. Expanding the cultural horizon within which mainstream economics has limited economic discourse until now is the intellectual challenge that we intend to take up.

We have many debts of gratitude incurred during the preparation of this book. Our first thought goes to our students at the University of Bologna, Bicocca in Milano, and Tor Vergata in Rome: from our many encounters with them these pages were born, grew, and matured. Then there are our colleagues and friends who with generous attention have followed the various stages of our work. Here we particularly want to recall Elettra Agliardi, Helen Alford, Michele Bagella, Stefano Bartolini, Giorgio Basevi, Kaushik Basu, Roberto Burlando, Emanuela Carbonara, Lorenzo Caselli, Roberto Cellini, Andrew Clark, Francesco Daveri, Carlo D'Adda, Pompeo Della Posta, Sergio De Stefanis, Giovanni Dosi, Mauro Gallegati, Sergio De Stefanis, Viviana Di Giovinazzo, Giulio Ecchia, Gianluca Fiorentini, Benedetto Gui, Luca Lambertini, Fabrizio Marchesini, Massimiliano Marzo, Giuseppe Mastromatteo, Cristina Montesi, Natalia Montinari, Vera Negri Zamagni, Luigi Paganetto, Fausto Panunzi, Luigi Pasinetti, Vittorio Pelligra, Alessandra Pelloni, Gustavo Piga, Pierluigi Porta, Tommaso Reggiani, Pierluigi Sacco, Carlo Scarpa, Roberto Scazzieri, Francesco Silva, Alessandra Smerilli, Luca Zarri, and Alberto Zazzaro.

Finally, we express our sincere and grateful appreciation to Michael Brennen for his valuable assistance in the hard work of translation and to Giovanni Antonio Forte for his tireless assistance in preparing the final manuscript.

Chapter 1

Economics: what it studies, with what methods, and how it evolved

1.1 What is a science?

For scholars of economic science (that is, economists), economics is a science, but in what sense can we speak of economics as a science?

To answer that question we must first answer a more general question: *what is a science*? If by science we mean a rational *body of knowledge* shared by a community of scholars that enriches over time through critique and subsequent revisions, then without doubt economics is a science, just as are philosophy, biology, and mathematics.

If instead we understand science to be *knowledge based on facts*, developed with the empirical or scientific method, then doubts begin to arise whether economics is really a science. Even though economics has always sought to imitate the natural sciences (such as physics) and to base its theories on *facts*, it cannot be considered an exact science that is able to provide answers and give valid interpretations in any historical era. Because it deals with people's behaviors and decisions in a given social context, it must adapt to the time and place in which those decisions develop.

1.1.1 Economics is a social science

Historical data and statistical research can be used in the natural sciences as a reliable and safe basis for making predictions. For example, we can predict in advance the moon's motion — barring extraordinary interference such as the passage of a meteorite — since it will follow the same orbit today as yesterday. Predicting the future in economics is more difficult because it studies the behavior of human beings who can change their decisions at any time; that is why it is more similar to philosophy than to physics.

Unlike a mathematician or a physicist, an economist cannot formulate a law that is valid for all times and places; what the economist can formulate is a **tendential law**, or a relationship that is true in most cases.

The Microeconomics of Wellbeing and Sustainability. https://doi.org/10.1016/B978-0-12-816027-5.00001-X

Empirical research in economics is doubtlessly important, but it is frequently used by economists as a rhetorical tool to persuade the opinions of the public, politicians, or their colleagues. However, the data they present always refer to the past, while the predictions requested of economists are about the future — a future that is never the same as the past, given the high number of variables that influence human behavior.

1.2 The investigative method of economic science

Different paths can be followed to collect the information useful for developing a theory.

*Proceed from the particular to the general, or the **inductive method**. Example: observing the fall of an apple led Newton to formulate the laws of universal gravitation.*

*Proceed from the general to the particular, or the **deductive method**. Example: from Newton's law I deduce that not only does an apple fall, but that objects attract each other.*

This is why economists find it more appropriate to follow a logical course that is the result of a *combination of the inductive and the deductive methods*: Starting from an observation in reality (the inductive method) they formulate abstract assumptions of human behavior, such as rationality, pursuit of their own self-interest, and so forth; on the basis of these assumptions they deduce laws in light of which (the deductive method) they attempt to explain individual economic facts that, since they are inserted into a given social context, are not entirely predictable.

The typical reasoning of economic science is: "if...then."

Example: if the price of gasoline rises, then on average its consumption will decrease.

On the basis of these considerations, we can say that

economics is a science based on facts that has the goal of generating models that indicate tendencies on which predictions are then based.

1.3 What is an economic model?

In a certain sense, all sciences (including philosophy or theology) make use of models, or simplified representations of reality. Economics also makes use of formal models using mathematical, graphic, and geometric languages.

To better understand what a model is, consider a map or a diagram of a mountain. Such representations do not depict the "real" mountain, nor are they photographs of the mountain, but rather they are simplified representations of the real mountain that only note a few of its essential characteristics, such as altitude, shelters, or woods. They overlook many others (abandoned cabins, bushes) that are not considered relevant to the map's users (e.g., hikers or hunters) who are not interested that there is a farmer's tool shed at mile marker such-and-such, while they are interested in knowing where there is a shelter or a village with water and food.

Something similar happens with the models that economic science uses. When an economist wants to study someone's cookie consumption behavior, she is not interested in the color of his eyes or his height, but in his income and his tastes in food. Here too she uses a "map" — a model — that includes a few characteristics and ignores others.

Some may ask why a more complete model or map, the most realistic one possible that includes every defining element of a mountain or a consumer, is not useful.

Actually, were the map too "real" it would not be very useful, just as a "real" photo of a mountain that did not indicate its paths and their altitude changes would not be very useful.

Taking a photo requires engineers — not scientists — to build a camera, just as making a map requires cartographers who have a theory about what is useful to a hiker entering new territory, such as altitude changes, paths, and so forth. Similarly, in economics journalists, sociologists, and writers are quite effective at describing consumption in all its aspects; however, studying the energy consumption choices of a country's families this year requires turning to economists. In fact, after developing a theory to identify a few key variables they only focus on those few (as do cartographers), which they then use to build a model with which to understand things not commonly visible to the naked eye.

*An **economic model** is a theoretical scheme that represents the basic elements of one or more phenomena one wants to study.*

One last consideration: paths and altitude changes are not visible to the naked eye when looking at a photo; reflection and scientific work are required to first "see" them, and then make them known to everyone. Every science is truly such when, thanks to study and research, it is able to see and make visible things that are not obvious.

An economic model is a good model and the economist who defines it is a good economist, when, due to the model, first the scholar and then the society are able to see things that were not previously visible.

If all of reality were comprehensible by paying close attention with the naked eye, by simple observation with the senses and with common sense, there would be no need for science. The social and civil value of science, not just of economics only, is to make us see something more and different.

1.4 The ethical responsibility of the economist

In the first half of the 19th century the economist and philosopher John Stuart Mill defined economics as a science that generates *tendencies*. By this the English economist meant that, while in the natural sciences scientists' theories do not alter the behavior of the objects studied (with a few important exceptions in particle physics), *in the social sciences a relationship of mutual influence exists between theories and actual behaviors, in the sense that economic theories about human behavior have an impact on the behavior itself, at times modifying it to a significant extent.*

Prior to Copernicus the planets in their orbits behaved exactly as they do today, and they obeyed the law of gravity before Newton discovered it. However, if a prominent economist writes an Internet article today announcing that the stock market will crash tomorrow, his prediction, even if wrong or made in bad faith for speculative reasons, can actually affect stock prices tomorrow, since there is a relationship between predictions and their fulfillment. This is the source of the *civil and ethical responsibility of the economist*, and of the social scientist in general.

Political economy is not a theoretical discipline in the same sense as in, say, philosophy. To clarify this, the great economist J.M. Keynes liked to say that economists must think and act like dentists! In effect he was saying that economists cannot behave like naturalists. The latter are quite interested in knowing why, for example, a certain species of animal becomes extinct, but that cannot worry him or draw him in personally beyond a certain level. The economist as well is interested in explaining why certain people are unable to find work, or why certain companies fail, and so forth, but her work is not finished until she can show how her model or theory might offer — even indirectly — suggestions for courses of intervention or for actions of one sort or another that might improve the situation. If this element is missing we might talk about mathematical economics or of philosophy of economics, both of which are useful and interesting, but certainly not about political economy.

This characteristic of our discipline sheds light on a special dimension of the responsibility of the scholar who studies economic questions, that of considering the use and implementation of the results of scientific practice in economics and making these known to non-specialists. Hans Jonas wrote that

Just how much this "scientific asceticism" has harmed a proper understanding of the nature of political economy and its functions is evident to all, and the recent 2008 economic and financial crisis is a sad confirmation.

Jonas, 1984

So what are the goals of the suggestions for action that political economy provides? They aim to improve the well-being of people who live in society. The well-being we are referring to clearly does not include just its material components, but its immaterial and spiritual components as well, for the simple reason that the needs of mankind are both material and spiritual, and the types of goods that serve to satisfy each are different. One or the other type of need will be prevalent in a given society in a given historical period, depending on its stage of development. In the early stages of development, when capital accumulation has not yet reached a critical threshold, the prevalent needs will be material; it is thus normal that economics appears to be the science that is concerned with how to increase people's material well-being. However, beyond a certain stage of growth the problem for economics essentially becomes that of the quality of life, or which categories of goods and services the citizens of an advanced society want to have produced and distributed. In large measure this is the big question regarding the choice of a development model from among all those that are technically feasible.

With some simplification we can say that while the economic problem of industrial societies primarily has to do with choices in conditions of material or natural scarcity — so much so that all countries that have wanted to industrialize have been constrained to follow a single development path, although with well-known local variations — the economic problem of post-industrial societies, which many are by now, is mainly that of understanding how the various members of civil society can freely decide the composition of the set of goods to produce (whether more private use goods or more goods for public use, or more hard goods or more personal services) and the way the goods are provided. Indeed, the well-being we derive from consuming a good or service does not depend solely on its intrinsic characteristics, but also from the way it is offered to us and our degree of participation in the choice itself. Ultimately we can grasp the difference between material and spiritual well-being by pointing out that for material well-being "more is better," in that having more things or consuming more goods means living better, but that is not true when referring to spiritual well-being, or happiness. As we will see consumerism in and of itself does not make people better off or make them happier.

1.5 From dismal science to hopeful science?

One of the most unpleasant names economics has earned in the past is that of the "dismal science." One of the main causes of this unfortunate definition was determined by the association of the discipline with Malthus' well-known predictions that, given a geometric population growth in the face of a linear growth in food resources, over time the quantity of goods available to each individual would gradually decrease, and the future of the earth would be marked by poverty and overpopulation.

Fortunately Malthus' prediction turned out to be wrong, as he underestimated the progress of technology that — even in a growing population — increased labor productivity such that it increased, rather than decreased, both agricultural productivity and per capita income. In more general terms, which is also applicable to Malthus' reasoning, the label "dismal science" originates in the fact that economists are able to grasp constraints and interdependencies between different variables, and they quite frequently point out the limits or negative indirect consequences of projects or initiatives motivated by the highest ideals.

In many historical periods it was often thought that giving attention to a positive goal for humanity, expressed by proclaiming a universal principle, promulgating a constitutional or ordinary law, or creating a particular rule (e.g., work for all, abolition of child labor, identifying an optimal fixed exchange rate, or determining a guaranteed minimum wage) was sufficient to insure the proposal's success. Economists frequently have entered the debate in such circumstances by bringing to light constraints and interdependencies between variables, which in fact made fulfilling the ideal proposal impossible if the relationship between the forces in play in the reality of the market obstructed it.

For example, economists point out that proclaiming a universal or a constitutional right to labor is not sufficient in and of itself to guarantee work for all. The principle does not produce the desired effects if market conditions are not actually created that are able to generate sustainable jobs over time. Furthermore, economists emphasize that laws abolishing child labor in a developing country can make them worse off (driving them toward prostitution or sloth) if the conditions are not created for better work alternatives that are viable, such as higher salaries for families that consent to supporting education expenses for their children, subsidies or financing *in toto* by the state for educational expenses for families, and so forth. Finally, economists bring to light that fixing an optimal exchange rate that does not correspond to the market supply and demand equilibrium drives economic agents to disregard the rule and create an informal market in which the exchange rate reflects the real purchasing power relationship between two currencies.

Does this mean that economists have no ideals, or perhaps instead, motivated by their ideals, that they make an extra effort to try to confirm that their idealist principles are compatible with and applicable to factual reality? The so-called dismal science often conceals a "pragmatic idealism" among those who are not satisfied with merely stating an ideal, who do not relent in their efforts to confirm that the ideal is really compatible with and feasible in actual socioeconomic life.

Considering current examples when states enact financial laws, is the economist—finance minister perhaps less motivated by idealist reasons when she stresses that spending constraints prevent devoting too many resources to a worthy cause, pointing out how additional resources destined for that purpose must be taken away from another equally worthy cause? Or by emphasizing that there is a compatibility problem in directing resources to a given purpose not only at the present time, but in other times as well, thus highlighting the effects on future generations of today's decisions on public debt or the environment?

Economics has recently begun regaining a passion for themes such as the determinants of happiness, rediscovering one of the motivations that lay at the origins of studies in the discipline (see Chapter 12). In this regard, one of the more informative phrases that documents the attention that classical economists gave to this theme is found in a fragment from an interchange between two giants of economic thought. Commenting on Adam Smith's work, Malthus stated that "The professed object of Dr. Adam Smith's inquiry is the nature and causes of the wealth of nations. There is another inquiry, however, perhaps still more interesting, which he occasionally mixes with it, I mean an inquiry into the causes which affect the happiness of nations."

Philosophers and social scientists have always discussed happiness. What is new today is the high level of renewed interest in these studies within economics, determined largely by the opportunity of having large data sets available in which it is possible to measure the effects of different variables on people's self-declared happiness or life satisfaction. The saying "the things that count cannot be counted" highlights the difficulty of understanding and measuring areas such as happiness; however, empirical studies on happiness developed during recent decades, based on the vast bulk of new data available, somewhat reduce the impact of that statement. Above all, these studies indicate how economics is coming to understand the importance of an integrated approach, in which individual preferences (which, as we will see, form the basis of several chapters that study behavior in consumption, production, and choices between work and free time) are empirically tested rather than being assumed *a priori* on the basis of a particular philosophical approach, ultimately giving greater weight to people's statements (although subject to rigorous checks) over philosophers' conventions.

These remarks on studies in the economics of happiness, which we will address in more detail in Chapter 12, serve here only to conclude our introductory remarks on economics and its recent developments. Economics is evolving from the dismal science (which is really a science that studies interdependencies and constraints on human action in accord with the principle of "pragmatic, embodied idealism") to a science that, beyond playing this foundational role, is passionately turning again to consider in increasing detail the determinants of human flourishing.

1.6 Attention to interdependencies: opportunity cost

An introductory chapter in a textbook on microeconomics must shed light on some key aspects that are foundational for all the analyses developed in subsequent chapters. Without question, one of these is opportunity cost. Recalling the question addressed in the preceding section, one of the reasons economics is perceived as the dismal science is that it can bring to light constraints, obstacles, or critical elements of problems to solve, which hurried and less analytical reflection would not glimpse.

One of the most important of these is **opportunity cost**. We usually think that market price determines the cost of a given action, good, or service, and in the absence of a price its cost is zero. To the contrary, the principle of opportunity cost teaches us that *everything has a cost, even things that cost nothing in terms of a monetary price.*

The matter is very simple. Common wisdom tends to see our pocketbook, or the spending limits our budget places on our choices, as the only constraint, or cost, on our actions. As we will see in later chapters, in reality there are at least two basic constraints on human action: the boundary of technological possibilities and time. Time is probably the most restrictive constraint because it cannot be modified either by the growth of available material or by technical and scientific progress. We can in fact loosen our spending constraints by becoming wealthier, but we cannot prolong the number of hours in the day — although with progress in medical science we can slowly and progressively extend the length of our lives. Time constraints are because that it is almost never possible to do two things simultaneously, and thus every choice we make, even if directed into an activity without monetary cost, precludes another that we could have done during the same time.

In reality, if we pay attention we realize that the more our available economic resources increase, the relative price of time with respect to money increases; that is, the most important constraint becomes that of time, and time becomes more precious than money. It is no accident that as individual income grows in wealthy societies, giving of one's money increasingly tends to replace giving of one's time. For people who have good economic possibilities and are very busy, time is worth much more than money. For the same reason, a highly paid manager will be inclined to pay much more to reduce the time required to go from one place to another, and thus will be more likely than a university student to travel by plane rather than train, or on a high-speed train rather than a slower one.

For the same reason, the cooking practices of prior generations (except, of course, those of professional chefs) tend to increasingly shift toward recipes that require less time to prepare. To become aware of this, we need only compare our parent's culinary traditions with those of the current generation in terms of the time expended on food preparation. The opportunity to buy pre-washed salad at the supermarket, which costs up to nine times more than non-washed salad, is certainly new in this generation; it represents a classic case of a price premium with which we actually buy not a product, but a time savings.

Moving from examples to definitions, opportunity cost represents the value of what we give up when we make a particular choice. The most classic example of this (which we will consider in Chapter 9), is choosing to take an hour of free time during the day (supposing that we have the real possibility of using the same time for an hour of productive work). We need pay no one to make that choice, and thus we may think that the choice is free. In reality, by making that choice we give up an hour of work, and thus the opportunity cost of that hour of free time is represented by the money we would have earned had we devoted that hour to productive work.

1.7 The two phases of economic analysis: positive and normative

One of the characteristics that should always be kept in mind when analyzing an economic problem is the distinction between its positive and normative phases. By **positive phase** we mean the study of reality through factual analysis, and particularly of the correlations and relationships that exist between different economic variables. The **normative phase** necessarily comes later. It begins with what has been learned during the positive phase about the relationship between the different variables examined, and then evaluates which political economic initiatives to adopt that either aim at achieving a certain well-being goal or resolving a problem brought to light in the positive analysis phase.

The following discussion shows the fundamental difference between these two areas. In a certain sense the positive phase has greater objectivity, and at times is even free of value judgments, because during the analysis an economist must rigorously adhere to observing the facts and verifying the behavior of the variables under study without regard to her evaluation criteria. The normative phase is instead fully influenced by the researcher's value judgments and priority scale. Indeed, at the point where one suggests a certain policy aimed at directing the economic system toward a goal, one should have the intellectual honesty to state one's own scale of values, without pretending that the proposed policy solution is the only objectively valid one. In other words, during the normative phase an economist cannot hide behind a shield of presumed objectivity, taking advantage of the deeper knowledge of the situation he developed during the positive phase and declaring his as the best objective solution, based on a given scale of values.

To more fully understand what we have said above, consider a simple example. In the case of an analysis of the drug market, the positive phase concerns the evaluation between the basic variables of that market, such as the law of supply and demand for drugs, the factors that influence its supply and demand, and the effects of suppression policies used by police. From this point of view, a rigorous and objective observation during the positive phase is that fighting drug traffic and choosing to make drugs illegal increases the revenue of large criminal organizations. The observation originates from the fact that illegality changes the criminal organization that deals in a given substance into a monopolist, while the war against drugs increases the risks of those on the supply side, which motivates them to ask higher prices as a reward for the risks incurred. Furthermore, when drug seizures reach a certain level of significance and consistency, the supply diminishes, making it more scarce, and the equilibrium price increases, which in turn could make the supply even more scarce and raise the equilibrium price. It is clear that competition emerges among legal vendors when we abandon the prohibitionist mindset (one need only think of tobacco and alcohol), and the monopoly rents of criminal organizations dry up. What we have stated about the positive analysis phase might seem to favor the anti-prohibitionist choice. In fact, though, an economist limits herself to observing several phenomena while striving to be as objective as possible. To this point critics of the anti-prohibitionist choice should not intervene because we are still in the positive analysis phase, and no value judgment has yet been formulated regarding the choices to make to combat the situation.

As we have said, the normative phase begins after the positive phase. Given the relations between variables previously examined, some economists hold that the best solution to the drug problem would be anti-prohibitionism, arguing that its principal benefit is that of eliminating the nexus between drugs and criminality. With this move we clearly enter the normative phase; the proposed solution has no objective validity, since it depends on the scale of values adopted.

The implicit scale of values hidden behind this proposal puts primary emphasis on minimizing the social cost of criminal activity connected with drug trafficking (which includes not only the actions of large organizations, but also the petty crimes committed by addicts looking for the financial resources to buy their drugs). This choice may not be shared by others with different scales of values. For example, if one believes that part of the purpose of laws is to create social norms — that is, if a broad category of people thinks that legality tends to coincide with the morality of an action — drug liberalization could increase the number of addicts. This could lead those whose scale of values prioritizes minimizing the number who fall into drug addiction tend toward the prohibitionist choice.

Moreover, personal inclinations and one's position in society could drive different people to lean toward one or the other solution. For example, adults who are already culturally and psychologically "mature" and who are worried about the problem of security could be more oriented toward the anti-prohibitionist solution, while those who run drug recovery centers, or parents with adolescent children, may be more likely to favor prohibitionism.

Faced with various influences on personal positions, one of the more interesting criteria that should be adopted during the normative phase is the "veil of ignorance" proposed by John Rawls. Prior to making a decision for a given group of people, Rawls suggested that we divest ourselves of our subjectivity by imagining that a "veil of ignorance" prevents us from knowing which social group we are born into or we are part of (in our example, mature adults concerned about security or parents of adolescent children). What would our choice be in this case, knowing that there is a certain probability of our being part of one or the other group?

The principle of the "veil of ignorance" clearly induces a certain degree of caution, drawing us toward a choice that ensures against the worst outcomes of the random draw that would assign us to one social group or the other.

However, it does represent one of the more interesting criteria for confronting the problem of making public choices.

We can draw the following conclusion from our example: it is not possible to set aside either ethics or value judgments in economics. While the initial positive phase of observing facts in the field would seem more value free, the second normative phase necessarily entails them, and an economist would be shirking his duty to not admit that.

In reality, if we pay close attention, even the first positive phase does not in fact set aside ethics and value judgments. Reality is indeed multi-faceted, and the choice of a point of view from which to carry out our positive evaluation can also influence the subsequent normative phase. Returning to our example, a study on the social and individual costs of drug addiction, and on the probability of falling into addiction once taking drugs is no longer illegal, can already strongly bias the policy phase toward prohibitionism. In contrast, an analysis of the social costs of crime linked to drug trafficking can push toward a more favorable view of anti-prohibitionism.

In other words, a more careful analysis helps us understand how in reality ethics and value judgments exist even during the positive phase, which are linked to the choice of what to observe. The great British statesman Winston Churchill understood the point quite well when he asked his staff to bring him the greatest number of statistics possible; in this way, he stated, he would find one that was adapted to the *a priori* position he wanted to support. Churchill understood that the simple choice of what to observe could already significantly influence public opinion without having to rig the data.

In light of the above, it seems quite clear that economists cannot take refuge in a presumably neutral perspective, as pivotal moments in their activities either require the explicit formulation of a scale of values or are not exclusive of ethical considerations.

It is equally clear what the value of economists and our professional duty depends on. The added value we can bring to the discussion is to provide the greatest number of points for reflection that derive from the positive phase and spell out, with the greatest possible honesty, the options for public choices and their positive and negative consequences. We are not asked to remain necessarily neutral or refrain from passionately arguing for some choices over others. The important point is to do so properly, stating our scale of values up front and not exploiting our informational advantage in order to pass off the solution we have espoused as the most objectively valid one.

1.8 The theory of rational choices in the presence of constraints

When asking non-specialists for a definition of "economics" and "economist" we receive widely divergent responses. It is generally believed that an economist takes care of accounting and balancing budgets, or of broad topics such as debt, inflation, unemployment, and problems with productive companies. Economists may be the subject of jokes, such as the one in which after a dinner with friends, when it is necessary to equally divide up the bill, someone says "you're an economist, you do it!"

In reality, in studying the variety of problems the economist addresses we find that economics deals with almost all aspects of life. Although the core interest remains the changes in economic variables due to the behaviors of individuals in either production or consumption, and studying in depth the determinants of individual or collective choices of actions, we also realize that many factors that are not strictly economic decisively impact such movements.

For example, studying the behavior of economic agents and their choices in consumption, savings, and job offers we cannot ignore moral values, social norms, family dynamics, individuals' choices about free time, and educational choices. In large measure non-economic determinants have fundamental effects on economic choices, and conversely, economic choices have significant non-economic effects. When studying economics we end up working with the whole of life.

This broader perspective makes defining economics even more problematic. We might venture a different way of formulating a definition by starting from the method used rather than from the spectrum of topics covered.

A characteristic of modern economics is that it begins by reconstructing individual economic agents' behaviors (a *microfoundation*) in a model, even when defining the movements of aggregate quantities. Another common element is addressing all the problems these agents solve over the course of their existence as problems of constrained maximization, that is, as seeking the optimal solution to a given problem after having defined the desired goal and the constraints that limit the possibilities for action.

There is a common method that the vast majority of economists use to address the problem of consumers (maximization of their utility or preference function under spending constraints), workers (here too, maximization of their utility or preference function under the constraint of the inextensibility of the available time), and producers (maximization of the goal of profit by their companies under the constraint of the range of technological possibilities available in a given historical period).

Basically, this approach, defined as **constrained maximization**, requires few restrictive assumptions. Constraints on our initiatives are an unavoidable fact of our lives; they are an expression of our non-omnipotence and the limits of space, time, and technology that we run up against every day.

Hypothesizing that individuals set goals and seek to maximize them in the presence of these systemic constraints means nothing more than postulating the rationality of our actions, *meaning by "rational" the determination to pursue a goal in the most effective manner possible, once it is defined*. By looking at the method rather than at the vastness of topics covered, we can define economics as the **theory of rational choices in the presence of constraints**.

Having argued the soundness of our definition, we must necessarily try to understand the possible criticisms and challenges to it. For some, the hypothesis that individuals in general maximize their objective function in the presence of constraints is refuted by the diversity of motives from which different people act.

How can we state that this is the fundamental principle when we encounter humanitarian workers, missionaries, and masochists? Are humanitarian workers, missionaries, and masochists rational, and do they maximize? In theory, yes; for the humanitarian worker, whom we hypothesize carries out this work for purely altruistic reasons, the goal becomes that of maximizing the well-being of others, which she consistently pursues for that purpose. The same is true for the masochist who prefers to suffer physically or morally and who consistently pursues that end. Part of the criticism of the paradigm of rational choice in the presence of constraints is thus really the criticism of a vision of individual preferences that is too narrow and conformist; this can be resolved by accepting the possibility that such preferences can significantly vary between individuals.

Two other criticisms of the paradigm are trickier to answer. The first is that hypothesizing perfect rationality – almost a super-rationality – asks too much of individuals, in that it sometimes requires excessively logical and computational abilities. With the assumption of rational behavior economists in fact almost always ask too much of the agents in their models; they assume that individuals are capable of finding direction in a multitude of possibilities, effectively selecting information and having a reasoning and calculation ability that is probably above average. Recent laboratory experiments have found empirical evidence that confirm the soundness of the criticism, demonstrating how, in situations in which the required rationality appears to be excessive, people actually behave rather differently than the models predict.

So as the Nobel laureate Herbert Simon stated, in many situations we must partially modify the theory to accept that people, rather than maximizing their preferences, content themselves with satisfying them above a minimally acceptable level; when in their evaluation of all the available alternatives that threshold has been exceeded, they stop.

Another possible criticism, although probably less relevant, is that the reasons why people do not behave rationally do not depend on the difficulty of evaluating complex situations to the best of their abilities, but rather on truly irrational traits that are independent of the logical and computational difficulties linked to formulating a rational choice, which psychologists have long studied in depth. Among the possible examples, we recall the behavior in finance of "weak-hearted traders." These are investors who, when selecting their investments, choose to take on sizable risk – for example by investing significantly in equities – but when the market declines and they suffer a "virtual" loss, rather than keeping calm they irrationally decide to sell, even if there are real possibilities for a recovery. They do this not because of their inability to see the recovery, but uniquely due to the impossibility of psychologically sustaining the heavy "virtual" loss they are experiencing.

Another example, identified by C. Lowenstein in his study on individual preferences, is of consumers arriving at a restaurant with a large appetite. In many cases, what happens is that their appetites push them to order more food than they would were they keeping a cool head, even knowing that they will not be able to finish everything they ordered. Thus one type of rationality deviation can be explained by transitory compulsive attitudes, and along the same line of analysis, by true forms of dependence (lack of self-control is one of the more common forms of irrationality).

We could go on at length citing examples of violations of the paradigm of the rationality of individual behavior. All theoretical hypotheses, such as the theory of rational choices in the presence of constraints, have their limits. They are useful to the extent they are falsifiable, that is, to the extent the models are confirmed or refuted by reality, on which basis it is possible to effectively describe reality in both cases.

It remains the case that today the great majority of economists agree on the convention of the constrained maximization approach, and it is the point of reference from which to begin searching for new general paradigms.

It is basically an approach we can be comfortable with, and we can build our study of economic reality on that basis. An essential point we have sought to clarify from the beginning is that the paradigm in question does not include the additional restriction of having to choose a certain preference model, such as the traditional model of *homo oeconomicus*, which is based solely on a short-sighted form of self-interest. Later in the book we will call the approach that requires this assumption, which is actually a subset of the paradigm we just described, a *reductionist approach*.

In many cases, presumed violations of the rationality paradigm are actually violations of the assumptions of this preference model that originate from the inability to grasp the variety and wealth of individual motivations for acting.

Within a certain approximation, we can define economics as the theory of rational choices in the presence of constraints. We can also venture an attempt at defining economists and their general mindset.

Economists need not be dismal scientists; by reasoning from the definition of economics just set forth we can arrive at almost the opposite conclusion. If economics is the theory of rational choices in the presence of constraints, the mindset of an economist is necessarily that of a problem solver, someone who has a habit of analyzing problems, studying the preferences and motivations of the agents involved, and identifying realistic solutions — solutions that respect the constraints and interdependencies necessary to balance between various economic considerations and the use of time. When faced with a problem, an economist is not a fatalist who maintains that if a situation is not optimally resolved in the light of past experience, it should necessarily perpetuate forever. Nor is he content with setting out his own idealistic impulses by enunciating principles without concerning himself about how to actualize them in everyday reality. An economist thus cannot be a dismal scientist, because she tends to be an optimist who looks to the future with hope, having confidence in the possibility of rationally confronting the issues on the table and finding solutions to complex problems.

1.9 Microeconomics and macroeconomics

Two more fundamental concepts to absorb at the outset of our study are those of microeconomics and macroeconomics. By **microeconomics** we mean the analysis of the behaviors of single productive units or of individual economic agents. Microeconomics is thus concerned with the behavior of companies and individuals, giving particular attention to their consumption decisions and time use choices between work and free time. By **macroeconomics** we mean the analysis of the behavior of aggregate variables in the economic system and of the political economy choices implemented by local or national authorities regarding those variables. Macroeconomics thus concerns itself with the study of phenomena such as inflation, unemployment, public debt, foreign balance of payments, and the monetary, fiscal, and exchange policies that decisively impact these aggregates.

Until recently there was a clear distinction between these branches of economics. In fact, macroeconomists such as Keynes started directly from the statistical observation of the behavior of aggregate economic variables, and they developed their political economy prescriptions on that basis.

The microfoundation revolution in economic models has shrunk the distance between them. In the microfoundation models, macro variables such as consumption, savings, and investments are the result of the aggregation of the behaviors of individual economic agents and governments, and they are studied using the approach described in the previous section as the *theory of rational choices in the presence of constraints*. Thus the dynamics of these variables are not detached from individual behaviors, but are rather the result of individuals' choices combined with government policies.

In any case, the difference between the two branches is not wholly eliminated, and the choice between them depends on whether a scholar focuses attention on the dynamics of aggregate quantities or on individual behaviors. The adoption of a common methodological criterion is however a basic element: with the microfoundation of models, microeconomics and macroeconomics are much closer to each other than they once were.

Recalling what we said in the preceding section regarding the paradigm of economics as the theory of rational choices in the presence of constraints, we should consider whether the challenge to economists' traditional approach to formulating preferences and economic models is greater in microeconomics or macroeconomics.

The answer is easy. The phenomenon is much more widespread in microeconomics, which can focus attention on the detailed behavior of individuals or small groups. Since its basic characteristic is the aggregation of economic agents' behaviors, macroeconomics must necessarily be less discriminate, characterizing individual behaviors by hypotheses that apply to the majority of agents that decisively defines the trends in the macro aggregates. This is why macroeconomics frequently simplifies the problem of the diversity of preferences by defining a single "representative" agent and synthesizing everyone else's behavior to fit it. Recently, however, macroeconomics, constantly under pressure from theoretical and empirical studies that evince the variety of preferences and models of action, is increasingly sensitive to the problem; it is addressing the challenge by beginning to incorporate greater diversity into its models than a single representative agent, including at least the interaction between two or more agents with different preferences or behaviors.

1.10 Integration with other disciplines

One of the problems we will address in this book is the relationship between economics and the other social sciences. Prior to the modern era a holistic, integrated vision of various disciplines was considered one of the chief qualities to pursue, and the Renaissance geniuses were able to cover a range of topics, partly because the breadth of knowledge in the various branches of the sciences was still limited.

The scientific progress of recent centuries has led to an enormous expansion of the field of knowledge in every discipline, which has made it practically impossible to know them integrally. It is as if a "big bang" of knowledge that happened at the beginning of the Renaissance began a process of functional specialization that has had the merit of bringing about enormous progress in the various disciplines within every single field.

However, the downside of this extreme specialization is the fact that every discipline has developed its own specialized language among its "initiates," making communication between experts in different fields quite difficult. Even within a single discipline — say, economics — the knowledge in the subdisciplines is so extensive that, in order to be successful in their research economists tend to specialize in a sector (such as labor economics, international economics, industrial economics, and so forth) and to only slightly develop their knowledge of other sectors in economics. This is one of the reasons that explains the difficulty economists had in foreseeing the 2008 global financial crisis; it was a complex phenomenon that required connecting the economics of the securities markets, macroeconomics, and finance, and thus competency in at least three economic subdisciplines.

The problem with scholars being experts in minutia and the inability of disciplines to communicate among themselves ends ups having a negative impact on the ability of the disciplines to know the object of their study in depth and to be able to formulate sensible policy suggestions.

In the case of economics, ignoring the contributions of the social sciences similar to it, such as sociology and psychology, sharply limits its ability to understand the behavior of economic agents. The secret of many successful economists, some of them Nobel laureates such as George Akerlof and Daniel Kahnemann, has been to introduce solid research acquired from closely related social sciences as new elements in their discipline. As we will see in Chapter 12, studies in the economics of happiness are today a natural area of confluence for economics, sociology, and psychology, consequently it is a favorable field for fulfilling this new vision of collaboration among the disciplines. In a nutshell, economists have learned from sociologists just how important it is to compare notes with a group that considers itself their peers in evaluating individual well-being in a society, and from psychologists that preferences are anything but stable, and that the utility we derive from various goods is subject to adaptation processes that should be closely studied.

1.11 A three-dimensional approach

In Section 1.7 we developed the characteristics of the positive and normative phases of economics, emphasizing that in the normative phase is it is our duty to state the value criteria that guide the suggestions we economists propose as the solutions to a given problem. We thus think it appropriate to briefly mention in this introductory chapter the lively debate over the definition of the goals to pursue.

From this viewpoint as well we find indications of great turmoil and evolution. For many years the definition of the political economy goals to pursue (in the normative phase following a positive analysis) was typically unidimensional. What we mean by this is that main goals to achieve were defined in material terms aligned along the principle of maximizing the creation of aggregate economic value (that is, goods and services that have market value). To accomplish this goal the lode star was the growth of gross domestic product, which represents the total of the goods and services produced and sold in a given span of time (usually a year) by economic agents in a given country. A goal directly linked to GDP (Gross Domestic Product) growth is increasing workers' productivity, or their capacity to create monetizable goods and services in a given unit of time. Once a GDP growth target has been set, it is obvious that it can be met either by increasing the number of productive individuals (by pro-birth policies or by workers immigrating from other countries) or by increasing the productivity of the employed populace. Productivity growth is thus a microeconomic goal that follows directly from the goal of GDP growth when a populace and the number of those employed in it is stable.

The unidimensional approach accepted as a given the concurrence of the goal of GDP growth with the happiness of its citizens. That approach held that the task of economists was to maximize the available quantity of goods and services, leaving the treatment of eventual negative side effects on individual happiness to experts in other disciplines, such as psychologists or environmentalists. Over time the limits of this "modular" approach have become evident, in that in light of the principle of the strict separation of knowledge areas and functional specialization, experts concerned themselves only with their disciplines and their particular area of focus on the person (in our case, essentially, the individual as consumer, saver, and worker). This rigidly compartmentalized separation shows all its flaws when we find out that the various disciplines are closely interrelated. The non-economic consequences of economic choices are very important, and it is not possible to model and study the whole of human behavior without seeking to pull together its various parts, such as the economic person, the social person, and the psychological person.

From the viewpoint of defining goals to pursue, this progressive integration with other disciplines is becoming ever more urgent with the increasingly evident limits to the social and environmental sustainability of development. The **environment** is certainly the most urgent topic today. Natural scientists and economists have stayed on their narrow tracks for years, speaking incomprehensible languages. Economists, concentrating on the problems of creating economic value (GDP and productivity), took for granted the availability of natural resources (from reproducible goods such as wood, to non-reproducible goods such as oil, to non-reproducible public goods such as the climate), and above all they did not reflect deeply on the negative consequences in terms of the environmental sustainability of producing goods and services. Natural scientists, accustomed to considering the problem of balancing ecosystems and the scarce or non-reproducibility of some natural resources, and little accustomed to considering the Malthusian problem of ensuring increasing production for an expanding populace, have identified moderation in consumption as a goal; they also hold that the goal of unlimited economic growth is environmentally unsustainable. In a nutshell, economists have encouraged consuming more, while on the contrary natural scientists have encouraged consuming less. In this babel of knowledge, languages, and prescriptions, it is clear that the proper approach can no longer ignore being aware of other disciplines and their reasoning.

Today's most urgent problems of global warming and balancing ecosystems have generated significant movement in this direction, forcing economists to partly assimilate the language and knowledge of the natural sciences and to integrate the dimension of environmental sustainability into the old unidimensional goals. Thus taking the environmental balance into account, the traditional goal of increasing GDP and productivity becomes that of sustainable development, or increasing the energy efficiency of production — that is, the ability to create more economic value in parity with the use of non-reproducible natural resources.

However, these two dimensions are not enough. The increasingly attentive analysis of the interdependencies between economic and productive choices and the non-economic life of individuals has led economics today to focus attention on a third dimension to consider in well-being goals: **social sustainability**. To better understand this, economists increasingly consider whether the growth of per capita income is in service to people and their development or vice versa, that is, whether that growth goal is or is not compatible with creating the necessary social conditions so each person can flourish (a goal sometimes defined as the common good).

This is a problem that is anything but trivial; many times, accepting as a given that the outcome should be to increase GDP or productivity, the actions taken invade areas that are important for people's lives and happiness, such as the ability to invest in and build relationships, enjoy a stable professional work environment, and so forth.

The risk today is that the pendulum of public opinion, which is sensitive to the problems of social and environmental sustainability in development, could swing in the opposite direction and end up demonizing important dimensions such as growth or the creation of economic value. Adopting a three-dimensional instead of a unidimensional approach — that is, paying attention to the environmental and social sustainability of a development model — does not mean demonizing the creation of economic value. We recall yet again that economic value is a basic factor in overcoming the Malthusian challenge and eliminating hunger and malnutrition in the context of a growing world population. It is also obvious that the social dimension of creating economic value fundamentally contributes to the satisfaction of collective life. A growing GDP means not only growth in per capita income (hopefully well distributed across the populace), but also the availability of more resources for the social goods and services that are basic to individual life, such as the quality of health care, education, infrastructure, and so forth. Economic growth is thus a fundamental factor, but its social and environmental consequences can no longer be overlooked. This integrated goal, which is partly new for economists, will be one of the guiding criteria for our analysis of the behavior of economic agents and companies in the economic system.

1.12 Comparing Ptolemaics and Copernicans

In essence, we can see from the themes already placed on the table in this first chapter that the discipline of economics seems to be in a transition phase in which a consensus on the dominant paradigm is anything but settled. On the one hand, there are those we might call "Ptolemaic" economists who maintain that the essence of economic science consists in assuming people's self-interested preferences, arguing that this simplification of reality is reasonable and not too limiting; they negatively evaluate reflections on modifying the traditional preference structure. On the other hand, there are the "Copernican" economists who argue that the anomalies that refute the Ptolemaics' hypotheses are too obvious, systematic, and well-established. The Copernicans' goal is to rework the paradigm, since they consider the Ptolemaics' approach to be reductionist. They argue that the essence of the economic method is found in constrained maximization, or the theory of rational choices in the presence of constraints, which represents the true unifying factor in the study of various economic agents (consumers, workers, and companies); they accept the fact that individual preferences include many other components besides individual self-interest, such as altruism, an aversion to inequality, and so on. Finally, some Copernicans think this extended paradigm is unacceptable; even though it assumes broader views of individual preferences, there would still be so many violations of the economic theory that these would end up refuting the very idea that constrained maximization could be the guiding criterion of individual choices.

In the topics covered in this volume we will always start from the traditional mainstream analysis, explaining from time to time their possible inconsistencies or empirical refutations and seeking to illustrate the extensions that can progressively lead us toward the definition of a new paradigm.

One might argue that our approach is too demanding, requiring excessive effort of students. We do not see it that way. Ultimately, for many university students (we hope this is not the case for those using this book!) an introductory course is the only opportunity they will have to develop a basic economic culture. Furthermore, we maintain that a university's task is not to uncritically pass on techniques, but to stimulate a reflective attitude in students regarding the complexities of the problems discussed. With confidence in the fact that students' desire to learn can increase when presented with material engagingly described in all its complexity, in the following chapters we propose to go beyond illustrating the rudiments of standard techniques by offering critical reflections on what economics is today and what it is poised to become in the near future.

The evolution of ideas in economics

1.13 The schools of economic thought

As nearly always happens in European history, when there is a time of peace and economic growth economic theory evolves as well. It is no accident that what we might call modern economic theory emerged right around the mid-18th century, and that it appeared more or less simultaneously in various places in Europe.

As in the history of the arts and sciences, in economics as well the contributions of prominent thinkers are arranged along lines of thought called *schools*. The following sections give a brief overview of the classical economic schools, listing the main common elements of each.

By **economic school** we mean a group of economists who follow and develop the ideas of the same central founder, or who in any case share the same central lines of thought.

Before delving into each school, we should note in advance that although history books traditionally associate the emergence of political economy (and in Britain in particular) with the Industrial Revolution, in reality the world that gave rise to the new economic science of the 1700s was still an essentially agricultural world; the important new aspect was the expansion and internationalization of trade. Smith himself, who as we will see later is traditionally considered the father of modern economics, did not investigate, but rather anticipated industrialization. During his visit to the pin factory what captured his attention was not the machinery, but the way in which labor was divided.

Factories as we know them, with machinery and automation, did not yet exist, as craft work and agriculture dominated the European scene. However, all the prerequisites for the advent of the Industrial Revolution were in place, and economists were the first to realize that the world would quickly be radically changed.

1.14 Colonial expansion and mercantilism

In the historical period between the end of the 1500s and the beginning of the 1700s the first large modern states were formed. The consolidation of the great European powers (England, Spain, France, and the Netherlands) was accompanied by a series of economic interventions to support their commercial activities. All these contributions together were called "mercantilism."

This phenomenon, which was comprised of more than one school of thought, represented a set of techniques and rules of conduct for merchants and ministers of the economy.

Mercantilism is a set of rules, practical directions, and economic policy suggestions addressed to sovereigns to increase a country's wealth. Mercantilism held that *the wealth of a nation was measured by the quantity of gold and precious metals it possessed*; that is why mercantilists supported the reasoning of **colonial policy and protectionism**. Traditional societies were transformed from transient associations between individuals for the purpose of single business deals into permanent organizations to carry out large-scale, risky commercial activities. The first **mercantile companies** were formed; among the most famous were the British East India Company in 1600 and the Dutch West India Company in 1602.

The wealth accumulated in this way was then used to strengthen the military apparatus of the state, which in turn was a determining factor in the conquest of new territories and the assertion of economic supremacy over rival nations.

When precious metals began to flow into or out of a country in proportion to its sales or purchases of foreign goods, mercantilists suggested that sovereigns strengthen international trade, as the fundamental premise of mercantilism was to encourage exports and discourage imports. To attain this goal mercantilists suggested that sovereigns apply **trade protectionism**, a trade policy that states adopted to discourage imports (the purchase of goods from other states) through the imposition of heavy duties; the purpose was to prevent gold and precious metals from leaving the country.

International trade was considered a "zero sum game": enriching one country could only be accomplished by impoverishing others.

Thus in a trade exchange one party became wealthier (the party that increased the gold entering the country due to sales) and the other became poorer (the one that decreased its gold supply because it was spent to purchase goods not produced within its territory). It took centuries before this idea of market exchange disappeared (and it still has not completely vanished).

1.15 France and physiocracy: François Quesnay

An important classical school developed in France around the middle of the 18th century, known by the name of **physiocracy**. The term, which derives from the union of the Greek words *physis* (nature) and *kratos* (power), was coined to emphasize the basic thesis of this school of thought; it assigned productive power to nature, or to the fertility of the land, which through agriculture created greater wealth than that expended to produce it. The most representative person of this school of thought was François Quesnay, the court physician of Louis XV. He developed the first graphical representation of an *economic circuit*, comparing its dynamics to the flow of blood in the human body.

In particular, Quesnay associated the circulation of blood with the flows of products and money between farmers, landowners, merchants, and craftsmen. This thesis, first described in the *Encyclopédie* of Diderot and d'Alembert, was later perfected when the *Tableau économique* was published in 1758; in that work Quesnay laid out a systematic representation of a circular economic process of production and distribution that was accurate enough overall to consider it the first *economic model*. Despite the *Tableau économique* being a very elementary representation of an actual country's economy, physiocracy can be considered the first economic school (see Fig. 1.1) that attempted to define a true theory — an all-encompassing, abstract vision — of the economy.

The logic of the Tableau *was in fact based on simple but quite convincing ideas. The production process feeds itself through a circular, continuous flow of production and consumption that involves three social categories:*

agricultural producers *(the productive class). By their labor they created wealth (that is why they were called "productive"), which was determined by the portion of the crop that exceeded what was necessary to reseed to begin a new production cycle and to sustain themselves and their families; that portion was called the* produit net, *the net product or surplus. They sold this product to the other two classes and used the money received to acquire other means of subsistence, such as bread, and other means of production, such as tools;*

craftsmen *(the sterile class). They did not create a surplus, rather, they worked the raw materials purchased from the productive class and transformed them into tools and manufactured goods to sell to the productive class and the landowners.*

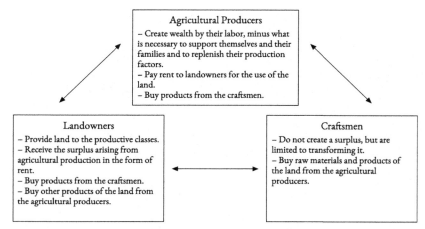

FIG. 1.1   The physiocratic model.

They too, like the farmers, used the proceeds of the sales of their products to support themselves and to continue production and trade;

landowners *(the unproductive class). They neither worked nor produced anything; their incomes were represented by land rents, or compensation for the use of the land, that they collected from the farmers that worked it. In any case, landowners played an important role in an economy because they spent the money received from rents to purchase food from the farmers and goods from the merchants. In this manner the landowner class played a fundamental "redistribution" role of the wealth produced by the entire society.*

Through the model represented in the *Tableau*, Quesnay brought to light that there are real flows (the circulation of goods) and financial flows (the circulation of money): flows of real goods only come from the land, and **economic growth** is possible only if the agricultural product obtained is greater than that necessary to reconstruct the means of production and ensure the subsistence of the populace. The excess product, or surplus, made it possible to incrementally increase the use of factors of production so as to obtain an even greater production in the future. Since land alone produced wealth (that is, by sowing a grain of wheat, 100 could be obtained in the harvest), *the physiocrats posited land as the basis of the wealth of a nation.*

Thus in difference with mercantilists, physiocrats were liberals; their motto was *laissez faire*, which later became so famous in the history of economic thought. It seems that the expression *laissez faire* was stated for the first time by the French merchant Legendre in response to a question by Colbert, Louis

XIV's finance minister, about what could be done for the country's industry: Colbert asked"Que faut-il faire pour vous aider?" "Nous laisser faire,"[1] Legendre responded.

That same system of taxation also had the merit of incentivizing the modernization of agriculture. To recover the money spent for taxes, landowners (who were primarily aristocrats) had reason to devise new technologies that, by increasing the net product of the harvest, would consequently increase their revenue.

Furthermore, the physiocrats were the first to consider **wealth as a variable flow** rather than as a stock of goods. What does that mean? In difference with the mercantilists who, as we have seen, measured the wealth of a country on the basis of the gold and precious metals it possessed, the physiocrats held that a country's wealth should be measured by the income (the *produit net*) an economic system was able to produce each year.

This distinction between stocks and flow remains basic to economics. Even today the wealth of a country is not measured by stocks — that is, on the basis of the gold held in bank vaults, or by the quantity of raw materials possessed or other material goods — but rather on the basis of its gross domestic product, or the quantity of goods and services a given country can produce in a year. GDP can be considered the heir of the physiocrats' original *produit net*, which as we saw measured the surplus a country produces from year to year. Despite the fact that the *Tableau économique* was a very elementary representation of a country's real economy, physiocracy remains the first economic school that attempted to define a true theory, or an all-encompassing abstract vision, of the economy.

1.16 The common elements of classical economic thought

Industrial capitalism spread through Europe between the end of the 18th century and the first half of the 19th century. Britain was the leading country in that era; the Industrial Revolution took hold there and then spread to the rest of Europe.

The invention of the steam engine, the exploitation of new forms of energy, and improvements in transportation led to profound changes not only in the economic sphere, but in the social sphere as well. Establishing the first industrial settlements and opening factories not only increased the production of goods that, thanks to new technological discoveries, could be produced in greater number at lower cost, it also transformed craftsmen into workers. Economic thought arose in this altered historical scenario. Below we summarize the common elements that, with appropriate caveats, represent the basic principles around which the economic theories of the various classical schools of thought developed. We will present these in more detail in subsequent sections.

---

1. "What can be done to assist you?" "(Leave us alone and) let us work." Loosely, Legendre's response has the sense of "Let it happen."

Economic liberalism. *Economic liberalism is the economic theory that rejects all intervention by the state, based on the principle that economic agents should be free to make the decisions they deem most appropriate.*

The "laissez faire" principle. *This presupposes a natural order in which an economic system, if left to itself, automatically tends towards full employment.*

The principle of self-interest. *Based on the principle of self-interest, by producing and trading to enrich themselves individuals contribute towards enriching society at the same time.*

Say's law (or the law of markets). *According to Jean Baptiste Say's law, a French economist (1767—1832), the production of goods and the consequent creation of income create demand that allows selling everything produced.*

The labor theory of value. *According to the labor theory of value, the value of a good depends on the amount of labor that went into producing it.*

The division of society into well-defined social classes. *Classical economics conceived of society as being divided into three major classes:*

Entrepreneurs, or Capitalists, *as the owners of the means of production. They organized production in exchange for compensation, called profit, which is the portion of the product that is due to the capitalist for having organized production and advanced the capital for paying workers' wages and purchasing raw materials to process. Profit is defined as a residual; that is, it is the difference between the proceeds from the sales of the goods produced on the one hand, and wages and rent on the other.*

Landowners. *They rented land to entrepreneurs and received compensation in return, called* rent;

Workers, also called the proletariat, *in that their children (prole) were their only property. They received a remuneration for work performed, called* wages. *Wages were set at a* subsistence level, *or the price at which wages tend to stabilize.*

As we will see, these principles are present, although with the appropriate distinctions, in both the Scottish and Italian classical schools we will discuss in the following sections.

1.16.1 Economists…But not just economists

A common characteristic of the founders of modern economics was a vision of the economy as a dimension of social life that was never separated from the others, and in particular from politics, law, and ethics; this is why economic analysis is also political and social analysis. At least a half-century passed before the economy began to be a separate, independent area from the others. Thus over time economic science has evolved somewhat like an hourglass: in the beginning its area of investigation was broad and ranged from analyzing human sentiments to political choices, then during the 19th century its field of observation was restricted, so that by the end of the century it became quite narrow. Since the turn of the 20th century, however, its fields of interest have again broadened, and the topics covered by economists are more or less the same as those covered by Smith and Genovesi — although with very different methods and tools (Frame 1.1).

1.17 The Scottish school: Adam Smith

Adam Smith, the philosopher and economist who was the most famous and prestigious proponent of classical economics, was born in Scotland in 1723 and lived until 1790. For several years Smith taught logic and philosophy at the University of Glasgow, giving ample space to law and economics in his lectures.

His most important philosophical work, *The Theory of Moral Sentiments* (1759), was not all that successful at the time of its publication, but recently it has been widely reconsidered by philosophers as well as economists. The central concept in the work is *sympathy*, that is, the ability to identify oneself with others' thoughts and situations. For Smith, sympathy is the basis of the moral judgments of approval or disapproval of others' behavior; it is also the basis of happiness, which in Smith's opinion originates when we attune ourselves with someone else's feelings.

Smith's most important economic work is *An Inquiry into the Nature and Causes of the Wealth of Nations* (1776). It is considered the first systematic text on political economy, through which Smith influenced economists throughout the 19th century, and in some respects it continues to inspire economists today. The work contains Smith's economic theory, which we summarize in the following key ideas:

> Wealth is not created either from gold or land, but from labor. *Smith developed a theory that distinguishes him from the mercantilists and the physiocrats. According to Smith, labor is the source of all wealth and the value of goods.*

FRAME 1.1 Praise for trade

The classical economists' idea of trade and commercial exchange in the 18th century is profoundly different from that of the mercantilists; indeed, they maintained that trade enriched all parties involved. A country that trades is not only wealthy, it is also civil, because trade by its nature requires a climate of trust and an absence of conflict, and thus it makes people more refined and virtuous. We find this reading in a passage from Adam Smith, the Scottish economist considered by many to be the father of modern economics:

Whenever commerce is introduced into any country, probity and punctuality always accompany it. These virtues in a rude and barbarous country are almost unknown. Of all the nations in Europe, the Dutch, the most commercial, are the most faithful to their word. The English are more so than the Scotch, but much inferior to the Dutch.

Smith, 1978 [1763], p. 538

We find a similar concept in the words of Antonio Genovesi, another economist who lived in Naples, in the far south of Europe; in 1754 he held the first chair of economics in history, entitled the "Chair of Commerce and Mechanics."

I have heard it said among us that we have no trade. This means that the 800,000 families in this kingdom do not form a civic body. Now anyone who says this is a person without a head.

Genovesi, 2005 [1765], I, ch. 16, § VI, p. 513

The jurist Gaetano Filangieri, who followed Genovesi's economic teachings at the Federico II University in Naples, also maintained that the market has a civilizing role in society. In fact, Filangieri held that it brings about and develops people's fundamental rights. Filangieri, as did Genovesi, espoused the Aristotelian vision of the economy. He held that happiness does not consist in the accumulation of wealth as an end in itself; to the contrary, a person should consider money exclusively as a *means* for living a comfortable life in order to be able to concentrate on what makes life good, that is, developing the civil virtues.

When [wealth] is only the fruit of conquest, when it is not the sweat of the farmer, the laborer, or the merchant that calls it forth, wealth necessarily corrupts people, foments idleness, and accelerates the ruin of the nations... But the present state of things is entirely different. Today it is no longer the spoils, the tribute of subjugated peoples, alliances sold, kings' lavish titles, which Caesar, Pompey, and the Roman patricians sold to the highest bidder — these are not, I say, the means by which the wealth of nations is called forth. Today the wealthiest nations are those where the citizens work harder and are more free. Thus wealth today need no longer be feared, rather, it is to be desired; the main purpose of the laws should be to call it forth, since it sustains people's happiness, political liberty outside the states, and civil liberty within them.

Filangieri, 2003 [1780], pp. 66–67

> *The annual labor of each nation is the basis from which we derive all of life's necessities and conveniences.*

Taking a cue from the physiocrats, Smith distinguished between productive and unproductive labor; it is no accident that this distinction appeared only after returning from a trip to France, although how he used it differed somewhat from the physiocrats.

Moreover, his concept of labor was that it is entirely mechanical and repetitive, which multiplies and amplifies the productivity of labor, and thus the wealth of nations; this was another significant concept introduced by Smith, even though it was not entirely unprecedented, as we also find it in Verri (Frame 1.2).

> The distinction between use value and exchange value. *As we have seen, Aristotle distinguished between two different uses of a good. A pair of shoes, for example, can be used for walking; in this case the shoes have a "use value." The same shoes, however, can be used not for walking, but to exchange for another good; in this case they have an "exchange value."*
>
> *Use value depends on the ability of a good to satisfy the need of a single individual, which is why it varies in relation to people's needs and tastes; for example, the same shoe can be variously appreciated by different people.*
>
> *Exchange value corresponds to the price of a good; it is based on objective data, since it derives from market supply and demand. Exchange value is thus more stable, since it depends on the labor necessary to produce it.*

According to Smith, these two values do not always coincide. To explain this he adopted the so-called "paradox of water and diamonds": water has high use value but no exchange value; the opposite happens with diamonds, which have a high exchange value but a very low use value (see Frame 1.3).

Economists subsequently called use value "utility," and exchange value "price." Given the variability and subjectivity of use value — and thus its unpredictability — Smith chose exchange value, which is more objective since it is tied to the quantity of human labor with respect to subjective utility. But which type of labor?

> Embodied labor and commanded labor. *According to Smith, the price of a good does not always coincide with the labor that went into making it.*
>
> **Embodied labor** *measures the value of a good based on the labor necessary to make it. This can only be true in what he called a "primitive society," that is, in a society that precedes the private ownership of resources, and in particular capital and land rent.*
>
> *For example, if it takes two hours to capture a beaver and four hours to capture a deer, we can state that the price of a deer is effectively twice that of a beaver. In this case labor, which we indicate by W (from "wage"), is equal to price, or W = P.*

FRAME 1.2 The pin factory and the division of labor

Smith noted that the production of goods was greatly facilitated by the division and specialization of labor.

To take an example, therefore, from a very trifling manufacture; but one in which the division of labor has been very often taken notice of, the trade of the pin-maker; a workman not educated to this business (which the division of labor has rendered a distinct trade), nor acquainted with the use of the machinery employed in it (to the invention of which the same division of labor has probably given occasion), could scarce, perhaps, with his utmost industry, make one pin in a day, and certainly could not make twenty. But in the way in which this business is now carried on, not only the whole work is a peculiar trade, but it is divided into a number of branches, of which the greater part are likewise peculiar trades. One man draws out the wire, another straights it, a third cuts it, a fourth points it, a fifth grinds it at the top for receiving the head; to make the head requires two or three distinct operations; to put it on, is a peculiar business, to whiten the pins is another; it is even a trade by itself to put them into the paper; and the important business of making a pin is, in this manner, divided into about eighteen distinct operations, which, in some manufactories, are all performed by distinct hands, though in others the same man will sometimes perform two or three of them. I have seen a small manufactory of this kind where ten men only were employed, and where some of them consequently performed two or three distinct operations. But though they were very poor, and therefore but indifferently accommodated with the necessary machinery, they could, when they exerted themselves, make among them about twelve pounds of pins in a day. There are in a pound upwards of four thousand pins of a middling size. Those ten persons, therefore, could make among them upwards of forty-eight thousand pins in a day. Each person, therefore, making a 10th part of forty-eight thousand pins, might be considered as making four thousand eight hundred pins in a day. But if they had all wrought separately and independently, and without any of them having been educated to this peculiar business, they certainly could not each of them have made twenty, perhaps not one pin in a day; that is, certainly, not the two hundred and fortieth, perhaps not the four thousand eight hundredth part of what they are at present capable of performing, in consequence of a proper division and combination of their different operations.

Smith, 1982 [1776], pp. 14—15

In every other art and manufacture, the effects of the division of labor are similar to what they are in this very trifling one; though, in many of them, the labor can neither be so much subdivided, nor reduced to so great a simplicity of operation. The division of labor, however, so far as it can be introduced, occasions, in every art, a proportional increase of the productive powers of labor.

Smith's position on the benefits of the division of labor merits further development and discussion. He enthusiastically evaluated the division of labor; indeed, he saw it exclusively as a means of increasing production. When the American entrepreneur Henry Ford began mass producing cars in the early 20th century, he applied the method of the division of labor as conceived by Smith. In so doing Ford was able to reduce the price of a car from 1000 to 600 dollars, while at the same time increasing production from ten thousand to one million per year. This success encouraged the spread of "Fordism," which for most of the 20th century became the organizational model of every factory.

Continued

Frame 1.2 The pin factory and the division of labor—cont'd

However, sociologists of labor have observed that the division and speciali-zation of labor are the basis of workers' alienation. Where a craftsman understands the entire production cycle, which depends entirely on his manual ability, the modern worker knows only a small fragment.

Smith, 1982 [1776], pp. 14–15

FRAME 1.3 The paradox of water and diamonds

In The Wealth of Nations Smith wondered how it is possible that water, which is so useful for life, had such a low price while diamonds, which are totally useless, had reached very high prices.

"The things which have the greatest value in use have frequently little or no value in exchange; and on the contrary, those which have the greatest value in exchange have frequently little or no value in use. Nothing is more useful than water: but it will purchase scarce anything; scarce anything can be had in ex-change for it. A diamond, on the contrary, has scarce any value in use; but a very great quantity of other goods may frequently be had in exchange for it." (Smith 1982 [1776], I.IV. p. 44–5). This paradox can be explained by introducing the concept of scarcity into the reasoning. Water is certainly necessary for life, but it is abundant; consequently it has a low value, despite its immense importance for the survival of the species.

When other figures are introduced into this "model" of the primitive world, for example capitalists who own the hunting tools (bows, arrows, etc.) and landowners of the forests where hunts are held, the price of the goods (beavers and deer) no longer includes just the labor in hunting hours necessary to produce them, but also a return on the capital and the land. These price components added to the embodied labor represent additional types of compensation, which from Smith onward are called respectively **profit**, or compensation of capital, and **rent**, or land compensation.

Thus in a society that has advanced beyond its primitive stages — what a few decades later Karl Marx would call a "capitalist society" — price no longer coincides with the embodied labor, or the "remuneration" of labor (i.e., wages, W) as it was called; it also includes profits (which we indicate by Π) and rent (R). In a market economy, the price will be equal to:

$$P = W + \Pi + R$$

Smith identified this algebraic sum as the **natural price**, or the simple cost of production of goods.

*The **natural price** of a good corresponds to its cost of production. This concept closely resembles the "just price" of St. Thomas Aquinas (we should not forget* *that Smith, a philosopher, knew well the works of Aristotle, St. Thomas, and all the debates on just price and usury).*

However, in the market the natural price is rarely the "market price," or the actual price of goods at a particular moment; the market price emerges from the intersection of the demand for a good with its supply (concepts we will take up later), which depends on various transient and local elements.

*The **market price** of a good corresponds to the effective price of a good on the market at a particular time.*

Using Newtonian terminology (at that time it was in vogue to metaphorically explain economic phenomena with terms taken from physics), according to Smith the natural price is the central price towards which the prices of goods "gravitate."

For example, if in a given year and particular place a vine disease occurs that greatly reduces their quantity, it is likely that the price of wine will increase in that area because there will be few bottles on the market (recall the principle of scarcity that drives up the price of diamonds). This increase in the price of bottles of wine happens in the market price, while the natural price, or the cost the winemaker must bear to bottle the wine, remains unchanged.

For Smith, price in a market economy does not embody labor alone, so he invented a new and somewhat mysterious term, **commanded labor**, which corresponds to the quantity of labor a good is able to "command," or purchase, on the market. What does that mean? If a pair of shoes costs 10 pounds sterling and labor costs a pound per hour, we can write:

$$P = 5(W) + 2(\Pi) + 3(R)$$

In this case the embodied labor is 5, but with the proceeds from selling the pair of shoes on the market, its owner will be able to "command," or buy, an additional 10 h of labor. This is why Smith wrote:

Labor measures the value not only of that part of price which resolves itself into labor, but of that which resolves itself into rent, and of that which resolves itself into profit

Smith, 1982 [1776], p. 46

This theory of value has generated thousands of articles, long disputes, and heated debates; it is also the basis of Marx's theory of the exploitation of workers.

Self-interest. *Another key concept in Smith is self-interest. In a famous passage in* The Wealth of Nations *Smith wrote:*

It is not from the benevolence of the butcher, the brewer, or the baker, that we expect our dinner, but from their regard to their own interest. We address ourselves, not to their humanity but to their self-love, and never talk to them of our own necessities but of their advantages.

Smith 1982 [1776], p. 26–7

According to Smith, this means that the market does not require "benevolence," or love of and for others; for it to function well it is sufficient that people look after their own interests.

Although at first glance Smith seems to offer a negative view of human nature, looking closely we see that he wanted to emphasize independence from the benevolence of our fellow citizens as a virtue; developing this virtue is made possible precisely by this new form of relationship in a market economy.

Since they are impersonal, market relationships allow us to satisfy our needs without having to depend on others' benevolence or magnanimity. This is why, according to Smith, **the market has a civilizing function**: it is a means that enables us to free ourselves from others without needing to depend on them in the same way beggars *depend* on others' benevolence for their lunch.

More generally, according to Smith the market liberates human beings from the servitude that was the basis of the feudal system, which on the contrary was characterized by a few benefactors (aristocrats, the clergy, and large estate owners) and many people (vassals and serfs) who were dependent on the largesse of the few.

As Smith stressed in *The Wealth of Nations*, the market allows us to depend on the many, and at the same time, on no one:

> *Each tradesman or artificer derives his subsistence from the employment, not of one, but of a hundred or a thousand different customers. Though in some measure obliged to them all, therefore, he is not absolutely dependent upon any one of them.*
>
> Smith, 1982 [1776], III.IV, p. 420

By seeking their own advantage ("their own vain and insatiable desires"), wealthy landowners employ servants, laborers, cooks, and craftsmen to produce lavish meals and luxury goods. This is why Smith maintained that the **market economy** is not only more efficient than the closed system of the feudal economy (recall the principles of the division of labor and free exchange), but it is also superior from an ethical point of view because it liberates people from dependency relationships, which were typical of the feudal era (whether to the clan, the feudal lord, or the head of the household).

However, Smith is equally aware that the market — this new form of relationship between anonymous and self-interested individuals — can impoverish social relations, and consequently produce unhappiness and loneliness. If for Smith it was sufficient that individuals pursue their own self-interest in order to bring about the wealth of the nations, in *The Theory of Moral Sentiments* he made it quite clear that

> *How selfish soever man may be supposed, there are evidently some principles in his nature, which interest him in the fortune of others, and render their happiness necessary to him.*
>
> Smith, 1984 [1759], I.I.1, p. 9

The widespread development of markets over the past two centuries clearly shows this collateral effect.

1.17.1 The invisible hand

For his self-interest based model to work, however, Smith needed an additional element. Who can assure us that many people (butchers, brewers, and farmers) seeking their various personal interests will in fact automatically produce social order, wealth, and general well-being instead of chaos, conflict, and widespread malaise?

To describe the benefits of free, self-interested individual initiative, Smith introduced the concept of the **invisible hand** ("they are led by an invisible hand to…without intending it, without knowing it, advance the interest of society," (Smith, 1984 [1759], IV.I.1, pp. 184–185)); this is an image we also find in 1751 in another author, Ferdinando Galiani of Naples, who was part of the classical school of economics.

The *emulation* of the rich and powerful by other citizens in their service is the primary passion that motivates people and entire populations; it is the most powerful mechanism for producing wealth and the common good. This desire to imitate others leads simple people to work ever harder so they can be able to one day afford the same wealth as the people for whom they work. Smith gave the example of the poor man's son who endures great fatigue, working night and day to be able to acquire greater talents than his competitors.

This passion to accumulate wealth — which, recalling King Midas' end, we might almost call morbid — rests on a psychological mechanism of which individuals are unconscious victims; Smith called the idea that the rich are happier, and thus that becoming more wealthy and powerful means being happier, *self-deception*. For Smith this idea was completely false, since the happiness of the wealthy is actually not much different from that of the poor.

Smith added, however, that behind the image of the invisible hand was a widespread sense of confidence in a "sound reason," which Smith sometimes called "Providence," that devised the world in such a way that individuals acting in their own self-interest contribute to the common good, or the wealth of the nation, without either wanting or knowing that they do so — as long as the economic and social system are well organized through appropriate institutions and laws that ensure fundamental rights (such as life, liberty, property, public order, and justice) and safeguard their free exercise.

1.18 The Neapolitan school: the civil economy of Genovesi and Filangieri

All the major capitals of the Italian Enlightenment, from Venice to Florence to Milan, were vital, important centers in developing the nascent science of economics; Naples, together with Milan, assumed a leading role. The

Neapolitan school of civil economy should be understood within the entire Neapolitan culture, which in the early decades of the 18th century was one of the most active and important in Europe. "**Civil economy**" was the expression that **Antonio Genovesi** chose for his principal economic treatise, called *Lezioni di economia civile* (Lessons in Civil Economy, 1765).

In this work Genovesi expressed the idea of the *economy as a place of civility and as a civilizing means for improving people's "well-living."* Indeed, a key term in the Neapolitan school was "trust," or better yet "public faith," which was considered the real precondition of economic development; this was absent in Smith, who as we recall also maintained that the market was a place of civility.

Indeed, in difference with Smith, according to Genovesi self-interest alone does not automatically lead to the proper functioning of the market. For example, Genovesi cited the disastrous situation of the Kingdom of Naples at that time; despite the fact that it was a populous nation with plenty of workers, with a mild climate and lands that readily adapted to growing various crops, and with good access to the sea, which was ideal for commercial trade, it had not progressed at the same pace as other European nations, or at least the other cities in the Italian peninsula.

Genovesi identified the reason for the poverty and unhappiness of the Kingdom of Naples as the lack of *public decency (buon costume)*, or the *basic civil virtue that consists of mutual respect and respect for the common good*, among its populace.

This concept was asserted anew a little later by the jurist **Gaetano Filangieri**, for whom the primary resources of a nation are "confidence in the government, the magistrates, and in other citizens." Thus for the civil economy tradition "public faith" was people's primary resource, and for economic development as well.

If it is in fact true that the expansion of markets contributes to developing the civil virtues in a populace, in *Scienzadellalegislazione* (The Science of Legislation, 1780) Filangieri emphasized that, for the civil economy, if public faith is not *cultivated* then markets do not develop and the economy remains at a standstill:

nothing is more necessary than public faith for widespread and ready commercial traffic...Confidence is the soul of trade...without which all the pieces that make up the edifice collapse on their own

Filangieri, 2003 [1780], lesson 10, ch. 10, p. 5

Genovesi also commented on the nature of trust:

This word fides *means a cord that binds together and unites. Public faith is thus the bond of families united in a shared life*

Genovesi, 2005 [1765], p. 751

And finally, happiness. Genovesi and the Neapolitans used the expressions "civil economy" and "public happiness" synonymously. For Genovesi, happiness is social in nature: *people can be wealthy even by themselves, but to be happy two or more are required.* This is why, if we wish to be happy, we must take the happiness of others to heart as well.

The following is the central passage from which we can immediately understand this aspect of Genovesi's idea of happiness:

You labor for your own interest. No person could act other than for his happiness; such a one would be less human. Yet do not desire to cause misery to others; if you can, and when you can, studiously try to make others happy. The more one works for one's own interest, so much the more, if one be not mad, must one be virtuous. It is a law of the universe that one cannot make oneself happy without making others happy

Genovesi, 1962 [1756], p. 449

Giacinto Dragonetti (1738–1818) is another relevant author of the Neapolitan School. His book 'Delle virtù e de I premi' (on virtues and awards, 1766) was translated in many languages (often together with On crimes and punishments of Beccaria), and cited by T. Paine in his Common Sense, a classic of America's independence.

1.19 The Milan school: Verri, Beccaria, and civil competition

In Milan, the nexus between civil life and public happiness became the central theme of the nascent Lombard school. Its main thinkers were Pietro Verri and Cesare Beccaria, and later Gian Domenico Romagnosi and Carlo Cattaneo; they made Milan one of the capitals of the Italian Enlightenment and the civil economy tradition.

Where public faith was the core theme of the Neapolitan school of civil economy, the Milanese school gave particular attention to the role of "**civil**

competition" in public happiness, as well as the importance of civil society being highly principled lest it perish or its political power collapse.

Pietro Verri, a contemporary of Genovesi, is without doubt the leading figure of this school. All the themes of the Italian classical economics tradition are present in his philosophical and economic thought. These are:

- the role of the virtues;
- wealth understood as a means, not an end;
- praise for trade as civilizing and peaceful;
- trust (or "good faith") as the precondition for developing trade.

In particular, two themes of the civil tradition were especially close to the hearts of the Milanese: the role of *just laws for public happiness* and *the importance attributed to the creativity and intelligence of the person* in creating the value of goods.

It is thus not surprising that Verri was the one who inspired the most famous book of the Italian Enlightenment, **Cesare Beccaria**'s *Dei delitti e dellepene* (*On Crimes and Punishments*), published in 1764, that launched the idea — revolutionary for its time — of the incompatibility between civil life and the death penalty:

> *The death penalty cannot be useful, because of the example of barbarity it gives men....It seems to me absurd that the laws, which are an expression of the public will, which detest and punish homicide, should themselves commit it, and that to deter citizens from murder, they order a public one*
>
> Beccaria, 1963 [1764], Paolucci, trans. p. 50

Beccaria's work greatly influenced the entire European Enlightenment; for example, reading this work led Pietro Leopoldo, the Archduke of Tuscany, to abolish the death penalty and torture in his realm on November 30, 1786, because "those things are useful for barbarous peoples."

Gian Domenico Romagnosi, another Milanese author who wrote alternatively on economics and law, was also convinced that no civil economy could exist without civil laws. *Incivilimento* ("becoming civilized") was the slogan of his economic and social vision, and in a certain sense the last word of the tradition as it transitioned into the 19th century. A good government should aim not primarily at economic growth but rather at civilizing its populace, since privileging economic growth over civil growth would necessarily mean producing breakdowns in society. Thus according to Romagnosi, it is better to have less economic growth but to do so *all together*, so that, thanks also to good laws, the civil virtues and public trust can sustain the impact of expanding economic interests.

> *The boundless yearning of the individual to become wealthy is moderated, although not weakened, by the ceaseless action of a well-constructed civil society, so that if on the one hand we see selfishness and boundless individual immoderation, on the other we also see participation and social equity.*
>
> Romagnosi, 1839

The second point typical of the Milanese school is no less interesting and innovative: the **role of creativity** and human intelligence. In the 19th century Carlo Cattaneo was primarily the one who developed economic thought that criticized British economists, who had identified productive factors as the key elements of economic growth. Cattaneo posited instead the intelligent person as the causal factor in economic development. In a passage from one of his 1859 studies, *Frammenti di filosofiacivile (Fragments of Civil Philosophy —* yet again that magical adjective, "civil"), we read:

> *There is no labor, no capital, that does not begin with an act of intelligence. Prior to all labor and capital…intelligence is what begins the work and, for the first time, impresses the character of wealth into them*
>
> Cattaneo, 2001 [1861], p. 58

With the Milanese school the emphasis on human sociality, which was primarily emphasized by the Neapolitan school, thus joined with the other pillar of Western, humanistic, and Christian culture: *the value of the person placed at the center of society and the economy*. The person is the one who, with her creativity and intelligence, enters into relationship with others and with things and confers value — and economic value as well — to goods; this was a surprisingly prophetic proposal for its time, and one that is very timely for ours.

Romagnosi and Cattaneo were the last prominent Italian proponents of the civil tradition. Due primarily to Francesco Carrara's work, after 1850 Italian economic thought distanced itself from its classical tradition, which was considered too unscientific and analytic in that positivism-influenced cultural climate, to turn its gaze to France and Britain; this eclipsed the Italian civil tradition, and that eclipse is only now coming to an end.

1.20 A century of Smithean economics

The history of economic thought shows that the Italian school is not what influenced the development of official economic theory; Smith was the central protagonist of the century that spanned from his 1776 work to the so-called "neoclassical revolution" of 1870; we will soon have more to say about that. Indeed, subsequent economic theories rest on the principles Smith systematically laid out for the first time.

1.20.1 Ricardo's theory of land rent

Among the economists who succeeded Smith, **David Ricardo** (1772—1823) was the most influential of his generation. The son of a stockbroker, he was enormously successful in the stock market. With the money gained from his speculative activity he bought various plots of land and lived comfortably off their rent for the rest of his life.

Ricardo's thought is fully situated in the classical setting Smith had opened up. As did Smith, he supported liberal ideas and the advantages of the division of labor, which extended from trade between individuals to trade between states. In the history of economic thought Ricardo is primarily remembered for his theories on international trade, that is, the **theory of land rent** and the **theory of relative costs** (which we will analyze in detail in Chapter 10, Section 9), through which he demonstrated the opportunities of international trade (which, as we recall, is one of the foundational principles of classical economics).

With his theory of land rent Ricardo rigorously demonstrated that had the British government not lifted a protectionist policy of grain import tariffs, the economy would have become stationary, and then gone into crisis, caused by *decreasing land rents*. He thus sided in favor of importing grain from France, which for centuries was a rival of Britain in the European panorama.

Let us now analyze Ricardo's theory of land rent more closely in the following logical steps:

1. Land, according to Ricardo, has the following characteristic: the first type of land cultivated (the most fertile) produces a quantity a of grain, the second (a little less fertile) produces a quantity b, the third (even less fertile) produces a quantity c, and so forth;
2. $a > b > c$, thus if foreign grain is not exported because the state has adopted protectionist measures and imposed import tariffs, it is forced to cultivate less fertile lands that are poorly adapted to agriculture (Ricardo called them "marginal"), yielding less grain;
3. The increased demand for arable land provokes an increase in the price of rent;
4. The increase in the demand for land and its greater difficulties in cultivation, because it is less fertile, entails employing more workers and provoking an increase in wages;
5. Since, as we saw in Section 1.16, profit is a residual — in our example determined by the difference between revenue from grain sales on the one hand, and salaries and rent on the other — in the end there is no profit, which, according to Ricardo and all the classical economists, is the only real driver of economic growth. The entire economic system would become stationary, and then go into crisis.

Through the theory of decreasing rents Ricardo provided the theoretical justifications in support of keeping imports open (of grain in the case of Britain in that era), which would have the effect of reducing rents and simultaneously of increasing profits, and thus savings and the accumulation of wealth. His economic theory also demonstrates his intellectual integrity, as he was a wealthy landowner.

According to the **theory of decreasing rents**, an increase in the quantity of labor employed for grain production results in a less than proportional growth in grain produced.

Ricardo applied the law of decreasing rents to land as a productive factor. Economists subsequently extended this law to all productive factors, that is, not just to land, but also to labor and capital. Achille Loria (1857−1945) was the most original and relevant economist taking on Ricardo's theory of rent one century later, claiming that in 20th century the most important conflict was not (unlike Marxists) wage vs profit but rent vs profit.

1.20.2 Malthus and population theory

Thomas Robert Malthus, a contemporary of Ricardo, was another protagonist of classical economic thought. Malthus, a priest in the Anglican church, is best known for his 1798 work *An Essay on the Principle of Population*. In it he laid out his **population theory**, according to which population grows more rapidly than resources.

Malthus's thesis is simple: food increases arithmetically (2, 4, 6, 8, 10…) while population increases geometrically (2, 4, 8, 16…). Malthus argued that if that is true (and the data seem to confirm his hypothesis), then natural and unstoppable population growth would lead to progressive impoverishment (Malthus, 2008 [1798]).

In the past, Malthus stated, such a collapse had been avoided due to wars, epidemics, and plagues that had decimated the population. Paradoxically, Malthus thought that the absence of such calamities would lead to the same outcome, in that an economic policy designed to shield the populace from the tragedies of wars and epidemics would lead humanity into poverty due to lack of food. So what should we do?

According to Malthus the solution was certainly not to prefer wars and epidemics (he was a priest, after all!), but to adopt means that would permit controlling demographics, such as recommending abstinence and inviting women to marry later, in order to reduce the birth rate.

Malthus' theory did not sufficiently account for technological development, which changed the progression rate in food production; however, his message regarding the relationship between population and food is coming back to the fore in the current environmental crisis due to the problems it causes both in food production and in population dynamics.

John Stuart Mill (1806–73) is another figure we should recall who impacted the history of economic thought in that era. He was an economist and philosopher who is also famous for being the first "feminist" philosopher in history. In his work *The Subjection of Women* (1869), he proposed giving women the vote, or universal suffrage, and the possibility of their entering the labor market to free them from dependence on their husbands.

Mill, the son of James Mill, a friend of Ricardo, took up **Jeremy Bentham**'s theories; Bentham was the founder of *utilitarianism*, a philosophical system centered around the concept of "utility," which heavily influenced neoclassical economics, as we will see in Chapter 8.

Mill distinguished himself from other classical economists in that, although he was a committed liberal, he maintained that the state should have an active role in the economy in support of the poor, education, and improving workers' conditions in the factories.

1.20.3 Marx and his criticism of the classical economic system

Calling the German author **Karl Marx** (1818–83) just an economist is reductive. He studied law, philosophy (he was part of the school of the German philosopher Hegel), and economics. He moved to Paris in 1844, where he began focusing on economics and on formulating his initial arguments on the *alienation* of labor. He returned to Germany, where in 1848 he wrote the *Communist Manifesto*. Expelled from Germany in 1849, he moved to London, where he worked for several years on writing the work for which he is best known, *Capital*; the first volume was issued in 1867. His critique of the system of classical economics is the central thesis of the work. His fiercest criticisms were directed against Smith's theory of value and his theory of profit, in which workers contribute only a part of the value of a good (*W*). Marx showed instead that the product of a day's labor is significantly higher than the wage paid to the worker by the capitalist; for Marx, *workers created the entire value of goods*. Based on that, he argued that profit is theft from the workers: capitalists appropriate for themselves the unpaid labor that Marx called a **surplus** (Marx, 1970 [1867]). Marx maintained that capitalism was thus a profoundly unjust system because it was based on the oppression of the working class by the capitalist class. For Marx, a communist society is a just society — that is, a society in which the entire value of production returns to the workers (Marx and Engels, 2008 [1848]).

We must not misunderstand Marx's criticism of Smith's theories of profit and the labor theory of value. In *Capital* Marx did not reject the principle that the value of goods is given by the labor necessary to produce them; on the contrary, he elaborated his theory of surplus value starting from the premise that the value of goods is essentially represented by the workers' labor.

Marx's criticism of the market economy is the most radical ever formulated in the history of ideas, which neither the development of capitalism during the last century nor the collapse of Communism have entirely refuted. This is why Marx continues to inspire the thought and action of many scholars even today.

1.21 Neoclassical economics

As we have seen, in the century following Smith economic science developed along the lines of Smith's seminal ideas; economics is about the wealth of nations rather than about individuals, growth, income, and international trade. However, economic science took a radical turn from 1870 to 1900 that left it greatly changed, almost distorted, so much so that it is called the **neoclassical revolution**.

Economic science became universal (for example, the American economists came on the scene), and under the influence of positivist ideology, adopted mathematics as its preferred language for expressing its methods. **Positivism** is a philosophical orientation that emerged in France and spread throughout the rest of Europe in the second half of the 19th century. It identifies knowledge based on empirical data and the scientific method as the sole legitimate form of knowledge about reality. Economists are no longer primarily philosophers — as were Smith, J.S. Mill, and Marx, for example — but rather mathematicians.

We summarize below the main elements of neoclassical economics.

Economists' main focus of study is no longer the wealth of nations, but the behavior of the individual. From an analysis of the system as a whole, such as labor, wealth, development, and trade, attention has shifted towards analyzing individual behaviors, such as choice, individual utility, and preferences. Where the classical focus of study was essentially the wealth of nations, the neoclassical focus is on individual satisfaction. This is why the name of the discipline changed from "political economy," which derived from the public nature of the subject matter, to "economics," or the science of choices.

Utility theory of value. The value of a good is no longer determined by the amount of labor necessary to produce it, as the classical economists thought, but from the utility that a person can obtain from it. The viewpoint shifts from the producer to the consumer.

The use of mathematics to represent economic theories. Until the neoclassical revolution the language of economists was prose or logic, not mathematics. At most one might find a few graphs or simple arithmetic formulas in their works, but discourse was the primary means used to persuade each other. When economists began using the language of mathematics it had two main effects. The first was that, due to the excessively technical expressions (differential and integral calculus) that economists began using to write their economics books, there was a progressive separation between economists and political philosophers. The second was that economics became increasingly similar to the "hard" sciences, such as physics, and distanced itself from its philosophical origins (consider Smith and Genovesi, both of whom were philosophy professors).

Economics as an experimental science. As a direct consequence of its desire to become closer to physics and biology, economics became an experimental science based on facts. This is why, beginning with the second half of the 19th century, statistical research greatly expanded in economics.

1.21.1 The British school

Different national schools arose between 1870 and 1874 that, while taking their particularities into account, follow the generic traits that characterize neoclassical thought. **William Stanley Jevons** (1835–82), **Francis Ysidro Edgeworth** (1845–1926) and **Alfred Marshall** (1842–1924) are the main representatives of the British school.

In particular Jevons' work, *The Theory of Political Economy* (1870), is considered the manifesto of the neoclassical revolution. It contains the core principles of neoclassical theory, some of which are still currently considered as indisputable, such as the first principle that *people act for the purpose of seeking their maximum utility.* Jevons adopted this principle from the utilitarian political philosopher Jeremy Bentham.

Edgeworth followed along the same ideas as Jevons' work. He too was greatly influenced by Bentham's utilitarianism. He constructed a mathematical economic theory that started from the premise that human beings are "pleasure maximizers" (i.e., the hedonic principle); on the basis of that principle he derived all other economic laws, such as demand, exchange, and production. The title itself of his most successful work, *Mathematical Psychics* (1881), well represents the orientation the "new economics" was acquiring by applying mathematical science to feelings of pleasure.

Alfred Marshall (1842—1924) was another key protagonist of British neoclassical economic thought in the timeframe we are considering. In difference with his two British colleagues, he was less inclined to adopt Bentham's utilitarianism and was closest to the British classical economists. In his influential textbook *Principles of Economics* (1890), he attempted with some success to find a middle ground between the classical school and the innovations introduced by neoclassical economists. Finally, we should not forget Wicksteed (1844—1927), particularly for his "non tuism" theory (Wicksteed, 1910).

1.21.2 The Austrian school

During that dynamic season of economic thought, Austria also became one of the countries contributing to the new economics, although with some qualifications. In particular, although sharing a subjectivist and individualist approach with the rest of the neoclassical movement, Carl Menger (1840—1921, the founder of the school) and those following him up to the philosopher and economist **Friedrich von Hayek** (who won the Nobel Prize for economics in 1974) adopted neither utilitarianism nor the use of mathematics.

This is why, from a certain viewpoint, including the Austrians with the other neoclassical economists is somewhat forced. Nonetheless, economic thought traditionally considers Menger's *Principles of Economics* the second basic work in the neoclassical revolution.

1.21.3 The Lausanne school

Lausanne, Switzerland is the third country of the new economics; **Léon Walras** (1834–1920) is the person of reference in this case. A mathematical economist, in his *Elements of Pure Economics* he rewrote economic science based on the model of Newtonian physics. Walras offered the most elegant theory of his generation, known as the *general theory of economic equilibrium* (equilibrium is a concept in static physics). For at least one hundred years his theory has been the basis of economic theory throughout the world. He was not strongly influenced by utilitarianism; his entire logical framework depends on the concept of "marginal utility," which we will consider in Chapter 3, Section 4.

1.21.4 Pantaleoni and Pareto

Maffeo Pantaleoni (1857–1924) was one of the main Italian neoclassical economists, authoring *Pure Economics* in 1889. Translated into English and Spanish, Pantaleoni's work was one of the most influential of his generation. He built his new science of economics around a single theoretical framework based on the philosophical premise of *hedonism*: agents seek to maximize pleasure or minimize pain.

Vilfredo Pareto (1848–1923) was without doubt the most important Italian economist of that era (and perhaps ever). Walras's successor to the chair of economics in Lausanne, Pareto profoundly changed neoclassical economic science.

In his *Manual of Political Economy* (1906), he abandoned all reference to pleasure, utility, and utilitarian philosophy, topics which were the basis of the economic theories of the early neoclassical economists. By introducing his theory of **indifference curves** (which we will consider in Chapter 3), he founded the new economics that inspired 20th century economists and continues to inspire contemporary economists even today.

Pareto also introduced a new criterion for evaluating an economic situation. Previously, neoclassical economists, strongly influenced by utilitarian philosophy, utilized a criterion known as "sum ranking" when evaluating economic alternatives. In that approach the utilities of the various individuals involved are summed, and the choice with the highest result is the one to prefer, independently of the distribution of resources within the group of people considered.

For example, imagine comparing two economic policy choices: eliminate taxes on a primary household, or reduce taxes on gasoline. We hypothesize that there are three groups in the economic system — workers (L), entrepreneurs (I), and retired people (P) — and that the estimated effects of the two policies are the following:

$L = +4$	$L = +2$
$I = +2$	$I = +2$
$P = +2$	$P = +3$
Sum $= 8$	Sum $= 7$

The sum of individual utilities in choice A, 8, is greater than choice B, or 7. Thus neoclassical economists would prefer the economic policy of eliminating taxes on the primary household.

Pareto opposed this criterion for choosing for the simple reason that, according to his theory, it is impossible to sum individual utilities on a single scale of values (as can be done with temperatures or weights) because each individual has his own scale of preferences.

For Pareto, in economics we cannot measure utility, but only individuals' tastes or preferences, which cannot be added, subtracted, or compared between different people: What sense does it make to say that Frank likes fish twice as much as Joan?

This is why Pareto introduced a new criterion, known today as "Pareto optimality," which we can define as follows:

> *A situation (an economic state, or the situation following an economic policy choice) is defined as* **Pareto optimal** *only if at least one person is better off and no one is worse off.*

So, returning to our example, if we apply the criterion of Pareto optimality we cannot state that choice A is preferable to choice B, because in choice A retired people (P) are worse off ($+2$) than their condition in choice B ($+3$).

Pareto's criterion has helped distinguish economic from political and ethical considerations. With Pareto the hourglass (the metaphor we used at the beginning of our discussion) reached its narrowest point and widened out again in the 20th century.

About half of contemporary economics (what we are studying in this book) derives directly from Pareto; this fact alone is sufficient to understand the influence he has had in the history of economic thought.

1.21.5 20th century economics

We will only briefly mention 20th century economics, since current courses on microeconomics and macroeconomics teach contemporary economics; that is why we need not give it much space. We should add notes on two economists who were too important to not at least mention: **Joseph Alois Schumpeter** (1883–1950) and John Maynard Keynes (1883–1946), who were both born in the same year Marx died. Schumpeter authored many important works in the economic as well as the political thought of the 20th century.

His most important economics work is *The Theory of Economic Development*, published in 1911. In this small book the great Austrian economist proposed one of the most evocative and relevant economic theories of the 20th century by distinguishing between **innovative entrepreneurs** and **imitative entrepreneurs**.

The innovator breaks a static state of affairs in which there are neither profits nor losses; taking economic advantage of a new idea — a new product, a new market, a new productive process — she creates added value and growth, driving the economy forward. Then like a swarm of bees, other imitator entrepreneurs arrive who are attracted by the new profit opportunity, making that innovation their own. From that moment on, it will become an integral part of the entire market and society.

The economic system returns to equilibrium until other innovators come on the scene who move the economic development stakes further out, thanks to a new cycle of the innovation—imitation process, which is the real virtuous circle that creates wealth and growth. For Schumpeter then, entrepreneurs are not exploiters who makes a profit at the expense of workers, as Marx maintained, but *innovators*; profit is their reward for their innovative capacity.

John Maynard Keynes was a British economist in the Marshallian tradition (the so-called "Cambridge School"). Along with the neoclassical and Pareto, Keynes too is associated with a "revolution" for having brought economics back to the pivotal themes that give central place to persons and their choices to maximize their utility.

In 1936 Keynes published the most widely read and influential economics book of the 20th century, *The General Theory of Employment, Interest and Money*. The central message of the work, which constituted an ideal response to the great 1929 crisis, is twofold. According to Keynes:

1. First, the economy fundamentally depends on psychological elements, on *animal spirits*, rather than on individual rationality. Expectations, moods, and fears are the emotional elements on which the entire economy rests. Capitalism is thus unstable, as the crisis of his time demonstrated.

The second element regards the central role of the government in a country's economy. After more than a century of optimism in the "invisible hand" — a central principle of classical economics, or the ability of markets to self-regulate without the need for outside interventions — Keynes demonstrated that the market requires government intervention, particularly in times of crisis, which is expressed in two main tools of political economy: monetary policy and public spending. We will engage these topics more extensively in the second part of this work.

During the final decades of the 20th century Keynes' crucial message and his distrust of the anarchy of markets were forgotten in favor of a much more thoroughgoing liberalism (that is, an absolute trust in the self-regulating forces of the market), primarily in the USA and Britain. At the beginning of the third millennium, partly due to new crises of capitalism coupled with environmental questions, there is renewed interest in Keynes' message and in a particular *active role of the government in the economy* — not to act against markets, but rather in service to their proper operation, as we will have occasion to see over the course of the following chapters.

Further reading

Beccaria, C. (1963 [1764]). *Dei delitti e delle pene [On crimes and punishments], trans. Paolucci, H., Upper Saddle River* (p. 50). Library of Liberal Arts.

Boldizzoni, F. (2008). *Means and ends: The idea of capital in the West* (pp. 1500–1970). Springer.

Edgeworth, F. Y. (1881). *Mathematical Psychics*. London: Kegan & Co.

Jevons, W. S. (2013 [1870]). *The theory of political economy*. New York: Palgrave Macmillan.

Jonas, H. (1984). *The imperative of responsibility in search of an ethics for the technological age*. Chicago: University of Chicago Press.

Keynes, J. M. (1936). *The general theory of employment, interest and money*. Macmillan Cambridge University Press, for Royal Economic Society.

Malthus, T. R. (2008 [1798]). *An Essay on the principle of population*. Oxford: Oxford University Press.

Marshall, A. (2013 [1890]). *Principles of economics*. London: Palgrave Macmillan.

Marx, K. (1970 [1867]). *Capital*. London: Lawrence & Wishart.

Marx, K., & Engels, F. (2008 [1848]). *The communist manifesto*. Oxford: Oxford University Press.

Menger, C. (1950). *Principles of economics*. Glencoe, Illinois: Free Press.

Mill, J. S. (1988 [1869]). *The subjection of women*. Indianapolis: Hackett Publishing.

Pantaleoni, M. (1898 [1889]). *Pure economics*. London, New York: Macmillan.

Pareto, V. (2014 [1906]). In A. Montesano, A. Zanni, L. Bruni, J. S. Chipman, & M. McLure (Eds.), *Manual of political economy*. Oxford: Oxford University Press.

Pasinetti, L. L. (2007). *Keynes and the Cambridge Keynesians: A'revolution in Economics' to be Accomplished*. Cambridge University Press.

Schumpeter, J. A. (1934 [1911]). *The theory of economic development*. translated by Opie R. Cambridge: Harvard University Press

Screpanti, E., & Zamagni, S. (2007). *An outline oh th History of Economic Thought* (2nd ed..). Oxford: OUP.

Smith, A. (1978 [1763]). *Lectures on jurisprudence* (p. 538). Oxford: Clarendon Press.

Smith, A. (1982 [1776]). In R. H. Campbell, A. S. Skinner, W. B. Todd, & Indianapolis (Eds.), *The wealth of nations, Adam Smith, an inquiry into the nature and causes of the wealth of Nations,The Glasgow edition of the works of Adam Smith*. Liberty Fund. pp. 14–15, pp. 26–27, I.IV, pp. 44–5, p. 46, III.IV, p. 420.

Smith, A. (1984 [1759]). In D. D. Raphael, & A. L. Macfie (Eds.), *The theory of moral sentiments, the Glasgow edition of the works of Adam Smith* (pp. 184–185). Indianapolis: Liberty Fund, I.I.1. p. 9, IV.I.1.

Walras, L. (2003 [1899]). *Elements of pure economics*. translated by Jaffé W. Oxford, UK: Taylor & Francis.

Wicksteed, P. H. (1910). *The common sense of political economy*. London: Macmillan and Co.

Chapter 2

The market

2.1 Market: an abused term

The word "market" may be the most used and abused term in contemporary economic and political debate. In lively discussions between opposing parties, we find on one side those who accuse their counterparts of not having enough market culture to understand that promoting markets can not only stimulate economic growth, but also eliminate positional rents and inefficiencies by promoting merit. On the other side there are those who say that in the current socioeconomic system we run the risk of tying every aspect of life to the law of the market god, with dire consequences for the weakest and commodifying every dimension of human life.

One of the goals of economics students should be to understand exactly what the term "market" means and to reflect on its strengths and limitations. Rather than starting from an abstract definition, let us consider a few types of markets we can observe in real life. The first are the street markets we see from time to time in cities, with colorful stalls selling various products and animated discussions between supply (the sellers) and demand (the buyers). Potential buyers discuss products and bargain with vendors. If they come to terms after haggling, the agreed price does not match the sticker price, which in any case is mutually advantageous. Indeed, if it were not, the transaction would not happen.

Another type of traditional market is an auction, with one seller and many potential buyers, which many readers may have seen at least once. In this case the supply side is represented by the auctioneer, who puts up a good for sale and declares a minimum auction price. The most interesting particular characteristic of an auction is the intense competition between buyers competing for the good by offering increasingly higher prices.

Finally, the spread of the Internet has brought about the creation of vast markets that are basically similar to those hypothesized by economic theory. Online auctions eliminate the constraint of spatial distance and expand the buying and selling audience for a given product to people connected by computer in different countries far distant from each other. The phenomenon of online markets is constantly expanding for highly standardized products for which there is no uncertainty about their qualitative characteristics. Auctions can be set up not only between buyers, but between sellers as well. This is one

The Microeconomics of Wellbeing and Sustainability. https://doi.org/10.1016/B978-0-12-816027-5.00002-1

of the systems with which public administrations can attempt to become more efficient and transparent in buying products. By setting up competition between different vendors they can reduce the risk of corruption (and of collusion between the buyer and seller to set higher prices beneficial to both), and they will certainly have better prices than those set by traditional purchasing methods.

The stock market itself evolved from a hawkers' market, where the verbal and gesticular abilities of the buyers physically present in the square were important, to virtual markets, in which everything happens by computer-generated buy and sell orders that so-called "market makers" match to determine the equilibrium prices that generate trades.

Through these specific examples we can see that all markets have some essential characteristics in common: supply, demand, supply and demand prices, bargaining, and equilibrium prices at which parties agree to exchange money for a good or service.

2.2 Stylized characteristics of the market

To study the characteristics of markets in detail we must begin with an analysis of how supply and demand are determined; to do that we will start with the **aggregate supply and demand curves** drawn in Fig. 2.1.

The x—axis measures the quantities demanded and supplied (Q); the y—axis measures the corresponding price (P). The **aggregate demand curve** (Q_D) has a negative slope; each point on it indicates the quantity of product

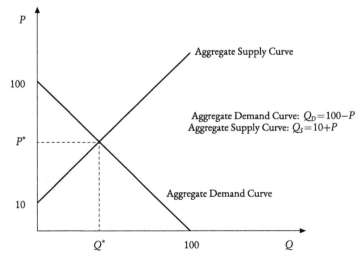

FIG. 2.1   Market equilibrium. *Note:* The equilibrium that determines the observed price and the aggregate quantity actually sold in the market is the intersection point of the supply and demand curves.

that buyers as a whole are willing to purchase at that price. The negative slope indicates that the quantity that the aggregate demand (i.e., demand by consumers as a whole) is willing to buy at lower prices is greater than at higher prices. The effect does not depend solely on the fact that consumers who had previously bought are willing to buy a greater quantity (an intensive effect), but also by the entrance of new consumers for whom the new price is now less than their maximum willingness to pay (an extensive effect). The relationship between price and quantity demanded is thus inversely related.

In difference with the demand curve, the **aggregate supply curve** (Q_S) has a positive slope. At each point it indicates the quantity of product that sellers or producers on the whole are willing to sell at that price. (For the sake of simplicity we assume that the producers and sellers are the same person, that there are no intermediaries, such as large retailers, between producers and the market.) The positive slope indicates that at higher prices the quantity that all sellers are willing to sell on the market is greater than at lower prices (Table 2.1).

That effect does not depend solely on the willingness of existing producers to make and sell more product at higher prices (the intensive effect), but also on the fact that, given higher prices, producers who had been idle because they were less efficient or had higher costs are now willing to produce and enter the market (the extensive effect). The relationship between price and quantity supply is thus positive.

The linear or non-linear shape of the supply and demand curves is a further element to consider; their shape depends on the type of mathematical function we hypothesize might represent the economic situation we are observing. Sometimes we will use linear supply and demand curves, at other times non-linear ones.

A basic element in analyzing the market is distinguishing **between individual and aggregate supply and demand curves**. In Fig. 2.1 we describe

TABLE 2.1 Quantity and price values for demand and supply curves.

Demand curve		Supply curve	
Q	P	Q	P
0	100	0	10
20	80	20	30
40	60	40	50
60	40	60	70
80	20	80	90
100	0	100	110

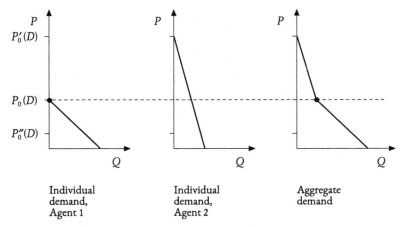

FIG. 2.2   The aggregate demand curve. *Note:* The market demand curve is the "horizontal" sum of individual demand curves.

aggregate supply and demand curves. These curves actually represent the sum or aggregation of the individual demand curves of each individual buyer (or seller) in the market.

In Fig. 2.2 we can see how a set of individual demand curves can be horizontally summed to give the aggregate demand curve.

The vertical intercepts of individual demand curves generally vary, which is significant. They indicate on the y−axis the **buyer's reservation price** ($P_0(D)$), or the maximum price an individual buyer is willing to pay for a unit of the good being traded. Considering the consumer's reserve price $P_0(D)$ (Fig. 2.2), if we set a price $P'_0(D)$ higher than P_0 then there is no demand; if we set a price $P''_0(D)$ lower than P_0, then the consumer is willing to buy more than one unit.

Understanding the relationship between individual and aggregate demand curves helps us better interpret the characteristics of the aggregate demand curve. The shape of the latter is much smoother because it represents the set of many individual consumers' choices, which vary widely among themselves. When the number of potential buyers entering the market is high, every small fall variation in price can cause a small increase in the quantity demanded. This is due to two basic effects: (A) **an intensive effect**, or the willingness of consumers who were already willing to buy units of the good at slightly higher prices to increase their demand for a higher quantity; (B) **an extensive effect**, or the possibility that a new consumer with a reserve price equal to the new market price will enter the market and decide to buy a unit of the product. The set of intensive and extensive effects thus determines the shape of the aggregate demand curve.

We see a similar phenomenon on the supply side. The aggregate supply curve is the horizontal sum of individual producers' supply curves. The individual supply curves show the quantity that individual producers are willing to sell at a given market price. In this case as well the vertical intercept of an individual supply curve indicates the **seller's reservation price** $(P_0(S))$, or the minimum price on the supply curve at which the seller is willing to put up a unit of the product for sale (In Chapter 4 we will find that the seller's reserve price is the marginal cost.).

Given the seller's reserve price $P_0(S)$, at a slightly higher price $(P'_0(S))$ the producer will be willing to sell more than one unit of her goods, while at a slightly lower price $(P''_0(S))$ she will no longer be willing to sell anything.

It will be obvious to the reader that, to keep the presentation simple, the traditional analysis of individual supply and demand curves is done with continuous curves rather than discrete or stepped curves. Continuous individual demand curves imply that it is possible to buy and sell infinitesimal units of a good. In most cases this is not possible in reality (e.g., one can buy 1, 2, 3 or more oranges but not fractional parts), so the proper representation would be a stepped individual demand curve, as shown in Fig. 2.3.

In that case the notion of a reserve price would be more obvious because it would be coupled with a discrete (rather than an infinitesimal) unit of the desired good. Consider, however, that when we talk about aggregate demand curves it makes much more sense to represent them with smooth curves, because in that case summing the individual choices of many economic agents means that, even for minimal price changes, the broader scale of units bought and sold on the x—axis, together with the generated intensive and extensive effects, always designate variations in the aggregate quantity demanded, even for very small price variations.

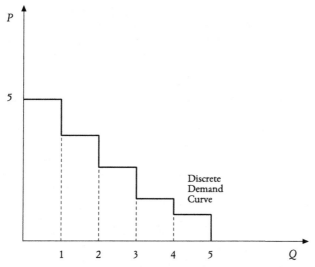

FIG. 2.3   The discrete demand curve. *Note:* The discrete demand curve faithfully represents all circumstances in which one can buy whole.

2.3 Movements along the curves and movements of the curves

The analysis we have carried out to this point allows us to identify the nature of **movements along the demand curve**. In this case we are not talking about real movements, but about points along the same curve that identify different quantities that the set of all buyers present in the market is willing to buy (e.g., Qd' and Qd'') at different prices (e.g., P' and P'').

It is even more interesting to analyze **movements of the demand curve** to the left or right, which shift it closer to or further from the origin. From a graphic viewpoint (Fig. 2.4) we observe that for a movement to the right, comparing demand schedule D with demand schedule D' at the same price, at the new demand curve D' the same set of buyers is willing to buy consistently more product than they would at the old demand schedule D.

What is the economic insight concealed behind this shift? There are many reasons why the demand curve can shift to the right. For example, an advertising campaign may have led to a change in consumers' tastes; the ad campaign made the product more attractive, and thus increased the overall market demand at each possible market price level.

Another cause of the demand curve shifting to the right is an increase in the real income of the populace, which automatically results in an increase in their purchasing power. This increase can drive an increase in consumption of various goods available in the market, thus generating the observed effect of shifting the curve. Note however that the literature studying the relationship

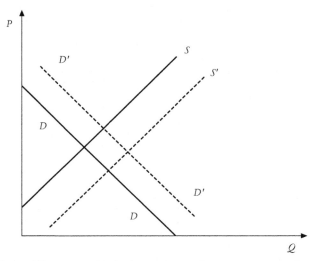

FIG. 2.4 Curve shifts. *Note:* Shifts in the supply and demand curves occur frequently in the market. Sometimes the shifts are parallel with respect to the original curves; in some cases, in addition to shifting on the Cartesian plane, they also change slope.

between income and consumption emphasizes that consumption is not solely or predominately determined by current income, but primarily by expected average future (permanent) income. Thus it can happen that the mere expectation of an increase in income (e.g., the government promising to reduce taxes) can shift the aggregate demand curve and generate increased consumption at the same price. Finally, a third cause of movement of the demand curve is determined by the possibility that the price of a good B that is a direct substitute for good A under observation may increase when part of the demand for A transfers to B; for example, a price increase for butter could increase the demand for margarine.

The same explanation applied in the opposite direction could justify a shift in the demand curve to the left; this could be due to a negative shock on tastes, a reduction of real or expected future income, or a price reduction for a product that is a direct substitute.

The same reasoning applies to the supply curve.

Movements along the supply curve are not actual movements, but points on the same curve that identify the various quantities that the set of producers present in the market is willing to sell (for example, Q'_s e Q''_s) at different prices (for example, P' e P''). To explain the positive slope of this curve we should recall that the quantity of goods that sellers are willing to put on the market at a given price fundamentally depends on the technology and the cost structure of the companies that produce the goods. If the price rises from P' to P'', companies with higher production costs will find it opportune to enter the market (an extensive effect), while companies already in production will find it opportune to continue producing an even greater quantity of products (an intensive effect).

Shifts in the supply curve indicate from a graphic viewpoint that for a shift to the right, comparing supply schedule S with supply schedule S' while maintaining the same price at S', the set of sellers is willing to sell consistently greater quantities of the product. The economic interpretation of such shifts is completely different from the case of a demand curve. One possible reason for the curve to shift to the right could be a technological innovation in the sector that reduces production costs, allowing companies to produce the same quantities at lower costs. In this case companies already present in the market that maximize profit will find it opportune to offer greater product quantities, and companies with costs that previously kept them out of the market will be able to begin production. Another explanation could be a cost reduction of the material necessary to produce the good.

2.4 Market equilibrium

Having developed our understanding of the characteristics of supply and demand curves, we can now examine one of the fundamental properties of the market, that of successfully determining an equilibrium price and quantity as a spontaneous result of decentralized negotiations between individual participants.

The market equilibrium price ($p*$) corresponds to the price at the intersection of the supply and demand curves. This is defined as the market clearing price, or the price capable of «clearing» any excess supply or demand. The expression means that at the equilibrium price there is no «excess» or unsatisfied quantity demanded or supplied.

To substantiate our reasoning, we provide a synopsis of the effects of combining supply and demand variations on equilibrium prices.

1. In the case of a demand curve shift to the right (due to a positive shock on consumers' tastes, an income increase, etc.) and a supply curve shift to the right (due to technological innovation or cost reduction), the two positive effects on quantity tend to be additive, which leads to an increase in the quantity exchanged. The effect on price of the former is positive and the latter is negative, and they tend to counterbalance each other.

2. In the case of a demand curve shift to the right (due to a positive shock on consumers' tastes, an income increase, etc.) and a supply curve shift to the left (due to an increase in production costs in a given sector, caused for example by increasing scarcity of production inputs), the two positive effects on price are additive, and the final effect is largely positive. The effect on quantity of the former is positive and the latter is negative, and they tend to counterbalance each other.

3. In the case of a demand curve shift to the left (due to a negative shock on tastes caused by a substitute good entering the market that is more convenient or of better quality, income reduction, etc.) and a supply curve shift to the left, the two effects on price (negative for the former and positive for the latter) move in opposite directions and tend to counterbalance each other. The overall change in price depends on which of the two effects predominates, while the quantity exchanged will certainly decline.

4. In the case of a demand curve shift to the left and a supply curve shift to the right, the two negative effects on price are additive, and the final and unequivocal effect is that prices drop significantly. The effects on quantity tend instead to counterbalance each other.

2.5 Problems relative to administratively defined non-equilibrium prices

To better understand the definition of excess demand, we can compare the case of an equilibrium price $p*$ to a situation in which there is a non-market clearing equilibrium.

A classic example of a non-market clearing equilibrium is **administered or politically determined prices**. In many eras in many countries around the world, in order to ensure that the poorest have the opportunity to buy the products needed for subsistence, governments have set prices by law that are artificially lower than market clearing prices.

In Fig. 2.5 the administered price is $\overline{P}$ and is lower than the market clearing price, or $\overline{P} < P^*$. As is evident from the diagram, in this case the administered price does not clear the market, leaving excess demand on the table. That is, at price $\overline{P}$ there is a gap between supply and demand, in that the quantity that all buyers are willing to buy in those conditions—$Q_D(\overline{P})$—is greater than all sellers are willing to produce and sell—$Q_S(\overline{P})$. What we observe is basically the natural consequence of movements along the curves explained in the previous section, where we stated that, at lower prices, the quantity demanded by the market increases and supply decreases. The combination of these two phenomena creates the gap between supply and demand.

Our models and the graphs that represent some of their aspects are only abstract simplifications of reality; a few specific examples can help us better understand them. While no one can observe excess demand or a non-market clearing price in nature, we have all lived through or observed the consequences of such a situation. The visible effect of excess demand is a waiting line. When the quantity offered is scarcer than the quantity demanded, and consumers are aware of this state of affairs, their natural behavior is to

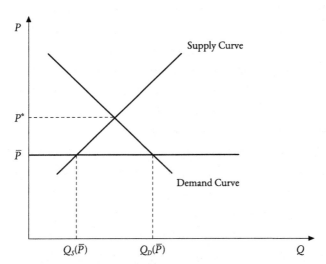

FIG. 2.5   Non market clearing administered prices. *Note*: In the case of a price imposed by law, for example a politically set price for food, the administered price $(\overline{P})$ is lower than the equilibrium price (P^*). This creates excess demand and rationing, in that some potential buyers' demand for a good will not be satisfied. The excess demand is equal to the difference between $Q_D(\overline{P})$ and $Q_S(\overline{P})$. Rationing and excess demand create waiting lines (knowing that not everyone will be able to obtain the good, buyers form lines to avoid being too late) and empty storefronts once the limited quantity available runs out.

compete for the few goods available. The rational strategy to adopt is to try to be among the fortunate few who can buy at least one or part of the available products; to be sure of that, it is necessary to arrive early and wait in order to take precedence over competing consumers (Frame 2.1).

If you have ever had occasion to ask someone from one of the countries behind the Iron Curtain — where the practice of administered prices was widespread — what one of the more negative aspects might have been of life in those countries prior to their transition to capitalist systems, you might have heard something like this: one of the most unbearable aspects was to leave home and find a two block long line to buy bread or basic food, only to frequently find the storefronts empty and products sold out by the time it was their turn.

The other visible characteristic of administered prices is empty storefronts, which is closely correlated with the lines. If the quantities produced are less than the quantities demanded, they will be quickly snatched up and the storefronts will never be full; once the subset of consumers is satisfied for whom there is product available, those arriving afterwards will find empty shelves.

Administered prices are not just a historical artifact of true socialist countries; they exist today in many market economies in particular sectors. One of those areas is healthcare. In this case as well the principle of the free market (and thus market clearing prices freely determined through negotiations between supply and demand) conflicts with the need to ensure healthcare

---

FRAME 2.1 The rationality of waiting lines

A line is a typical phenomenon in all situations in which there is an excess demand for goods or services. Examples we probably know are the waits prior to having a blood test in a public hospital, or lines of parents, both of whom work, to enroll their children into a school that provides a limited number of full-time places. Forming a line has a cost — an opportunity cost, obviously, because it costs nothing to get into a line in the above cases. In many of these cases the reader may have wondered if there were alternative solutions that could avoid these costs, such as a drawing from among everyone who wants that particular good or service. The advantage of the line over a drawing is that it allows participants to express their willingness to pay for a given good. A drawing is blind and does not discriminate between those who have a greater or lesser need for what the good or service can offer. By means of a line, someone who has an extreme need for a service can instead significantly increase her possibility of obtaining it by paying a higher opportunity cost and getting in line first. However, there are concomitant factors that can limit this aspect; for example, someone may badly need a service but be in a physical condition that makes it particularly burdensome to wait in a long line.

services at affordable prices for all citizens, including those who are less well off, thus guaranteeing access to a primary public good such as health. This is why public health prices are artificially low, below market equilibrium prices. Again, the effect is the same as a waiting line in which users compete for priority of service by using a system of tickets with consecutive numbers.

To solve the problem the possibility of being able to make an appointment by phone is useless, although they are available in many cases. While adopting such a strategy avoids lines at clinics to receive care or make an appointment, as in the past, the problem of "virtual lines" is anything but solved. Everything might seem to be resolved by a telephone call, but the problem of excess demand translates into appointments that may be months out from the call, in complete contradiction to the urgency of the need for treatment — when the response is not actually that all available appointments are filled and to call again in a few months when appointments have opened up again. Emergency rooms are a fast track for urgent care, but they too are frequently congested with people who are trying to circumvent the waiting lines and receive free care even when their conditions are not serious. That is why people are triaged as soon as they arrive at the emergency room and classified by their level of seriousness; in mildly serious cases they are placed in a waiting line or even given a numbered ticket.

When discussing the problem of non-market clearing equilibriums, and particularly in the case of administered prices previously described, it is very important to be able to distinguish the *positive* phase from the *normative* phase; in Chapter 1 we identified this ability as one of an economist's basic methodological competencies. It is difficult to refute that the discussion on the relationship between artificially low prices, waiting lines, and empty store-fronts is by its nature part of the positive phase. From this observation the normative judgment does not automatically follow that we should unequivocally preclude all use of administered prices. As the reader will recall, value judgments come into play in the transition between the positive and normative phases, and the matter is more complex than it might appear. Those who maintain that the efficiency of the market — its ability to spontaneously determine equilibrium prices that reflect demand side tastes and economic abilities and supply side technological and productive capacities — is the fundamental, unique value to preserve will be proponents of policies contrary to administered prices. Those who maintain that ensuring basic goods and services to the less well-off, who do not have the means to buy at market prices, could instead favor a policy of administered prices in some key sectors. The search for solutions that are able to bring together the principle of market efficiency with the universal availability of goods and services is the real frontier for bringing everyone into agreement and taking the best of both supply side policies. A possible solution that can resolve the limitations of the two previously described alternatives would be to leave the market free to determine prices while supplementing the purchasing power of the less well-off with subsidies. Even this solution, which seems impeccable in principle, conflicts with the reality of the difficulty of identifying the less well-off and efficiently providing them with subsidies.

An opposite example of a non-market clearing price could be fixing an administered price artificially higher than the equilibrium price. To a certain approximation, the agricultural policy adopted by the European Economic Community from the post-war era until now is an example of such a price policy (although in the last decade the Community's political strategy has sought to partially modify this policy by integrating it with environmental issues and territorial oversight).

The problem is illustrated in Fig. 2.6. The horizontal line corresponding to price P_W^* indicates the global equilibrium or market clearing price of a given agricultural product, while price P_{EU}^* indicates the equilibrium or market clearing price of the same product (e.g., milk, grain, oranges, etc.) within the European Union countries; for the sake of simplicity the global supply and demand curves are not shown. As we can see, the European equilibrium price is higher than the global price. This essentially reflects supply side factors, or higher production costs of European farming companies than the rest of the world (due to the fragmentation and smaller sizes of European companies with respect to companies in the USA, and due to higher labor costs with respect to the countries of the global South). At the beginning of the post-war era the Community authorities gave precedence to protecting European agriculture over the efficiency of the free market; the latter would have allowed European consumers to buy goods at lower prices, but to the detriment of the survival of European agriculture as it was then structured. They supported their strategy on the basis of the principle of "food sovereignty": according to the Community's authorities, for security reasons it was better for the member countries not to be dependent on food produced abroad.

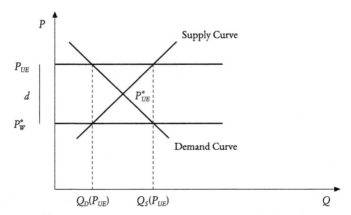

FIG. 2.6 Administered price higher than the equilibrium price.

At that point there were two possible courses for adhering to that principle. The British course suggested lowering the price of goods sold by European farming companies to the global price and making up the difference between P_W^* and P_{EU}^* with a direct subsidy to growers for each unit sold. The French course proposed instead to impose a customs tariff equal to or greater than the difference in order to make foreign goods less affordable than European goods. Given the tariff, the final price at which producers outside Europe would have been able to sell, after covering the cost of the customs duty, was P_W^* plus the cost of the tariff; thus their final price to the consumer would have been equal to or greater than the European price. The French option won out, which initiated a policy of tariffs along with export subsidies. The tariff was set at levels above the difference between the foreign price and the European price $\left(d = P_{EU}^* - P_W^* + x\right)$, and the internal price for European growers became an administered price set above the European market clearing price at $P_{EU}^* + x$ so it would be competitive with respect to the price of foreign goods burdened by the tariff. At the same time, the export subsidy policy established that European products could benefit from a subsidy, equal to, for simplicity, $s = P_{EU}^* - P_W^* + y$ when exported to foreign markets. In this way, by appropriating the subsidy European growers were able to offer a lower price than P_W^* when exporting their goods, thus effectively competing with local products in foreign markets. Within the European Union the administered price above the market equilibrium price $P_{EU} = P_{EU}^* + x$ was obviously not a market clearing price. Fig. 2.6 clearly illustrates that in this situation there was a surplus, or excess supply, $Q_D(P_{EU}) < Q_S(P_{EU})$, with producers willing to put more goods on the market than consumers demanded. The excess supply, rather than leading to lines and empty storefronts as in the case of excess demand, gave rise to overproduction. Some may remember pictures of tractors destroying mountains of unsold oranges, or free distributions of Community butter at certain times of the year. An alternative use of the surpluses was to use them for free food aid in the case of famines in African countries, which on the surface seemed to respond to the humanitarian crises. This action, which seemed inspired by the best of intentions, actually ended up causing other problems. Not only did the import tariffs preclude access to European markets by African producers, which would have allowed a substantial number of them to rise above the poverty threshold, but even supplying food aid for famines, although laudably intervening in the immediate problem, seriously damaged production in areas around the crisis zones: offering products at unbeatable prices — zero! — eliminated the demand for local production. Only today is it becoming evident that the proper way to intervene in limited scale emergencies is to buy products from producers in the area, usually in such cases with the help of money collected from the international community, rather than flooding local markets in the crisis zone with free goods from abroad.

Even in the case of Community agricultural prices, which were administered prices above the market price, the non-market clearing equilibrium had evident effects, such as production surpluses, higher prices for European consumers, and making it impossible for foreign producers in the poorest countries to improve their lives by exporting to European markets.

2.6 Dynamic adjustment toward equilibrium

2.6.1 The stability of an equilibrium

One of the more interesting questions relative to **market equilibrium** is the dynamic analysis of adjustments toward equilibrium. For an equilibrium point to be defined as *stable*, it must have the property that, starting from any point off equilibrium, things must return to equilibrium. To give a trivial example borrowed from physics, think of a ball placed at any point in a sink that slopes toward the drain. The ball will tend to go toward the drain and remain there (as long as the drain is smaller than the ball). The location above the drain thus represents a stable equilibrium point in a model (the model studying the movement of the ball in a particular type of container represented by the sink).

Does an analogous "virtuous adjustment" market mechanism exist that can take the system toward the equilibrium point, regardless of the starting point? The answer is yes, under certain restrictive conditions that also depend on the slopes of the two supply and demand curves.

Suppose we begin from the situation of the administered price described above — that is, a price below the equilibrium price — and imagine that the government has decided to abandon the policy of administered prices, leaving prices to be defined by the dynamics of the market. The first supply reaction in the face of excess demand, which in the past would have resulted in waiting lines and empty storefronts, would be to raise prices and the quantities offered. Suppose, however, that the new offered market price (sellers do not know the market clearing equilibrium price) turns out to be slightly above equilibrium. In this case we would have a surplus, and sellers would directly ascertain that at the new price they freely set the quantity demanded is less than the quantities produced and made available. At this point the sellers, reflecting on the fact that part of their merchandise remained in stock unsold, would partially rectify the situation by offering a slightly lower price. Through these progressive adjustments in response to observable phenomena caused by excess supply or demand, in the end the market would arrive, under several conditions relative to the slope of the curves, at the equilibrium price P^* that would clear the market and eliminate all excess supply and demand (Frame 2.2).

By studying this rudimentary, simplified adjustment dynamic, we have discovered another basic property of the market, that of spontaneously arriving at an equilibrium price in a decentralized manner; there is no need for a planner to embark on the impossible mission of gathering information on the tastes and possibilities for all consumers and then deciding how much every supply side agent should produce and sell. Every attempt at constructing planned markets of this type has always failed, precisely because it is impossible for planners to have control over such extensive information on supply and demand dynamics.

FRAME 2.2 Planning mishaps and the story of Fernando de Noronha

All textbooks state that the market is a splendid tool that can bring the supply and demand proposals of countless individuals into alignment, without the need for a centralized approach or an auctioneer, and by means of a price that allows a certain number of transactions to happen. These proposals are in turn dependent on consumers' tastes, technological production capabilities, and limits on the availability of resources.

To understand well this positive function of the market, consider the example of an actual episode on Fernando de Noronha, a beautiful Brazilian island; it is a natural, unspoiled paradise with splendid beaches and exceptional marine fauna.

Arriving on the island for a two day stay, two Roman tourists were immediately led to a sort of hangar along with other tourists. The island authorities politely asked the tourists to provide their documents with information about their stay and to kindly wait an hour in the hangar to hear the natural beauties of the island described. In the meantime, the island's tour operators studied the tickets and decided the best itinerary to propose to the various visitors. Favorably impressed by the kindness of the locals, but also a bit annoyed at the loss of time and the need to stay enclosed in the building without being able to start visiting such a naturally beautiful place, the tourists awaited the outcome of the evaluation while images of plants and animals scrolled across a screen — which they could have seen at home on their televisions or computers. Finally, after an hour the outcome of the evaluation was announced. For the Roman tourists the local tourist agency, taking their limited stay into account, came up with the ingenious proposal of visiting the one "historic" site on the island: a cannon dating from 1700 located in the center of the only inhabited spot on the island. Thanking the officials for their enlightened counsel, the two Romans hastily bid farewell to go find rooms, rent bicycles, and begin touring the island's beaches on their own.

The problem of Fernando de Noronha's tourist office is very similar to what a planned, non-market economy could run into — that is, an economy that decides from on high what consumers should consume and what companies should produce. As our example illustrates well, if we extend it to a much broader scale, it would require a colossal effort that would be costly in both time and resources, and with absolutely counterproductive outcomes due to the limited, insufficient information available to potential planners. Without any organization or planning, the market reconciles the encounter between supply and demand by means of the price system.

2.6.2 What can we observe about the behavior of markets over time?

Up to this point we have studied the market with the aid of supply and demand curves, analyzing their characteristics and movements and defining an equilibrium price. But what do we actually observe in the market? Certainly not supply and demand curves. What we can actually see is a sequence of equilibrium prices as they develop over time; from those prices we must be able to reconstruct what happened, that is, the changes in the underlying supply and demand that led to setting those prices. Our reasoning thus applies to the vast majority of markets in which prices are not administered. That is not a trivial task, because in some cases there can be multiple ways of interpreting the data. Let's take an example that can help us understand this. In Fig. 2.7 we observe the dynamics of prices for Brent crude oil from 1970 to 2010.

The reasons for the variations in the prices observed in the chart are generally those specified in Section 2.3. We can divide up the chart and consider several well-defined subperiods. The first major event we observe is the spike in prices corresponding to the first great oil crisis in 1974, meaning that there was a sharp increase in the equilibrium price. In this and all other cases that follow, we notice that our interpretive tools always provide two possible alternative or partially reconcilable explanations. In a specific instance a price increase can be caused either by a sharp increase in demand (a right shift in the demand curve) or by a reduction in supply (a left shift in the supply curve), or even both concomitantly. When a given observed phenomenon can be explained by multiple causes, we find ourselves faced with an observational equivalence dilemma.

In our case we must ask ourselves if there was a sharp increase in the demand for oil in 1974. This can typically happen in contexts of strong economic growth in which companies increase their demand for energy, as it is one of the most important factors for production; it can also happen in contexts in which

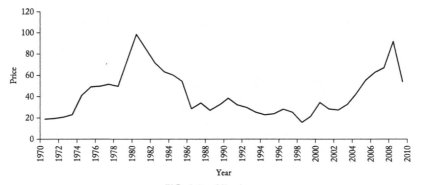

FIG. 2.7   Oil prices

there is a significant increase in the number of motorists, and thus a significant growth in the demand for fuel. Nothing like that happened in 1974 to justify such a sharp price increase. The phenomenon can in fact be fully interpreted from the supply side. The new event was the decision by the main oil producing countries to create a commercial cartel, OPEC, to limit production quotas by member countries in order to drive up prices. OPEC's reasoning, which made it convenient to raise prices, was that the economies of industrialized countries could not do without oil as an energy source, at least in the short to medium run. Thus the low sensitivity of oil demand to price would result in a less than proportional decrease in consumption with respect to the price increase (see the explanation of the concept of price elasticity at the end of this chapter). Knowing the history of those years, we can conclude that the 1974 spike in crude oil prices can be exhaustively explained from the supply side.

After 1974 the price tended to drop slightly, but in 1979 a second price surge coincided with the second oil crisis. Once again, OPEC's actions and supply side shifts explain the event.

This brings us to the 1980s, when we observe that prices dropped sharply and stabilized. How might we explain this new dynamic in the market equilibrium price? With the tools available to us, we know that a drop in price can be caused either by a reduction in demand (a demand curve shift to the left) or by an increase in supply (a supply curve shift to the right). In our specific case both happened, although the latter was definitely the more substantial of the two (although partly explained by the former).

On the demand side, Western countries began reacting to OPEC's strategy by deciding to partially modify their production technologies to limit their dependence on oil (thus a progressive reduction in demand). Although this action had a limited effect, it played a key role in causing a change in OPEC's strategy. The OPEC countries understood that it was not a good idea to change the quantity produced so as to cause the price to be either too high or too low. If the price were too low, the income to the oil producing countries would be insufficient. Were the price too high,[1] as happened in the two crises during the 1970s, it would have the effect of initiating energy conversion processes, with medium run consequences for the producer countries. On the one hand, it would make it easy for industrialized countries to modify their production technologies to save energy, setting up the conditions for a future reduction in demand. On the other hand, it would make the exploration and production of new oil fields economically feasible in non-OPEC countries with potentially exploitable oil reserves; the costs of such development would be rather high, thus it would not be practical when the price of the final product is not high. The OPEC countries came to understand that with high crude prices the

---

1. Note that this happens only indirectly, in that OPEC can control the supply of oil through decisions to limit production rather than its price. In fact, knowing the demand reaction, deciding how much to produce also means deciding the market price.

development of new reserves could increase non-OPEC production, which would cause an increase in supply and end up reducing the cartel's chances of controlling the market.

In the 1980s OPEC decided to not overtighten the noose by keeping prices in a medium range, thus avoiding the problems described above with prices that were either too low or too high. This situation of relative calm in the oil market lasted until a few years ago.

In Fig. 2.7 we can see that the situation changed, and oil prices have begun rising again in the last few years. Beginning our interpretive scheme again, we wonder what happened: was there a reduction in supply or an increase in demand? Might it be that OPEC decided to put a more aggressive strategy in place as it did in the 1970s, knowing well from the lessons of the 1980s the risks that such a strategy would entail in the medium run? The answer is no. The current price increase should be read primarily in light of a strong increase in demand. A new phase of global growth and the aggressive entrance of new emergent economies on the scene profoundly altered the situation and set the conditions for a strong increase in the demand for oil, both as an energy source for industrial production and in consumption as fuel by a growing number of motorists, primarily in emergent countries. In the background there were also those talking about structural limits in the oil supply, in that the discovery of new oilfields was not keeping pace with demand pressure. Other analysts argued that such concerns were overblown, commenting wittily that the Stone Age and the Iron Age did not come to an end due to stone or iron running out. The odds seemed favorable that Oil Age would not end for the same reason, but probably by the discovery of a cleaner alternate energy source that might possibly be equally available to all countries.

The history of oil prices in recent decades, with its spikes, drops, and subsequent increases in the last few years, is an exceptional laboratory for reading contemporary economic history and studying the function of the market, and the laws of supply and demand in particular.

2.7 Benefits and limitations of the market

Having analyzed the basic characteristics of markets from a theoretical point of view, along with specific examples to help us bring theoretical knowledge into factual reality, we can now proceed to our first evaluation of the upsides and downsides of the market, which we will consider in greater depth in later chapters. One of the purposes of an introductory economics course is to give students the minimal elements to be able to define a glossary of the more important terms at the center of the socioeconomic debate. In newspaper articles or TV talk shows we usually hear a few quips or quick slogans for or against the market. An economics student who has studied the first principles of the subject should already be able to develop more complete, structured arguments on the benefits and shortcomings of the market, while avoiding platitudes and superficial slogans.

2.7.1 The benefits

The first benefit of the market is that it is a quasi-miraculous tool that, because it is a decentralized and spontaneous mechanism, provides a solution to the demands of however many buyers and sellers one might want. Price is the factor that brings about this equilibrium, which thus has an important informational function. As illustrated by what we studied in the preceding section, price movements up or down signal variations in the tastes or purchasing power of the demand side or changes in the supply side, such as the entrance of new producers or changes in technology or production costs.

As we have pointed out, attempting to entrust the task of harmonizing buyers' and sellers' requirements to a "benevolent planner" has failed every time it has been tried. No planner is able to efficiently collect and manage such widespread detailed information on consumers' tastes and abilities to pay or succeed in knowing their reserve prices and demand curve slopes. Even if she were hypothetically able to possess this information, no planner would be able to coordinate the actions of various producers to bring to market the precise quantities corresponding to the aggregate demand at the price she set (Frame 2.3).

Thus the market plays a wholly spontaneous and decentralized role of eliminating any excess supply or demand by means of the equilibrium price, reached through free negotiations between parties. Of course, this mechanism does not always function instantly, requiring gradual adjustments at times. That happens particularly when the information exchange is slow between suppliers and buyers. The exchange of information is very quick in virtual markets, since the interactions between supply and demand happen immediately.

The second benefit of the market is that it brings about mutual satisfaction through exchange. A transaction made at a given price has the advantage of

---

FRAME 2.3 The example of the market for beachhouses

Beach bathhouse operators set subscription prices for cabins and umbrellas at the beginning of the summer season, and during the season they can tell if their prices are equilibrium prices. The presence of excess demand compared to the available places indicates that prices are too low, while in contrast, rows of empty beach umbrellas suggest that prices are too high. The managers have two possibilities: (A) note what they observe now and set a different price scheme for next season (a slow adjustment), with the risk that demand could change in the meantime due to changes in taste or income; (B) try modifying prices by offering mini subscriptions during the current season (a rapid adjustment). The latter choice could be blocked by commercial regulations that limit their options to alter conditions during the current season.

increasing — or at least not decreasing — the well-being of both the buyer and the seller. Given the knowledge we have acquired so far, consider the following. For an individual consumer who has an opportunity to buy at the equilibrium price P^* a unit of a good for which his reserve price is $\overline{P}_D > P^*$, the benefit from the purchase of the unit is exactly the difference between $\overline{P}_D$ and P^*, or the difference between the maximum price he was willing to pay for the unit (the reserve price $\overline{P}_D$) and the market equilibrium price P^* (Fig. 2.8).

A similar logic applies to the producer, for whom the benefit from the exchange is given by the difference between the market price P^* at which she can sell the unit and her reserve price $\overline{P}_O$, or the minimum price at which she would be willing to sell it.

At this point we can define the consumer surplus as the area under the triangle $Q^*\left[\overline{P}_D - P^*\right]/2$, or the sum of the differences between the reserve price and the market price for all consumers who buy the good at equilibrium (area A). The producer surplus is the area of the triangle $Q^*\left[P^* - \overline{P}_S\right]/2$, or the sum of the differences between the market price and the minimum sale price at which the producers in the market would be willing to produce (area B).

As Adam Smith pointed out quite effectively in his well-known example of the butcher, this important outcome is not due to the benevolence of the consumer or the producer, but rather on the ability of the market to bring together their personal interests to the advantage of both. In Smith's example, we can find meat at the butcher shop every morning and buy it at a reasonable price to satisfy our desires as consumers, not because of the butcher's

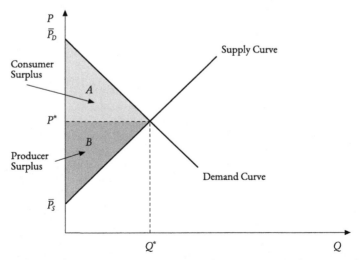

FIG. 2.8 The benefits of exchange. *Note*: The benefit to the consumer from the exchange is equal to area A of the triangle, and the benefit to the seller is area B of the triangle.

benevolence, but because of his personal interest to earn money and his willingness to make an advantageous transaction. The fundamental role of the market in this case is to transform, through competition, the individual self-interests of a large group of consumers and producers into a socially useful outcome that increases everyone's satisfaction, or at least does not reduce anyone's satisfaction.

A third and last benefit of the market can be understood historically if we interpret it, along with the parallel emergence of the modern capitalist system, as evolving from the feudal era.

Relationships between individuals in feudal times were generally hierarchical and based on subordination, which frequently became forms of semi-slavery. With the advent of the market, the relations between contracting parties standardized and became anonymous and impersonal. If we consider the previous historical situation, this can represent a benefit rather than a limitation of this new way of economically organizing society (Frame 2.4).

2.7.2 Limitations

In contrast with the benefits listed in Section 2.7.1, it is also appropriate to emphasize the limits of the market. First, while it is true that the market can be

---

FRAME 2.4 Smith in Practice. It is not from the benevolence of ski resort operators …

Consider someone who returns to skiing after many years away from it. An astute economic observer who is accustomed to noting changes in how markets operate will immediately spot several things. First, skis have changed, continuing the evolution of a trend to make them more user friendly; the skis themselves make skiing much easier. The innovation from this viewpoint are the so-called carved skis; they are not long and rectangular, and with recesses in the middle, which makes it easier to ski in a curve. This adaptation has the benefit of increasing demand from potential skiers, and readers may have noted that the maximum age at which one can ski has markedly increased. Second, the annoying practice of having to pass one's lift ticket through a turnstile slot has been superseded. Thanks to the introduction of a magnetic zone on the tickets, it is sufficient to put the ticket in one's pocket and bump against the turnstile to open it. Third, the lifts are larger and faster, at least in the major resorts, and thus able to carry more people to the top of the slopes in less time.

Paraphrasing Smith's famous question, do we owe these innovations benefiting users to the benevolence of the resort managers? Not necessarily, although we cannot exclude that forms of benevolence and reciprocity may exist in market transactions. The described improvements can be due to their interest in increasing demand and attracting new skiers to their resorts, in competition with others.

Thus we do not owe these innovations to the benevolence of the companies managing the ski resorts or the ski makers, but for most and decisive part to the incentives that emerge from market competition.

a step forward in democracy and in leveling the relations between the various levels of society, it is equally true that democracy is founded on wealth-weighted voting. From an economic view, this means that on the demand side, those with deeper pockets, or a greater spending capacity, have a greater say.

Another basic limit of the market, which is related to this, is its inability to carry out a redistributive function. In other words, while it is true that a market transaction is by definition an exchange of mutual advantage (or at least a non-decrease in satisfaction) between individuals who freely choose to do so, it is unable to act against possible disparities in agents' initial conditions. As an example, consider the extreme example of illegal organ sales. If a poor person decides to sell one of his kidneys and a wealthy person buys it, assuming there is no coercion behind the seller's choice, the transaction remains a voluntary decision among parties who decide to participate solely because it leads to an improvement over the initial conditions for each. However, certainly in this case the market took note of an initial disparity between the wealthy person and the poor person without acting on it, and it was unable to intervene in any way to counter the misery that drove the seller to such a desperate choice.

This extreme example brings a basic problem to light. Is it necessary to impose limits on markets, or should we leave open the possibility for anyone to sell anything, on the basis that an unforced transaction is the free will of the parties in any case, thus indicating an improvement for both? In the case of the trade in human organs, it is clear that ethical concerns prevail that drive us to prevent such a choice that is dictated by poverty and carried out in a moment of desperation that the seller could later regret. But what should we regulate in less extreme situations than this?

Another interesting example is the decision by Calcutta's political authorities to distribute land to the poorest in the region, with the constraint that it not be sold for a long time. The paternalistic intent in this case was to prevent detrimental transactions between the new landowners and potentially wealthier parties. However, if the owners wanted to convert this new wealth into fungible assets to then use to increase their satisfaction (e.g., to buy investment goods to start a new non-agricultural business), why prevent them from doing so?

A third important limitation of markets is that the extraordinary result of either not worsening or improving everyone's situation through competition between individually self-interested parties is valid only within narrowly restrictive conditions. As we will see, this astounding outcome does not happen for these cases:

— public goods;
— negative externalities;

- limitations to new producers entering the market;
- imperfect information;
- lack of perfect homogeneity of products exchanged.

In the presence of all these exceptions (the presence of at least one of them is almost a rule of reality), the market requires interventions by authorities to limit the potential negative effects on some categories of citizens.

A fourth basic limitation of the market is its consequences on the social and moral norms of a society. It is true that the free market has demonstrated that it can contribute extraordinarily to economic development; one need only consider the results of the quasi-natural experiment of the two Koreas that were at the same level of development and living standards at the beginning of the post-war era, and which are now in very different positions. However, some authors maintain that the market and the values it promotes can progressively deteriorate the social and moral fabric of a community. Hirsch and Marx, among others, argued that the market reinforces values such as greed and self-interest and promotes anonymity in interpersonal relationships. Moreover, by "commodifying" every aspect of human life, the market ends up undermining such basic values of the social fabric as the gift, altruism, and interpersonal trust. In his work on the social limits of growth, Hirsch observed that the market is depleting the moral legacy of the past. Following this line of thought to its ultimate consequences, the aforementioned limitations of the market would end up undermining its own foundations, because qualities such as interpersonal trust (even though they are not reinforced but rather dissipated by the market) are absolutely indispensable for its proper operation (as we will explain with the trust game in Chapter 6, Sections B.1 and B.2). Many economists have countered the extremism of Hirsch's and Marx's proposals by criticizing their idealization of a golden age prior to the Industrial Revolution and its significant moral heritage (recall our point on the benefits of the transition from the feudal to the capitalist era). Thinkers such as Polanyi, although recognizing the soundness of the dangers pointed out by Hirsch, have argued that the market culture itself generates reactions and "antibodies" in society that counter the presumed tendency toward moral decadence. For example, socially responsible companies demonstrate that the market can enhance values. We will return to this point in Chapter 11 when we discuss corporate social responsibility. Other authors go even further and argue that the market itself has a positive rather than a negative cultural heritage. The economist Benjamin Friedman's summary of these arguments in his book on the moral consequences of growth is significant in this regard. The following passage summarizes well the concepts developed by the author:

> *Economic growth — meaning a rising standard of living for the clear majority of citizens — more often than not fosters greater opportunity, tolerance of diversity, social mobility, commitment to fairness, and dedication to democracy [...] But when living standards stagnate or decline, the moral fabric of citizens tends to*

deteriorate, and consequently, we see a decline in tolerance and of openness to
and generosity toward the poor and disadvantaged.

B. Friedman, *The Moral Consequences of Economic Growth*, New York,
(A) Knopf, 2005, pp. 4.

Friedman's reasoning is based on an important argument, which is the typical misconception that the economy is a zero sum game. It is a common idea among part of the public that the economy is like a poker game in which one player's winnings necessarily correspond to the losses of the other players, such that the algebraic sum of the winnings and losses on the table must be zero. In other words, poker is not a game that creates added economic value above what is placed on the table at the beginning of the game. The economy is not like that, however. As we will see in Chapter 13, in periods when the global economy is not stagnant the volume of goods and services sold in each country and in the world increases by a certain percentage each year, creating new wealth. As we will see, this has happened nearly every year since the post-war years until now. Friedman's statement emphasizes that economic growth — at least when it is widespread and not concentrated in the hands of a few — makes people more tolerant of others. On the contrary, a stagnant economy in which the volume of goods and services does not grow from year to year is truly a zero sum game, which provokes feelings contrary to tolerance, generosity toward the least, and openness to others. If in fact the game is zero sum, then the slice of the pie that goes to someone else means less pie available for me, and others are perceived as rivals to beat.

2.8 Does the market evolve spontaneously, or should targeted institutional interventions guide it?

A key discussion point on the market is its presumed naturalness. Common wisdom identifies the market with the total spontaneity of economic life, and thus with laissez faire or non-interventionist policies; the less economic activities are regulated, the closer we are to a true market economy. That idea is completely wrong. The market is a very delicate institution that requires a certain framework of rules to be able to operate, such as respecting sales contracts between two parties, protecting property rights, an absence of risk of property expropriation by the state, the quality and promptness of the civil justice system in all situations in which one of the two parties is not able to perform certain contractually established provisions, and so forth.

Thus the first belief to refute is that if left to its own spontaneous evolution the market will naturally drift toward the sort of competition between firms that ensures its primary benefits. As we will see in more detail when we discuss the world of production and market equilibriums between companies in a given sector (Chapters 4 and 5), we could say that in many cases the market, particularly in sectors with economies of scale, has monopolistic or oligopolistic tendencies. Thus if left to itself it will naturally tend not toward free competition but toward the dominant companies that are able to take advantage of regulatory or natural positional rents forming a cartel (for example, in situations where there are a limited number of business licenses in certain fields).

That happens because companies are not at all equal, nor do technologies spread so rapidly that they become assets common to all producers to level their costs. Finally, the inability of various countries' judicial authorities and police to defeat criminal activity makes it such that the minimum price rule cannot always be the sole, fundamental criterion on which to base market transactions. Outside a framework of legal rules, the minimum price rule can paradoxically end up favoring the most unscrupulous companies that launder criminal money (thus obtaining capital at zero cost) or those that operate below the minimum standards for environmental or labor regulations.

2.8.1 The emergence of solidarity products overcomes one of the limits of the market

It is interesting to observe how the recent spread of socially responsible products has overcome one of the historical limits of the market. It is a singular experience to observe how a movement that originated as a strong criticism of the functioning of the economic system ended up shedding light on its unexplored potentials.

Let's start from its beginning. Over the course of the 1960s in Holland, several producers decided to build a new product supply chain through the emerging fair trade movement with the goal of overcoming several limitations of the traditional supply chain. Those limitations made it difficult for the lowest level producers to acquire a substantial part of the value created by the final sale of the product. Using the example of coffee, by "supply chain" we mean the entire sequence of productive processes that leads from the harvest and sale of the raw beans, their transportation to the processing industry that takes care of the roasting, to the final sale to the consumer after passing through various intermediaries. In the traditional supply chain the contracting power of the farmers is low because it stops at the first link in the chain with the sale of the raw beans. They are quite frequently near the poverty threshold, and it is particularly difficult for them to obtain a greater portion of the final value of the product. To help them do that, the fair trade inventors created an alternate supply chain in which the raw material producers are paid up to two times more than in a traditional supply chain. To avoid the trap of a fixed subsidy, the supply chain designers invest part of the resources resulting from the sale of the final product to finance healthcare, education, professional training, and technical assistance; this gives the primary producers the opportunity to increase their productivity and to play a greater role in the market, which allows them to escape their poverty.

Due to these "costly" characteristics of the lowest producers receiving a greater share of the value and the investments to promote their increased inclusion in the productive circuits, fair trade products sell on the final market at prices that are no lower, and often slightly higher, than traditional products. Despite that, many consumers decide to buy them because they recognize the social value embodied in the products.

Beginning in tiny niche markets, the phenomenon of fair trade products has grown enormously from its origins, to the point of reaching notable market shares in some product areas, such as attaining 47% of banana sales in Switzerland and 20% of the ground coffee sold in the UK in 2005. In many British and American universities, many "colonial" products, such as sugar, tea, and coffee, are fair trade products.

Beyond the debate over the effectiveness of this initiative, which we will consider in later chapters, what interests us here is its enormous symbolic value and its reflections on the very concept of the market. Fair trade products are indeed a true innovation that opens a new way of thinking about consumption, which ends up broadening the functions of the market itself. We stated earlier that one of the main limitations of the market was its inability to heal social problems and the unequal distribution of initial resources with which agents enter the market. Traditional wisdom has it that, through exchange, the market achieves the mutual satisfaction of the parties starting from their initial conditions.

Using an incisive example, in an exchange between a desperately poor person and a rich person the market slightly increases the satisfaction of both by making the desperate person and the wealthy person somewhat more satisfied, but it cannot intervene in the causes that make the poor person so poor by increasing his opportunities to enter a more dignified role in society.

With the introduction of fair trade products, or products with some socially responsible content, this is no longer true, at least in principle, because consumers have the opportunity to "vote with their wallets" to socially promote those on the margins of the economic system. Buying fair trade products not only makes the desperately poor less poor, it also contributes to removing the causes of such poverty.

This is an important innovation (inspiring similar initiatives and imitation from mainstream profit maximizing companies) that extends the possibilities of the market, although it is obvious that the market alone cannot solve the problems of poverty and exclusion in economic systems. Beyond the effectiveness of the intervention in the particular situation of producers involved in the supply chain, the ability to act in a complementary manner to political institutions' actions and to make companies and institutions more sensitive to these topics can be an important element of leverage and inspiration (Frame 2.5).

FRAME 2.5 The washing machine salesman

Once upon a time there was a salesman selling truly remarkable washing machines. He knocked on the doors of a little village that had not yet been touched by Progress; once he was received, he extolled the qualities of his product, recounting how it could improve the inhabitants' quality of life and happiness. He usually began his presentation with a detailed analysis of the functions of the washing machine and how it would lessen the time spent on household chores, freeing up time for leisure and interpersonal relationships and reducing the fatigue of daily life. After this opening statement, the inhabitants of the village usually lit up and began to fantasize about the improvement the appliance would make in their standard of living. Once past this first moment of enchantment with the washing machine before them as the instrument and symbol of the magnificent fortunes of Progress, taking advantage of the presence of this Man of Progress while he was in their homes, they timidly proposed other instances that would be very important to them. "Could we also have an appliance so we can have hot water in our houses every morning? And one that relieves us of the drudgery of washing dishes by hand?" At this point the salesman was stumped for a moment: the only appliance his company had in the warehouse ready to sell was the washing machine. However, after a moment of perplexity he came up with a brilliant solution, which he foisted onto his listeners with his remarkable oratory ability. "No problem! You can use the washing machine to meet those needs!" he emphatically exclaimed without hesitation. "The washing machine is the symbol of human progress, and it will relieve people of every burden of daily life!" Persuaded by the salesman's skill, at least half the citizens of the village bought a washing machine. Convinced by his verbal abilities, they used it not only to wash clothes, but to perform all the other important tasks the salesman had assured them it would be able to accomplish. So the villagers began putting their plates in the washing machine and attempting to use its water to take hot baths. However, the water was not at all hot, and the plates were all smashed when the agitator began to operate. Anger rose in the village, and the furious inhabitants began to speak ill of the washing machines in the village. Some of the angrier villagers began to kick and destroy theirs, forgetting in their ire the honest service performed by the washing machine in its real function of washing clothes. The villagers' satisfaction level with their washing machines was at an all-time low. Persuaded by the bad publicity about the washing machines from those who had bought one, no one among the other villagers wanted to buy one for themselves. At first the washing machine salesman tried to continue his work by knocking on doors of houses he had not yet called on. They greeted him with a scowl, and hardly anyone let him in. In the end he was forced to flee the village to avoid the wrath of its inhabitants.

Some enthusiasts who sing the market's praises risk producing the same effect as the washing machine salesman, with the result of depriving some villages of the real but limited benefits of market mechanisms. As we have emphasized, the market has the great value of fixing an equilibrium price through the interplay between the supply and demand of a very large number of market participants, and without the need for an auctioneer. The market defined price is a good indicator that conveys information about the relative scarcity of a good and about

Continued

Frame 2.5 The washing machine salesman—cont'd

consumers' preferences, while properly directing the choices to allocate factors of production toward this or that product. While the market is particularly suited to perform certain functions, problem arises when we want to make it do something other than — remaining with the theme of our tale — wash clothes, pretending that it can bring hot water into our homes or wash dishes. The market does not resolve the problem of public goods, such as healthcare, education, defense, and the quality of the environment; if these are left to spontaneous individual decisions, they are produced in fewer quantities than are necessary. To fully achieve its potential through competition, the market requires that the various actors have equal weight and dignity. This is a highly fragile condition, and in many situations, such as natural monopolies or positional rents, the market cannot guarantee its preservation; rather, it must be sustained and promoted by specific oversight authorities (such as antitrust regulators) charged with opposing large companies' attempts to collude and limit access to the market by new actors. Furthermore, the market is a neutral tool with no morality of its own. Economic and moral value do not coincide, thus in certain morally delicate sectors we frequently decide not to let the market manage it. Finally, to function well the market requires perfect information, but information is itself a public good that paradoxically is not sufficiently produced if entrusted to the laws of the market alone.

In conclusion, returning to the lesson of our tale, those who complain about the lack of a market culture must understand that this dearth depends in part on forcing certain views of the market as a wonder-working cure-all for all the socioeconomic problems that beset us. A more realistic evaluation of the potential and limits of the market would avoid turning it into an idol, which would be counterproductive to appreciating what the market can do (Becchetti, 2009).

Appendix

Further analysis of supply and demand curves: the slope and elasticity of the demand curve

Analyzing a curve in a graph requires the two fundamental concepts of slope and elasticity. Applying our discussion to an economic relation we have already studied, consider again an aggregate demand curve.

A first element to consider in describing its characteristics is its slope, or inclination. Mathematically the slope is measured by the ratio between the variation in the quantity on the y-axis corresponding to a given variation on the x-axis, or symbolically, $\Delta y/\Delta x$.

Following Alfred Marshall's teaching, to simplify our reasoning it is helpful to invert the order of the values on the two axes by putting prices on the x-axis and quantities on the y-axis. The values of y will represent quantity demanded and the values of x will represent the price level. This convention helps us because we know that in the demand curve economic agents make

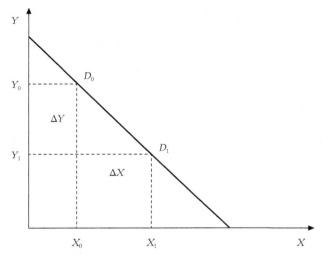

FIG. 2.9 **The slope of the demand curve.** *Note:* The slope of the demand curve is determined by the ratio between ΔX and ΔY. In the case of linear demand curves the slope is the same over its entire length.

decisions on the quantity demanded (since buyers cannot set prices), and this is the variable that reacts to prices (Fig. 2.9).

Briefly summarized, for a variation from D_0 to D_1 along the curve, the slope is equal to $PE = \Delta Y/\Delta X$, where $\Delta Y = Y_1 Y_0$ and $\Delta X = X_1 - X_0$. In the specific case of the demand curve (see Fig. 2.9) the slope is clearly negative, because higher prices (positive ΔX) correspond to a willingness from the demand side (negative ΔY) to buy less product overall. The negative slope of the curve is greater if the absolute value of $\Delta Y/\Delta X$ is greater. From a graphic standpoint a negatively inclined curve has a greater slope when it is steeper.

Taking instead the aggregate demand curve as an example, we observe that the slope is positive ($PE = \Delta Y/\Delta X > 0$) because when prices increase (positive ΔX) there is a corresponding supply side willingness to sell a greater quantity on the market (positive ΔY). In the case of a positively sloped curve, such as an aggregate supply curve, from a graphic standpoint the slope is greater the less the curve is flat.

The limit of the slope depends on the size of the units measured on the x and y axes. Thus with the simple ratio described above it is not possible to compare different phenomena that are independent of the adopted scales of measurement. To avoid this problem it is necessary to divide the slope by a scale variable of the observed phenomenon. In so doing we can move from slope to **elasticity**.

Considering the preceding example of movement along the demand curve from point D_0 to D_1, we have three different possibilities for measuring elasticity. The first is to use the initial value as the element of scale; in this case the elasticity is equal to $\eta = [\Delta Y/Y_0]/[\Delta X/X_0]$. Alternatively, we can use the final value as the base; in this case $\eta' = [\Delta Y/Y_1]/[\Delta X/X_1]$. Finally, it is possible to use the average value between the initial and final values, or the so-called "arc elasticity", thus $\eta'' = [\Delta Y/(Y_1 + Y_0)/2]/[\Delta X/(X_1 + X_0)/2]$. The three methods described are used in situations in which we want to evaluate the elasticity of a curve for a given good in the presence of a discrete variable (from D_0 to D_1).

We obtain even greater information when we measure the elasticity of a curve at each point. In this case, given that we are not examining the situation at a specific point on the curve, the only important difference is the transformation of a discrete variation (ΔY or ΔX) into an infinitesimal variation, and thus the transformation of the ratio between discrete variations $\Delta Y/\Delta X$ into a derivative dY/dX (we assume for simplicity here that X is the only variable affecting Y, or that the total and partial derivatives coincide), which by definition is the limit of the incremental ratio, or the limit of the variation in Y for a variation of X which tends toward zero and is thus infinitely small:

$$\frac{dY}{dX} = \lim_{\Delta x \to 0} \frac{\Delta Y}{\Delta X} \tag{2.1}$$

In the case of the elasticity of a point, our formula becomes $\eta^* = [dY/dX]/[X/Y]$. The other significant change in the formula regards the base values against which to compare the increments in y and x. By having everything on one point, there is no longer a problem of having to choose between the initial point, the final point, or the average of the two. The scale values are thus simply the values of x and y that correspond to the point at which we calculate elasticity.

To interpret the concept of elasticity let us consider again the basic formula $\eta = [\Delta Y/Y_0]/[\Delta X/X_0]$ and note a very simple fact: the two terms between brackets are simply the percentage changes in Y and X. Thus elasticity can be read as the percentage change in y as x changes. This premise allows us to arrive at the key insight that can help us easily understand the concept of elasticity and its economic significance. It is basically the response of one variable to changes in another, which we can classify in three ways: proportional, less than proportional, and more than proportional.

Let's consider again the demand curve and an example of a 30% increase in market prices. We talk about a proportional demand reaction if a 30% drop in demand results from a 30% increase in prices; in this case we have unitary elasticity (that, is, the absolute value of the elasticity is equal to one or ($|\eta| = 1$). We see instead a less than proportional reaction if demand drops less than 30% ($|\eta| < 1$); in this case the demand function is conventionally defined as **inelastic**. Finally we have a more than proportional reaction if demand drops more than 30%; in this case ($|\eta| > 1$) the demand curve is conventionally defined as **elastic**.

So what is the basic economic significance of elasticity? It is about reactivity, or just how reactive demand is to changes in price. For example, when the price of gasoline increases, the quantity demanded will probably not change much, at least in the short run, because gasoline has few substitutes; this defines an inelastic curve. In contrast, when the price of a certain type of pasta increases, the quantity demanded will probably drop sharply, because that sort of good is easily substituted. With these two examples we have also clarified a determining factor for elasticity: the substitutability of the good in question. The more substitutable a good is with other goods, the more sensitive it will be to price because we can readily substitute it in our baskets of goods. Regardless of the substitutability of a good with near perfect alternates (for example, substituting spaghetti with rigatoni for a type of pasta), the substitutability of a good with others that are similar is also important (for example, substituting meat for pasta). The greater the possibility of finding substitutes, the more a good will be sensitive to price changes.

Further reading

Bowles, S., Carlin, W., & Stevens, M. (2017). *The core team, the economy, economics for a changing world*. London: Oxford University Press.

Becchetti, L. (2009). *Oltre l'homo oeconomicus. Felicità, responsabilità, economia delle relazioni*. Città Nuova: Roma.

Friedman, B. (2005). *The moral consequences of economic growth* (p. 4). New York: A. Knopf.

Goodwin, N., Nelson, J. A., Ackerman, F., & Weisskopf, T. (2005). *Microeconomics in context*. Boston: Houghton Mifflin.

Chapter 3

The theory of consumption

3.1 The income circuit

Introducing a summary scheme of how an economy works is a good way to begin our study of individual behaviors in economics — that is, choices made by consumers, producers, and individuals about how to allocate time between work and leisure. We will consider and illustrate the diagram in Fig. 3.1, which in contemporary terminology is called an "income circuit." It is a sort of "hypertext," or better yet, a "hypergraphic," given that its content is essentially graphic; when "clicking" on each element text, windows open that give insight into the economic phenomena that lie behind that element (see Section 3.2).

The ovals refer to agents in the economic system, classified by the role each one plays. One identifies the family (or households), and the other identifies companies (or production units). Keep in mind that what determines one's classification in one of the ovals is the role one plays, not necessarily a

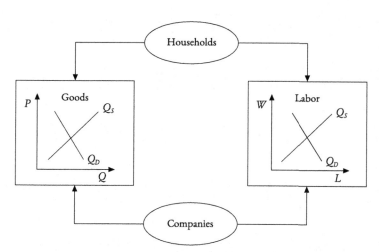

FIG. 3.1   The income circuit. *Note:* In its simplest form, the income circuit includes two ovals, two supply and demand graphics, and a series of arrows that connect them. On the one hand there are households that demand goods and supply labor, and on the other hand there are companies that offer goods and demand labor.

The Microeconomics of Wellbeing and Sustainability. https://doi.org/10.1016/B978-0-12-816027-5.00003-3

difference in identity. In other words, the same individual, apart from necessarily being part of a family unit (even if composed of a single individual), can also be an entrepreneur. As we know well, companies — particularly if they are not very small — have complex organization charts. For the sake of simplicity, but without losing generality, in our case we will carry out our analysis using the simplest possible model of a company led by a single entrepreneur. The individual in question will certainly be someone capable of acting and making decisions in both ovals as an entrepreneur and as a member of a family unit. The squares contain a concise, stylized depiction of the operation of the markets for goods and labor. In the **income circuit** the basic characteristics of the markets we saw in Chapter 2 are shown. In the first we observe supply and demand curves for goods that intersect, determining at the intersection point the quantity supplied and a market clearing equilibrium price. In the second we also find supply and demand curves, but in this case they are about supply and demand for labor. By following the direction of the arrows that connect the ovals to the squares, we find that decisions made by both households and companies in the ovals underlie the supply and demand curves for both the goods and labor markets.

Focusing attention on households, we discover that their decisions determine the demand for goods and the supply of labor. Looking in turn at the companies, we find that their choices are the basis for the supply of goods and the demand for labor. Returning to households, we see how the income circuit has the advantage of essentially summarizing the two tasks of consumer and worker that an economic agent performs.

We also observe in recent years that the decision that determines the characteristics of the demand for goods is no longer narrowly defined as consumption, but more extensively as a vote with one's wallet (as also indicated by Samuelson and Nordhaus in their economics textbook). This expression signifies the political and symbolic importance of consumption. This is not simply about an action we take while looking for the best price/quality ratio, but rather about a gesture that is not without ulterior value in a market in which companies sell lifestyles and status, rather than mere objects, by messages conveyed through advertising. A phenomenon such as fair trade products, or products that incorporate particular social and environmental contents, help us understand the potential of a vote with one's wallet, which — beyond quality and price — can also reward the social behavior of the company selling the product when that behavior aligns with the buyer's social preferences.

Another interesting characteristic of the income circuit is that it emphasizes the centrality of consumption in the economic system. Consumption and market demand are what decide the destinies of companies and the economy. Thus the real power of the market economy is not, as people believe, in the hands of the large companies, but rather in the citizen-consumers who vote with their wallets in their daily purchases. The problem is that this power is atomistic and decentralized. Decisions by individual consumers obviously do not have an impact on companies' behaviors. However, even the choices of small groups of consumers can have an impact and become quite influential, in that they express a potential market share; such groups are highly attractive to companies that stake their competitiveness and survival on the basis of even minimal purchases by various market segments.

Summarizing briefly, a new definition of the market emerges from the income circuit as a virtual place in which decisions by households and companies comprise a solution of a mutually advantageous equilibrium price for those involved in exchange (see the concepts of producer and consumer surplus defined in Chapter 2).

An important element in this figure is that there are two circuits, one real and the other monetary. The real one is represented by the supply and demand for goods and labor; the monetary one is represented by the quantity of money exchanged in every transaction in both markets. In goods market exchanges, the consumer gives the seller what the market defines as the monetary equivalent of the value of a good. In labor market exchanges, the company gives the worker a salary, which the market defines as the monetary equivalent of the value of the labor performed.

The increasing necessity of integrating social and environmental sustainability problems in economic discourse invites us to reflect on a third circuit as well, a circuit in which we measure natural resource use and production waste requiring subsequent disposal. Consumption and production are not neutral processes with respect to the environment; goods produced and consumed do not simply disappear without modifying in any way the environment in which they were produced. Scrap material and industrial waste from the production process and household trash from consumption remain as a result of every production process and of consumption; these wastes must be disposed of to reduce potential damage to the surrounding environment.

In addition, the production process also consumes energy by using energy either from renewable sources that are not at risk of exhaustion, such as solar or wind, or from non-renewable sources that are at risk of exhaustion, such as coal or oil. It is thus necessary to pay attention to the consequences that exchanges in the two main circuits have on the third circuit; we will discuss this in more depth in Chapter 13 when we talk about growth and the environment.

3.2 The income circuit as a hypertext

The income circuit, in addition to summarizing how the economy works, can be viewed as a hypertext that can be a starting point to understand the logic of the structure of this textbook. In this sense, Chapter 2 can be seen as the text window that would appear by "clicking" on the supply and demand graph in the income circuit (Fig. 3.1). In that window we develop the meaning and characteristics of the illustrated supply and demand curves, their origin and connection to individual supply and demand, and much more information regarding the overall functioning of the market. Much of the rest of this book can be seen as an in-depth study of what happens along the arrows that connect households and companies in the ovals to markets in the squares.

Beginning with the arrow that links households to demand, we now propose studying **consumption theory**. By considering the goals, constraints, and choices of individual agents it is possible to define their individual demand curves, and then, by summing them horizontally, to define the aggregate demand curve. We will then address the topic of **production theory** by studying the goals, constraints, and choices of the production units that underlie the definition of their individual supply curves that, summed horizontally, determine the aggregate supply curve (Chapter 4). We will then proceed with the analysis of strategies and constraints underlying companies' **labor demand** by following along the labor demand curves of individual companies and their horizontal sum aggregation. Studying production requires more in-depth development because it is substantially different from consumption theory. While interactions between individual consumers' choices do not require particular development, interactions between individual producers' choices will require a detailed study of the dynamics of various forms of markets, such as perfect competition, monopolies, and oligopolies, as well as studying the possible complex strategic interactions between production units by using game theory (Chapters 5–7).

We will then study the individual choices that underlie the labor supply curve. We will start with economic agents' choices between work and free time, from which, by defining strategies and constraints, we will identify the individual **labor supply**; by summing these horizontally we will derive the aggregate labor supply (Chapter 9).

3.3 The theory of consumption

Let's start by navigating along the four branches that begin from households and firms in the income circuit hypertext and asking ourselves what underlies the demand for goods. In discussing the market we have already stated that the aggregate demand for goods is simply the horizontal sum of individual demands. We also considered a few basic traits of individual demand by developing the concept of a reservation price (the maximum price at which a consumer is willing to buy the first unit of a given quantity of a good) and by emphasizing its diversity, which in turn depends on the diversity of consumers' tastes.

Now with the theory of consumption we will discover what underlies the individual demand curve. Classic macroeconomics did not ask this question at all; rather, it began by directly observing the dynamics of aggregate consumption and making assumptions about the aggregates that did not require studying the behavior of individual consumers. The advancement of economics knowledge requires today that we consider the dynamics underlying aggregate consumption, laying out in detail a reasonable and acceptable explanation that links consumers' preferences, the constraints they face, and their methods of choosing, and then depicting their individual demand curves (which cannot be done haphazardly); the aggregate demand curve can then be depicted as a reflection of the individual curves.

A **microfounded theory of the consumer** thus requires: (a) a hypothesis of consumers' preference structures, (b) identifying possible constraints on their ability to act, and (c) a rationale that guides their choice criteria.

Regarding the first point, the simplified approach that textbooks tend to follow is this: reduce the complexity of an n-dimensional problem (relative to the n goods a consumer must choose to buy in a given unit of time) to a problem of choosing between two goods (which is thus tractable in a traditional two-dimensional form). The traditional approach subsequently involves specifying a utility function whose arguments are the quantities of potentially purchasable goods. Point (b) is identified as consumers' available monetary resources that are the fundamental constraints on their actions. Consumers cannot spend more than their available resources, which, compared to prices, define the limits of their consumption possibilities. Regarding point (c), we then proceed to solve the problem of consumers' choices assuming the hypothesis of rational behavior, which is understood as behavior that maximizes their utility functions given their constraints.

The simplified consumer problem is thus the choice between two goods in the presence of a budget constraint. In order to make that choice we must construct a utility function in which increases in the quantities owned of the two goods increase consumers' satisfaction. After having understood the standard approach, we will "challenge" it by explaining the limitations of its assumptions and illustrate the problem of anthropological reductionism in economics; this is due to a conception of the individual based solely on the principle of self-interest, which does not take into account a number of other fundamental motives of human action, such as the value of relationships or moral duty. We will develop a more detailed discussion of the consequences of a less reductionist approach in Chapter 13, where we will review the most relevant results in the recent literature on the empirical measurement of the determinants of life satisfaction. In so doing we will evaluate whether the hypothesized a priori preferences regarding the behavior of economic agents coincide with those derived from empirical analysis.

3.4 The problem of maximizing consumer utility

The utility function $U(x_1, x_2)$ is a relation that maps the correspondence between the consumer's satisfaction level and the quantities of the two goods purchased. Holding the consumption level of the second good fixed for the moment, we can observe how the utility function is depicted in the two-dimensional space as a function of the variations in the first good alone

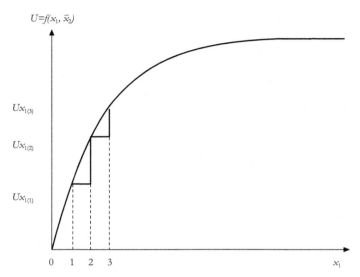

FIG. 3.2 **Diminishing marginal utility.** *Note:* the graph represents the change in consumer utility when varying the units of good 1 consumed while the quantity consumed of good 2 remains constant ($\bar{x}_2$). Utility increases with increasing consumption of the good x_1, but the increases gradually become smaller.

(Fig. 3.2). The graph illustrates the classic concave shape of such a function, which indicates how satisfaction levels gradually decrease with the consumption of successive units of the good. (This is obviously a reasonable hypothesis, rather than an absolute truth, defined by economists at a time when psychologists emphasized the same phenomenon in their discipline). If we observe the change in utility produced in the transition from the availability of one unit to two units of the good $\Delta U_{(2-1)} = Ux_{1(2)} - Ux_{1(1)}$ we note that, given the hypothesis of the concavity of the utility function, the change in utility is greater than that produced in the transition from, say, the availability of the second to the third unit of the good $\Delta U_{(3-2)} = Ux_{1(3)} - Ux_{1(2)}$.

We define this variation in utility determined by the consumption of one additional unit of a good as **marginal utility**, which we represent analytically as $MU_1 = \Delta U / \Delta x_1$.[1] Since the choices of the shape of the functions used in economics serve to illustrate economic insights, the choice of the concave

---

1. The Δ symbol indicates a discrete, non-infinitesimal change in an entity. As is well-known (see the Appendix to Chapter 2, Eq. [2.1]) if we make such a variation infinitely small we have the definition of a derivative, thus the marginal utility becomes nothing more than the partial derivative of the utility function with respect to one of its arguments (good 1) $\frac{\partial U}{\partial x_1} = \lim_{\Delta x_1 \to 0} \frac{\Delta U}{\Delta x_1}$ Note that in difference with Eq. (2.1) in Chapter 2, the function has two arguments, and thus to represent its changes with respect to just one of the two it is necessary to use the sign of the partial derivative rather than the sign of the total derivative.

function clearly expresses both graphically and mathematically the well-known law of **diminishing marginal utility**.

The meaning of this law becomes quite apparent if we consider food consumption. If we have an appetite, the first unit of a certain good gives us enormous satisfaction, which tends to gradually decrease for successive units until we are satiated; an additional unit beyond that point can actually reduce our satisfaction level or even result in a negative change in utility. The point of satiation can be depicted in a utility function graph by identifying its highest point, which corresponds to a certain quantity of the good x_1; beyond that point the utility function begins to decrease (Fig. 3.3) (Frame 3.1).

3.4.1 Cardinality and ordinality of the utility function

One of the biggest problems that the economic literature has had to face concerning utility functions is that of **cardinality** and **ordinality**. The problem of cardinality has to do with the difficulty of assigning meaningful quantitative values when comparing interpersonal utility, and even between different baskets of goods for the same person. The traditional measures we use in the exact sciences have an objective meaning; for example, a meter corresponds to a certain fixed distance, and its multiples refer to and have a precise relation to the base unit. However, it seems difficult to assign a number to our degree of satisfaction relative to our consumption of various units of goods. Considering again our original graph in Fig. 3.2, what values should we assign to the y-

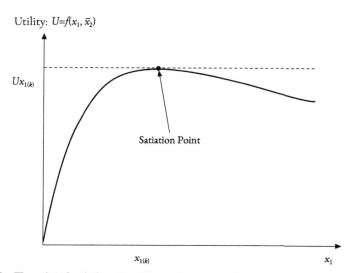

FIG. 3.3 **The point of satiation.** *Note:* The graph represents the change in consumer utility when changing the quantity consumed of good 1 while holding the quantity consumed of good 2 constant $(\bar{x}_2)$. In this case, there is a satiation point for good 1 (with utility $Ux_{1(k)}$), beyond which the marginal utility of good x_1 becomes negative.

FRAME 3.1 The law of increasing marginal utility

Readers can have some fun ascertaining under what circumstances and for which goods the law of diminishing marginal utility appears to be valid. As we will see when we analyze this very particular category of goods (see Chapter 12), it does not seem applicable to "relational goods" such as friendship, the value of which generally increases rather than decreases with the frequency of encounters with the friend (which would be analogous to consuming a good).

Generally speaking, this represents a reasonable approximation when we speak of traditional goods, with one notable exception. There is a type of individual for whom the law of marginal utility operates exactly the opposite, even in the case of consuming some traditional goods: collectors. If we reflect on it carefully, we can observe that the value of a collection grows as the number of objects of the same sort in it increases. Instead of gradually having less value, in this case the additional units have an equal or greater value because they increase the value of the collection. One could object that collections contain objects that are of the same kind but that are not identical, so in the case of a collector the law of diminishing marginal utility is still respected when we consider it as applying solely to additional identical units of the exact same kind.

---

axis? In other words, what is the degree of satisfaction relative to our consumption of the first unit of a good (2, 4, 8)? Is a level 8 satisfaction double that of level 4? And, provided we could reasonably fix such levels, can it be compared to those of other individuals?

Faced with such a puzzle, the Italian economist Vilfredo Pareto devised an alternate solution that compares different baskets of goods ordinally rather than cardinally. To understand the concept of ordinality we can start with a very simple example. When we observe a two-year old girl holding a doll in each hand and we show her a puppet, she might react two different ways: she may throw the dolls down and grab the puppet, or she may hold onto her dolls and care nothing for the alternative. In both cases the child clearly expresses, at least at that moment, an ordinal preference between the two "baskets of goods"; that is, by her choices she indicates which of the goods she prefers. So by observing the choices individuals make we can verify whether they prefer one or the other basket, and we find out how they rank their preference criteria for various baskets.

The theory of utility, and the possibility of using it to effectively compare different goods or baskets of goods, is based on a few fundamental principles defined as axioms.

Before stating these axioms we should note that the following operators are used in preference theory, $>$ (preferred) and $\succeq$ (weakly preferred), which are analogous to "greater than" and "greater than or equal to" in algebra.

The first axiom is **reflexivity**, which states that basket A is weakly preferred to itself $(A \succeq A)$. The second is **completeness**: given two baskets A and B only two possibilities exist: either $A > B$ or $B > A$; if both conditions apply simultaneously, it means that the individual is indifferent between the two baskets. The third axiom is *transitivity*: given three baskets A, B, and C, if $A > B$ and $B > C$, then $A > C$. Reflexivity, completeness, and transitivity make it possible to apply ordinal utility theory to all goods or baskets of goods. The fourth axiom is **monotonicity** (more is better), and it applies only if we are in a preference space without satiation points. This axiom states that a greater quantity of a good is always preferable to a lesser quantity.

The reader may be misled into thinking that these axioms are trivial or incomprehensible, but in reality that is not the case. The first two imply that people express their preferences consistently and that irrelevant alternatives do not count when comparing the two baskets of goods (Frame 3.2).

3.4.2 Indifference curves

We now turn our focus on the consumer from utility functions to **indifference curves** (Fig. 3.4). We begin by returning to our utility function for two goods,

---

FRAME 3.2 An example of violating the axioms

Numerous experiments have shown that the axioms are not always satisfied. People can find it difficult to compare two different goods when they are evaluated on more than one of their characteristics. The usual example Robert Frank mentions is an individual who must find a place to live. It has been shown that when the choice is between an apartment that is closer to downtown but more expensive (good A) and an apartment much further from downtown but much less expensive (good B), buyers split between the two choices by a certain percentage (let's suppose 50%/50%). If the real estate agent decides to visit a third apartment on the same street as the first but that is slightly farther from downtown, more expensive, and in worse condition (good C), 75% of buyers will then opt for the first possibility and 25% for the second more distant but much cheaper apartment. In other words, no one chooses the third possibility, but the comparison between the three shifts some buyers from the second to the first apartment. The explanation for this paradox is that people have difficulty choosing between good A and good B, while the easier choice between the second and third apartments (B and C), in which the second is clearly the better choice due to its characteristics, pushes people in the direction of the second. This type of behavior violates the principle of the "independence from irrelevant alternatives"; that is, good C is an irrelevant alternative to the comparison between the first two apartments and should not influence the choice between A and B. However, the third apartment creates an inconsistency in the comparison between the first two that violates the principle of completeness, and 25% of buyers change their choices between the first two apartments even though their characteristics did not change.

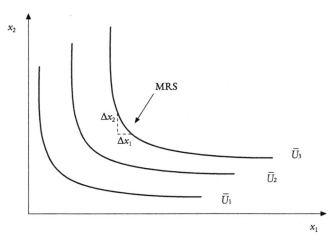

FIG. 3.4 Indifference curves. *Note:* We measure the quantity consumed of good 1 on the horizontal axis and the quantity consumed of good 2 on the vertical axis. As indifference curves move away from the origin, they allow reaching higher levels of satisfaction because the quantities consumed of one or both goods increase. The marginal rate of substitution (MRS) indicates how many more units of good 1 one must have if one does not have a certain quantity of good 2 to remain on the same indifference curve − that is, to maintain the same level of satisfaction.

$U(x_1, x_2)$, which we can imagine in three-dimensional space as a spherical cap, with the vertical axis represented by utility values and two axes on a plane represented by the quantities of the two goods. Intuitively we can think of indifference curves as what we get by horizontally cutting the spherical cap and taking into consideration the edges of the slice we just cut. Following this image, the graph that depicts the change in utility while varying the quantities consumed of one good and holding the other good fixed is the vertical section of the spherical cap. Formally, indifference curves are the locus of points that express different combinations (or different baskets) of two goods x_1 and x_2 that are capable of generating the same level of satisfaction for the economic agent in consideration. That is, the agent attains the same level of satisfaction at every point along the same indifference curve. In Fig. 3.4 (a horizontal section of the utility spherical cap) the values on the x-axis and y-axis are represented by the quantities consumed of the goods x_1 and x_2. In it we observe different indifference curves, each of which identifies a different degree of satisfaction. Indifference curves express different degrees of satisfaction, and in particular, as we gradually move farther away from the origin of the axes, we find indifference curves that allow attaining higher levels of satisfaction. To take a specific example from our graph, the indifference curve $\overline{U}_1$ is closer to the origin of the axes than $\overline{U}_2$, thus the points on it indicate baskets of goods that give less satisfaction than the ones consumable on indifference curve $\overline{U}_2$. Indifference curves are part of a much broader family of level-indicating

---

FRAME 3.3 A limitation of the standard theory

A basic limitation of the traditional theory of the consumer is that it is based on the concept of utility of choice, which overlooks the problem of the utility of experience. That is, it posits that a person's utility depends solely on the type and quantity of available goods but does not include the circumstances and lived experience that led the person to choose such goods, nor does it include the purposes for which the goods were acquired. For example, given a person's preference structure, ten roses always give the same level of satisfaction whether they were stolen or bought as a gift for a special person, and independently of the effort and sacrifice necessary to make the purchase.

---

curves used in many other fields. Perhaps isobars are the best-known among them, or the curves that identify points of identical atmospheric pressure; we see them surrounding the high pressure A and low pressure B areas in weather forecast maps. Other examples are isobathic and contour lines that respectively measure ocean depths and the heights of mountain peaks in particular types of geographic maps (Frame 3.3).

3.4.3 The marginal rate of substitution

The **marginal rate of substitution** is a fundamentally important concept that measures the slope at a point on the indifference curve. Formally, for discrete intervals the slope of the indifference curve is equal to $\Delta x_2/\Delta x_1$, which has a precise economic meaning. It indicates the additional quantity of good 2 (Δx_2) one must have to maintain the same level of satisfaction when one is deprived of a certain quantity of good 1 (Δx_1). This is why the slope of the indifference curve is called the marginal rate of substitution. As we consider indifference curves, which have the traditional shape shown in Fig. 3.2, we observe that, as we move along the curve from left to right using the expression ($\Delta x_2/\Delta x_1$) introduced above, the marginal rate of substitution *decreases* in absolute value.

To illustrate the economic significance of this characteristic, we will start from a point very near the vertical axis (point 1) on the indifference curve. There we find that it corresponds to a basket that includes a great many of good 2 and few of good 1. At this point the marginal rate of substitution is very high because only a few units of good 1 exchanged for many units of good 2 are sufficient to allow us to enjoy the same level of satisfaction. Moving to the right we can go to a point near the x-axis at which the y-axis value is very low (point 2). In this case the situation is just the opposite: given the abundance of good 1 in our basket and the scarcity of good 2, the possibility of having one more unit of good 2 is worth many units of good 1. Expressed in terms of $\Delta x_2/\Delta x_1$, the absolute value of the marginal rate of substitution is much lower, thus

FRAME 3.4 The mathematics of the marginal rate of substitution

It is possible to analytically explain in simple terms why the slope of the indifference curve is given by the derivative of good 2 over good 1. Movements along the indifference curve identify changes in the quantity of the goods that will maintain the level of consumer satisfaction unchanged. That is mathematically equivalent to calculating the total differential of the utility function by setting it equal to zero. We also remind the reader that the total differential is the operation that describes the changes in value of a function when changing its arguments.

From a mathematical point of view, considering the traditional form used in this chapter, that is equivalent to:

$$dU = \frac{\partial U}{\partial x_1} dx_1 + \frac{\partial U}{\partial x_2} dx_2 = 0$$

where the first term on the right of the equal sign indicates how much utility varies following a change in good, and the second term changes in response to the variation in the good. Setting the net change in utility to zero indicates that we are moving along the same indifference curve, or that the changes in the quantities of the two goods do not change the overall utility level.

Solving for dx_2/dx_1 we obtain:

$$\frac{dx_2}{dx_1} = -\frac{\partial U}{\partial x_1} \Big/ \frac{\partial U}{\partial x_2}$$

which is the slope of the indifference curve. From this we derive that the slope of the indifference curve, or the marginal rate of substitution, is equal to the ratio between the marginal utilities of the two goods.

the marginal rate of substitution represents the *relative value of the two goods in terms of a consumer's tastes*. Its tendency to decrease closely depends on the hypothesis of diminishing marginal utility, the implications of which we presented and discussed at the beginning. If increasing the number of units of a good one owns gives decreasing satisfaction with each additional unit, it follows that the utility of a scarce good is much greater than that of an abundant good. We leave to the reader (see Chapter 2) the freedom to consider in which life circumstances this law applies and when it is instead violated (Frame 3.4).

3.4.4 Choosing the optimal combination of goods

What we yet lack to solve the consumer's problem is to take constraints into consideration. As we pointed out in Chapter 1, the common thread that links all problems of optimal choices (the choices that underlie the arrows in the income circuit) is constrained maximization, or choosing optimally in the presence of constraints. While to this point we have depicted the relationship between purchasable goods and consumer satisfaction as happening in the most effective possible manner, now we must introduce spending limits due to budget constraints. To do this we will write a simple relationship between the prices of goods (p_1 and p_2), the available income (m), and the quantities purchased (x_1 and x_2)

$$m = p_1 x_1 + p_2 x_2 \tag{3.1}$$

In this equation, we have total consumer expenditure on the left hand side, and total expenditure for good 1 (the first addendum) and good 2 (the second addendum) on the right hand side. Now we need to draw this constraint in the same Cartesian plane in which the indifference curves are located. To do this we simply solve the expression for the value of x_2 by rewriting it as

$$x_2 = \frac{m}{p_2} - \frac{p_1}{p_2} x_1 \tag{3.2}$$

The **budget constraint** is thus a segment with its y-axis intercept equal to the ratio between income and the price of good 2 (m/p_2), with its slope equal to the ratio of the prices of the goods (p_1/p_2), and the x-axis intercept equal to the ratio between income and the price of good 1 (m/p_1) (Fig. 3.5). The insight behind the values of the two intercepts is quite simple. If we are on the y-axis, that means that we have decided to consume only units of good 2, so our spending frontier will be equal to our total income divided by the price of good 2; similar reasoning applies to the x-axis intercept. Considering the first case, we could actually buy fewer units of good 2 than m/p_2, but m/p_2 represents the

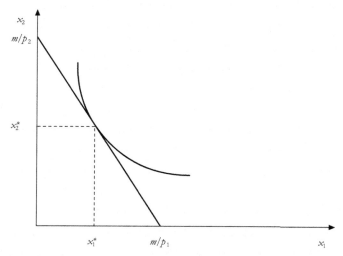

FIG. 3.5 The optimal choice. *Note:* The consumer's optimal choice (purchasing quantity x_1^* of good 1 and quantity x_2^* of good 2) corresponds to the tangency of the indifference curve and the budget constraint; this is the only point that satisfies maximizing utility while respecting the budget constraint.

maximum number of units of good 2 we could buy with the given income at that price. Thus the significance of the budget constraint is that it is also the *boundary of our expenditure opportunities*. This means that once the constraint is depicted, all points inside it are attainable, because that implies spending less than m, but less desirable than those on the boundary, at least as long as we are in a preference region in which the satiation principle does not apply. On the other hand, all points above the constraint cannot be reached because that would entail spending more than is possible given the consumer's wallet. The optimal choice must thus lie at a point along the boundary.

At this point, having identified the budget constraint and indifference curves we can graphically solve the problem of the consumer's optimal choice. The solution is intuitively simple (Fig. 3.5). Starting from the hypothesis that the consumer wants to maximize his degree of satisfaction, and taking into account his spending constraints, the best option would be to pick a point on the boundary of spending possibilities (on the segment of the budget constraint) that is tangent to the indifference curve that is farthest from the origin of the axes. In so doing it is possible to attain the maximum possible satisfaction while respecting the limits of the purchasing possibilities dictated by the consumer's wallet. Graphically the consumer's optimal choice will be at the tangency point between the budget constraint and the indifference curve.

Studying the characteristics of that point, we discover that the slope of the indifference curve there is by definition equal to that of the straight budget line. We know that the slope of the indifference curve is given by the ratio between the changes in the disposition of the two goods at each point that allows them to remain on the indifference curve; this is the *marginal rate of substitution*, which expresses the relative value of the two goods in terms of the consumer's tastes (Fig. 3.4). Observing the expression $m = p_1 x_1 + p_2 x_2$, we note that the slope of the budget constraint is instead equal to the price ratio of the two goods, or p_2/p_1. Thus at the optimal point:

$$-\frac{\delta x_2}{\delta x_1} = \frac{p_2}{p_1} \qquad (3.3)$$

The ratio between the prices of the goods must be equal to the marginal rate of substitution. The intuition is that at the optimal choice point the relative value of good 2 with respect to good 1 must be equal in terms of both tastes and prices. To give a simple example, if on a certain point of the curve good 2 is worth twice (in terms of taste) that of good 1, and the price of good 2 is less than twice that of good 1, we are not on the optimal point, and we should increase consumption of good 2 and reduce consumption of good 1 to increase our satisfaction. In other words, if good 2 is worth more than twice as much as good 1 and costs less than twice the price of good 1, we can exchange good 1 for good 2 in the market and increase our well-being, since the relative price we assign to good 2 in terms of our taste is higher than the market price.

However, when we increase the quantity of good 2 in our basket of goods while simultaneously reducing good 1, by the law of diminishing marginal utility the marginal utility of good 2 decreases and that of good 1 increases. Thus the relative taste/price gap between good 2 and good 1 tends to close up, which progressively leads toward the equilibrium price.

Note that there is a unique optimal choice only when an indifference curve has a strictly convex shape. A curve is strictly convex when, in connecting any two points of the curve with a straight line, we obtain a segment that is above the curve at every point (except the ends, which are on the curve). The reader can ascertain that for strictly convex indifference curves there is a single point of tangency with the straight budget line, and thus there is a single optimal choice. If indifference curves are instead simply convex they may have straight sections, so the principle of the uniqueness of the optimal choice is not necessarily met (see Fig. 3.6A). Non-convex indifference curves are instead characterized by concave sections, and in this case as well there is not a unique optimal choice (see Fig. 3.6B).

Having discussed the characteristics of the optimal choice, we can make a few observations about the characteristics of the model we used. One might ask why there is no possibility for saving in this basic reasoning. After all, when making choices we can be happier by not spending everything we could and setting aside savings for the future. The answer is that the model is very simple and only has one time period, so saving makes no sense in such a context. Additionally, when using the same approach for multi-period models the goods x_1 and x_2 can be identified as current consumption and savings (or future consumption). The model is indeed flexible enough to include the possibility of choosing between consuming and saving.

How is it possible to use this model when moving from the simplified case of two goods to the reality in which we choose between n goods? The solution criterion remains the same, but the problem is that with more than two goods

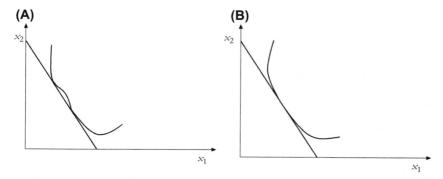

FIG. 3.6 (A) **Non-convex indifference curve.** (B) **Non-strictly convex indifference curve.**
Note: In Fig. 3.6A the non-convexity of the indifference curve entails two optimal points. In Fig. 3.6B the non-strict convexity entails multiple optimal points.

the optimal choice can only be obtained mathematically and cannot be depicted graphically. From a graphic standpoint we can see two dimensions well, and three with difficulty, but not more than that.

3.5 Do consumer rationality and constrained maximization perhaps imply that consumers look only at price when choosing products?

Does the model we have built imply that consumers' sole guiding criterion is to buy the cheapest goods? Absolutely not. The criterion is to maximize their satisfaction based on their preference structures rather than always choosing the lowest price.

Consider an example. The two goods in question (x_1 and x_2) could be represented by two types of restaurants when choosing how to allocate a monthly budget (or the part of it we decide to allocate to eating out): a pizzeria with reasonably priced dishes frequented primarily by young people, and a nouvelle cuisine restaurant in which the portions are sophisticated, quite pricey, and not abundant.

For a young person trying to maximize the quantity of food consumed for the money spent, the pizzeria is definitely greatly preferred over the nouvelle cuisine restaurant. So let's imagine that the optimal choice in which the highest indifference curve is tangential to the budget line occurs in an area of the graph in which the consumption of meals in the pizzeria is significantly higher than those in the nouvelle cuisine restaurant. For an adult with good income possibilities just the opposite could happen. When seeking out fine food, and possibly for modest quantities that do not put one's waistline and health at risk, preferences will be much more oriented toward the nouvelle cuisine restaurant. Another important reason for explaining the adult's choice is that one of the basic elements in consumption, which is frequently over-looked by economists, is seeking status or social prestige. Going often to a nouvelle cuisine restaurant confers prestige; being seen in a pizzeria for young people confers much less status. Consequently, let's imagine that for someone with good financial resources the optimal choice at which her budget constraint is tangent to the highest point of her specific indifference curves happens in an area of the graph in which the optimal consumption share of meals at the nouvelle cuisine restaurant is much higher than the share of meals in a pizzeria for young people.

The different choices of the two consumers described in our example are perfectly compatible with the criterion of constrained maximization, but not with that of looking for the lowest price; they simply reflect the diverse preferences of the two individuals. They also highlight the fact that many characteristics can guide consumption preferences, and that frequently our budget serves not so much to buy more goods, or goods with certain physical characteristics, but rather their symbolic or immaterial elements.

To take another very interesting example, let's start with the results of a study carried out in an Italian hospital. Alongside a traditional automatic coffee vending machine, a vending machine was installed with fair trade coffee that had a 15% higher price than the traditional one.

The study showed that a consistently higher proportion of consumers decided to buy the fair trade coffee instead of the traditional coffee, even though they could directly verify the price difference since the machines were near each other. This is another interesting example that once again demonstrates our assertion. Consumers' choices do not follow solely the criterion of the best price, rather, they combine it with other criteria. Choices such as these that might seem anomalies according to traditional rules are perfectly compatible with the assumptions of the theory of rational choices in the presence of constraints, or the principle of constrained maximization. The difference between the consumers who buy traditional coffee and those who buy fair trade coffee does not lie in the fact that the former are rational and the latter are not, but is due rather to the difference in their preference structures. For fair trade consumers, satisfying their desire to contribute to producers' socioeconomic progress is worth more than the 15% higher price they paid, so choosing the fair trade product gives them greater satisfaction than the traditional product.

Transferring our example yet again to a graphic representation of the optimal choice on the indifference curve graph, we can imagine the goods x_1 and x_2 to be a normal coffee and a fair trade coffee. Consumers give a certain weight to the two goods in their utility functions in accordance with their preferences. In a certain sense, within these preferences there are primary, immaterial arguments to their utility functions — self-interest, sensitivity to the conditions of those around them, the desire to combat others' poverty, a sense of guilt, and so forth — that explain the value they attribute to buying the two goods in their utility functions. For consumers whose primary concern is self-interest rather than other-regarding motivations, or who do not consider the fair trade initiative to be valid, the optimal solution will be the one in the corner in which all the budget allocated for coffee will be used to buy traditional coffee. (The reasoning is graphically depicted in Fig. 11.2 in Chapter 11 on social responsibility).

All consumers who attribute some value to fair trade, and who have preferences that are not solely self-interested, will make an optimal choice that includes combinations of the two goods, and thus a non-zero quantity of fair trade coffee, if not the choice to buy just fair trade coffee.

We could continue with many other interesting cases, such as choosing between low-cost and traditional airlines, or teenagers choosing between brand name and off-brand sneakers. The important point is to understand that the reasons for consumption are multifaceted, and that an act of consumption is a *vote with one's wallet* with fundamental symbolic connotations; beyond merely buying the cheapest product, consumption is a way of expressing our personalities by buying products that reflect our lifestyles. If this were not true, we would see advertisements presenting arguments solely for a good's price and the characteristics that define its quality. Instead, in many cases advertisements mention neither of these two aspects.

3.6 How we derive individual demand curves

3.6.1 Price-consumption curves

Up to now we have graphically defined the optimal choice, but we have not yet arrived at the analytical basis of an individual demand curve. By solving a constrained maximization problem either by substitution or through the use of an auxiliary function called a "Lagrangian" function, we will discover that, in addition to defining the characteristics of the optimal choice point, the problem immediately leads to deriving a demand function for the given good relative to its price and the consumer's income. However, we can also arrive at the same result graphically.

Let's start with a graph with quantities of good 1 on the x-axis and of good 2 on the y-axis on which we draw a map of indifference curves and a budget constraint (Fig. 3.7). Point A, where the budget constraint is tangent to the indifference curve $\overline{U}_1$, is the optimal choice for our consumer. The projections from this point on the x-axis and y-axis give us respectively the optimal x_1^* and x_2^* values chosen by the consumer. Now let's imagine a price increase of good 1 from p_1 to P_1', where $P_1' > p_1$. What effect will the price increase have on the

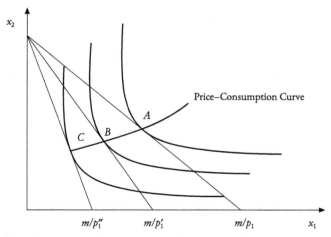

FIG. 3.7   The price-consumption curve. *Note:* Increasing the price of good 1 shifts the budget constraint (i.e., the horizontal intercept shifts to the left) and generates new tangency points with indifference curves that are incrementally closer to the origin. The set of these tangent points represents the optimal basket of goods given the various prices of good 1, while the union of these points indicates the price-consumption curve.

budget constraint? The intuition is that the consumer's spending possibilities will shrink, and if he decides to consume just good 1 he will be able to afford fewer units of it, since in the meantime his income did not change. This intuition corresponds mathematically to a leftward shift of the budget constraint intercept on the x-axis from m/p_1 to m/P'_1. In addition to the intercept change, the slope of the constraint changes from p_1/p_2 to P'_1/p_2. The y-axis intercept does not change. With the new budget constraint drawn, we find that it corresponds to a new optimal choice point for the consumer (point B), or a new tangency point between the modified budget constraint and a new indifference curve. We obtain two new optimal consumption values of the two goods, $x^{*'}_1$ and $x^{*'}_2$, that correspond to this point. We can continue this exercise by changing the price of good 1 to $P''_1 > P'_1$ and finding the new optimal choice C.

By following the previous reasoning we will find the new optimal values for the two goods, which correspond to the tangency points between the modified budget constraint and the new indifference curves, that we will call $x^{*''}_1$ and $x^{*''}_2$ for price P''_1. Without realizing it, through this exercise we are gradually constructing the consumer's demand curve. By joining all the optimal points we obtain, we can in fact define the **price-consumption curve** as an intermediate step (Fig. 3.7). What we have in the price-consumption curve is a map that links the price of good 1 and the optimal choices of goods 1 and 2. Recalling that the demand curve is a map that links the optimal choices of a good as a function of changes in its price, in the price-consumption curve we have all the elements to extract a demand curve by isolating the information relative to the variations in the price of good 1 and the optimal choices for it that correspond to its price changes (Fig. 3.8). Thus

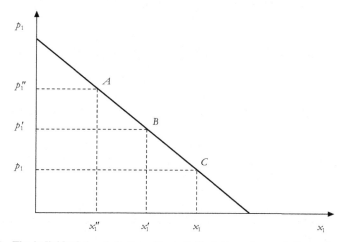

FIG. 3.8 The individual demand. *Note:* The individual demand curve indicates the consumption choices of a good (x_1) in relation to the various price levels (p_1) resulting from a consumer's optimal choice.

by using the graph alone we have arrived at the individual demand curve, which is the final goal of our analysis of the theory of the consumer. Starting with our reflections on a consumer's preferences and the choices she must resolve daily, this theory gives us a way to explain the demand for goods, which is a fundamental characteristic of markets.

3.6.2 Income consumption curves and Engel's law

By means of a similar exercise we can observe the change in a consumer's optimal choices in relation to changes not in price, but in her income. Starting with the usual graph of indifference curves, we first observe the effects of a positive change in income (from m to m', where $m' > m$) on her budget constraint (Fig. 3.8). Intuitively, a change in income should imply an increase in her consumption possibilities, and thus a shift of the consumption possibility boundary farther away from the origin of the axes. That intuition corresponds to what we can express mathematically. The value of the two intercepts on the x and y-axes increase from m/p_1 to m'/p_1 and from m/p_2 to m'/p_2 respectively. The slope of the budget constraint (p_1/p_2) does not change because it does not depend on income. Thus a change in income causes the budget constraint to shift *in parallel* to the previous budget constraint, either toward the origin of the axes if income decreases, or away from the origin if income increases. Analogously to the price-consumption curve, here we can identify the new optimal point that corresponds to the new budget constraint, which indicates two new optimal quantities of the purchased goods ($x_1^{*'}$ and $x_2^{*'}$). With subsequent income increases we obtain $m''' > m'' > m'$, and we calculate the optimal choices for goods 1 and 2 in relation to the modified available incomes ($x_1^{*''}$ and $x_2^{*''}$ for income m'' and $x_1^{*'''}$ and $x_2^{*'''}$ for income m'''). By connecting the optimal points in the graph, we obtain a map that links different income levels and the respective optimal choices of goods 1 and 2. In this manner we have drawn an **income consumption curve** (Fig. 3.9).

At this point we can separate out from the income consumption curve the relationship between different income levels and the optimal choice of just one of the two goods. In this way we obtain the **Engel curve** (named after the Belgian statistician Ernst Engel, who first defined its properties at the end of the 19th century), or the curve that identifies the relationship between income level and the optimal choice of a good. Starting with the Engel curve, we can conventionally identify two different demand behaviors for a specific good in relation to income changes.

We have an **inferior good** when, with an increase (or reduction) of income, its quantity demanded increases (or decreases) less than proportionally (for example, income doubles and there is a less than 100% increase in the consumption of the good, or income is halved and the reduction in consumption of the good is less than 50%). We have a **superior good** (or a **luxury good**) when, with an increase (or reduction) in income, the quantity demanded increases (or

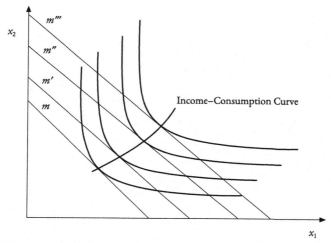

FIG. 3.9 **The income consumption curve.** *Note:* the income consumption curve is made up of the set of points at which each indifference curve is tangent to the respective budget constraint, each of which corresponds to a different income level. All the budget constraints have the same slope but different intercepts.

decreases) more than proportionally (for example, income doubles and the increase in consumption of the specific good is greater than 100%, or income is halved and the reduction in consumption of the good is greater than 50%).

Engel curves are very important because they give us a means to study the evolution of our consumption habits (and consequently of our customs) with changes in the standard of living. From a historical perspective, by considering the gradual increase in per capita income in all high-income countries during recent decades we can evaluate which were inferior goods and which were luxury goods. To verify this, one need only observe the evolution of the share of income spent for such goods. In fact, the definition of an inferior good (a less than proportional increase in consumption with changes in income) implies a progressive reduction in the share of income spent on them as income increases. On the contrary, the definition of a luxury good (a more than proportional increase in consumption with changes in income) implies a progressive increase in the share of income spent on them as income increases. The study of such aggregate dynamics in high-income countries shows that food goods are treated as inferior goods. We can immediately understand this. When income increases, it is not used to buy more food; rather, the increased purchasing power is used for items such as leisure time, vacations, entertainment, and so forth. A progressive reduction in the share of food consumption, known also as Engel's Law, is thus an important indication of an increase in the wealth of a given populace or country. This is such a regular pattern that it is also used in studies on poverty. In developing countries it is quite difficult to derive where individuals are with respect to the poverty threshold simply by measuring their income. In fact, the presence of non-monetary and informal exchanges, of self-consumption (consumption that does not pass through markets or the acquisition of goods through the use of money), and of self-production (such as using the products of one's own farm animals and the produce of one's own garden, or fruit trees near one's home) makes it quite difficult to evaluate the relationship between declared income and poverty conditions.

At this point the relationship between income and food consumption is a reliable indirect indication. If the share of expenditures for food is very high, we have a very precise indication of poverty conditions, in that people must allocate all their monetary income to satisfy their primary needs. On the contrary, if even with very low incomes the share of expenditures for food consumption decreases, we have an indication that the people in question are not in poverty because alternative forms of exchange to market exchanges, such as self-consumption, self-production, an informal trade circle, gifts, barter, and so forth, allow them to exceed the poverty threshold.

3.7 Slutsky's equation

Once we are familiar with the effect of changes in price and income on the problem of the consumer's optimal choice, we can address a slightly more complex topic that is very important in consumption theory.

We will start again with our graph that identifies the optimal choice at the tangent point between the indifference curve and the budget constraint (which we identify as corresponding to the point with the optimal consumed quantities x_1^* and x_2^*) by studying again in greater depth the effects of a price change. For example, let's suppose we begin with a price reduction for good 1 from p_1 to p_1', where $p_1' < p_1$ (Fig. 3.10). As we have already learned, this price change expands the spending opportunities for the consumer, which shifts the budget constraint farther away from the origin of the axes. More specifically, the horizontal intercept increases (from m/p_1 to m/p_1'), and the slope changes (from p_1/p_2 to p_1'/p_2). Corresponding to the new budget constraint we obtain a new optimal point (B) that determines an optimal choice for the two goods identified in the quantity $x_1^{*\prime}$ and $x_2^{*\prime}$.

Focusing our attention on good 1, we discover that the change from x_1^* to $x_1^{*\prime}$ conceals two separate effects:

- the first is due to the change in the price of the good that we will call the **substitution effect**;
- the second is due to the consumer's reduced purchasing power that we will call the **income effect.**

How can we parse the overall effect into these two components and evaluate their dimensions? We only need one simple step to achieve our goal.

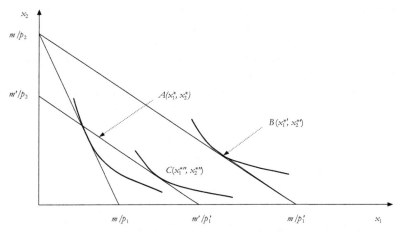

FIG. 3.10 Income effect and substitution effect. *Note:* The graph analyzes the effect of a price reduction for good 1 from p_1 to p_1'. In its overall effect the price change causes a reduction in consumption of good 1 equal to $x_1' - x_1$. This change can be broken down into a substitution effect $(x_1'' - x_1')$ and an income effect $(x_1'' - x)$.

Here it is necessary to construct a hypothetical budget constraint, that is, one that does not coincide with an actual income and price situation in reality. This budget constraint must have the following graphic properties:

a) it must pass through the initial optimal point (the one at consumption x_1^* and x_2^*);
b) it must be parallel to the new budget constraint (the one at consumption $x_1^{*\prime}$ and $x_2^{*\prime}$).

The economic insight follows. What we are doing is constructing a hypothetical situation in which the prices in force are those following the price change in good 1 (p_1', p_2), while income remains what would allow us to buy the old optimal basket of goods (x_1^*, x_2^*) with the new prices, or in mathematical terms, $m' = p_1' x_1^* + p_2 x_2^*$. This hypothetical budget constraint is particularly important because comparing it with the new post-price change budget constraint allows us to precisely identify the loss in income or purchasing power implicitly caused by the price reduction of good 1. We can now identify a third optimal choice at point $C(x_1^{*\prime\prime}, x_2^{*\prime\prime})$ on the hypothetical budget constraint. The difference between $x_1^{*\prime}$ and $x_1^{*\prime\prime}$ identifies the income effect, or the consumption change in good 1 due solely to the loss of purchasing power implicitly caused by the price reduction for good 1. The difference between $x_1^{*\prime\prime}$ and x_1^* instead allows us to determine just the substitution effect, or the consumption difference in good 1 caused by the good's price change, **net** of the change in purchasing power or income implied by the changed price. In fact, if we think about what we have done, constructing the hypothetical budget constraint in this case allowed us to exactly eliminate the effect of the change in purchasing power compared to the previous optimal choice.

Summarizing, we have: an initial optimal choice $\left(x_1^*, x_2^*\right)$ that is a function of prices p_1 and p_2 and of income m; a final choice after the price change in good 1 $\left(x_1^{*\prime}, x_2^{*\prime}\right)$ that is a function of the prices p_1', p_2 and of income m; an hypothetical choice $\left(x_1^{*\prime\prime}, x_2^{*\prime\prime}\right)$ that is a function of prices p_1', p_2 and m', where m' is the income that allows buying the old basket of goods at the new prices.

We can identify for good 1 the overall effect of the change $\left(\Delta x^{TOT} = x_1^{*\prime} - x_1^*\right)$ that can be broken down into the change caused by the substitution effect $\left(\Delta x^s = x_1^{*\prime\prime} - x_1^*\right)$ and the change caused by the income effect $\left(\Delta x^m = x_1^{*\prime} - x_1^{*\prime\prime}\right)$.

As in the case of Engel's Law, we can now classify consumption goods according to their characteristics in terms of income effects and substitution effects. To do this it is convenient to divide the income effect and the substitution effect by the change in the initial price that caused it.

The following types of goods are defined:

a) **normal goods**, or those for which the substitution effect and the income effect (divided by the initial change Δp) are negative. Thus for a normal good $\Delta x^s/\Delta p < 0$ and $\Delta x^m/\Delta p < 0$

b) **inferior goods**, or those for which the substitution effect is negative but the income effect is positive. Thus for an inferior good $\Delta x^s/\Delta p < 0$ and $\Delta x^m/\Delta p > 0$;

c) **Giffen inferior goods**, or those for which the substitution effect is negative but the income effect is positive, and the income effect is larger than the substitution effect so as to generate an overall positive effect. Thus for a Giffen good, $\Delta x^s/\Delta p < 0$ and $\Delta x^m/\Delta p > 0$ with $\Delta x^{TOT}/\Delta p > 0$.

It will not have escaped the reader's attention that the *substitution effect is always negative*. Recall that this statement does not refer simply to the change in the optimal quantity consumed (Δx^s) but rather to the ratio of the change in quantity divided by the change in price $(\Delta x^s/\Delta p)$. Due to the substitution effect, when the price of a good increases the quantity consumed decreases, and vice versa, when the price of a good drops the quantity consumed increases. The ratio between the two changes is negative in both cases. The economic insight behind this result is that, at the same purchasing power, and thus regardless of the implicit change in purchasing power caused by the price change of a good, the demand for a good is always inversely related to its price.

The sign of the income effect is not always negative, as is the substitution effect. It is negative for normal goods and positive for inferior goods and Giffen goods (which, as the reader will note, are a subset of inferior goods). What happens in the case of normal goods is that their consumption is directly related to changes in purchasing power. If purchasing power decreases (as happened in our example of an increase in the price of one of the two goods), the effect this has on the consumed quantity is negative, thus the ratio between a positive change in price and a negative change in quantity is negative. By the same mechanism, if purchasing power increases (in the case of a drop in price for one of the two goods), the effect generated is that of an increase in the quantity consumed of a normal good.

The opposite happens for Giffen goods. An increase in purchasing power has the effect of reducing the quantity consumed of the good, while a decrease in purchasing power has the effect of increasing it. The sign of the income effect is thus positive and carries greater weight on quantity than the substitution effect, which changes the sign of the total effect to positive. The name "Giffen good" was established in honor of the British economist who first studied this apparently paradoxical phenomenon, without however fully working it out. Observing the consumption habits of the Irish during the great famine at the end of the 18th century, which claimed many victims, Giffen noted that in correspondence to the income decline caused by the great famine the consumption of potatoes increased, while potato consumption started declining when the situation recovered. To explain the anomaly it was necessary to break it down into an income effect and a substitution effect, which the Russian economist Eugene Slutsky did in 1915. Giffen's research thus teaches us that there exist necessary primary goods for which consumption tends to increase in poverty conditions and tends to decrease in conditions of economic prosperity.

3.8 Further thoughts

3.8.1 Prices and information

The analysis carried out so far has led us to the following conclusion: *Once we have defined our tastes for different products* (and as we have seen they can vary much more than we might think, leading us to prefer higher priced fair trade coffee to normal coffee), the substitution effect indicates that a price increase (decrease) for one of these goods causes, net of the income effect, a decrease (increase) in the quantity consumed. That applies to each individual product, including fair trade coffee and nouvelle cuisine restaurants. However, there is an underlying condition that, if removed, can knock down all our carefully constructed reasoning. In the basic model of the consumer we have studied, we have assumed that the consumer has perfect information about the characteristics of goods up for sale.

In reality this is not at all the case, with the exception of highly standardized products. If we leave a context of perfect information, the relationship between price and quantity changes can actually invert in some circumstances. We are basically thinking about our behavior as consumers who live in a world of **information asymmetries**, or situations in which people have different levels of information. When we buy products that are important to our health, such as food, do we always look for the cheapest products? How many of us prefer the name brands instead of buying the cheapest discount brands? Why do we violate one of the fundamental conclusions in the theory of the consumer?

The very simple reason is that, in having imperfect information about the quality of a product, we interpret price as a signal of quality (and even more so when the brand has a good reputation): the higher the price, the higher the expected quality of the good.

3.8.2 Consumer theory and anthropological models

What is the conception of the person that underlies the standard theory of the consumer? To respond to this, consider that the most recent developments in the theory of the consumer indicate two different paradigms relative to economic agents' behavior. The results we have obtained to this point are valid if we refer to both paradigms.

The first paradigm is that of *restricted rationality*, or *rationality with respect to means*. Consumers are aware of their budget constraints, and their preferences are directed only toward pursuing their own interest; that is, their satisfaction increases as the quantity of goods or services increases, and they are indifferent to others' preferences. Rationality consists of pursuing, in the most efficient manner possible, the goal of attaining the maximum utility level that is compatible with their constraints. The constrained maximization approach explained in this chapter is consistent with this paradigm.

The second paradigm is that of *rationality with respect to goals*. Consumers are always aware of their constraints, but in difference with the prior case the structure of their preferences is much more varied. Beyond self-interest, they may also have elements of altruism (concern for others' utility in their own utility functions), paternalism (or goods within their utility functions that others enjoy, which in their view make the latter happy), inequality aversion (too great a gap between their and others' consumption levels reduces their own utility), or reciprocity (they feel satisfaction when reciprocating what they have received from someone else). In this case rationality consists of pursuing, in the most efficient manner possible, their broader goals that are compatible with their constraints. The constrained maximization approach explained in this chapter is thus compatible with this paradigm as well, which differs from the first in its greater elasticity in its conception of individuals' utility functions. To give a specific example, the altruist who aims to maximize others' satisfaction is perfectly rational and simply has a different preference structure.

Although there are numerous behavioral anomalies with respect to the model of constrained maximization, as we will see later, we can generally consider that the principle of rationality in its broader version, and less so in its restricted version, can satisfactorily represent the average behavior of individuals in the market.

The predominance of the principle of rationality with respect to goals over its restricted version has been demonstrated by very many laboratory and natural experiments that document how people are motivated not by self-interest alone, but also by traits such as reciprocity, aversion to inequality, pure and impure altruism, moral duty, and by the desire to make others happy.

3.8.3 Intertemporal consumption

The common assumption in all the examples developed in this chapter is that the economy has only one time period. This explains why it is "rational" for consumers to spend all their money on consumption goods without saving anything. The money obtained as income has no value in and of itself, but only as a means of exchange that allows buying goods that increase consumers' satisfaction.

An interesting extension of consumption theory allows us to carry out some simple reasoning on the choice between present and future consumption by extending the temporal horizon to two periods, without abandoning our two dimensional graph. The situation now changes radically because if there is a second period, saved income has value because it allows us to increase our future consumption.

In Fig. 3.11, consumption in the present period is represented on the horizontal axis (C_1) and consumption in the second period on the vertical axis (C_2).

Each consumer has a certain resource provision consisting of her income in the current period (m_1) and the income she will receive in the second period (m_2).

Note that in the absence of the possibility of lending or borrowing, the consumer's budget line cannot reach the horizontal axis (Fig. 3.11).

The consumer will not in fact be able to consume more that his income m_1 in the current period. However, he will be able to decide to save part of his current income so he can consume more than his income during the second period. In the absence of the possibility of lending and borrowing, the money saved will earn no interest. The maximum possibility for future consumption, which corresponds to the vertical intercept, will thus be equal to $m_1 + m_2$.

Interestingly, the possibility of lending or borrowing at a given interest rate r—which is a first hint of a financial market in this very simple basic model — improves consumption opportunities because it allows extending the budget line from the current resources point to the horizontal axis and increasing spending opportunities in the future period when the consumer decides to save (Fig. 3.12). To simplify our explanation we assume that there are no financial intermediaries or brokerage fees, so the lending and borrowing rates are the same.

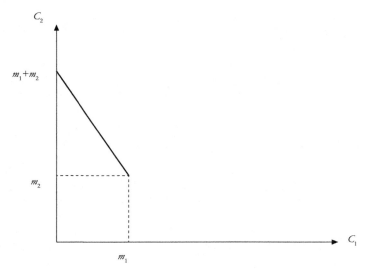

FIG. 3.11 The consumer budget constraint in the absence of the possibility of lending or borrowing.

The significance of the interest rate r is that it is the variable that defines the time value of the money transferred, rewarding those who hold back from consuming part of their income now with a payback and "penalizing" those

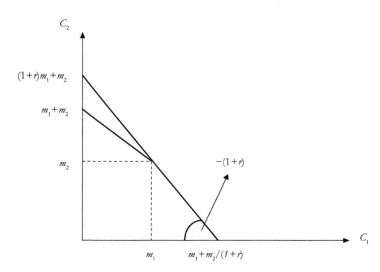

FIG. 3.12 The possibility of lending or borrowing a loan significantly increases the possibility of consumer spending.

who want to consume now more than their available income. An income m_1 saved and transferred into the second period is in fact worth $m_1(1 + r)$, while a demand to advance future income m_2 to now will be "penalized" and discounted at the same interest rate. A consumer who wants to borrow to have future income available now will only receive $m_2/(1 + r)$.

In light of the above, we can observe that the budget constraint we have used until now must be appropriately adjusted to take into account the new situation in which individuals can save and make loans. That is, they can save income not spent in the first period and obtain a return on it, or request money by taking out a loan to consume more in the first period than they could by spending their current income.

In essence, the intertemporal budget constraint becomes:

$m_1 + m_2/(1 + r) = C_1 + C_2/(1 + r)$ (the present value of the budget constraint)

Or, if we multiply everything by $(1 + r)$

$m_1(1 + r) + m_2 = C_1(1 + r) + C_2$ (the future value of the budget constraint)

Given this budget constraint, it is possible to represent it in Cartesian space considering that:

$$C_2 = m_1(1 + r) + m_2 - (1 + r)C_1$$

Note that the horizontal intercept is equal to $m_1 + m_2/(1 + r)$, that is, if the person decides to consume everything today, she will be able to use the current period income (m_1) plus her discounted income from the second period. The vertical intercept is instead equal to $m_1(1 + r) + m_2$. This implies that if she decides to consume everything in the second period, she will be able to use the income in the second period plus the income from the first period which, since it was saved, will yield a return determined by the interest rate, and will thus be equal to $m_1(1 + r)$. The slope of the budget line will instead be equal to $-(1 + r)$.

We can now generically represent the consumer's utility function as $U(C_1, C_2)$. Using the methodology described in the preceding sections, it is possible to derive the consumer indifference curves and represent them in Cartesian space.

The solution to the problem of consumer maximization under an intertemporal budget constraint is at the tangent point between the intertemporal budget constraint line and the indifference curve that is furthest from the origin of the axes. The consumer is thus located at the point on the budget frontier that allows him to reach the highest level of satisfaction possible given his spending constraints.

We will thus have two possibilities (Fig. 3.13). If the tangent point is to the left of the available resources point, the consumer will find it optimal to lend his money by saving part of his current income to consume more than his future income in the second period. If instead the tangent point is to the right of the available resources point, the consumer will find it optimal to take a loan

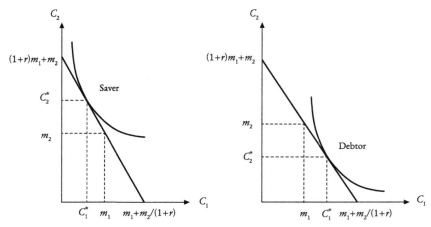

FIG. 3.13 *In the case of a saver, the result is $M_1 - C_1 > 0$; in the case of a borrower, the result is $M_1 - C_1 < 0$.*

and use part of his future income to consume more than his current income in the first period.

We can now analyze how the situation changes when the interest rate changes from r to r', where $r' > r$. If the interest rate rises, the budget line rotates around the endowment point and becomes steeper. With the new interest rate it is still possible for the consumer to have the same combination of present and future consumption that exactly equals the income received in the two periods. If she decides to take out a loan to consume more today, she will pay a higher interest rate and her spending possibilities will be reduced. If she decides instead to lend her money, she will benefit from the higher interest rate and acquire a higher yield from her current saved income. In this case we can intuitively note that if the consumer thought it optimal to lend at the current interest rate r she will continue to do so, attaining a higher indifference curve at the new interest rate r' and increasing her satisfaction. In the case in which she is a debtor, we cannot say whether she will become a saver at the new interest rate, even though it will certainly reduce the quantity she consumes compared to the first period. Now we will analyze the case of an interest rate reduction from r to r'', where $r'' < r$. The line rotates around the endowment point and becomes flatter. This is because if the consumer decides to take out a loan his purchasing possibilities will increase due to the lower interest rate. In the opposite case in which he becomes a lender, his spending opportunities are lower than the situation prior to the rate change, since with the lower rate the yield on his saved current income is lower. In the case of a reduction in the interest rate, if the consumer is a borrower he will remain a debtor in the future. On the contrary, in the case in which he is a lender we cannot say whether he will become a debtor, although he will certainly reduce his future consumption level (Fig. 3.14).

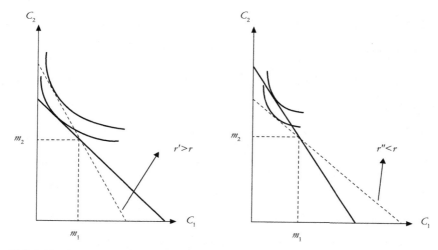

FIG. 3.14   Changes in the interest rate. *Note:* On the left side is the case of an increase in the interest rate from r to r', which corresponds with an increase in satisfaction for a creditor consumer. On the right side is the case of a reduction from r to r'', which corresponds with a reduction in satisfaction for a lender. Although not shown, we can easily intuit that in the first case a borrower's well-being decreases, while in the second case a borrower's situation improves.

Further reading

Mas-Colell, A., Whinston, M., & Green, J. (1995). *Microeconomic theory*. Oxford: Oxford University Press.

Samuelson, P., & Nordhaus, W. (2010). *Economics* (19th ed.). New York: Mc Graw Hill.

Chapter 4

The theory of production decisions

4.1 The economic problem of production

4.1.1 What it means to produce in economics

Any economic system, whatever its social and institutional structure may be, whether capitalist or otherwise, must provide for the satisfaction of its members as well as perpetuate itself over time. To produce means to *transform* resources of one type or another, which we call *inputs* or *factors of production*, into goods and services we call *outputs* or *products*. The latter may be directly consumable, in which case we will talk about *consumption goods*, or they may serve to produce other goods, in which case we will talk about *means of production*. Inputs can be *primary resources*, or factors of production that are not the result of prior production processes, such as labor, land, or raw materials, as well as the means of production obtained from other processes, or capital goods such as factories, machinery, and so forth.

In economics the process of transformation should be understood as the **transformation of value**, rather than transformation only in a physical sense. Production is thus the transformation of nails, wood, and glue into a table (transformation in a technical sense), transporting coffee from Brazil to Italy (transformation in space), storing grain in a silo (transformation in time), and finally a store selling products to the end consumer (transformation in mode). Beyond the specific differences between these forms of transformation, what they always have in common is the creation of value.

The task of the economic theory of production is to study the relationship between the value of the inputs placed into the production process and the value of the outputs obtained. In difference with an engineer who would tell us *how* inputs are transformed into outputs, an economist is more interested in researching the conditions under which the value of the outputs is greater than the value of the inputs. The relationship between inputs and outputs depends on both the *technical relationships* prevalent in the economic system, such as the state of technological knowledge, the quality of human capital, the structure of the territory in which production takes place, and the *social*

The Microeconomics of Wellbeing and Sustainability. https://doi.org/10.1016/B978-0-12-816027-5.00004-5

relationships in which the production process takes shape. It is not hard to understand that it is one thing for production to take place in a capitalist company, while it is quite another if it happens in a cooperative company, a social company, a public company, or a non-profit company. As we might guess, with prevalent technical relationships remaining equal, the results of productive activity in terms of value will vary depending on the type of company under consideration.

4.1.2 Short run and long run

Alfred Marshall made famous the important distinction between the short run and the long run. Plants play a leading role among the inputs in modern production processes. By *plant* we usually mean the factories, offices, or areas where production activity is carried out; it also includes all the items that are part of the capital investment, as well as a certain part of the labor inputs employed in management and controlling tasks.

The **short run** is a time frame in which we assume that the plant used for a particular production will remain fixed, although the intensity of its use may vary. A plant that is available in the short run is the result of investment decisions made and implemented in the past; those decisions may have changed, but not in the immediate future, since modifying a plant takes time. However, it is possible to vary the rates at which inputs such as raw materials, energy, and workers are deployed, since their availability in the short run is not entirely determined by decisions made in the past. Changes clearly take place in plants and production techniques even in the short run, but the effects of such changes are modest relative to its initial conditions, such that it does not seem unreasonable to ignore them.

The short run is thus a time period that is short enough that it does not permit anything but marginal adjustments to the production capacity of the plant, and yet long enough to permit changes to production levels by varying the use of one or more input variables: a blast furnace can operate 24 h a day as long as multiple work shifts are available.

Note that the short run does not have an exact time duration; it could be a month, a quarter, or a year, which will vary depending on the type of production process involved. The short run for a steel mill will probably be longer than the short run for a manufacturing firm.

The **long run** is defined in difference with the short run. It is distinguished by a situation in which all inputs are variable, and the company must thus also choose the plant it will use to carry out its production plan. As we might guess, in a long-run situation — in addition to the problem of arranging for all the inputs needed for the plant — a company must solve a typical investment problem by choosing the size and type of plant that is best suited to current and prospective market situations.

4.1.3 Production technology and Pareto efficiency

In every society the legacy of knowledge regarding how one achieves a certain output from certain inputs constitutes the **available technology**, which is the whole of the production process, or the set of production technologies available in a given historical period. Now we will introduce the important notion of **Pareto efficiency**. Consider any two techniques α and β that are part of the same technology. By comparing them it may result that, with respect to β, technique α: (1) produces the same output levels but uses fewer of some inputs without using more of other inputs; (2) uses the same quantities of all inputs but produces a greater quantity of some outputs without reducing the quantities of other outputs. We would then say that α *is efficient with respect to β*. That is the notion of efficiency credited to Vilfredo Pareto.

This is different from **engineering efficiency**, which we find used in studying power generating plants, for example. Due to the equivalence of all forms of energy, both the input and output of a plant can be measured in the same unit of measure — in kilowatt-hours, for example. It follows that its efficiency is defined by the input-output ratio, which is a pure number, i.e. with no logical dimension. (Due to the inevitable presence of internal energy losses, efficiency will always be less than 100%.)

The situation is quite different in economics, where there is no single unit of measure with which to make equivalent measurements of the inputs employed and the outputs obtained. And yet, the notion of Pareto efficiency makes it possible to compare alternative production techniques without having to express inputs and outputs in terms of value; therein lies its relevance and extended application in economics. However, note that the notion of Pareto efficiency is not an objective measure in the sense that engineering efficiency is; Frame 4.1 explains why.

We will not consider the problem of *substitutability among outputs*. For space reasons we will only consider the *single production* case, in which a company is dedicated to producing only one output. In reality, however, with the same production process a company tends to obtain two or more outputs, such as cars and trucks, for example.

4.2 The entrepreneur

4.2.1 The distinctive traits of entrepreneurship

So who is responsible for carrying out production, given that production is a typically human activity and that animals do not in fact produce? The entrepreneur. All economists, from 15th century Civil Humanism (we have in mind Benedict, Cotrugli, Coluccio, Salutati, Albertanus of Brescia, and Antoninus of Florence) to Adam Smith, Alfred Marshall, and Joseph Schumpeter, were unanimous on this point: entrepreneurship is essential to the very existence of the market economy. (A command economy, such as the Soviet bloc until

FRAME 4.1 Why Pareto efficiency is not a neutral criterion for production purposes

It is a common error in economic reasoning to assume that Pareto efficiency can incontrovertibly and objectively define whether one production process is superior to another, regardless of the goals the producer wants to pursue. An intuitive way to understand why this is not the case is to consider Wight's (2009) thought experiment, appropriately adapted.

In a hospital far out in the countryside, a doctor has ten doses available of a life-saving serum. One night two buses arrive; there are ten people in each one, all of whom need the serum. In bus A, the people are in such a condition that if they receive the serum their lives will be saved. Those in bus B however have a 50% possibility of remaining alive even after having received the serum. The doctor must decide to whom he should administer the life-saving serum. In economic terms, he must efficiently allocate a scarce resource – the ten doses of serum. To whom will he give them? Clearly, he should give them to those in bus A, because by so doing he will save ten human lives rather than five, as would happen were he to opt in favor of those in bus B.

The situation changes, and the doctor is informed that the passengers in bus A, whose average age is 80 years, have a remaining life expectancy of five years; the passengers in bus B are 5 year old children, and they have a remaining life expectancy of 80 years. If the doctor wants to act efficiently on the basis of this new information, to whom should he give the doses of serum? Obviously to the people in bus B, because in so doing he maximizes a total number of 800 years of life: $80 \times 10 = 800$. Were he to distribute them to the people in bus A, the additional years of life would be 50: $5 \times 10 = 50$. Thus if the criterion for choosing is to "maximize the number of human lives," it will favor the people in bus A; if however the criterion is to "maximize the years of life," the choice will fall to the people in bus B.

To complete the thought experiment, now let's suppose that the ten doses are not owned by the hospital, but rather by a private pharmacy that sells them to whoever offers the highest price; in that case the choice would certainly favor the 80 year old people because they can pay, while the 5 year old children cannot pay. Thus if the goal is to maximize revenue, the doctor will act efficiently by assigning the ten doses to the passengers in bus A.

What does this story tell us in essence? That despite what we tend to think, the criterion of efficiency is not a criterion for making an objective decision. We can talk about efficiency and allocate resources on that basis *only after having set the goal we want to achieve*. Efficiency is thus a means to a given end rather than an end in itself. It is clear, then, that when using efficiency to compare economic performance between different types of companies – for example a capitalist company, a cooperative company, and a social company – we must first take into account the goal the company aims to achieve, whether maximizing profit, social utility, the common good, or something else (adapted from J. Wight and J. Morton (2007)).

FRAME 4.1 Why Pareto efficiency is not a neutral criterion for production purposes—cont'd

The following are the main questions we now want to resolve:

if more than one technique is available to a company to produce a given output, how can we choose the optimal combination of inputs? This is a problem of *substitutability between factors of production*;

if the quantities used of all the inputs vary in the same proportion, what is the output level obtained? Will it vary by the same or by a different proportion? This is the problem of the *scale of production*. Remember that this is a problem that arises only in the long run, since all inputs − including fixed inputs − must vary in the same proportion.

1989, can do without entrepreneurs; it needs only savvy politicians and diligent officials.)

But who is an entrepreneur? There are three fundamental characteristics that distinguish such a person:

Propensity to risk. An entrepreneur is someone who loves risk − calculated risk, obviously. This means that an entrepreneur moves into action without yet knowing what the outcome of her activity will be; she is a little like an explorer who pushes into new territory without a map. The bureaucrat, one the other hand, merely applies a procedure he already knows before his work begins.

The ability to innovate. An entrepreneur is not someone who limits himself to replicating what others have already implemented. He is thus someone who competes to expand the boundaries of production possibilities. In this sense an entrepreneur is an agent of change, which may have to do with a product (*product innovation*), a production process (*process innovation*), or of internal organization (*organizational innovation*). Essentially, an entrepreneur is someone who can build a bridge between the knowledge production in university research centers and other institutions and its application in companies, where it is transformed into technological progress (see Frame 4.2).

Ars combinatoria, or the art of combining things together. Similar to an orchestra conductor, an entrepreneur must understand the abilities, strengths, weaknesses, and above all the motivations of her coworkers so she can organize the production process in a way that favors the harmony of individual actions. When an entrepreneur is deficient in this art the company becomes a place of more or less heated conflict, which leads to suboptimal outcomes, and at times to its ruin. (Keep in mind that the ability to bring things together is an art, not a technique that one can learn from a textbook; that is why not all entrepreneurs are equally talented.)

> **FRAME 4.2 Innovativeness**
>
> A passage taken from Italo Calvino's *Invisible Cities* illustrates well the concept of innovativeness.
>
> > Marco Polo described a bridge, stone by stone. "But which stone holds the bridge up?" — asked Kubla Khan.
> > Marco responded, "The bridge is not supported by this or that stone, but by the arch they form."
> > Kubla Khan remained silent, thinking. He then added: "Why are you talking to me about stones? I only care about the arch."
> > Marco responded, "Without stones, there is no arch."
>
> Innovating means arranging things, such as the stones, into new shapes and new forms of order. Creating something new requires thought that holds together matter and form, physical structures and functionality. But above all, it requires not being afraid of the future, not fearing that the bridge might collapse. An innovator is someone who nourishes hope, who does not at all believe that the future will be disruptive just because we do not control it.

Clearly, these three elements are variously present in different measures in real world entrepreneurs. And in fact some are successful and some are not. That depends on a number of factors that are not just personal in nature. For example, some cultures facilitate entrepreneurship and an attitude toward risk more than others. These are cultures based on the idea of development and of integral human progress. There are social systems that favor the art of bringing things together in companies more than in others; it is practically impossible to create harmony in a company if there are deep inequalities in the distribution of income and wealth. The important point to keep in mind is that the entrepreneurial role requires all three of these elements in some manner and to some degree, otherwise we are talking about bureaucrats, administrators, managers, or something else.

Why is it so important to insist on the art of bringing things together, particularly today? We can answer that immediately. Every time different people carry out tasks that are interdependent — a consequence of the division of labor — a coordination problem emerges. Interdependence can be of two types: *technological* or *strategic*. In the first case, the characteristics of the production process itself determine how coordination should happen. The typical example is an assembly line, and more generally, the Fordist system. In the Fordist "factory" or office, coordination happens quickly: the hierarchy and a system of incentives and penalties are sufficient to the task.

Today, however, reality is dominated by strategic interdependence. "Strategic" means that the behavior of each part of an organization depends to a great extent on the expectations of others' intentions and behavior. In such cases, coordination is a "meeting of minds," in the words of Thomas Schelling, an American Nobel laureate economist. The famous late 19th century writer Gilbert Chesterton described well the distinction between an entrepreneur and a manager or corporate executive when he clarified the difference between the act of building and the act of creating. He wrote: "The whole difference between construction and creation is exactly this: that a thing constructed can only be loved after it is constructed; but a thing created is loved before it exists." The true entrepreneur is thus a creator in this precise sense, rather than merely a builder.

4.2.2 Types of companies

The question arises: what might we say about the ultimate purpose entrepreneurs have in mind for them to do what they do? Traditional economic theory has a ready answer: the goal of a company is to maximize profit. But that is not correct because, as reality demonstrates, companies can have many goals. Maximizing profit is indeed the typical goal of a for-profit **capitalist company**, which then proceeds to proportionally distribute the profit earned among all those who provided capital. This is the dominant, but not the only form of company in our market economies.

The goal could in fact be to maximize the net income that the company distributes proportionally among its members on the basis of the labor each provided. This is what happens in **cooperative companies** in production; these are quite widespread in Europe, and in a particular way in Italy, which we will discuss in Chapter 10.

Finally, the goal could be to maximize the social utility associated with production activity. This is what happens in non-profit **social companies** and **public companies**, which we will also discuss in Chapter 10.

The point to emphasize is that entrepreneurial activity is not defined by the goal pursued, but by the three attributes mentioned above. People must be left free to choose their goals, and that choice depends in turn on their motivational system. There are entrepreneurs who are motivated solely by *extrinsic motivations* — such as profit — while some are guided by *intrinsic motivations*; for the latter, profit or net income is a means to pursue goals of a social nature. The Nobel laureate Muhammed Yunus wrote: "a social business is designed and operated as a business enterprise, with products, services, customers, markets, expenses, and revenues — but with the profit-maximization principle replaced by the social-benefit principle."

We conclude by stating that the company is a *genus* that includes different *species* within it: capitalist, social, cooperative, and public. Thus a truly liberal economic system that respects the principles of liberty cannot encourage or discourage one or the other company model at the fiscal and normative levels. In this regard the European Parliament's 19 February 2009 legislative resolution on the social economy constitutes a decisive milestone (see Frame 4.3).

FRAME 4.3 The European Parliament's Resolution 2008/2250 INI on the Social Economy

The European Parliament,

A. whereas the European social model is built mainly upon a high level of services, goods and jobs generated by the social economy with the support of forecasting and innovation capacities developed by its promoters,

B. whereas the social economy is based on a social paradigm which is in line with the fundamental principles of the European social and welfare model, and whereas the social economy plays a key role today in preserving and strengthening that model by regulating the production and supply of numerous social services of general interest, ...

D. whereas the wealth and stability of society derives from its diversity, and whereas the social economy actively contributes to that diversity by improving and reinforcing the European social model and by providing a distinctive business model, which enables the social economy to contribute to stable and sustainable growth, ...

F. whereas the social economy represents 10% of all European businesses, with 2 million undertakings or 6% of total employment, and has great potential for generating and maintaining stable employment, due mainly to the fact that those activities, by their very nature, are not likely to be delocalized,

G. whereas social economy enterprises are usually small and medium-sized enterprises (SMEs) contributing to a sustainable economic model, under which individuals are more important than capital, and whereas such enterprises are often active in the internal market and therefore need to ensure that their activities comply with the relevant law,

H. whereas the social economy has developed from particular organizational or legal business formations such as cooperatives, mutual societies, associations, social enterprises and organizations, foundations and other entities in each of the Member States; whereas the social economy covers a range of concepts used in the various Member States such as "the solidarity economy" and "the third sector," and although those concepts are not considered to form part of the social economy in all the Member States, comparable activities sharing the same features exist throughout the European Union, ...

J. whereas the social economy gives prominence to a business model that cannot be characterized either by its size or by its areas of activity, but by its respect for common values, namely, the primacy of democracy, social stakeholder participation, and individual and social objectives over gain; the defense and implementation of the principles of solidarity and responsibility; the conjunction of the interests of its user members with the general interest; democratic control by its members; voluntary and open membership; management autonomy and independence in relation to public authorities; and the allocation of the bulk of surpluses in pursuit of the aims of sustainable

FRAME 4.3 The European Parliament's Resolution 2008/2250 INI on the Social Economy—cont'd

development and of service to its members in accordance with the general interest,

K. whereas despite the increasing importance of the social economy and of the organizations that form part of it, it remains little-known and is often the target of criticism stemming from misguided technical approaches; and whereas lack of institutional visibility is one of the most important obstacles that the social economy faces in the EU and in some of its Member States, which is due in part to the peculiarities of national accounting systems, ...

Resources needed to achieve the objectives

[...]

34. Calls on the Commission to ensure that the features of the social economy (its aims, values and working methods) are taken into account when devising EU policies and, in particular, to incorporate the social economy into its policies and strategies in the sphere of social, economic, and enterprise development, especially in connection with the "Small Business Act" for Europe (COM(2008)0394); asks that when the social economy is affected impact assessments are carried out and the interests of the social economy are respected and given priority; urges the Commission, in addition, to look again at the possibility of setting up a social economy inter-service unit linking the relevant directorates-general;

[...]

41. Calls for programmes to be set up that will encourage experimentation with new economic and social models, to initiate framework research programmes, by including social economy subjects in calls for proposals under the Seventh Framework Programme, to envisage the use of a "multiplier" applied to the official statistics and to introduce instruments for measuring economic growth from a qualitative and quantitative point of view;

[...]

42. Calls on the Commission and the Member States to include a social economy dimension in the establishment of Community and national policies and in EU programmes for enterprises in the fields of research, innovation, finance, regional development and development cooperation, and to support the establishment of social economy training programmes for EU, national and local administrators and to ensure the access of social economy enterprises to programmes and actions for development and external relations;

[...]

43. Urges the Member States to make provision for training projects involving higher education, university and vocational training courses designed to create awareness of the social economy and of business initiatives based on its values.

4.3 The production function

4.3.1 The short-run production function

Assuming for the sake of simplicity that the production process has only one output — the value of which we indicate with y — *the short-run production function is the set of efficient techniques to produce the output quantity y by using the quantities L (labor) and M (material) of the input variables in the time frame considered, given the fixed size of plant K.*

Symbolically:

$$y = f(L, M, \overline{K}) \tag{4.1}$$

which we read as follows: output y is a function of L, M, and $\overline{K}$.

Now we will consider the problem of *sub (a)* — substitutability between inputs — starting from the case in which there is only one input variable. That is, we assume that L is the only variable factor: the company has a given quantity of material to use and a given plant, and labor is the only input that can vary to obtain different output quantities. In this situation, Eq. (4.1) can be written more simply:

$$y = g(L) \tag{4.2}$$

to indicate that y varies as L changes, given M and K. We call Eq. (4.2) the *function of the total product of L.* Geometrically, one of its possible forms is that of Fig. 4.1. Since L is an essential element in production, the curve starts from the origin because if $L = 0$ then $y = 0$ as well. The trend and the position

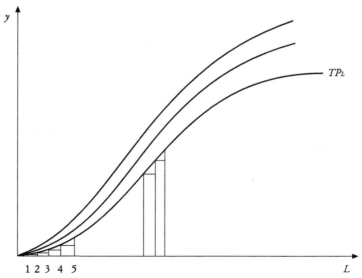

FIG. 4.1 The function of the total product of an input variable.

of this curve clearly depend on the quantities used of the other inputs; this is why a family of curves of the total product of labor is plotted in Fig. 4.1. In order to grasp the economic significance of the sigmoid shape of the curve of the total productivity of labor TP_L it is necessary to introduce the concept of the marginal productivity and the average productivity of an input.

4.3.2 The law of diminishing returns

We define the **marginal productivity of an input variable** — which in the present case of labor we will indicate with P'_L — as the change in output due to a very small change of the input under consideration, with the use of all other inputs remaining constant. Symbolically:

$$P'_L = \frac{\Delta y}{\Delta L}$$

We define the **average productivity of an input variable** as the ratio between the output obtained and the overall quantity used of the input, with the use of all other inputs remaining constant. Symbolically:

$$APL = \frac{y}{L}$$

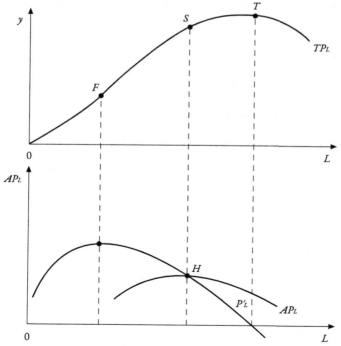

FIG. 4.2 Total, average, and marginal product of an input variable.

With these definitions as a base it is now easy to derive the marginal and average productivity curves for an input once its total productivity curve is known. Fig. 4.2 geometrically illustrates the connection in question. As we can see, up to the point that the curve TP_L is convex (point F in Fig. 4.2) the curve P'_L is ascending; from the point at which TP_L begins to be concave, P'_L begins to descend. Finally, when TP_L reaches its maximum point (point T in Fig. 4.2), P'_L goes to zero (the curve P'_L intersects the x-axis).

The curve AP_L is also bell-shaped like the curve P'_L, except that AP_L ascends until point S of TP_L. In other words, the maximum point of the curve AP_L — point H — is shifted to the right with respect to the maximum point of P'_L. This reflects the fact that average productivity, like all average variables, takes into account all the units used of a factor rather than just the last unit, as is the case with marginal productivity.

Finally, we observe that the curve AP_L reaches its maximum at the point where it intersects the curve P'_L, or point H in Fig. 4.2. This is a general property that links any average variable with its corresponding marginal variable: *the average variable reaches its maximum or minimum value at the point at which it equals the corresponding marginal value*. In the case in question the variable in play is productivity; we will later consider cost and revenue, but the rule remains the same.

The shape of the curve TP_L in Fig. 4.2 reveals an important economic law: **the law of diminishing returns**. Studying agricultural production, Ricardo observed that different quantities of labor, with the help of certain quantities of other inputs, such as agricultural equipment, fertilizer, and so forth, could be employed on a given plot of ground. Ricardo pointed out that in producing agricultural goods it is possible to vary the proportions of land and "complex labor" — labor and capital — employed. That is how Ricardo came to the law in question: with the quantity of land under cultivation remaining fixed, increases in production resulting from equal increments in the use of successive amounts of complex labor increase at first and then decrease. In other words, the average and marginal productivity of labor trend higher at first and then decline, as shown in Fig. 4.2.

4.3.3 The variability of two inputs

Let's now assume that there are two input variables, which we will indicate by L and M. Our production function thus becomes:

$$y = h(L, M) \tag{4.3}$$

given the plant $\overline{K}$ as before.

To geometrically represent Eq. (4.3), it is helpful to use a graph with the quantities employed of L and M indicated on its axes. In this way we obtain curves named **production isoquants** (see Fig. 4.3). Each curve represents all efficient combinations of the use rates of L and M that yield the same output

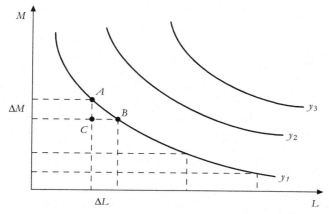

FIG. 4.3 Production isoquants.

level y. Fig. 4.3 depicts a typical map (or family) of isoquants derived from production function (Eq. 4.3). A few observations are appropriate:

- since the production function is by definition the set of efficient techniques, an isoquant is a curve descending from left to right, meaning that if we want to maintain the output level unchanged, when the use level of one input increases, the use of the other input must correspondingly decrease.
- every isoquant is associated with an output level, which increases the farther it is from the origin of the Cartesian axes ($y_1 < y_2 < y_3$);
- two or more isoquants can never intersect: if this were the case the efficiency property would be violated;
- the isoquants drawn in Fig. 4.3 are convex with respect to the origin. Why? To answer that, consider the ratio between the change in M — which we indicate by ΔM — that is necessary to compensate for the change in L — which we indicate by ΔL — to remain on the same isoquant, y_1. The ratio $|\Delta M/\Delta L|$ defines the **(marginal) rate of substitution** $MRS_{M,L}$ between M and L, which is the degree of substitutability between the two inputs for the purpose of obtaining a given output volume. (Note that MRS is always a negative number: that is why we place it between two vertical lines to denote the absolute value.)

The convexity of the isoquant implies that as we gradually substitute M with L, increasingly greater quantities of L are needed to compensate for the reduction of an equal amount of M. With careful consideration, we see that this is the direct consequence of the law of diminishing returns described above. Indeed, we can easily show that: $MRS_{M,L} = P'_L/P'_M$. Consider Fig. 4.3.

To go from A to B, we can think of moving from A to C, thus losing the amount $P'_M \Delta M$ of output. Since the decrease in output must equal its increase, given that A and B lie on the same isoquant, it must be: $-P'_M \Delta M = +P'_{L\Delta} L$, and thus $MRS_{M,L} = \frac{P'_L}{P'_M}$.

4.3.4 The long-run production function: returns to scale

We now turn to the problem *sub (b)*, in which we will study production laws in a long-run context in which all inputs are variables.

The expression **returns to scale** refers to the relationship between changes in output and the *equiproportional* variations of all inputs. The term "scale" qualifying the term "returns" indicates that the only thing that changes is the production level, while the *structure* and the characteristics of the process remain unaltered.

Assume the long-run production function is given as $y = f(L, M, K)$, and assume that we start from a level of input use such that the output produced is y^0.

Now increase all three inputs by the same proportion — doubling them, for example. If we discover that the output increases by the same proportion — that is, it doubles — then we talk about *constant returns to scale*; if the output more than doubles, then we talk about *increasing returns to scale*; if the output increases less than double, we talk about *diminishing returns to scale*.

What do the different types of returns to scale depend on? The most frequent cause of increasing returns to scale is that of **technical indivisibility**. While it is true that a process can always be doubled (or tripled, etc.) it is not always possible to halve the intensity of an operation. Two workers with two shovels can produce double that of one worker with a shovel, but a part-time worker with a "half-shovel" produces nothing; this is an example of factor indivisibility.

A second cause of returns to scale consists of *economies due to the three-dimensional nature of space*; these are **static** returns to scale. Consider the area–volume relationship of a cube with sides x. The total surface area is equal to $6x^2$, while the volume is equal to x^3. If the side of the cube doubles $(2x)$, the surface area increases by four times $(24x^2)$ while the volume increases by eight times $(8x^3)$. So if the production capacity of a plant depends on volume while its cost depends on area, the cost of production will increase less than proportionally to production. Consider an oil pipeline: its carrying capacity can be quadrupled by doubling its diameter, while construction costs are linked to its diameter, not its capacity.

A third factor that generates increasing returns to scale is the *economy of specialization*: higher production levels allow a greater division and specialization of labor, with consequent productivity increases and a reduction in costs. The introduction of the assembly line, automation, and learning by doing are all examples of the economy of specialization. These are the so-called **dynamic** returns to scale, which have very little to do with factor indivisibility.

4.3.5 Diseconomies of scale

We should point out that nothing we have said so far implies that a large company is always preferable to a small one. Indeed, it may be that in certain production sectors or in certain historical periods the importance attributed to economies of scale in an abstract sense does not materialize, or even that diseconomies of scale happen due to:

- limits on the availability of inputs, for example, a limited labor supply: increasing the scale of production may lead to higher labor costs due to the need to ensure that the necessary labor is available;
- purely technical considerations: increasing a plant's production capacity of individual units may lead to increased tension and/or friction that requires more expensive materials;
- management problems: controlling and coordinating operations in large plants can be difficult to resolve;
- conflicts: it is a readily ascertainable fact that large organizations can increase conflicts between workers and owners, or between owners and managers; furthermore, the complexity of large organizations can sometimes lead to significantly higher organizational costs.

It is thus up to empirical research to determine on a case-by-case basis whether economies of scale as a whole outweigh diseconomies of scale, taking into account also the historical and institutional context in which the company or sector operates. In theory it does not seem plausible to formulate a "law" on the matter; that said, in light of common sense we can conclude that sectors such as basic chemicals and steel exhibit economies of scale, while in the service sector, such as banking, the empirical evidence seems to suggest that there is limited room for increasing returns to scale. This accounts for the fact that regional banks (such as credit unions and saving banks), if well managed, can yield comparatively better results than large commercial banks, particularly in times of crisis.

4.4 Production costs

4.4.1 Types of production costs

The analysis carried out so far has only considered the system of technical constraints in which production takes place. We have said nothing so far about economic constraints, such that at this point we are not able to indicate the point on a given isoquant at which a company will choose to produce a given level of output. In other words, we do not yet have a criterion to choose between alternative efficient techniques. To solve this type of problem we must introduce the new economic category of **production cost**, which is defined as the sustained monetary outlay to purchase the resources necessary to carry out production.

We will assume that: (*a*) the company acquires all inputs at prices that do not depend on the quantities purchased; (*b*) the company can buy all inputs in the quantities required. These assumptions imply that the market for production factors are in perfect competition (see Chapter 5); (*c*) the company carrying out the production process operates in such a way that it chooses *the production technique that minimizes costs*. It follows that the production cost of a given output level, given input prices and technology, is the *lowest cost* at which that given output level can be attained.

In the short run, output is a function of the use levels of variable factors and of the services provided by a plant that are available to the company. Production cost thus depends on both the cost of using variable factors and the cost of acquiring the availability of the plant. We call the former **variable costs**, since they vary according to the output level. They include the cost of the raw materials consumed in the course of the production process, the cost of running the machinery, direct labor costs (production workers), and the decline in the value of the equipment due to its use in production. We call **fixed costs** the costs that the company would bear even if there were no production, since these costs are relative to past decisions made when it was decided to purchase the plant. Fixed costs include maintenance not connected to the use of the plant, insurance costs, general administration costs, depreciation attributable to the short run in consideration (this component of fixed costs should not be confused with the wear and tear on the plant due to its use, which, as indicated above, is part of the variable costs), the remuneration for entrepreneurial labor, and the financial capital invested in the plant.

This last cost component is **normal profit**, which is by nature an *opportunity cost*: An entrepreneur decides to make a financial investment that allows her to become part of a particular branch of activity because she foresees making a "normal profit" that is at least equal to what she could have made by directing the financial investment elsewhere.

Indicating the total short run costs by TC, we can write:

$$TC = TFC + TVC \tag{4.4}$$

where TFC is the total fixed cost and TVC is the total variable cost.

Taking the ratio of total costs to the quantity produced, we obtain the **average total cost**, ATC. From Eq. (4.4), dividing both sides by y, we obtain:

$$ATC = \frac{TC}{y} = \frac{TFC}{y} + \frac{TVC}{y} \tag{4.5}$$

The average total cost is thus equal to the sum of the average fixed cost $AFC = TFC/y$ and the average variable cost, $AVC = TVC/y$.

Finally, we define **marginal cost**, which we indicate with C', or the change in total cost due to a very small variation in output level. Symbolically:

$$C' = \frac{\Delta TC}{\Delta y} \tag{4.6}$$

Clearly, marginal cost only takes into account the variable component of the total cost, given that the change in fixed cost is by definition zero in the short run.

What happens when we shift from the short run to the long run? The only thing we need to keep in mind is that we drop the distinction between fixed and variable costs, for the simple reason that over the long run all costs are variable, including for plants. A company will choose one plant in particular from among those that technology makes available to it, one that best corresponds to its growth expectations while keeping market conditions in mind.

4.4.2 Short-run cost curves

We will first consider the case in which labor is the only input variable, L. Variable costs thus reduce to the payments made to acquire that input. In this circumstance, cost curves are derived directly from the corresponding productivity curves, once the price of the input variable is known. That is, the average variable cost curve is taken from the average labor productivity curve, and the marginal cost curve is taken from the marginal labor productivity curve.

When labor is the only factor that varies, the unit price of which is the wage rate indicated by w, AVC:

$$AVC = \frac{TVC}{y} = \frac{wL}{y}$$

and since average labor productivity is given by y/L, from the previous equivalences we derive: $AVC = w/AP_L$. Thus the average variable cost is equal to the ratio between the price of the single input variable and its average productivity, a ratio also known as the labor cost per unit of product (LCUP).

The marginal cost will be:

$$C' = \frac{\Delta TC}{\Delta y} = \frac{w\Delta L}{\Delta y} = \frac{w}{P'_L}$$

since the cost increase due to a production increase equals the amount spent to purchase additional units of the input variable. The marginal cost is thus equal to the ratio between the input variable price and its marginal productivity. Once we know the average and marginal productivity curves, we can immediately derive the average variable cost and the marginal cost curves. Fig. 4.4 is taken from Fig. 4.2. The full correspondence between the curves of the two graphs deserves attention: Where the marginal productivity curve reaches its maximum point, the marginal cost curve is at its minimum point. The same applies to the average curves. In addition, when a productivity curve is increasing, the corresponding cost curve is decreasing and *vice versa*. Finally, the marginal cost curve intersects the average variable cost curve at its lowest point, just as the marginal productivity curve intersects the average productivity curve at its highest point.

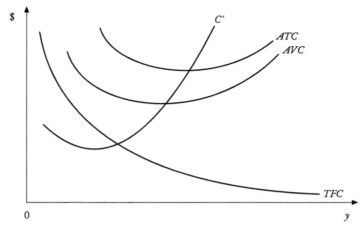

FIG. 4.4 Average and marginal cost curves.

What about fixed costs? The total fixed cost is by definition constant in the short run. Thus the average fixed cost curve will be an *equilateral hyperbole* as shown in Fig. 4.4. Summing the two curves AFC and AVC vertically we obtain ATC.

A final important observation. In Fig. 4.4, the marginal cost, average total cost, and average variable cost curves are U shaped; this shape reflects the laws of diminishing returns. Within a given plant, there is first a phase of increasing productivity of the variable input, and thus of decreasing costs, followed by a phase of decreasing productivity, and thus of increasing costs. Between these two phases there is a point at which the average costs are at their minimum. When this point is reached, we say that *the plant is being optimally used.* Every plant is designed to function in combination with a certain number of variable inputs. If the plant is used to produce a lower output level than it was designed for, it is clear that it cannot be used at its full potential, thus costs will be higher than they could be. Similarly, if the plant is over utilized there will be congestion, with a consequent drop in productivity and an increase in costs. Thus for every plant there is an output level at which the average cost is at its lowest.

4.4.3 Two variable inputs: choosing the optimal combination of factors

When there are two input variables, to derive the cost curve we must solve a new problem. If in fact there are two variable inputs, it is necessary to establish the criterion by which a company can proceed to implement the optimal combination of variable factors. To this end it will be useful to introduce the notion of an **isocost line**, along which the combinations of the two variable

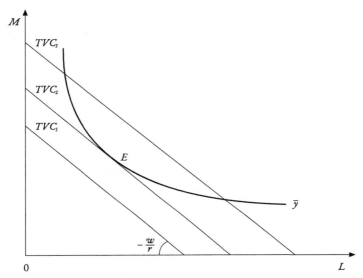

FIG. 4.5 Minimizing the total cost and choosing the optimal technique.

factors used have the same cost. Indicating the unit cost of labor by w and the unit cost of the other input variable M by r, the isocost line equation can be written as:

$$TVC = wL + rM$$

Fig. 4.5 represents a generic isocost line with a slope given by the ratio w/r, and its distance from the origin is measured by TVC, the total variable cost. The same mathematical properties apply to the isocost line as apply to the budget line in the problem of consumer choice, so we need not repeat that here.

The solution to the problem of choosing the combination of inputs — and thus the technique — that allows obtaining a given output at the minimal cost can be conveniently expressed geometrically. Fig. 4.5 represents a family of isocost lines and the isoquant relative to the chosen output level $\bar{y}$. As we can see, the solution we are looking for is at the tangent point E between the isoquant $\bar{y}$ and one of the isocost lines, TVC_2. Any point other than E would entail a greater expense to produce $\bar{y}$, or as in the case of TVC_1, $\bar{y}$ could not actually be obtained.

Since the slope of the isocost is given by the ratio of the prices of the inputs, w/r, and the slope of a point on the isoquant is simply the marginal rate of substitution between the two inputs, the tangent point E must have the following relationship:

$$MRS = \frac{w}{r}$$

On the other hand, since the *MRS* is equal to the ratio between the marginal productivity of the two inputs, then at *E*:

$$\frac{P'_L}{P'_M} = \frac{w}{r} \tag{4.7a}$$

or

$$\frac{P'_L}{w} = \frac{P'_M}{r} \tag{4.7b}$$

In conclusion, all the points along the isoquant denote efficient techniques; however, only technique *E* is *optimal*, that is, that minimizes the cost of production. We can thus state that the *optimal technique, that is, the optimal combination of factors, is the one in which the ratio between the marginal productivity of the two inputs equals the ratio of their prices, or the one that equalizes the weighted marginal productivity of the inputs.*

The rule we have derived now allows us to analyze the effects of changes in the prices of the inputs. A non-equiproportional change in the prices of the two inputs entails a change in production technique; the company should replace the more expensive technique with the less expensive one. In what direction does that substitution happen? The substitution between inputs proceeds along the lines that *the input with the lower relative price should be used more extensively, and vice versa.* So if *w* decreases while *r* remains unchanged, the company should employ more workers and less *M*: that is clearly confirmed in Eq. (4.7b). In fact, if *w* decreases P'_L will also decrease, which means that *L* should be used more than *M*.

We are now able to give the solution to the problem we started out with. To arrive at the total variable cost curve, we need only draw a family of isoquants and a family of isocosts on the same graph; we will then look for the tangent point of each isoquant with an isocost line (see Fig. 4.6). By joining these tangent points we obtain the *company expansion path*, which is a curve that indicates the minimum cost to produce successive levels of output. But this is precisely the meaning of the total variable cost curve. So, to produce y_1 the minimum total variable cost is TVC_1; to produce y_2 the minimum total variable cost is TVC_2, and so on. The *TVC* curve is thus derived from the company's expansion path. What shape will the variable cost curve have? We have seen that in the case of two variable inputs the relationship between their marginal cost and marginal productivity is the same as what we saw in the case in which there is only one variable input. We conclude that in the present case as well, the short-run curves for average and marginal cost have the typical *U* shape.

4.4.4 Long-run cost curves

Over the long run, as we know, the company can choose the use rate of all inputs, thus there are no fixed inputs that can constrain the company's production

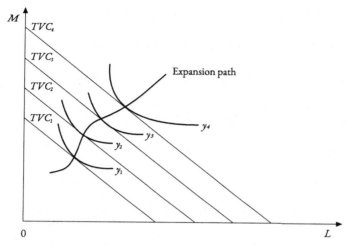

FIG. 4.6 The company expansion path.

capacity if they become unavailable. In a long-run situation, how does the company choose the plant that best suits it? The problem arises from the fact that every plant has an output level that can be produced at the minimum average cost. This is because the larger the plant, the higher the fixed cost, which has a higher impact on the average cost for low production levels.

To clarify this, we will assume that the company can choose between three different sized plants: small, medium, and large. The small plant implies an average cost curve such as AC_1 in Fig. 4.7A, the medium plant implies AC_2, and the large plant implies AC_3. If the company expects to sell an output level that does not exceed y_1, it will certainly choose the small plant. If it expects to sell an output level between y_1 and y_2, it will opt for the medium plant. Finally, if it expects to be able to sell an output level greater than y_2, it will choose the large plant.

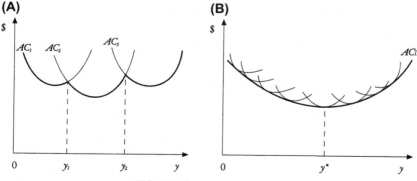

FIG. 4.7 Long-run cost curves.

If after having opted for the small plant the company must produce output greater than y_1, it will do so at a higher cost than it would have borne had it initially bought the medium plant, and so forth. Along the lines of this reasoning, we conclude that the curve marked in bold in Fig. 4.7A is simply the **long run average cost curve** for the case in which there are only three plants. If we now assume that there are an infinite number of plants available instead of three, the stepped curve in Fig. 4.7A becomes a smooth curve (see Fig. 4.7B). Mathematically, it is the **envelope** of the short-run cost curves, and it denotes the long-run average cost curve AC_L.

Why does the AC_L curve also have a U shape, similar to the short-run average cost curves? The answer given by traditional theory is that it depends on the law of returns to scale: Up to a certain output level y^* the average cost decreases as the plant size increases, due to increasing returns to scale; above that output level, the average cost begins to rise as the size of the plant increases due to decreasing returns to scale, which are caused primarily by organizational factors. Organizing a large company does in fact entail specific costs to coordinate, supervise, and monitor the corporate hierarchy, among other things.

4.5 Economies of scale

A distinctive characteristic of production in modern economic systems is the use of processes that are only implemented at high output volumes; their salient characteristic is that they are more efficient than small scale operations. The expression **economies of scale** designates all the factors that make unit costs at high production levels less than unit costs at lower output levels. What brings about economies of scale? Two distinct types of economies of scale are usually noted: *real* and *financial*.

For example, financial economies benefit companies that are able to pay lower prices for the inputs it uses, due to the fact that increasing the scale of production also increases the quantities demanded for inputs. Examples of financial economies of scale are lower prices for raw materials, lower costs for outside financing, lower costs to transport and distribute the output, and so on. As we can see, these are cost savings *outside* the company, because they have to do with bargaining power in the input markets.

Real economies of scale are associated with reductions in input quantities used when a given company increases output levels. Consider the following examples.

- Starting any production process always requires a certain monetary outlay; the higher the production level, the less that outlay impacts each unit of output. In other words, this is a typical *fixed cost effect*. The initial fixed costs include the cost of installing machinery, fine tuning the equipment, product line costs, and so on.

- Another example of real economies of scale is *economies of reserve capacity*. A company always maintains a certain reserve capacity so output is not interrupted in the event of a machine failure. A small company that uses, say, only one machine will need to maintain another to ensure against the risk of interruptions; a company that uses four machines certainly does not need eight machines to cover itself; six or so should be sufficient. The same applies to the repair workforce. The situation of *economies of reserves* is similar. Raw materials reserves increase when output increases, but in general the amount of reserves — which cost the company to maintain — vary less than proportionally with respect to output.
- *Increasing returns to scale*, which we have already discussed, are ultimately another important cause of real economies of scale.

A final remark. Economies of scale should not be confused with *economies of scope*. When a company is able to produce more than one good — that is, it can implement a *multi-product production* — it can happen that by producing several products together the overall costs can be lower at the same output levels than the sum of the production costs for each output considered by itself.

4.6 External costs and opportunity costs

Before concluding this chapter, we should clarify an important point. To this point, when considering production costs we have always referred to the costs borne directly by the company; these are so-called **internal costs**.

It is clear, however, that production activity always produces external effects — sometimes positive, sometimes negative — that have an impact on those not involved in the activity itself but who are affected by it. We call such cases positive or negative *externalities*, which give rise to **external costs** to the company (which we will specifically consider in Chapter 8.)

Smoke from a factory chimney is a classic example of a negative externality. The process chosen by the factory produces smoke as a by-product, which afflicts those nearby who breathe polluted air or damages a farmer's crops in an adjacent field. An example of a positive externality is a beekeeper who benefits from meadows adjoining her property, when the bees feed on the pollen in the flowers that grow on land belonging to another company.

When there are external costs, the **private cost** borne by the company is less than the **social cost**, which is the sum of the private cost and the damage to those who suffer from negative externalities. The result is that the company will tend to push production beyond the level it would were it to take into account the external costs of its activity. In the absence of corrective measures and/or interventions by a public agency, production levels tend to exceed those that are socially desirable; the case of environmental damage is just one of many examples, although it is presently the most worrying one.

The other important distinction to keep in mind is between **accounting costs** and **economic costs**. The former are the costs that give rise to monetary outlays or movements of cash when the company must buy on the market the inputs it needs to carry out its production plan. However, there are also inputs the company uses and finances with its own risk capital — the capital it derives from past savings, in addition to the capital contributions of its owners. By using its own funds the company pays no interest, as it would have to do were it to take out a bank loan.

Although using its own funds does not produce an accounting cost, such use is not free, as one might think. The reason is that by employing its own risk capital in that way, the company foregoes the benefit it would have obtained had it decided to lend out those same resources by making a financial investment of one sort or another on the capital markets. The *opportunity cost* measures the next best alternative the company gives up when making a choice. This is an extraordinarily important concept in economics that was first introduced by the Austrian economist Karl Menger in 1871.

The **economic cost is the sum of accounting costs and opportunity costs**. The economic way of reasoning requires that when a company must decide whether or not to start a given production process, it must pay attention to the economic costs, not just the accounting costs.

Further reading

Goodwin, N., Nelson, J. A., Ackerman, F., & Weisskopf, T. (2005). *Microeconomics in context*. Boston: Houghton Mifflin.

Menger, K. (2007 [1871]). *Principles of economics* (J. Dingwall & B. F. Hoselitz, Trans.). Auburn, Alabama: Ludwig von Mises Institute.

Schelling, T. (1960). *The strategy of conflict*. Cambridge, MA: Harvard University Press.

Wight, J. (2009). Teaching economics. In J. Peiland, & I. Van Staveren (Eds.), *Handbook of economics and ethics*. Cheltenham: Elgar.

Wight, J., & Morton, J. (2007). *Teaching the ethical foundation of economics*. New York: NCEE.

Yunus, M. (2007). *Creating a world without poverty*. New York: Public Affairs.

Chapter 5

Perfectly competitive markets

5.1 The problem of supply

5.1.1 The benefits of production

Knowing the cost function of a certain production process is a necessary but insufficient condition for a company to be able to decide on the most desirable quantity of the good to produce. Where in the previous chapter we discussed *how* production is done, in this chapter we will focus on *how much* to produce. For that we must turn our attention to the benefits of production, just as in the previous chapter we focused on the costs of production.

We need to preface that discussion with two considerations. First, the benefits of productive activity can be *internal* and *external* to the entity in which the process takes place. External benefits are those associated with a given production process that have an impact outside the company on the territory where the process takes place, such as other companies, local communities, and civil society organizations. A **socially responsible company** (which we will discuss further in Chapter 11) is one that is concerned not only with generating internal benefits for itself (those that benefit it exclusively) but in benefitting others as well. Alexis de Tocqueville, in his masterful 1835 book *Democracy in America*, grasped this point well when he wrote regarding the newly rich: "In their intense and exclusive anxiety to make a fortune they lose sight of the close connection that exists between the private fortune of each and the prosperity of all."

The second consideration concerns the motivations that drive economic agents to act in one way rather than another; these can be **extrinsic and intrinsic**. For example, we can devote ourselves to study either because we believe that a degree will offer better job opportunities and a higher income or because we are convinced that intellectual activity is worth pursuing as an end in itself. In the first case, the study will only produce *extrinsic benefits*; in the second case, it will produce *intrinsic benefits* as well. It goes without saying that in reality students are motivated by both, although in different proportions in relation to multiple factors, such as education received in the family, the quality of instruction, the personalities of the instructors, and so forth. Finally, there is a third type of motivation underlying economic action that is less

The Microeconomics of Wellbeing and Sustainability. https://doi.org/10.1016/B978-0-12-816027-5.00005-7
139

common than the previous two but of great practical relevance. These are *transcendent* motivations, in which we act in a certain way because we want to produce benefits that are advantageous to others. This is the case of the pure altruist, or more generally, of those who are moved to action by a specific vocation; we will consider this extensively in Chapter 10.

The above also applies to entrepreneurial activities. As we noted in Section 4.2 of Chapter 4, there are entrepreneurs who only have extrinsic motivations and are thus interested solely in the extrinsic benefits of their activity, called "profit." Other entrepreneurs also have intrinsic motivations and are able to distinguish between *what is useful* to achieve profit as a goal and *what is worthwhile* as an end in itself. A *civil entrepreneur* is one who leads a company in a way that makes extrinsic and intrinsic motivations harmoniously compatible. Here we mention just a few names of entrepreneurs who have worked in Italy, such as Adriano Olivetti in Ivrea, Alessandro Rossi in Schio, Ernest Solvay in Rosignano, and Gaetano Marzotto in Valdagno.

The two considerations just discussed lead us to the following conclusion. If we want to understand a company's decision-making process — why it makes certain choices rather than others — we cannot ignore the motivational system of the entrepreneur and her co-workers. The reason is easy: if they have only extrinsic motivations, it is clear that they will only pay attention to the extrinsic benefits of production and will thus make decisions, particularly in organizational matters, in a certain way rather than another. The list could go on.

Why does traditional theory not consider this distinction and its ensuing consequences? That is readily answered: the theory assumes that a capitalist company is the only type that can populate the market. Given that this type of company has maximizing profit as its sole purpose, and given that a capitalist entrepreneur is guided only by extrinsic motivations in his actions, it follows that traditional theory will only pay attention to internal, extrinsic benefits. In Chapters 9—13 we will expand our knowledge by studying other forms of companies than the purely capitalist type.

In the meantime, we would like to cite the following statement by Adriano Olivetti, which tells us that we can be capitalist entrepreneurs with intrinsic motivations: "We all believe in the unlimited power of spiritual forces; we also believe that the only solution to the current political and social crisis in the Western world is to give these spiritual forces the opportunity to develop their creative genius. We cannot talk about civilization if even one of these essential forces of the spirit is absent: truth, justice, beauty, and above all, love" (Olivetti, 1960, 489).

5.1.2 Perfect competition

At this point we have sufficient knowledge to address the problem of how much to produce. Just as in the problem of how to produce we used the criterion of minimizing economic costs in order to choose the optimal production technique from among the efficient ones, analogously the criterion that allows us to determine the optimal production quantity is that of maximizing the **net benefits**, which equals the difference between total benefits and total production costs. If the company is capitalist, the costs and benefits will only be those that are internal and extrinsic; if the company is a cooperative or a social company, then the other cost and benefit categories we have discussed must be taken into consideration.

In what follows we will consider the case of a capitalist company operating in a perfectly competitive market. For such a company the net benefit coincides with **economic profit**, which in turn is the difference between economic costs and revenues. Economic profit is thus different from **accounting profit** precisely because it also includes economic costs and revenues.

Before we go any further, this would be a good time to remind ourselves of the elements that make up a perfectly competitive market. Augustin Cournot, a French economist, has the distinction of having introduced the theory of a perfectly competitive equilibrium. The notion of equilibrium that he developed in his 1938 work *Recherches* is partial, in that it refers to the price and quantity variables in a market isolated from the rest of the economy. Cournot's approach was taken up and perfected by Alfred Marshall, who defined a perfectly competitive equilibrium as the state a market would be in if all decision-making entities, and companies in particular, were devoid of market power. To be precise, a market is perfectly competitive in which:

agents are maximizers: producers who transform inputs into outputs maximize economic profit within cost constraints; consumers who buy the outputs maximize their utility function within their income constraints; agents' decisions in the market are independent of each other; there are no coalitions or collusion, and production and consumption decisions do not create external effects;
the number of buyers and sellers is sufficiently high that no one is able to exert a significant influence on the quantities bought or sold in the market; the intensity of competition in the market is measured by the number of players in a certain sector, from which it follows that agents are price-takers;
producers and consumers have complete information about the possibilities of production and consumption, thus there are neither uncertainties nor information asymmetries between agents.

As we will see, every deviation from one or more of these ideal market conditions leads, depending on the case, to monopolistic competition, either to monopoly or oligopoly. In this sense we can state that the theory of perfect competition constitutes a sort of benchmark against which other market structures can be defined and analyzed, which we will discuss in the next chapter.

One final important observation. Competition is the flip side of resource scarcity: only in a world without either material and/or immaterial scarcity would there be no need for competition. There is competition even in command economies — as were those of the Soviet bloc until 1989, the year the Berlin Wall fell — but of a different sort than what is prevalent in market economies. Thus the question to address is not whether or not to abolish competition, which is impossible, but to decide which type of competition we want to incline toward, either **positional** (the current prevalent form) or **cooperative**. We will focus on this in Chapters 10 and 11.

5.2 The revenue function

In a market economy, a capitalist company produces goods that it dedicates itself to selling on the market, and the receipts from product sales constitute *revenue*. Under conditions of perfect competition, an individual company cannot influence the price at which it sells its product. Indeed, were it to try to charge a higher price than its competitors it would not be able to sell anything, given that buyers, who have perfect information about market conditions, would turn to the companies with the lowest prices for their purchases. On the other hand, if the company were to lower its sales price in its attempts to sell more, it would not be able to satisfy all potential clients, since, given its size, it cannot produce above a certain upper bound.

The result is that in perfect competition each company can sell its desired quantity at the current market price, such that the *demand curve for a single company* is a (semi)straight horizontal line, as shown in Fig. 5.1A. This curve is located at a height corresponding to the market price (p^*) that results from the intersection of the market demand curve, D, and the market supply curve S (see Fig. 5.1B).

We thus have the following:

1. **total revenue** is $TR = py$;
2. **average revenue** is $AR = TR/y = py/y = p$;

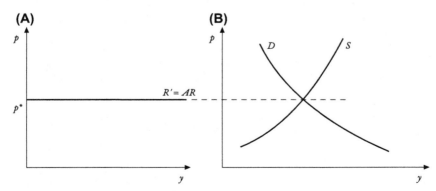

FIG. 5.1 Revenue functions in perfect competition.

3. **marginal revenue,** $R' = \Delta TR/\Delta y$, is also equal to p, since, for the reasons mentioned above, by selling one more unit the company would take in an amount equal to the sale price of the product.

We have discovered that in perfectly competitive conditions both marginal revenue and average revenue equal the sale price: $p = AR = R'$. From what we have said, it becomes important to not confuse the demand curve for a single company (see Fig. 5.1A) with the market demand curve (see Fig. 5.1B). (Note that the scale used to measure quantity in the two graphs in Fig. 5.1 is necessarily different.)

5.3 Profit maximization in the short run and the supply curve of a single company

We now have available all the elements to solve the problem of the capitalist company, which is, as we recall, to maximize profit. Indicating total profit by π we have:

$$\pi = TR - TC$$

where TC is the total short-run cost. In view of the fact that the normal profit rate, being an opportunity cost, is already included in the total cost calculation, π is a residual, or what remains to the company after it has paid for all the inputs used in production; thus π is extra profit collected by the company's owners.

The problem now is to determine the level of y that yields the maximum difference between revenue and costs. Fig. 5.2 illustrates the situation by representing the average and marginal cost and revenue curves. To the left of point E the extra profit is not maximized, since each unit of output to the left of y^* entails a marginal revenue that is greater than marginal cost. In other words, to the left of y^*, by increasing sales by one unit, revenue increases by p dollars and cost by C dollars, so revenue increases more than cost and profit increases.

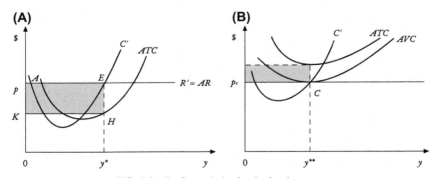

FIG. 5.2 Profit maximization in the short run.

On the other hand, production levels above y^* incur a marginal cost greater than marginal revenue, so its extra profit is not maximized. Therefore:

if $C' < R' = p$, the company should expand production;
if $C' > R' = p$, the company should reduce production;
if $C' = R' = p$, the company is maximizing its extra profit.

Note that, $C' = R'$ at point A as well, but by selling one more unit revenue increases more than cost $(p > C')$, so A does not indicate a maximum profit point for the company. In fact, to condition $C' = R'$ we must add the condition in which curve C' cuts curve R' from below. Finally, we observe that the gray area in Fig. 5.2A indicates the extra profit, obtained by multiplying the optimal quantity y^* by the difference between average revenue (which equals the price) and average cost. The area of the rectangle $0y^*Ep$ represents total revenue, while the area of the rectangle $0y^*HK$ represents total cost.

A company that produces the output level that allows it to maximize its extra profit in the short run is said to be in **short-run equilibrium**. However, stating this does not imply that it necessarily attains positive profits; that happens only if its ATC is less than the current price. It could in fact happen that the current market price p, although less than ATC, exceeds AVC, giving the company an incentive to continue production. Indeed, for $p > AVC$ the company recovers, although only partially, a part of fixed cost or normal profit. The company would have a reason to cease production only if the market price were not able to cover the average variable costs.

Technically, the point at which the company is able to cover its variable costs is called the *shutdown point*, or point C in Fig. 5.2B. If the market price were to drop below p_c in Fig. 5.2B, the company would not be able to cover its variable costs and would thus find itself forced to stop production. It might be able to temporarily remain on the market if it foresees a price increase in the not too distant future. In that case the company would record losses, but it could accept them in view of future improvements.

We have thus identified the optimal production quantity for a given market price, or the quantity that maximizes the company's extra profit. By repeating this operation for all possible market prices we derive the company's **short-run supply curve**. From what we said in Section 5.2, it is clear that it *coincides with the portion of the marginal cost curve situated above price p_c*. The quantity supplied is zero if the market price is less than p_c; if the price were p_c, the company would supply the quantity y^{**} (see Fig. 5.2B); if the price were p, the quantity supplied would be y^* (see Fig. 5.2A).

5.4 The perfectly competitive company in the long run

What changes when we consider the long run? Essentially nothing, except that the average cost and marginal cost curves to consider are those for the long run.

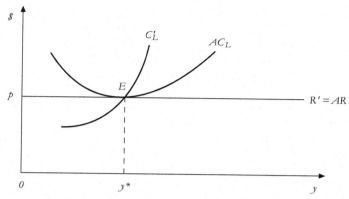

FIG. 5.3 The long-run supply curve for a single company.

Fig. 5.3 illustrates the **long-run equilibrium** for a single company operating in a competitive market. There are three conditions that must be satisfied in such an equilibrium:

the company produces its output $y*$ at the minimum unit cost: the price line, which is also the marginal revenue line, is tangent to AC_L at its minimum point. That means that in that situation, the company takes maximum advantage of the production possibilities of its plant;

at point E, the average cost equals the average revenue and thus the total cost — the area of the rectangle $0y*Ep$ — equals the total revenue, or the area of the rectangle $0y*Ep$. That means that the extra profit is zero;

at point E it is also true that the marginal cost and marginal revenue are equal, which, as we know, is the condition that must be satisfied to maximize profit.

In conclusion, long-run competitive equilibrium for a single company has the following parities: $p = R' = C_L' = AC_L$. Furthermore, from the preceding we can derive that the company's long-run supply curve coincides with the section of the curve C_L' that is above the minimum point of the average long-run cost curve AC_L. In fact, if the price drops below p, as indicated in Fig. 5.2, the company will not be able to cover its total costs, and its output will be zero; keep in mind however that in the long run a company must cover all its costs, since the distinction between fixed and variable costs disappears over the long run.

It is interesting to note that at each point of the **long-run supply curve** the following double equality holds true: $p = C_L' = C_B'$, where C_B' denotes the short-run marginal cost curve; this confirms that maximizing long-run profit presupposes maximizing short-run profit.

5.5 The supply of a good in a competitive industry

We define the *short-run supply* and the *long-run supply* of a certain good to be the horizontal sum of the respective short- and long-run supply curves of the companies operating in the market. As we know, in the short run the plants are a given, and new companies cannot enter that industrial sector. At the same time, the companies that operate in it cannot leave it, in the sense that they cannot divest themselves of their plants in an economically advantageous manner, even if they choose to produce nothing. Since we are working with a perfectly competitive market, no company alone is able to control overall supply; individual companies must consider price as a given. As we know, if a company were to sell at a price above the current market price, its sales would go to zero. On the other hand, if a company can sell any quantity of the good at a given price, it certainly has no reason offer a lower price.

In short, the *short-run supply curve of a competitive industry* is the *horizontal sum* of the supply curves of companies operating in the industry, as shown for example in Fig. 5.4. For simplicity's sake let's suppose there are only two companies operating in the industry, A and B. S_A and S_B are the short-run supply curves of A and B respectively; S is the industry supply constructed by summing the supply levels of the companies at each price level.

In the long run companies can adapt their plants to the level deemed optimal, as well as enter or leave the sector. Consider the case illustrated in Fig. 5.5. Fig. 5.5A depicts the supply curve of a competitive company in the case of a U-

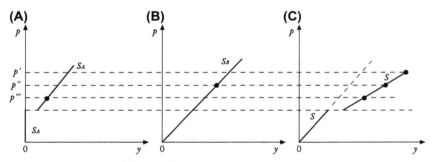

FIG. 5.4 Short-run individual and market supply curves.

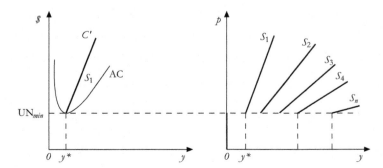

FIG. 5.5 Long-run supply curves.

shaped average cost curve. In Fig. 5.5B we depict what the curve would look like if there were only one company in the industry. We call S_1 the supply curve for an industry with one company. S_2 is the supply curve of an industry with two companies, which is obtained by summing the supply of the two companies with the same supply curve, or the same curve depicted by S_1. Similarly we could obtain the curves S_3, S_4...S_n. It can be shown that as the number of identical companies n increases, S_n will tend to be more and more flat.

Fig. 5.6 depicts a graph that illustrates the determination of the number of companies in the presence of a decreasing demand curve, which we indicate by D. Supposing that the industry is perfectly competitive and that two companies operate in it, equilibrium will be at E_2. But the equilibrium price at E_2 is greater than p^*, or the price corresponding to the minimum average cost: the profits obtained by the two companies in operation will attract a third company into the industry. At the new equilibrium set at E_3 the price is lower, and profits are lower but not negative. However, the entry of a fourth company into the industry entails that at price p^* there is excess demand: there is no equilibrium for S_4. Thus long-run equilibrium in the simple example considered here only allows three companies to operate, and the *competitive industry supply* is equal to the abscissa of E_3.

As demand increases, the number of companies n present in equilibrium increases in the industry. For a large enough n, the supply curve for the industry will be approximately horizontal, with levels equal to the minimum average cost. The equilibrium *profit* for each company is then *approximately zero*. This conclusion is based on the assumption that there are no alternatives for the company to employ its entrepreneurial abilities. One could argue however that utilizing those abilities entails some sacrifice or *opportunity cost*.

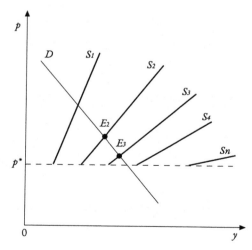

FIG. 5.6 The number of companies in long-run equilibrium.

That allows identifying the **normal (non-negative) profit** for any given industry, which is the minimum profit that is barely sufficient to keep the companies in business.

5.6 Market equilibrium in perfect competition

In the previous section we derived the supply curve of an industrial sector with the assumption that the average cost curves do not change when new companies enter the sector. If a competitive industry has constant costs, the sector's supply curve is horizontal at a level equal to the minimum average cost. Before discussing the equilibrium of an industrial sector, this is a good time to specify what happens when the assumption of constant costs is abandoned.

Suppose there is a demand side shock in the market for the i-th good such that $D' > D$ (see Fig. 5.7); there may have been an income increase for consumers, a population increase, tastes may have changed, or something else. Corresponding to the intersection between D' and S, price p'_1 is greater than the minimum average cost. In the short run, this will increase profits of the companies — let's say there are n of them — operating in the market, which will attract new competitors ($n' > n$). The short-run supply curve *will shift to the right until it reaches a new price level* (p_2) such that profits are zero. This is because at that price level average costs must be minimized to ensure that the flow of businesses entering the sector stops. However, if the increased factor demand by companies operating in the market leads to an increase in factor prices, this could push up the average cost of long-run production for each company. Let AC' be the new average cost curve. The new minimum long-run equilibrium price (p_2) will thus be higher than the equilibrium price reached in the case of invariant average costs.

The new equilibrium (p_2; y_2) will be located above and to the left with respect to the constant cost equilibrium; it will be part of the demand curve for

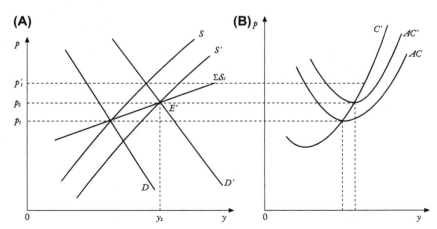

FIG. 5.7   The sector supply curve with increasing costs.

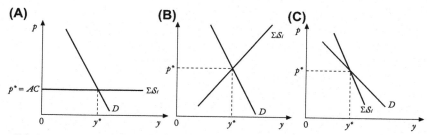

FIG. 5.8 Partial equilibrium: (A) constant costs; (B) increasing costs; (C) decreasing costs.

the sector with increasing costs, which can be obtained by infinitely repeating this simple exercise in comparative statics. Fig. 5.7 shows an increasing supply curve for the industry. The case of an industry with decreasing costs — due perhaps to the prevalence of economies of scale — is fully symmetrical.

Once the sector supply curve is constructed, we need only place it with the aggregate demand function of good i to determine the partial equilibrium of the i-th market. Fig. 5.8 shows the equilibrium of the three cases of constant, increasing, and decreasing costs.

As we can infer from Fig. 5.8A, changes in the quantity demanded have no effect on the price, unlike what happens in the other two cases. In an industrial sector with constant costs there are no production factor price changes when varying the quantity produced, and possible long-run price changes are solely attributable to changes in technological conditions. Such changes might be due to exogenous innovations and inventions, or innovations that do not originate from specific research and development by the company. In long-run equilibrium companies' extra profits are zero, which means that the mechanism that regulates companies entering and exiting the sector no longer functions.

This result with truly paradoxical aspects merits careful attention: capitalist companies, all of which aim to maximize their respective profits, only succeed in obtaining a normal profit in long-run equilibrium because extra profits are eliminated. This is as if to say that they are fighting for a goal that will never be attained. This is the content and the meaning of Smith's famous theorem of the **invisible hand**, which we discussed in Chapter 1. The secret (so to speak) of the theorem is all in the condition of perfect competition in markets, yet this is the condition that ensures such a wholly unexpected result. Thus when we see companies or groups of companies that are actually making extra profits — sometimes very large ones — this means that, in some way or another, perfect competition has been either abolished or severely limited, despite all the rhetoric. We will see how this can happen in Chapter 6.

Summarizing, we can state that:

in an industry with constant costs, the long-run equilibrium price is determined solely by the state of technology and input prices —that is, by cost conditions and *not* by demand conditions. Additionally, the overall output level, and thus the number of companies, is determined by market demand: the greater the demand, the greater the number of companies. Finally, the long-run supply curve for the sector is a horizontal line at the level of the minimum point of the long-run average cost curve of a representative company;

in an industry with increasing costs, the long-run equilibrium price is determined by both cost and demand conditions, which increases when the quantity produced is increased. Additionally, the number of companies in the sector is obtained by dividing the sector output by the output that corresponds to the minimum point of the average long-run cost curve of a representative company. Lastly, the long-run supply curve for the sector is an ascending curve;

in an industry with decreasing costs, the long-run equilibrium price is determined by both cost and demand conditions. Additionally, the equilibrium price decreases over the long run when the quantity produced increases; that is, the long-run supply curve for the sector is a descending curve.

From the analysis we have developed, it follows that the long-run supply curve for the sector is not necessarily ascending; as we have seen, it can be horizontal or even descending. We cannot state *a priori* which of the three conditions should be considered the most plausible or probable; that question must be established on a case-by-case basis, with specific reference to the type of sector under consideration. What we can state in general is that *there is no long-run supply "law"* that sets forth a direct relation between price and quantity produced; in the same way we could speak — although with reservation — of a "law" of demand.

5.7 Social well-being in a single market

When we consider the equilibrium in a single market we can evaluate how the preferences of the agents operating in the market are satisfied. More specifically, we can provide an aggregate indicator, which we will call **social well-being** (W), of the performance of that single market. Transactions involve two types of agents, sellers and buyers, whose interests conflict: the former seek to maximize their profit, while the latter seek to buy the desired quantity at the minimum price.

Let's consider a single consumer, and let's suppose that her individual demand function is described by the following pairs of price and quantity values:

p	10	9	8	7	6
y	1	2	3	4	5

Furthermore, let's suppose that the price at which consumers can buy the good is 5.

As we mentioned earlier in Chapter 2, Section 2.7, the **consumer surplus** is the difference between the sum the consumer is willing to pay (which depends on her preferences and her budget constraints) to obtain a certain quantity of merchandise and the sum she actually pays when she buys it. If we measure this difference in monetary units, with reference to the preceding example, then her consumer surplus is given by $5 + 4 + 3 + 2 + 1 = 15$, since she would be willing to pay 10 (instead of 5) when she buys the first unit, 9 (rather than 5) for the second, and so forth.

We can generalize the above and aggregate the surplus for all consumers. If we consider the total demand for a good, the consumer surplus (S_C) will be given by the area under the demand curve and above the horizontal line corresponding to the purchase price p^*; see Fig. 5.9. If the demand curve is linear, S_C will be equal to the bounded area of the triangle.

We will now turn our attention to producers. As we know, their goal is to maximize profit; the relevant indicator of **producer surplus** is given by the sum of *gross profits* (gross of fixed costs) they earn in equilibrium.

We are now in a position to define social well-being in the context of an analysis of partial equilibrium. If there are n companies, we can say that:

$$W = S_C + \sum_{i=1}^{n} \pi_i$$

that is, social well-being is equal to the sum of the surplus for all consumers and the gross surplus for all producers.

We can visualize W in the case of a perfect competition equilibrium, which is geometrically identified by the intersection between the aggregate demand curve and the aggregate supply curve (see Fig. 5.10).

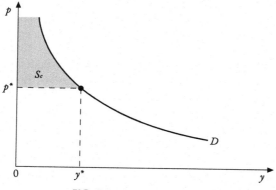

FIG. 5.9 Consumer surplus.

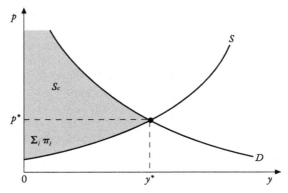

FIG. 5.10 Social well-being in a single market.

As we know, in perfect competition the supply curve coincides with the ascending section of the marginal cost curve. Thus profits (gross of fixed costs) result from the sum of the difference between p^* and the marginal cost of the various units that are produced and sold, or the area indicated by $\sum \pi_i$ in Fig. 5.10. The knowledge of consumer and producer surplus plays a practical role every time a public authority (for example, a city or a regional government) must decide how and where to invest available resources, whether to build — say —a swimming pool or a bike path. In such cases, the option chosen will be the one that maximizes social well-being W.

5.8 Market competition is not a competitive sport

We know well that competition is intimately linked to the market economy: there can be no market where there is no competition, although the opposite is not true. In a competitive economy, the outcomes of the economic process do not follow from the will of some oversight entity — as was the case in planned economies, in which the prices of goods and services, their quantities, employment levels, and so forth were decided politically *ex ante* — but by the *free* interactions between many agents, each of which *rationally* pursues their own *objective* good within a well-defined set of *rules*. Let's grasp the meaning of these four key words.

Stating that their interaction must be free means that no agent can be constrained by force or by a state of necessity that deprives him of the freedom to decide. Thus people reduced to slavery, totally uninformed agents, or the absolutely poor do not satisfy the condition of voluntary participation that is required by the competitive system. The qualification "rationally pursues" posits economic agents' ability to calculate — that is, the ability to both evaluate the costs and benefits of the options in play and adopt a criterion as the basis for making a choice. Note however that, contrary to what one might read or hear, this criterion does not necessarily have to do with maximizing profit. It is not true that market competition presupposes accepting the profit logic, a logic by which operating profits must be distributed only to the capital holders in proportion to their contributions.

This brings us to clarify the meaning of the third key word. The goals the players pursue in the competitive game may be self-interested or altruistic, symbolic or material, and they may be for the short or the long run. What matters is that each player have a clear goal he intends to pursue, otherwise the rationality requirement would remain unsatisfied. Finally, competition requires well-defined rules that all participants know and that can be enforced by some authority outside the competitive process itself. This might be the state, a supra-national entity, or an agency within the civil society that is equipped to meet the need. There are two fundamental rules. The first is a rule that prevents the concentration of power in the hands of one or just a few economic agents; this is the specific role of various antitrust laws. (The first such law was the American Sherman Act, which was passed in 1891. This was a law that sought to recover, at least partially, the spirit of Adam Smith's teachings against government commerce policies that serve only to strengthen the existing power system.) The second is a rule that prohibits fraud and deception; this is the goal of legislative and administrative provisions that require transparency in commercial operations and bring discipline to companies' corporate governance.

Clearly, in reality the rules are not always respected or enforced. This explains the plurality of competitive models encountered in practice and the variety of outcomes in terms of the well-being that competition can bring. Regarding the first point, we talk about perfect competition when no agent has even a minimum of market power, that is, the power to *directly* influence the economic process. Otherwise, we talk about imperfect competition, which has different and increasing degrees of imperfection: monopolistic competition, oligopoly, and monopoly. Regarding the second point, here we recall the so-called "theorem of the invisible hand" attributed to Adam Smith, although G. Vico in his *Scienza Nuova* (*New Science*, 1725) and F. Galiani in his *Della Moneta* (*On Money*, 1750) had reached the same conclusion, albeit less directly and clearly. As we noted above, the theorem shows that in a context of perfect competition, individuals seeking their own purposes, interacting among themselves while complying with the rules discussed above, generate mutually beneficial outcomes that no one had foreseen and thus were not part of anyone's intentions. This is a well-known case of the mechanism of the beneficial consequences of human actions that no one had in mind, the so-called **mechanism of unintended consequences of intentional action**. What is usually never brought to light is that the benefits of competition vary depending on the types of agents who participate in it. Competition between capitalist enterprises is one thing; competition between cooperative enterprises is another. There is competition in both cases, but the final outcomes are substantially different.

One final consideration. When discussing market competition we should be wary of the by-now common analogy between competition in the market and competition in sports, a comparison we often find in public debate and even in many textbooks. This analogy is parsed in various ways: the metaphore of the market as a contest comes from the etymology of "competition" (which derives from the latin"cum—petere" to struggle together), the victory of the best as an image of meritocracy, corruption (doping) that leads to failure in both sports and markets, the work team as a squad, the manager as a coach, and so on.

This is not to deny that a few of the images do capture some aspects of truth, such as the image of the team, or doping; however, it is even more true that when we use a sports image to represent market competition we are making a serious mistake that leads inexpert scholars off-track and sends an image of the market that does not correspond to reality.

This is for at least two reasons. First, the market—sports competition comparison leads, more or less consciously, to consider market competition as a zero-sum game, that is, a game like poker in which A's losses are equal to B's winnings. Unfortunately this error is one of the most common in political and cultural debates in the media, and it is one of the most deeply-rooted prejudices that is very difficult to eradicate, even among economists.

We might call this error the "mercantilist vice," since this was the type of error economists of the 17th and 18th centuries (called "mercantilists") committed when thinking about international trade. They imagined and described it as a relation in which one party won (the one importing gold) and the other party lost (the one exporting gold). Every time we commit this old error yet again today, we view market exchange as an essentially redistributive problem similar to dividing a pie: If A's slice is bigger, B's is smaller, and vice versa. From Adam Smith onward, however, one of the fundamental demonstrations of modern economics has been to shed light on market exchange as a positive sum game in which all partners in an exchange improve if we increase the size of the pie. This concept is somewhat counterintuitive; that is why for centuries distinguished scholars and philosophers failed to grasp this basic aspect of market competition. Ricardo first demonstrated this theorem mathematically in 1817, followed by Edgeworth in 1871, but the insight was already at least a century old; it was quite clear to the founders of the civil economy, for example.

It is true that in certain cases market exchange can become a zero sum game, or it can be perceived as such by economic agents. But — and this is the point — if or when the market becomes a zero sum game, we find ourselves in a pathological rather than a normal situation. That happens when a market economy or a company does not create wealth, when partners are not seen as co-laborers, as happens in a poker game. Many express this mutual advantage as a "win-win" game, which is an unfortunate expression because it remains within the metaphor of winning a contest. In reality there is a coherent way to understand "win-win," but that is not how it is used; rather, it is to understand economic exchange as a team action. Traditional economics in fact uses the concept of a team to indicate a work group within a company, but it does not use it for market exchange. Actually, we could perfectly represent the relationship between a vendor and a client, or a plumber and the head of a household, as a team, giving them an image that is closer to reality: We cooperate to reach a common goal that benefits both. Market competition is a complex interplay of cooperation and competition.

Finally, there is a second error, which is to see market competition as a competition sport. We make that mistake when we understand competition as a contest between companies in which one tries to "beat" the other. We say that company A's purpose is to beat company B (or F or D), and in so doing the (unintentional) result of a company's action reduces the product cost for consumer X (and so contributes to the common good). This is similar to a sporting contest in which athlete A's purpose is to beat her competitors, and as an indirect result to break the previous record. Although one might doubt that competition in sports is only like this, in any case this view of competition is not that of the market — at least in how it actually works — or of the civil economy tradition.

Indeed, from our perspective company A's goal is not to beat B, but to satisfy consumer X's needs as best it can. The fact that company B leaves the market because it does not satisfy X's needs better than A is not A's goal, but merely an unintended side effect of its actions. What is the difference between these two ways of seeing the situation? The difference is precisely in understanding, interpreting, and living out the market as a cooperative game, rather than as a contest in which one wins and the other loses. Today there are in fact significant studies that show that countries and cultures that see the market as a zero sum game grow less and badly compared to cultures in which the market is understood as creating wealth for all agents involved in exchange. The market, our shared life, and politics depend on how we imagine them — on our *culture* — and thus on what we want them to become.

Further reading

Cournot, A. A. (1838). *Recherches sur les principles mathématiques de la théorie des richesses [Researches on the mathematical principles of the theory of wealth]* [1897, Macmillan].

De Tocqueville, A. (2007 [1835]). In J. P. Mayer (Ed.), *Democracy in America* (G. Lawrence, Trans.). Garden City, NY: Doubleday, 1969.

Edgeworth, F. Y. (2004 [1871]). *Early mathematical economics 1871–1915*. Routledge.

Frank, R. (1994). *Microeconomics and behavior*. New York, NY: McGraw-Hill/Irwin, a business unit of The McGraw-Hill Companies.

Galiani, F. (1977 [1750]). *Della Moneta [On money]* (P. R. Toscano, Trans.). Department of Economics, University of Chicago by University Microfilms International.

Ricardo, D. (2001 [1817]). *On the principles of political economy and taxation* (1st ed.). Kitchener: Batoche Books (London: John Murray).

Vico, G. (1948 [1744]). *Scienza Nuova [New science]* translated from the third edition by T. G. Bergin & M. H. Fisch. New York: Cornell University Press, Ithaca, 1948.

Chapter 6

Non-competitive markets and elements of game theory

6.1 Markets in which companies have power over prices

6.1.1 How non-competitive markets come into existence

It may be helpful to recall the characteristics of the economic model of perfect competition developed in the preceding chapter:

- a company considers the price of the goods it sells as a given, and it sells its entire production at that price; the company is thus a price-taker and a quantity-adjuster;
- production technology has the property that it generates U-shaped cost curves in both the short and the long run;
- the role of an entrepreneur, all things considered, is trivial; like a robot, he cannot do anything except set the quantity that is advantageous for him to produce given input prices, output prices, and the production function.

While in a perfectly competitive market a single company can freely increase its sales at the current price, in an imperfect market the sales flow a firm can expect to achieve is inversely correlated to the product price; that is, there is a trade-off between the saleable quantity and price. From this it follows that, in a perfect market, the price drops under the impersonal action of market forces only if a great many companies all seek to increase their sales at the current price at the same time. If the market is imperfect, sales can increase if just a single firm individually changes its price. In the second case, the decision to lower the price is *preliminary* to the attempt to increase sales, and it is also a *non-anonymous* decision.

To grasp an important difference between perfectly and imperfectly competitive markets, consider a sector in which production is in equilibrium. If the price of goods rises, sellers earn a higher than normal profit. Depending on whether the entrance of new companies is: (*a*) perfect, (*b*) very easy, or (*c*) difficult or impossible, there will be different predictable outcomes. In case (*a*), after a certain time the overall supply will tend to increase and the price to decrease until profit returns to a normal level; this is what happens in perfect

The Microeconomics of Wellbeing and Sustainability. https://doi.org/10.1016/B978-0-12-816027-5.00006-9

competition conditions. Case (*b*) is what distinguishes areas of economic activity characterized by *monopolistic competition*. Case (*c*) is what defines a *monopoly*. Finally, if it is difficult for new companies to enter the sector, and if the size of the companies operating in the market is such that none of them can ignore the behavior of the others, we are in an *oligopoly*.

What are the reasons that can help us understand the gradual transformation over time of competitive markets into non-competitive markets? There are two main causes; we will examine each in turn.

6.1.2 Technical progress

The prospect of earning extra profits motivates a capitalist enterprise to achieve ongoing technical innovations in view of the fact that, for at least some amount of time, it alone will be able to take advantage of the new technology. If all companies are so driven, however, that tends to produce a result that ultimately stops the process by which new companies enter the market. Suppose we are in a long-run equilibrium situation in which each company has achieved its optimal size. The total supply is given by the quantity resulting from the optimal size multiplied by the number of companies. We know that there are forms of technical progress that allow production efficiency increases — and thus lower production costs — only if a company increases its output levels, either by introducing new plants or by hiring more workers.

An increase in the size of a firm driven by these types of technical progress would have no effect on the competitive structure of the market if:

1. it is uniform across all sectors of the economy;
2. the increase in labor productivity is not caused by greater than proportional increases in company size;
3. the income increase due to increased productivity leads to a proportional increase in the demand for the various goods.

If these conditions are met, the result would be a proportional increase in overall demand and in each company's optimal quantity, such that the number of companies would remain unchanged. However, this is not the case in reality, with the result that technical progress tends to increase the optimal quantity of individual companies more than aggregate demand increases. This leads to fewer companies and a drive toward concentration. Firms that innovate more quickly create problems for the rest. Not only that, but the company that is successful as a result of either process or product innovation can more readily absorb companies in difficulty. When this happens, there are fewer companies on the market, and those that remain find themselves in a position to be able to influence prices by manipulating the quantity they supply and/or obstructing the entry of new potential rivals.

6.1.3 Changes in the composition of consumption

We turn now to the second main cause. Productivity increases brought about by innovation and/or technological changes translate into increases in purchasing power, which allows an expansion in consumption. However, we know from Engel's analysis of demand that an expansion in consumption is always accompanied by changes in its composition: we do not consume more of the same goods, rather, we consume other goods, or at least those we think are different. With this, another condition for the existence of a perfectly competitive market fails. Due to a lack of product homogeneity there is room for *product differentiation*, and with it the possibility that a company can increase its economic power by protecting its market share both through changes in the product's characteristics and through sales development, such as advertising and ancillary services.

What are the consequences? When products are differentiated, a potential entrant in the market must choose the products it wants to produce, and consequently the commercial activities with which it intends to develop its products. This actually means launching a new product on the market, which will appear different to consumers from products offered by other enterprises, if for no other reason that the brand is different. Commercial activities entail costs that are not proportional to the volume of activity engaged. This creates *substantial commercial economies of scale*, which have nothing to do with changes in production plants. The indivisibility of research and advertising expenses (advertising must reach a certain level to be effective) and the indivisibility of the product distribution network are the most important causes of commercial economies of scale.

It is now easy to imagine how such economies might lead to consolidating several companies into a group, and particularly how they might discourage potential competitors from entering the market. Nor should we overlook the financial reasons. A large enterprise or an established business can more readily obtain the financial means necessary for technological restructuring or new marketing ventures due to its easier access to capital markets, privileged relations with the banking system, financial economies, and so forth. As we can see, when product homogeneity is lost, the freedom to enter the market is always impeded to some extent.

6.2 Market forms and branches of economic activity

What might we say about the correspondence between market forms and branches of economic activity?

- Conditions close to perfect competition are the norm in the primary goods and agricultural production sectors; there are no significant barriers to entry for new companies and products are in large part homogeneous.

- The situation is very different when selling these products in both wholesale and retail. For the retail trade the following factors can play a role in product differentiation: (*a*) consumer preference for a point of sale location; (*b*) lack of knowledge by consumers of buying opportunities; (*c*) *product-specific differentiation* (the fact that each seller is able to distinguish her product from those offered by rivals in such a way that buyers retain some form of loyalty). On the other hand, there are also specific barriers to entry in the wholesale trade. For example, the appropriate licenses are required, specialized equipment is necessary (refrigerators, warehouses, transportation), a network of relationships with production centers, and so on. This explains the large difference between *consumer prices* (retail prices) and *producer prices* (wholesale prices), which can be partly explained by commercial distribution costs. Such differences quite often reflect real monopolistic gains. In the commercial distribution sector the predominant market form is monopolistic competition.
- Many services have characteristics similar to those of the retail trade. Hotel, transportation, and professional services are highly differentiated. On the other hand, companies that produce consumer goods often differentiate themselves by advertising and other types of sales promotions. As a result, each company, whether in services or production, ends up securing a certain market niche in which it is able to exert some control. These are cases of **monopolistic competition**. If in such circumstances a firm succeeds in erecting significant and enduring barriers to entry, then it is a case of **monopoly**. There are many factors that can explain the emergence and/or consolidation of such barriers (see Frame 6.1) However, if the entry

---

FRAME 6.1 Origins of entry barriers

In 1956 Joe Bain introduced a by-now classic taxonomy of the causes of non-institutional barriers to entry, which traces their origin back to three circumstances:
1. product differentiation;
2. cost advantages in absolute terms by companies already present in the industry;
3. economics of scale.

Subsequently George Stigler proposed a more general definition, according to which "A barrier to entry may be defined as a cost of producing (at some or every rate of output) which must be borne by a firm which seeks to enter an industry but is not borne by firms already in the industry." This definition highlights that an essential element of entry barriers is an asymmetry that benefits existing companies with respect to potential competitors.

barriers are not absolute and if there are few existing companies of substantial size such that each is forced to take the others' decisions into account, then we speak of a **differentiated oligopoly**.

- In sectors that produce intermediate goods, such as chemicals, machinery, electricity, cement, and so on, the entry obstacles mentioned above are rarely found, because the products — with the possible exception of machinery — are sufficiently homogeneous. Here the entry barriers are more connected to economies of scale, having to do with the fact that average production costs drop as production levels increase. But large enterprises require heavy financing and capturing significant market share. That is why there is a tendency toward concentration; a small number of companies control almost all production, and the rest is divided among possibly even many small firms. It is precisely in such cases that there are forms of a *concentrated oligopoly with homogeneous products*. The **concentration ratio**, expressed as the percentage of sales made by the largest *n* companies (where *n* is usually a number between 3 and 10) out of total sales, is an indicator of the degree of concentration in a certain branch of industry. In a perfectly competitive market the concentration ratio is close to zero. In the case of a monopoly, the ratio is 100%. If we consider the cement sector, we find that its concentration ratio fluctuates around 80%.

- Finally, we will point out the case of a **natural monopoly**, found in every situation in which the nature of the product and/or the size of the market are such that they do not allow more than one company to take advantage of economies of scale. Typical examples are transportation, communication, electricity, and so forth. In these cases, a single unified network of plants allows taking full advantage of the substantial, increasing returns to scale. In general, natural monopolies are regulated by public authorities, or *public utility monopolies*, which intervene to prevent consumers from being exploited by the company. In essence, we can state that a firm enjoys a monopoly position when no potential rival's decisions can influence its actions. When these conditions are not met, the company is in an oligopolistic situation.

The essential difference between a monopoly and an oligopoly is not the number of companies operating in a given market (if anything, this is a consequence) but in the fact that the monopolist's decisions take into account only cost and demand information and not its rivals' possible reactions, which is the case in an oligopoly. Ultimately the criterion of the number of companies cannot be taken literally to judge whether a given market structure is monopolistic or oligopolistic. Rather, the presence or absence of *interdependence* distinguishes the two forms of markets.

6.3 Monopoly

6.3.1 Equilibrium in a monopoly

As with any capitalist firm, the monopolist's goal is to maximize profit. Compared to what happens in perfect competition, here the novelty is represented in the revenue curves:

a) a company operating in a perfectly competitive market can sell any amount of output without influencing the market price, so its average and marginal revenue curves coincide and are horizontal lines;

b) a monopolist, however, can increase the quantity sold only be lowering the price. This is due to the fact that the monopolist's demand curve is nothing more than the market demand curve, which descends from left to right. On the other hand, the drop in price necessary to sell one more unit of a good impacts all units. It follows from this that the additional revenue from the sale of one more unit of the good — the marginal revenue — is less than the price that represents the average revenue.

The demand curve (which is also the average revenue curve) and the marginal revenue curve are shown in Fig. 6.1. As can be seen, the marginal revenue curve is always positioned below the demand curve. Given that, the amount a monopolist must reduce the price to sell more depends on the price elasticity of the demand for the good (see Frame 6.2):

- if $|e| = 1$, that means that a 1% price increase leads to a 1% demand decrease such that there is no change in total revenue, so marginal revenue is zero;

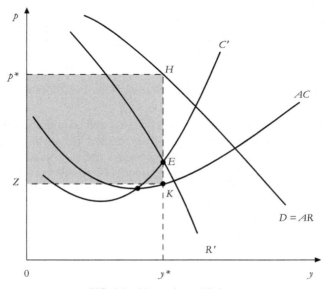

FIG. 6.1 Monopoly equilibrium.

FRAME 6.2 The relationship between elasticity and marginal revenue

We can express the relationship between elasticity and marginal revenue as follows:

$$\Delta R = p|\Delta y| - y|\Delta p|$$

where Δp indicates the change in price and Δy indicates the corresponding change in quantity. Dividing both sides by Δy, we have:

$$\frac{\Delta R}{\Delta y} = p - \left|\frac{\Delta p}{\Delta y}\right| y$$

Recalling the price elasticity formula, we obtain:

$$R' = p\left(1 + \frac{1}{e}\right) \quad \text{or} \quad R' = p\left(1 - \frac{1}{|e|}\right)$$

If the demand curve is linear, this shows that the slope of the marginal revenue curve is *double* that of the demand curve, and the quantity at which $R' = 0$ corresponds to a price that is half the price at which sales are zero.

Let $p = a - by$ be the demand equation. We will then have: $R = p \cdot y = ay - by^2$, which is a parabola with upward concavity. Differentiating with respect to y, we obtain $R' = a - 2by$, which is the equation for a straight line that has the same vertical intercept as the demand curve and double its slope.

- if $|e| > 1$, then a certain price decrease causes a greater than proportional increase in demand, such that total revenue increases when larger quantities of goods are sold, and marginal revenue is positive;
- if $|e| < 1$, the result is just the opposite.

We assume the cost curves have the familiar U shape, just as in the case of perfect competition. Fig. 6.1 depicts the usual average and marginal cost curves.

As we know, the rule that ensures profit maximization requires making marginal cost and marginal revenue equal:

$$C' = p\left(1 - \frac{1}{|e|}\right)$$

This condition can be rewritten as follows:

$$\frac{p - C'}{p} = \frac{1}{|e|}$$

The difference between price and marginal cost, divided by the price, is known as the **Lerner index**, or also as **mark-up**. From the mark-up formula we conclude that at the monopoly equilibrium position the elasticity of demand must be greater than 1 (in absolute value). In terms of Fig. 6.1, the condition is satisfied at point E, called the **Cournot point**, or the point corresponding to the quantity y^*. The price at which this quantity will be sold is read on the demand curve p^*. The total extra profit is represented by the area of the rectangle $ZKHp^*$. (As we know, normal profit is already included in the average cost.)

A monopolist can make two different decisions: either fix the price and accept selling the quantity the market is willing to buy, or fix the quantity produced and sell it at the price set by demand conditions; it cannot simultaneously attempt to set both price and quantity. If the monopolist is able to maintain over time the entry barriers it has set up, it will succeed in earning extra profits even in the long run; otherwise, over time the monopolist's power will disappear.

6.3.2 Monopoly and social well-being

In general we can state that, for the same cost curves, the monopoly price will be higher and quantity produced will be lower than in perfect competition.

Clearly such a state of affairs, while benefiting the monopolist, harms the consumer. So, regardless of the resources a monopolist must spend to maintain its monopoly position, the presence of monopolies brings about a loss of social well-being. It can be shown, in fact, that the monopolist's higher profit does not compensate for the loss of consumer surplus. (Recall that social well-being is the algebraic sum of the producer surplus and consumer surplus.) That explains why, particularly in cases of natural monopolies, public authorities frequently intervene by either performing or managing the activity in question themselves or regulating the price the monopolist is authorized to charge. This is what happens in electric, gas, water, and other such services. Generally speaking, the common goal of regulatory policies is to ensure that the monopolist's revenue is limited to covering its costs plus a normal profit.

We should note that if technological indivisibility and/or technical progress were to take certain forms, a monopoly could produce more and sell it at a lower price than its competition. While it is true that a monopolist sells at a price greater than marginal cost, the possibility available to it of accessing operations on a vast scale allows it to produce at a lower average and marginal cost. The monopolist's margin is still present, but it is less than the cost reduction it could attain by using a different technology.

The important point to emphasize is that the presence of economies of scale can lead to *unstable* situations in markets that are initially perfectly competitive. A company that succeeds in attaining a size sufficient to deploy a large-scale process produces at lower average costs than its rivals; it is thus able charge a lower price, which allows it to expand its market share to the point that it becomes a monopolist. One the other hand, if demand is sufficiently high with respect to the economically minimum level of a large-scale process, it is quite possible that the market will slide toward some form of oligopoly.

6.3.3 Price discrimination

Price discrimination is a very common practice to increase profits in a monopoly; the idea is to sell the quantity identified by $C' = R'$ at different prices in different market segments.

When is this possible? The *first* condition is that consumers' preferences, income, or geographic location are different than where a good is supplied. In other words, there must be different price elasticities in different market segments such that the market for the good can be subdivided. The *second* condition is that the various market segments must be separated, in the sense that arbitrage (buying in the segment where the price is lower and reselling in a segment where the price is higher) is not possible. This is why price discrimination is found most often in providing services, such as health, transportation, or entertainment, where the nature of the product is such that it is impossible to resell it.

Price discrimination policies help explain phenomena such as *dumping*, or selling a good in a foreign market at a price below cost. If a firm enjoys a monopoly power in its internal market while it has many rivals in foreign markets, it will be convenient for it to isolate the internal and external markets from each other and charge different prices in each.

Intertemporal price discrimination is another form, in which the same product is sold at different prices at different times. The most frequent example is seasonal sales, or introducing a new durable good at an initially higher price and lowering the price later.

Arthur C. Pigou (1920) identified three types of price discrimination:

1 **First-degree price discrimination** happens when a vendor charges a different price for each unit sold, such that the unit price is equal to the maximum amount a buyer is willing to pay for that unit. There are obviously formidable information requirements to be able to practice first-degree price discrimination, in that the vendor must know the exact demand curve of each individual. First-degree discrimination is also called *perfect discrimination* in that it allows a monopolist to appropriate the entire consumer surplus.

2 **Second-degree discrimination** happens when the unit price depends on the number of units bought rather than the identity of the buyer. Examples of second-degree discrimination are discounts based on the quantity purchased. When the price varies with the quantity purchased according to a rule that *is the same for all buyers*, we also speak of *non-linear prices*. All other conditions being equal, a monopolist's profit with second-degree

discrimination will never be less than what it would earn by charging a uniform price.

3 **Third-degree discrimination** happens when different consumers pay different prices, but the unit price is constant (i.e., it does not depend on the volume purchased). Examples of third-degree discrimination are those in which different prices are reserved for particular groups of buyers, such as pensioners, students, or military personnel. The profits a monopolist obtains with third-degree discrimination are never less than a monopolist that charges the same price in different markets.

6.4 Monopolistic competition

6.4.1 Equilibrium of an imperfectly competitive company

Edward Chamberlin (1933) coined the term "monopolistic competition" to include all the market forms between perfect competition and monopoly. Joan Robinson (1933) preferred instead the expression "imperfect competition" for the same markets. The market structure in question has the following characteristics:

- competition between companies, each of which ignores other companies' reactions to its own actions;
- freedom of market entry and exit;
- the goods produced by different companies are heterogeneous but perfectly interchangeable.

The first two characteristics show the competitive aspect of this market form; the third shows its monopolistic aspect. Indeed, due to product differentiation each company succeeds in winning over a market segment in which it can exercise some market power. It is thus a price-setter rather than a price-taker, as happens in perfect competition. However, its discretion in setting prices is not unlimited, as happens in a monopoly, since each company must always take into account the competition from close substitutes offered by rival companies.

It is now easy to derive the equilibrium conditions of a company in monopolistic competition.

Consider Fig. 6.2A regarding the price p and output y of the short-run equilibrium for a representative firm (R' is the marginal revenue, ATC is the average total cost, y^* and p^* are the equilibrium output and price, and D is the demand curve for an individual company).

The necessary condition for maximum profit is that $R' = C'$, where the marginal revenue is less than the price, as in the case of a monopolist. In the case of Fig. 6.2A this condition is satisfied at y^*. Price p^* corresponds to that quantity on the demand curve. In this situation the company earns an extra

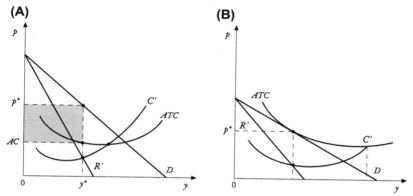

FIG. 6.2 Monopolistic competition: (A) short-run equilibrium; (B) long-run equilibrium.

profit represented by the dashed area in Fig. 6.2A (recall that normal profit is already included in the *ATC* curve).

The presence of extra profits will attract new companies into the sector. This in turn will influence the revenue of companies already operating in it, for the obvious reason that each firm sells less at each price level when new brands are marketed; consequently, the demand curve for an individual company will shift to the left, as the same number of buyers must now be divided up among a higher number of companies. That will clearly reduce the extra profits of the existing companies. The process of new companies entering the market will continue until a company's expected demand curve becomes tangent to its average long-run cost curve. As shown in Fig. 6.2B, in this situation extra profits are zero since the price equals the average cost.

6.4.2 Comparing monopolistic competition with perfect competition and monopoly

In perfect competition, as we know, in the long-run equilibrium position we have $C'_L = R' = CM_L = p$. In monopolistic competition, instead we have shown that $C'_L = R'$ and $p = CM_L$ but $p > C'_L$. In other words, the price is higher and the output is lower than in perfect competition. Actually, as we can deduce from Fig. 6.2B, even in the long-run position production is not at the minimum average cost, since the output y^*_M is less than y^*_C, or the output that corresponds to the average minimum cost.

Thus if each firm were to produce the quantity y^*_C, the entire market could be served by fewer companies and the total cost would be less, with the result that fewer productive resources would be used. In essence, the loss of efficiency in resource use encountered in monopolistic competition is due to the fact that, because of product differentiation, there are "too many" companies operating in the sector, and each produces an output that is less than optimal.

So there are "too many companies that are too small." The typical example of this is the retail trade.

This criticism suffers from a weakness, which Chamberlin himself pointed out: it overlooks the fact that differentiation is linked to consumer preferences, who are often willing to pay a higher price in order to have the possibility of choosing from among different varieties of the same type of good. This is as if to say that product diversity comes at a price. Said another way, the possibility of actually being able to make a choice is a positive argument in consumers' utility functions, who show that they increasingly appreciate its value. Regarding the comparison with a monopoly, note that over the long run extra profits are zero in both perfect and monopolistic competition. A monopoly enterprise, however, can earn extra profits even over the long run as long as it is able to maintain the entry barriers it set up for its protection. Finally, we observe that resources are inefficiently allocated in both a monopoly and in monopolistic competition.

6.5 An oligopolistic market

6.5.1 Its distinctive characteristics

An oligopoly is a market structure in which several companies operate, but none of them have a negligible market share (as happens in perfect competition). Every oligopolistic enterprise is thus able to exercise a certain influence on the relevant price and/or quantity variables and is aware that other companies operating in the sector can, by their decisions, do the same. The distinctive nature of an oligopolistic structure is that there is **strategic interaction** between companies; such interaction is absent in a monopoly and in perfect competition, in which companies, taking price as a given, behave atomistically.

Consider a duopoly, or a market in which there are only two suppliers and multiple buyers. In addition to company A, another company B produces and sells an identical product as its rival. Suppose the two companies know the behavior of the good's consumers, summarized by the demand function $p = f(q)$; p indicates the price and q indicates the total output, which is equal to the sum of q_A and q_B, representing the production levels of the two companies A and B respectively. For the sake of simplicity, assume that production costs are zero. If each company independently chooses its output level to maximize its *profits* (indicated by π), then firm A chooses q_A to maximize $\pi_A = pq_A = f(q_A + q_B)q_A$. As we see, π_A also depends on q_B; that is, A's optimal output level choice is no longer independent of the output level simultaneously chosen by the other company, as it is in perfect competition. Thus there is no demand curve for an individual company in an oligopoly; the quantity of product an oligopolist can sell at a certain price depends on what its rivals do. This is why an oligopolist can never know *with certainty* the market share it will have.

One final observation. Just as not all monopolistic enterprises need be large, the same is true for oligopolistic companies. Two grocery stores in an isolated area are certainly small with respect to the supermarkets in a large city, and yet the logic of how they operate is typical of a duopoly. At the same time, we speak of an oligopolistic market even if the number of companies involved varies, on the condition however that the same interdependence exists between them.

There are two historical phases in the economic study of oligopolies. In the first, the analysis was carried out with the help of the same tools used to study competition and monopoly. While recognizing that an oligopolistic enterprise's decision-making process is far more complex than other firms, scholars such as A. Cournot (1838), J. Bertrand (1883), Y. Edgeworth, E. von Stackelberg, and others reduced an oligopoly to a particular case of a monopoly market by making assumptions that greatly simplified the problem. Their crucial assumption was that, when making decisions about its own production, a company assumed that its rivals would not modify their own output levels — that is, that they would not react at all. The second phase was distinguished by its use of game theory in studying oligopolistic behavior. The second phase began in 1944 when O. Morgenstern and J. von Neumann published their seminal work *Theory of Games and Economic Behavior* (see Appendix A to this chapter).

6.5.2 The Cournot model

Although Cournot was not familiar with game theory, as we just noted, we can conveniently lay out his model using the conceptual apparatus of the theory. Cournot considered two companies that compete with each other in extracting water of equal quality from two wells near each other; we are thus faced with a variable sum non-cooperative game between two players with complete information, in which each firm simultaneously chooses the quantity to place in the market.

To complete the description of the game, we must specify the set of players' choices and payoffs for each pair of strategies the players chose. Cournot assumed that the variables to be chosen were the *output levels* of a homogeneous good; the payoffs were instead expressed in terms of profits, which the companies intend to maximize.

The two companies produce with the same cost function $C(q_i) = 2q_i$, $(i = A,B)$, for which the marginal cost is $C' = 2$, and the inverse demand function (i.e., price as a function of output) is given by $p = 9 - Q$, where $Q = q_A + q_B$.

The profit function of company A is thus given by:

$$\pi_A = pq_A - 2q_A = (9 - q_A - q_B)q_A - 2q_A$$

from which, deriving with respect to q_A and setting the first derivative to zero, we obtain:

$$q_A = (7 - q_B)/2$$

which represents company A's **reaction function**, (R_A). We see clearly that the reaction function decreases with respect to the output level of the rival firm; similarly, company B's reaction function R_B is given by $q_B = (7 - q_A)/2$. The two reaction functions are shown in Fig. 6.3.

Point C geometrically identifies the **Cournot equilibrium**, which corresponds to the intersection of the two reaction curves. The maximum profit conditions for the two companies are satisfied only at that point. From an algebraic point of view, the coordinates of point C (which belongs to the bisector of the first quadrant, since we are dealing with a symmetrical equilibrium) are given by $q_A^* = q_B^* = 7/3$, from which $Q^* = 14/3$ and $p^* = 13/3$. The equilibrium profits are thus equal to $\pi_A^* = \pi_B^* = 49/9$. If we use the formula from Section 6.3 to calculate the mark-up (which is the ratio of price minus marginal cost and price), we obtain $(p^* - C')/p^* = 7/13 = 1/|e|$, from which we can specify the absolute value of the demand elasticity corresponding to the Cournot equilibrium. It turns out that $|e| = 13/7$.

What would a monopolist do that operates with the same technology and faces the same demand curve? Calculating the monopolist's equilibrium according to the procedure presented in Section 6.3, we obtain $p_M^* = 11/2$, $q_M^* = 7/2$ and thus $\pi_M = 49/4$ and $(p_M^* - C')/p_M^* = 7/11$.

These results confirm that the mark-up in a monopoly is greater than in a duopoly, and that the monopolist's profit is greater than the total profits in

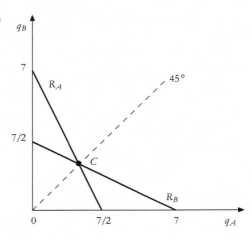

FIG. 6.3 The reaction curve in the Cournot model.

Cournot's duopoly (that is, $\pi_M > \pi_A + \pi_B$, where π_M denotes the monopolist's profit). This means that, considered only from the companies' side, Cournot's equilibrium is not Pareto efficient. In fact, if the two firms were to collude they would act like a monopolist and obtain a greater profit.

Two concluding observations. First: are we sure that a Cournot equilibrium always exists? No, because it could happen that the two reaction curves never intersect in the positive quadrant. Cournot avoided such a possibility by assuming zero production costs and the linearity of the demand function.

Second: the Cournot game has echoes of the Prisoner's Dilemma (see the appendices to this chapter). In fact, each company has an interest in increasing production in order to increase its profits, but in so doing it puts its rival at a disadvantage. Since every increase in output reduces the price consumers are willing to pay for the good, it thus reduces the other's profit.

6.5.3 Bertrand's model

Nearly a half-century after Cournot published his work in 1833, J. Bertrand proposed a duopoly model that was destined to become one of the most influential contributions in the studies of forms of markets. Basically, Bertrand rejected the core hypothesis of the Cournot model — that companies compete on quantity — and instead accepted the hypothesis that the choice variable is *price*. Keeping Cournot's other assumptions of product homogeneity and constant marginal costs, Bertrand's equilibrium means that price is equal to the marginal cost. Let's give an account of this important result.

Consider two companies that both produce at the constant marginal cost C'. We want to show that in Bertrand's equilibrium $p_A = p_B = C'$, where p_A and p_B indicate the prices set by companies A and B respectively. Let's proceed by absurdity and suppose that the two firms initially set two prices that are equal but greater than the marginal cost. In this case, each company would have an incentive to reduce its price, thereby taking all its rival's customers and making higher profits. If both companies engage in such a price war, the process can only end when $p_A = p_B = C'$.

It would not in fact be advantageous to sell at a price lower than C', because that would entail negative profits. On the other hand, a situation in which $p_A > p_B$ cannot represent an equilibrium, because the company with the higher price would not be able to sell anything, given that consumers would turn to the rival; it would find it advantageous to set a price slightly lower than the other company's price. The latter would in turn lower its price below its rival, and so forth.

We have thus shown that $p_A = p_B = C'$ in the equilibrium of a non-cooperative game in which the strategic variable is price.

- Several points deserve attention.

- Bertrand's equilibrium is the only Nash equilibrium in prices (recall that Cournot's equilibrium is the only Nash equilibrium in output levels).
- Bertrand's equilibrium is insensitive to the number of companies, in the sense that even if we had $n > 2$ companies, and all of them produced at the marginal cost C', in equilibrium all companies would set the price equal to C'. Furthermore, Bertrand's equilibrium is insensitive to the elasticity of demand.
- Market shares are indeterminate. When companies charge the same price, consumers are indifferent in choosing one seller or another, and Bertrand's model cannot specify the output sold by each producer in equilibrium. The fact remains that, regardless of its market share, in equilibrium no producer obtains positive extra profits.
- If the two companies produce at constant but different marginal costs, then Bertrand's equilibrium is such that the company with the lower marginal cost sets a slightly lower price than its rival's cost, thus taking the entire market and obviously earning positive profits. That is to say, if $C'_A > C'_B$, then in Bertrand's equilibrium $p_A = p_B = C'_A - \alpha$, with α positive and as small as desired. That means that in equilibrium $q_A = 0$, given that no consumer would find it convenient to turn to company A, which cannot sell at a price less than C'_A; company B would serve all consumers, earning a profit equal to $\left(C'_A - \alpha - C'_B \right)$ for each unit sold.

The truly surprising point about Bertrand's equilibrium is that it is the same equilibrium that emerges in perfect competition. In other words, despite the fact that the supply is concentrated and that enterprises have the power to influence price, there are no extra profits. *Price competition in a homogeneous market among a "few" companies that produce at the same marginal cost generates the same equilibrium that would be observed in a market with "many" companies that are price-takers.* This shows just how important it is to define the variable that is the object of competition between companies; whether we choose price or quantity makes a big difference.

Moreover, Bertrand's result helps us understand why companies do not engage in price wars in oligopolistic markets: they know that in the end all of them would end up taking a loss. Note however that if the products are differentiated, this result no longer applies. In that case differentiation gives each firm a market power that translates into extra profits. That is, differentiation mitigates the consequences of price competition, and so in equilibrium the price charged by each company is greater than its marginal cost.

6.6 Incentives for collusion and cartels

6.6.1 Oligopolistic collusion

As is Cournot's equilibrium, Bertrand's equilibrium is Pareto inefficient. There are in fact pairs of values (p, q) that ensure higher profits for both producers, just as happens in a monopoly. Fig. 6.4 represents such situations in geometric form. The curve in Fig. 6.4 indicates all the combinations of maximum profits that two identical companies can obtain in a duopoly with homogeneous products, such as the one described above. Point B, which coincides with the origin of the Cartesian axes, represents Bertrand's equilibrium; point C represents Cournot's equilibrium. If we take point C as a reference, the gray region represents the possible combinations of π_A and π_B that are greater in a Pareto sense than the profits obtained in Cournot's equilibrium. If they were to collude rather than compete with each other, they would try to reach a point in the gray region where they would both make more profit.

Note that *collusion can also be tacit*, that is, it can emerge from repetitions of a non-cooperative game such as we saw with Cournot. In that case, the companies end up choosing *as if* they had entered into an agreement to maximize their joint profits.

When the collusive outcome is instead the result of an explicit agreement between producers, then we speak of a **cartel**, which is a direct agreement (although frequently secret, and thus illegal) between oligopolists that aim to maximize their joint profits either over the entire sector or by subdividing the market between the parties to the agreement. A cartel can include many companies in different countries, such as OPEC (the Organization of Petroleum Exporting Countries).

If a cartel groups together all the suppliers of a homogeneous product, it is in fact comparable to a monopoly enterprise with multiple plants. If the goal is to maximize their joint profits, then under certain conditions the cartel can consider the market demand curve as *its* demand curve, and the horizontal sum of the marginal cost curves of the individual firms as *its* marginal cost curve. At this point the cartel proceeds to set the quantity and price by applying the

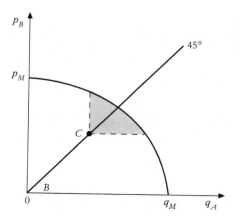

FIG. 6.4 Pareto inefficiency of the Cournot and Bertrand equilibria.

monopoly rule that equates marginal cost and marginal revenue. How then is the product quantity so identified divided up among the various companies?

A necessary condition for efficiently allocating the quantity to produce is that the marginal costs be the same for all companies involved. Otherwise, the cartel could increase the overall profits by reducing the market share assigned to companies with higher costs and at the same time increasing the production quota for companies with lower costs. It may even happen that a cartel allows one of its firms to not produce and still participate equally in the division of the profit. This happens when production by companies with high costs, if they were allowed to produce, would end up exerting a depressive effect on the market price.

6.6.2 The instability of cartels

The so-called ideal distribution of overall production among the members of a cartel rarely happens in practice. Very often the allocation is decided on the basis of past sales levels, or on the basis of the production capacity at the time the collusive agreement is signed. In other cases the market is divided on the basis of the geographic distribution of consumers. In such cases both the price and quantity of the product produced may well differ from firm to firm. In general, however, the distribution of profits is an essentially conflict-ridden problem, and laborious negotiations are inevitable to resolve it. This is why cartels are often unstable.

Another important source of instability in cartels arises from the incomplete information of its members. In particular, as we know from the Prisoner's Dilemma game, in many situations of oligopolistic interaction each player retains a unilateral incentive to act opportunistically. It is true that a cartel is a solution to a cooperative game — one that stipulates a binding agreement, with sanctions in the case of defection — but it is also true that in reality the actions of the partners are not precisely observable. That leaves room for opportunistic, self-interested actions that undermine the cartel's cohesion. Let's look at a simple example in Fig. 6.5 that illustrates this possibility.

Consider a group of producers that has set the cartel's equilibrium on the basis of the estimated product demand (curve D) and its production costs — that is, price p_M, total quantity q_M, and the individual production quotas. If all producers operating in the sector belong to the cartel, then the result coincides with a monopoly equilibrium.

Now imagine a cartel member that, in accordance with the agreement, tries to sell the quota assigned to it; it expects to be able to sell at the unit price p_M. Suppose instead that the market is inclined to absorb that quota only at a price $p < p_M$. What might happen? There are three possibilities:

a) one or more cartel members may have brought more to the market than they were assigned, such that the actual supply is equal to q^*, and the

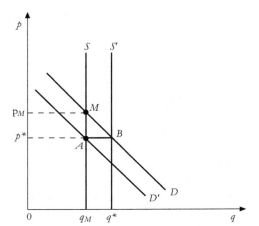

FIG. 6.5 The instability of a cartel.

resulting price from the intersection of curve D and the inflated supply curve S' is equal to p^*;

b) no cartel member violated the agreement, but demand fell (or the estimate erred on the high side), so the real demand curve D' intersects the supply set by the cartel (curve S) at point A;

c) a member produced more than expected and demand decreased, so the new demand curve (between D and D') and the new supply curve (between S and S') intersect at one of the points on segment AB, all of which are of the order of p^*, the observed price. Now if one of the "loyal" members believes that the reason for the price drop is the first or third possibility, it will find it opportune to violate the agreement by also trying to produce and sell more than what is permitted by the agreement. In other words, the imperfect observability of the relevant economic variables and of the cartel partners' behavior can incentivize actions that lead to the cartel's dissolution.

6.7 Contestable markets and market structure endogeneity

The theory of contestable markets proposed in the early 1980s by W. Baumol, J. Panzar, and R. Willing is an interesting attempt at an *endogenous* determination of the entry and exit conditions for companies in the market. Let's see what that means. As we have noted, to this point we have assumed that the market structure (competitive, monopolistic, or oligopolistic) was a *given* in a model. That simplified the analysis, but it leaves open the problem of explaining how a certain market structure comes into existence. The theory in question aims to give an explanation of market structure endogeneity that starts by considering cost and demand conditions. In particular, the theory of contestable markets sets conditions in which it is impossible to prevent entry into the market, such that it works in fact as if it were perfect competition.

That result is obtained by introducing the following hypotheses:

- all companies have access to the same production technology;
- there may be economies of scale (and thus fixed costs), but there are no unrecoverable investments (from which so-called *sunk costs*, or **unrecoverable costs**, originate);
- companies already present in the market cannot instantly modify prices; the reaction time of companies present in the market is longer than the reaction time of potential entrants.

In Baumol's words, "A contestable market is one into which entry is absolutely free, and exit is absolutely costless." So, a market is contestable if the threat of market entry by a potential rival constrains incumbents to act *as if* the potential competitor were already an actual competitor. The theory is thus a generalization of the perfect competition model; the price-taking assumption peculiar to perfect competition is replaced by the possibility of market entry and exit. The notion of *free entry* should be understood in George Stigler's sense, that is, as the absence of cost discrimination with regard to potential entrants. *Free exit*, however, should be understood as the absence of costs and friction to a company that wants to leave the market.

What are the practical consequences of contestability? To answer that we need to define the notion of *sustainable industrial configuration*, which is the price vector and output vector whose components refer to each operational enterprise, such that the following two properties are satisfied:

1. overall production is equal to demand, and no company incurs losses;
2. a potential entrant cannot obtain positive profits by setting a price lower than the firms already in operation.

From the definitions of contestable markets and *sustainable* industrial configurations, it follows that *sustainable* configurations alone are also in equilibrium. Indeed, in the presence of contestable markets, the non-sustainability of a certain market structure would trigger a market entry process, which would consequently alter the final industrial configuration. Whether a given market structure is sustainable or not clearly depends on the shape of the cost and demand curves.

We indicate average cost with AC. Fig. 6.6A illustrates the case in which a monopoly is *not* a sustainable industrial structure. If the monopolist were to choose a price $p < p_1$ it would not be able to produce all the quantity demanded except at a loss. In the case in which $p > p_1$ a potential entrant would find it worthwhile to enter the market and produce quantity q_1 at price p_1. Finally, if the monopolist were to choose p_1, entry would still be profitable for an entrant producing an output level equal to q_0 at a price between p_0

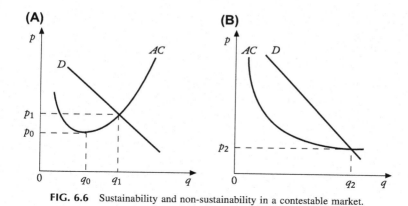

FIG. 6.6 Sustainability and non-sustainability in a contestable market.

(equal to the average minimum cost) and the price charged by the monopolist (p_1).

Fig. 6.6B illustrates the case in which a monopoly *is* a sustainable market configuration. Since the demand curve now intersects the average cost curve in the section in which it is decreasing, an entrant will not find it profitable to offer any output at a price lower than p_2. In fact, for $p > p_2$ the entrant's sales would be zero; on the other hand, for $p < p_2$ its profits would be negative. As we can see, in this case the monopolist cannot exploit its so-called market power; that is, it cannot set a price that allows it to obtain extra profits. The presence of extra profits would immediately attract the entry of rivals that could obtain positive profits by slightly reducing the price below the price charged by the monopolist. This circumstance shows the role that *free entry* plays in restraining the company in the market from inefficiently allocating its resources.

The theory of contestable markets is a useful industrial policy testing ground for advocates of liberalization policies. In particular, a normative corollary follows from the theory that public intervention should aim to remove possible barriers to entry and increase the degree of market contestability, limiting direct intervention to non-sustainable cases.

However, this conclusion should be accepted with a certain caution, as it is necessary to ascertain that there are no sunk costs in the case under consideration. As empirical evidence indicates, the sunk cost assumption is quite unlikely. In many businesses production requires investments that can only be partially recovered; additionally, there is a certain delay before consumers respond to price changes, and companies need time to calculate and implement price changes. This is why in practice the theory has fewer possibilities for application than its authors perhaps imagined.

6.8 Innovations and dynamic competition: Schumpeter's approach

6.8.1 Creative destruction

Until now we have assumed that monopolistic or oligopolistic enterprises make their decisions in a given technological context — and in fact the technology must be a given in order to make it possible to define a company's cost curves. But a capitalist firm, whatever the market form in which it operates, is constantly searching for innovations that allow it to make greater profits than what existing technology allows.

In the well-known seventh chapter of his work *Capitalism, Socialism, and Democracy* (1942), on one hand Schumpeter attacked the empirical importance of the concept of perfect competition and its theoretical use in economics, while on the other he outlined several characteristic traits of how many markets function in a modern capitalist system. Two of Schumpeter's propositions in particular are relevant here. The first identified different types of competition than price competition: "But in capitalist reality ... it is not that kind of competition which counts but the competition from the new commodity, the new technology, the new source of supply, the new type of organization ... which commands a decisive cost or quality advantage and which strikes not at the margins of the profits and the outputs of the existing firms but at their foundations and their very lives (Schumpeter, 2003)."

The second proposition qualifies the first, drawing attention to potential competition. Needless to say, this type of competition operates not only when it is actual, but when it is a constant threat as well; it disciplines even before it attacks.

The originality of Schumpeter's contribution lies in having identified the consequences of a specific type of competition between companies operating in a non-competitive market, as indicated in the evocative title of Chapter 7: *The Process of Creative Destruction*. Schumpeter identified innovation, be it in a process or in a product, as the distinctive trait of a capitalist society that constitutes the main factor of economic development. It is what makes the difference from a "stationary equilibrium" situation in which the economic system functions by simply reproducing what was produced and consumed in the past.

Even if perfectly competitive conditions were achievable, it is not a given that they would be socially desirable. This is because "A system—any system, economic or other—that at every given point of time fully utilizes its possibilities to the best advantage may yet in the long run be inferior to a system that does so at no given point of time, because the latter's failure to do so may be a condition for the level or speed of long-run performance." (Schumpeter, 2003, p. 83).

Innovations are what organically transform the economic system; they incessantly revolutionize economic structures from within, destroying the old and creating the new. "This process of Creative Destruction is the essential fact about capitalism. It is what capitalism consists in Schumpeter (2003, p. 83)." In short, for Schumpeter a company's success is not the result of optimizing a static calculation under certain conditions; rather, it derives from the firm's ability to plan and implement a strategic course based on technological innovations. In other words, however much a company might seek to grow its profit by acting on the quantity sold, it will not be able to achieve great results by controlling that quantity within the scope of a *given technology*. Rather, attaining higher profits will be pursued by introducing *innovations*, or changes in the technology.

It follows from the above that when we talk about market forms that are not perfectly competitive (in which competitors must all accept the market price), we must take into account that while such forms may exclude perfect static competition, they do not exclude **dynamic competition**, as we could call the competition between companies competing in a process of introducing and disseminating innovations. Of course, dynamic competition can be more or less intense in the phase of *introducing innovations* and the phase of *disseminating innovations*, and we would do well to recall that both phases are necessary to be able to talk about competition.

6.8.2 Dynamic competition and the nature of profit

An interesting result that emerges from the literature on Schumpeter's argument concerns the nexus between dynamic competition and the nature of profit. This means that a market form without any of the requirements of static competition cannot for that reason be regarded as an obstacle to dynamic competition. Not only that, it has many more possibilities of developing in market forms that statistically are perfectly competitive. In this regard we should keep in mind that, in most cases, innovations almost always lead to a company increasing in size. One of the basic characteristics of technological progress is that it often results in a lower unit price, on condition that the quantity produced increases.

For example, mass production methods and automation are advantageous, in the sense of lowering unit costs, only if production happens on a much greater scale than what was required by older technical methods. That is why large enterprises are quite frequently the organizational form of production that allows systematic development of the innovation process. In a market structure such as perfect competition, in order for there to be a great many companies they must all necessarily be small; such a structure would confine production within an extremely narrow technological horizon, or in any case much more restricted than what is possible by market forms in which enterprises can become quite large.

The notion of dynamic competition gives us a way to grasp the nature of profit, understood as gain that emerges from exploiting the possibilities of change in a dynamic context. For Schumpeter as well as post-Keynesian scholars, profits exist because the system is never in perfect competitive equilibrium — and the fact that the economy is never in equilibrium is anything but pathological. It is indeed the entrepreneur seeking technical innovations who has the specific task of systematically disrupting the competitive equilibrium.

By innovating, an entrepreneur erects monopolistic-type barriers around herself and derives a profit advantage from them. Profit is then understood as *the reward for this innovative role*. On the other hand, the gaps between companies' ability to appropriate the opportunities offered by technological progress are in many cases the result of interactions between the power to control technological knowledge and market power accumulated through a series of learning processes and accumulated research investments.

The problem that arises in practice is that all too often our industrial systems know how to effectively manage innovation only when it already exists, but they find it difficult to create new innovations. What should we do in such situations? When considering such questions, we understand why a firm cannot cease asserting its identity regarding its values, culture, and social relations, as well as its technology and resources. This is the Renaissance way of thinking typical of Italy in the 16th century, which gave rise to the so-called **"Leonardo's workshop"** model in which apprentices worked closely with a master. That model is being revived today, so much so that there are those who insistently speak of the necessity of returning to "Renaissance management," or "humanistic management" (as Americans call it) as a replacement for the American engineer Frederick Taylor's now obsolete "scientific management" theory of the early 20th century.

Appendix A: an introduction to game theory (by Alessandra Smerilli)

Introductory concepts

A game is played out every time people interact strategically with each other.

Game theory studies what happens when people interact and behave rationally and strategically.

Game theory is the study of mathematical models of cooperation and conflict between intelligent and rational individuals.

Rationality: each agent maximizes his expected utility compared to some belief.

Intelligence: each agent understands the situation in which she is involved, knowing that other agents are also intelligent and rational.

There are many types of games: card games, video games, sports games (such as soccer), and so forth.

We will consider games in which:

— two or more players participate;
— there are decisions in which strategy counts, or the set of moves a player intends to make;
— the game can have one or more results;
— the final result or win for each player depends on the strategies chosen by the other players, thus there is a strategic interaction.

When the only two editors in a city choose the price of their newspapers, knowing that their sales are jointly determined, they both participate in a game. Readers who buy the papers are not players in the game, since they do not know the effects of their actions on the editors' behavior. The best way to understand which situations games can represent is to give a few examples. Consider the following:

— OPEC members choose their annual production;
— two producers, one of nuts and the other of bolts, decide whether to use the metric or the American system.

Games that do not fit this case are excluded, such as lotteries (in the case of slot machines, where there is only one player who plays against chance, strategy is not important) or games without strategic interaction, such as solitaire.

Historical remarks

Game theory entered economics with the publication of Von Neumann and Morgenstern's *Theory of Games and Economic Behavior* in 1944. That massive text remains extremely important because it introduced the idea that conflict can be mathematically analyzed, and it lays out the necessary analytic tools. The development of the conceptual apparatus of the *Prisoner's Dilemma* (Tucker, unpublished) and Nash's publications on the definition and existence of equilibrium (1950, 1951) laid the foundations for the modern theory of non-cooperative games. Game theory applied specifically to economic reality began to take shape from 1953 onward. Until the mid-1970s game theory remained an independent branch with little relevance for standard economics, although with the important exception of Schelling's 1960 book *The Strategy of Conflict*, which introduced the concept of a focal point. Since 1970, when economists began studying in depth the behavior of rational agents with limited information available, information has been the central theme of many models. When the behavior of individual agents was finally placed at the center of attention, the temporal sequence in which they act began to be explicitly considered.

The description of a game

Cooperative and non-cooperative games

It is important to note from the outset that altruistic attitudes are not in any way expected from players in cooperative games; that is never assumed, because the basic hypothesis is that everyone pursues their own interest. If a player's interest is in doing good to his neighbor, that results from his degree of satisfaction in doing one thing instead of another; the key point remains that doing good pleases the player, and that is what guides his actions.

The unit of analysis in non-cooperative games is an individual who seeks to attain the best result for herself, given the constraints and the rules. If the players choose "cooperative" behavior, that happens because it is in the interest of each individual player.

Cooperative game theory studies the formation of coalitions precisely because they can be advantageous for the individual players. Cooperative games are characterized by the types of coalitions a group of players form, whether different coalitions produce different outcomes.

Non-cooperative theory seeks instead to explain individuals' choice mechanisms on the basis of individual reasoning, without alliances between individuals. The idea of analyzing games by studying the formation of coalitions between individuals is due primarily to Von Neumann, while it was Nash who gave impetus to non-cooperative theory (provoking Von Neumann's rather irate criticism).

Games with complete and incomplete information

A player has complete information when she knows who the players are, the available actions for all players, all the possible outcomes, and what information each player possesses.

Games with perfect and imperfect information

Information is perfect if at every moment in the game a player whose turn it is to decide knows all the decisions made to that point.

Static and dynamic games

In dynamic games, behavior depends on what happened in the past. In static games the players move simultaneously.

Glossary

Players: agents who make decisions with the goal of maximizing utility by their actions.

Nature: an actor in a game that is not a player and that takes random actions at a specific point in the game.

Action: a choice (a_i) hat player i can make.

Set of Actions: $A_i = \{a_i\}$ constitutes the entire set of actions available to a player.

Strategy: s_i is a rule that indicates to a player which actions to choose at every point in the game.

Set of Strategies: $S_i = \{s_i\}$ is the set of strategies a player can implement.

Payoff: the utility or gain a player receives after all players and nature have chosen their own strategies and the game has been played.

Equilibrium: $s^* = \left(s_1^*, \ldots s_n^*\right)$ is a combination of strategies made up of the optimal choice for each of the n players in the game.

Axiom of Rationality: the assumption underlying game theory is that all players act rationally, that is, no player chooses an action if another is available that allows him to obtain better results.

Common Knowledge: information is common knowledge between two or more players if they are aware of it, and if they know that the others know that they are aware of it, and so forth.

Normal form games

In the representation of a normal form game, each player simultaneously chooses a strategy, and the combination of strategies chosen by each player determines each player's gain.

The normal form representation of a game specifies:

the players;
the strategies available to each player;
each player's payoff for every possible combination of strategies.

Let S_i be the set of strategies available to player i, and let s_i be an element of that set. Let $(s_i, \ldots, s_n)$ be a combination of strategies, one for each player, and let u_i be the utility function of player i: $u_i(s_i, \ldots, s_n)$ is player i's gain if the players choose the strategies $(s_i, \ldots, s_n)$.

Definition: the normal form representation of a game with n players specifies the strategy space of players $S_1, \ldots S_n$, and their utility function is $u_1, \ldots, u_n$. We denote such a game with:

$$G = \{S_1, \ldots, S_n; u_1, \ldots, u_n\}$$

These types of games can be represented as a matrix as follows:

		P2	
payoff		C	NC
P1	C	−1, −1	−9, 0
	NC	0, −9	−6, −6

Players:

P1 (player row)
P2 (player column)
$S_i = \{C, NC\}$
$u_1(C,C) = -1$
$u_2(C,C) = -1$
$u_1(C,NC) = -9$
Etc.

Examples of noteworthy games
The battle of the sexes

Mario and Anna would like to go out together. Mario would prefer that they go to the soccer game together instead of the ballet; Anna would prefer the ballet to the soccer game. However, both prefer to go out together rather than remain alone.

Anna

		Soccer	Ballet
	S	2, 1	0, 0
Mario	B	0, 0	1, 2

Zero-sum games

In a zero-sum game, the sum of the payments received by all players equals zero, whatever strategy they might choose.

The following example is the representation of the Rock−Paper−Scissors game:

P2

		R	P	S
	R	0, 0	−1, +1	+1, −1
P1	P	+1, −1	0, 0	−1, +1
	S	−1, +1	+1, −1	0, 0

Variable sum games

Two automobile manufacturers simultaneously decide to launch a new model on the market. Each one is considering whether to offer financing (F) to its customers; doing so could increase their market share, but it would involve some cost. Both companies would prefer not to offer financing, but each fears the other will do so. Suppose that the expected benefits for the companies are as follows: if both offer financing, 400 for each; if neither offers financing, 600 for each; if one does and the other does not, 800 to the former and 300 to the latter.

The normal form of the game is as follows:

P2

		F	NF
P1	F	400, 400	800, 300
	NF	300, 800	600, 600

Nash equilibrium

Definition

Nash's concept of equilibrium, published in 1950, is so widespread that when we talk about equilibrium in games with no further qualification, we can assume that we are talking about a Nash equilibrium. *A combination of strategies s^* is a Nash equilibrium if no player has an incentive to modify their own strategy if others do not change theirs.*

In the example represented in the previous diagram, we see that the combination of strategies (F,F) is a Nash equilibrium. To understand the definition, let's put ourselves in the place of player P1: if we move in the (F,F) situation, with a payoff of 400, do we have an incentive to change strategy if P2 does not change hers? No; if P1 were to choose NF, he would collect 300 instead of 400. For reasons of symmetry, the same discussion applies to P2.

The following is the mathematical definition of a Nash equilibrium:

$$\pi_1\left(S_1^*, S_2^*\right) \geq \pi_1\left(S'_1, S_2^*\right)$$

$$\pi_2\left(S_1^*, S_2^*\right) \geq \pi_2\left(S_1^*, S'_2\right)$$

$$\forall i \pi_i\left(S_i^*, S_{-i}^*\right) \geq \pi_i\left(S_i', S_{-i}^*\right)$$

where π_i is the utility function of player i with respect to the combination of strategies S.

In the battle of the sexes game, the two Nash equilibria are (S,S) and (B,B).

A Practical Method for Calculating the Nash Equilibrium.

For every possible strategy by player 2, the best response by player 1 is shown; for every possible strategy by player 1, the best response by player 2 is shown. The cells of the payoff matrix where both have a "best response" are Nash equilibria. The following tables show in sequence the calculation of the equilibria.

P2

		S	C	D
P1	A	1, 0	1, 2	0, 1
	B	0, 3	0, 1	2, 0

P2

		S	C	D
P1	A	1, 0	1, 2	0, 1
	B	0, 3	0, 1	2, 0

P2

		S	C	D
P1	A	1, 0	1, 2	0, 1
	B	0, 3	0, 1	2, 0

So in this game, the equilibrium is (A,C).

Characteristics of a Nash equilibrium

The Nash Theorem: Every finite game always has at least one Nash equilibrium (in mixed strategies).

- There may be multiple Nash equilibria for a game.
- The Nash equilibrium is not always Pareto-dominant with respect to other outcomes.

(An outcome is Pareto-dominant over another if its associated payoffs are greater than the payoffs of the second outcome.)

As an example, consider the game economists know best: the **Prisoner's Dilemma**, introduced by Tucker in 1951. Two criminals who committed a serious crime are held in separate cells. The public prosecutor, however, only has the necessary proof to charge them with a petty crime, for which the penalty would be a year in jail.

Each of the two prisoners is told that if they confess to the more serious crime, they will be *set free (0 years)*, while the accomplice would be sentenced to *20 years*. If they both confess, each would receive an intermediate sentence of *5 years*. If neither confesses, they will be sentenced to *1 year* each. What would you do if you were in the place of either?

Let's represent the game in normal form.

P2

		Confess	Not Confess
P1	C	$\underline{-5}, \underline{-5}$	$\underline{0}, -20$
	NC	$-20, \underline{0}$	$-1, -1$

As we see, the Nash equilibrium is (Confess, Confess), so in equilibrium the two players would each receive 5 years in jail, while if both decide not to confess, they would receive 1 year each. Thus in equilibrium both are worse off than they would be had they decided not to confess.

Extended form games

The extended form of a game specifies all the moves and the order in which they happen. The extended form is thus better adapted to analyzing dynamic games, but static games can be represented in extended form as well.

An example:

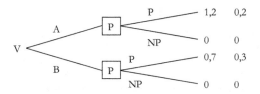

The main characteristics of a dynamic game with complete and perfect information are:

- decisions are made in succession;
- all the preceding decisions are known prior to making the next decision;
- the players' payoffs for every possible combination of actions are public knowledge.

A player's *strategy* is his complete plan of action, which specifies a feasible action by the player in any circumstance in which the player might find himself.

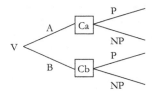

For player 1, actions (A or B) coincide with the strategies.
For player 2:

Strategy 1:
    If V plays A, play P;
    If V plays B, play P; **(P,P)**
Strategy 2:
    If V plays A, play P;
    If V plays B, play NP; **(P,NP)**
Strategy 3:
    If V plays A, play NP;
    If V plays B, play P; **(NP,P)**
Strategy 4:
    If V plays A, play NP;
    If V plays B, play NP; **(NP,NP)**

Information Set: for a player i, at any point in the game this is the set of game nodes within which she believes she can find the node actually reached. The player cannot distinguish between the various nodes in an information set.

In the example, V has one information set and C has two information sets.

A *subgame* of a game in extended form:

a) begins at a decision node n, which is an information set with one element;
b) includes all the terminal decision nodes that follow n in the tree (but not those that do not follow n);
c) does not intersect any information set.

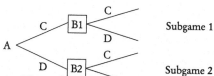

The solution to an extended form game. The way to find the solution, or which path will be traversed in an extended form game, is called the **backward induction** method. For example, the game given in the beginning of this section unfolds in two moves. In the first, the Vendor (V) must decide whether to set a high (A) or low (B) price. In the second, the consumer must decide whether to purchase (P) or not purchase (NP).

How do we solve the game? Player 1 (V) moves first; to decide which move to make, he must imagine how player 2 (C) will react to his move. The game then resolves by beginning at the end with a technique called "backward induction." Player 1, assuming that player 2 will act rationally, wonders: if player 2 were on the upper path, what would she do? She must choose between P, which yields a payoff of 0.2, and NP, which yields a payoff of 0; she will surely select P. If she were on the lower path, she would choose P for the same reason (0.3 > 0). Player 1 knows that by selecting A, he will receive a payoff of 1.2, and by selecting B he will receive 0.7, so it is rational for V to choose A.

Let's formalize the reasoning:

- we move backwards along the tree;
- when player 2 must decide, her problem is: $\max\limits_{a_2 \in A_2} u_2(a_1, a_2)$

Suppose that for every a_1, player 2's optimization problem has a single solution, which we can call $R_2(a_1)$. This is the *reaction* of player 2 to player 1's actions.

Since player 1 has all the information available, he can resolve player 2's problem and should foresee player 2's reaction to every action player 1 can make.

Player 1's problem thus becomes:

$$\max\limits_{a_1 \in A_1} u_1(a_1, R_2(a_1))$$

If the solution to the problem is a_1^*, then:

$$\left(a_1^*, R_2\left(a_1^*\right)\right)$$

is the backward induction solution to the game.

Perfect Nash equilibrium in subgames. In extended form games, the perfect Nash equilibrium in subgames is equivalent to the Nash equilibrium. A Nash equilibrium is perfect in subgames if the players' strategies constitute a Nash equilibrium in every subgame.

An example:

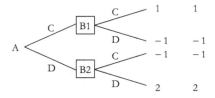

Strategies for player 2:

1. (C,C)
2. (C,D)
3. (D,C)
4. (D,D)

The perfect Nash equilibrium in the subgames is thus: (D, (C,D)).

Appendix B: trust in game theory

The trust game and the paradox of trust

The trust game, or investment game, in its basic form is a sequential game in which two players participate, the trustor and the trustee. The game is non-cooperative, which implies that the two players cannot agree on the behavior to follow, or analogously, there are no contractual clauses that allow the two players to reach an agreement that shields them from the risk of abuse or the other party violating the agreement. The simplest form we will work with here is the single iteration game, while keeping in mind that experimental variations exist in which the game is repeated for several iterations.

The dynamic of the game is shown in the following figure, where the two black dots represent the sequential decision nodes for the two players. In the top part of the figure we represent the first player's decision node — the trustor — who receives a sum equal to 10 units (let's suppose 10 dollars) and she must decide on a sum x (a number from 1 to 10) to give to the second player, the trustee. The game rules establish that what the trustor gives the trustee is automatically multiplied by 3, so the trustee receives $3x$. The second player, having received the total multiplied by 3, may in turn decide to return an amount y (between 0 and $3x$) to the first player.

So the final payoffs will be:

$10 - x + y$ for the trustor
$3x - y$ for the trustee

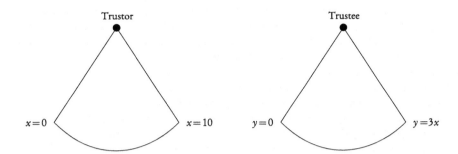

The more an economic game succeeds in identifying a fundamental characteristic of a real, everyday socio-economic problem, the more meaningful it is. The trust game quite faithfully captures the fact that interpersonal relationships in daily life, especially if we consider relationships that have economic consequences, frequently happen in conditions of *anonymity* and *asymmetric information*; that is, we do not know the counterpart with whom we must close some type of agreement, and thus whether we can trust her or not. They can also happen in conditions of *contractual incompleteness*; that is, we cannot defend ourselves from the risks of anonymity and information asymmetry by drawing up such perfect and detailed contracts that they can cover all possible cases and contingencies to protect us from abuse by the counter-party. In this scenario, any type of socio-economic relation (e.g., the decision between two co-workers to cooperate, to trust a product in a commercial transaction, etc.) requires that one of the two parties have sufficient trust to take the first step and make himself vulnerable to the other, accepting the risk of taking an action that may have negative consequences in terms of time and/or money in the event the counterparty does not reciprocate the trust shown. According to what the game implies, however, if the trust is reciprocated the cooperation between the two creates **superadditivity**, or an outcome that is greater than the sum of the individuals' allocations (in our example, the multiplication by 3 of the amount given by the trustor).

It is easy to understand how this can happen if we apply the game's design to labor relations in productive organizations. In such organizations it is as if trust games were constantly being played out, because to carry out complex tasks it is necessary to organize labor groups among co-workers who have different and non-overlapping abilities, such as marketing, technical, business, and legal expertise. In order for the work to be carried out, each one must share their personal knowledge with the others, running the risk that their contribution will be appropriated by others. Only if the various team members overcome the fear that others will not reciprocate the trust shown will it be possible to build an operational work group that will generate a greater level of knowledge than the sum of the members' knowledge and create an excellent result for the firm. Working together creates superadditivity for at least two reasons. First, by exposing our knowledge to others and exerting the effort to make ourselves understood and respond to objections, we learn better what we know —or think we know. Second, by bringing different types of knowledge together it is possible to create more complete and articulated knowledge than that of the individual participants.

Going back to our basic game, we observe that if the two players act by following the logic of *homo oeconomicus* and maximize their own utility, and each expects that the other will act like *homo oeconomicus* and follow the same logic, the final equilibrium of the game will be $x = 0$ and $y = 0$, and the sum of the payoffs of the two players — the overall value created by the game — will be 10 (the initial amount). This is the outcome of the game corresponding to the lowest possible level of trust by the trustor and the expectation of reciprocated trust by the trustee. In fact, with $U(\text{trustor}) = 10 - x + y$ and $U(\text{trustee}) = 3y - x$, the trustor, expecting that the counterpart will act like *homo oeconomicus* by maximizing his payoff and thus returning nothing of what he received, will find it optimal to give nothing to the trustee. These two choices — the choice by the trustor to give nothing, which entails a forced choice by the trustee who will have nothing to return — is also the equilibrium of the game, or the Nash equilibrium.

Let's see what might happen instead if to the contrary the players exhibit team behavior by adopting a rule to divide equally and draw their utility from the sum of the payoff, or the overall value generated by the game. The trustor would give all 10 dollars, which becomes 30 dollars the trustee would receive; the trustee in turn, abiding by the criterion of dividing equally, would give half to the trustor. Each of the players would finish the game with 15 dollars. Both would finish the game with a greater payout that ensured by a Nash equilibrium. The social result would be much higher and would multiply the initial amount by 3 (according to how the rules of the game were constructed). The lesson we can draw from comparing the two solutions (a Nash equilibrium and a team equilibrium) is that the lack of trust by the trustor and the lack of trustworthiness by the trustee lead to a suboptimal result, not only from a social point of view, but from an individual point of view as well. This is why the game we are analyzing identifies a paradox of myopically self-interested rationality — the behavior of *homo oeconomicus* — if we assume that both players are like that.

Beyond the theoretical solutions, what do the empirical results indicate? The vast case history of experiments with this game, carried out with different types of players and putting real money into play, show that players' average behavior differs from that of *homo oeconomicus*. The percentage of trustors who give nothing is very low (almost always less than 10%) when the game is played only one time, and only slightly higher if the game is repeated. In general, the trustor offers an average sum between 3 and 5 units, and the trustee returns something similar.

So if players' behaviors diverge from the paradigm of *homo oeconomicus*, what are the possible motivations (apart from maximizing one's own payoff) that drive them? In the case of the trustor, the motivations identified are those of *strategic altruism, pure altruism, aversion to inequality*, or *betrayal aversion* (the fear of being betrayed by the other player). In *pure altruism*, the trustor's utility function includes not only her own payoff, but, with a certain weight, the payoff of the trustee as well. Thus the optimal choice is to give something to the other player. A motivation similar to pure altruism can be that the trustor enjoys his ability to create wealth, or the fact that his move allows increasing the total resources on the plate of both players.

In **strategic altruism**, the trustor gives to the trustee because she expects that her trust will yield a return — that is, that the trustee, in receiving the amount multiplied by 3, will return a greater sum of money than what he receives. It is possible to clearly identify the presence of this motivation by asking the trustor what she expects the trustee to return before knowing the final result, then comparing her response with the amount actually given to the trustee.

In **aversion to inequality**, the trustor perceives a disutility arising from the positive distance between his and the trustee's result. For example, he may be uneasy at the possibility that he might have everything and the trustee nothing.

Finally, *betrayal aversion* reduces the propensity of the trustor to give part of what he has to the trustee so he will not have to suffer the disutility of opportunistic behavior by the trustee.

What instead drives the trustee to return something? The primary motivations can be *pure altruism, aversion to inequality*, and *reciprocity*. Note that, given the context of a single iteration of the game, strategic altruism plays no role because the game ends with the trustee's move, and her generosity cannot generate a counter-response by the trustor. As to the third motivation hypothesized for the trustee, reciprocity, this is the assumption that people find it useful to respond tit-for-tat, or to respond positively to positive behavior and vice versa. In the empirical and experimental literature there are a great many cases that prove the relevance of this type of preference.

The Genovesi version of the trust game

The version of the trust game considered above is based on the idea that an individual's interest or disinterest in others is a *question of individual preferences*. Saying that a person *A* has an interest in another person *B* is equivalent to saying that A prefers that *B*'s consumption or well-being be greater; consequently, *A* is willing to sacrifice part of his own consumption or income to improve *B*'s situation.

From this perspective, which we find today through much of economic science that studies non self-interested behavior, being truly social means having other-regarding preferences, and thus being willing to sacrifice part of one's own advantages in order to benefit others.

In contemporary economic theory, social or other-regarding preferences normally translate into an assumption of altruism, or one person's positive interest in the consumption or well-being of another. Recently more specific models have been developed, often based on experimental laboratory evidence. For example, Fehr and Schmidt (1999) and Bolton and Ockenfels (2000) have theorized that people (or at least some) have preferences that are sensitive to the differences in their and others' incomes, or they are "adverse to inequality." Rabin (1993) has instead proposed that people have preferences for "reciprocity," which motivate them to reward those who have been kind to them and to punish those who were not kind in a previous round of interaction in a sequential game. What is common to these types of models is that what makes preferences social is the willingness to sacrifice one's own interest to reward or punish others.

The game underlying these models is the trust game, the original structure of which can be represented as follows:

The trust game: payoffs are material rewards, not preferences

The Trust Game: payoffs are material rewards, not preferences

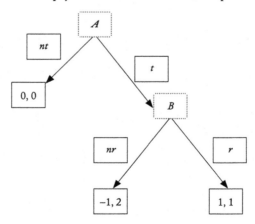

Standard rational choice theory does not provide for the possibility that *A* will rationally trust *B*, since it considers that if *A* were to choose to trust (*t*) she

would know that B in turn, comparing 2 with 1, will choose not to reciprocate, which means A would have a reward of -1 (which is less than 0, the status quo). Thus the only equilibrium in a game that does not repeat is (0,0): A finishes the game with the first move *nt*.

The theory of social preferences provides for the possibility that A can rationally trust B, since if A believes that B has social preferences (for example, he might want to reward A at his own expense because she was kind and had trusted him), A could play t with the expectation that B might play r due to his social preferences, thus attaining the equilibrium (1,1), *which is better for both than the status quo of* (0,0).

This theory seems to be in line with Antonio Genovesi's vision of the civil economy, but there is actually an important difference. Rabin's theory (and *strong reciprocity* theories in general) provide that in a game such as the Prisoner's Dilemma it is possible to reach the cooperative outcome, because they include this type of preference (and thus the payoff in the game).

So where is the difference with Genovesi's theory? If we analyze the theory of *social preferences*, we can state that the relationship between people does produce *de facto* mutual benefit. But the point is that the *intentional* content of the relationship according to the theory is not mutual advantage but rewarding or punishing the other based on one's preferences. In such models and games there is no idea of "joint action" or "mutual benefit" among the parties involved; they remain individuals who are totally indifferent to each other.

However, if we draw inspiration from a theory like Genovesi's, we can tell a different story about the trust game and trust phenomena. The basic idea is that Genovesi suggested moving from an I-based theory of mutual indifference (which in essence the Smithian or standard theory and the theory of social preferences are) to a we-based theory in which everyone asks "What should we *do*? What is the best course of action for *us*?" We have actually seen this, a vision along the lines of what today is called "team reasoning" or "**we-thinking**." How might a trust game read if we were to adopt the *we-thinking* perspective?

Look again at the representation of the trust game; in that diagram we emphasize two outcomes, (0,0) and (1,1).

The Genovesi version of the trust game

The Genovesi Trust Game

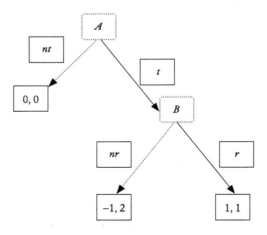

A Genovesi-type perspective suggests to players that the proper and civilly beneficial way of looking at the game is to compare (0,0) and (1,1) as if they had to maximize a sort of social well-being and function as if they were a single person. Faced with the choice between (0,0), (−1,2), and (1,1) they would certainly choose (1,1), since the sum is greater in that case (2 > 1). A society functions well when it sees the civil market game as the transition from a status quo of non-cooperation to one involving mutual advantage. No one would stop to consider opportunism in the second phase of the game, because were this sort of individualistic concern to prevail, fear would block agents at (0,0) in a sort of Hobbesian state of nature.

Intentions play a central role in this theory, as in Rabin, but here they are what we might call "collective" rather than individual intentions.

If both players know that the combination of trust actions by A and reciprocal actions by $B(f_a/r_b)$ is "better for us," the game becomes a joint effort to obtain a common outcome under the assumption that the two reason in the same way, that they feel themselves to be a "team" in a certain sense. There is no sacrifice, only a renunciation of opportunism, on the basis of the common awareness that opportunism pins them both to the status quo. B is not rewarding A for her kindness — that is, choosing to reciprocate A's kindness — but rather her intention to work together for a mutually advantageous outcome. Of course, it is important that each player have good reasons to think the other is not an opportunist, since when that happens the whole edifice of the civil economy fails, and economic development with it — as history has shown and continues to show, even in Genovesi's own country.

The difference between a Genovesi-style theory and social preferences theory might seem of little relevance, but in reality when we analyze the most ordinary market relationships it is not. In ordinary market relationships, each agent benefits from his participation in the market. But according to the idea of morality and sociality in Rabin's theory and in strong reciprocity in general, a baker is neither "social" nor "moral" if he chooses to simply sell his bread to those who ask for it (instead of not selling it), since he makes no "sacrifice" in that choice. Likewise, his customers are not "moral" when they buy bread, and that's that. In social preferences theory, which today is increasingly present in works that try to give a moral content to the economy, true reciprocity has no place in "normal" market transactions unless someone makes a sacrifice. "Civil" bakers are not enough; bakers are required who reward and punish, at their own expense, their "anonymous" customers. We are thus always in a theory of the market as a morally neutral zone in which we cannot experience genuinely social relationships in normal cases. The civil economy thinks otherwise and considers the market economy as civil in and of itself, since meeting to exchange in an attitude of friendship rather than opportunism is already a moral reality.

The distinction between a Genovesi-style theory of market sociality and social preferences theory is important for analyzing cases in which the operation of the market depends on trust. Consider a context in which contracts are not enforceable, in which there are no institutions to ensure that the other party will do her part, even when she has an incentive to be opportunistic when performing a contract. Imagine all the sequential cases (and probably not repeated) in which one party must act before the other, such as having to first deliver the goods and then be paid. How do we explain that in many such cases transactions take place normally, despite the prediction of the standard theory? Social preferences theory would explain it (as happens in the trust game) by asking B to reward A (who trusted her in the first move) by giving up part of her gain for A's benefit. Although in this case the relationship is mutually beneficial, in that the exchange takes place, B is asked to sacrifice part of what she gained for A, provided that B is sufficiently averse to inequality or sensitive to A's motivations. From this it follows that the theory makes a radical distinction between economic exchanges that take place through enforceable contracts and those in which such contracts cannot be made; pure self-interest is at work in the former, and altruism and sacrifice in the latter. This distinction seems to require too much, in that it requires us to relegate market "morality" to environments that are too mean-spirited, requiring stop-gap sacrifices in an otherwise immoral normality.

Let's summarize what we have said. The conventional way of understanding market relationships is characterized today in economic theory and sociology by two opposing positions: markets in contrast to sociality, and self-interest in contrast to altruism. These contrasting views do not perfectly overlap. For example, there are economic analyses of markets in which agents act on the basis of social preferences, and there are reductionist theories that explain even the most intimate relationships in terms of maximizing self-interest. That notwithstanding, the conceptual framework of contemporary economic theory does not offer a way to conceive of individual relationships that are *at once* mutually beneficial exchanges in which neither party need be altruistic and give up a slice of its economic benefit and genuinely interpersonal interactions that have moral value because of their social content. And yet the absence of such a conception impoverishes our understanding both of the market and of human relations in general.

Indeed, if we remain within contemporary economic theory, we are not able to describe market relations as a genuine form of reciprocity solely for the fact that they are oriented toward mutual benefit. How many pages have been written by philosophers and sociologists (such as Karl Polanyi) to argue that "true sociality" begins where purely market relations end! The end result is that markets and the world itself are less and less human. Conversely, economic theory (and in a certain sense all of social theory) is not able to explain non-market relationships as mutually beneficial relationships, such as those among families and friends, as if to say that if an exchange is mutually beneficial then it immediately becomes something much less noble, and the relationship becomes a mere contract and somewhat mercenary.

Further reading

Baumol, W., Panzar, J., & Willig, R. (1982). *Contestable markets and the theory of industry structure*. New York: Harcourt Brace.

Bertrand, J. (1883). Book review of theorie mathematique de la richesse sociale and of recherches sur les principles mathematiques de la theorie des richesses. *Journal de Savants, 67*, 499–508.

Bolton, G., & Ockenfels, A. (2000). ERC: A theory of equity, reciprocity and competition. *The American Economic Review, 90*(1), 166–193.

Chamberlin, E. (1933). *Theory of monopolistic competition*. Cambridge, MA: Harvard University Press.

Fehr, E., & Schmidt, K. M. (1999). A theory of fairness, competition and cooperation. *Quarterly Journal of Economics, 114*(3), 817–868.

Hirschman, A. O. (1970). *Exit, voice, and loyalty: Responses to decline in firms, organizations, and states*. Cambridge, MA: Harvard University Press.

Milgrom, P., & Roberts, J. (1992). *Economics, organization and management*. Pearson.

Neumann Von, J., & Morgenstern, O. (1944). *Theory of games and economic behavior*. Princeton University Press.

Nash, J. (1950). The bargaining problem. *Econometrica, 18*(2), 155–162.

Nash, J. (1951). Non-cooperative games. *Annals of Mathematics, 54*, 286–295.

Pigou, A. C. (1932). *The economics of welfare* (4th ed.). London: Macmillan.

Rabin, M. (1993). Incorporating fairness into game theory and economics. *The American Economic Review, 83*(5), 1281–1302.

Robinson, J. (1933). *The economics of imperfect competition*. London: Macmillan and Co.

Schelling, T. C. (1981). *The strategy of conflict*. Harvard University Press.

Schumpeter, J. (2003 [1942]). *Capitalism, socialism, and democracy* (p. 84). New York: Routledge.

Taylor, F. W. (1911). *Principles of scientific management*. New York and London: Harper & Brothers.

Chapter 7

New theories of the firm

7.1 New lines of research in the study of the firm and markets

A significant, although not unique, characteristic of modern capitalism is the success of the large enterprise. This has led to two important consequences: (*a*) the work required to manage corporate processes has become increasingly complex, such that it is entrusted to professional managers; (*b*) since each investor's optimal portfolio tends to be diversified among the shares of many companies for obvious safety and security reasons, a shareholder has neither the ability nor the interest to closely follow the affairs of an individual company in which she has invested. In view of all this, managers in large public enterprises end up exercising the power to set corporate policy guidelines, since they are freed up from close oversight by the shareholder-owners.

This situation was first documented in an important 1932 work by A. Berle and G. Means, *The Modern Corporation and Private Property*, a book that represents the standard of reference for all so-called *managerial theories* of the firm. For the first time, that work presented and argued the thesis of the *separation of ownership and control* of the enterprise.

A second line of research associated with Herbert Simon highlighted a particular novelty of a modern firm. Its goal is almost never to maximize profit, but rather to find a *satisfactory* level of profit, for the basic reason that a company's behavior in the market is guided by **limited rationality**. The *behavioral theory* of the firm is based on this premise.

A third line of research seeks on the one hand to explain why business organizations are created: Why do agents feel the need to find alternative forms of exchange to bilateral relationships between independent individuals, which are typical of market exchanges? On the other hand, it seeks to resolve the many problems of decision coordination and information communication that vex large corporate organizations in particular: How can internal corporate problems be resolved that arise from the divergence of interests between those to whom the power of control is delegated and those who retain ownership of the business?

To grasp the novelty of these three lines of research, it is essential that we first understand well the meaning of the terms "contractual incompleteness"

The Microeconomics of Wellbeing and Sustainability. https://doi.org/10.1016/B978-0-12-816027-5.00007-0

and "information asymmetry." As we will see, when contractual incompleteness and/or information asymmetry are present, **constraints imposed by incentives** are essentially the same as **constraints imposed by resources** in solving corporate problems. If information and/or individual actions are not precisely known, it is not sufficient to look to resources and/or technology alone, as we did in the three previous chapters. We must additionally examine **incentive schemes**: to achieve efficient results, appropriate incentives must be provided for individuals so they will properly disclose the private information they have and/or adopt the appropriate behavior strategies. At the same time, however, giving economic agents incentives does not always have the desired effect. In fact, it often happens that giving a company manager monetary and non-monetary incentives conditions his behavior to such an extent that it creates perverse outcomes; we will also consider that in this chapter.

7.2 Complete contracts and competitive markets

Most of the problems that arise in economic relationships have to do with agents' motivations. Individuals pursue multiple interests, which rarely align with each other. So how should we determine which actions to take, and how should tasks be distributed among individuals? How should we determine who should make decisions? How should we set up the various communication channels between the parties involved?

In what follows we will continue to assume that people operate solely on the basis of what they perceive to be in their individual interest (in Chapter 10 we will abandon even this anthropological hypothesis). The problem to resolve is thus how to make sure that when economic agents act they take into account not only the consequences that directly affect them, but also those that affect others to a greater or lesser degree.

A similar goal is achieved in practice through agreements, through which people recognize that changing their behavior is in their mutual interest. Similar agreements include the types of actions each party must take, the payments to be made, the rules and procedures that will be followed in the future to make decisions, and the behavior that each party can expect from the others. In a market economy, such agreements typically take the form of *contracts*, which may also be informal and implicit. The latter are voluntary agreements (thus mutually beneficial) between rational agents, formulated to adapt to circumstances and individual necessities, that function like formal contracts.

In principle, if a contract were **complete** the problem raised would not exist, because such a contract would be capable of specifying what each party must do and of defining how costs and benefits should be distributed in every possible circumstance, including those in which the terms of the contract are violated. In such a situation it is obvious that each party finds that the best choice is to respect the contract's terms.

But what is required for the **completeness of a contract**? Three conditions must be satisfied:

- each party must be able to foresee all the circumstances that could emerge over the course of the contractual relationship. Furthermore, the parties must be able to accurately describe those circumstances in order to determine in advance the contingencies under discussion; they must also be able to recognize which of the predicted circumstances have actually occurred;
- the parties must be able to define and agree on the best course of action in each possible circumstance;
- once the terms of a contract have been accepted, the parties must be sure to perform them. This aspect consists of two elements. First, the parties must not subsequently want to renegotiate the contract, otherwise the awareness that they will renegotiate at a later time could deprive the original agreement of its credibility and thus prevent it from ensuring the desired results. Second, each party must be able to determine if the terms of the contract are being respected, and if they are violated, each must have the will and the possibility of obtaining the agreed performance.

We now understand why it is actually almost impossible to write a complete contract. Our limited ability to foresee eventualities, the imprecision of language, the costs of calculating solutions, and the costs associated with drafting a plan — in a word, agents' *limited rationality* — imply that not all circumstances can be evaluated. Unforeseen cases inevitably arise over the course of complex interactions, and when that happens the parties must find a way to adapt to them. Such adaptations introduce the possibility of **opportunistic behavior**, including non-compliance.

The fear of opportunistic behavior may reduce the trust necessary to attain efficiency. For example, a farmer may be reluctant to trust a group of workers to harvest a crop out of fear that the threat of a strike during the season will make him vulnerable to demands for wage increases. He may even choose to plant less in order to be able to employ only family and friends. In general terms, incomplete contracts whose enforceability cannot be fully guaranteed create an *imperfect ability to bind the parties* to its terms.

Even when a certain situation can be perfectly anticipated and the agreements are binding, prior to the conclusion of the contract one of the parties could obtain *private information* that interferes with the practicability of an otherwise efficient agreement. In the used car market, for example, sellers have better information on the cars than buyers, which makes buyers skeptical of the quality of the cars.

Even when there is no private information before the conclusion of the contract, later there may be inadequate information to determine if the contract's terms have been fulfilled, or such an assessment may be too onerous. This could also open the possibility for opportunistic behavior, and advance recognition of such problems limits the types of contracts that can be concluded.

In short, the individual interests of the parties to a contract may not always be compatible with each other. Opportunistic behavior thus prevents efficient exchanges from taking place. The problem then becomes overcoming these difficulties to the extent possible, which implies recognizing that individuals' opportunistic behaviors limit what can be effectively attained. This is why it is necessary to design schemes that take into account the **constraints imposed by incentives**. This requires investigating the various sources of imperfect contracts, their consequences, and their possible remedies. To conclude, while it is true that contracts are tools to protect the interests of the contracting parties, it is equally true that when they are incomplete new problems arise. In order to grasp the consequences of such circumstances (Frame 7.1) it is necessary to introduce the distinction between **observable actions** and **verifiable actions**. The former can be noted by agents who are different from those who carry out the action; the latter, beyond being observable, can also be tried before an arbiter (a judge, for example).

7.3 Asymmetric information and opportunistic behavior

7.3.1 Adverse selection

Consider a case in which two agents enter into some form of negotiation in order to settle a matter of common interest. If only one of the two agents has access to the relevant information, or only one is able to evaluate the costs and benefits consequent to implementing the various strategies, then we are in a

---

FRAME 7.1 The consequences of contractual incompleteness

Consider two agents who wish to exchange a good that the buyer values at v and the seller values at c (where $c < v$). The two parties have complete information on the good in question, but suppose that the delivery of the good and payment for it cannot happen simultaneously; that is, payment may be made either before or after receiving the good. Finally, suppose that the exchange, the actual delivery of the good, is observable but not verifiable. With this assumption, a binding contract that states the seller's duty to deliver the good and the buyer's duty to pay a price p (where $v > p > c$) cannot be enforced. If the delivery precedes the payment, the buyer can always deny having received the good and not pay for it; on the other hand, if the payment precedes the delivery, the seller can always declare that the good was delivered even if that is not true. If the parties, aware of what has happened, were to commit themselves to a judge's decision to settle a possible dispute, they would not find it advantageous to carry out what would have been a mutually beneficial transaction in any event (given that $c < p < v$).

situation of *asymmetric information*. There are two main types of problems caused by asymmetric information, although they are not the only ones. The first concerns **pre-contractual opportunism**, known as adverse selection; the second concerns **post-contractual opportunism**, known as moral hazard.

The term *adverse selection* originates from the insurance field. A frequent example of adverse selection is car warranties; new cars are typically sold with a warranty that the manufacturer will pay for any problem, apart from routine maintenance, that arises during a certain time period. Some car manufacturers have experimented with selling an optional extended warranty that covers repairs for longer periods. Clearly, people who expect to use their cars much more will be the ones who buy the extended coverage. Those who expect to use their cars simply for carrying passengers on well-maintained roads in normal weather conditions will be less inclined to buy an extended warranty.

Adverse selection is a problem of *pre-contractual opportunism* that arises due to one of the parties having *private information* when considering its usefulness *before* completion of the contract. This is why we also talk about **hidden information**. The used car market is the best-known case of adverse selection, first considered by George Akerlof in 1970 (see Frame 7.2).

FRAME 7.2 The market for "Lemons"

Consider the market for used cars, supposing that there are two type of cars offered: high-quality cars (A) and low quality cars (B). Suppose that each type B car owner values his car at $1000; this is the minimum price he would accept to sell the car. Similarly, $2000 is the valuation a type A car owner places on it. Buyers' valuations, or the maximum price they are willing to pay, are instead $1200 for a type B car and $2400 for a type A car.

If buyers were able to observe the quality of the car (which is known to the owner alone), then type B cars would sell for a price between $1000 and $1200, while type A cars would sell for a price between $2000 and $2400.

What happens if buyers cannot observe a car's quality and thus must estimate it, which is what actually happens? Consider the case of asymmetric information regarding the quality of the used car. Suppose a buyer has an equal probability of considering a type A or B car, and thus the buyer is willing to pay the average value (or expected value) for the car; that means that the buyer is willing to spend $1800 ($= 1/2 \times \$1200 + 1/2 \times \$2400$). The problem is that this price will only attract those who own lemons, given that the minimum selling price for a type A car is $2000. On the other hand, if the buyer were sure she was buying a lemon, she would not be willing to spend $1800, since the equilibrium price for lemons would be between $1000 and $1200. If the market price were between these two extremes, only poor quality cars would be sold, and buyers would correctly expect to only find poor quality cars. Summarizing, type A quality cars would not be traded on the market, despite the fact that buyers' valuations (or $2400) would exceed those of the sellers (or $2000).

What are the main consequences of adverse selection types of asymmetric information? That there cannot be a price at which the supply of a good equals the quantity demanded. The problem is that since supply costs cannot be obtained from sellers, the price must be the same for all buyers, regardless of the costs of providing service to individual customers. The only buyers willing to pay a certain price are those who, on the basis of their private information, believe that the price is advantageous.

These customers will tend to be the ones who are the most expensive to satisfy. If there are administrative costs, then the price must increase so much that even those who value the product the most would not find it worth buying. Any price less than what allows covering costs will attract only those whose supply cost does not exceed revenues. Consequently the market disappears, even in the case in which, in the absence of private information, exchange would guarantee a mutual opportunity for gain. The solution that has actually emerged is for an agency outside the market to certify the product quality. In such cases we speak of a market failure, in the sense that market forces alone are not able to lead to a mutually advantageous agreement.

The type of information imperfection considered above can be usefully framed in a case study originally explored by George Stigler, who classified goods or services in a market into three categories corresponding to three increasing degrees of buyers' lack of information.

- **Search goods**: goods or services whose existence on the market is not always known to all buyers, but whose quality can be known *before* the purchase, after some research: for example, a suit, a house, or a newspaper.
- **Experience goods**: goods or services whose qualities can be known only *after* the purchase and after its use or consumption: for example, a car or a restaurant meal.
- **Credence goods**: goods or services whose qualities *are not* perfectly identified even after their purchase or use: for example, the accuracy of a medical diagnosis or therapy, the quality of legal counsel, or the effectiveness of a university course.

7.3.2 Moral hazard

Moral hazard is an expression that indicates a form of *post-contractual opportunism* caused by the unobservability of certain actions, which allows an agent responsible for executing a contract to not follow its terms in order to gain an advantage. Such behavior is not considered by the competitive market model, for the obvious reason that it assumes that transactions occur in goods and services exchanges with known and observable characteristics, such that the parties can always verify, without cost, compliance with the terms of the contract.

The term moral hazard also originated in the insurance field, where it indicates the tendency by policyholders to change their behavior in order to obtain reimbursements provided by the policy. In general, when an agent finds it advantageous to act unethically — hence the expression "moral hazard" — there will always be negative consequences for someone else. For example, having insurance coverage can make people less attentive when taking the necessary precautions to avoid or minimize damage. If the necessary precautions could be defined in advance, and subsequently observed and accurately measured, then the insurance contract could be fulfilled. However, they are frequently not observable and verifiable, which makes it impossible for it to be a truly binding agreement; that is, the contract may require maintaining a certain behavior, but the insurance company is not able to verify compliance. This is why moral hazard phenomena are often referred to as **hidden action** cases. If a driver were liable for all damages caused by her driving, she would probably drive much more cautiously than when she is insured.

Similarly, health insurance coverage makes overconsumption of prescription drugs and/or diagnostic tests much more likely (as happens in the United States, for example). In each of these cases, the coverage provided by the policy changes the behavior of those insured in ways that are more costly for the insurer.

Moral hazard problems arise in any situation in which someone — a supplier, customer, employee, or whoever — whose behavior cannot be verified at zero cost, and whose interests do not coincide with those of his counterpart, may be tempted to act inefficiently or manipulate information in his possession to induce others to make inefficient choices.

Nearly every situation characterized by moral hazard can be formalized in terms of an **agency relationship**. This expression refers to instances in which an individual (the *agent*) acts on behalf of another (the *principal*), with the supposition that the former is acting to promote the latter's interest. The moral hazard problem arises when the agent and the principal have different interests, and the principal is not able to easily recognize if her agent's work is actually carried out in her interest. Agency relationships are quite widespread: a doctor is a patient's agent, an employee is a company's agent, the board of directors is an agent for a company's owners, and so forth. However, moral hazard problems also arise when there is no true principle; consider a work team in which one of its members only pretends to work, causing harm to the others.

What solutions are there to moral hazard problems? We see two.

1. A first solution is to increase the resources dedicated to monitoring and verification. Sometimes this consists of preventing inappropriate behavior by directly stopping it before it occurs. For example, public enterprises in the United States cannot publish their financial statements until they have been verified by auditors who are independent from the company;

prospectuses describing investments for which money will be solicited from the public must be approved by a government agency. Health insurance companies can require that their policyholders get a second opinion prior to paying for expensive treatments on the basis of a single doctor's recommendation. Workers often must have a timecard stamped that records their movements, and they are subject to various penalties if they arrive late or leave early.

2. A second solution, widespread in some sectors, is to require paying a deposit to guarantee the services to be performed; these are sums of money that are withheld if the work is inadequately done. For example, contractors often pay a deposit that is retained if the project is not completed on time and in the prescribed manner. Paying a deposit can be an effective expedient to create the desired incentives; the problem is that individuals often do not have the financial resources necessary to pay an adequate deposit. This is particularly relevant when the gains obtainable from misconduct are high and the probability of being discovered is low; in such cases the deposit should be quite high.

7.4 Managerial theories of the firm

7.4.1 Baumol's model

The attention economic theory has focused on the role of managers has increased apace with the emergence of large enterprises. In 1910, the 100 largest companies in the Western world controlled no more than 15% of the total value added in their respective markets; 50 years later, that percentage had tripled.

W. Baumol, R. Marris, and O. Williamson created the first and best-known models of the managerial approach to the theory of the firm. We should note, however, that Berle's and Means' initial insights were taken up and further developed by the American economist Kenneth Galbraith in the early 1960s. He observed that the emergence of bureaucratic organizations is a central characteristic of industrial development, which led to the emergence of a managerial *technostructure* within large companies. This is a management group that monitors the management of the firm; it is primarily interested in the survival of the organization to maintain and increase its power.

Beyond explicitly taking into account the separation between ownership and control, managerial theories of the firm have the following characteristics in common.

- *Extension of the Time Horizon.* As we know, the traditional analysis of a company is based on a single time period. An enterprise has the goal of maximizing profit in the current period, and the analysis is carried out assuming that the various periods are independent of each other.

Managerial theories of the firm operate over a multi-period horizon, in the sense that when an enterprise must make choices, it takes into consideration not just the current period, but some number of future periods as well.

- Two considerations make this extension necessary. First, there is a close connection between the decisions made in different periods. As an example, if a firm wants to expand in future periods, it must already begin to apply particular price and sales promotion policies; in other words, current profits could be sacrificed to obtain a future expansion. Second, a modern corporation understands that a certain growth rate is a condition of survival, such that it becomes necessary for it to plan for expansion and include future periods within the scope of its decisions.

- *Maximizing Behavior.* All these models adopt the principle of *constrained maximization*. There may be differences between the models in exactly how they specify the firm's objective function, but all arrive at an equilibrium solution in the same way.

- According to Baumol, managers maximize the value of sales under a given profit constraint, since growing the company at the fastest pace possible allows it to increase its bargaining power. As long as the current profit is at the minimum level sufficient to satisfy shareholders, managers have an interest in increasing the size of the organization, even if that means giving up maximizing its profit.

- Baumol's model can easily be illustrated in graphic terms (see Fig. 7.1). The production that allows maximizing the total value of sales is A, at which point marginal revenue is zero. (The curve TR, which represents

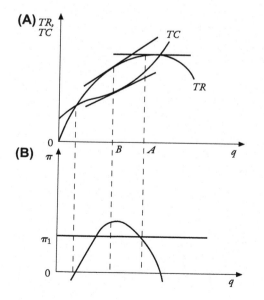

FIG. 7.1   W. Baumol's model.

total revenue, is obtained from a linear demand curve.) According to traditional theory the optimal quantity would be B, at which point marginal revenue equals marginal cost. So the possibility of maximizing sales depends on the minimum acceptable level of profit for shareholders and lenders (π_1). If this level is less than or equal to π_A, A will be the chosen output; otherwise, the minimum profit constraint becomes an operational part of the decision, and the company will choose a lower production and a higher price. According to Baumol there are two possible types of equilibria. In the first the profit constraint provides no effective barrier to sales maximization ($\pi_1 \leq \pi_A$), in the second it does ($\pi_1 > \pi_A$).

- *The Role of the Stock Market.* The existence of the stock market exerts a great influence on an enterprise's actions. On the one hand, the market is a funding source; indeed, for large enterprises, issuing shares or debt securities is one of the regular forms of raising funds. On the other hand, the stock market provides an ongoing valuation of a company through share price trends. The stock market exerts an influence both on the shareholders who retain control of a company and on its managers. The controlling shareholders keep watch over the value of their shares, and they thus have a direct interest in seeing the company's market value grow. The situation may be partially different for managers. They may not have a direct interest in the market value of the firm, since they do not necessarily own shares; rather they see the stock market as the place to tap for funds for expansion, and thus they want the market to view the company in the most favorable light.

- To that end they will be careful to make annual dividend payments regularly and in sufficient measure to satisfy shareholders' expectations; otherwise it could be difficult to place new shares and procure funds when needed. Managers can only have an indirect interest on the share price; indeed, if the share price on the market were to fall too low, the possibility would arise for outside financial groups to buy shares until they gain a controlling interest, which would jeopardize administrators' independence. Managers are thus preoccupied with the share price not as owners, but primarily to reduce the risk of takeovers.

7.4.2 Capital markets and the role of takeovers

Capital markets play many roles. They allocate scarce resources to various agents who request them, they provide signals for managers' investment decisions, and they are a form of control over managers' actions. Let's consider this last role at some length.

Takeover theory, first developed by Marris, states that the market for corporate control can get to the point that neither the market competition for inputs nor the market for outputs can ensure the elimination of inefficient firms. If investors become aware that profits could be increased if different management strategies were pursued, they could try to buy a controlling interest in a company and implement new strategies to pursue higher efficiency levels.

The growing number of takeovers during the 1980s and 1990s was an effective test environment to analyze the conflicts of interest between managers and shareholders, which stimulated a renewed theoretical interest in the subject. The traditional evaluation of takeovers, as formulated by Marris, maintains that the threat of a takeover serves primarily to discipline managers: Failing to maximize profits reduces the value of the enterprise on the stock market, which draws investors and/or outside entrepreneurs (predators) to buy the firm and replace the executive management team with the goal of increasing its performance.

Grossman and Hart (1980) made the first formal study of the disciplinary role of takeovers. The authors emphasized that when the operating environment of a company changes, the contracts that initially govern the relationship between shareholders and managers become obsolete. This gives managers the opportunity to make inefficient decisions and appropriate part of the company's value. Takeovers can then increase efficiency by enabling a third party, the predator, to take control of the company and to establish a new contract that is better adapted to the new situation. The disciplinary role of takeovers stems from the effect of this renegotiation on managerial behavior: Managers will be more cautious in making decisions that would be advantageous for themselves but that would reduce the value of the firm and increase the convenience of a takeover. However, the empirical evidence shows that, rather than being punished, managers normally receive a "**golden parachute**" severance package when they are removed after a predatory takeover.

7.4.3 Costs to predators and perverse effects of takeovers

Takeovers never happen at zero cost to predators, who have an incentive to bear the costs of a takeover only if they think they can make sufficient profits. There are two main factors that can reduce predators' incentives.

1. *The Free-Rider Problem.* Grossman and Hart pointed out that the potential problem of *free-riding* can cancel their incentive. In the event of a takeover, shareholders may not want to divest their shares so they can benefit from the share price increase induced by the transfer of ownership. On the other hand, the predator can obtain a profit only if the bid price for the shares is less than their price after the change in ownership; she cannot buy the shares and make a profit on them at the same time. A possible solution to this problem is *capital dilution*, or the possibility, as provided for by the corporate charter, that the new controlling shareholder may either issue new shares or sell part of the company's assets to another company under her control under conditions that disadvantage minority shareholders.

Since dilution increases predators' revenues, it also increases the probability of successful takeovers.

2. *Resistance by Managers.* Managers can try to make a takeover difficult by appealing to regulatory authorities over commerce and trusts (such recourse is frequent in the United States and Great Britain) or through various other disruptive actions (known as *poison pills* in financial jargon). If this does not work, they can collude with the predator and buy out his shares in the company (if he already owns some) at a premium over the market price in return for him signing an agreement that prevents him from owning the company's shares for a certain time. The other shareholders who do not participate in the agreement can be disadvantaged by this defensive maneuver, since the takeover did not go through and the company bought the predator's shares at a price above the market price. Clearly, managers' resistance can be mitigated by offering adequate severance packages.

With this we can understand Scherer's observation (1980) that "the available evidence provides at best only weak support for the hypothesis that takeovers generate an effective disciplinary mechanism against departures from profit maximization."

We should also note that the threat of a takeover can also have perverse effects on incentives. Rather than inducing managers to make the necessary structural changes, a takeover threat can drive them to act short-sightedly and sacrifice long run benefits in order to increase short-run profits. That can happen because: (*a*) managers are not very astute and make decisions that reduce future cash flows in favor of current cash flow (short-sighted managers); (*b*) stock markets are not fully efficient and undervalue future profits to the detriment of present profits (short-sighted markets). There is abundant empirical evidence for (*a*), but the same cannot be said for (*b*).

7.5 Optimization and "satisficing" in the enterprise: behavioral theory

As the reader will have noted, the models for the managerial approach are all indebted not only to the separation of ownership from control, but also to organizational theory. The latter is doubly linked to H. A. Simon, whose original scientific contribution (*Administrative Behavior*, 1947) is characterized by the vastness of its application, which goes well beyond the scope of the theory of the firm.

Simon's thought indicates that the traditional way of conceiving how a firm works is sterile and misleading, because (*a*) it leads to applying optimization rules even in situations in which it is not possible to attain equilibrium, or that equilibrium does not actually exist. That is because companies, like any other agent, act on the basis of **bounded rationality**; (*b*) there are important behavioral results that are characteristic of transitional states but that disappear in equilibrium, which can be properly analyzed only in terms of the underlying dynamic mechanism. The company's behavior on the market will be guided by the rules of **procedural rationality**, which consists in defining rational behavior procedures that have little to do with the rules of constrained maximization.

The ideas and system of categories developed by H. A. Simon gave rise to the *behavioral* theory of the firm, which was originally due to the work of R. Cyert and J. March (*A Behavioral Theory of the Firm*, 1963). The central objective of the authors' work was to study the decision-making process of a "large multiproduct firm under uncertainty in an imperfect market." In particular, it was Cyert and March's interest in the organizational problems created by the internal structure of a large managerial enterprise that led them to view the enterprise not as a single decision-making unit with a single goal, but rather as an organization with multiple decision-making units with multiple goals.

More precisely, the firm is conceived as a coalition of different interest groups, or *stakeholders* (such as managers, workers, shareholders, customers, suppliers, and banks) who are connected to its activities in various ways, each with its own goal. For example, workers want high salaries, good working conditions, and good pensions. Managers work toward high salaries, power, and prestige. Shareholders aim for high profits and an expanding corporate capital.

Thus the *first* step in the behavioral theory of the firm is to analyze the process by which the demands of the different groups are formed, which is carried out by identifying the key variables in the company's decision-making process. The *second* step is to study the ways in which the demands of the various groups (which are in conflict among themselves, because individuals usually have different goals than the firm as an organization) succeed in finding mutually compatible goals. These demands, which in practice take the form of levels of aspiration, will depend on how these levels have been achieved in the past, the demands obtained by similar groups in different companies, prior levels of aspiration, and the expectations about the future of the enterprise. The process of forming these levels of aspiration and how they are satisfied are what make the behavioral theory dynamic. The *third* stage concerns the precise identification regarding its output levels, inventories, sales, the market share controlled by the company, and profit. And here as well the goals take the form of levels of aspiration rather than of a rigid constrained maximization. This is because the company "satisfices" rather than always seeking to maximize its performance in every situation.

As we can see, the characteristic element of the behavioral approach to the theory of the firm is to interpret the enterprise as a complex organization that is designed to endure over time. It is a complex structure that does not merely respond mechanically to commands from on high. The phrase "from on high" may have a slightly ironic meaning, as if the leaders of the company resembled the gods, as if voices came from the clouds. As an alternative, we would say "executive management." While it is true that top management always makes the final decisions, it is also true that these decisions take into account what other groups in the firm think. Thus corporate behavior can be viewed as the result of trade-offs between various classes of stakeholders.

7.6 The neo-institutionalist theory of the firm

7.6.1 Coase's view of the firm

We now turn to the third line of research mentioned at the beginning of the chapter. The most original and interesting explanation for why firms exist is due to the British economist Ronald Coase. In his famous 1937 article, *The Nature of the Firm,* Coase wrote that "The main reason why it is profitable to establish a firm would seem to be that there is a cost of using the price mechanism (Coase, 1937)." In other words, using the market entails costs that gradually increase as the number of agents involved increases. The basic idea is that negotiating a contract between two or more parties is costly, that is, that there are *transaction costs*. In general transaction costs are classified as **costs due to contractual incompleteness** and **coordination costs**.

- We know that the presence of uncertainty makes stipulating complete contracts expensive; we need only think of the agency contracts we looked at in the previous chapters, in which the presence of information asymmetries made a first best solution impossible. More generally, as we saw when discussing contractual incompleteness, there are costs linked to the necessity of foreseeing all eventualities that might happen and including them in the contract. Sometimes that is not possible because there are so many such eventualities. The parties must then define a new contract every time something unforeseen happens, but defining contracts entails considerable legal costs.
- Moreover, the fact that a contract is incomplete can place one of the parties at the mercy of another party's opportunistic behavior. As we will see shortly, this happens primarily when an individual must make a **specific investment** in order to participate in a transaction, that is, an investment whose value is high for that particular transaction, but that would have little value in different transactions. Once the investment has been made, if an occasion arises to renegotiate the contract the investor could find herself forced to accept much worse conditions than those that made the investment advantageous. This happens because her investment has a very low value outside of that particular transaction, so it is not advantageous for her to reject the new contract even though it provides worse conditions than those previously agreed to, since rejecting it would make her even worse

off. Since this opportunistic behavior is anticipated, the result will be a very low or even no investment.

- *Coordination costs* derive from the necessity of bringing all participants into agreement. It is natural to expect that these costs will increase as the number of parties increases. The "cost of using the price mechanism" that Coase referred to can be identified, to a first approximation, as this category of costs. Consider a situation in which the production of a certain good happens through the market interactions of n independent individuals. Each of them must individually contract with all the others, and the number of bilateral agreements necessary is equal to the combinations of n elements, or $n(n - 1)/2$. However, if production happens within a firm, each of the n participants need only enter into a single contract with the owner or his representative, so only $n - 1$ bilateral agreements are necessary. If we start from the assumption that each contract entails a certain cost, the second choice will be considerably more efficient. With five individuals, Fig. 7.2 shows that ten bilateral agreements would be necessary. In a company, however, one person becomes the central agent (E), and a total of four contracts is sufficient to bring all the parties into relationship.
- Given the types of transaction costs identified here, it makes no difference if the contracts happen within a company or on the market. The only advantage to organizing production in companies is because fewer contracts are necessary.
- Despite its simplicity, this analysis introduces two crucial problems. First, the fact that there is an individual in a firm who has the task of coordinating and entering into the various agreements implies that this person is invested with *authority*: that person has the power to accept a potential contractor or not and to set the terms of the agreement. Second, what are the criteria for deciding who will be invested with this authority? More explicitly, what is the link between *authority* and *property rights*?

7.6.2 The nexus between authority and property rights

The question arises: what are the criteria for deciding who will be delegated this authority? In their foundational 1986 work *The Costs and Benefits of*

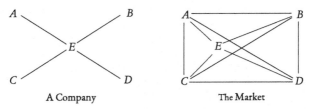

FIG. 7.2 Bundles of contracts in a company and on the market.

Ownership: A Theory of Vertical and Lateral Integration, Grossman and Hart state that authority, understood as the power to decide in every possible situation not defined in advance, is implicit in the very definition of *property rights*. According to the definition chosen by the two authors, property is characterized by a twofold power: the power to exercise all *residual rights of control*, or to decide everything that is not explicitly included in the contract or not specified by applicable laws, and the power to retain the *residual management rights*. Consider the first type of power.

The concept of residual management rights would not make sense in a world of complete contracts, because there would not be any "residual" circumstances or events (or none considered up front). However, since contracts are almost always incomplete, referring to the right of ownership to settle disputes and "complete" contracts greatly simplify transactions.

That said, the new theory of property rights is focused on defining the field in which such rights play a fundamental role. We have repeatedly stated that economic transactions in a modern market economy are characterized by contractual incompleteness, which can create considerable problems in the case of specific investments. On the other hand, this is not the only relevant characteristic, since the fact that individuals and capital goods are *heterogeneous* plays an important role.

The importance of the heterogeneity of individuals and capital that participate in the production process has recently been taken up by Williamson, although we can already find references to this in Marshall's and Schumpeter's theories of the firm. Capital and particularly individuals are generally not fully substitutable, as they have specific characteristics. Thus it is possible for **complementary relationships** to be established between individuals and capital goods that bring about a true "network of technological interdependencies," as in the previously described case of a production team.

Indeed, capital goods are built with certain characteristics to satisfy particular production requirements, while individuals mature their abilities through interaction with capital goods and with other people engaged in the same production process. On the other hand, it happens frequently that these are *specific* abilities, that is, they are useful only in certain contexts in relation to the particular capital goods and people with whom these individuals interact. It follows that the contributions individuals or capital goods make to the production process depends, to a greater or lesser extent, on their interactions with other specific individuals and capital goods.

How can we reconcile this with determining a firm's limits? Grossman and Hart start from a new definition of a firm; they no longer see it as simply a bundle of contracts (as in Coase), that is, as a legal way to resolve the problem of transaction costs. *A firm is now seen as a set of activities, capital goods, and indispensable skills to carry out the production process.*

If we start with the problem of specific investments, the difficulty of imposing penalties for contractual non-compliance implies that the efficient solution would be ensured if whoever made the investment also owned the business in which the specific investment is made. For example, General Motors (GM) needed a new plant to build steel frames. It could build it itself. In this case, the problem of opportunistic behavior would be solved since the investor receives all the surplus generated by its own investment, and it is not subject to anyone else's opportunistic behavior. In a certain sense, GM's actual solution of buying Fisher Body is close to what we indicated in this example; by buying Fisher, GM owned the investment.

In other words, if there are two agents A and B, and A owns a business in which B will make a specific investment, the efficient solution requires that A and B integrate, or that B buy the business in which she is investing.

This is true even if B's specific investment is in **human capital** rather than a physical input; the efficient solution would require that B become the owner of the business into which she would be making the specific human capital investment of her knowledge and acquired abilities. Human capital investments require careful consideration because a worker's specialization, while increasing his value and bargaining power on the market, can also have adverse effects when it becomes too high. While an investment in human capital is advantageous for the firm because it increases productivity, it may not be so for a worker; she could find herself constrained within that particular work with few possibilities of using her skills elsewhere if something unforeseen happens, such as the enterprise failing, or if restructuring makes her knowledge unneeded. As a result, a worker may have little incentive to make such an investment even if the costs are borne entirely by the firm. The efficient solution is when the investor and owner are the same.

On the other hand, that integration does not have only advantages, as it might seem from what we have said; there are also significant costs. Consider the case in which both agents, and not just one, make an investment: to whom should authority be attributed in this case, or, more precisely, who should become the owner of both investments and decide the proportions in which the surplus should be divided?

In the simple example given, B is the only one who made an investment. Transferring the power to decide A's behavior to B makes it optimal for B to invest a socially efficient quantity of resources.

It is different if A as well as B must make a specific investment for a certain transaction to be possible. Assigning A the authority to influence the set of B's choices, while improving A's investment decision from a social point of view, has an adverse effect on B's decision, in the sense that it reduces his incentive to invest an efficient quantity of resources.

So we are faced with a trade-off. The preferred solution would be found by comparing the costs and benefits of every possible allocation of property rights. If the inefficiency of A's choice caused by transferring the property to B exceeds B's inefficiency if A were to become the owner or buy B out, then the second solution would be preferable, and vice versa if not. The problem, however, is that neither solution allows reaching a first best solution; one of the two agents will always invest a suboptimal quantity of resources. So since the solution is inefficient in any case, it is worth reconsidering the *non-integration* solution we previously discarded because it is not desirable from a social point of view. If the inefficiency linked to such a strategy were less than that of the other two possible strategies (*A* buying *B* and vice versa), then it would be the preferred option and would become the ownership structure.

7.6.3 Grossman, Hart, and Moore's theory of property rights

What might we make of these solutions if we take complementary relationships into account, beyond technological interdependencies between individuals and specific capital goods? Hart and Moore (1990) studied this problem by extending Grossman and Hart's analysis in two directions.

The authors confirmed the results presented to this point that if only one agent must make an investment, he should own the assets that comprise the company. However, they explicitly introduced a second reason that justifies attributing ownership of an asset to a specific agent. Suppose that an individual need not make a specific investment, but rather has crucial knowledge and skills that make her indispensable for an economic activity. In other words, any *coalition* of agents that does not include her cannot obtain a surplus in production above what can be attained when she participates. According to Hart and Moore, a **coalition** is a set of individuals and capital that are technologically interdependent; the set may also include the final consumers of the good produced. Consumers exert their influence through market demand, and they thus determine the specifics of the product supplied.

More precisely, we can say that *n* individuals and *m* capital goods form a coalition when the value they jointly produce by collaborating in production is greater than the sum of the values of what the same individuals and capital can produce *separately*. To clarify the concept, a coalition can be an industry that is vertically integrated from the extraction of the raw materials to the distribution of the final product. Alternately, the employees of two companies who exchange know-how and information can form a coalition, even if they operate in separate sectors.

This last example is illuminating and helps us more clearly define the concept: in a coalition, all individuals *cooperate* in order to obtain a common result. As the term itself suggests, the members of a coalition all tend toward a common goal, and they cooperate to pursue it as efficiently as possible. Returning to our initial discussion, if an individual is indispensable to carry out a certain activity, he should belong to the coalition that performs it; furthermore, he should also either be its owner or have the residual right of control over the activity, and thus have *authority* over the other members of the coalition.

So what happens if there are several indispensable individuals in a given production process? They should be *joint owners* and manage the activity according to some criterion of collective choice (the rule proposed is a majority). A very interesting implication of this is that it makes possible considering and analyzing alternative forms of ownership to that of the traditional capitalist enterprise, and it provides the theoretical justification for the existence of non-capitalist firms, such as social companies and cooperative enterprises.

In short, given the exogenous nature of the distribution of abilities among the members of a society, technological interdependencies, the potential of investing in the human capital of each individual, and the stock of fixed assets, Grossman, Hart, and Moore (GHM) show that the allocation of control over fixed assets is efficient if: (*a*) *within every coalition those who are the least substitutable in the production process are also the owners*, and (*b*) *these owners make the maximum contribution to the total surplus through their initial investments*.

This result has similarities and differences with J. Schumpeter's analysis of the capitalist firm set out in his well-known 1942 work *Capitalism, Socialism and Democracy*. According to Schumpeter, assigning control of production to particular individuals is not justified by the fact that they have the ability to carry out tasks that others cannot do, but rather because they know how to use those abilities to innovate; that is, they can alter the way factors are combined and modify labor techniques or organization while choosing the most socially efficient solutions. The new theory of property rights is thus in full agreement with the Schumpeterian idea that the uniqueness of entrepreneurs lies in their human capital investment contributions to the production process. At this point, however, the two theories diverge.

To Schumpeter's argument the new theory adds: (*a*) the scarce substitutability of abilities and (*b*) the nexus of technological interdependence established between people and the machines they use. As an extreme case, the GHM theory shows that if an individual is indispensable for using a machine, in the sense that the machine would be of little use in the production process without her contribution, it is efficient for her to own it even though her human capital investment is nil.

Moreover, unlike Schumpeter's approach in which an entrepreneur's mindset distinguishes him from others, Grossman, Hart, and Moore do not take these personality differences into account: everyone, without distinction, can make investments in human capital and thus become less replaceable, *but*, some invest more than others or are more determined than others. However, the theory in question does not explain why that happens, which is an important limitation.

7.7 The organizational dimension of the firm

7.7.1 Forms of companies and governance structures

The expression *form of a company* indicates the organizational structure of a firm or group of firms, such as the number of hierarchical levels, the definition of discretionary power or authority delegated to individuals placed in the various hierarchical levels, and the channels through which the enormous amount of information necessary to carry out production is sent.

Choosing a particular organizational form shapes the entrepreneurial responses to the opportunities and constraints available in a given time and place, such as technologies, markets, financing, legal conditions, actions by public authorities, and the company's internal and external managerial resources.

The different forms of firms in a country's industrial system are one of its distinctive traits, and they are an important indicator of its level of economic development. This can help us understand why certain organizational forms are more widespread than others in advanced economies, and why the size and complexity of enterprises have so markedly increased over the last century.

The explanation for this is that companies are created and develop in response to increasing transaction costs. In his 1975 work, Williamson argued that production is organized within a firm, rather than on the market, whenever transaction costs are lower in a corporate environment than on the market. On the other hand, the economic historian Alfred Chandler (1982) stated that organizational changes have played an extremely important role in the success of large enterprises during the last century of industrial history. Chandler analyzed the development of managerial structures in large US enterprises and identified a well-defined time sequence. Initially companies were organized along the **unidimensional model** (*U-form*); the various business activities, such as production, sales, and so forth were separate functional units; Fig. 7.3A represents this situation. Each unit had either a specific production or service function to perform for the benefit of the whole firm. Each unit had a director who reported directly to executive management; executive management in turn coordinated and managed all the different corporate activities. Managers were organized hierarchically; the head of the company at the top of

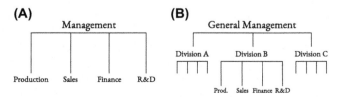

FIG. 7.3 Company forms: (A) unidivisional; (B) multidivisional.

the pyramid oversaw the heads of the various corporate departments, who had no discretionary power.

This corporate form had the advantage of allowing each division to take advantage of possible economies of scale. However, the efficiency of this organizational form decreases as the size of the firm increases in both scale and range of production. The unidivisional form is efficient when the company operates in a single geographic market or produces a single product.

When it expands into multiple geographic markets or increases its production range, it becomes extremely difficult for a central management to process all the information flowing in from the various markets, and thus to coordinate all the internal and external resources overseen by a specific unit. Consider what happens in a sales department; as the company expands into new markets, the number of distributors increases. If the firm is expanding its product lines, managers must work with several markets in which customers have different requirements, and the agreements with and directives given to distributors are necessarily different. Similar problems are encountered if an enterprise expands into different geographic markets, particularly if they are foreign, given that foreign markets have different demand characteristics and laws governing corporations. Central management must face similar problems for all the divisions, with the risk that the amount of information and the number of decisions to manage will become excessive.

In Chandler's view, the greatest problem due to overloading managers is that long-run strategic planning is neglected. It is easy to understand why: managers' performance is judged based on results attained over a certain time period, typically in the short or medium run. In the absence of time or resources, it is in their immediate interest to let go of decisions that would only influence results over a long time span.

The answer to the problems we have outlined is to change the organizational structure to a **multidivisional form** (*M-form*), which is shown in Fig. 7.3B. In this organizational model, there are multiple units or divisions within an enterprise, each one of which is functionally structured. Each division is fully independent of the others and is built around a specific market (e.g., national and international divisions) or product. In this way a corporation can manage an enormous volume of operations and information, even if it is quite large, because the operational decisions for each unit are made by the division's managers; executive management for the entire company can then focus exclusively on strategic long-run decisions, such as investment planning or resource allocation across the various operational divisions.

In a multidivisional enterprise, division heads have the power to make decisions about how to manage their own unit; they are not part of the general corporate management. Division heads work directly with the production or sales unit, and they have access to first-hand information that has not been filtered through various hierarchical levels, as happens in unidivisional companies. In addition, each division is a *cost center* from an accounting standpoint; this makes it easier to verify its performance, and thus managers' compensation, which enhances the use of incentives.

Finally, a multidivisional form makes it easier to coordinate and control the company's activities. In an unidivisional company the heads of the various units operate by different criteria. Suppose that executive management intends to reach a certain profit goal. Those in charge of sales must adopt certain price or marketing strategies, those concerned with production must adopt certain production processes and purchase raw materials from certain suppliers, and so on. All these policies must be defined by executive management and incorporated into directives that subordinates in the various units must simply obey. So it is possible to imagine the complex coordination problems that centralized management must face, and as the company grows it might not be able to effectively resolve them.

In essence, the multidivisional form is a combination of *decentralization* and *concentration*. This follows from setting up "natural decision units," to use Williamson's expression, in the sense that the parts that interact intensely are combined into divisions, which then remain separate from all the other parts with which they have no or limited relationships. The operational divisions enjoy a high degree of autonomy, almost as if they were separate enterprises, while executive management is responsible for control and verification; its ultimate goal is to ensure compatibility between results at the division level and those of the overall organization.

7.7.2 The holding company

A third organizational form Chandler identified is the **holding company** (**H-form**). This is a group of companies in which different businesses coexist, either because there are too many to form a multidivisional company (which would have an excessive number of divisions), or because they are too different technologically for it to be possible to control and coordinate the managerial aspects of the entire complex. Each participating company retains an independent legal identity, and top management no longer uses an internal hierarchy as the means of controlling them. In other words, a holding company resembles a multidivisional firm without an executive management.

We can distinguish two types of holding companies based on the type of control available to its management.

- The first type is the **loose holding company**; as the name suggests, it is characterized by the lack of a single entity that controls it. Among the various firms in a loose holding company, there is a dense network of privileged relationships in which information and know-how are exchanged, managers move between the companies, intermediate products are exchanged, and so on.

- Since the companies in the group are absolutely equal, no one can exercise any influence over the decisions and actions of the others. This type of organization presupposes the existence of strong bonds of trust between the parties, trust that leads to stable and continuous cooperation over time.
- A famous example of a loose holding company is the Japanese *zaibatsu*, a form that has been highly studied in the literature; participating companies independently define their strategies and internally reinvest their profits according to each one's specific requirements and development pace, while maintaining close, cooperative relationships among themselves.
- The loose holding company is present in many industrial companies in the United States and Europe, particularly in Italy. In the United States, connections between large companies are quite common that are maintained by their membership on the boards of directors of various companies, either at the same time or in succession. Perhaps the most illuminating example in Italy is Mediobanca, which is the hub of a dense network of financial participations between private groups.
- The second type is the **tight holding company**, which is closer to a multidivisional enterprise. In this case, the companies are part of a hierarchical organization that is directly or indirectly managed by another company, which in turn is controlled by a single economic entity. The hierarchical organization implies an authority relationship that is usually exercised and justified by shareholdings in the subordinate companies. This type of group gives top management the possibility of reducing its financial liabilities. In the event that a subsidiary fails, the controlling shareholder only risks the capital invested in that particular company. On the other hand, if that production unit were a division of the parent company, the parent would be liable for the entire loss.

7.8 Alternate conceptions of the firm

7.8.1 The company as a commodity and shareholder value

To close this chapter we want to draw attention to the fact that since the end of World War II microeconomic theory has developed three different ways of looking at an enterprise: **as an association**, **as a coalition**, and **as a commodity**. The first conception sees the firm as a special community, organized to endure over time, in which various stakeholders participate, such as workers, investors, customers, suppliers, and the geographical territory, and cooperate among themselves to reach a common goal. Note that this is the idea behind the American "corporation," which in its inception was a non-profit entity whose governance was adopted from the Benedictine and Cistercian monasteries. The corporation is a good in itself, and as such it cannot be left to the caprices of the market, and of the financial market in particular.

The conception of the firm as a coalition developed from Nobel laureate Ronald Coase's pioneering 1937 contribution; as we have seen, his argument was that the firm emerged to save on transaction costs, or the costs of using the market. As we know, every market negotiation entails specific costs, so there is a reason for a company to exist as long as transaction costs exceed the operating costs of ownership. The justification for the emergence of the company is thus functionalist.

Finally, beginning in the 1970s the idea took shape of the firm as a commodity, and as such it can be bought and sold just like any other commodity; this is the dominant view today. It is thus nothing more than a "nexus of contracts" that, depending on the convenience of the moment, are signed by multiple parties, all of whom seek to maximize their individual gain. If in fact the firm is nothing more than a commodity, it is clear that the only class of stakeholders that merits attention are the shareholders, for the obvious reason that to sell something there must be an owner, and whoever pays the price to buy a company becomes its owner.

What provoked the transition from the first to the third conception of the company? This transition began to take shape when institutional investors — such as mutual funds, pension funds, and insurance companies — that owned over 50% of the capital of all corporations listed on a stock market in the world imposed the rule on managers that a company's financial return must be equal or greater than its rival companies. Even if the return is high but somewhat less than the competition, the company should be restructured, sold, or closed. But what about those who, after working in the company for even a long time, are fired or laid-off? For the theorists of the firm as a commodity this is not a problem for management, but rather one that pertains solely to the state or private philanthropy.

What are the practical implications of these different conceptions of the firm? The most important of these concerns the ultimate goal the entrepreneur pursues. If the firm is seen as an association destined to endure for a long time in the market, then clearly its only objective to pursue is to maximize long-run profit. To that end, both the human and environmental sustainability of the company must be at the center of management's concerns, which must engage the problem of making the most appropriate investment in human capital for its workers and of establishing fruitful, reciprocal relationships with other stakeholders, such as customers, suppliers, and local governments.

If instead the firm is conceptualized as a commodity, it is obvious that management's goal should be to maximize value for its shareholder-owners. To that end a short-run perspective, or *shorttermism*, will prevail, and with it the principle of shareholder value. This is the principle that leads to pushing up stock market share prices and assigning free cash flow — the cash that remains after paying operational, financial, and fiscal costs — to shareholders. In order to improve expected returns, as we know, shareholder-owners must have management's diligent collaboration. To induce managers to work toward the same goal, they are offered a compensation scheme that is tied to the return on capital; stock options are the best-known tool to that end, although they are not the only one. If management does not then perform, share prices will fall and the company will pass to other hands that will meet that need in one way or another. Note that this would be the result even if the company were hypothetically profitable in the long run. The devastating financial and economic crisis that began in 2007 in the United States is a consequence − certainly not the only one − of the pervasive and uncritical acceptance in economic and financial environments of the principle of shareholder value as the guiding principle of corporate action. As the facts have demonstrated, the consequence could only be disastrous.

As Sumantra Ghoshal, the famous guru of corporate strategies and a professor at the London School of Economics, wrote:

> *If companies exist only because of market imperfections, then it stands to reason that they would prosper by making markets as imperfect as possible … by creating barriers to entry and by managing the interactions with their competitors. It is market power that allows a company to appropriate value for itself and prevent others from doing so.*

(Ghoshal, 2005)

7.8.2 The problem of organizational planning

A highly important practical consequence that stems from the way the firm is conceptualized concerns the problem of organizational planning. This is the problem of how best to structure the organization to implement the strategies defined by the board of directors, given that structure should follow strategy rather than vice versa, as often happens. There are three key principles that can ensure the best fit between strategy and organizational structure:

a) *a complementary relationship between organizational variables.* This happens when the action of one variable increases the benefit or advantage of other variables' actions. This complementarity ensures that the value of the overall effect is greater than the sum of the effects of individual variables;

b) *flexibility.* An organizational system is flexible when changing (or not changing) one element of the structure does not compromise its performance; otherwise it is rigid (consider an assembly line);

c) *a spirit of initiative and cooperation.* A spirit of initiative speaks of an entrepreneurial attitude and the capacity to act without having to discuss every detail with one's superior. By cooperation we mean the ability to carry out actions whose purpose is to promote the common goals. It may happen that, in order to draw attention to its own initiative, one part of the structure may not cooperate or may outright boycott the other parts. And vice versa, it may also happen that, out of a love for the spirit of cooperation, some may not assert their own talents and thus stifle their creativity.

If we think of the firm as an entity destined to endure over time (the company as association), the problem of organizational planning clearly becomes one of management's chief tasks. Every senior manager inspires his own particular style of leadership that reflects his personality and his system of values. However, there are some organizational principles that are common to any managerial role:

1. a tendency to go beyond a task-oriented logic in favor of a goal-oriented perspective. That requires that a manager have the ability to manage the economic capital together with the **relational capital** within the group. A manager who is a respected leader promotes a positive and harmonious work environment; facilitates ways for people to express and share their abilities; initiates and spreads a transparent communication style; reduces the hierarchical distance with those who work under her; supports open and flexible ways of sharing and imparting responsibility;

2. a tendency toward *participative* management. Its particular characteristics are linked not only to hierarchical roles, but to its capacity for dialogue and positive tolerance toward differences. A dialogue is one of the most important managerial tools; although it can initially be uncomfortable because people's cognitive maps and symbolic codes are different, participatory management allows people to grow and express their skills. Indeed, personal liberty and common goals encourage responsibility and consistency. From this perspective, a manager is person-oriented and team-oriented rather than toward individuality;

3. *sharing experiences* increases the identity of the group, because it allows them to feel that they are active participants and that the various members see themselves reflected in the others, which initiates valuable learning processes. Sharing experiences requires structured times for narrative and debate, which capitalizes on these shared events toward the defined goals. Moreover, the delicate game of exchanging thoughts reinforces the sense of belonging, improves relational skills, and supports and rewards reciprocal support skills. All this presupposes that special attention be given to the means of communication.

As we will see in Chapter 10, making a work environment satisfying, a place where people discover not only that they are respected but that also facilitates personal growth, is the ultimate goal of post-Taylorist organizational planning — as long as there is a desire to see the firm as an association of persons oriented toward producing value.

7.8.3 Connective capital and company development

A concept recently introduced into the lexicon of managerial disciplines is "connective capital." It denotes the fact that in current historical conditions the strategic factor in a company's success is not just the human capital embodied in individuals, but also their ability to work as a team by engaging in relational exchanges.

Thanks to such exchanges, it becomes possible for each person's tacit knowledge to circulate among all the team members.

In the 1960s, the American philosopher Michael Polanyi introduced the by-now famous distinction between codified knowledge and tacit knowledge. The former is what can be transmitted by means of codes, such as books, protocols, and manuals; someone studying a text comes to possess knowledge that was initially in the mind of its author. Tacit knowledge is instead knowledge that can only be transmitted by direct personal contact. Consider what happened in a workshop like Leonardo da Vinci's, with its interactive relationships between masters and apprentices. But even today, a young surgeon or artist needs direct contact with a master. Connective capital measures an organization's capacity to mobilize and draw out the dispersed tacit knowledge present in each person.

We should keep in mind that while codified knowledge was more than sufficient for the Taylor model to work well, and which led to an appropriate insistence on public education, in the post-Taylorist production model inaugurated with the third Industrial Revolution tacit knowledge is what is most needed. Empirical evidence has confirmed that a successful firm today is one that manages to accumulate the highest level of connective capital.

How do we do that? We find an eloquent, memorable response in Adriano Olivetti's address to the workers in Pozzuoli on the occasion of opening a new company factory on April 23, 1955:

> *Can an industry take on purposes? Are these found simply in the level of profits? Beyond its evident rhythm, is there not something more fascinating — a destination, a vocation — even in the life of a factory? … The Ivrea factory, although operating in an economic environment and accepting its rules, has turned its purposes and its primary preoccupations to the material, cultural, and social elevation of the place where it was called to operate, launching that region toward a type of new community in which there is no substantial difference in purposes among the protagonists of its human affairs, of its history made day by day, to assure a future to the children of that land and a life more worthy of being lived.*

(Olivetti, 2012, pp. 28−29)

At a time when the positivist idea was broadly accepted that the dynamics of cause and effect were sufficient to understand the world, Olivetti did not hesitate to state that a company that wants to consider itself civilly responsible cannot avoid questions regarding the purpose for which something is done, or why it is considered good. It is interesting to compare Olivetti's words with what David Hevesi wrote in the *New York Times*: "I'm saddened and offended by the idea that companies exist to enrich their owners ... That is the very least of their roles; they are far more worthy, more honorable, and more important than that. Without the vital creative force of business, our world would be impoverished beyond reckoning." (2008)

Further reading

Akerlof, G. A. (1970). The market for "lemons": Quality uncertainty and the market mechanism. *The Quarterly Journal of Economics, 84*(3), 488–500.

Berle, A. A., & Means, G. C. (1932). *The modern corporation and private property*. New York: The Macmillan Company.

Chandler, A. D., Jr. (1977). *The visible hand*. Cambridge, MA and London: The Belknap Press of Harvard University Press.

Coase, R. H. (1937). The nature of the firm. *Economica, New Series, 4*(16), 386–405.

Coase, R. H. (1960). The problem of social cost. *The Journal of Law and Economics, 3*, 1–44. The University of Chicago Press.

Coase, R. H. (1988). *The firm, the market, and the law*. University of Chicago Press.

Cozzi, T., & Zamagni, S. (2004). *Istituzioni di economia politica*. Bologna: Il Mulino.

Cyert, R., & March, J. (1992 [1963]). *A behavioral theory of the firm*. Englewood Cliffs, NJ: Prentice Hall (reprint, Oxford, UK: Blackwell).

Ghoshal, S. (2005). In J. M. Birkinshaw, & G. Piramal (Eds.), *Sumantra Ghoshal on management* (p. 15). Harlow: Prentice Hall.

Grossman, S., & Hart, O. (1986). The costs and benefits of ownership. *Journal of Political Economy, 94*.

Grossman, S., Hart, O., & Moore, J. (1990). Property rights and the nature of the firm. *Journal of Political Economy, 98*, 1119–1158.

Hart, O., & Moore, S. (1990). Property rights and the nature of firm. *Journal of Political Economy, 98*(6), 1119–1158.

Hevesi, D. (2008). Michael Hammer, business, writer, dies at 60. *New York Times*, September 5.

Michael Porter, E., & Mark, R. Kramer (2011). Creating Shared Value. *Harvard Business Review, 89*(1-2), 62–77.

Nicita, A., & Pardolesi, R. (2008). Il Nobel che fece l'impresa. Coase e il governo delle regole incomplete. *Mercato, concorrenza, regole, 3*, 427–467.

Olivetti, A. (2012). *Ai lavoratori*. Roma: Edizioni di comunità.

Scherer, F. M. (1980). *Industrial market structure and economic performance*. Houghton Mifflin, Business & Economics.

Schumpeter, J. (2003 [1942]). *Capitalism, socialism, and democracy*. New York: Routledge.

Williamson, O. E. (1987). *The economic institutions of capitalism*. London: The Free Press, a Division of Macmillan, Inc.

Chapter 8

The utilitarian view of welfare economics

8.1 What is welfare economics?

8.1.1 Utilitarian ethics

In his 1920 work *The Economics of Welfare*, the British economist Arthur C. Pigou, a student of Alfred Marshall, wrote: "The purpose of this volume is to attempt a partial study of the causes affecting economic welfare in actual modern societies. ...What we wish to learn is, not how large welfare is, or has been, but how its magnitude would be affected by the introduction of causes which it is in the power of statesmen or private persons to call into being." As we can see, the purpose for welfare economics is in economists' attempts to build bridges between theoretical analysis and solutions for socially significant problems by suggesting appropriate forms of intervention to public authorities.

And, just as do individuals, public authorities must also make choices concerning how to best use the resources available to them. In any given time period the amount of available resources is fixed, which always creates problems of choice; if more resources are allocated to a given project, there will be fewer to implement another project even though it is relevant and important. Such choices clearly impact many people's living conditions; some will gain, while others will lose. The question then arises: What can an economist say about the greater or lesser desirability of a given change or a given decision when those directly concerned are not in unanimous agreement?

A common distinction in economics is between an *analysis of the consequences* of a given policy and a *judgment* about its desirability. The former is called **positive economics**; the second is called **normative economics** (see Chapter 1, Section 7). When a question arises about how the equilibrium price of a good might be influenced by the introduction of a tax, we are in the area of positive economics. Equally, when considering how a tax on income might influence the welfare of the poor and the rich, this too is a positive investigation. Normative economics is instead concerned with *evaluating* the consequences of a given measure for the purpose of arriving at a judgment on the merits of the measure in question.

The Microeconomics of Wellbeing and Sustainability. https://doi.org/10.1016/B978-0-12-816027-5.00008-2

Welfare economics is part of normative economics; its purpose is to provide criteria by which it is possible to formulate judgments on alternative economic policy plans. For example, is it good or bad for society to proceed with constructing a nuclear power plant? It is clearly not possible to find an objective rule for expressing an incontrovertible judgment, for the obvious reason that any rule is based on a **value judgment**. One person may think a society spends too much on national defense, while another may think exactly the opposite, but that does not mean we cannot say something sensible about the desirability of alternative policies for a society. In many cases, very weak value judgments are enough to allow us to choose between various proposals. Not only that, it is also important to bring value judgments to light that are implicit in statements such as "Policy M is superior to policy N." This helps us understand the ethical assumptions on which certain statements and positions are based.

Traditional welfare economics was built on the philosophical foundation of *utilitarianism*, the stream of thought linked to the work of the British philosopher Jeremy Bentham; it is still dominant today. There are three fundamental premises of utilitarian ethics.

The first concerns the *evaluation of alternative situations*, which states that the only proper basis for such an evaluation is the welfare or satisfaction that agents derive from the actions being evaluated. This first component of utilitarianism is called *welfarism*. For example, it gives no weight to human rights as such; these are taken into consideration only to the extent they produce utility.

The second premise regards the *basis for choosing actions*, stating that actions should be evaluated solely on the basis of their consequences. No consideration is given to agents' intentions (as does Kantian deontology, for example) or to motivations other than those that improve welfare. This second component is known as **consequentialism**: The value of an action is wholly determined by the value of its consequences, whatever the intentions of the agent or circumstances that produced it. If the consequences are good, if they increase welfare, then the action is judged to be ethically good, and *vice versa* in the opposite case.

Finally, the third premise concerns how to combine individuals' welfare, stating that the criterion for aggregation should be the sum of each individual's welfare. This third component is called *sum-ranking*: alternative social states should be evaluated by considering the sum of individual utilities associated with them. No attention is given to how total utility is distributed among individuals in alternative projects, say, X and Y. Within the scope of utilitarianism, social justice has no value in and of itself. It does not matter that one social group receives much and another receives little when a particular policy is implemented. What matters is that the sum of the individual utility gains due to project X is greater than that of project Y.

Over time these three pivotal principles of Benthamist doctrine have been subject to various formulations and interpretations. In particular, with the rise of ordinalism in economics, the third principle has been replaced by the Pareto criterion. Yet another is the important and well-known distinction between *act utilitarianism* and *rule utilitarianism* introduced by Roy Harrod in 1936. Finally, John Harsanyi (1977) laid the foundations of *neoutilitarianism* with the distinction between "ethical preferences" and "personal preferences."

8.1.2 The old welfare economics

A central point of Benthamism is the idea that utility is a variable that can be measured cardinally. Individual utilities can then be summed, and the sum provides a measure of social welfare. The best-known expression of this line of thought is found in Pigou's work we mentioned previously.

But what does applying Bentham's criterion require in specific cases? Simply this: the possibility of **comparing interpersonal utility**; society must be able to compare one person's improved welfare with another person's diminished welfare. Assume that there is a community composed of three people whose utility functions are U_A, U_B and U_C. The collective welfare is thus expressed as $W = U_A + U_B + U_C$. According to Bentham's criterion, $\Delta W > 0$ if and only if $(\Delta U_A + \Delta U_B + \Delta U_C) > 0$. It could happen that a policy being evaluated from a collective welfare point of view might have the result $\Delta U_A > 0$, $\Delta U_B > 0$, $\Delta U_C < 0$, but despite that, $(\Delta U_A + \Delta U_b) > |\Delta U_C|$. The collective welfare would increase, but C would be worse off than before. Applying Bentham's criterion, the policy would be approved, which implies that the welfare improvement enjoyed by A and C exceeds the decrease in C's welfare.

The problem is that — apart from ethical considerations that C might deserve special consideration due to a disability — applying this criterion necessarily supposes that utility is a cardinal quantity. So what is the unit of measure we should use to express various individuals' utility? It simply does not exist, because utility, understood as the capacity for goods to satisfy needs, is a subjective attribute.

To tell the truth, scholars of the old welfare economics were aware of the fact that there could not be an objective method to compare different people's levels of subjective utility. However, they overcame their hesitation by considering that utility comparisons were not between individuals but between *groups* of people, such as rich and poor, young and old, men and women, because it seemed reasonable to assume that there were significant *average* differences. But that sleight of hand could not last long, and in fact it did not.

We will consider the profound differences between utility and happiness in Chapter 12. In the meantime, an effective way of grasping the ultimate consequences that follow from the utilitarian philosophical system is to reflect on the famous fable of the ant and grasshopper in the 1987 version by M. Hollis and E. Martin (Frame 8.1).

FRAME 8.1 The Tale of the Ant and the Grasshopper Revisited (Legrenzi, 1998).

All summer long the grasshopper consumed and the ant invested. "You are acting quite irrationally," said the ant. "When winter comes you will regret it."

"I will be very unhappy, but I am acting rationally," the grasshopper replied. "Being rational coincides with being happy, and at the moment my pleasure exceeds my future pain. Come join me and sing in the sun!"

The ant responded, "In my opinion, being happy consists in maximizing my utility over the whole of my existence. Unhappiness and happiness have a constant weight, so to be rational, I need to get busy and invest for the winter."

Winter came; the grasshopper was hungry and asked the ant for help.

"I would like to help you," the ant said, "but since I am rational and self-interested I cannot prefer your welfare to mine; you have nothing to give in exchange. Don't you feel guilty for singing all summer?"

"Very guilty, just as I anticipated," the grasshopper responded. "But now is now, and at the time I acted rationally. You are the one who is irrational in refusing to help me."

The ant though about that, but it only had enough food to finish the winter. "For me, now is my entire life, but I can help you in another way. Do you see the leaves on that Epicurean tree? They are delicious and nutritious, but after a while they will make you sick. I cannot eat them because I calculate happiness over the entire span of my existence, but for you the ecstasy of the moment supersedes your future unhappiness."

So the grasshopper ate the leaves and ended up getting sick.

"Was it worth it?" the ant asked the dying grasshopper?

"It isn't worth it *now*, but it was *then*," the grasshopper responded.

The ant said, "I need to tell you something, but I don't know if it is good news for you or not. There is an antidote!"

"Quickly! Quickly!" the grasshopper exclaimed.

"I am not sure you can use," the ant responded, "because at first it will make you feel very bad before it cures you."

"Tough news," the grasshopper sighed, "given that I cannot invest in my future happiness. Farewell."

The grasshopper died, and the ant lived a dull existence, avoiding situations in which happiness could become future unhappiness.

Now very old, it thought "It is sad to almost never be able to do what I want, but leading a happy life makes for a very short existence."

8.1.3 The Pareto criterion and the new welfare economics

In the transition from the old to the new welfare economics during the 1930s the concept of cardinal utility was abandoned and, in particular, interpersonal comparisons of well-being were rejected. Since utility expresses the satisfaction of individual preferences, all that is required is that agents be able to order their preference systems — which is simply ordinal utility. But how can judgments of social welfare be formulated if we drop the sum—ranking criterion?

The **Pareto criterion** provides the answer: A configuration of heterogeneous — and thus incomparable — variables is optimal when it is impossible to increase one of the variables without decreasing another. In the specific case of social welfare, the Pareto criterion assumes the well-known formulation in which a certain configuration is *optimal when it is impossible to increase someone's welfare without decreasing someone else's.*

As we can see, this criterion allows us to evaluate alternative social states with no need to appeal to interpersonal utility or welfare comparisons; all that is required in practice is to determine if every individual's situation is improved or worsened. Then we would say that social state *a* is **Pareto superior** to social state *b* if and only if at least one individual is better off in *a* than in *b*, and that no one in *a* is worse off than in *b*. **Pareto optimality** thus denotes the state of affairs in which there is no opportunity to find a solution that is Pareto superior to the one under consideration. It is immediately clear that the Pareto criterion is of no help as a criterion for choosing in all the cases in which it is necessary to evaluate or weigh the benefits to some and the burdens on others. For example, if I prefer bread to cookies and I only have cookies, while someone else prefers cookies to bread and has only bread, then a bread-for-cookies exchange would obviously lead to a Pareto superior situation. However, if I take someone else's bread illegally, that cannot be judged as a Pareto improvement, even if the bread staves off my death by starvation and the other person is only slightly harmed by the loss of a little bread.

The Pareto criterion thus incorporates a particular value judgment: **axiological individualism**. That judgment exclusively identifies the good of a society with the well-being of the individuals in it. This is certainly a legitimate position; there are however ethical systems that attribute moral importance either to society as such or to groups within it (such as social classes, for example) that is different from what is attributed to individuals. Compared to such systems the Pareto criterion is at best inadequate, if not completely meaningless.

Even accepting the anthropological assumption of individualism, the Pareto criterion is a long way from being a complete criterion for economic policy, because Pareto ordering of the states of the world is *incomplete*. Indeed, the Pareto criterion does not allow us to say anything about the level of superiority of one situation over another if both are Pareto optimal, much less to choose between alternative situations that could well be Pareto superior compared to an initial situation, but that imply variations in the well-being of different individuals.

Finally, although income distribution is a fundamentally important question in formulating judgments of alternative arrangements in an economy, the

Pareto criterion can say nothing about the distribution of economic welfare among individuals. In general, there are as many Pareto optimal situations, which cannot be compared among themselves, as there are possible income distributions. This means that the Pareto criterion makes a sharp distinction between the allocational efficiency of a particular economic configuration and judgments about its fairness. And yet, questions about income distribution and resource allocation tend to be inseparably linked in practice.

Despite all these limitations, the notion of Pareto optimality is highly regarded and widely employed in economic science. We will discover the reason for this in the next section.

8.2 The two fundamental theorems of welfare economics

8.2.1 Walrasian general equilibrium

In two well-known 1951 contributions, Kenneth Arrow and Gerard Debreu demonstrated there is a close correlation between a Pareto optimal allocation of resources and the allocation of a competitive equilibrium.

The *first fundamental theorem* of welfare economics states that every general competitive equilibrium is Pareto optimal; the *second theorem* states the reciprocal result that given any Pareto optimal allocation, under certain conditions it is always possible to find a way of distributing resources among individuals such that the relative Walrasian equilibrium allocation coincides with the given allocation.

As we can see, taken together these two theorems establish a sort of one-to-one correspondence between perfect competition and Pareto optimization. Thanks to them, the Smithian invisible hand ceases to be an evocative metaphor and becomes a theorem rich with political consequences, the ideological and now also scientific justification of *laissez faire* as a political economy program. The first states, in essence, that the perfectly competitive mechanism is non-wasteful: it does not squander resources. The sense of the second theorem is that the market mechanism is unbiased: through an appropriate redistribution of resources it is possible to pursue any Pareto optimal state as a competitive equilibrium.

To grasp the sense of the above, we must first clarify what is meant by a Walrasian general equilibrium. A Walrasian general equilibrium is a particular configuration of input and output prices in which:

all consumers buy outputs and sell inputs in order to maximize their utility within their budget constraints;
all companies buy inputs and produce outputs they will sell;
all companies maximize their profit within their cost constraints;
supply equals demand in all markets.

The basic goal of Walrasian theory is to show how voluntary exchanges between well-informed individuals (that is, who possess all relevant information regarding the characteristics of various goods), who are mutually disinterested (that is, they are only interested in pursuing their own well-being), and rational (who make choices that maximize their objective functions), lead to an organization of production and exchange that is efficient and mutually beneficial. The particular problem is that the only form of social interaction it admits is what takes place in the market through voluntary exchange. Other means of attaining an economic order are not considered, much less allowed. Any other means, such as trade unions, pressure groups, cartels, and so on, would violate the basic requirement of perfect competition.

By interacting in the market individuals give rise, wholly unintentionally, to ordered exchange relationships through market prices. To discover how agents who act atomistically are coordinated by the market, from which an economic order emerges, it is necessary to show how prices are determined in such a way that the activities and initiatives that efficiently satisfy agents' needs become advantageous.

A very simple way grasping the meaning of competitive equilibrium is to use an Edgeworth box, an analytical tool widely used in economics.

8.2.2 The Edgeworth box

Consider an ultra-simplified economy made up of just two individuals A and B, two goods X and Y, and with no production processes — in other words, an economy in which the only economic activity practiced is exchange.

Let (A_X, A_Y) and (B_X, B_Y) *be the initial allocations* of goods to each of the two agents. Whatever form the exchange takes, the total quantity of good X will be distributed among the two individual such that $A_X + B_X = X$ and $A_Y + B_Y = Y$, precisely because we are considering a pure exchange economy.

Now construct a rectangle — the "box" — whose sides are of length $X = 10$ and $Y = 8$, the overall quantities of the goods available to the two agents. In Fig. 8.1, we represent A's situation by referring to the origin O_A and to B's situation by referring to the origin O_B, which is rotated $180°$ with respect to O_A. Any point inside the box can be interpreted as an allocation of the total quantities of the two goods (10_x and 8_y) between the two individuals. For example, point C indicates that A has 3_x and 6_y, while B has 7_x and 6_y. Moving from one point to another in the box means reallocating the goods such that the increase in the quantity of a good for one equals the decrease of the quantity of the same good for the other. We can thus say that each exchange between A and B results in a reallocation.

Now suppose that point C represents the initial distribution of the two goods between the two agents. We indicate A's indifference curves, which are convex with respect to the origin O_A, by A_1, A_2, and A_3, and B's indifference curves which are convex with respect to the origin O_B, by B_1, B_2, and B_3 Since the indifference curves A_1 and B_1 intersect at point C, the marginal rates of substitution (MRS_{xy}) of the two curves measured at that point differ from each

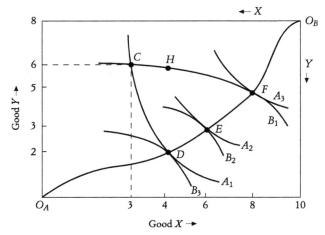

FIG. 8.1   The Edgeworth box in a pure exchange economy.

other. Starting at point C, A is willing to exchange 4_y for 1_x, moving to point D on A_1, while B would be willing to accept 0.2_y for 1_x, moving to point H on B_1. Symbolically, $MRS^A = 4$ and $MRS^B = 0.2$. Since A is willing to give up a much greater quantity of Y than is necessary to induce B to give up 1, there is room for an exchange that would benefit either one or both individuals. That is true whenever $MRSA_{xy} \neq MRSB_{xy}$, exactly as is the case at point C.

So, if starting from C, A exchanges $4y$ for $1x$ with B, A will move from C to D along the same indifference curve A_1, while B will move from C on B_1 to D on B_3. That is, B will "cash in" on all the gain in the exchange, while A's welfare position remains unchanged. At point D, the indifference curves A_1 and B_3 are tangent to each other, and thus their marginal rates of substitution are equal; this highlights the absence of further gains to be made from exchange. In fact, at point D, the amount of Y that A is willing to exchange to obtain one more unit of X is exactly equal to what B asks to give up a unit of X. Any further exchange would worsen one or the other's situation with respect to the situation they attained at D.

On the other hand, if A were to exchange $1y$ for $5x$ with B, A would move from C on A_1 to F on A_3, while B would move from C to F along the same B_1. In this case, A would accrue all the advantages of the exchange.

At point F, $MRS^A_{xy} = MRS^B_{xy}$, and there is no further advantage from exchange. Finally, if A exchanges 3_y for 3_x with B and arrives at point E, both subjects improve their welfare positions, since E lies on the indifference curves A_2 and B_2. So, starting from point C — which does not lie on the curve DEF — both agents can gain from the exchange by moving to a point where D and F meet. Where the process of exchange will lead depends on the negotiating strength of the two agents; if A's negotiating strength is greater, the final point will be closer to F, such that the greater portion of the total gain will go to A.

Points such as D, E and F, at which the indifference curves are tangent to each other, are called "contract points." The line that unites all these points is the **contract curve** — $O_A DEFO_B$ — in Fig. 8.1. Note that these tangent points exist because the indifference curves are convex and the field is dense (that is, the number of indifference curves is infinite). The important characteristic of the contract points is that, for each of them, there is no other situation preferred by one of the two agents that is not less preferred by the other. Said another way, the following condition is satisfies at each contract point: $MRS^A_{xy} = MRS^B_{xy}$.

Starting from an initial allocation such as C, the negotiation process will end when a point is reached along a segment of the contract curve that is delimited by the two indifference curves passing through C. Having reached the contract curve, neither agent can improve her welfare position without worsening the other's. (Do not forget that the assumption of the voluntary nature of the exchange always applies; neither can be forced to engage in exchange if they do not see an advantage in it.)

8.2.3 The first welfare theorem: a competitive equilibrium is Pareto optimal

We are now able to grasp the import of the first theorem. For the sake of simplicity, we will limit ourselves to the case of a pure exchange economy in which consumers have a certain initial allocation of goods. We specifically want to see if consumers maximizing their individual calculations leads to an efficient distribution of goods.

Consider two consumers A and B and two goods (X, Y) with market prices of p_x and p_y. As we know, in order to maximize their own utility each consumer will initiate trade with another until both of their marginal rates of substitution for their goods equal the ratio of the prices of the goods. Since the prices of the goods are the same for both consumers, the following condition will be met in equilibrium.

$$MRS^A_{x,y} = \frac{p_x}{p_y} MRS^B_{x,y} \tag{8.1}$$

Having identified the equilibrium condition, now we need to show that it is Pareto optimal. The Edgeworth box will be useful to that end. Inside the box we show both consumers' indifference curves, as in Fig. 8.1. We already know that only the points along the contract curve satisfy the condition of Pareto optimality, and that every allocation off that curve can be improved with additional exchanges of goods. But the contract curve is formed by the tangent points of the indifference curves for the two consumers, or the points at which the slope of the indifference curves is the same. In other words, the following condition is met at each point on the contract curve:

$$MRS^A_{x,y} = MRS^B_{x,y} \tag{8.2}$$

Since Eq. (8.2), which describes the Pareto optimal allocations, is contained in Eq. (8.1), which identifies the general equilibrium for a pure exchange economy, we have shown what we wanted: *a competitive equilibrium is Pareto optimal.*

8.2.4 The second welfare theorem: Pareto optimality and income distribution

To attain general equilibrium, consumers must be able to earn incomes that allow them to buy the quantities of the two goods identified by a point on the contract curve where condition in Eq. (8.1) holds, such as point E in Fig. 8.1. Each consumer's income depends on the initial distribution of production factors between the agents, or the quantity and prices of the labor and capital each possesses. By multiplying the quantities of labor and capital each consumer possesses by their corresponding prices, we can know their budget constraints. Depending on how the initial resource distribution is set between the two individuals, there will obviously be a different combination of outputs produced, and consequently a different general economic equilibrium configuration. In other words, determining the exact point on the contract curve depends on the initial allocation between the agents, which is not surprising. We know in fact that all the points on the contract curve are Pareto optimal, but the point on it that the market mechanism will select depends on the initial resource allocation available to the agents. As a result, in general equilibrium the quantities of the two goods the two agents consume, and thus their welfare level, will depend on this initial data point.

As we can readily understand, the problem that arises at this point is no longer a problem of efficiency but of distributive justice. Let's see what the second fundamental theorem has to say about this. Let ω be the initial allocation of goods: $\omega = (\omega_{ax}, \omega_{ay}, \omega_{bx}, \omega_{by})$. As we can infer from Fig. 8.2, ω gives a distinct advantage to A. Let Z be the relative competitive equilibrium to ω. However, an allocation such as V — which also lies along the contract curve, and is thus efficient — seems preferable to Z from a fairness point of view. The

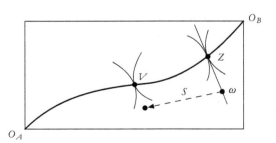

FIG. 8.2 The second fundamental theorem of welfare economics.

question then arises, given ω, can the competitive mechanism lead the economy to an allocation such as V? The second fundamental theorem of welfare economics provides an affirmative response.

Imagine that an authority exists that can make cash transfers between individuals (a central bank, for example). Each agent has an "account" with this bank that lists the value of the goods they possess. We will thus have:

$$p_x\omega_{ix} + p_y\omega_{iy}, i = A, B$$

The bank is authorized to modify individuals' accounts with a quantity S_i that can be either positive or negative. The budget constraint of the ith agent thus becomes:

$$p_xV_{ix} + p_yV_{iy} \leq p_x\omega_{ix} + p_y\omega_{iy} + S_i$$

Clearly, the bank will seek to favor a more fair allocation by assigning an $S_i > 0$ to those disadvantaged by the initial allocation and an $S_i < 0$ to those who are judged to be too "rich." Once these transfers have been made, the agents can negotiate among themselves and the market mechanism will again be able to resume its function as an efficient resource allocator. The problem is thus: given an initial allocation $\omega = (\omega_a,\omega_b)$ and a desired allocation $V = (V_A,V_B)$, does there exist a transfer vector $S = (S_A,S_B)$ and a price vector $p = (p_x,p_y)$ such that each individual can maximize her utility function $U_i = (i = A,B)$ while respecting her budget constraint $p_xV_{ix} + p_yV_{iy} \leq p_x\omega_{ix} + p_y\omega_{iy} + S_i$? The affirmative answer is the content of the second fundamental theorem. Assume that the agents' U_i are egocentric, that they are only increasing, and that the indifference curves are convex. Let V be any Pareto optimal allocation for which $V_{ij} \geq 0$ for all i and j. There then exists a vector of S transfers and a vector of prices p such that (V,p) is a Walrasian competitive equilibrium. (Obviously the algebraic sum of the S_i must equal zero.)

Note carefully what the second theorem specifically assumes for its validity: The aforementioned bank or government agency must know not only the initial allocations for each individual, but their utility (or welfare) functions as well. Otherwise the agency would not be able to precisely determine the S_i transfers. But if the agency knows all that, why bother with market interventions? Could not the State arrive directly at the allocation V in Fig. 8.2 without using the market? The answer is necessarily yes. Herein lies the paradox. While the second fundamental theorem is invoked to support the argument that the State must avail itself of the market, it is valid only in circumstances in which there is no need to use the market as a distributive mechanism. Recently this paradox has contributed in no small measure to weakening former certainties about direct interventions by the State in the economy.

A second observation concerns the specific use of the second theorem in the new welfare economics to validate separating problems of *efficiency* from problems of *fairness*. As an allocation tool the market aims for efficiency. If the distribution of well-being and income resulting from competitive bargaining is deemed unfair, then the initial allocation of goods and resources should be revised through lump-sum transfers. This means admitting that there is a **dichotomy** between the **production** of wealth and its **distribution** among those who contributed to generating it, and thus intervention by public authorities is justified only in this second phase rather than the first.

A final important note on the purposes of the argument, which we will develop in subsequent chapters. The first theorem tells us that the coordination of agents' economic decisions is carried out solely and exclusively through the market price mechanism. It follows that intersubjective relationships play no role, and thus there is no need for any relational approach to solve the problem of coordination. On the other hand, the message of the second fundamental theorem is that once the State (or some other public agency) has adjusted individuals' initial allocations, it can stand aside and leave the price mechanism alone to carry out its coordinating role. In essence, taken together the two theorems assure us that anonymity and impersonality in transactions are more than sufficient to reach a Pareto optimum. We will see later that this is not at all the case, and why.

8.3 Utility-possibility frontiers and the invisible hand

Now consider Fig. 8.3, which depicts the contract curve relative to an exchange between two individuals A and B. The stretch $a - b$ includes all the Pareto optimal allocations that can be attained by starting from w_1 through a process of free exchange between A and B. The same is true for stretches $b - c$, $c - d$, and so forth.

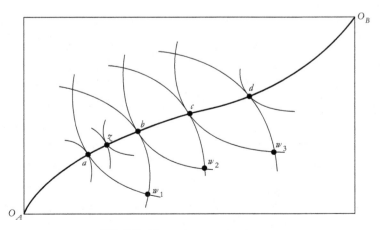

FIG. 8.3 The exchange contract curve.

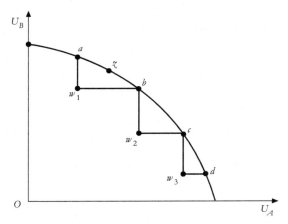

FIG. 8.4   Utility-possibilities frontier.

To make the connection clearer between initial conditions and the end result on the contract curve, it is useful to define the **curve, or frontier, of possible utilities**. However, see Fig. 8.4, where the utility levels for the two agents A and B, indicated by U_A and U_B respectively, are represented by indices that are not comparable. The utility-possibility curve or frontier contains all the combinations of A's and B's utilities that lie along the contract curve in Fig. 8.3. Depending on the initial distribution of the two goods, different utility combinations result for the two agents. The curve has a negative slope due to the fact that it contains the Pareto optimal allocations: An increase in the utility of one can be achieved only at the cost of a decrease in the other's utility. On the other hand, the concaveness of the curve reflects the assumption of diminishing marginal utility for A and B.

Let w_1, w_2, and w_3 indicate alternative initial conditions. As can be seen in Fig. 8.4, from each of these points it is possible to reach only a limited number of positions on the frontier as a solution belonging to the set of points in which neither agent incurs utility losses. For example, if we start from w_1, we will end up at a point on the segment $a - b$; as we know, exactly where will depend on A's and B's negotiating abilities, or on random factors.

In light of what has been said, we can now understand why the two fundamental welfare theorems taken together establish a one-to-one correspondence between a Walrasian competitive equilibrium and a Pareto optimality.

However, pay attention to what is necessary for this conclusion to be valid. First, the markets must be perfectly competitive. Otherwise, if there were monopolies, asymmetric information, or some other flaw, reaching a Pareto optimal position would require the intervention of a State agency or another type of authority to regulate the functioning of the markets. Second, it is necessary to posit that redistributing the initial allocations according to the second welfare theorem can happen within a political process whose operating laws can be adjusted *ad hoc*. This almost never happens in reality, since redistributing resources and income typically creates conflicts; social groups from which resources are taken to redistribute could successfully oppose such government interventions. From these two considerations it follows that not all allocations represented on the curve of feasible utilities can be attained due to market imperfections, political barriers, or other reasons. Thus the **attainable utilities frontier** will always be located below the feasible utility frontier.

8.4 The social welfare function and arrow's impossibility theorem

We can now understand why the Pareto criterion is of no help to us when there are utility conflicts between individuals, conflicts of the sort that arise as we move along the utility-possibilities frontier. In such cases, what is needed is a rule that allows us to coherently order both the points on the utility-possibilities frontier and those on two or more frontiers. A complete and coherent ordering of social states is called a *social welfare ordering*; when it turns out to also be continuous, we will speak of a **social welfare function** (*SWF*). This is a function, $W = f(U_A, U_B)$, of agents' utility levels such that a higher value of the function is preferred to a lower one. This is also known as the *Bergson—Samuelson social welfare function*, from the name of the Swedish economist, Abraham Bergson, who first introduced it in 1938, and the American economist Paul A. Samuelson, who studied its properties in depth.

Clearly, an *SWF* represents the value system that a social decision-maker — whether a parliament, a government, a benevolent planner, or whoever —

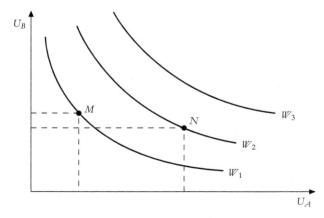

FIG. 8.5 Social indifference curves.

maintains that it should accept. Fig. 8.5 represents a map of *social indifference curves* for a generic *SWF*.

Note immediately that the knowledge of the social welfare function allows us to make an assessment of projects or changes that leave both winners and losers on the field. In Fig. 8.5, a change from M to N increases social well-being in the sense that it leads a society to a higher indifference curve. This is true even if group B loses due to the project in question being carried out, and even if no actual or hypothetical compensation is taken into consideration. The sense of the discussion is that the preferences of the social decision-maker are such that, taking into account A's and B's interests in play, social state N is judged to be superior to M. Obviously, another social decision-maker could have preferences that lead him to judge social state M as superior to N.

In Fig. 8.6 we have drawn a generic frontier of possible utilities together with the map of the social indifference curves in Fig. 8.5. The maximum attainable social well-being corresponds to the tangent point between the frontier and the highest indifference curve (point M). In this way we have reduced a very high number of possible general equilibria to a single equilibrium that represents the maximum level of social welfare $-$ W_2 $-$ that the economy can attain compatible with its available resources and technology. This is the **optimum optimorum**, or the best of the Pareto optimums. However, note carefully that the point of maximum social well-being depends on what underlies the *SWF*; that is, it depends on the particular set of value judgments that are incorporated into the *SWF*. It would thus seem that the method suggested by Bergson and Samuelson is able to resolve the basic problem of welfare economics. But, reflecting carefully on it, that is not the case. Indeed, the concept of the *SWF* has a serious shortcoming, summarized as follows. In accordance with the ordinal rule, the criterion of sum-ranking is not applicable when constructing an *SWF*. We need another method to formulate an *SWF* that starts from the knowledge of individual preferences

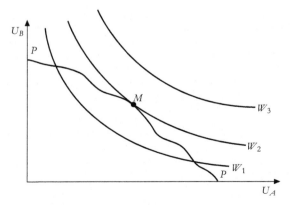

FIG. 8.6 Determining maximum social welfare.

alone. Yet, in a famous foundational 1951 work, Kenneth Arrow demonstrated that, except for trivial cases such as when all individual preference functions are identical, there is no *SWF* capable of satisfying a minimal set of reasonable axioms. This is the substance of the well-known **Arrow impossibility theorem**.

Let's clarify this. Each of *n* individuals has a defined preferential order of the set of social states. An *SWF* is thus a transformation from the set of all logically possible *n*-way individual orderings R_i to the set of all possible preference orderings of various social states. Stated symbolically: $R = F(R_1, R_2, \ldots R_n)$.

When deciding the order between social states x and y, let's suppose that the only information available is that the ith agent prefers x to y and the jth agent prefers y to x. However, we have no grounds on which to suppose that someone might want to be i in state y rather than j in state x; we know nothing about that.

Given that, Arrow demonstrated that no social choice function exists that is able to satisfy the following minimal requirements of consistency and morality:

> *unrestricted domain*: the domain of a social welfare function must include all logically conceivable profiles of individual orderings, meaning that paternalism is not admissible;
>
> *completeness and transitivity*: R must exhibit the same rationality characteristics of individual preference functions — that is, it must be complete and transitive;
>
> *independence from irrelevant alternatives*: the social choice of a given set of alternatives must not be influenced by the way in which individuals order alternatives that are not part of that set;
>
> *Pareto conditions*: if all individuals prefer x to y, then x must be socially preferable to y, which is another way of interpreting the principle of unanimity;
>
> *nondictatorship*: there must not be a dictator, or someone who invariably manages to impose her preferences on others.

The difficulty lies in the fact that, at least for some configurations of individual preferences, the attempt to satisfy these requirements creates an order of social preferences that does not respect the property of transitivity, just as happens with Condorcet's well-known paradox of majority voting. So we have a choice of either one or the other; either we give up at least one of Arrow's social choice axioms, or we give up ordinalism in order to allow using an information structure that goes beyond the mere consistency of individual preferences and their aggregation into a social choice function that depends solely on individuals' orderings.

The result of Arrow's work is highly important, because it demonstrates how indispensable ethical and rational properties that are entirely reasonable when considered separately end up creating paradoxical results if put into practice together.

8.5 Market failures

8.5.1 Externalities

In previous chapters, on several occasions we came across situations in which market mechanisms were not able to produce the expected outcomes. In particular we encountered different cases in which, for one reason or another, market forces did not ensure that the results promised by the two fundamental theorems of welfare economics would be achieved.

Such cases are called "market failures" in the literature. Consider the main types:

1. in pursuing their own goals, agents produce either positive or negative effects that affect others, without the market mechanism being able to filter them. This is the case of *externalities*;
2. agents who participate in a transaction are not able to coordinate among themselves how to divide the gains obtainable from exchange, or how to divide up the costs of a business that tends to benefit everyone. These are the cases of *public goods* and property held in common, or the *commons*;
3. the existence of monopolistic or oligopolistic market structures does not allow the market to attain the results promised by the two theorems of welfare economics;
4. agents do not have sufficient information available to allow them to take advantage of all mutually beneficial opportunities. This is what happens in cases of *information asymmetry*.

We have already discussed situations like those in points 3 and 4; in what follows we will focus our attention on the problems raised in points 1 and 2. We will first consider the case of **externalities**, or the effects − beneficial or harmful − that affect someone else's production or consumption and are not reflected in the prices paid or collected. We are talking about *external effects* in all cases in which: (a) the consumption choices of some influence the utility levels that others derive from their consumption choices; (b) the production functions of some companies are influenced by the production decisions of other companies.

Smoke from a factory chimney is a classic example of a negative externality. The production technique used by a factory produces smoke as a by-product that is "consumed," so to speak, by those who live near the factory and breathe the smoke-polluted air. Another readily available example of an externality, this time positive, is given by the fields surrounding a beekeeper's property, in that the bees can feed on the pollen from the flowers that grow in other people's fields. But the most interesting example is that of the industrial districts and cooperative districts that so clearly characterize Italian experiences.

Given the existing definition of property rights, or the rights and obligations of those who engage in economic activity, externalities exist when the party responsible for producing the smoke is not required to compensate the consumers damaged by its activities, or the fields' owners have no way to be paid for the advantages accrued by the beekeeper.

The presence of positive externalities, known as *external economies*, or negative externalities, known as *external diseconomies*, implies that market allocations are not efficient, in the sense that individuals' choices are made based on prices and costs that do not reflect the actual value of the resource utilized. In the example of the smoke-emitting factory, the producer acts on the basis of the costs of its activities, or the **private cost**, which is less than what it would have to bear were it required to pay compensation for the damages it causes to the neighbors, or the **social cost** (the sum of the private costs and the damages sustained by others). The result is that it will tend to push production beyond what would be optimal were it to take the externalities, or the social cost, into account. These are due to imperfections in the operation of the market mechanism.

In consumption, an external effect is a *direct* effect of one agent's consumption on the utility levels of another agent — direct in the sense that it does *not* operate through the price mechanism. If one agent's consumption influences the well-being of another agent through the price mechanism, that is, when B offers a higher price than A would pay for a certain good, the economy is operating as predicted by the two fundamental theorems of welfare economics. If B obtains a large quantity of the good at A's expense, because B is willing to pay more, then the competitive mechanism favors B, as expected. If B's consumption instead directly influences A's utility, then the price mechanism does not provide sufficient signals to consumers. When consuming a certain good, B considers only her level of utility and, given the prices in effect, chooses the actions that maximize her utility function U_B. However, her actions have a direct impact on U_A, and the price B pays for the good does not reflect this effect on A. In other words, the price mechanism does not properly signal B about the overall costs and benefits of her decisions, and the final distribution of goods is not a Pareto optimal allocation.

It can thus be argued that the two fundamental theorems of welfare economics are only able to take into account the types of interactions that can be absorbed by the price mechanism. When there are either consumption or production externalities, prices are incapable of properly informing decision makers; this leads to less than optimal situations in market outcomes, precisely because prices send misleading signals about the allocation of resources.

8.5.2 Taxes, subsidies, and the Coase theorem

The previous discussion does not mean that the existence of external effects nullifies the function of the market. The solution for correcting the inefficiencies caused by externalities is to introduce the appropriate corrective measures of *taxes or subsidies*, which Pigou had already anticipated in 1920. If in the process of consuming or producing an agent damages others, he should be required to pay a tax commensurate with the damage he caused; if he benefits others, he should receive a subsidy.

Consider the case of a production externality in which there is a divergence between the private cost and social cost, as in the example of the smoke-producing factory. The company that operates in a perfectly competitive market and that produces a certain good x is in equilibrium when its marginal cost equals the price; that is, $C'_x = p_x$, where the first term represents the *private cost*. Obviously, C'_x does not include the cost of pollution since it is external to the firm.

Now suppose that the environmental agency is able to estimate the marginal cost of the pollution the company produces. In such an event the marginal social cost C'_{Sx} is given by the sum of the marginal private cost C'_x and the marginal external cost C'_{Ex}:

$$C'_{Sx} = C'_x + C'_{Ex} \tag{8.3}$$

If [8.3] is valid, then $p_S < C'_{Sx}$, so resources are not optimally allocated. In particular, when the private cost is less than the social cost, determining the optimal production level based on marginal costs leads to overproduction of the good associated with the negative externality; that is, the divergence between private and social cost signals a distortion in resource allocation.

As can be readily understood, the tax the polluting company should pay should equal the marginal external cost. In this case, C'_{Sx} can be thought of as the sum of the marginal private cost C'_x and the tax commensurate with the externality. How should the revenue from the collected tax be used? Pigou suggested that it be used to compensate those who were harmed or to finance the construction of depollution plants.

As is evident, the weak point of the Pigovian solution lies in the practical difficulty of quantifying the value of the pollution damage linked to the externality. Ronald Coase suggested a different way of correcting the consequences of externalities by using the market mechanism itself.

In his well-known 1960 essay *The Problem of Social Cost*, Coase proposed an alternative approach based on the consequences exerted by the property rights structure on the results of economic interactions.

The basic idea is that when agents have complete information, and when there are no transaction costs (all the costs related to the negotiation and conclusion phases of private contracts), the negative consequences of externalities can be corrected by means of the market mechanism itself, with no

---

FRAME 8.2 The Coase Theorem Beyond Coase.

But the "Coase Theorem," a term coined by Coase's University of Chicago colleague George Stigler, took on a life of its own. Economic policy analysts on the political right began treating "zero transaction costs" not as a heroic simplifying assumption, but as a plausible policy goal. For example, one Heritage Foundation blogger invoked the Coase Theorem in 2010 as supporting the proposition that "the government has to define property rights and then get out of the way and trust the market."

Coase himself hated this. "I never liked the Coase Theorem," Coase said on the EconTalk podcast last year. "I don't like it because it's a proposition about a system in which there were no transaction costs. It's a system which couldn't exist. And therefore it's quite unimaginable."

Coase believed that high transaction costs sometimes justify government regulation. "There is no reason why, on occasion ... governmental administrative regulation should not lead to an improvement in economic efficiency," Coase wrote (The Firm, The Market, and The Law). "This would seem particularly likely when, as is normally the case with the smoke nuisance, a large number of people are involved and in which therefore the costs of handling the problem through the market or the firm may be high."

https://www.washingtonpost.com/news/wonk/wp/2013/09/04/the-coase-theorem-is-widely-cited-in-economics-ronald-coase-hated-it/

---

need to resort to or invoke other organizational principles. Coase demonstrated the following theorem: *if the parties involved are able to freely negotiate among themselves (i.e., transaction costs are zero), an optimal resource allocation will be attained that is independent of the initial distribution of property rights, and with no intervention by the State.* We can thus state that to the extent the initial resource allocation can be subject to negotiation among the parties, without any limits, then the initial allocation is not relevant for efficiency (Frame 8.2).

Consider the case of a factory that emits pollution and a community that suffers the damage and which also owns the right to clean air. The community can alienate this right by selling pollution "permits." Each permit would allow the factory to produce an additional unit of output and the pollution that comes with it. The community would continue to sell permits as long as the marginal benefits of selling one more exceed the marginal costs of the increase in pollution. As we can see, the idea underlying the Coase Theorem is that individuals can freely make their rights a matter of negotiation, just as if they were any other good. This is why we can state that the Coase Theorem extends the rules governing the exchange of goods to exchanging the ownership of rights.

The relevance of the Coase Theorem lies in the fact that the presence of market failures in itself does not constitute a sufficient reason to justify public intervention. The role of the State should be confined to defining appropriate property rights among agents, thus there would be no need for taxes, subsidies, or administrative controls. Since the Coase Theorem states that negotiations between private parties would allow reaching an efficient arrangement if transaction costs were zero, the State should rather direct its interventions toward reducing such costs as much as possible.

As has been observed, the Coase Theorem is more robust than the first theorem of welfare economics. Just as does the latter, the Coase Theorem states that if everything is negotiable, including property rights, then Pareto efficient outcomes are ensured. But in difference with the first theorem, it requires no assumption of convexity, price-taking, or complete markets. All it requires is the absence of any barrier to negotiation. Since it is tautological to state that if agents negotiate efficiently that the outcomes of the negotiations will be efficient, then the Coase Theorem makes practical sense only if we have reason to believe that efficient negotiations are actually possible in reality.

Unfortunately, the vast literature on negotiation theory confirms that the efficient outcomes promised by the Coase Theorem only apply in relatively special cases with just a few agents and in the absence of information asymmetries. Additionally, negotiations between economic agents may be interrupted or fail. Negotiation generally involves a situation in which a surplus exists to be distributed between the parties by an agreement, but where no prior single criterion exists for dividing it among the parties. Negotiations are thus inevitably complex processes in which strategic behaviors are strongly present.

Recognizing the strategic nature of negotiations between rational agents leads us to reject the idea that a simple exchange of property rights is sufficient to address market failures caused by externalities, to say nothing of the cases in which attributing property rights is problematic in itself. What are the criteria for allocating property in the atmosphere or the oceans? Who would own the property rights to a river?

The Coase Theorem thus does not seem conclusive when it comes to questions of the opportunity for or the necessity of public interventions when there are externalities. However, this does not detract in the least from the theoretical relevance of this important result.

8.5.3 Public goods

Consider what is held to be an extremely important limiting case for externalities: the production and consumption of public goods. Interest in this category of goods traces back to an original 1844 work by J. Dupuit, a French engineer, for the purpose of measuring the utility of public works, in which he clearly grasped the characteristics that distinguish public or collective goods. A **pure public good** is identified by two typical characteristics: the absence of rivalry in consumption and the absence of excludability from its benefits. Let's clarify this.

Absence of rivalry in consumption of a good means that many people can simultaneously benefit from the good without reducing the utility they draw from its consumption. Think of sunlight, television programs, and viewing a landscape. The well-being of someone using these goods is not influenced by its concomitant use by other consumers.

Absence of excludability means that when the good is made available for some consumers, it is not possible or economically advantageous to exclude other consumers from benefiting from the good. Excludability can be either technical or economic in nature. The first lies in the good's physical characteristics; think of a system of television stations that serve a given area. The second derives from the high costs incurred to exclude some people from using the service. Think of the light of a streetlamp or the protection provided by security devices, and so on. Public goods are a limiting case for externalities. Indeed, their consumption by one consumer appears in every other consumer's utility function. It is thus evident that when public goods are present, the conditions that will ensure Pareto optimality cannot be the same as the ones we have already seen. A first problem posed by the presence of public goods is the aggregation of individual demand curves. While the aggregate demand curve for private goods is obtained by horizontally summing individual demand curves, in the case of a pure public good the aggregation must be done vertically rather than horizontally. In essence, it is necessary to ask each individual not what quantity she is willing to buy at each price level, but what price she is willing to pay for each quantity.

The individual demand curves are shown in Fig. 8.7A and B, which are *vertically* aggregated in Fig. 8.7C. Note that the quantity consumed is E for both individuals A and B, while the equilibrium price is given by the sum of the prices that individuals are willing to pay (and which are not necessarily equal).

Two other problems arise with public goods. The first of these concerns determining the optimal quantity of a public good to produce. The solution available for this is known as the **Samuelson condition**: *The sum of the*

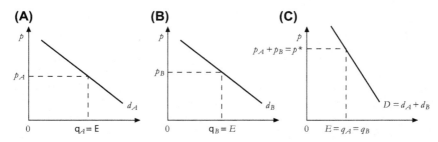

FIG. 8.7   Vertical aggregation of demand curves of a public good.

marginal utilities that each agent draws from the consumption of the public good must equal to its marginal cost.

There is a second major problem as well: How should we finance them? This problem is of central importance to a public economy. Let's see why. In perfectly competitive markets, an individual consumer cannot influence the price of goods and thus adjusts the quantity purchased of a private good in order to match the marginal utility of purchasing that good to its current price. Since in equilibrium the price of a good equals its marginal cost, the well-known condition of Pareto optimality is satisfied. That does not hold true for public goods.

The marginal cost of the benefits conferred by a public good is in fact zero, due to the fact that there is no rivalry in consumption, so it seems optimal to extend their availability to the entire community. However, the community must also finance its cost. If every consumer were to pay the same amount (for example, the total cost divided by the number of consumers), then the consumers with the lowest marginal utility would prefer to not consume the public good. This is clearly sub-optimal in view of the fact that the additional consumption by an individual does not increase its total cost. It follows that the optimal condition would require that each consumer pay a price equal to her marginal valuation of the public good. If this were the case, then the so-called **Lindahl equilibrium** would be attained (from the name of the Swedish scholar who first formulated in 1919 the scheme subsequently elaborated in 1954 by Paul Samuelson).

We are now able to grasp the substantial difference between a Lindahl equilibrium and a Walrasian competitive equilibrium with private goods alone. While in the latter agents have an obvious advantage to correctly disclose their preferences, a Lindahl equilibrium is vulnerable in this respect. What undermines the practicality of the payment scheme required by a Lindahl equilibrium is the **problem of "free-riding"**, or consumers who take advantage of collective consumption by not adequately participating in their financing. (The expressions "free-rider" and "free-riding" refer to someone who uses public transportation without buying a ticket, counting on the fact that the cost of the ride will be paid for by others.) Indeed, faced with a request to disclose the quantity consumed of a public good and his consequent utility, a consumer has an incentive to conceal his true utility and not reveal his real preferences in order to pay a lower contribution. But it is obvious that the presence of free-riders leads in the end to a sub-optimal supply of the public good, because there will be insufficient funds to pay for it.

The free-rider problem is partially resolved by *club goods*. This is an intermediate class of goods between pure public goods and private goods, in that their use is excludable; only those who are willing to pay can enjoy their benefits. An example would be buying a ticket to see a soccer match.

The aforementioned problems also arise in the case of the "commons," or common property goods such as a common grazing pasture, a historical center, and so forth. The problem that arises in such cases is that agents seeking their own interest interfere with each other to the extent that they would be collectively better off only if their behavior were constrained by some rule of conduct. However, no one has an interest in restraining themselves, with the result that in the end, as the Prisoner's Dilemma illustrates (see Chapter 6, Appendix A), everyone is worse off.

8.5.4 Merit goods

In addition to public goods there is another category of goods, called *merit goods*, that, although they are private goods, generate strong positive externalities when they are consumed. Attributing **merit** to something has obvious ethical connotations and assumes that individuals are not fully able to perceive the public utility associated with the consumption of particular goods or services without a more or less lengthy experience in using them. As examples, recall the obligatory nature of certain vaccinations, certain medical examinations, a minimum education, or certain forms of assistance.

In 1959 Richard Musgrave provided a summary on the concept of merit goods, stating that some goods or services were so meritorious (or demeritorious) in certain situations as to consider abandoning the principle of consumer sovereignty.

If there were no specific legal obligation, not all parents would send their children to school or would have them sufficiently vaccinated. Generalizing briefly, the fact is that in many circumstances individuals do not know the best way to satisfy their own needs or to feel good about themselves. In our advanced societies instances of complex well-being increasingly emerge that often leave individuals disoriented. It is in such circumstances that the problem of an adequate supply of merit goods arises.

Many goods and services that increase a system's competitive capacity can also be added to the overall category of merit goods, because they impact the productivity of production factors. In general these are infrastructure goods such as the construction of road networks, good schools, appropriate and far-sighted urban planning, new railway lines, an opportune product quality certification center, a social aid office, disease prevention, and so on. As we can see, their role is to increase the direct or indirect advantages and opportunities of the economic system under consideration. Such goods and services are sources of widespread externalities that can stimulate economic, social, and cultural development of a given community.

Reconsidering the concept of an externality and extending it to an entire society, it is possible to escape the strict dichotomy between public and private goods. By so doing it is possible to explicitly consider the wide range of *mixed goods* in which a private component fulfills the utility of those who directly enjoy it, while a public component generates external effects on others who do not directly enjoy the ownership of the good or service in question. A classic example is education. This service is characterized by a private component that defines the quantity of the good directly enjoyed by individual i and by another component that resonates through the entire community to the extent that the benefits of i's intellectual growth extend to others, which contributes to increasing the cultural level of the entire society. Even money is a mixed good, since it has both a private and public dimension.

8.6 The market and distributive justice

One of the most disturbing limits of the market mechanism is its inability to ensure an income distribution that can somehow be judged fair among everyone who contributed to producing it.

Welfare economics has always recognized that the distributive outcomes of market processes may not be compatible with the rules of fairness a society adopts for itself. The ultimate sense of the second fundamental theorem is precisely to provide a criterion for evaluating the relative efficiency of the redistributive policies meant to achieve a certain result.

In recent years there has been added awareness that income distribution can be a special type of public good in certain aspects. From this perspective, the market should not guarantee fair distributions for the simple reason that solidarity creates benefits within society as a whole but that are external to individual agents. Left to its automated processes, the market then "produces" less redistribution than would be "efficient" or socially desirable, due to the phenomenon of free-riding. As we can see, this is an application of the general principle that the welfare of a society is a *de facto* public good when it originates from the preferences of the individuals who make it up, given that the contribution a single individual can make toward accomplishing the public good by his attention to others is so small that the incentive to do so is lost.

It may be interesting to recall that Jacob Viner proposed considering distributive equity from the viewpoint of the public good rather than the more traditional ethical and political view when he observed that "distributive justice with which [voters] are tolerably content" is a necessary condition for the vitality of the market system. Indeed, one of the salient characteristics of the market game is that it admits no upper or lower limits on *ex post* outcomes; the upper limit could be that all the wealth ends up in the hands of one individual, with the lower limit being no income for other individuals. So it is reasonable to suppose that there may be a majority of risk-averse people who do not accept the possibility of ending the market game at the bottom due to bad luck. It follows that in democratic societies the guarantee of a *minimum income level* for everyone becomes a necessary condition to ensure the efficiency of the system. It is now known that economies with high income inequalities (such as in third world countries) grow at a lower rate than those with a more equitable distribution.

Moreover, highly unequal income distributions threaten the social sustainability of a system. Indeed, there has been a growing awareness that the societies in which we live are complex systems that simultaneously have equal rights but unequal wealth. We are at once members of the "citizenship club," in which we recognize each other and we are obliged to recognize each other as equal (one person, one vote), and members of the "market club," the rules of which reward and punish transactions whose logic is different from what shapes the relationship between equal citizens. The most familiar tensions are the ones between *rights of citizenship* and *property rights*; between rights and opportunities; between having equal freedom to do or have something and having different basic abilities to do or have something. If each of us is worth at least as much as anyone else as a member with equal dignity in the "citizenship club", then the problem lies in the fact that the different endowments of resources and opportunities in it makes the unequal value of its equal liberties futile or irrelevant.

This means that **economic democracy** and **political democracy** cannot diverge too far or too long, or the very foundations of the market system would be dangerously affected. This is the justification for public interventions that supplement the market mechanism without replacing it.

One final consideration. When speaking of distributive policies, it is important to distinguish between inequality and poverty. When there is a criterion to identify the so-called **poverty threshold**, everyone whose income is below that threshold is considered to be poor. The poverty threshold or line can be defined in *relative* terms compared, say, to average per capita consumption, or in *absolute* terms by defining a minimum basket of goods that identifies the basic necessities for a person. The *International Standard of Poverty Line* sets the poverty threshold for a two-person household equal to the average value of per capita consumption. For households with more than two members, poverty thresholds are calculated by applying an *equivalence scale*. These scales allow comparing different households by applying appropriate correction coefficients.

Having clarified that, we might be tempted to think that poverty reduction policies might serve to reduce inequality, but that is not necessarily true. For example, some anti-poverty measures might suggest income transfers to those just below the poverty line and neglect those with even lower incomes. Poverty reduction policies of this sort would increase inequality in society, even though they can reduce the level of poverty.

Atkinson's theorem (1970) is an important result in the topic of income distribution. It demonstrates that with decreasing marginal utility of income and an equal capacity by individuals to enjoy income, transferring income from the wealthy to the poor produces a utility gain for the poor that exceeds the decrease in utility of the wealthy. It follows that social wellbeing increases when moving from a less egalitarian to a more egalitarian income distribution.

8.7 Forms of public intervention and government failure

Having grasped the reasons for which there is room for public intervention in the economic sphere, the question arises: How should the State operate to efficiently achieve its goals? As does any other economic agent, the State must choose between many strategies for action. It can directly intervene, provide incentives to the private sector to do something, decree that private parties must act in determined ways, or adopt some combination of these. Let's consider some examples.

Faced with a known market failure — say, a lack of medical care — the government could intervene directly, perhaps by nationalizing healthcare. The same applies for other sectors, such as electricity, certain areas of basic chemicals, and so on. Sometimes direct intervention does not result in the State producing the good itself, but by buying it from the private sector. If the government has reason to believe that there is a market failure in supplying low-income housing, it can intervene by buying housing built to certain specifications from private contractors.

As an alternative to direct action, the state can provide incentives to try to alter the functioning of markets in a pre-determined way. It could grant subsidies to farmers to support their income or to redirect their production choices. It could refrain from taxing profits for a certain number of years to provide incentives to companies to invest in new equipment. Finally, it could grant tax breaks to incentivize companies to hire certain categories of workers, such as unemployed youth, disabled people, and so on. All these actions place the State in a position to manipulate the price system in order to achieve purposes judged to be socially necessary.

For various reasons, it can happen at times that the private sector does not react at all, or in the desired manner, to government incentives. There may also be some concern that granting subsidies is too costly. In such situations the government may direct the private sector to do something under the threat of administrative or even criminal penalty. Consider the requirement that car manufacturers produce cars with anti-pollution devices, or that companies provide accident insurance for building permits in a certain neighborhood to contribute to the construction costs for its local school.

The fact that government intervention in such cases does not result in an increase in the State budget does not mean that these measures are without costs. These costs may fall indirectly on workers, companies, or consumers, and they can be quite high.

Demonstrating the possibility of a space for public intervention based on a market failure argument is certainly a necessary but not a sufficient condition to legitimize such interventions. What is required is that the government be able to implement what market forces cannot attain at a "reasonable" cost. This is the most significant contribution of the latest economic research on **government failures**. In fact, the British philosopher H. Sidgwick had already warned over a century ago that "It does not of course follow that wherever laissez-faire falls short governmental interference is expedient; since the inevitable drawbacks and disadvantages of the latter may, in any particular case, be worse than the shortcomings of private enterprise." (Sidgwick, 1901, p. 414).

This basically states that where the invisible hand of the market does not succeed in transforming private vices into public virtues, the visible hand of the government does not necessarily succeed in transforming government vices into public virtues. This is the sense in which the expression "government failure" should be understood, which was made popular by economists such as Stigler and Friedman of the **Chicago school**, and the **public choice school** of Buchanan and Tullock.

Indeed, we cannot forget that the government must also respect budget constraints. The funds that government spends to implement its projects must come from somewhere, either by taking resources destined for other purposes or by raising taxes. There is no reason to believe that government action in and of itself costs less than when done by private operators. This implies that public intervention must also be subject to efficiency evaluations; the public interest objectives that the government pursues cannot dispense with the necessity of respecting the constraint of efficiency.

We find one or more of the following causes at the root of various cases of government failures.

- As we have seen, the problems posed by imperfect and asymmetric information to market operations also apply to the public sector of the economy. For example, the absence of information is what prevents applying all the techniques for fixing prices to correct the lack of competition caused by various natural monopoly situations. More generally, the point is that when considering alternative allocations the government is always constrained to make use of existing markets with their possible imperfections and/or incompleteness.
- Principal–agent types of agency problems also vex, perhaps primarily, the public sector. Think in particular about *bureaucracy* and the typical rent-seeking behaviors of bureaucratic structures, which, among other things, generate real influence costs. The part that the category of externalities plays in the theory of market failures is played here by the category of **internalities**, or the punishment and reward systems prevalent in non-market organizations, the role of which is to favor the interests of those who work within the organization. To give just one example, think of the job openings to rise in the organizational hierarchy that are reserved for those who already work in the organization.
- It is well-known that government agencies frequently create internalities that have nothing to do with the public purpose they claim to pursue. Just as the existence of externalities indicates that there are costs and social benefits that do not enter into the calculations of private decision-makers, the

existence of internalities indicates that there are costs and benefits in public decision-makers' calculations in government agencies that take precedence over considerations of the public good. Whether government failures attributable to internalities are greater or less than market failures attributable to externalities is a question that can only be resolved empirically.

- In many situations, public regulation has actually contributed toward creating or protecting monopoly positions, enabling the companies so favored to operate inefficiently, waste resources, and impose higher prices than necessary, beyond the actual intentions of the government authorities who enacted the regulation. This point of view is quite widespread, for example, among scholars who have analyzed the behavior of American airline companies. It is no coincidence that air transportation in the United States is one of the foremost recent examples of the transition from tight public price controls and qualitative standards to substantial *deregulation*.

In conclusion, combining the most important results of the studies on market and government failures over the last quarter century, we can conclude that *the choice between the State and the market is not a choice between perfection and imperfection, between perfect markets and imperfect government, or vice versa. Rather, we have choices between types and degrees of imperfection and types and degrees of failure.* This is why, beyond the necessary technical knowledge, a great deal of wisdom is needed when making specific choices on matters of State intervention in the economic sphere, paying particular attention to the fact that what may be optimal in a given historical context may not be so in another.

8.8 From the welfare state to the welfare society

In 1919 several major industrialists in the United States, among them David Rockefeller, Henry Ford, and Andrew Carnegie, signed an agreement that launched an initiative that shortly afterward would be called *welfare capitalism*. On the strength of the *restitution principle*, the basic assumption of this agreement envisaged that companies should take responsibility for the destiny of the well-being of their dependents and their families. In this way the company gives back to the surrounding community part of the profits it earns in its business. The principle is inscribed in the DNA of American culture that it is necessary to return after the fact part of what has been obtained, thanks to the community's contribution to productive activity. Welfare capitalism immediately had some success in the United States, but it did not take long for its Achilles' heel to become evident: it did not satisfy the requirement of universal coverage. If a citizen had the good fortune to work in one of the companies that was a signatory to the agreement, he would have the certainty of being able to benefit from the conferred services; that would not be true if he worked somewhere else.

That is why exactly twenty years later in 1939 in England the well-known economist John Maynard Keynes wrote, in an essay entitled *Democracy and Efficiency*, that if welfare is desired as the model of social order it must be universal rather than particular; it is not possible to cover only a few categories or groups of citizens. On the basis of this insight Lord William Beveridge, a member of the English Parliament, succeeded in having the famous "Beveridge Report" approved during wartime in 1942; this was the origin of the National Health Service, free assistance to the handicapped and elderly who were not self-sufficient, and free education for all until a certain age. This was the beginning in England of the well-known model of the welfare state: the State, not the company, must take care of the well-being of its citizens. In this regard Beveridge's phrase has become famous: the State must take responsibility for citizens "from cradle to grave." This model is an authentic triumph of civilization, which certainly cannot be denied. It first spread throughout England, and then to the rest of Europe. In contrast, the welfare state never took root in America; instead there was welfare capitalism, a model that Americans were, are, and will always be fond of.

After several decades, the welfare state model also began to show its own double Achilles' heel. The first is financial sustainability. If welfare services are to retain their quality, their costs grow over time, and general taxation is the primary means the State has at its disposal to cover those costs. For taxes to be sufficient to cover the entire expense, the tax pressure would come to well over 50%, which would worryingly reduce GDP. It is clear that if the resources to finance the welfare state were to come exclusively from general taxation, the fiscal pressure would only increase; from a political perspective, that would jeopardize a country's democratic system.

The second factor underlying the crisis of the welfare state is the bureaucratization of the system; we use the word "bureaucratization" in a technical sense to mean the standardization of the ways in which needs are met. The problem is that people's needs cannot be standardized. A trivial example may explain the asymmetry that separates people's different needs from the uniform coverage provided by various services. Two people with the same disease and the same diagnosis may have different reactions to the same drug. What may work well for one may not go well at all for another, since different human bodies respond differently to the same type of treatment. This is why social services are always surrounded by an aura of discontent. Citizens' low regard for public services, at least in Italy, is closely linked to their lack of implicit quality, although the explicit standards of codified quality are high.

That is why over the last 15 years there has been discussion about transitioning from the welfare state model to the *welfare society* model. In this system the whole of society, and not just the State, must care for the well-being of its citizens. Parallel to this concept, the principle of **circular subsidiarity** has begun to emerge. If society as a whole should provide universal care for all those who live in it, it is clear that it is necessary to bring the three spheres that make up the whole of the social triangle into relationship. These are the sphere of public agencies, or the State, regions, communities, and various para-state entities; the corporate sphere or the business community; the sphere of organized civil society, such as various associations, social co-operatives, NGOs, and foundations. The idea of circular subsidiarity is this: the three spheres must find ways to systematically interact to plan the services that need to be provided as well as manage them.

The advantage of adopting the welfare society model and its principle of circular subsidiarity lies in the possibility of rising above the two aporias of the welfare state we previously discussed. First, with this model it would be possible to find the necessary resources from the business world. When we say that "resources are lacking" the reference is to public resources, rather than to private resources that, on the contrary, are present and continually increasing. The point is that until now no one has thought to tap the resources available from the corporate world in order to channel them toward supplying welfare services. Second, the presence of the public institutions becomes fundamental in this system, as the must be vigilant to ensure that assistance is universal. The danger of some social groups being excluded from benefiting from services must always be kept in mind. The world of the civil society that we continue to call "nonprofit" or the "Third Sector" — although it would be better to speak of civil society organizations — occupies a special place in the triangle, because it is a repository of specific knowledge. Who better than an association of volunteers can know if there are particular needs to be met in a neighborhood? Such information can only come from those who work closely with people at the local level. Moreover, these people are in a position to be able to ensure ways of governing that can raise their implicit quality.

This is why circular subsidiarity will prevail as the model for the near future. There is only one alternative to this model, which would be to return to welfare capitalism, to the liberal welfare model that entrusts to companies the task of satisfying citizens' needs according to their inclination toward social responsibility. If we insist on keeping the old welfare state model alive, over time we will end up with welfare capitalism, which would be a true paradox. To avoid falling into this dangerous service vacuum, it is necessary to aim toward the model of the welfare society, in which companies, public agencies, and citizens along with their organizations contribute in proportion to their abilities and give what they are able on the basis of well-defined partnership agreements.

Appendix

ABSTRACT

This Appendix illustrates that the market "fails" when common goods — goods that are rivalrous but non excludable — are present. That is, the decentralized spontaneous equilibrium created by individuals' choices who maximize their utility leads to overexploitation of the common good, a phenomenon also called "the tragedy of the commons." It outlines different versions of the characteristics of the social dilemma behind the above-mentioned market failure with the Prisoner's Dilemma and the Deer Hunt. It also proposes some solutions that outline the concept of "we rationality" and discusses the potential role of social contracts and the civil society.

Economic science and commons

You can gather mushrooms only on predetermined days. Even on days when you are lucky you cannot be greedy. Residents cannot gather more than 5 kg of mushrooms, and non-residents no more than 3 kg. Only whole mushrooms can be gathered. When picking them, we recommend extracting them with a slight rotation, covering the small hole in the ground, and cleaning them on the spot with the help of a knife; this will avoid depleting the nutrient layers in the ground to the benefit of the whole forest.

This is one of the many municipal regulations on harvesting mushrooms. What do these rules mean? Why are such detailed rules necessary? Are individuals' intelligence and rationality not sufficient? This case can be a simple and effective way to enter into the topic of common goods, their nature, and their possible destruction.

The underlying idea of the private consumption/common good relationship on which economic science is based is more or less the following: A civil society in which everyone simply pursues their own interests normally works well (or rather, compared to other systems), because taking care of one's own interests is an expression of citizens' civil virtue. In essence this is the idea within Adam Smith's metaphor of the "invisible hand," the most famous metaphor in economic thought; everyone pursues their own private interests and society providentially finds itself with the common good.

There is, however, a very serious problem. The ethical legitimization of exchange and this virtuous vision of self-interest, seen as an expression of prudence, functioned and continues to function in simple societies in which the good of the individual is also directly the good of everyone, and in which goods are mostly private, such as washing machines, sandwiches, shoes, and computers. If goods become *common*, the discourse become terribly complicated. It so happens that *the virtue of prudence is no longer automatically a market virtue*, since it is no longer true that seeking one's own private interest produces the common good as well; that is, what is good for an individual produces common bad.

The biggest change in globalized postmodern societies has to do with the topic of common goods, which are becoming the rule rather than the exception. Indeed, we have entered the era of common goods. Today the quality of development of peoples and the earth certainly depends on shoes, refrigerators, and washing machines (the classic private goods), but much more on common goods or bads, such as greenhouse gases and the exploitation of natural resources.

In 1911 Katharine Coman wrote a first analysis of common goods, or the commons, while Garrett Hardin's 1968 essay *The Tragedy of the Commons* is the best known work on the topic. As they are commonly defined, common goods are rivalrous but non-excludable consumption goods, such that the advantage that each one derives from their use cannot be separated from the advantages that others also derive from them. That is, the benefit that an individual takes from the common good manifests *together with*, rather than *against*, that of others, as happens in private goods, but it also does not manifest *regardless* of others' benefits, as happens with the public good. Examples of common goods are non-renewable energy sources, forests, lakes, seas, environmental goods, water, landfills, and the level of trust in financial markets (the recent financial crisis can be understood as a tragedy of trust as a collective good).

Hardin begins his analysis with the statement that in the management of many collective phenomena there are situations we can call "tragedies," or "tragic choices." In its original Greek meaning, the word "tragedy" indicates situations in which there is no optimal solution, because every choice entails high costs; thus in a tragedy there is no optimal choice that is best for everyone or from all the perspectives from which we can view it. In the case of population growth, the environment, and collective or common goods − the commons − the tragic situation is the conflict between individual liberty and conserving common resources. It is as if the coin with which we pay for having conquered freedom, and the absence of hierarchical and priestly mediators, is the destruction of the common resources on which our communities depend for survival and the resources we live on, such as the environment or water.

To better understand what common goods are and the problems linked to them, recall the classic example of a group of herders who share the use of a pasture to which each one can freely bring his cows to graze. Hardin showed that the best choice from a purely economic interest perspective is for each herder to increase his herd in the pasture by one animal. In this case the advantage for a single herder is +1 (one more cow), while the decrease in the common good, the pasture grass, is only a fraction of −1, because the loss of grass is divided among all the herders that use the pasture. The individual benefit of increasing the use of the common good is thus greater than the individual cost. This is what leads to each herder's incentive to increase his herd until the pasture is destroyed. At some point each herder doubtlessly becomes aware of the loss of the common good, but it is generally too late, because once a critical point has been passed the destructive process of the common good becomes irreversible. Individual awareness comes only when a critical threshold has been surpassed, but by then it is often too late, because paradoxically it can happen that the *race to seize the remaining resource* only increases, which is destined to become increasingly scarce.

The value of Hardin bringing this to light is that it defined a scenario that can occur anytime when working with a commons when a selfish rationality comes into play that is not capable of trusting and cooperating with others.

In light of what we have said, it should be clear that a common good is considered to be a hybrid between a public good and a private good; in difference with a public good, it is characterized by rivalry in consumption, and in difference with a private good, it is characterized by non-excludability, which is the source of the tragedy.

The central problem in the economic theory of public goods is the tendency not to produce public goods if relying on economic rationality and the market, because that triggers the well-known "free-riding" problem (as game theory makes evident).

The tragedy of common goods is instead the destruction of goods that already exist; if it is true that if economic theory describes both of these as "Prisoner's Dilemmas," destruction becomes the double of non-production. The common goods that Hardin wanted to emphasize are common resources that cannot be easily reproduced once they are destroyed, because they are non-renewable; this is true for much of the natural environment, but it is also true for trust between people, community relationships, and ancient conventions, which once destroyed do not rebuild themselves. We will now analyze common goods in depth through game theory.

In the language of game theory, the tragedy of the commons is essentially a type of "Prisoner's Dilemma" with n players. That is, there is a rational strategy for an individual maximizing her utility, but if that same strategy is followed by all the other rational agents it produces inefficient results both collectively and individually.

To enter the well-known logic of the Prisoner's Dilemma, consider the hypothetical case of Anna and Bruce, who both fish in the same lake. The strategies the two players have available are "Limited Fishing" and "Unlimited Fishing"; how might they reason? In the following chart the game is summarized, with an indication of the various payoffs.

		Anna	
		Limited	Unlimited
Bruce	Limited	3 3	1 4
	Unlimited	4 1	2 2

The tragedy of the commons described as a prisoner's dilemma

For both players, the dominant strategy is "Unlimited Fishing." This leads to a Nash equilibrium with the pair of strategies "Unlimited Fishing," which corresponds to a payout of 2 for each player. It is obvious that this equilibrium is not Pareto efficient; both could improve their payoffs if they were to adopt the strategy "Limited Fishing," with which they could obtain a payout of 3. In our example each player will fish too much, and in so doing they will soon come to the end of the common resource. A variant of this game can be to introduce the possibility of repeating the game, even an infinite number of times. However, we don't know if the final outcome would be different or not.

If individuals are not short-sighted, on the basis of what had been learned from past tragedies, we might think that the prisoners have a personal interest and incentive to "escape from prison" and cooperate without the need of legal or external enforcement by judges, courts, and so on. Although it cannot be entirely discarded, this solution does not seem particularly useful for understanding the history of how real communities resolve tragedies of the commons.

A further development of a solution to this individualistic and rational vision is a proposal to privatize the collective good by subdividing it into many small private pieces, such as a forest, a park, or a river. Actually, subdividing a forest into many individual plots should not always be demonized or criticized as antisocial. Consider the many cases — some of which have been studies in the literature[1] — of managing common goods in some areas of the Trentino or Emilia-Romagna in Italy, where forests and lands are managed by systems that are a combination of communitarian and individual elements; each family has a piece of the common good, but community criteria are followed for subdividing and using the forests and lands and for dividing profits.[2] However, the crucial point is that many basic common goods, such as ozone and water, are not divisible, and thus it is necessary to find collective solutions to the problem.

---

1. in particular, see the works of Marco Casare (2007).
2. an important aspect of these centuries-old conventions is that it is impossible to restore them once they are destroyed.

There are in fact other possible solutions, as we will soon see

First, it is worth emphasizing the fact that we could improve the semantics of game theory applied to the tragedy of the commons by using other games, such as the "Deer Hunt." This game is used to describe a cooperation problem, in which there are two or more deer hunters. Hunting the deer requires cooperation, and thus the necessity of joint action in which each person's part is essential in order for everyone to reach their goals. The reciprocity required to hunt a deer thus has an uncertain outcome; no player can control any other player, as there is no possibility of coercively enforcing the contract. Hunting a small rabbit by oneself has a certain outcome, although it is less rewarding than a deer. The certainty in hunting rabbits is that it does not require others' cooperation. The structure of such a game follows. Recall that in this game "Limited" is equivalent to "Cooperate," while "Unlimited" is equivalent to "Do Not Cooperate."

The tragedy of the commons described as a deer hunt

This game has two Nash equilibria: "Limited—Limited" (cooperate—cooperate) and "Unlimited—Unlimited" (do not cooperate—do not cooperate), even though a payoff of 4 for both is associated with the first and a lower payoff of 2 with the second. Deciding to chase and hunt a rabbit a hunter comes across while following the deer's trail (which is a choice of do not cooperate) produces a lower but certain payoff of 2. Doing one's part in hunting the deer and resisting the temptation to take the certain rabbit that crosses one's path while proceeding toward the goal of the common hunt produces a greater result of 4, *but only if the others keep the agreement* and do not chase a rabbit. In this sad second case, those who continue to unilaterally follow the deer will not succeed in hunting it alone (due to its "production technology") and will end up empty-handed. Thus loyalty to the initial agreement *is more profitable but more fragile* because, in difference with rabbit hunting, it wholly and demonstrably depends on others' choices.

		Anna	
		Limited	Unlimited
Bruce	Limited	4 4	0 2
	Unlimited	2 0	2 2

Such a game is different from the Prisoner's Dilemma for at least two reasons. First, here we have not one but two equilibria. It is advantageous to hunt the rabbit *if* someone else hunts a rabbit, and hunt the deer (and thus cooperate) *if* the others hunt the deer. Do Not Cooperate/Unlimited is a better equilibrium if we take *risk* as a variable, since 2 is smaller than 4 but certain; the equilibrium Cooperate/Limited is optimum if we look at the *payoffs*, which are higher but riskier. Second, in such a game the greater payout of 4 is not obtained by someone who exploits others' cooperation (free-riding, as happens in the Prisoner's Dilemma); the maximum payoff goes to risky mutual cooperation. Why is a game such as the "Deer Hunt" preferable to the Prisoner's Dilemma to describe the tragedy of the commons cooperation, in difference with most economics textbooks?

First, because the game better highlights the true nature of free cooperation between human beings, which is more profitable than opportunism, *but is also relationally riskier.* As long as cooperation remains free, it is not individually irrational, as in a Prisoner's Dilemma, but only more risky and fragile, since it is linked to others' responses we do not control. Moreover, the relational structure of the Deer Hunt better illustrates the idea of stability (because it is an equilibrium) of free cooperation once it is chosen. If we begin with (4,4), there are no incentives to deviate either individually or collectively from mutual cooperation, as we see in the satisfying stories of conventions that, once established, evolve and endure for centuries (Ostrom, 2006).

However, although we will lose something, in the remainder of this Appendix we will continue to use the Prisoner's Dilemma as the basic game for reasons of continuity with the vast majority of economic analyses of the commons because, for what we want to say in the following pages, either game is suitable. It is still worth keeping in mind that the history of the description of the tragedy of the commons is more complicated than the Prisoner's Dilemma. Now we will look at other possible solutions to the problem of the commons.

The other two classic solutions are the *social contract* (à la Hobbes, in which a Leviathan is created by an artificial pact), and the *ethical individual.*

The Hobbesian solution commits everything to the State, which creates a system of sanctions and the institutions to implement them. Rational agents understand that unless they restrain their individual liberty they will not be able to coordinate among themselves, get out of the tragedy, and reach a better result for everyone.

The social contract

The Nash equilibrium is "Limit–Limit," which is also Pareto efficient. The payoff is greater than the others, even though this time the maximum benefit, a payoff of 3, is less if compared to the case in which there is no State and there is full liberty. The "Unlimited" strategy is linked with a lower payoff, because now in the case in which a player does not limit herself, there is a payoff penalty.

		Anna			
		Limited		Unlimited	
Bruce	Limited	3	3	0	4-2
	Unlimited	4-2	1	2-2	2-2

So the Leviathan is created by a social contract, but at the price of individual liberty. The decisive element against this solution, in addition to renouncing liberty, is that it cannot be implemented today in the most important commons; given their global nature, there is no possibility of establishing a social contract and a Leviathan on that scale (fortunately!). Who today can create an enforcement system to force compliance with any agreements that might be stipulated by the major world powers? The failures of the accords on CO_2 emissions, the exploitation of seabeds, and international public goods are facts that speak much more eloquently than any theoretical discourse.

The third solution aims toward *ethical individuals*, whether of Kantian or other inspiration, partly as a reaction against the untrustworthiness of top-down solutions. In this solution agents internalize ethical norms, such as "Do not pollute the environment," for example, and follow them because they know that once the norms are internalized they will be happier following that moral conduct.[3] This solution, which is not an alternative to the first, but rather complementary to it — even though not automatically so[4] — consists in the formation of an ethical individual in which agents attribute intrinsic value to the choice to limit themselves in consuming common goods (a value that is added to the game matrix).

If we measure this intrinsic value with ε, and if this value is large enough (>1 with our payoffs), an agent can decide to limit her consumption of common goods, even if she is the only one to do so, as can be seen in the following chart:

The intrinsic rewards game

In this case Anna has an environmental ethic and limits herself in consuming the commons, even if she is the only one to do so and Bruce does not. At the same time, Anna's results depend on Bruce' response; in material payout terms she will obtain $1 + \varepsilon$ or $3 + \varepsilon$ on the basis of Bruce's behavior. The intrinsic

---

3. From a technical point of view, it is as if people changed their preferences over time to also include the public good in their objective functions; in this way the *common* good also becomes a *private* good, thanks to internal rewards and penalties that make ethical behavior preferable to unethical behavior.

4. As the Swiss economist Brunto Frey has shown (1997), the use of external sanctions can crowd out intrinsic motivations.

reward (ε) makes her choice to cooperate unconditional, but others' responses influence the results she obtains. This follows a logic that can be defined as "unconditional reciprocity": when intrinsic motivations are strong one does not depend on others' *choices*, but one depends on others for the *results*.

		Bruce	
		Limited	Unlimited
Anna	Limited	3 +ε 3	1 +ε 4
	Unlimited	4 1	2 2

Individual ethics are certainly important and are co-essential, but today a further step is required. In this solution, which in any case is highly important and co-essential for any serious solution to the problem of the commons, the center is the *individual*; in the other, the center is the *State*.

What is missing in this account of possible solutions? The great missing component is the *civil society*, which is a reality we cannot define either as a State, a market (whether self-interested or capitalist), or purely as a summation of individual private matters.

So what does it mean to take civil society seriously on the topic of water, and more generally on the commons?

The We-rationality

Saying "culture" means not just changing individuals' values, but changing to a different perception of the problem that points toward "us." Another role of culture is not only to shape individuals with intrinsic values, but also to form a common vision of the problem, one that starts from the ground up in an awareness of a bond between people that reasons in terms of "us."

If Anna thinks in terms of "us" she may prefer to limit herself all the time, since, whether Bruce limits himself or not, the sum of the cooperation is always greater: 6 (3 + 3) > 5 (4 + 1) just as 5 (1 + 4) > 4 (2 + 2). Here the sum of the payoffs is interpreted as a measure of the common good, as a sort of function of collective well-being that coincides with the function of individual well-being, as suggested by the British economists Michael Bacharach and Robert Sugden in their theory of *we-rationality*. The typical reasoning of someone who looks at the world from a "we" perspective is this: "Better me than no one. Although I know I risk being exploited by others' free-riding, I prefer my single contribution to the common good to the situation in which no one contributes, and I can hope that it brings about reciprocity."

		Bruce	
		Limited	Unlimited
Anna	Limited	3 3	1 4
	Unlimited	4 1	2 2

Obviously, if people have both intrinsic rewards (ε) and the "we framework" it is even easier to engender cooperation. It frequently happens in peoples' lives that with the passing of years ε is reduced, but the sense of "we," or the good of the community, increases with maturity.

How many "we" people should there be, and/or how many people who always cooperate due to ε? From game theory studies (see Bruni, 2008), today we know that there are two preconditions: (1) if there are some who have a very high value of ε and who hold out longer in crises, and (2) if the "we" cooperators are somewhat sophisticated — for example, they punish altruistically and not at a high cost — then it is possible that a small quota of "we" people can "invade" a large populace over time. In fact, we know from history that cultural changes often result from highly motivated and well-informed minorities. Obviously, the legal, social, institutional, and political systems greatly influence both individuals and the "we framework."

The role of civil society

In a recent article, Amartya Sen, probably the most influential political economist today on environmental policies and human rights, emphasized that the topic of the "global commons," such as water, "Rather, the important issue is that today — right now — the developed countries take up an unequally large share of what are called 'the global commons' — the common pool of air, water and other natural space that we collectively can share." (Sen, 2010, p. 565). As we noted in the previous section, it is obvious that the Hobbesian solution of the State that penalizes offenders cannot be implemented, particularly for the global commons. That does not mean that the heads of governments (and especially those who elect them, who are often quite short-sighted) should not do all they can to reach a global agreement with sanctions, but this does not seem to be either the simplest or the only solution. But there is more: billions of independent people, not just heads of governments, use the global common goods today, all of whom maximize their own goals. Coordinating and setting limits on all these people would be an arduous, if not impossible, task. From this perspective, the individual and educational ethical dimensions become important, although this alone is not *the* solution.

And yet something should be done, because a new global social agreement between free and equal citizens — and not only those in the G20, but potentially everyone — who limit themselves in using common resources is too urgent. This would be a different agreement from a Hobbesian solution, which tends to be illiberal, or one made between heads of governments, families, or clans. This new global social agreement should be an agreement of fraternity, after equality and liberty. Modernity has conquered the latter two, creating democracy and human rights, but they alone have revealed themselves to be incapable of managing the common goods on which much, if not nearly all, of our present and future depend. *Liberty* and *equality* speak of individuals; *fraternity* is the principle of modernity that speaks of *bonds* between people. Without such bonds, and without recognizing that we are all linked to each other because we insist on using the same common resources, we will not successfully avoid a tragedy of the commons.

All this has very concrete implications. If we do not want water, public lands, parks, and many other common goods to be managed either by the State or by the capitalist or for-profit market (for the reasons just discussed), then we must recognize and assign an important place to civil society in the areas of the economy and business.

We are convinced that a shared solution to this crucial theme will not be found until we give a central place to this "excluded third," the civil society, and its economic expressions. Indeed, why not imagine and implement a solution for managing water similar to what emerged from civil society regarding care, poverty, and mental illness? Thirty years ago these sectors, which are other forms of common goods, were entirely in the hands of the State and of families. Today, a large part of these services are in the hands of thousands of social cooperatives. These are the so-called social or civil enterprises, which are motivated by social and solidarity purposes rather than profit. Social entrepreneurs emerged as an expression of civil society; although they did not expect high returns on their invested capital, they wanted and knew how to use their entrepreneurial talents to manage common goods; entrepreneurs are essential for efficiently managing scarce resources. All this was possible — at least in the most virtuous cases, not all obviously — thanks to a new alliance or pact between the market, the public, and civil society. The public is well represented, but it is an equal partner with entrepreneurs and communities.

For many common goods we can imagine a similar solution. With appropriate laws (as happened in Italy in 1991 with the social cooperation law) we can give life to new social enterprises to manage water that are the fruit of an alliance between the public, companies, and civil society. This does not mean prohibiting by law that social enterprises can earn profits, partly because significant capital is required, but rather setting limits on them; these would not be non-profit, but low-profit companies. Provision should be made in these for pluralistic forms of governance with multiple stakeholders involved in decisions, establishing deep bonds with local communities that have an interest in water management. Social enterprises, which some call community or communion companies, are the solution to managing common goods; this is true not just for water, but for public lands in cities (such as parking), energy, and the environment; it is a solution that is perfectly aligned with the principle of subsidiarity.

Conclusion

History has seen many moments in which communities, societies, and peoples have been at a fork in the road that separates fraternity from fratricide — two roads that have been adjacent and intertwined since the time of Cain. At times, we have chosen the path of fraternity; at others, perhaps the more numerous, we have chosen the path of fratricide. We face this fork in the road today, and we must do all we can to go in the direction of fraternity. The future of our species is at stake, and — perhaps — we still have time to take the right road. But how? The response remains inevitably open.

In any event, the civil message committed to these pages is twofold. From a first perspective, we must conclude that if we want to escape from the dilemmas and the tragedy of non-cooperation, we must develop multi-dimensional strategies, such as a new agreement with clear, fair, expressive, and shared rules, reinforce and cultivate individual motivations (ε) and never take them for granted, and develop a "culture of we," with appropriate incentives, rewards, and governance choices.

At the same time, we have also proposed a second element, although rather quietly: we must recognize that we cannot escape the traps of non-cooperation and mistrust except by fully embracing the vulnerability of civil, economic, and organizational life. True reciprocity emerges only by recognizing our *mutual vulnerability*; we escape the tragedy of the commons only by accepting the fact that we escape the major tragedies, which could become deadly, by accepting and incorporating the little daily tragedies of betrayed reciprocity and of others' missed and inevitable responses — the "good pains," as Martha Nussbaum (1996) called them — on which our flourishing necessarily depends.

Further reading

Arrow, K. J. (1951). Alternative approaches to the theory of choice in risk-taking situation. *Econometrica, 19*, 404–437.

Arrow, K. J. (1960). The problem of social cost. *Journal of Law and Economics, 2*.

Arrow, K. J. (1963). *Social choice and individual values*. London: J. Wiley & Sons.

Bruni, L. (2008). *Reciprocity, Altruism and Civil Society*. London: Routeledge.

Casari, M. (2007). Emergence of endogenous legal institutions: Property rights and community governance in the Italian Alps. *The Journal of Economic History, 67*(1), 191–226.

Coase, R. H. (1937). The nature of the firm. *Economica, New Series, 4*(16), 386–405.

Coase, R. H. (1960). The problem of social cost. *Journal of Law and Economics, 3*, 1—44 (The University of Chicago Press).

Coman, K. (1911). Some unsettled questions of irrigation. *American Economic Review, 1*(1), 1—19.

Frey, B. S. (1997). *Not Just for the Money: An Economic Theory of Personal Motivation*. Cheltenham: Edward Elgar Publishing.

Hardin, G. (1968). The tragedy of commons. *Science, 162*(3859), 1243—1248.

Legrenzi, P. (1998). *La felicità*. Bologna: Il Mulino.

Nussbaum, M. (1986—2001). *The fragility of goodness, luck and ethics in Greek tragedy and philosophy* (1st ed.). Cambridge University Press.

Ostrom, E. (1990—2003). *Governing the commons. The evolution of institutions for collective action* (1st ed.). Cambridge University Press.

Pigou, A. C. (1932). *The economics of welfare* (4th ed.). London: Macmillan.

Sen, A. (2010). Sustainable development and our responsibilities. *Notizie di Polteia, 26*(98), 129—137.

Sidgwick, H. (1901). *Principles of political economy* (3rd ed., p. 414). London: Macmillan.

Chapter 9

The theory of Homo reciprocans

9.1 Labor supply in traditional theory

Following the approach developed in Chapter 3, which focused on the theory of consumption, we can easily derive the labor supply curve for an individual whose behavioral logic is that of the well-known *homo oeconomicus*. The easiest way to solve the problem is to imagine a person who must decide how to divide his available time between work and leisure. For the sake of convenience, suppose that the agent in consideration only has income from work, which is used to buy a consumer good, and that both the labor and the consumer markets are perfectly competitive. To simplify the analysis, suppose that there is a single consumption good (which can be thought of as a composite good, or a basket of goods in fixed proportions). The agent's budget constraint is thus:

$$pc = wn \qquad (9.1)$$

where p is the price of the good, w is the nominal salary, c is the consumption (expressed in physical terms), and n is the time worked.

If t is the amount of free time, considering the choice as made on a daily basis and measuring the time in hours, then $t = 24 - n$. Thus [9.1] can also be written as:

$$pc + wt = 24w \qquad (9.2)$$

We can interpret [9.2] as follows: the consumer sells all her initial allocation of free time (24 h) and obtaining an income of $24w$, which she then spends to buy the consumption good and to repurchase the free time she wants to enjoy. Naturally, what we have just described are not actual exchanges; in reality the consumer-worker only offers the work time desired on the market. Correspondingly, the cost of the repurchased free time is obviously not a true cost. It is instead an **opportunity cost**, or income the agent gives up to enjoy the free time.

Graphically the budget constraint is a straight line that has an x–axis intercept (the axis on which we measure free time) at 24 and has a slope equal

The Microeconomics of Wellbeing and Sustainability. https://doi.org/10.1016/B978-0-12-816027-5.00009-4

to w/p. Note that the x—axis intercept is independent of prices. Indeed, the agent can always decide not to work (and so, without other income sources, not to consume), whatever w and p might be.

Suppose the consumer-worker's preference between consumption and free time can be represented by the utility function $U(c,t)$, which has the usual properties. Corresponding to this utility function we have a map of indifference curves in the *plane* (t,c), which are assumed to be continuous, decreasing, and convex. By virtue of the assumption of rational behavior, the equilibrium point is along the budget constraint at the point where it crosses the outermost indifference curve. The equilibrium point corresponds to the tangent point between the straight line of the budget constraint and the indifference curve (see Fig. 9.1).

Note that the position of the budget constraint is completely determined once w/p is given, which is the actual salary expressed in units of consumption goods. In other words, only relative prices are relevant to a rational agent's decisions. Indeed, when the nominal salary and the price of the consumption good vary in the same proportion, the worker's real salary — his purchasing power — remains unchanged, such that he has no reason to change his labor offered.

Without a loss of generality, it is thus possible to posit $p = 1$. This assumption is simply the choice of a unit of measure; in particular, it serves to express all quantities in units of the consumption good. Technically this is a *normalization* condition. Given this normalization, w directly represents the real salary, which graphically is the slope of the budget constraint.

What is the effect of an increase in real salary w on the labor supply? As we have said, if we modify w the x—axis intercept of the budget constraint does not move. Instead, the slope of the budget constraint changes; more precisely, if w increases the budget constraint rotates clockwise (thus upwards) by pivoting on the x—axis intercept.

FIG. 9.1 The choice between consumption and leisure time.

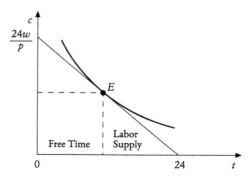

First, the traditional *substitution effect* is at work, which operates through a change in the slope of the budget constraint. If w increases, the substitution effect makes the labor supply increase and reduces the consumption of leisure time.

Second, the traditional *income effect* is in operation, which in this context we could define as the **employment income effect**. Given the initial labor supply, the increase in salary increases the consumer's real income; on the assumption that free time is a normal good, this increases the consumption of free time and reduces the labor supply.

If leisure time is a normal good, the income and substitution effects move in opposite directions, so the labor supply (which is equal to the time available minus the free time consumed) can increase or decrease. We can be sure that the labor supply will increase corresponding to a real salary increase only if free time is an inferior good. Consequently, if the substitution effect is greater than the income effect, then the individual labor supply curve is increasing with respect to real salary. If the weight of the two effects is reversed, then the curve is decreasing. Of course, as Paul A. Samuelson noted, there is no reason to think that one effect will dominate the other at every salary level; in other words, it is not a given that the labor supply function is monotonic with respect to salary.

On the basis of the above, it is easy to understand how for a certain interval of salary values between 0 and $\overline{w}$ a labor supply curve can be ascending from left to right, while for another interval of salary values greater than $\overline{w}$ the curve can be descending (see Fig. 9.2). If leisure time is a normal good, it is clear that the income effect alone leads to a decrease in work time with an increase in w. However, a higher w means that the cost of free time is also higher. (The cost of free time is measured by the salary the agent gives up.) So with an

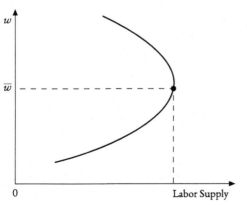

FIG. 9.2 An example of a labor supply curve that bends backwards.

increase in w, free time becomes a relatively costlier good, such that, due to the substitution effect, an increase in w entails less free time and more work time.

The two effects thus operate in opposite directions when w changes, such that the net effect will depend on which of the two is the dominant effect. When w is low, leisure time is not a particularly attractive good, so the substitution effect will be dominant. So if we start from a low w, subsequent increases in it slowly entail more work and less free time. On the other hand, when w is quite high, free time becomes the more attractive good, and the income effect will be dominant, with the result that successive increases in w will translate into more free time and less work. The empirical evidence seems to suggest that over the long run the income effect prevails, while the substitution effect prevails in the short run.

9.1.1 Of pyramids and hourglasses: the labor question today

In the previous section we laid out the traditional theory of labor supply. While it was able to adequately represent the market situation at the time of the first and second industrial revolutions — at the end of the 18th and 19th centuries respectively — it is no longer able do so. Let's try to understand why.

A metaphor can help us understand the nature of the current employment problem. Until the advent of globalization and the third industrial revolution, the productive order could be ideally represented by a pyramid. At the base there were routine tasks which required no particular skill or training investment to do them. Moving towards the peak there was a sort of stratification of tasks that proceeded in parallel with how far one's education had progressed. Those with college degrees were nearly certain to occupy, sooner or later, a medium or even medium-high position. Those who showed particular talent and competence reached the top of the pyramid, where there were few places, since labor-intensive organizations did not need many people to think big and do forward-thinking planning. Since knowledge was predominately codified rather than tacit, it was sufficient to bring a few people together in the top positions who could translate into practice Taylor's famous rule of "one man, one job" — consider an assembly line, for example.

Today the pyramid has become an hourglass. The lowest level is more or less the same; that is, today as yesterday there is a need for those who must carry out standardized tasks, which are mainly entrusted to immigrants. The difference between the two shapes has to do on one hand with the middle level, where there are very few places in an hourglass, and on the other hand with the higher levels that, unlike a pyramid, now occupy the top of the hourglass. Today the fact is that in a post-Fordist era, the world of labor tends to privilege either many experts and highly specialized people or those who accept taking positions at the lower levels of the labor hierarchy. What is gradually contracting is the demand at the intermediate skill and/or specialization levels. Note that this is happening not only for those who are employed but for the self-employed as well; consider what is happening in the professional arena. This is why there has been a highly visible loss of power — and not just economic — in the middle classes.

Many proposals have been put forward to meet this need. They range from policies to improve bringing labor supply and demand together to labor policies to create new jobs in the service sector. Others propose aiming to integrate young people into the labor market by professional training and apprenticeships. Still others advance the idea of balancing labor market guarantees, where the gap is too wide between the flexibility of temporary work offered to young people and the rigidity of permanent employment reserved for adults. Finally, some suggest increasing the funds for social shock absorbers and applying tax reductions and/or credits for employing young people.

These and many other proposals are certainly valid and on target. However, they are not sufficient to meet the current challenge, for the simple reason that such measures aim at the effects rather than the deep causes of the plague of unemployment and unemployability. Nor should we think that all job aspirants should have the qualities and/or skills to reach the upper levels of the hourglass. If work is for people, if it serves as a constituent factor in our identity, we cannot accept that only the super-efficient and the super-qualified are able to enter the labor market. When we come to understand this, we are compelled to try daring new courses of action. What we need to do, by appropriate interventions, is to encourage labor freed up from the capitalist sector of the economy — which can never absorb more than 75%—80% of the workforce — to transfer to the social sector of the economy. The product of the social sector of the economy is characterized by the fact that the work carried out in it is different from employed wage labor. When Fordism was considered the only form of labor within the modern horizon, employed wage labor could rightly be the prototype of labor tout court. It was then inevitable that self-employment, cooperatives, associations, and other forms of independent labor were thought of as exceptions. Today the opposite is true. New workers and new types of work are outclassing traditional employed labor. Year after year the large historical manufacturing enterprises lose around 1% of their employees, while the number is constantly increasing of those who work with atypical contracts — which before long will be typical — in these new types of work. This is why it necessary to launch a robust social economy sector to ensure that this "freed-up" labor can be absorbed. We must stress in every way possible that business is the high road to create jobs, not the public administration. But note well that private capitalist companies are not the only type that can create work; social enterprises — those whose guiding principle is reciprocity — can create work as well.

That is possible on one basic condition: that the overflow of actual demand be directed towards the production goods for which the social economy has a specific comparative advantage. As we increasingly hear stated, there is a specific demand for quality of life underlying the new growth model, but the demand for quality goes well beyond a mere demand for well-made manufactured or agricultural goods. Rather, it is a demand for creativity, care, service, culture, and the commons. In other words, the quality referred to is not so much that of consumption products, whether goods or services, as it is for quality in human relationships.

There are three conditions that must be satisfied to allow reapportioning consumption expenses between material and immaterial goods, and between commodities and common goods. The first brings into question the cultural matrix of society, because changes in the basket of consumption goods pass through lifestyle choices, which in turn depend on the prevalent culture. The second condition is to free up the world of social entrepreneurship from all the bureaucratic constraints that obstruct its operation. This is about preparing new financial instruments to finance the birth and development of social companies, such as social impact bonds, solidarity bonds, crowdfunding, and so on. Third, it is urgent that we accelerate the transition from redistributive welfare to generative welfare. Indeed, because generative welfare is involved with people's capabilities rather than simply their life conditions, it is able to create work. One empirical data point: at the end of 2012, there were 434,840 people working in Italian social enterprises, to which another 1,200,000 people should be added who work in various types of cooperative enterprises.

9.2 How to select workers with a "vocation"

The standard labor supply theory assumes that workers are motivated by salary and the material benefits of compensation, on the idea that work is a "bad," or a means to obtain a salary, which is instead a "good," where more is preferable to less. Work is thus not a source of utility in itself, but a "bad" that workers must endure in order to obtain the "good" represented by payment for work.

Such a theory of work, although it does represent many actual work dynamics, cannot fully satisfy us if we want to understand different organizational realities and the complexity of human motivations.

Psychology and empirical observation abundantly show us that, particularly in a so-called "post-Fordist" society, it is also a place where workers' human development can be realized, and — at least in some professions — the work itself is also a source of compensation, since working is also a good (and not just a bad). To study the labor supply of workers with intrinsic motivations, we must imagine a more complex objective function that also contains symbolic and value terms that are added to salaries.

Our starting assumption is that the managers of a civil firm are interested in hiring people with a "vocation" — not just employees who are prepared and able to do the work, but people who are just as prepared and who *additionally* feel the mission and values of the organization to be their own. We assume that the organization has already tested the qualifications and professional competence of the candidates who applied. To give an example, a cooperative that is working to bring disabled people into the labor market will not want to choose managers and workers who are just technically capable; rather, it will want to hire people who, beyond being technically qualified, have a certain dose of "vocation." That vocation leads them to approach these disadvantaged people with an attention and care that no contract could impose by sanctions or incentives. Often the market success of such organizations depends primarily on the fact that their customers are looking for and recognize precisely that "plus," which they may not see in a public system or for-profit firm.

Our first theoretical building block is George Akerlof's famous article *The Market for Lemons*; published in 1970 (Akerlof, 1970), it was one of the most influential economics articles of the 20th century. We consider it here to develop a discussion on organizations and motivations. The basic idea of that short article (which, among other things, earned the author a Nobel prize) is the ancient Gresham's Law: *bad money drives out good*. Gresham's Law refers to the phenomenon, common in the *ancient regime*, that occurred when two currencies circulated in a given territory, both of which had the identical ability to satisfy debts but that were considered as having different intrinsic values. In such cases the money that people considered as having less worth — the "bad" money — circulated rapidly because everyone wanted to get rid of it, and the "good" money was instead hoarded at home.

Thanks in part to Akerlof, today we know that this law is quite general in scope, applying not only to currencies but to a wide range of economic — and as we will see — even motivational phenomena. In his work Akerlof went to the root of Gresham's Law, showing that the reason for such a market malfunction (selecting the worst currencies) was essentially due to an *information* problem, and in particular a problem of *asymmetric* information between the contracting parties: The party offering money in exchange for goods knew whether the money about to be used in a contract was good or bad, while the party receiving the money did not know how to distinguish the two types of money. The good money was driven out of the market because there was only one price for both the good and the bad money. Given the common knowledge that there was a certain probability of encountering a bad currency in an exchange, and without being able to recognize the two, the currency exchange rate (or price) was lower than it would have been with only good money. So those who had good money would not accept the exchange offered because they considered it unfair, while — and this is the point — those who had bad money had strong incentives to use it, because the price offered was greater than the "right" price for that money. The analogy between asymmetric information and Gresham's Law is only partial because the difference between the good and bad currencies is observable (for example, by their difference in weight). It is true that the phenomenon that Gresham — and still earlier Copernicus — observed was of a substantially different nature than the phenomena that interested Akerlof.

The example Akerlof used in his article is how the used car market works, an example we have already illustrated in Chapter 7, Section 3.

We will recall here the conclusions of Akerlof's reasoning, which presented several aspects, all of which were problematic.

First, someone with a good car will not be able to sell it unless she accepts a lower price than its value (and thus completing an economically inefficient exchange).

Second, only poor quality cars will be found in the used car market.

Third, someone looking for a good used car will not be able to find one on the market, because he knows that only clunkers are available.

Finally, the very fact that someone is trying to sell a used car is interpreted as a signal that the car is a clunker.

In this case the market fails due only to a question of information; if there are potential buyers and sellers for good cars, they will not be able to find each other in the used car market. This mechanism explains, for example, why the price of a new car drops significantly in the used market if it is put up for sale just a few days after having bought it; in such a case the loss of market value is normally much greater than just the car's deterioration or physical obsolescence.

Akerlof's results have been applied to many, many different situations, from match-making agencies (just the fact that people sign up for a match-making service "signals" that they are of low aesthetic or relational quality), to insurance (how can a company avoid that only the imprudent take out theft insurance?), to the labor market. In the latter case, if a company does not know how to recognize the ability and the will to work of those it interviews and offers a salary of 300 (on the basis of a conjecture that if they hire a "good" worker she will return 400, while if they hire a "bad" worker who is less skilled or willing she will only return 200), Akerlof's theory tells us that only "bad" workers will apply for that job.

After Akerlof, economic theory devised various solutions to correct for these failures (which were more in the theory than in the market) due to information asymmetry. These solutions can be divided into two large families: those centered on *supply* (workers who offer their labor, a private individual who puts a car up for sale, etc.) and those based on *demand* (companies that want labor, dealers who used cars, etc.). The supply models identify the solution to the problem in some sort of "signal" a seller can send buyers to show their above-average quality. A typical signal in the labor market is education; having a degree can signal companies that the applicant is better than those without a degree, and thus deserves a higher salary. In the used car market sellers can offer a warranty that sends a costly — and thus credible — signal that the car they are guaranteeing is above average, such that the buyer is inclined to pay a higher price.

If we look at organizational realities, and in particular at Values-Based Organizations (VBOs), we understand that using signals is a normal practice when selecting staff. Over time volunteer workers are often hired by the organization; their having volunteered in the organization reduces the information asymmetry and signals their intrinsic motivations. Time spent working with associations listed in a candidate's curriculum vitae is an element that weighs heavily when selecting personnel. The supply side solutions suggested by the theory are more interesting for the discussion in the next chapter regarding civil enterprises and VBOs. Staying with the topic of choosing personnel, think about the mechanisms an organization can use to avoid choosing "clunkers."

A first theory regarding salary policy is widely discussed in the economic literature. If there is information asymmetry, the employer can pay a *higher* salary than the expected value, hoping to not choose only poor quality workers who will not make an adequate commitment. Using the same example as before, if a firm offers a salary higher than 300 (perhaps close to 400) there will be some probability that there will be good *as well as* bad candidates among those who apply. However, this theory, which is widespread today, is based on a crucial hypothesis: that the monetary salary is the only incentive, the only "carrot," to which workers respond. Workers are considered to be unidimensional individuals. In such a theory there is no room for other types of symbolic or values-based compensation, which are instead quite important in VBOs.

What happens when we deal with organizations looking for people who are also intrinsically motivated? The association also finds itself in an asymmetric information situation with new candidates, and the association is interested in choosing qualified people who *also* have intrinsic motivations, for the reasons we laid out at the beginning of the chapter. Let's see some possible solutions to the problem.

9.3 "Getting more by paying less"

To enter a little into the merits of the models that include non-monetary or immaterial components —models that entered the economic literature several years ago — imagine that a firm assumes that a good candidate, one with a "vocation," is not interested just in the salary or material incentives (as the standard theory assumes); she also attributes an intrinsic value to the activity in which she is asking to work, an intrinsic value that is part of the satisfaction (or utility) she would draw from the work for which she is applying.

The preferences of a "good candidate" (in this case a person with intrinsic motivations) can be represented by the following utility function: $L = \alpha W + (1 - \alpha)M$, where W is the salary, M is the intrinsic compensation she draws from performing the activity typical of that VBO, α is the weight attributed to salary, and $1-\alpha$ is the weight she assigns to the intrinsic motivations. Assume that this weight is inversely correlated with the weight attributed to salary. In other words, we could state that the vocation translates into an *intrinsic compensation* (non-monetary or material) she derives from performing that particular work. So we assume that the worker has *both* intrinsic motivations (the vocation) *and* instrumental motivations (the salary), but with different weights. A "good worker" would thus be someone who attributes a value greater than zero to the intrinsic component, while a worker without a vocation, as assumed by the standard theory, only attributes value to the salary she receives.

When the motivation is present, the salary amount is not the only determining factor for candidates. We can define a "vocation" as an individual's desire to directly engage in an activity which he considers as having value in itself.

For Heyes (2005) there are two conditions that must be met in order to define a worker as intrinsically motivated for a given job:

motivated workers go beyond their duty in carrying out their work;
they do a particular work because they draw pleasure from the activity, and this pleasure translates into accepting a lower salary.

This is why a higher salary can attract the wrong type of person. So in situations with asymmetric information, offering a lower salary becomes a means for the company to motivate good candidates to self-select.

Let's draw some initial conditions from this family of models for selecting vocations.

If the salary offered by the VBO (W^*) is below the market (W), when a worker accepts the lower salary, his accepting the offer indicates in itself that he has a level of intrinsic motivation greater than zero, since the difference in well-being between the salary he could obtain on the market (W) and the salary he accepted from the VBO (since $W^* < W$), is compensated by the intrinsic satisfaction the work gives him; the "compensation gap" is thus filled by the happiness of living out his vocation. If for example a worker were willing to work with no salary, perhaps as a volunteer, that would show that all the well-being he derives from that particular work comes from the intrinsic compensation of the "vocation."

If instead the VBO offers candidates the market salary ($W^* = W$), then in and of itself compensation, understood as a means, provides no guarantee that motivated workers will be chosen. In this case the VBO could pay *rents* to motivated workers (that is, not "exploit" their intrinsic motivations), because there is no good reason to think that "good" workers would not accept a higher salary such that only "bad" workers would be chosen.

So if an organization offers a salary below the market, it can be certain (at least in a context without structural unemployment[1]) *that it will not choose any workers with a level of intrinsic motivation equal to zero.* Moreover, it knows that the more it reduces the salary, the more the workers chosen will have a high intrinsic component (if they accept), and it also knows that if it were to offer zero salary it would have workers whose only motivation is intrinsic. A survey of managers' actual salaries in the social economy offers a strong empirical confirmation of this conclusion. This conclusion is not all that different from that hypothesized by the standard theory (the so-called "efficiency salaries"), with the significant difference that in this case to attract the best workers the organization should pay them *less* (rather than *more*, as the standard theory maintains) with respect to market salaries.

Finally, if an organization is looking for people motivated solely by intrinsic motivations, to be consistent with this theory it should not pay salaries. In such cases gratuitousness would select the best people, as in the case

---

FRAME 9.1 Blood donations.

In 1970 the British sociologist Titmuss (1970) showed that the British blood donation system based on non-profit organizations, in which blood was donated rather than sold, was more efficient that the US system, where blood was normally sold. The insight of the explanation of the greater efficiency of the British system was based on the adverse selection process; that is, people selling blood may be those who need the money more and whose health is generally below average. More recently, Bruno Frey (1997) cited the example of blood donations in the US which, due to a lack of supply, is forced to resort to the for-profit market, but it maintains a strict separation between the donation and for-pay systems. Following this model, organizations should ideally consider volunteer workers as a separate genus from those who are paid, with compensation, professional qualifications, and various responsibilities. If the two markets overlap, the phenomenon of crowding-out can easily occur. From this perspective, gratuitousness does not correspond to a zero price, but to an infinite price.

---

1. Things become more complicated in a labor market with unemployment, since it is not a given that the candidate without a "vocation" has a better actual salary alternative than one who gives it up. In this case, for example, offering candidates a lower salary than current market conditions could attract normal workers (those without a vocation) who are willing to work for a lower salary than the reserve because they are unemployed. In such a market setting, a low salary policy cannot be used as a means for selecting motivated candidates.

of blood donations, in which donated blood is of a higher quality than that bought on the market (Frame 9.1).

These initial conclusions open up significant perspectives on the importance of voluntary work, or why organizations that focus on gratuitousness alone succeed in attracting good people who are particularly motivated. These are the conclusions reached by the models that have in common the slogan *getting more by paying less*, regarding selecting non-profit managers or British healthcare salary policies (noting in particular that the best nurses are the lesser paid ones) (Frame 9.2).

FRAME 9.2 The feminist critique.

Some economists direct interesting criticisms against the "pay less and get more" theories (Nelson, 2005). These theories argue that the genuineness = sacrifice equivalence has long been a cover for domination and exploitation within the family, which, on the basis of a theoretical argument, has now been shifted from these models in favor of lower salaries in the healthcare professions, which are still held mainly by women. According to this critique, lower salaries in the non-profit sector would only allow women who are economically independent or who have wealthy husbands to cultivate that vocation, while women with greater economic needs would be forced to accept work without fulfilling their aspirations.

The crucial assumption in these theoretical models is that there is a *direct proportionality between the genuineness of the motivations and the willingness to sacrifice material benefits* (i.e., salary). However, we should ask ourselves whether we are sure that accepting a low salary is the proper test for measuring intrinsic motivation or someone's vocation. We will return to this at the conclusion of the chapter, where we will complicate and enrich the operational solutions proposed by this family of models.

9.4 When intrinsic motivations come into conflict with monetary incentives

A first complication of the discussion to this point takes into consideration the theory of the so-called "motivational crowding-out effect."

The theoretical structure of the models we have analyzed so far is based on an assumption in economics that is as common as it is demanding. That is, it is assumed that workers' two goals, a material goal (a salary, W) and an immaterial goal (intrinsic compensation, M), are independent of each other and are additive. However, the empirical evidence shows us that in reality this assumption is not so innocuous, especially when we are working with values and activities related to a "vocation." That is the Swiss economist Bruno Frey's argument. His 1997 book *Not Just for the Money* was a study entirely devoted to this type of situation, in which he documented much empirical evidence and numerous experimental data that showed the existence of this type of crowding-out of intrinsic motivations.

Frey's crowding-out theory is also an application of Gresham's Law: The *bad money* (in this case material incentives) *drives out* (or displaces) *the good money* (intrinsic motivation).

With data in hand, Frey showed that a monetary compensation can in certain cases reduce focused commitment to an activity rather than increase it, particularly when it comes to activities in which there are aspects that involve a "vocation" where intrinsic motivations are relevant. Psychologists offer various explanations for the displacement effect. According to Deci and Ryan, monetary compensation impacts the self-determination and self-esteem of those who are intrinsically motivated, because when a salary or monetary compensation are involved a person considers money the *motive* for why she works. The underlying insight is simple. People do not always know how to give a monetary value to their activities. For example, if we were to ask a mother or a missionary about what the monetary value might be of helping a child or listening to a poor person, they would probably respond "I haven't the faintest idea." We would hear the same response from our children when asking them the monetary value of clearing the table. However, if at a certain point we were to start paying them five dollars for clearing the table, it is possible and probable that they will start to attribute a value of five dollars to that activity. If we were to do the same for the mother or the missionary and offer them an economic figure for their activity, it is highly likely that they would consider the money as devaluing or disregarding their commitment (even if the sum of money were quite high). A similar phenomenon happens, although to varying degrees, every time we start to pay volunteer workers or when we use incentives for the environment, and more generally in situations in which civil virtues are in play. Note that in such situations the money reinforces the intrinsic motivation if it is perceived as a gift, rather than a price; this is the phenomenon that Frey described as "crowding-in."

This is the theoretical basis Frey used to explain the data that show that while a salary *increase* can have both positive and negative effects on performance (the net effect will be positive if the incentive effect of the salary increase compensates the displacement of the intrinsic motivations), transitioning from gratuitousness or free labor to some form of monetary remuneration seems instead to systematically have negative effects on workers' commitment. A consequence of this theory is the difficulty, or even impossibility, of returning to gratuitousness once we have started paying volunteers, without decreasing the workers' well-being (Frame 9.3).

For example, the utility function would be rewritten as follows: $U = \alpha W + (1 - \alpha)M(W)$. The form of $M(W)$ is important for the model's predictions. If we hypothesize that the function $M(W)$ has a negative and monotonic slope, every salary increase (W) reduces the intrinsic motivation

FRAME 9.3 Further development.

Regarding the utility function of workers with "vocations," another possibility is to consider two distinct trends in the function that depend on the starting point. If we start from $W = 0$ (volunteer work), every positive increase in W reduces intrinsic motivations. If instead we originally started from $W > 0$, the net effect of a salary raise on performance is uncertain. As we have seen, this is the common argument about the operation of incentives on motivations. Finally, we can complicate the discussion by assuming that the function $M(W)$ has an angular shape, that is, that a salary decrease can act on motivations and utility differently than an increase in salary. Increasing the incentives significantly displaces motivations, while reducing incentives increases motivations only a little or not at all. This assumption would seem consistent with the well-known experiment by Gneezy and Rustichini (2000). In the Haifa preschools that were the focus of their study, introducing a fine for parents who were late picking up their children increased the delays because it reduced intrinsic motivations, while when the fine was canceled the delays did not return to their prior levels. In this case the elasticity of the rigid side of the angular curve was actually zero.

component; conversely, a salary decrease increases the motivational component.

Although they shed light on several important phenomena, even these evocative and important conclusions from the models showing motivational crowding-out are not fully satisfying. Why? To give an example, think of a young volunteer worker who, after having married, finds herself forced to look for paid employment. Knowing of her intrinsic motivations, the organization in which she works could easily offer her paid employment so as not to lose a worker with a "vocation." In this case it seems implausible that there would be motivational crowding-out effects. More generally, a theory that posits an endemic conflict between intrinsic and monetary motivations cannot be taken seriously, as if civil life were a zero sum game between the economy and authentic sociality. That is the problem to which we now turn our attention.

9.5 What is a work "vocation"?

At the end of this analysis of the process of choosing people with a vocation, when considering these models an open question remains: Why should a vocation be associated with a willingness to accept a lower salary? What is the theoretical justification for this hypothesis?

The cultural hypothesis associated with these models is the ancient and deeply rooted idea (which dates back at least to Adam Smith) that genuine sociality and intrinsic motivations are not compatible with normal economic dynamics. So if we want introduce such practices into the market, it is necessary to reduce their characteristic economic components to make room for genuineness. Even the motivational crowding-out models share a similar premise: Instrumental motivations (working for a salary) and genuine motivations (working for a vocation) are in conflict with each other, and each tends to drive out or displace the other. In our view, such a reading incorporates a cultural flaw in considering that the economic and genuine dimensions are in structural conflict. We do not believe that this conflicting vision between a vocation and economic compensation is a positive message for the economy or for society; it certainly is not for those who operate from the perspective of the civil economy, in which the market is seen as one part of civil society. In this respect Geoffrey Brennan, an Australian economist (2001), proposed an interesting model that differs in part: Don't pay less, but structure the salary in such a way that makes it relatively more attractive to someone with a vocation. In the case of university professors, which was the subject of his study, he noted that to make candidates self-select it was necessary to offer a below-market salary, but at the same time make up the difference with various fringe benefits (e.g., research funds) that are only selectively appreciated by those with an academic vocation. Brennan divided potential candidates into two categories: *true* Scholars (*S*), "who place a high value on academic pursuits", and "Expedients" (*E*), "who are motivated mainly by the full income (including leisure) that the academic life affords."

From our perspective this research track is interesting because it does not conclude that there is a necessary incompatibility or conflict between a vocation and the market.

"Socrates" — a person with a vocation — is not paid less, but *differently*, with more complex and sophisticated incentives, in order to lead candidates to self-select. This seems to us the course to follow, although in the case of VBOs the key question becomes: What are the forms of compensation that attract the right people so they choose to apply? Research funds can be a good tool for university professors, but what are the fringe benefits to use for a cooperative or an NGO? Our proposal is that we should go beyond the idea that fringe benefits are only material (such as research funds) and move in the direction of identifying symbolic and relational forms of compensation that do not make up for the lower salaries, but that are added to them as means of self-selection.

Indeed, we should note that organizations are not alone in asymmetric information situations when looking for workers; *there are also workers with vocations* (Socrates) *who are looking for the right organization to turn to.* The "symbolic" signal thus has a dual nature: it allows a company to signal its values and candidates to select themselves. In this sense the organizational culture and governance of VBOs seems to us to be fundamental. If the value-based mission is clearly evident and the ideals are high and accountable, these facts are important signals that attract people with vocations. Is it not true, and evident to everyone, that when an organization or community expresses high ideals that it attracts quality people, and when it has a crisis of ideals it attracts lower quality people? Actually, we should honestly conclude that when an organization begins to no longer attract "Socrates," its values crisis is already in an advanced state, and it may already be too late. Difficulty in attracting people with a vocation is a symptom (not the cause) that the organization's ideals are no longer visible from outside.

In short, the mission and corporate culture are what become the real self-selecting signal for new candidates. When candidates without a vocation apply, that says that the general culture of the organization is no longer attractive, and it must work at this foundational level of identity if it wants to transform that vicious circle into a virtuous circle.

Finally, we have an uncomfortable question at this point in the discussion: Are we sure a vocation is a stock character trait that exists in people *before* they start work, or is it possible to imagine that a vocation may be partly endogenous in the work activity itself? For example, we could distinguish between people's preferences for the work prior to beginning it and their attitudes towards the work once they have begun. To give an example, think again of the market for university professors. When choosing them is it necessary to identify a vocation (for example, dedication to students and to research) by offering a lower salary, or might we assume that once the professors are hired they will recognize that one obligation of a good teacher is to engage in research and devote oneself to one's students?

We would like to leave this question open without a clear and definitive answer. On the one hand, people's stories, cultures, and identities are different, and the word "vocation" expresses this diversity; not everyone will spend 40 years healing the sick, or dedicate their lives to searching for new galaxies, or give their lives to the poor. On the other hand, it is also true that there are many other things that bring people together beyond these differences, such that someone — particularly someone who is young — can flourish if incorporated into energetic and positive organizations, or wither and become cynical and opportunistic if that is the organizational culture.

9.6 "Homo reciprocans"

9.6.1 The principle of reciprocity

In the preceding paragraphs we have seen that interpersonal relationships and their motivations also have significant effects on economic performance. *Reciprocity* is a relational form that is particularly analyzed in contemporary economic theory, but it was already present at the beginning of the civil economy tradition.

Reciprocity is certainly the most important social norm in civil life. The entire dynamic of life in common, from the micro to the macro level, can be read as a network of relationships that are highly diverse among themselves, but that have some norms of reciprocity as their common denominator.

Reciprocity comes from the Latin phrase *rectus-procus-cum*, which means "that which goes and in turn comes back." Aristotle can be considered the first theorist of reciprocity when he identified *antipepontos* (reciprocity) as the basis of life in common, from the market to *philia* (friendship between equals), and it was the basis of justice as well. Communities stay together on the basis of reciprocity norms, which are the great cohesive force of life in common. Even today in the disenchanted West it remains true that human communities, from the family to the nation, grow when positive forms of reciprocity prevail. These are the forms that give rise to cooperation and civil developments, such as contracts, markets, mutuality, friendship, and love — thus when its negative, destructive forms such as conflicts, wars, revenge, and retaliation do not gain the upper hand. Negative reciprocity is what fills the courts and destroys people's lives when they retaliate without hesitating to spend money and years of their lives, when an act of forgiveness would be sufficient to break the chain of destructive and senseless reciprocity.

There are two broad type of reciprocity, direct and indirect. **Direct reciprocity** has the following structure: $A \rightarrow B$, $B \rightarrow A$. That is, a person (A) gives or does something for person (B), who in turn responds to the same person on the basis of how she acted and what she did. What is exchanged between A and B can be of equivalent value; this is the form of reciprocity typical of contracts. It can also be of unequal asymmetric value, in which case we are considering other forms of reciprocity, such as friendship, relationships within the family, community, and many others.

In each case, however, for reciprocity to endure over time, A must consider B's response to A adequate (even if not necessarily equivalent) if reciprocity is to evolve and become a social norm. Indeed, reciprocity is often a repeated interaction, and the adequateness of the responses is a necessary condition for the relationship to endure over time, since if one of the parties in the relationship feels exploited by the other the reciprocity will not endure and will instead degrade into pathological forms of relationship.

However, there are other forms of reciprocity that are quite important both for social and economic life; these are the forms of **indirect reciprocity**. There is a twofold structure to indirect reciprocity. The first form of indirect reciprocity is of the type $A \rightarrow B \rightarrow C \rightarrow$. A does something for B, and A's actions affect how B in turns treats a third person C, without there having been any direct relationship between C and A. This relational structure is the basis for much of the educational process in the family. Many internal organizational dynamics also depend on indirect reciprocity, which is the basis of both the organizational culture that is created over time and the spontaneous cooperation between people. We are more likely to stop and pick up a young person looking for a ride if we were hitchhikers when we were young. Much of the success of micro-credit, community finance (such as savings banks and rural funds), and the so-called "time banks" are based on these norms of indirect reciprocity.

The second form of indirect reciprocity is of the type $A \rightarrow B, C \rightarrow A$. A acts in a particular way towards B, and in a later moment that first action influences an outside person C, who saw how A acted towards B but was not directly affected by it, which affects C's direct relationship with A. Similar dynamics are very important in the most ordinary events of economic life. In particular, some laboratory experiments have shown that people's *motivations* —the "why?" — play a significant role in both direct and indirect reciprocity. For example, consider a customer (C) of a company or a bank (A) that interprets the bank's philanthropic actions for a social project (B) as merely a means to increase profits; this customer could also penalize the company's social projects. There is a similar discussion when customers interpret social balances, social reports, and so on as reputational tools designed *solely* for the purpose of increasing profits. Obviously the opposite and more common case also exists when customers reward companies and banks they consider to be *genuinely* interested in the common good.

Much of the success of social responsibility campaigns depends on how the various stakeholders read the intentions of the protagonists. Human beings are the only animals capable of attributing meaning to their own and others' actions; this is why reciprocity plays out not only at the level of actions, but also of intentions. "Objective" facts are not enough; we want to understand the relational and motivational message they incorporate. A gift can express gratuitousness and recognition, but also the will to dominate the other (we should always keep in mind that a relationship with the Mafia frequently begins with a "gift," which, once accepted, is forever binding).

Economics has always been interested in reciprocity, but only in the past two decades it has become a specific topic of interest for economists. The traditional neoclassical treatment of sociality and reciprocity in economics presents problems, and it should probably be complicated and enriched from at least two perspectives: (a) an action without conditions is not considered as an act of reciprocity, but of definite altruism or, in other cases, simply as foolish; (b) other forms of relationship that are different from reciprocity are defined as selfish, or in any case as non-reciprocity. These two points clearly emerge when we consider a key quote from one of the foundational essays on the theory of *strong reciprocity*:

> *It is important to distinguish strong reciprocity from terms like 'reciprocal altruism' and 'altruism'. An altruistic actor is unconditionally kind, i.e. the kindness of her behavior does not depend on the other actors' behavior. A reciprocally altruistic actor, in contrast, conditions her behavior on the previous behavior of the other actor. Yet, while a reciprocally altruistic actor is willing to help another actor although this involves short run costs, she does this only because she expects long-term net benefits. ... If player B is an altruist she never defects even if player A defected. Altruism, as we define it here, is thus tantamount to unconditional kindness. In contrast, if player B is a strong reciprocator*

she defects if A defected and cooperates if A cooperated because she is willing to
sacrifice resources to reward a behavior that is perceived as kind. ... The
kindness of a strong reciprocator is thus conditional on the perceived kindness of
the other player. Since a reciprocal altruist performs altruistic actions only if the
total material returns exceed the total material costs we do not use this term in
the rest of the paper. Instead, we use the term 'selfish' for this motivation

Fehr, Fischbacher, and Gächter (2005, p. 5).

A "civil" theory of reciprocity must set itself the goal of surpassing these limits, both of which are crucial in the dominant theory of reciprocity typical of the "social preferences" approach.

9.6.2 Other approaches to reciprocity

The spread of the use of the category of reciprocity in economics is linked to the emergence and development of experimental and behavioral economics over the last 30 years, which has shown the relevance of behaviors that diverge from what conventional economic theory predicts. Recognizing the novelty of this way of working with reciprocity does not mean that theories assuming non self-interested or altruistic behavior have been lacking in economic science. Several economists at the end of the 19th century (Pantaleoni, for example) hypothesized that agents, while not abandoning the traits of *homo oeconomicus*, could act non self-interestedly in an economic sphere as well. But such behavior was not considered significant in explaining economic interactions, for which the simple but realistic assumption was sufficient that when agents act in the market they do not have the well-being of others or of humanity in mind, but rather their own and their family's advantage. This new stage of studies was primarily driven by empirical and experimental analysis, which provided robust, ample evidence of behavior not motivated by self-interest. Cooperative choices revealed in interactive experiments like the Prisoner's Dilemma, including non-repeated or one-shot games, were among the first anomalies studied. The explanations of such anomalies concentrated on several hypotheses. Sugden (1984) was one of the first theoretical models, which applied to voluntary contributions towards public goods; it explained the logic of a contribution on the basis of the assumption that each agent has an idea about what amount he would like to see from others.

If the actual contribution is equal to or greater than this value (ε), then the agent has a moral obligation to contribute at least ε: "I shall call this the principle of reciprocity" (Sugden, 1984). Sugden's model is part of a way of explaining the emergence of reciprocity on the basis of a "moral rule" category; there are no references to economic rationality to explain the emergence of cooperation, and the ethical norm is considered an alternative explanation to economic rationality. In other words, a social norm is rational in a different sense than how neoclassical economic science understands it as individual and instrumental maximization; here agents do not make calculations for every single choice, but rather they adhere — always on a rational basis — to an ethical norm that guides them in a wide range of action. In every instance it remains within the scope of *conditionality*; the social reciprocity norm is not without conditions on how other players respond. Many early studies on reciprocity thought it was altruism, but they quickly became aware that simple altruism did not explain the anomalies when compared with the laboratory evidence; they needed more sophisticated relational and motivational hypotheses.

This is the source of the theories from the 1990s about *aversion to inequality, trust responsiveness, warm glow, team-thinking,* and others (see Bruni, Gilli and Pelligra, 2008 for an overview). Rabin was one of the first authors to bring the concept of reciprocity into play in 1993, although the key word in his theory was *fairness*. In his classic essay in *American Economic Review*, we read in the first few lines that "people may care not only about their own well-being, but also about the well-being of others. Yet psychological evidence indicates that most altruistic behavior is more complex: people do not seek uniformly to help other people; rather, they do so according to how generous these other people are being" (Rabin, 1993, p. 1281). According to this theory agents are not indiscriminately generous or ungenerous towards others, but rather their own reciprocal actions are conditional and selective:"Indeed, the same people who are altruistic to other altruistic people are also motivated to hurt those who hurt them" (Rabin, 1993). Analyzing *intentions* is particularly important in Rabin's work.

He laid out a series of simple equations in his model that he used to explain how an agent tries to understand the other's *intentions* and so *judge* the other's *degree of kindness*. The average player gives half of her initial stock. In repeated games, however, towards the middle of the rounds the levels of giving begin to decline, until the last stage in which no one gives anything. Some explain this behavior as "learning," supposing that in the early rounds players do not understand that it is to their advantage not to give anything, but as the game proceeds they learn that not giving is the rational (or dominant) strategy. But this explanation does not account for the fact that when the game begins again with the same players (the so-called "re-start effect") the giving level goes back to about half their initial stock.

Furthermore, in experiments conducted primarily by the Zurich school, when players are assured that punishing agents who defect will gain them nothing in the future, because the games are not repeated and there is random matching, *retaliatory behavior* is still evident. This would seem to respond to the possible objection by those who say that punishing defectors is strategic and instrumental for their own gain, and thus explainable in terms of pure self-interest, without bringing up reciprocity.

Even if the current debate on reciprocity captures various important realities of life in common, we must recognize that it is not sufficient; we must look more deeply. Above all, we must keep in mind that the relationship between reciprocity and economics is an expression of the particular way that economic science sees sociality. As we know, the *only type* of sociality economists have traditionally analyzed is *instrumental* sociality. All other non-instrumental forms of sociality were considered as a sort of background against which economic choices could be represented, but they were essentially instrumental and undisturbed by the relational setting in which they were carried out. Economic science has assumed that self-interest is the general motivation for economic transactions, and that anonymity is a normal characteristic of markets (think of the perfect competition model, for example). It also recognized non-economic environments in which human beings carry out their own social and civil dimensions, such as family, friends, volunteer work, and so forth, which are sustained by other motivations, but it left to others the study of the more complex relational dynamics that developed in these areas.

Such reductionism and "division of labor," in which each discipline took its own "slice" of the human person, no longer holds up today. Remaining just within economic science, economists increasingly share the view that it is neither methodologically proper nor descriptively effective to assume that economic relationships take place on a constant social substrate. Interpersonal dimensions can in fact be significantly determined and influenced by economic factors; here we have in mind the development of markets that tend to erode the spaces once occupied by "relational goods," which are created as by-products of non-market interactions (see Chapter 12). On the other hand, the quality of relational life has important economic effects. On the basis of robust and widespread empirical evidence, we know that people placed into work environments that are attentive to the quality of relationships also have a better work performance; on the other end of this spectrum we find "mobbing," or group bullying.

Experimental and behavioral economics have been showing for years that to properly understand relevant economic phenomena it is necessary to introduce categories into the analysis such as "sincerity" and "genuineness" (two expressions we use here as synonyms of non-instrumentality); the presence of these in agents and others greatly influences their interactions. Even at a purely theoretical level there is a growing interest in quintessentially relational aspects in order to explain not just behavior outside the market (such as family choices, which economic theory has traditionally studied), but also truly pro-social behavior *within* ordinary market dynamics, such as when we are working on voluntary contributions to public goods, for example. The experimental evidence shows that in many of these phenomena the motivations underlying behavior and the dynamics in relationships create "anomalies" in agents' behaviors; influenced by similar dynamics, they choose strategies that for economic theory are not individually rational, because they are superseded by other strategies that are even more rational.

If we look at non-instrumental human relationships while remaining within the conventional way of conceiving of the market and economic interactions, we are forced to classify such behaviors as deviations and anomalies. Reciprocity is at once one and many. In order to understand and serve civil life with economic and social theory, it is necessary to have a pluralist, non-ideological way of viewing human reciprocity and to know how to parse it on several levels, ranging from contracts to gifts. We should read the various forms of reciprocity as tending to be complementary rather than in conflict among themselves, since life — including social life — is nourished and enriched by diversity.

Further reading

Akerlof, G. (1970). The market for lemons: Quality uncertainty and the market mechanism. *Quarterly Journal of Economics, 84*(3), 488–500.

Brennan, G. (2001). Selection and the currency of reward. In R. Goodin (Ed.), *The theory of institutional design* (pp. 256–275). Cambridge: Cambridge University, Press.

Bruni, L., Gilli, M., & Pelligra, V. (2008). Reciprocity: theory and facts. *International Review of Economics, 55*(1-2), 1–11.

Bruni, L. (2008). *Reciprocity, altruism and civil society.* Routledge: London.

Bruni, L. (2006). *Reciprocità. Dinamiche di cooperazione.* Mondadori: economia e societàcivile. Milano: Mondadori.

Deci, E. L., & Ryan, R. M. (1985). *Intrinsic motivation and self-determination in human behavior.* New York: Plenum Publishing.

Fehr, G., Fischbacher, U., & Gächter, S. (2002). Strong reciprocity, human cooperation and the enforcement of social norms. *Human Nature, 13*(1), 1–25.

Frey, B. S. (1997). *Not Just for the Money: An Economic Theory of Personal Motivation.* Cheltenham: Edward Elgar Publishing.

Frey, B. (2005). *Non solo per denaro.* Milano: B. Mondadori.

Gneezy, U., & Rustichini, A. (2000). Fine is a piece. *Journal of Legal Studies, 29*(1), 1–17.

Heyes, A. (2005). The economics of vocation, or Why is a badly-paid nurse a good nurse? *Journal of Health Economics, 24,* 561–569.

Hirschman, A. O. (1970). *Exit, voice, and loyalty: Responses to Decline in firms, organizations, and states.* Cambridge, Mass.: Harvard University Press.

Kolm, S. (2008). *Reciprocity: An economics of social relations.* Cambridge, New York: Cambridge University Press.

Nelson, J. A. (2005). *Interpersonal relations and economics: Comments from a feminist perspective.* In B. Gui, & R. Sugden (Eds.), *Economics and social interaction: Accounting for interpersonal relations* (pp. 250–261). Cambridge: Cambridge University Press.

Pelligra, V. (2007). *I paradossi della fiducia,* Bologna, Il Mulino.

Rabin, M. (1993). Incorporating fairness into game theory and economics. *The American Economic Review, 83,* 1281–1302.

Sugden, R. (1984). Reciprocity: The supply of public goods through voluntary contributions. *Economic Journal, 94,* 772–787.

Titmuss, R. (1970). *The gift relationship.* London: New Press.

Weisbrod, B. (1998). Modeling the nonprofit organization as a multi product firm: A framework for choice. In B. Weisbrod (Ed.), *To profit or not to profit. The commercial transformation of the nonprofit sector.* Cambridge: Cambridge University Press.

Weisbrod, B. (2002). Volunteer labor sorting across industries. *Journal of Policy Analysis and Management, 21*(3), 427–447.

Chapter 10

Not just for profit: civil enterprises and values-based organizations

10.1 The non-capitalist company

Organizations that do not pursue profit are certainly not new. In fact, if we look at history — and not just Western history — the economy and companies normally operated for reasons that were not merely or primarily economic. Arsenals were created to support wars, abbeys were created to praise God, and the Franciscan banks (the *Monti di Pietà*) were created to care for the poor in Italian cities in the 15th and 16th centuries. Merchants' activities were deeply interwoven with the civil, political, and above all religious life of their times, such that the motives that drove them in business were much more complex than just maximizing profit. In the modern era the *cooperative movement* that developed, particularly in Europe, was and still is today a great non-capitalist economic experiment, since the motive behind this form of enterprise is not profit, but rather mutuality, through which the needs of its members and the community are met (particularly in the so-called "social cooperation" movement that emerged in Italy in the early 1970s). The non-capitalist nature of cooperatives is not limited to its different motives or non-monetary purposes; rather, it is expressed in its democratic and pluralist governance. The principle of "one person, one vote," for example, is very different from that of capitalist companies, in which voting is on the basis of the share of capital each stockholder owns, or "one share, one vote."

From a certain point of view, over the last three centuries the Western economic system has freed itself from its religious and symbolic presuppositions, and companies have increasingly concentrated their focus on maximizing profit, which has brought about the capitalist economic system. In capitalist economies, however, it is still true that most companies even today pursue various goals, not just profit, despite the fact that most economics textbooks continue to state that the sole goal of the firm is maximizing profit. When family or small to medium firms (which are the vast majority of companies in all Western countries, particularly in Italy) engage in the market,

The Microeconomics of Wellbeing and Sustainability. https://doi.org/10.1016/B978-0-12-816027-5.00010-0

they act in a complex web of social, community, and political motivations, and not solely in the pursuit of individual profit.

An overly simplistic and summary way of expressing this diversity of relationships to profit, or money, is to distinguish between for-profit companies (the vast majority) and non-profit companies, which are normally considered the exceptions that prove the rule. We do not believe this is a good way of viewing contemporary economic reality; that is why we will develop a different approach in this chapter.

There has been vast theoretical reflection produced in recent years on the phenomenon of non-profits, and here is certainly not the place to give an account of the broad range of such studies. Most of the contributions analyze the phenomenon within so-called *market or government failures*. The problem from which economic theory starts to approach non-profits is to understand how such strange creatures, whose main goal is not to maximize profit, can survive in a market that is increasingly global and competitive. Most of the studies on non-profits assume that consumers are indifferent about the source of products (whether State-owned enterprises, private for-profits, or private non-profits) and *ceteris paribus*, they chose the good offered at a lower market price.

This methodological premise assumes that consumers do not take the source of the good or service into account when choosing, but only the best combination of price and quality. In other words, in healthcare, education, and grocery shopping, when consumers choose products, they consider the *motives* behind the business to be irrelevant. This raises a problem of identifying a criterion for deciding whether to entrust a particular good or service to the State, to the market, or to non-profits, since there are no business activities that should intrinsically be provided by the market, the State, or the non-profit sector. Economic theory has developed several models to make such choices that are generally associated with market failures (see Chapter 8). The classic cases of market failures are due to public goods, asymmetric information, and externalities. In particular, in order for the efficiency hypothesized by neo-classical economics to be attained, agents must have perfect information regarding prices and product characteristics. In some types of exchange these assumptions are not met, and there is significant *information asymmetry* among the parties. A typical example is what often happens in healthcare, in which the patient almost always has an *information deficit* with respect to the doctor. For example, the patient does not normally have the means to judge whether one therapy is objectively better than another, whether a drug will work or not, and so on. In these types of situations the market price system does not guarantee an efficient allocation of resources, because the prices for goods do not reflect consumers' marginal utility and/or producers' marginal productivity; here too the market "fails." Some theorists state that in the presence of deep information asymmetry consumers prefer to rely on non-profits, which offer greater guarantees than for-profit firms.

However, that raises the following questions: Why do non-profits work better than the government when there are market failures? Should not the State be able to offer greater guarantees than non-profits? Why are non-profits alone efficient when there is information asymmetry or public goods? The answer frequently given is that non-profits can more readily find information than the State or for-profits. The *costs of finding information* are lower in a network of informal relationships, such as those that develop in non-profits; people tend to reveal their preferences more clearly when they think they will not be used for monetary purposes. In our view such a justification for the presence and role of non-profits is too weak. We can draw a few conclusions from the preceding discussion. The more an economy is affected by market or government failures, the greater the role of non-profits. An economy in which the market and government functioned perfectly would have no need of non-profits, because market mechanisms would resolve all economic problems. It is immediately clear that this argument does not satisfy us.

10.2 Beyond the third sector and non-profits

The usual divisions between non-profits and for-profits, or between the first, second, and third sectors, conceal very precise cultural views of what the firm, profit, and the market are. For example, consider the Third Sector. What do we mean by "Third Sector"? Prior to the post-modern turn (which happened in the West during the last two or three decades of the 20th century, when a process accelerated that had started in modernity itself), Europe, and through its influence many other democratic regimes in the world, had implemented the dual family—State model for care and assistance. The family took care of much of the task of caring for children, the elderly, and the sick. When problems arose that were too burdensome or complicated, or in cases of poverty or the failure or absence of the family, the State intervened with hospitals, schools, nursing homes, and so forth.

The welfare state is based on this model; it in turn was the replacement for the pre-modern model founded on the family—community division, when the community existed but there was no State, or it was too weak. As did many other states with a Catholic cultural background, such as Spain, France and South America, Italy had developed a hybrid or three-part model of family—community—church. In the absence of the State the church took care of the poor and sick, creating complex systems of care, thanks especially to its many social charisms in people such as Vincent de Paul, Cottolengo, Francesca Cabrini, and Don Bosco. In many contexts these systems created the conditions for the development of the social State between the 19th and 20th centuries.

In these countries the social model of the State emerged from crises in the community and the church. With the emergence of the market economy, the community atomized and transformed into "society." With the development of the liberal secular State, many of the church's social works were dismantled and appropriated, and the State replaced the church, first in education and then in healthcare. This was a gradual process of substitution that reached its pinnacle in the second half of the 20th century.

The model of the "third" sector emerged from a new twofold crisis, this time with the traditional family (which tends to be hierarchical and unequal) on one hand, and the State on the other. Following the significant feminist movements, and with changes in lifestyles increasingly centered around individual rights and desires, the family could no longer carry out many traditional care services for children, the elderly, and the disabled. Partly due to a legitimate request for subsidiarity by civil society, but primarily due to the unsustainability of costs, the State could no longer satisfy the new needs for social care and assistance. The Third Sector emerged in response to the vacuum created by the retreat of the State and the family.

Despite a rich civil history of cooperative movements, mutuality, fraternal organizations, associations, and intermediate organizations, by the end of the 20th century in a certain sense it was necessary to reinvent civil society in order to respond to new needs.

"Third Sector" is an expression that emerged in the Anglo-American world, and it indicates a clear vision of the economy and society. The sector that provides services in care, workforce reintegration, social cooperation, as well as NGOs and associations, are neither a "state" (and so far so good, since these organizations are comprised of private individuals, although they work in close relation with the public administration) nor a "market," thus they are a "third" sector. The **social economy** (a synonymous expression), or the **private—social economy**, is thus considered a well-defined area of the economy; just as there are transportation, tourism, and art sectors, there is a sector in which there are people who provide care, assistance, and social services. Even *voluntarism* (see Frame 10.1) is normally considered part of the social economy. However, compared with other sectors in the economy, the world of social services is called a "third" sector because it lies *between* the State and the market. This "thirdness" thus implies the idea that the *market* is something very specific, and above all different from the *social* dimension. Indeed, for such an ideological vision the market is synonymous with personal interest, and the firm is an entity that can only aim at maximizing profits; as a consequence of this view, people who are motivated by other social, relational, values-based, or symbolic passions *cannot* launch companies, much less be agents in the market. But all that is simply a cultural impossibility that contributes to feeding a partial and ideological theory of economic agents in civil society.

That is why these are also called "no profit" organizations, while organizations whose goal is profit are considered normal. According to this vision, which we call the "Anglo-American" view of the firm and the market, the purpose of a company is to maximize profit, and everything else is either a

---

FRAME 10.1 The definition of a social enterprise according to the European EMES network

A social enterprise is an entity that:
1. is independent of the public administration and other private entities;
2. carries out production according to entrepreneurial principles, such as continuity, sustainability, and quality;
3. in difference with conventional enterprises, pursues an explicit social purpose that produces direct benefits for an entire community or disadvantaged people;
4. excludes seeking the maximum profit for those who hold the risk capital; rather, it is prompt to seek a balance between a just compensation for at least some of its productive factors and the possible benefits for those who use the goods or services produced.

It is thus an enterprise that can involve several types of stakeholders in its ownership and management, from volunteers to financiers, that maintains strong ties with the territorial community where it operates, and that draws the resources it needs from money and labor donations based on its recognized merit, as well as from the market and private demand.

According to data in the *2009 Social Enterprise Report* produced by the Iris Network, there are 15,000 social enterprises in Italy, with 350,000 employees, 10 billion euros turnover, and around 10 million users. This is a sector that could still grow significantly. According to the ISTAT estimations, there are 500,000 companies (11% of the total) and 1.5 million employees (8.1% of total employment) that operate in sectors such as healthcare, social assistance, culture, sports, and recreation, areas of activity that are particularly promising for starting new entrepreneurial initiatives with a social purpose.

---

means or a constraint. The goal is to maximize profit, and being subject to certain social constraints, whether legislative, fiscal, or civil, is a price to pay to achieve profits. From this typically Anglo-American perspective, there is nothing intrinsic in the for-profit firm; reputation, social responsibility, attention to the environment, and so on are not sought because they have value in themselves, but because they are part of a medium to long-run profit orientation. The civil economy tradition has much to say on these topics that is very different.

10.3 Social firms and civil firms

Those observing the relationship between the economy and society today are aware that a more mature civil society does not ask companies to simply produce wealth, make low-cost quality products, pay taxes, and respect the law; it also asks them to take on tasks that until a few years ago were considered the responsibility of the State, churches, or the family. On the other hand, civil society is asked to become efficient in ways that public opinion did not previously consider to be among its tasks. Citizens want the human relationships concealed behind products to be brought to light so the rational kernel within the mystical shell may be *revealed*, in Marx's expression.

This demand for the relationships underlying the market to become visible again is eminently met by many social economy experiences, such as fair trade, but the phenomenon is even more widespread than that. For example, we find it in the strong tendency to reduce the supply chain for food products, as well as in banking and finance. Citizens today require greater social responsibility from the economy and from themselves.

This process began in the 1950s, but only in recent times — partly due to the strong impetus of the global environmental crisis — has it surpassed a critical point and reached the general public and political institutions. The phenomenon is thus diverse and multi-faceted, more so than is evident from the increasingly abundant literature on the topic. A first macroscopic element from which to begin an analysis of this phenomenon is the progressive process of convergence toward the center. On one hand companies formed within the liberal, capitalist tradition, under pressure from consumer movements, have started paying attention to social aspects; on the other, associations formed with a clear social vocation feel the need today to become companies and face typical market dynamics head-on.

The term **social enterprise** (which in the 20th century many labor experts considered simply an oxymoron) well summarizes this encounter between these two organizational cultures, which — as we will see — actually originate from and trace back to visions of the market and society that are quite far apart. This is a phenomenon that encompasses two distinct traditions: capitalist enterprises that move into the social sector, and social organizations that become companies.

However, first consider a preliminary question: Are we certain that *socially responsible companies* (which we will consider in depth in Chapter 11) are a new reality in today's economic and social panorama? Or instead, as many critics think, when we talk about a socially responsible company today are we only saying something obvious or banal, or in any case nothing new? Indeed, some authors think that the firm as an institution has always been socially responsible, since it was conceived and developed within the social realities of laws, people, and rules of the game to be respected. This criticism is similar to the criticism regarding the "novelty" of globalization: The market economy, it is said, emerged with a natural vocation to globalization, and what we are seeing now is nothing more than the evolution of an ancient process, so there is nothing really new about it. The novelty would instead be essentially technological or quantitative, not cultural or qualitative.

In fact, if we look at the history of capitalism from the 19th century — if we do not want to actually go back to markets in medieval times or the late Roman Empire — perhaps we might take the critics' side. Many entrepreneurs and merchants took care of non-economic or social aspects as part of their business. Consider the large enterprises that emerged between the 19th and 20th centuries that took an interest in housing for their workers, schools for their children, summer camps, and that built churches, study centers, and football fields. Italian capitalism includes hundreds of moments that are both new and old in corporate social responsibility (or CSR), as well as social entrepreneurs, from Rossi in Vicenza to Olivetti in Ivrea; in the 20th century even Fiat and Pirelli took on social roles that were outside the economic sphere alone.

Actually, there is an important difference between the old and the new forms of corporate responsibility. The social actions of early industrial capitalism, or the large Ford-era enterprises, started primarily from the top down; the company owner was the one who, *if* and *when* he wanted, somewhat paternalistically bestowed services on his workers that went beyond their salaries. Thus his own personal moral convictions were what drove him to take care of social aspects — or in other cases, the fear of a socialist revolution. Today the process is essentially bottom-up; the CSR movement today does not *primarily* emerge from shareholders' or managers' initiatives, but in response to pressure that originates in civil society and is directed toward companies. While early "paternalistic" capitalism was a process within firms (that is, between workers and owners, frequently with the mediation of trade unions) whose sole interlocutor was the State and the law, today the social responsibility of companies originates from outside; citizens protest about companies well before and independently of companies' workers or employees.

The **environmental issue** is undoubtedly the starting point that triggered a process that is now invading a growing number of social areas, including rights, democracy, and social justice. In the current CSR debate high emphasis is placed on the self-regulation and free initiative of managers and owners to engage socially responsible processes, processes that are not and cannot be imposed by law. This remains a controversial topic, since there is a dialectic relationship between free initiative and legal obligation. But if we look at what normally happens in responsible companies, especially the large ones, they develop socially responsible practices perhaps in anticipation of or as a response to external pressures.

In order to grasp the real innovations within the CSR movement we need to look for them in depth, particularly in a radical change happening in how modernity understands the relationship between the economic and the civil.

We have already said that the CSR phenomenon, especially in Europe, is a result of crises in the social welfare State and the family (and more generally in the community), in that the State is withdrawing from social dimensions and the traditional family is no longer able to provide care services. While this twofold movement has produced a new phase of lively engagement in civil society in Italy in the last 30 years, it has also created a vacuum that today is

---

FRAME 10.2 Sports as a relational good

To go straight to the point we will begin with sports. This is a less demanding topic than care services, and it will help us easily approach the topic of this chapter. In traditional society playing or "producing" sports, or watching or "consuming" sports, were essentially relational goods; social relationships were produced and consumed. Even when buying a ticket, going to the stadium is not buying a normal market product. Sports today are less and less relational and more and more a standard market good that is produced and consumed by the normal rules of the market. For example, watching a game at home on cable is no longer a relational good. What are the medium to long-run consequences of this? The day when everyone watches a soccer game from home and no one, or too few, goes to the stadium, the good the market will offer is the dismal and unsustainable spectacle of watching a game behind closed doors (with the bleachers filled with cutouts for a pretend public), which would spell the end of soccer. The market must make sure such a result is never attained in sports and in the various areas of economic and civil life.

---

increasingly occupied by social enterprises that go into care services, education, healthcare, sport, and so forth (see Frame 10.2). But if companies are entering these areas, this immediately raises the question: Can the traditional logic of the firm — that of seeking profits within constraints — be sufficient to make the firm a "responsible" institution that is a "friend of society," one to which dimensions of life well beyond the economic dimension can be entrusted?

To a first approximation, from the perspective of the civil economy we could summarize a company's responsibility as follows: *for a firm to be socially responsible means it must know how to recognize that there are passions, ideals, and human relationships that are not commodities and cannot be reduced to commodities.*

For example, a soccer policy that is too interested in television rights and less interested in getting people to the stadiums (perhaps by reducing prices and making them safer) is a short-sighted policy. But if the mass media show only the "evils" in the stadiums, highlighting only its "costs" (the violence and risks) rather than its "benefits" (relationships and being with others with the same passions), they do a disservice to the sport, the economy, and in the long run to society. Such reductionism should certainly be avoided for the common good, but also for the good of the firm.

A civilly responsible enterprise is a company that knows when to stop itself at the right point in the process of transforming relationships, human passions, and relational goods into commodities, a process that is inexorable in market societies today. It is a company that knows and learns that without gratuitousness the company itself will implode, because its gratuitousness, its passions and ideals, are where the market, wealth, and profit are regenerated. Gratuitousness is the stem cell of what it means to be human in all areas of life. Obviously the civil sustainability of economic development and the company itself is not just the responsibility of the business world. Businesses have their specific responsibility, but civil institutions, citizens, and the media also have their responsibilities. An economic world that loses contact with gratuitousness has no future as an *economy*. Why? The main reason is that it no longer attracts lofty vocations. If a company becomes merely a business and leaves its passions at the door it will attract people of low relational and human quality, and thus bad managers and workers. Profit and money as incentives are too weak to motivate people's highest and most powerful energies. When we respond only to monetary incentives, liberty has already been reduced to something of little value—if it is true that only where there is true gratuitousness is there true liberty. This is why good firms that value ideals, passions, and gratuitousness are important, in that they increase personal and collective liberty. Liberty can neither be produced nor purchased, but all wealth emerges from it: "I tell you that virtue is not given by money, but that from virtue come money and every other good of man, public as well as private" (Plato, *Socrates' Apology*).

10.4 The nature of the capitalist enterprise

In this section we will consider how the modern political economy views the firm. To do that we will dwell on one specific central aspect of CSR, which is the important process of democratizing or "flattening" the governance of the firm; this is certainly one of the places where the CSR debate is most lively and relevant. This process conceals another mediator (in addition to the price mechanism) that modern economics invented to manage the ambivalence of human relationships and being hurt by others: the **hierarchy**.

A strong contradiction exists today within liberal capitalist economics and within the current CSR tradition that arose from it, which we can formulate in these terms: Despite the fact that modern economics is deeply linked to the principles of equality and liberty, why is the firm — the economy's primary institution — built on the principle of hierarchy, which was the main pillar of the feudal world that the market wanted to bring down? In responding to this question we will identify the principal features of the two traditions that energize the CSR movement today.

In its basic structure, Western pre-modern society was an *unequal society* in which relationships were primarily vertical rather than horizontal, because they were based on the centrality of the hierarchical principle. When a society is based on the principle of hierarchy the principle of equality is inactive, since hierarchy is the opposite concept of equality.

But what is a hierarchy?

The anthropologist and philosopher Louis Dumont, a student of Marcel Mauss, a theoretician who studied the nature of gifts, dedicated much of his work to studying hierarchical societies (Indian societies in particular) in comparison to modern egalitarian societies. He defined hierarchy as "a ladder of *command* in which the lower rungs are encompassed in the higher ones in regular succession" (Dumont, 1980, 65, emphasis original). The original meaning of the word and of the concept is religious in nature. The Hindu castes in India or the Catholic Church are ideal places to observe in order to understand the essence of a hierarchy. There is a close tie between hierarchy and *liturgy* (and its related initiation rites), which becomes the means by which the hierarchy carries out its role of transmitting spiritual goods from the higher to the lower ranks. This hierarchical structure of the world establishes an absolute relationship between the ranks of the hierarchy, such that the lower levels cannot have access to the highest order except through the intermediary just above them. The lowest orders (the laity, for example) can have contact with God only through the mediation of their superiors. The only way to come into contact with spiritual goods is through the successive mediation of the higher orders.

Now we will turn to the role of a hierarchy in capitalist firms.

"Hierarchy" and "authority" are logically distinguishable concepts (although various authors use the terms in very different ways from one another). No organization can function without a principle and a practice of authority, while a hierarchy is just one particular *form* for exercising authority. A hierarchy is a formal mechanism for exercising **authority** that is typical of a social system characterized by "superior" and "inferior" people or officials, who thus are not "equals." In particular, power is the ability to obtain behavior from another without his consent, and authority is the legitimate power that is recognized as such by those involved. A hierarchy in itself does not entail sharing power. For Max Weber, whose theory of authority remains an unsurpassed reference point even today, power includes "the probability that one actor in a social relationship will be in a position to carry out his own will despite resistance, regardless of the basis on which this probability rests" (Weber, 1980, p. 53). Authority, on the other hand, consists in "the probability that certain specific commands (or all commands) will be obeyed by a given group of persons" (Weber, 1980, p. 212) (Frame 10.3).

Authority needs a basis for legitimacy, which in Weber's theory can be charismatic, traditional, or legal. A large enterprise resorts to legal authority, which is why it makes use of a bureaucratic administrative structure, and thus it needs the hierarchy. This is why the legal authority of large bureaucratic enterprises is not substantially different from the authority typical of military societies (Frame 10.4).

In smaller firms and organizations that are characterized by personal relationships, legal authority alone is not enough to manage relationships. We know for example that one of the secrets of success of small and medium

FRAME 10.3 Hierarchy

For Dumont, hierarchical societies have three characteristics that are theoretically distinguishable, but that appear together in actual societies. They are:

society is ordered by castes, groups, or classes;

there are detailed rules to ensure the separation of the various classes;

there is a strong division of labor and an interdependence that derives from it.

So what we see is an interesting tension between separation and interdependence as the basis for every hierarchical society. Dumont makes the highly important point that these three elements can all be traced back to a radical pure—impure distinction, which is essential and basic in all traditional Indian culture: the more pure the person, the higher she is on the hierarchical scale. What do pure and impure mean in a caste culture and in ancient traditional cultures (such as Jewish, Greek, and so on) in which we find several constants regarding impurity? The pure—impure pair is a means for managing the fear and risk of contagion from the other. The word "caste," introduced by the Portuguese in the 16th century, means "unmixed." There are many variants in the caste system, from the five basic Indian castes to the myriad sub-castes divided by occupation and role, but there is one constant: the two classes at the opposite poles of society, the Brahmin and the Untouchables (the pariahs), the highest and lowest, between which all the others are located. As Dumont stated, purity and its opposite, contamination, constitute the foundation of the hierarchy (pure is superior to impure), its separation (pure and impure must remain separated), and the division of labor (the inferior serve the superior). The risk of contamination is thus a threat to the caste system itself and its social order. According to Dumont, hierarchical societies (or caste societies —for Dumont a caste society is the archetype of every hierarchical society) are holistic (the group is what exists and counts, not the individual members of the group), while egalitarian societies are individualistic (groups have value only if created and chosen freely by individuals). The individual is "born" only when he exits the caste system by becoming *samnyasin,* or an ascetic. There are thus strong similarities between the caste system and a capitalist enterprise.

companies is precisely in their "charism" and the authority that charism imparts to the founding entrepreneur (this is why the process of inter-generational change is always delicate in such organizations). In some organizations that have a high rate of horizontal participation, such as associations and cooperatives, authority must have a different basis than Weber's three bases, one that is more consonant with democratic practices in which the community holds the authority and delegates it to its representatives.

The enterprise hierarchy is also based on the need to make rapid, efficient choices; this is similar to a ship navigating difficult waters, in that without a hierarchy it does not move ahead and sinks. In emergencies, participation in choices is a cost that can become too high and unsustainable. However, we are convinced that if we want to understand the function of the hierarchy in

FRAME 10.4 John Stuart Mill and cooperation

John Stuart Mill was the first economist to emphasize this ambiguity of market versus enterprise in modernity, stating that in the liberal society of his time two important institutions of the feudal world remained, the capitalist enterprise and the family, both of which had survived the commercial society revolution. This was the reason for the later Mill's sympathy for the cooperative movement (which in the last years of his life, thanks in part to the influence of his future wife, Harriet Taylor, became true enthusiasm); Mill and other contemporary English economists, John Elliot Cairnes in particular, saw this as a necessary social and cultural process to make productive organizations more fraternal and egalitarian. Mill's fight for women's suffrage to create equality and liberty within the family came from this insight. This is the message of his wonderful book *The Subjection of Women* (1869): "the only school of genuine moral sentiment is society between equals. ... The moral training of mankind will never be adapted to the conditions of the life for which all other human progress is a preparation, until they practice in the family the same moral rule which is adapted to the normal constitution of human society" (Mill, 1976) In fact, for Mill the capacity for cooperation and a dedication to reciprocity are the basic anthropological characteristics that make possible both family and social life: "The peculiar characteristic, in short, of civilized beings, is the capacity of co-operation; and this, like other faculties, tends to improve by practice, and becomes capable of assuming a constantly wider sphere of action" (Mill, 2006). This was the anthropological basis for his well-known prophecy about the future of the capitalist enterprise: "Accordingly there is no more certain incident of the progressive change taking place in society, than the continual growth of the principle and practice of cooperation" (Mill, 2006). From this we can develop a more general historical reflection. Liberal thought within the British liberal economic tradition in the second half of the nineteenth century had begun a process that aimed to extend the same anti-feudal revolution to the internal governance of the enterprise that markets were accomplishing outside the corporation. This endogenous process of the democratization of the enterprise, along lines that were markedly different from the parallel French movement, came to a halt when confronted with the radical shift in socialist thought. Authors such as Mill, and to varying degrees Alfred Marshall and the British school of political economy (particularly the Cambridge school), had imagined a socialist path for the company, which should accept the need for the horizontal and participatory structure of the cooperative culture, including in its profits. However, this process ceased in the early twentieth century, partly due to the radical, revolutionary drift in the socialist and communist movements. The fear of a socialist or communist shift has thus contributed toward blocking the process of the natural socialization of the traditional enterprise, which could lead to the internal evolution of a market economy. Democratizing the company became synonymous with non-liberal cultures; it is thus no accident that the debate on corporate social responsibility within the capitalist world only resumed (or at least reached critical mass) after the collapse of the Soviet system.

capitalist enterprises, the "ship" metaphor is less central than an "immunity" metaphor and the pure—impure pairing.

So here we have come to a first conclusion that is of some importance.

From a certain point of view, there exists a close continuity between a large capitalist enterprise and the market: both see themselves as surpassing the *communitas* toward *immunitas*, because both the bureaucratic hierarchy and the spontaneous coordination of prices function without having to enter the dangerous territory of a face-to-face relationship with a personal "Thou." Both the capitalist firm and the market are two systems to avoid being wounded by the other; as we shall see, this too is in radical difference with the civil cooperative tradition.

Apart from this perspective it is not easy to understand why a capitalist enterprise, the fundamental institution of the market economy, was based, and in many ways is still based today, on the primacy of the hierarchical principle: The hierarchy is instrumental in guaranteeing the same immunizing effect as the mediation of the market.

10.5 The Paradox of the capitalist enterprise

While economic theorists argued that market relationships are horizontal, free, and symmetrical, requiring no recourse to hierarchical principles (except for an external mediating authority to guarantee property rights and enforce contracts), the modern capitalist enterprise instead stands out as a hierarchical community. The market mechanism certainly needs authority as well, but its nature and structure are different; beyond the two parties, between whom the hierarchical principle does not operate, there is an external judge; the presence of this judge, whose presence guarantees effective enforcement, means that contracts and agreements can be drawn up. The absence of authority and enforcement would lead to inefficient outcomes; in fact we know from game theory that cooperation emerges when there is an effective enforcement system. However, it is not the hierarchical principle that is at work but the principle of authority, which is external to the parties involved in the contract.

The economist Luigi Zingales wrote:

> *The term governance is synonymous with the exercise of authority, direction and control. These words, however, seem strange when used in the context of a free-market economy. Why do we need any form of authority? Isn't the market responsible for allocating all resources efficiently without the intervention of authority?*

> Zingales and Luigi (1998)

Marx immediately grasped the profound asymmetry — and thus the real lack of freedom and equality — in the capital—labor relationship within the capitalist enterprise, which he saw as emblematic of every exploitative relationship. We should note however that market relations are not necessarily exploitative, although it is also true that they are not always encounters between peers.

In his classic 1937 article *The Nature of the Firm*, Ronald H. Coase showed that the market and the corporation are two alternative institutions, one based on the principle of the contract (and therefore on the system of prices) and the other, essentially, on the hierarchical principle, or on the system of control. A company forms and develops on the basis of empirical and theoretical evidence that, due to transaction costs, the market is a costly mechanism. It is not always efficient in managing complex, necessarily incomplete relationships, and above all those that endure over time. Hierarchy and control have their own costs: moral hazard, adverse selection, and free riding are all costs linked to the distrust inherent in the hierarchical principle, unless it is balanced by other principles. In a hypothetical world of complete contracts, at the limit we could even do away with the institution of the corporation (were it relatively more expensive), leaving just the market. But complete contracts do not in fact exist in relationships within organizations.

In difference with a contract, which is based on a principle of exchange between peers, the hierarchical mechanism has an asymmetric structure: There is a "principal" and an "agent." It is no accident that agency theory is still the theoretical model for organizations most used by economists. The principle that governs the relationship between the principal (the company) and the agent (the manager, for example) is a "hierarchical contract," an oxymoron that in one phrase states two things that in classical thought could not logically exist together: what binds the manager to the firm or property is a contract, but the relationship is asymmetrical and subject to the hierarchical principle. The same holds true in the internal relations between managers and employees: within very broad limits set by contract, the hierarchy governs ordinary relationships *within* the organization.

Organizations also work with other forms of relationships, such as those that develop over time and can be represented as "repeated games" (which allow various forms of cooperation) or the effects of reputation. However, the hierarchical principle still remains central to the concrete reality of capitalist enterprises, including the fundamental role that shareholders have with respect to other stakeholders. Certainly those who interpret the company as the result of a social contract between stakeholders do not want to deny the centrality of the hierarchical principle in governance. This is the approach of economists who try to interpret the company on the basis of John Rawls' theory of justice: The company is a little society whose members (the stakeholders) enter into a social contract behind a veil of ignorance.

The modern capitalist enterprise is thus constructed on the hierarchical model (partly because it emerged in the pre-modern era) in imitation of a military society, the Church, or the society of the *ancien régime*. Consequently it is not in tune with the flattening inherent in the market that is required for it to function efficiently. The reason is that the hierarchy ensures a common life based on *immunitas*, just as the anonymous market does.

All personnel economic theory and agency theory are worthy attempts to foresee, mitigate, and minimize the "wounds" we inflict on each other in face to face encounters, exactly as in market theory.

The CSR movement also developed with the intent of unlinking this paradoxical dualism between the company and the market, but — and this is the point — without calling *immunitas* into question. On a cultural level it perfectly succeeds: the market/business, equality/hierarchy, and horizontal/vertical dualities go hand in hand with a consistent, well-oriented goal of mediating the I-Thou relationship.

This is a process entirely within the liberal tradition of classical political economy, and the British tradition in particular.

In Chapter 11 we will consider a question that emerges naturally from what we have discussed so far: Is CSR the *only possible* socially responsible business culture?

10.6 From the market to the company, from the company to the market

The civil economy conceives of the market as a large scale cooperative operation. Cooperation, collaboration, and mutual assistance are what comprise the basic characteristics of the market culture in this thought tradition, rather than competition and greed.

In this ancient tradition the market is a way of properly compensating the virtues, rewarding human cooperation, and thus creating the common good; it is critical of and in polemic with the human relationships that were typical of the feudal world. In the 18th century there was no theoretical reflection on the firm, but when the topics of the firm and of entrepreneurs became central in the 19th and 20th centuries, the civil economy tradition gave a great deal of attention to cooperation and cooperative enterprises, which were seen as a means for cooperating, just as in the market.

The current CSR debate expresses and incorporates all these old cultural tensions.

As we have already noted, the tradition originating from Smith, the founder of the theory, rests its theoretical underpinnings on separating the market from society and on market exchange as based on self-interest and *immunitas*; that is, the company is seen as a small *societas*. Instead, the civil economy denies the need to separate the market from society, since it sees the economic sphere as a place to exercise the civil virtues and reciprocity as a foundational principle in economics as well; the company is seen as a little *communitas*.

These different principles endure even today in the two cultures of social responsibility under discussion.

The liberal-capitalist tradition starts from the market based on the contract, seen as the locus of civilization because it is based on horizontal and symmetrical relationships, and imports the virtuous, horizontal, contractual, anonymous, and impersonal relationality of the market into the firm. In this sense it leaves *communitas* to move toward *societas*.

The tradition of the social-cooperative economy does exactly the opposite: it starts from cooperation and from associations based on the principle of reciprocity, understood as communities composed of equal persons in solidarity with each other, and it seeks to export the virtuous sociality of the cooperative into the market and the civil society, to "commonize" the market and the civil society.

The basic tendency of the CSR movement in liberal capitalist culture is to extend the contract, the typical instrument of the market, into the company; this is the basic idea of those today who see the company as a multistakeholder liberal society arising from a Rawlsian social contract under a veil of ignorance. The entry of the contract — the sole truly civil, egalitarian, and modern form of relationality, because it is based on free consent — into the company complicates and undermines the centrality of the hierarchy. In general, all of stakeholder theory (which not by chance is of North American origin) moves exactly in this direction.

The social-cooperative tradition has instead sought to democratize the operation of the market by utilizing, for example, the principle of redistribution (the tax system of the European welfare states) to realign the starting points of market contracts; the market is not seen as a naturally free and equal environment, but rather as based on asymmetrical relations of power, exactly as in the capitalist firm. With this we can understand how for this cultural tradition there is no substantial contradiction between the market and the company, as is typical of the liberal tradition. Rather, the only form of good, civilized production is cooperative and associational.

The typical cultural products of this tradition are the welfare state at the level of both society and the market, and trade unions at the level of the capitalist enterprise. Both of these are expressions of the intent to obstruct and correct the unjust social relationships concealed in capitalist market relationships, both inside and outside the firm,[1] as well as to address the "hand-to-hand combat" of a painful one-on-one mediation (as was, and still is to some extent, typical of mediation by trade unions).

The relationship between trade unions and businesses, for example, is not primarily contractual, but in the language of Albert O. Hirschman (1970), of

---

1. Actually, the emergence of the welfare state has a more complex history. It is not just the result of cooperative reflection, but of the action of Christian social charisms, the German debate on the social market economy, and English socialism (in which Mill's thought carried great weight). The fact remains that the European cooperative experience had a significant role in the design and development of the twentieth century welfare state.

voice, or protest, that traditionally is typically a tool used in politics rather than in the market economy (Crivelli, 2009). In other words, where it could the civil economic tradition (which in this aspect is in league with the social economy tradition) sought to create solidarity-based egalitarian organizations, such as cooperatives, associations, and so forth. With regard to the market and the capitalist firm, it sought to restrain their operation by inserting elements such as taxation and unions, which are typically political, into capitalism. The social state emerges from the social critique of capitalism, both from its starting points and the failure of the logic of the contract, rather than from an internal development within capitalism itself, as happened with philanthropy (which, not by chance, is typical of the North American model).

The development of the cooperative movement in consumption on one hand, and in savings on the other, is exactly the expression of a cultural action plan designed to bring cooperation into the market and the economy in the three macro areas of production, consumption and savings. The theorists of the cooperative movement envisioned an entire economic system based on the principles of cooperation and association: here it still retains its prophetic voice, though also the fragility of a construction that is too large and complex.

10.7 For-profit and for-project firms

We are approaching the conclusion of this chapter, so we will attempt to summarize the discussion to this point by comparing corporate social responsibility, or CSR, with corporate civil responsibility, or CCI, which is a comparison that goes beyond the firm alone as an institution.

With a simple (and simplified) diagram we will try to represent the standard U.S. or capitalist model, as we have called it, of corporate social responsibility as follows:

(a) the objective function, or purpose, of a for-profit firm is to maximize profit (Π);

(b) the main (although not the only) constraint that a firm must respect in maximizing profit is to attain certain standards of social, environmental, and labor responsibility and minimum ethical standards (S) to satisfy the stakeholders who are not shareholders.

With the usual geometric language of microeconomics we can draw Fig. 10.1, where a company uses its own production factors (X,Y: labor, capital, technology, knowledge, and so on) to maximize profit under a social responsibility constraint.

In this standard case the objective function of the firm is profitΠ, which is given by the indifference curves; the constraint (the line in the graph) is its social responsibility, such as paying taxes, respecting the law, and having good relationships with civil society and trade unions.

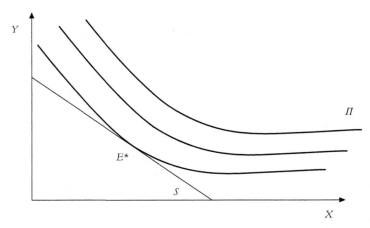

FIG. 10.1 **CSR.** *Note:* The goal of the "standard" firm (indicated by the indifference curves) is to maximize profit (Π) within a social constraint.

The main goal of this firm is to satisfy a particular stakeholder (the shareholders), and the main interests of the other stakeholders are *constraints*. So if the price of social responsibility drops (perhaps because it relocates to less socially demanding countries), the set of possibilities expands and profits increase.

Obviously, the literature and history tell us that the goal of real for-profit companies is more complex and other variables are involved, such as the reputation of managers. The fact remains however that social responsibility is not normally a purpose or an intrinsic value of business, but rather is understood as an external constraint; this is all within the Smithian tradition that sees the market as a place for legitimate self-interests, but not of full sociality.

> *If instead we want to represent the idea of the civil responsibility of a firm, we could simply invert the discourse:*
>
> *the goal of a company is to develop and implement a project over time;*
>
> *economic and efficiency conditions are constraints to be respected. Profit is a signal that the project is working, and efficiency is seen as ethical behavior, because in a world in which resources are scarce, efficiency has a moral component.*
>
> *In Fig. 10.2, the objective function is now the growth and development of the project (the indifference curves), while the constraint (the straight line) is economic efficiency.*

This is how the civil economy tradition sees the firm and the market. Each company can be understood as a "project company," or as a "for-project"

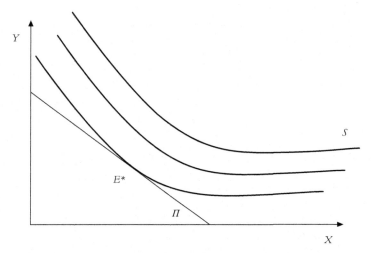

FIG. 10.2   CSR. *Note:* Now the indifference curves represent the project, and the line represents the efficiency constraint.

company, and efficiency and economic performance are signals that the project is working and constraints that must be respected if the project is to develop and be sustainable over time.

Furthermore, only from this theoretical perspective can we legitimately state that a non-profit enterprise (in ordinary language) is truly a company, even though it is social or civil: It is a company because it proposes to develop a project under an efficiency constraint.

A hospital, school, or museum can be **civil enterprises**, since their purpose is not to make money but to heal the sick, educate and train, or promote an artistic culture while operating in the market under efficiency constraints. But even an artisan is a civil entrepreneur if her purpose is not to make profits selling violins, but to make violins within a budget constraint that allows her to make a decent living. In the same way, a social cooperative, an operation supported by a religious order, a company in the Economy of Communion, an ethical or a cooperative bank, or a fair trade project are civil entrepreneurs.

A bank, for example, should eminently be a civil enterprise, since we should not think that the purpose of a bank should be to earn profits for its shareholders (and with other people's money). Is not the radical and generalized transformation of banks into speculators one of the foremost causes of the economic crisis in our time?

The economist M. Yunus — a Nobel Peace laureate and the founder of the Grameen Bank, one of the most interesting financial innovations of the 20th century — has repeatedly stated that in today's market economies and complex societies *access to credit is a fundamental human right*, since without this recognized right people are not able to fulfill their own plans and escape the many traps of poverty. If this argument is true — and we are convinced it is — then speculative banks should be the exception rather than the rule in market economies, if for no other reason that the products banks manage always have a high social risk, since so many interests are at stake (among which are families' savings). This is why a banking sector that generates high profits indicates a pathological condition in a civil economic system. It is no accident that banks from the *Monti di Pietà* to cooperative banks were thought of in the civil tradition as companies whose purpose was not to earn money, because there were so many different interests they had to meet.

Banks and civil finance are institutions with high social value and high responsibility; due to the plurality of interests they must balance, they cannot be left to the risky game of maximizing shareholders' profits. The new and more thorough financial market regulations that many hope for move in the direction of recognizing that banks have a social responsibility, which has been lost in recent decades, despite an exponential growth in risk estimation tools and ratings agencies.

But we could push even further and state that all companies, beyond their fields of business and their legal forms, are *civil* if and to the extent they produce products (whether industrial, commercial, touristic, artistic, or cultural) and try to create added value while efficiently operating on the market. If they do not do this, we could simply call them *uncivil*. The only difference between a large industrial enterprise that is recognized as being in the civil economy tradition (such as Olivetti, for example) and an artisan or a social cooperative is in their organizational and technical ways of operating, not in their nature or culture.

Indeed, there are few purely speculative organizations, and above all they do not last long, as the economic crisis we are struggling to put behind us has forcefully shown us. The Swiss economist Bruno Frey has recently highlighted that the average lifespan of speculative American insurance companies and investment funds that were overrun by the financial crisis was just a few years; the medieval Benedictine abbeys in Central Europe instead endured nearly five centuries on average. If a nation's economy manages to hold up during the great crisis we are living through, it certainly will not be primarily due to the financial and speculative capitalism of the large enterprises and banks, but rather to the social fabric of small firms rooted in local territories that must struggle and innovate daily to survive; they have often inherited the implicit culture and knowledge that grew around abbeys and convents. We do not consider them to be very far from the organizations we will call VBOs in the next section.

All these considerations may seem only a matter of words; in reality it is a matter of culture, well-being, and malaise, and thus a matter of life, which we cannot avoid.

10.8 Values-based organizations (VBOs)

The so-called values-based organizations (VBOs) have a particular significance within the range of not-for-profit firms. We introduced this term in the last chapter, which today is beginning to be used to indicate organizations — such as associations, NGOs, social enterprises, companies in the Economy of Communion — whose motivational inspiration (or that at least motivated their formation) is neither primarily profit nor instrumental dimensions, but rather a values-based motive, a *mission*, or a "vocation" that in various ways originates from the intrinsic motivations of its founders. When we speak of a mission, or intrinsic motivations, or a vocation, we are also talking about *gratuitousness*, if it is true — and this is our working hypothesis — that we enter the realm of gratuitousness every time we work with behaviors that are practiced because they are good and are valuable in themselves, prior to and independently of the material results they bring about, at least in the short run.

There is no commonly agreed definition of VBOs; in general they are normally identified with religious organizations. The expressions *values-based organizations* and *mission-driven organizations* are used in the international literature to indicate VBOs. According to **Molteni (2009)**, these organizations' motivating values can take several forms. They may be in the type of activity they carry out, or in the motivations for which an organization was established (such as a company that is created to include disadvantaged people in the production process), or in the way a business is run, which regards its governance or organizational structure. In our view these characteristics must be present in a VBO, although in degrees and different combinations. For example, it is difficult to imagine values-based motivations that do not then combine with an appropriate organizational or governance structure, since the "new wine" of a values-based mission normally needs "new wineskins" that are appropriate to hold the wine so it can mature over time.

In this book we refer to VBOs as organizations that have at least three elements, one of which is linked to the organization and its members.

1. The activity an organization carries out is normally an essential part of its identity, because its activity sources from a vocation that represents its values, identity, and mission.[2] While the owners of a capitalist enterprise can normally change business fields if they deem it advantageous, a VBO is created for a specific purpose that is inextricably tied to the organization.

---

2. Here the work should be thought of in a broad sense. For a social cooperative, for example, there can be different specific activities that change over time (laundry, assembly, etc.), but by "activity" we mean the re-integration of disadvantaged workers into the workplace, which is the mission of the VBO. In other cases — religious institutions, for example — the relationship between the mission and its works is even stronger.

In other words, the activity carried out in a VBO cannot practically or logically be separated from the results it wants to achieve. *Its activity is thus integral to the purpose for which it works.*

2. The organization's identity is an essential element, although, as with any identity, it is constantly and dynamically evolving together with its environment and its history. It is not a formal or abstract factor, rather, it is deeply bound to one or more people who share, and in a certain sense embody, the "vocation" and the values of a given VBO. We will call these members, who are frequently but not necessarily the founders of the VBO, *intrinsically motivated* people.

3. These intrinsically motivated members have the characteristic of being relatively less reactive to price signals (such as salary or extra work hours) than other less motivated members, but they are more sensitive to the VBO's values; that is why they are the first to protest. They thus play the role of "guardians" of the identity and quality of the organization's values, protesting when the organization goes through a crisis.

To understand the peculiar nature of a VBO, consider what it is not. For example, it is not a speculative enterprise whose purpose is to seek profit, and whose activity is merely a means of optimizing something external and without intrinsic value that is distinct from the activity itself. Such an organization is by definition solely instrumental, in which its employees respond only to material incentives, and no particular "vocation" is asked of them beyond their technical skills and that they respect their employment contract.

When VBOs have the three characteristics we just listed, they can be NGOs, environmental, educational, or care organizations, social and civil enterprises, and cultural associations. We thus understand that not all non-profit organizations are necessarily VBOs.

The primary goal of every VBO is to evolve and grow without losing its identity, which is bound to the VBO's survival in the medium to long run.

Anyone who works in the social economy field or in organizations with a mission that goes beyond profits knows well that success and harmonious growth in such organizations depend mainly on a limited number of people (often some of the organization's founders) who play a key role because of the particular motivations that drive them; we call these "intrinsic" or values-based motivations. These people influence the organizational culture *directly* with their choices of management and rules, and, particularly important for our analysis, *indirectly* as well, through their behavior, which other less motivated people imitate. If some of these key figures leave the organization (perhaps because new management does not reflect the original values), there are often cumulative effects that can trigger a process of deteriorating values in the organization. An important safeguard against such deterioration is the loyalty of its motivated members, which can be increased by pluralistic and participative governance.

The ideal type of VBO we have in mind could be a primary school run by a religious congregation that intends to continue its activity *only if* and *while* its most motivated teachers (the nuns, for example) see that the school's quality aligns with their spirituality and charism. Another VBO example would be an environmental NGO created by a few people trying to protect several endangered bird species. When the NGO grows, it is essential that it maintain its original vocation, a vocation incorporated in a very special way in the culture of the founders and in those who particularly feel the VBO's mission to be their own.

From the perspective of the civil economy, VBOs are full-fledged companies that enrich economic and civil life by their presence in the market.

10.9 The difficult innovations of a civil enterprise

Before concluding this chapter dedicated to companies that are more complex than those motivated purely by profit, there is more we can say about the market, VBOs, and civil entrepreneurs. We begin not from a economist from the past, but from one of the classical mainstream economists, David Ricardo. In 1817 this great British economist formulated one of the first real economic theories, which is still relevant today.

In previous theory, and in mercantilism in particular, trade and exchange happened when there were "absolute" advantages. If Britain and Portugal have the following cost structure, then specialization and international trade are advantageous (Table 10.1).

Ricardo demonstrated that *even in cases where there were only "relative" advantages*, trade is *advantageous for both* (Table 10.2):

Ricardo showed us that even in a world in which Britain is more efficient than Portugal in both sectors, it can be advantageous for Britain to specialize in the sector *where is relatively the strongest (where it has a comparative advantage)*. The point is that even in this case trade with the weakest *benefits the strongest as well*. The classic example is that of a lawyer who, although she can type faster on her computer than her secretary, still has an advantage in hiring a secretary and concentrating instead on her legal work; this is the well-known concept today of "opportunity cost." Just as in the case of Britain, in hiring a secretary who is not as fast as she is the lawyer is not offering aid or

TABLE 10.1 Absolute advantages (numbers express costs).

Britain	Portugal
Cotton products: 5	Cotton products: 8
Wine: 6	Wine: 5

TABLE 10.2 Relative advantages.

Britain	Portugal
Cotton products: 5	Cotton products: 8
Wine: 6	Wine: 7

charity, rather, she and the secretary both benefit from the exchange. When the market includes the weakest and turns it into an opportunity for the common good, for the good of all and of each one, then it is playing its civilizing role.

Why is this theory significant for VBOs? Consider the important innovation of the emergence of social cooperation in Italy. Disadvantaged people who are included in companies often become opportunities for mutual benefit, even for the companies that hire them, rather than being a "cost" or an act of charity. (There is also public participation in the costs of hiring these people, which is nearly always socially efficient.) Disabled workers were essentially seen as a cost or a burden by companies and trade unions; **social cooperation** was truly innovative when ways were found for these disadvantaged workers to become a resource for companies as well.

In such cases the persons who are "helped" feel that they are in a reciprocity-based relationship, which is an expression of greater dignity. They do not feel they are being helped, but rather that they are agents in a contract that is mutually beneficial, and so they feel themselves more free and equal. Even a person affected by Down syndrome can participate in a mutually advantageous contract with a company, although it requires truly innovative abilities by civil entrepreneurs. Mutual advantage is always a possibility, but it does not happen automatically or always; it requires creativity and much more, but when it happens the market becomes a true instrument of inclusion and authentic human and civil growth. In fact, a benefactor's sacrifice is not always a good sign for those who receive the help, because it can express a power relationship that may be concealed by good faith.

Civil entrepreneurs should give themselves no peace until the people included in their VBOs feel themselves to be *useful to the company* and to society, rather than assisted by a philanthropist. Consider **micro-credit**. Bringing the excluded into the banking system was one of the principal economic innovations of our time. It liberated people — women in particular — from poverty and exclusion much more efficiently than many international aid interventions. If an intervention does not help *all* parties involved, it can hardly be of real help for *someone*. If I do not feel benefited less than I benefit someone else, the other will rarely feel truly benefited by me, especially when the relationship endures over time. Diversity is the law of life, enabling relationships that do not deteriorate, but rather grow in mutual dignity.

10.10 In praise of diversity

In this chapter we have focused on what we have called "civil" enterprises, and thus of organizations, stating that not all companies and organizations are equal.

Economic science, however, gives scant attention to organizations other than capitalist enterprises; when it does give them a little attention, families, churches, the State, and multinationals are essentially treated the same way. There is today a particularly dangerous and pernicious aspect in the theory, and particularly the practice, of organizations, which we might call organizational "reductionism" or "isomorphism."

What are we talking about? It is the tendency to treat all forms or organizations as essentially similar, which is quite pronounced in Anglo-American environments. Schools, hospitals, multinationals, cooperative companies, universities, and a soccer team are all considered as expressions of the genus "organization," so the methods of understanding and treating them are always the same.

In our experience we have known consultants who have organized the same course in organizational theory for managers of for-profit companies and for nuns who are bursars for religious communities, based precisely on this organizational theory. There are obviously many common elements between a commercial enterprise, a cooperative, and a religious community; however, we are convinced that a "good" organizational theory should *focus primarily on the small differences* that exist between one organization and another. Humans and chimpanzees share 98% of their DNA, but the 2% is precisely what matters if we want to study and understand language, economics, and life in community.

Today the culture of globalization carries with it a radical tendency to flatten and standardize organizational tools, but if we do not give that 2% its proper importance we cannot identify the decisive elements in each organization, which we call its culture, identity, values, and mission. The organization in a social cooperative may only differ from a capitalist enterprise by 2% or 10%, but if consultants and managers treat both organizations the same way and with the same tools, they cancel centuries of history, liberty, and civilization and often lead them along unsustainable paths.

Life grows and is nourished by diversity; this is one of the important messages of biology. A civil society grows well when it makes life possible in several organizational forms, respecting and supporting their specific characteristics and cultures.

Democracy and social and economic liberty are guaranteed by a plurality of organizational forms. When an economy and a society pardon values-based organizations if they become speculative enterprises, or if they must close down due to "bad" consultants or managers, the entire economy and society become the poorer for it. When different organizations originating from different realities exist in an economy and a society, with many VBOs among them, life is richer, and the social ecosystem thrives with biodiversity, cultural variety, and life.

In Europe and Italy, civil societies and economies are still characteristically heterogeneous in their traditions and cultures. Standardizing market cultures inexorably leads to the commercialization of civil life, which carries a serious threat to democracy. The purpose of this chapter has also been to at least point out that different company cultures, such as those in civil enterprises, cannot be viewed simply as culturally and economically backward, and as such destined to give way sooner or later to for-profit firms. Even the economic forms of production are cultures. We must populate all aspects of humanity with life, with people, and thus the economy as well. Economics and finance are too important to leave them only to the experts.

The current crisis is also the result of a culture that, since it is based on a sharp distinction between the economic and the civil, has abandoned economics and finance and left them in the hands of experts. It is not sufficient to ask banks and companies to be responsible with the tools of their responsibilities; it is necessary to populate the economy with people and revitalize global markets. Many of the banks and companies affected by bankruptcies during this time of crisis had drawn up magnificent CSR documents (such as social budgets). Companies and banks will again be truly responsible when they turn again toward the city, and the city turns again toward them.

Further reading

Bruni, L., & Smerilli, A. (2015). *The Theory of Value Based Organizations. An Introduction.* London: Routledge.

Coase, R. (1937). The nature of the firm. *Economica, 4*(16), 386–405.

Dumont, L. (1980). *Homo hierarchicus* (p. 65). Chicago: The University of Chicago Press.

Mill, J. S. (1976 (1869)). *The subjection of Women Longman.* London: Green, Reader and Dyer.

Mill, J. S. (1848). *Principles of political economy with some of their applications to social philosophy.* London: J.W. Parker, West Strand.

Rawls, J. (1971–1975). *A theory of justice.* Belknap: Harvard University Press.

Weber, M. (1968). *Economy and society.* New York: Bedminster Press.

Weber, M. (2005(1930)). *The protestant ethic and the spirit of capitalism.* translation by Parson, T., Taylor & Francis e-Library.

Zamagni, S., & Zamagni, V. (2010). *Cooperative enterprise: Facing the challenge of globalization.* Edward Elgar Publishing.

Zingales, L. (1999). Governance. In *New Palgrave dictionary of political economy.* London: Macmillan.

Zingales, L. (1998). Corporate governance. In P. Newman (Ed.), *The new Palgrave dictionary of economics and the law* (Vol. 1, pp. 497–503). London and New York.

Chapter 11

Corporate social responsibility

11.1 The reductionism of the traditional approach to viewing the firm

As emphasized in Chapter 10, economists' traditional approach to the theory of the firm usually stops at what we discussed in Chapters 5—7. According to this approach, there is essentially only one type of productive organization, which follows the criterion of profit maximization; on this basis, it carries out its decisions on the choice of production inputs (capital, labor, raw materials, energy, semi-finished goods) and the level of output. The profit maximization principle has an important implication: the primary goal is the size of the slice of the value the company creates that is received by the one who organizes production (the owner—manager in the simplified version). The entrepreneur (or the shareholders in large public enterprises) is the *residual claimant*, or the one who has the right to what left over from the value created after all production factors have been paid. The fact that one stakeholder is privileged with respect to others has its logic in the particular nature of that stakeholder. A basic element in the creation of a firm is the decision to assume entrepreneurial risk by providing financial resources that will be lost if the business fails. In a certain sense the right to the residual is the reward and the incentive that motivates an entrepreneur to risk his own resources. However, shareholders are not the only ones at risk in a business. In some ways workers risk much more because their skills are less diversifiable than shareholders' money, in that shareholders can diversify their portfolios among several investments. Thus if a business fails, it can harm workers more than shareholders. Moreover, as we learned in Chapter 10, production is much more complex than the simplified model adopted in textbooks, because it involves and influences a wide range of stakeholders both inside and outside the company. Indeed, the company does not produce only goods and/ or services as outputs that can be sold on the market; at the same time it also creates cultures and relationships, modifying the social conditions and the environment in which it operates. It is neither possible nor convenient when starting a business or running a company to separate the first and most visible aspect of production from the second.

The Microeconomics of Wellbeing and Sustainability. https://doi.org/10.1016/B978-0-12-816027-5.00011-2

A fundamental problem for a firm modeled according to the traditional approach is that the goal of profit maximization, which fully satisfies the shareholders' desires, can conflict with the demands from other stakeholders.

To give just one example, technological progress or a crisis in its business sector can make a company's staff redundant. In such a predicament, restructuring the company with a reduced staff, although it harms the well-being of the laid-off workers, can be shorter and less costly than the process of retraining the workforce to increase profits. The conflicts between a firm's shareholders and its customers are more subtle but just as far-reaching. In a context in which the company has market power, it may find it advantageous to raise prices, reducing consumer surplus and increasing its profits. If we consider that most relationships between companies and customers develop in a context of asymmetric information, the conflict becomes even more bitter because customers are not able to verify whether a company is reducing their surplus and increasing its own. While it is true that in many cases there is the possibility of verification after a certain amount of time, the reputation and penalty mechanisms are not always effective enough to create a deterrent so the company does not repeat such behavior.

Possible conflicts among companies, suppliers, and employees are equally understandable. In the first case, the firm has an interest in setting up bidding among their intermediate goods suppliers, putting them in competition against each other and limiting their possible profits. In a globally integrated market, if the bidding happens in emerging or developing countries and the company does not concern itself with verifying whether suppliers respect conditions concerning the dignity of labor or environmental protection, it is highly likely suppliers will be drawn to violate those principles in order to win the supply contract. Moreover, suppliers can be driven to invest to specialize in a very specific technology that is necessary to produce components for the parent company, with no assurance that the relationship will not end and their specialized investment will be lost because it was too specific to that relationship.

So how is it possible to reconcile the principle of profit maximization with various stakeholder claims? Economists typically adopt a twofold approach to solving this problem. Companies need not worry about reconciling the creation of economic value and social well-being, but simply dedicate themselves to maximizing profits and satisfying shareholders. Other stakeholders should be defended and represented by political institutions and organizations (for example, trade unions in the case of workers), and, ultimately, by redistributive policies. According to the traditional approach, a socioeconomic system with strong representative and political institutions is capable of creating the necessary checks and balances, in the form of laws and regulations, that can harness companies' animal spirits and direct them on a path of economic value creation that does not generate negative side effects (externalities) on other stakeholders, but rather that indirectly redirects the wealth created back into the institutions. This is the so-called "trickle-down effect," expressed well by the aphorism "a rising tide lifts all boats."

Essentially competition, reputation, charitable institutions, and regulators that avoid regulatory capture can reconcile a company's attitude of maximizing profit with the well-being of society. The problem is that these three conditions are so demanding that they can never be fully realized, particularly in global markets where it is easy to find countries with low quality institutions and where the regulation hurdle is set quite low. That is why this belief seems to have been crumbling for some time, and there are a growing number of voices asking companies to increase their social responsibility by internalizing their externalities and managing the potential conflicts of interest they risk creating between various stakeholders. In response, companies seem to be increasingly sensitive to the problem. To cite just a few summary data, a 2017 KPMG report noted that CSR reporting is standard practice for 75% of the 4,900 surveyed large and mid-cap companies in the world. The 2018 report on *Socially Responsible Investing Trends in the United States* indicated that the US-domiciled assets under management using SRI strategies grew to 12 trillion at the start of 2018 from 8.7 trillion at the start of 2016 (an increase of 38%), reaching the share of 1 dollar out of 4 in US assets under management (https://www.ussif.org/files/Trends/Trends%202018%20executive%20summary%20FINAL.pdf).

Why has social responsibility become fashionable and exploded now? The answer is that the global integration of markets has made the system of checks and balances we described above much more fragile. While in the 1970s there was a balance of power, regulations, and laws that could ensure the rights of the various stakeholders in the predominately domestic economies of developed countries, that is not true today when companies locate important parts of their production in poor or emerging countries in which the institutions, laws, and regulations supporting the social and environmental sustainability of production are weak or non-existent. It is one thing to ask a company to be socially responsible or go beyond what is required by law in a developed Western country where there is (there was?) ample and broad protection for workers. It is another thing to ask this of countries torn apart by conflict in which anarchy reigns, and in which in many cases the State is far from implementing even one of the minimum conditions that ensure its authoritativeness and existence, or the monopoly on the use of force.

Given all that, what do we mean exactly by corporate social responsibility, and how can we ascertain and evaluate companies' socially responsible behaviors in concrete terms?

11.2 The definition of CSR

The criteria adopted by the principal international ratings agencies, such as Domini and Ethibel, can help us formulate a summary definition of CSR in terms of a **partial change in a company's "objective function,"** with a transition from maximizing shareholder wealth to maximizing the well-being of a group of stakeholders that includes, in addition to investors, its employees, suppliers, local communities, consumers, and future generations.

Thus the corporate social responsibility approach reduces the role of shareholders by stating that their satisfaction must be reconciled with that of a series of other stakeholders. It is clear that this new approach does not necessarily reconcile with maximizing profit. The latter implies that a company's sole goal (or at least the goal to which all others should be subordinated) is to satisfy shareholders and compensate them for their risk capital. In principle, in a world in which strong institutions and rules exist that can eliminate negative environmental and social externalities arising from a company's business, maximizing profit might not be all that far from the criterion for corporate responsibility. To give a more specific example, if strict rules exist to protect the dignity of labor and the environment, simply respecting the law could allow a company that aims to maximize profit to act within the limits of environmental and social sustainability. Since we are a long way from such a world, there is a profound difference between a traditional company and one that embraces the criteria of corporate social responsibility.

To fully understand how this different hierarchy of priorities might actually work, it may be appropriate to start from how KLD[1] − one of the principal rating agencies that assess the degree of corporate social responsibility for companies listed on American stock exchanges − has defined them.

Determining these criteria happens in two phases:

a. selecting a series of implementation areas, and
b. defining particular behaviors that make a company more or less responsible in each area. In the classification we are evaluating, the following areas are considered:
   1. relationships with local communities;
   2. employee relationships;
   3. the environment;
   4. product quality;
   5. corporate governance;

---

1. Kinder, Lydenberg, and Domini Research & Analytics, Inc. (KLD) is a research company that provides valuation tools to fund managers who intend to include social and environmental factors in their investment decisions. KLD was acquired by Risk Metrics Group in 2009. Criteria similar to KLD's, which we have adopted as a reference, have been adopted by other rating agencies, such as Vigeo.

6. human rights;
7. protection of diversity;
8. business activities in controversial sectors.

From this classification of areas it is already possible to understand the stakeholders to which the principle of corporate social responsibility is primarily addressed: workers, consumers, local communities, suppliers, and more generally the community and future generations through attention to the environment.

A first classic area of action is in **relationships with local communities**. A socially responsible company that operates in a certain territory sets itself the goal of transferring part of the economic value it creates to supporting local philanthropic initiatives. One way of interpreting this way of working is that a company's ability to create value is made possible and is facilitated by the territory in which it operates. This is why the company feels the need to *give something back* to the territory. We should also keep in mind that in a global economy in which intangible resources are increasingly important, and a company's reputation becomes a crucial strategic advertising tool, a socially responsible company's reference community for social initiatives expands geographically and ends up including populations in distant countries.

Second, in the area of **relationships with workers**, attention is not only on their wages, but also on a series of non-monetary factors that can significantly contribute to the quality of their life in the company. In particular this area includes criteria regarding participation in the company's profits and decisions, initiatives to reconcile home and work life, job safety conditions, and protecting employees' health.

Third, one of the central themes in corporate social responsibility is obviously the **environmental sustainability** of production activity. In the income circuit extended to the environmental effects of production (Chapter 13) we will observe that, beyond producing goods and services, companies generate harmful emissions and waste that have a negative impact on the environment. Consistent with this observation on production, the fundamental CSR themes in this area are production waste management, the environmental quality of production processes, controlling emissions, and active involvement in innovative environmental policies.

Fourth, the area of product quality reminds us that CSR should not be confused with a generic philanthropic attitude. Since consumers are included among stakeholders, being socially responsible also means providing quality products that meet their expectations. As is well known, in a context of perfect consumer information about the product's characteristics, the sole criterion of valuation becomes the relationship between price and quality. In a more realistic situation of asymmetric information, a low price can become suspect, and consumers want to be reassured that the company's products are of good quality, or at least that they are properly priced. This becomes even more important as the consequences of buying a poor quality product become more serious; consider the repercussions on consumers of buying poor quality pharmaceuticals, food, or financial services, and over the medium to long run as well. So social responsibility in this area becomes an important signal to consumers about a company's commitment to quality, which can have significant positive effects on consumers' health and on the demand for its products.

Fifth, the area of **corporate governance** is currently the least thoroughly developed in KLD principles, contrary to what happens in the economic literature. One of the main elements considered in this area concerns the gap between managers' and workers' salaries regarded as an index of poor corporate governance. More need to be done in the future to deepen our understanding of the sensitive topic of just how effective corporate governance, or the set of rules and institutions that regulate corporate life, is in resolving conflicts of interest between management, small shareholders, bond holders, workers, and so forth.

Sixth, the area of **human rights** addresses the possible social consequences to local communities of relocating a company's production facilities. Evaluating the respect for workers' rights is central to this aspect, not only in a company's home country, but also and primarily in the countries where it transfers part of its production, as well as in the foreign companies that supply intermediate inputs or to which part of production is subcontracted.

Seventh, the topic of **diversity protection** verifies whether a company guarantees equal opportunities for all, with particular regard for including women, ethnic minorities, the disabled, and so on.

The eighth and last area is a company's possible **business activities** in sectors considered to be in stark contrast with the principles of social responsibility. The KLD classification we are considering includes tobacco, pornography, gambling, firearms production, and nuclear energy.

Starting precisely from the last evaluation area, it is clearly evident that the definition of CSR criteria depends on a particular culture's value judgments. To give a few examples, Islamic ethical investment funds add alcohol and pork production to the list of controversial sectors. The American approach is much harsher toward the tobacco industry than is Europe, the British are particularly attentive to animal rights, and Catholics include the protection of life before birth as a fundamental criterion.

It is important to understand that CSR is not based on wholly objective criteria, and that part of it inevitably reflects the cultural differences between religions (such as Christianity, Islam, and Hinduism) and cultural approaches (such as giving priority to healthcare, animal rights, etc.). Nonetheless, some basic criteria, such as the environment, protecting the dignity of labor, human rights, engagement in social causes, and consumer protection by now seem to be universally shared, and they represent the core and the least common denominator of corporate social responsibility.

11.3 The debate among economists on corporate social responsibility

It is remarkable to note that while the literature on the firm presents many scientific contributions on the topic of corporate social responsibility, economists give little attention to the subject. As we have said, the main reason is that the standard portrayal of the corporate model adopted in economics textbooks by definition shows companies as profit maximizers, while the problem of market failures, such as negative externalities or the insufficient production of public goods, is usually addressed through political intervention.

Milton Friedman's famous objection to corporate social responsibility is clearly a product of this approach. The well-known Nobel laureate wrote that managers who run companies should focus solely on respecting the mandate shareholders have entrusted to them by maximizing profits, and thus the yield per share. For Friedman, any deviation from this goal is a violation of the fiduciary mandate managers receive from risk capital holders, and as such they are liable for legal action by shareholders. In essence, a manager who gives attention to social and/or environmental responsibilities is considered to be someone who abuses the income streams generated by the company that rightly belong to shareholders. We should not simplistically think that Friedman completely ignored the problem of squaring economic development with social well-being. His approach simply holds that, in a framework of strong rules and institutions, the energy of entrepreneurial animal spirits is properly channeled along lines that create economic value, while the strength of the system of controls, rules, and institutional interventions reconciles this value creation with the well-being of society.

In such a context there is a minimal concept of corporate responsibility that is limited to respecting the law. However, as we have already noted, the entire system crumbles when we reasonably recognize that a globalized economy does not have sufficiently strong controls, rules, and institutions to achieve this goal in either high or low income countries. Furthermore, we would do well to remember that the contribution companies make to the creation of value for society is not profit, but added value. The added value pie created can then be divided among the various stakeholders, and profit is the slice that goes to shareholders. Confusing profit with creating value means confusing the size of the pie with the slice that goes to each of its beneficiaries.

Another objection typical of the criticisms of corporate social responsibility comes from Michael Jensen. He states that the criterion of CSR is too complex to be able to apply, and so it easily lends itself to arbitrary interpretations by managers, which increases the risk that they might abuse a company's cash flow. Jensen observed that the criterion of maximizing profit concerns a single simple indicator, profit, which is easily verifiable and measurable (or at least under the constant scrutiny of financial analysts for publicly traded companies), while CSR requires weighing a series of different indicators (at least one for each of the eight areas considered in the previous section) by attributing weights that are necessarily arbitrary. For example, how should we bring together and weigh corporate environmental performance with labor relations?

This type of objection clearly has little basis. The simplicity of an indicator is not what establishes its validity, but its pertinence. This would be similar to a doctor who, faced with the necessity of formulating a complex diagnosis based on several factors, chose to look at only one because it is simpler to measure. Edward Freeman made a strong case for CSR by arguing that, realistically, the effectiveness of a company's operation depends on the consensus of the many stakeholders that are in relationship with it. From this perspective, the choice to be socially responsible would minimize transaction costs with its stakeholders; thus it would not actually be a noble choice but rather a matter of cost, as the optimal solution in view of the risk of sustaining costly conflicts with its various stakeholders. To give a concrete example of what we mean by the expression "transaction costs with its stakeholders," consider that during 2005 publicly traded American companies paid a total of over 9 billion dollars in settlements for lawsuits against customers and shareholders. The social reputation of a company and the trust that various stakeholders have in it is thus an important asset to safeguard.

This consideration is absolutely clear when looking in depth at the banking sector. One of a bank's strategic success factors is the trust its customers place in it. A crisis of confidence in a credit institution can lead customers to withdraw their savings, cause bond issues to fail, or to drastically reduce consensus favoring the option of directing employment termination benefits or severance pay to pension funds (which are managed by the banks) in order to build up supplemental pensions. The greater the occurrence of financial and banking crises, the less customers trust them and the more they choose the first option of withdrawing their money.

Publicly traded banks must necessarily maximize the interests of their shareholders, and in many cases this can come into conflict with customers' interests when in non-perfectly competitive markets, such as the banking sector. For example, banks may be tempted to sell their customers financial products on which their margins are the highest even if they are not the best possible choice for them, or they may raise the management fees on their accounts, counting on the fact that the monetary and/or opportunity costs are high for customers to close their accounts and open accounts at a new bank (and on a psychological reluctance to leave the bank). Finally, banks may decide that carry trade operations (borrowing at a low interest rate to buy higher rate instruments on the market) are more convenient for the purpose of maximizing profits than extending credit to companies. A clear, strategic choice toward social responsibility by a bank can help customers eliminate these suspicions and increase confidence in the bank, which is the fertile soil in which a bank's business can prosper.

One final interesting reflection from the economic literature comes from the French economist Jacques Tirole. He clearly observed that creating profit can be weakened by a company's CSR choices, given that it is defined as shifting a firm's focus from the priority of satisfying shareholders to satisfying a broader audience of stakeholders. If a company is publicly traded, and if there are rules in force that favor owners in property disputes — as is increasingly common — then a socially responsible company is clearly in a weakened position. In fact, it would be easy for a corporate raider to argue that the company is "inefficient" (obviously from the perspective of maximizing profits) and propose herself to the shareholders as a possible new manager with a plan to increase its profits and the value of its stock. The raider could thus easily rake together enough shares on the market to become its new owner, modify the company's strategy, and abandon its CSR choices.

Tirole's observation is fundamental to the relationship between types of companies and social responsibility, to which there are two possible responses. A socially responsible company can decide to stay out of the stock market (most of the companies that have set social goals have made this choice) or to accept the challenge and seek to demonstrate to shareholders that the CSR choice will ultimately benefit them, for the reasons laid out by Friedman.

More generally, companies that choose CSR face a challenge represented by the following questions. Does not CSR place their survival at risk? What is the relationship between CSR and profitability?

When there is a strongly negative relationship between CSR and corporate profitability, it is indeed clear that the risk of not surviving would alienate many companies from choosing CSR, even when their choice is not instrumental (that is, not motivated solely by the desire to increase profits). Any entrepreneur interviewed on the subject would say that his first social responsibility is to keep his employees employed.

The next section will try to address this topic in detail by illustrating all the major consequences to corporate profits when choosing CSR.

11.4 Can socially responsible companies overcome the challenge of economic sustainability and survival in the market?

The survival instinct is one of the main determinants of the actions of any natural or social organism. When we speak of corporate social responsibility, we must first ask ourselves if the choice allows a firm to survive and compete on the market. Indeed, when faced with this new situation, many entrepreneurs' reactions are primarily defensive. CSR seems like a chimera in the face of the harsh law of competition in a global economy, with fierce competitors that benefit by producing wherever labor costs less and environmental regulations are less severe. The question of the "profitability" of CSR, or the net results of its effects between costs and benefits, thus becomes central.

Using a biological metaphor, it is as if a new type of organism — a socially responsible company — were being introduced into an ecosystem. The question we set for ourselves in this section (and the next, in which we will discuss a particular type of social enterprise) is how to modify the system's balance. We can envisage three different orders of outcomes: the new organism succumbs, it successfully survives, or it actually contributes to modifying the characteristics of existing organisms. To be able to identify the final outcome of this "experiment," we must carefully re-examine the CSR areas and their specific characteristics as described in Section 11.2 and examine their impact on a firm's costs or revenues.

From this examination we conclude that CSR implies **certain costs** in the face of at least five potential benefits.

The certain costs are obvious. In nearly all areas considered, the greater attention to stakeholders entails greater costs to the company. In relationships with workers, all the initiatives considered related to improving the economic and non-economic aspects of its employees involve monetary outlays. The processes related to introducing or enhancing more environmentally friendly production processes that are designed to reduce polluting emissions or wastes are costly. Another cost is related to the attention given to local communities through philanthropic initiatives. Finally, in the area of human rights, greater attention to the working conditions in companies that provide intermediate production inputs imply greater costs, because it entails the choice of not always or necessarily accepting the lowest price supplier, but rather the most advantageous supplier that respects the criteria of the dignity of labor and of environmental protection. The only two characteristics that can create earnings for a company are attention to product quality, when it is rewarded by consumers in the market, and by setting a maximum limit on the compensation gap between managers and employees when it is applied by containing managers' salaries.

However, in the face of these certain costs there are at least five potential benefits that are more than capable of compensating for them.

11.4.1 Consumers voting with their wallets

Companies that choose CSR can be rewarded by socially responsible consumers who vote with their wallets. As we have previously emphasized, if consumers' anthropology were that of *homo oeconomicus*, the product with the lowest price would always win the competition. On the contrary, many questionnaires, laboratory experiments, and actual choices by consumers indicate that a substantial proportion of consumers will reward socially responsible products, and that they are inclined to pay a higher price to buy them than for traditional products. The reason for this is that consumers exchange a monetary sacrifice for non-monetary gratification.

Consider two examples. Fair trade products such as coffee, bananas, and chocolate generally cost somewhat more than normal equivalent products, and yet the market shares of these products have risen, reaching notable levels in just a few years in several specific sectors. Similarly, in the banking field there are several credit and microfinance institutions that propose that savers reduce the interest rate on deposits and the yield on bonds they hold so this "discount" can be used to finance socially significant initiatives, such as capitalizing microfinance startups in the Global South, credit to workforce reintegration cooperatives, and so on. No saver following the criteria of *homo oeconomicus* would accept this option, and yet the share of savings these financial institutions capture is constantly growing.

So a first potential benefit of choosing CSR stems from the greater ability of the firm to satisfy consumer tastes and socially responsible savers. Interviews conducted in every country in the world tell us that the potential for this first type of positive effect is much greater than what has been attained so far. One of the reasons for this growth is that people are becoming aware that this new way of parsing the world, of voting with one's wallet, does not require particularly high levels of altruism, but rather simply a little farsighted self-interest. Buying a product from a company leading the way in environmental responsibility means voting for a market with less pollution and fewer health problems for consumers. Buying from a company leading the way in social responsibility means voting for a more favorable labor market when consumers take on the role of workers. It is highly likely that with improved quality information about CSR people will progressively overcome this form of "masochism" caused by not fully appreciating the consequences of their consumption decisions on their own well-being. The problem is to successfully convince skeptical consumers of the actual social value of a good or service that they cannot directly measure. If everyone were to decide to use their votes with their wallets to reward companies on the frontiers in their ability to create economic, social, and environmental value, the world would change.

Businesses are increasingly aware of peoples' sensitivity to the social and environmental impacts of their choices. They have learned that such sensitivity translates into a greater willingness to pay when these factors are incorporated into the price. They also know that their choice to be socially responsible costs them in terms of production processes that are more attentive to the environment, greater monetary and non-monetary benefits for employees, and so forth. A carefully devised solution would be to condition the choice of greater social or environmental responsibility on consumers' support (Frame 11.1).

11.4.2 Product quality signaling

We have already pointed out that consumers are one of the categories of stakeholders to which a socially responsible company gives greater attention,

---

FRAME 11.1 The case of the airlines

Some airlines offer two prices for their tickets: the standard price and a slightly higher alternative price, stating that the additional money will go toward financing policies that compensate for their pollution emissions, such as reforestation projects. In this way, the higher cost of an environmentally responsible policy is already covered by the higher spending by sensitive consumers.

The approach can be sketched as follows. The individual demand of traditional consumers is such that their reserve price for a plane ticket is 100. The individual demand function of "responsible" consumers is the same in the case of a traditional product but shifts upwards in the case of a product that has environmental sustainability characteristics, such as a commitment to reforestation. In this case the reserve price of responsible consumers rises to 120. The optimal policy for the airlines that allows them to extract consumers' "social surplus" is thus to offer the traditional product at 100 and the one that includes the commitment to environmental sustainability at 120.

---

and that product quality is one of the action areas of social responsibility standards. Even for consumers who are not particularly interested in the other aspects of social responsibility, such as philanthropy, care for the environment, protecting workers' rights in the parent company and its suppliers, and so on, social responsibility is an important signal about the quality of a company's products.

Once again we should recall that in the real world perfect information, which is one of the primary starting assumptions on which the model of perfect competition is built, is constantly violated in that producers and sellers of goods and services have much more accurate and detailed information than consumers about the quality of what they offer. In a world in which information is imperfect, many of the dogmas of perfect competition are actually overturned. If the lowest price is the compass that guides consumers' choices in perfect information (those who are not particularly attentive to questions of social responsibility), when information is imperfect price becomes a signal of quality, and a lower price is seen as suspect because it creates the fear that a product is less reliable.

Faced with this information barrier, a company's choice of social responsibility can be read as a signal that it gives greater attention to its customers, which can increase consumers' trust in the company and its products. It is no accident that today CSR is most widespread in the sectors in which there are greater risks to consumers from poor quality products, such as banking and food.

11.4.3 Minimizing stakeholder transaction costs

As previously mentioned, during 2005 publicly traded American companies paid a total of over 9 billion dollars to settle lawsuits with their own investors. This is why the leading multinationals, along with traditional economic and financial risks, have closely evaluated and long included so-called "ethical risk" in their risk management courses, or risks arising from possible legal disputes with various stakeholders.

From this perspective, a company's social responsibility can reduce risky behavior and significantly improve stakeholder relations, markedly limiting ethical risk and its consequences in terms of expected costs to the company. This third potential benefit essentially coincides with Freeman's arguments in favor of CSR as an optimal choice for minimizing friction, or maximizing relational quality, with stakeholders (Frame 11.2).

11.4.4 Environmental innovation

A fourth potential benefit arises from the possible effects of applying environmentally friendly production processes. Firms that have long followed this course, and which are thus ahead in innovating and learning from productive experience, are able today to benefit from significant energy savings, because one of the strategies for adopting environmental sustainability is to increase

---

FRAME 11.2 An abundance of public warnings

One of the most unusual curiosities for a traveler arriving in the United Kingdom is the incredible number of signs and warnings. For example, in an elevator a voice says to pay attention to the doors closing; while walking in a public building where the floor is being cleaned there is a sign that says "Attention. Wet Floor," and sometimes the added phrase "Slippery when wet," which seems absolutely unnecessary. At many stops on the subway, another voice reminds passengers to "Mind the gap." The list could go on.

Why are there many more signs and warnings in the United Kingdom than in, say southern European countries?

One way to view it is that British authorities have a much more paternalistic attitude and maintain that they should advise citizens how to behave. A more careful interpretation suggests that citizens' and consumers' associations are much more aggressive in defending their rights, and that lawyers have greater incentives to bring lawsuits in their favor, thanks to the possibility of earning a percentage of the compensation paid when a trial is over. This is precisely the principle of *minimizing transaction costs with stakeholders* that contributes to explain why in these countries the public authorities or insurance companies find it preferable to post many more warnings.

the energy efficiency of production, which reduces energy consumption to equal the economic value created. Additionally, in a scenario in which concerns about environmental sustainability due to global warming are becoming ever more pressing, it is legitimate to expect increasingly stringent environmental regulations on corporate behavior. Being at the forefront in this area can be the source of an important competitive advantage. To give just one well-known example, the Japanese car producer Toyota started to invest in hybrid or fully electric engines a long time ago; it is now reaping the benefits of this strategy of being at the forefront of the car industry, which is moving in that direction.

11.4.5 Increased worker productivity

One of the more interesting and partly unexplored benefits from CSR is its impact on worker productivity.

First, increasing workers' economic benefits can have significant effects on their productivity. The economic literature usually considers the causal relation that goes from productivity to compensation, but not the inverse relation in which productivity can be influenced by compensation. With the advent of efficiency wage theory and gift exchange theory, the approach changes radically. **Efficiency wage theory** illustrates that better paid workers are more reluctant to engage in low productivity behavior and are more inclined to greater collaboration with the employer, because the cost of being fired is higher when wages are higher (the loss to workers is higher if their labor contracts are terminated). Furthermore, better paid workers have fewer incentives to voluntarily leave the employer to find work elsewhere, which reduces the risk that a company will invest in employee training for nothing if they take the benefits of that education to a competitor. Obviously, the explanations offered regarding efficiency wages are particularly valid in settings in which companies can fire workers without incurring high costs.

To give a specific example, one of the areas in which it is advantageous to follow efficiency wage theory suggestions is with caregivers or domestic workers. This is an area in which conditions are very close to those of a free market, and an employer who does not ensure decent working conditions runs the daily risk of losing a worker who is attracted to better working conditions. It is better to pay a little more than run the risk of having to repeatedly bear the cost of looking for people to hire.

Beyond the relationship between working conditions, extrinsic motivations, and productivity, there is another equally important channel that links CSR with intrinsic motivations and labor productivity. In an economy in which creativity, the ability to innovate, and continually place new product versions on the market to satisfy customers' changing tastes become increasingly important qualities, the relationship is consolidated between intrinsic motivations on the one hand and the productivity of creative workers and their know-how on the other. While intrinsic motivations may not have been very important to screw in a bolt, they are fundamental to winning over workers' hearts and leading them to maximize their creative commitment.

Intrinsic motivations have rules all their own. Among other things, they are nourished by harmony between workers' values and the company's values. From this point of view it is clear that if a company does not limit its social purpose to making the highest profit possible, but instead sets itself to reconciling creating economic value with creating social value and broadening its horizon to pursue goals with high social value, it is better able to win over the hearts and minds of its employees and increase their productivity.

It is interesting to note that not only are the beneficiaries of possible philanthropic initiatives among the stakeholders who are the main recipients of CSR, but also the firm's employees who can introduce them; by choosing CSR, a virtuous circle is set in motion that increases intrinsic motivations, job satisfaction, and productivity.

A closing reflection on the relationship between the certain costs and the five sources of possible benefits leads us to consider three possible situations for a socially responsible enterprise regarding the relationship between CSR, profitability, and survival in the market.

We speak of **strong sustainability** when the net balance between costs and benefits is positive, without considering the support of responsible consumers among the benefits. In this case a socially responsible company has no need of consumers' generosity and sensitivity in order to make the CSR choice sustainable. For example, this type of sustainability is fundamental to a company that sells intermediate products; it will have difficulty "monetizing" votes with wallets, since it will be difficult to reach end consumers with its social responsibility message.

On the contrary, we speak of **weak sustainability** when consumers' generosity and sensitivity is essential to determining a positive balance between costs and benefits.

We speak of **unsustainability** when the balance between the certain costs and the five sources of potential benefits is negative.

11.5 Is CSR sustainable? The evidence of the facts

Of the three possible cases of strong sustainability, sustainability, and unsustainability, which actually prevails in factual reality?

Before describing and commenting on some common elements of the numerous empirical investigations on the topic, we would do well to clarify that there can be no unequivocal answer. Empirical analyses are the most accurate and rigorous way of studying what happened in the past, but they are scarcely able to predict what will happen in the future. According to a famous saying, an economist who uses her knowledge of empirical data to venture into such a difficult task is like someone trying to drive his car by only looking in the rearview mirror.

At the root of the difficulty — or better yet, the impossibility — of identifying a single correspondence in the relationship between social responsibility and a company's performance lies the **indeterminacy problem**. This principle states that it is not possible to establish unequivocal and immutable laws because the object we are observing changes and evolves. The individuals and enterprises that are the subjects of our observation not only alter their behavior over time, but they respond optimally to the political economy initiatives set by public authorities. Among other things, that implies that formulating correct scenarios on how a certain model might operate would require incorporating assumptions about how interested agents would respond to variations introduced in their situations by public authorities' political and economic policy choices. The indeterminacy principle applies even more stringently to analyzing the relationship between corporate social responsibility and profitability. If we reexamine the sources of potential benefits arising from choosing CSR, we realize that the primary element of uncertainty depends on the response of socially responsible consumers and savers. The greater the number who "vote with their wallet" and reward products that incorporate social value, the greater the probability that companies that move in that direction will show improvements in their earnings. More succinctly, if the condition of strong reciprocity (i.e., the profitability of choosing CSR net of the participation of responsible consumers) does not apply, the success of socially responsible companies depends on us (Frame 11.3).

A key element that makes us think that people's support of such initiatives will increase rather than decrease in the future is that voting with one's wallet is not so much an act of altruism as it is of *far-sighted self-interest*. Those who can grasp the interdependence between corporate social and environmental responsibility and their own future know in fact that the consequences of not *voting with their wallets* fall directly on themselves. A lack of attention to the environment fuels pollution and global warming, with direct effects on the health of the populace and the stability of the climate. A lack of attention to the dignity of the person and the persistence of wide gaps in well-being between different areas of the planet fuels the desperation of those who seek to clandestinely enter the wealthiest countries, which creates a formidable competition with their own labor force from unskilled manual labor at rock-bottom prices, which puts acquired rights and protections at risk.

Those who vote with their wallets do so far-sightedly by rewarding companies at the forefront of creating combined economic, social, and environmental value. They support the innovations that help the economic system pursue "three-dimensional" efficiency by creating economic value in a way that is socially and environmentally sustainable.

FRAME 11.3 The hat vendor

To make it easy and fun to understand the principle of indeterminacy, it may be useful to recount a famous anecdote.

A hat vendor made his usual daily journey from the village where he lived to the market where he went to sell his products. He carried a sack with him that contained all his hats. As happened every day, he had to go through a stretch of tropical forest along his route. Arriving at the edge of the forest he stopped for a few moments to rest from the heat, taking shelter under a tree and setting down his sack full of hats. Suddenly some monkeys climbed down from the tree and stole most of the hats, carrying them up to the treetops. In a fit of anger the hat seller threw his own hat on the ground. To his great surprise, the monkeys imitated him and threw down from the trees the hats they had just taken as spoils. Surprised but happy, the hat vendor collected his hats and went on his way.

Many years later the hat vendor's grandson plied the same trade as his grandfather, and he found himself on the same road. Arriving at the edge of the forest, he followed in his grandfather's steps, stopping to rest under the same tree and setting down his load of hats. Suddenly several monkeys climbed down from the highest branches, stole some hats, and climbed back up to the treetops. The young hat vendor remembered the story his grandfather had told him as a child, and he violently threw his own hat to the ground as if he were irritated. At that point a monkey dropped down from the tree, scooped up that hat as well, and scampered back up to the treetops, mocking the hat vendor and saying "Did you think you were the only one with a grandfather?".

This is an example of the indeterminacy principle that can be applied by analogy to the social sciences: the agents in the models we build not only can vary their behavior, they are also capable of strategically responding to our moves, which risks bringing our choices to naught.

Having set out these premises, we can quickly assess several basic trends in the empirical results accumulated to date. In general, the work carried out has been done to answer two main questions.

What is the relationship between corporate social responsibility and corporate financial performance?

What effect does choosing social responsibility have on the stock market performance of publicly traded companies?

11.5.1 What is the relationship between CSR and financial results?

Answers to this first question come from analyses from different time periods and countries, and they do not give unambiguous indications. In many studies socially responsible companies seem to outperform, or at least not perform worse than traditional companies, but there are also studies that show negative results.

The general tendency is that the impact on performance is more positive when evaluated in terms of revenue per employee or value added, and less positive when considering profits and profitability of the shares. This seems wholly consistent with the very definition of corporate social responsibility as shifting the goal from maximizing shareholder wealth to satisfying the interests of a broader stakeholder audience. Net of the effect of any further value created by the CSR choice, changing the goal implies a redistribution from shareholders to other stakeholders. Socially responsible companies thus tend to create greater or equivalent economic value, but they distribute less to the shareholders and increase the slice allocated to other stakeholders.

If we look beyond purely economic value added to performance measurements that include social and environmental externalities created by these companies' business activities (for example, "full added value," which considers consumer surplus as a performance factor), the results of the comparison are decidedly in favor of socially responsible companies.

11.5.2 What effect does choosing social responsibility have on the stock market performance of publicly traded companies?

The evidence so far would seem to anticipate a negative correlation between CSR and financial market performance, but studies on the topic do not confirm this hypothesis. From a purely theoretical view, if we place ourselves on the side of managed investment funds, there are three potential costs arising from investing in socially responsible securities. The *first* is that if we adopt criteria for excluding non-socially responsible securities, we limit the scope of our investment horizon, which reduces the possibilities for portfolio risk diversification. The *second* is that obtaining information on companies' social responsibility is an additional cost in monetary terms or in human resources who must dedicate time to the task. The *third* is that, on the assumption that an investment fund has exclusion criteria for companies that do not satisfy certain social standards, there is a possibility that a socially responsible company in the portfolio will alter its strategy and end up below the minimum standard. In that case, to be consistent with the fund's general policy the portfolio manager must sell those shares, which may not be advantageous at that moment.

The impact of these three costs is actually much less than one might think. The first type of cost rapidly tends toward zero as the horizon of investable socially responsible securities expands. On the basis of standard correlation matrices between standard securities, it has been calculated that if there are around 200 securities to choose from, one runs out of possibilities for further diversification. Since ethical investment funds are generally international in scope and are able to choose from a vast range of securities, the problem does not exist as long as the selection criteria are not particularly stringent and restrictive. Finally, the second and third types of problems are components that have a very limited impact on a fund's performance and management costs.

Having exhausted the matter from a theoretical point of view, what we observe in the data analysis is that ethical funds generally do not have significantly lower yields than traditional funds, and they quite often have lower risk profiles. When the analysis is configured from the view of risk-adjusted yield, which is the most correct performance indicator, ethical funds can take pride in superior performance.

The tendency to have lower risk profiles can be explained on the basis of two factors. The first is that socially responsible companies significantly reduce so-called *ethical risk*, or the risk of conflict with stakeholders; such risk can translate into high losses to a company as a consequence of losing law-suits. In practice this tends to support Freeman's argument that choosing social responsibility is perfectly rational for a company, as it minimizes transaction costs with stakeholders. The second factor is determined by the different na-tures of those who invest in the two types of funds. Shareholders who invest in ethical funds are primarily institutional investors, or in any case "patient" investors who are not looking for short or very short run capital gains; they perceive a non-monetary satisfaction in remaining invested in an ethical fund, so they are less prone to move their money around to follow the market. The data is confirmed by the dynamics of the net savings flows that invest in the funds; traditional funds are much more variable, with ups and downs, while ethical funds are much more stable.

The combination of these two factors result in a lower observed risk in the ethical funds.

In conclusion, the impact of choosing CSR on performance depends not only on consumers' and savers' responses, but also on the types of indicators considered. By the very nature of CSR, the least favorable comparison variable with these types of companies is profit, which as we have seen is anything but negative. The relative performance of socially responsible companies tends to be better when we consider the creation of economic value, or added value, and the risk-adjusted stock returns.

The reduction of some risk profiles and a more equitable distribution of the value created among stakeholders are typical characteristics of socially responsible companies, which seem to ensure very positive results in terms of the sustainability of their competitive advantage over time.

The evaluations we have carried out in this chapter allow us to give an unconventional answer to the question of the advantage to shareholders of choosing corporate social responsibility. Since the value of an investment in risk capital, or in a simple stock share, is given by the three parameters of return, risk, and liquidity, it may turn out that choosing CSR is paradoxically preferable for a shareholder, even with a relatively low stock return. If in fact the lower risk compensates for the lower return, the socially responsible in-vestment can be advantageous even from a purely economic point of view, without considering the additional non-monetary gratification. In some cases a high social responsibility rating — understood as an indication of a company's prudent behavior that pays attention to all stakeholders and not solely toward creating shareholder value at all cost — can even be a more reliable indicator of low financial risk than the classic financial ratings. This is what the 2008 financial crisis teaches us, in that many of the companies that ended up in the eye of the storm had low ethical ratings but excellent financial ratings.

11.6 The problem of asymmetric information in CSR: social responsibility is not an "experience good"

As we have discussed, choosing CSR entails certain costs in contrast with five types of potential benefits. In such a situation, if it is difficult for consumers to verify CSR choices, a company can be strongly tempted to state that it is socially responsible but act differently in order to avoid paying the costs of CSR. Unfortunately, the problem of asymmetric information exists, or different information between two parties regarding a good or service in a transaction, and it is one of the more difficult problems to resolve. Indeed, part of the asymmetric information between the buyer and the seller can only be resolved by actual consumption experience. Such goods are called *experience goods*, which consumers must use in order to overcome an initial information asymmetry. To give an example, when a new ice cream shop opens its doors, its potential customers do not know if the ice cream is of good or bad quality. The first purchase thus happens "in the dark," but immediately after tasting it, or at least after a relatively few samples, consumers will be able to eliminate the asymmetry and evaluate the product quality. So regarding the problem of perceived enjoyment, ice cream is an *experience good*. (It may be beyond customers' ability to evaluate the quality relative to the health effects of the ingredients used in it.)

Unfortunately, CSR does not have these characteristics. If a shop sells fair trade coffee or an organic product, its customers must trust the products' social responsibility characteristics, and repeated purchases do not contribute to reducing the asymmetric information problem. In other words, someone why buys 10 sacks of coffee is no more informed about the social responsibility of the product than someone who buys only one sack.

In light of the above, we can understand why the temptation to cheat about CSR can be high. The suspicion alone that this could happen paradoxically ends up undermining consumers' trust and risks frustrating virtuous companies' efforts.

Faced with this problem, there are two possible solutions: certification seals and reputation.

The certification seals are stamps or logos affixed by certifying agencies that ensure compliance with certain product standards; these agencies are companies that were created to resolve the problem of asymmetric information. The financial results of a certifying agency are made up of costs and revenues, just like any other company. Its costs are determined by the expense of verifying product standards (in our case, the social responsibility of the company producing a good), as well as the operating expenses required to either affix or monitor the use of the certification seal. Its revenues are determined by a small percentage of the sales price of each product that the seller pays the certifying agency for its certification services. The system works as long as the agency maintains its reputation. If a certification were discovered not to be true, it would lose consumers' trust and no seller would be willing to pay part of its income to the certifying agency.

In principle, the reputation system can operate without certifying agencies. Consumers must know that the benefits to the company stating that it is socially responsible would diminish if it were to act improperly, and thus that it will do all it can to ensure that its statements correspond to reality. Despite that, affixing a certification seal makes the association between a producer and social responsibility much more clear and visible.

The reputation system has some limitations. For example, it is valid only in cases in which customers repeatedly buy from the seller. Only in such a case are customers able to punish a vendor in the event of improper behavior by breaking off the relationship and not buying anything from it in the future. Even in the absence of a repeated relationship with a customer, the reputation principle can still be effective if the responsible company is identified and the news of what happened spreads and negatively impacts the demand for its product by other consumers. However, in many cases the relationship is not repeated, information does not spread well, and the reputation principle does not apply.

11.7 Next generation social firms: a particular type of socially responsible company

In this textbook we began from the traditional model of a company whose purpose is to maximize profit. Reflecting on the relationship between a company and its various stakeholders, we concluded that this strategy can end up establishing a clear hierarchy among stakeholders in terms of satisfying their interests: shareholders come before all others, such as customers, workers, suppliers and their labor, local communities, and so on.

In introducing corporate social responsibility, we established that its essential principle consists precisely in changing this hierarchy, in particular by giving greater attention to satisfying stakeholders other than shareholders. The companies that adopt the criteria of social responsibility are in many cases very large publicly traded companies that must harmonize the principles of satisfying shareholders by growing profits and satisfying other stakeholders. This is precisely why we developed in some depth the problem of the relationship between CSR and its profitability consequences by detailing the pros and cons related to this choice.

Moving along an imaginary axis of changes in the relationship between stakeholders' strengths, on the far left we find companies maximizing profits; moving gradually to the right, we find for-profit companies that opt for CSR and traditional social cooperatives. Further along we find the so-called "pioneer" social companies that leverage people's "wallet votes" and are thus able to bring about virtuous patterns of socially responsible imitation among their competitors in the market; they create social capital and transform social responsibility from a residual issue into a truly competitive factor.

By the term **"pioneer" social enterprises** we mean companies that, although operating in sectors that are traditionally subject to competition and the laws of the market, differentiate themselves from their profit-maximizing competitors by a different hierarchy of values that envisions the goal of social advancement at the top. These companies emerged from the traditional social enterprises of consumption and production cooperatives and social co-operatives. Traditional cooperation emerges when groups of workers decide to build an organization that can create benefits for themselves by selling and distributing products at low prices in order to increase their purchasing power (a consumption cooperative), or through a work organization that can maximize the demands of the co-workers (a production cooperative). In a second phase, cooperatives broadened the scope of their beneficiaries and adopted a socio-welfare goal (type A social cooperatives) or the goal of reintegrating disadvantaged workers into the workforce (type B cooperatives).

The difference between the next generation social firms, the pioneers, and traditional social cooperatives is the expansion of the targeted beneficiaries beyond just the associates (or traditional mutuality) and service recipients in the local territory, even to the point of including distant recipients who live in marginal conditions in developing countries (or expanded mutuality). Another distinctive element is their ability to cause other people to become more socially responsible and to follow their examples.

The next generation social companies are not non-profit, in the sense that they do not have a legal structure that prevents them from making profits, but they are also not for-profit firms — that is, they can earn profits, but profit is not the main reason they exist.

Several major examples of pioneering companies are microfinance financial institutions (or at least those that act according to these principles), ethical banks, Economy of Communion companies, fair trade and solidarity importers, and the "world shops" that exclusively sell such products.

11.7.1 Microfinance

The primary goal of microfinance institutions is to extend access to credit to those outside the banking system, or those who are not able to provide the traditional guarantees necessary to obtain credit from a traditional bank because they have either insufficient or no collateral. Muhammad Yunus, the founder of the **Grameen Bank**,[2] the best-known microfinance institution, defines himself as a social entrepreneur; the primary goal of the institution is to facilitate access to credit by the broadest possible group of individuals without collateral, who are often very poor.

The entire microfinance experiment is still rapidly expanding. The UN declared 2005 the International Year of Microcredit. The data from the *Microcredit Summit Campaign* at the end of 2012 show around 3652 microfinance institutions (MI) in the world reporting data, which on the whole have reached 205.3 million recipients, 137.5 million of which are among the poorest. Considering an average family as having five people, microfinance has reached around 677.5 million poor people.

Among existing microfinance institutions today, around half of them follow the same priority hierarchy as the Grameen Bank, and they can thus be considered pioneer social enterprises. The other half, which includes Bancosol, another large microfinance institution, has the goal of making a profit, although they perform the same type of activity as the Grameen Bank in expanding credit to those outside the banking system. The difference between the two types of microfinance institutions is in the lend ingrates offered to borrowers; the profit-oriented institutions' lending rates are much higher. In this case, their profit maximization approach clearly results in a wealth transfer from customers to shareholders.

The controversy between the two types of institutions has recently become quite acrimonious. A profit-oriented microfinance institution such as Compartamos sets annual lending rates even as high as 100%, stating that their social responsibility consists of extending access to credit to new groups of marginalized individuals and reducing the cost of credit for customers of moneylenders, who set even higher rates. Compartamos pays its shareholders from its high profits, and it is thus able to attract resources from individual savers and investment funds dedicated to microfinance.[3] What seems clear is that microfinance institutions such as Grameen pay more attention to their customers in terms of interest rates, but they have less ability to attract risk capital.

We should immediately clarify that the lack of profit orientation of microfinance institutions such as Grameen does not at all coincide with a lack of attention to creating economic value; indeed, profit is nothing more than the share of economic value a company creates that goes to shareholders.

---

2. In its early history the Grameen Bank survived thanks to subsidies by private foundations; only over the last few years was it able to reach the goal of self-sufficiency by attaining moderate profits. Today the Grameen Bank is present in around 73,000 villages, and it has around 7 million customers.

3. The founder of the Grameen Bank, Muhammad Yunus, has recently sharply criticized this behavior, saying that it casts a shadow on the concept of microcredit as a tool to promote the well-being of the least.

Microfinance is one of the most interesting means for creating economic value, particularly when the loans are destined to start small entrepreneurial businesses. These new entrepreneurial companies, which could not be started without a loan, will in turn create profits, and thus new economic value.

Consider an example. If a saver invests 100 dollars in a microfinance institution, in the medium run can initiate a loan volume that is greater than the savings invested due to the deposit multiplier mechanism (the multiplier is equal to the inverse of the percentage of the funds retained by the bank as a reserve). Assuming a multiplier of 10, the initial 100 dollars will feed a total loan circuit of 1000 dollars. Assume that this amount finances 10 loans of 100 dollars each that finance the startup costs for entrepreneurial projects with a 30% return. The final result is that the savers' initial 100 dollars resulted in a total value of 1300 dollars, which is the sum of the value created by the financed investment projects. At the same time, savers did not lose their money and the bank made a profit determined by the difference between the lending and the deposit rate net of its operating costs. Assuming the loans were made to individuals outside the banking system who would not have been able to finance their entrepreneurial projects without a microfinance institution, microfinance had the benefit of promoting social inclusion by bringing people on the margins of society into the production circuit, conferring dignity and a role in society on them.

11.7.2 Ethical banks

Other examples of social market enterprises are the ethical or alternative banks that have adopted social and environmental impact as the basic principles of their business, using these principles as their primary criterion for choosing projects to finance once the constraint of economic sustainability has been met (consider the case of **Banca Etica** in Italy). Ethical or alternative banks, or all the other banks that belong to the worldwide network of the Global Alliance for Banking on Values, do not aim to maximize profits, but rather social value, which obviously must be created within the constraints of economic sustainability. At the same time, they are neither non-profit nor profit maximizing institutions, in the sense that their business and legal structure allows them to make a profit, even though that is not the business's primary goal.

We should note in this regard that not all legal forms of companies are equally adapted to this end. Recalling Jean Tirole's argument in Section 11.3, a bank with such goals would put itself in a very weak position by choosing to become a public corporation listed on a stock exchange. That does not mean that social firms cannot exist as public corporations, on the condition that the weight of its internal shareholders is counterbalanced and moderated by appropriate statutory rules.

In such a case it could easily fall prey to a takeover by outside groups aiming to make it more efficient, or it could easily attract risk capital holders capable of taking control of the bank and changing its primary purpose. This is not meant to reflect negatively on the stock market or on public corporations; rather, it serves only to emphasize that for each type of company and goal to pursue, some legal forms are better adapted than others to allow reaching the proposed goal.

11.7.3 Solidarity and fair trade

The third important example of a pioneering social enterprise is in solidarity and fair trade. This phenomenon emerged in the second half of the 20th century when a group of Dutch citizens decided to create a company to import products from ex-colonial countries, with the goal of building an alternate supply chain to the traditional ones. When this pioneering work began, the traditional supply chain in trading "colonial" agricultural goods, such as coffee, cacao, and bananas, was structured as follows. At the bottom there were a myriad of small, poorly organized producers whose standard of living was near the poverty line; because they had little bargaining power they sold their products at laughably low prices to a few intermediary oligopolists, who in turn transported and distributed the goods to their final markets. Quite often these intermediaries, beyond simply their market power, took advantage of having more than one economic relationship with producers. In a system with an informal credit market, the intermediaries often also financed the products, which ultimately increased their bargaining power and imposed conditions that would not allow producers to improve their standard of living. The intermediaries then sold the products on commodity exchanges or directly to processing companies who delivered them to consumer markets. The supply chain was quite long, and the small producers struggled to move up on it.

The model is not unique. There are other types of supply chains, some of which are vertically integrated with large agricultural firms that can control all phases of production. In general, though, the inability of small primary goods producers to move up the value chain is a constant element.

Fair and solidarity trade emerged with the goal of promoting more dignified conditions for producers by establishing more stable above-market payments to them. Additionally, the new importers committed to (a) resolving the liquidity problem by advancing favorable credit terms against the proceeds from the harvest; (b) investing in training initiatives and providing local public goods implemented by the first level associations that producers depend on to improve their standard of living; (c) ensuring that environmental sustainability is respected throughout the supply chain; (d) providing technical assistance to producers in order to increase their production skills and their access to global markets. By following the supply chain all the way to the producers, fair trade importers are forced to squeeze their margins. They do so by choosing to become non-profit companies and by creating a network of retail outlets — the so-called "world shops" — that sell their products exclusively. Even the final retailers are not able to make a profit; they often take the form of cooperative enterprises, and a significant part of their workforce is voluntary.

Even with these measures, the prices of fair trade products are generally higher than their traditional equivalents, but despite that they succeed in capturing growing market shares (see Chapter 2). Their growth is so strong that, from their initial positions as niche products, the market shares of solidarity products have reached noteworthy levels in several fields in particular.[4]

The key to this success seems to lie in fair trade importers' ability to mobilize consumers to *vote with their wallets* based on the social and environmental responsibility incorporated in their products. The most significant effect of their initiatives has been to trigger imitation by market competitors (including large multinationals). Once traditional competitors noticed consumers' appreciation for these products and their willingness to pay the "ethical premium" incorporated in them, they considered it worthwhile to respond by adding several products with similar characteristics to their own product lines. The interesting thing is that these competitors, which we will call partial imitators, have not at all abandoned their strategy of profit maximization. They calculated that, in a market in which there is growing attention to questions of social and environmental responsibility, from a profit point of view imitation was the best strategic response to fair trade importers coming onto the scene. One of the most important results of the arrival of these pioneers, these social market companies, has been that they have transformed social and environmental responsibility from a residual issue into a competitive factor that, along with others, is very much in play in inter-company competition. Traditional economic culture has only recently begun to understand the originality and innovation of this initiative. For many years the traditional attitude was predominantly critical, based on two fundamental considerations.

The first is that *a fair trade price is a distortion of the market*. Taking up the arguments we developed regarding the relationship between an equilibrium price and an administered price on the market, it considers the price paid to producers to be a violation of the free market that defines an artificially higher administered price than the equilibrium price, an error that creates excess supply and sends the wrong signals to producers.

The second is that *donations are superior to fair trade*. This argument states that the traditional mechanism of buying traditional products (which saves money if there is a negative price difference relative to fair trade products) plus a charitable contribution is more efficient than buying the fair trade product, even from the view of the social objectives pursued.

---

4. According to the 2005 data of the importers' association, fair trade products held 49% of the banana market in Switzerland and around 20% of the instant coffee market in the United Kingdom. Around 2009 the fair trade share of bananas sold in the United Kingdom jumped to around 25% following the entry of several large retailers, such as Sainsbury and Tesco, into the sector.

The answer to the first objection is twofold. First, the characteristics of the relationship between producers and intermediaries described above are not those of a competitive market. The traditional model of the market implicitly assumes the existence of a high number of both buyers and sellers, which prevents an imbalance of bargaining power between the parties. The market conditions described above more resemble those of a monopsony or an oligopsony, in which there is only one buyer, or just a few buyers, that can enforce their strategically superior position.

In a monopsony there is only one employer. The aggregate labor supply curve has a positive slope and an intercept at W_0. This means that at salary W_0 there is a single worker who is indifferent to entering the labor market or not. With a wage increase, the number of workers willing to be hired increases. Since the employer cannot discriminate because it must offer the same wage to everyone, it must pay all workers the salary of the last worker hired, or the highest reserve salary. The marginal cost thus has a positive slope that is greater than the aggregate labor supply, because hiring a new employee also increases "inframarginal" costs, or the wages paid to workers who have already been hired. The level of employment and the equilibrium salary in a monopsony $(O_M : W_M)$ are fixed at the point at which the labor demand equals the marginal cost, while in a competitive labor market equilibrium occurs when the labor demand equals the aggregate labor supply curve (E_C). Comparing the two equilibrium points clearly indicates that in a monopsony the employment level and the equilibrium salary are lower than in perfect competition $(O_M < W_C$ and $W_M < W_C)$. A political economy intervention that sets a higher minimum salary capable of bringing wages in a monopsony up to competitive levels improves workers' well-being by making wages comparable to those in a perfectly competitive market.

The monopsony model does not apply only to the mining regions of the British Industrial Revolution. Indeed, it is not necessary to assume that there is only one employer; there could also be geographically segmented labor markets and just a few employers who collude among themselves. These general characteristics easily apply to regional labor markets in developing countries; analogously, we can substitute workers with primary goods sellers and wages with the sale price of the primary goods to a distributor.

In a monopsony equilibrium (Fig. 11.1), the price is lower than under competitive equilibrium, and the suggested policy solution to re-establish a competitive equilibrium is precisely a higher minimum price equal to the price in perfect competition. The fair trade price is thus an initiative that moves in the right direction, although it is very difficult to know if it exceeds or remains lower than the competitive price.

The second basic difference from setting an administered price in a competitive system is that when we compare traditional and fair trade markets, we are not talking about two prices for the same product, but about the prices of two different goods. In a world in which consumers are increasingly

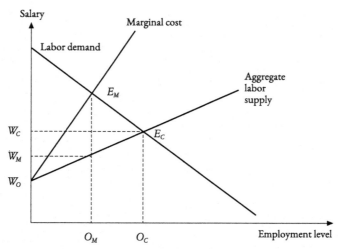

FIG. 11.1 A monopsony market.

attentive to small variations in the immaterial aspects of goods and their symbolic content, while a traditional good and a fair trade good are materially identical, they turn out to be different goods, each with its own supply and demand curve, and thus with its own equilibrium price. Fair trade coffee is a different product than traditional coffee (and both of them from an organic coffee), in that it is defined by a combination of qualitative and ethical characteristics that differ from a traditional product. Thus the introduction of fair trade products — which is partly represented by a non-market price, or better yet higher than the monopsony price paid to primary goods producers — and the extension of the principle to an increasingly broad range of products, such as textiles, hand-crafted goods, cosmetics, and a vast range of food products, are true horizontal innovations that can create a new series of goods that fill a gap in the market's ability to satisfy consumers.

To better understand this concept consider Fig. 11.2, which graphs the traditional and fair trade coffee indifference curves for a consumer with a certain degree of social responsibility. Prior to the introduction of fair trade coffee on the market, the consumer's optimal choice necessarily lies on the vertical axis (point *A*). The simple introduction of the new product allows the consumer to satisfy her social responsibility sensitivity by choosing to buy a combination of traditional and fair trade coffee. The optimal choice goes from point *A* to point *B*, touching an indifference curve that is farthest from the origin of the axes, which increases the degree of her satisfaction.

There is also a concise response to the second objection, which was: Why not follow the traditional course of purchasing a standard product, followed by a charity donation? The traditional course of buying standard products with

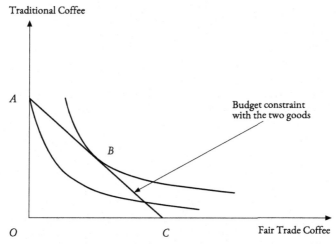

Traditional Coffee

Budget constraint
with the two goods

A

B

O   *C*   Fair Trade Coffee

FIG. 11.2   The optimal choice for a consumer with a preference for fair trade products.
Note: When only the traditional good is present the optimal choice is given by basket *A*, which
only includes the traditional good. If we introduce fair trade coffee as well, the budget constraint
becomes the line *AC* and the optimal choice is *B*, which lies on the highest indifference curve and
includes a mix of the two goods

additional charitable contributions cannot break the imbalance of market power between intermediaries and producers; fair trade can do that by extending
credit and by competing directly against local oligopolists in the distribution
channel. Additionally, aid does not bring about any imitation effects, so it does
not push traditional companies toward partial imitation and choices that are
more socially responsible. Fair trade directly rewards producers' work and
provides them with results that improve their positions, whatever their starting
conditions. Premium prices, technical assistance, and contributions to the first
level associations to promote training and local public goods are initiatives that
aim to promote producers' ability to compete in the markets on their own two
feet; this is a shift from aid to self-sustainability. This *modus operandi* avoids
the risk of having to terminate the initiative when the charitable funds run out.
Once producers can sustain themselves, they can put more effort into running
their businesses, and in the meantime new market outlets were created for their
products.

Returning to Chapter 2, recall that one of the main limitations of the market
is its inability to promote redistribution initiatives through exchange. We stated
that the market is traditionally seen as a "notary" that can only make transactions possible and record them, without being able to intervene in the dire
conditions of some of its participants or the inequalities in their endowments.
With the emergence of social market enterprises, fair trade, and all the imitators engendered by its emergence on markets, that is no longer taken for

granted and can be reconsidered. Thanks to this initiative, the market becomes a place where it possible to vote with one's wallet to support including marginalized producers. Fair trade is increasing the power of the market and is contributing to improving its reputation.

11.8 The effects of the entrance of social market firms: CSR becomes a competitive factor

One of the most surprising results of fair trade products entering the market is certainly the imitation effect on traditional profit-maximizing market agents.

To cite just one of the most significant anecdotes, on 7 October 2005 Nestlé, the large food company that has been the target of many criticisms and boycotts, issued a press release announcing the market launch of a fair trade instant coffee that was to be included in their product line. The decision was motivated by the awareness that the number of consumers oriented toward fair trade goods is continuously increasing, as is the revenue from such products.

Today the paradox is that revenue from fair trade products by imitators, such as large retail distributors, has surpassed the world shops, the pioneers that first sold these goods on the market. The largest seller of fair trade coffee today is the Starbucks chain, and Sainsbury, one of the largest British retailers, has announced that it will only sell fair trade bananas. Even the large producer Chiquita has announced the Rainforest Alliance, a social responsibility initiative that applies social responsibility criteria similar to those of fair trade.

It is possible to illustrate what has happened over the last few years with simple theoretical reasoning. One possible reference is the horizontal product differentiation model, first introduced by the American economist Harold Hotelling in the 1920s with his famous example of ice cream vendors at a beach.

In Fig. 11.3 the horizontal segment represents a beach with uniformly distributed bathers, one per point on the beach. The model assumes that each bather does not want more than one ice cream, and so has a unit demand. Two ice cream vendors sell a product that is identical in quality and price, and they must decide where to position their kiosks for the purpose of maximizing their market share (and consequently their revenues and profits if for the sake of simplicity we assume zero production costs). Since the quality and price of the goods they sell are identical, the only competitive element in play is the distance between bathers and the kiosks. This is a case of an oligopoly model with two companies — a duopoly — in which the strategic competitive variable in play is neither price nor quantity produced, but rather product location. Suppose that at the beginning the two kiosks are positioned at the points corresponding to 1/4 (the first vendor) and 3/4 (the second vendor) on the segment. Assume also that the second vendor makes the first move. In order to increase his market share, he decides to place himself near the first vendor, at 1/4 plus some small amount, thus taking about 3/4 of the market and leaving

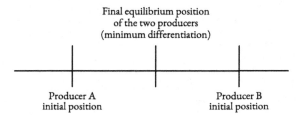

FIG. 11.3 **Horizontal product differentiation: Hotelling's model.** *Note*: To gain market share, producer *B* moves slightly to the right of *A*, thus acquiring all the consumers to his right, or about 3/4 of the segment. To recover market share, producer *A* moves to the right of *B* so she has the consumers on the right of the segment. *B*'s second move is obviously to move to the right of *A*'s new position. This repositioning proceeds until *A* and *B* end up exactly in the middle of the segment slightly apart from each other; in these equilibrium locations each will serve half of the consumers.

the first vendor about 1/4 of the bathers. At this point the first vendor's response is to move just past her competitor and place herself slightly ahead, retaking just under 3/4 of the entire market. The reader can continue to reflect on the competition dynamics of the model. What will be the equilibrium point determined by a pair of kiosk locations such that there is no profit variation for either vendor?

Hotelling showed that the equilibrium point corresponds to the "minimum product differentiation," where both producers are situated at the center at a minimal distance from each other, and each takes exactly half the market. Note that this market equilibrium does not coincide with the social optimum (i.e., the starting -$\frac{1}{4}$, $\frac{3}{4}$- location pair would have been better and optimal for minimizing consumers' distance from the nearest kiosk).

Hotelling's model talked about geographic location, but it has the merit that it can be applied to any sort of non-geographical space. Marketing teaches us that the positioning problem can be extended to an endless casuistry, given that it is possible to define the problem by constructing a multi-dimensional segment or plan and increasing the number of variables a company chooses for its competitive strategy, whether choosing a proof for beer among multiple competitors or for positioning a television program in a viewing schedule.

In applying Hotelling's model to the imitation problem in social responsibility, assume that for consumers the segment represents their sensitivity to social responsibility themes, and for companies it represents the willingness to incur costs for implementing social responsibility (see Fig. 11.4). Assume also that the competition between companies plays out on the dimensions of price in addition to ethical distance. More specifically, for fair trade products the axis measures, for simplicity and without lacking generality, the amount of money that sellers are willing to spend, thus increasing their costs, to promote development and inclusion among marginalized producers in the global South. For consumers, however, the

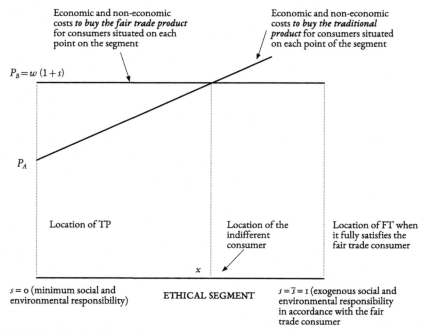

Economic and non-economic costs *to buy the fair trade product* for consumers situated on each point on the segment

Economic and non-economic costs *to buy the traditional product* for consumers situated on each point of the segment

$P_B = w\,(1+s)$

P_A

Location of TP

Location of the indifferent consumer

Location of FT when it fully satisfies the fair trade consumer

x

$s = 0$ (minimum social and environmental responsibility)

ETHICAL SEGMENT

$s = \bar{s} = 1$ (exogenous social and environmental responsibility in accordance with the fair trade consumer

FIG. 11.4 **The hotelling social responsibility game with asymmetric ethical distance costs.** *Note*: Assume that if consumers buy products from a company to their left on the ethical segment, those products are below their ethical standards, which entails a psychological cost. Buying products from a firm to their right means choosing goods that are above their ethical standards, thus there is no added psychological cost to the buyer. This explains why the cost to the consumer of a product by a traditional manufacturer (TM) is represented by a positively sloped straight line, while the cost of buying a product from a fair trade vendor (FT) is flat for all consumers positioned to its left.

distance between their position on the segment and the point of sale is the gap between their sensitivity to the problem from that of the company, or how much they think a company should transfer to producers in the global South and how much it actually transfers.

Consumers on the extreme left of the segment are not willing to pay anything toward this goal, and those on the opposite extreme are willing to pay a conventionally established maximum price. Prior to the emergence of the fair trade supply chain there was one traditional vendor on the market, a monopolist, located on the extreme left ($s = 0$ in Fig. 11.4), who maximized profit by serving all consumers at price P_A. This is not a socially optimal solution both for the usual problem of a monopoly in contrast to competition — extracting the surplus from consumers and producers and transferring it to the monopolist — but also primarily due to the impossibility for consumers to satisfy their value demands, particularly those on the far right of the segment.

Take into consideration that, in difference with the classic Hotelling model presented in Fig. 11.3, in the one we adapted to study the problem of social responsibility a company's moving to the right is somewhat like walking uphill. In other words, in the traditional Hotelling case a vendor entailed no costs when choosing a location, while in the case of social responsibility, moving to the right means investing an increasing sum in promoting the inclusion of marginalized producers in the global South, and thus increasing its production costs and squeezing its profits.

The new fact that triggers this competition is the entrance of a fair trade seller who, assuming for the sake of simplicity, positions itself at the far right of the segment ($s = 1$ in Fig. 11.4). The seller is a pioneering social enterprise that has the primary goal of transferring resources to marginalized producers in the global South, while respecting the constraint of its own economic sustainability. It thus uses a rational choice criterion, but not that of maximizing profit. To attain its goal, it accepts restricting its earnings, even to the point of zero, at the point where it decides to position itself, setting a price equal to its production cost (w) plus the transfer ws to the primary goods producers $[P_B = w(1 + s)]$, which is higher than the incumbent's price (P_A) that maximizes its profits.

The fair trade seller's entry modifies consumers' choices and market shares. As previously mentioned, consumers choose on the basis of two factors that negatively impact their utility: price and "ethical distance" (i.e., the distance between their sensitivity to social responsibility and that of a vendor). Limiting the mathematical treatment to the essentials and reflecting on the core of the problem, it is reasonable to assume that the consumers located closest to the extreme right of the segment find it advantageous to buy from the fair trade vendor rather than the traditional vendor, since for them the higher price is more than compensated by the reduced sensitivity distance between their and the company's convictions. The exactly marginal consumer (located at point x on the segment indicated in Fig. 11.4), who is indifferent to buying from one or the other vendor, sets the market share limits for the two competitors.

At this point, the profit maximizing incumbent, faced with a shrinking market share after the entrance of a fair trade pioneer, must try to respond. It is possible to show that if the marginal cost of a small step in the direction of social responsibility (determined by transferring some amount of resources above zero to marginalized producers in the global South) is less than the marginal benefit in terms of greater utility (determined by reconquering part of the lost market share, multiplied by the new per-unit profit margin that is slightly lower than the original margin), the best choice for the profit-maximizing seller is to become more socially responsible (Frame 11.4).

We wanted to keep the analysis of the problem necessarily simple in order to grasp the essential point: the imitative behavior of traditional producers. The model can obviously be made more complex with several insights. How does the equilibrium change with different assumptions about the cost of the ethical difference (linear, quadratic, and so on)? What happens with different

FRAME 11.4 Imitation

There are many examples of traditional enterprises partially imitating the pioneers. After the fair trade circuit began to sell its products and acquire small market shares, the traditional consumption cooperatives, such as Coop UK and COOP Italia, launched their own line of products with the same characteristics. In a 2005 press release picked up by the BBC, Nestlé decided to add a fair trade product to its product line, explicitly stating that it wanted to enter a very promising sector with great prospects for future growth. Sainsbury, one of the large British retailers, has chosen to sell only bananas sourcing from supply chains that follow fair trade practices. We should emphasize the different motivations by which pioneers and their imitators choose to make fair trade products. The former do so to be consistent with their primary goal of a social nature; the latter do so as a reaction to competition from the former and consistent with their goal of maximizing profits. That is why they choose to imitate to the point at which the costs of adding low profit margin items is more than compensated by the improvement in the company's image and its ability to attract consumers who pay attention to social responsibility profiles. Imitation is an important and socially desirable outcome for greater social and environmental responsibility in the economic system. However, what would happen if only imitators were to remain in the market?

assumptions about fair trade vendors' behaviors, such as maximizing their transfer to producers in the global South, or maximizing the transfer within the entire market, and thus positively evaluating competitors' imitations as well?

We can draw two important points from these extensions that economists have developed.

When consumers' tastes are dynamic and they have an increasing sensitivity to their consumption habits, an imitator can adopt a more aggressive policy in order to limit a pioneer's market share and the growth of consumers' sensibilities that negatively impacts its profits.

Finally, what is the optimal choice in fixing the location of the two players in the model for a national political authority that proposes to maximize consumers' well-being in the North with respect to the equilibrium that spontaneously emerges from competition between the two vendors? The interesting result in this case is that the transfer to the global South is greater in spontaneous competition than with public intervention. The explanation of this paradoxical outcome is that it depends on the lack of representation of the interests of producers in the global South in the choices made by public decision makers in the North, who solely maximize the preferences of their own electorate when choosing the proper balance between prices and social responsibility. In spontaneous competition between the two vendors, however, the pioneer's goal is to transfer to producers in the South, and this goal "infects" the traditional vendor.

The paradox of this extension of the model is that a duopoly produces more international social benefit than a market regulated by a domestic authority — which however has the sole goal of maximizing citizens' satisfaction in the North. In simple terms, when consumers are sensitive to social responsibility, the competition between a fair trade pioneer and a partial imitator overcomes the problems of governance and the lack of representation of the least in the political institutions in a global economy. Through the market, the combined action of fair trade pioneers and responsible citizens makes up for the lack of global institutions that are able to place people in different countries on the same level.

11.9 How competition changes in a global economy: the role of CSR

In order to explain the importance of the role of corporate social responsibility in the current economic context, we will start from the perfect competition model in a closed economy. In Fig. 11.5, as usual we draw a company's average and marginal cost curves and identify the long-run equilibrium points.

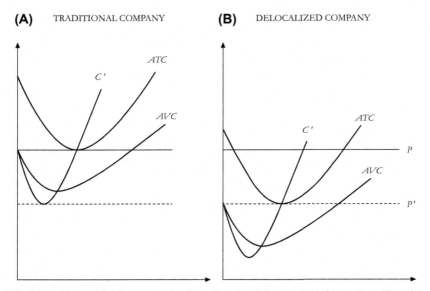

FIG. 11.5   Competition between a traditional and a delocalized producer. *Note*: The minimum average cost point P represents the long-run selling price of a good in a perfectly competitive market. The company that moves production to a country with lower environmental standards and fewer workers' protections is able to lower its production costs. The minimum point of the average cost curve shifts downward to P'. In this way, outsourced companies can put traditional companies out of the market if (as in the figure) point P' is below the minimum point of the average variable cost (AVC).

We also assume, as we expect should happen, that companies will respect the rules in force in their own countries and that their cost curves include the necessary costs to ensure the protection, security, and dignity of labor and to respect environmental regulations.

In the short run the price is equal to the marginal cost, but it is greater than the average total cost, so the company makes a profit. Over the long run, as new companies attracted by opportunities to make a profit enter the market, the overall supply increases (the supply curve shifts to the right), so if demand remains the same the equilibrium price falls. The new equilibrium point is where the price is equal to the minimum average total cost and companies' profits become zero (case A at price P).

A basic assumption underlying the entire model of perfect competition and its virtuosity is that companies all have the same cost curves. In a context in which information can circulate freely, the knowledge of production techniques should be a common asset, and companies should progressively take on similar characteristics. Setting aside trying to deal with all the possible violations of perfect competition that can impede its successful operation, such as externalities, public goods, information asymmetry, non-homogeneous products, entry barriers, and so on, we assume that the only deviation from the standard model is that companies initially operate in a closed economy and that the economy successively integrates with other countries' economies, allowing a producer to delocalize production to areas where there are lower environmental and labor protection standards. We also assume that companies will adopt such practices when moving operations to a country without a framework of rules that can ensure a minimally acceptable level of protection, even by the social standards of that country (case **B**) (Table 11.1).

From a graphic point of view, this implies that the effect of delocalization modifies the cost curve structure of this new type of company, and more specifically, that it shifts the cost curve downward compared to domestic production conditions. Companies that delocalize earn short-run profits and attain a long-run price (P'). It is equally evident that the price P' is less than the minimum average cost of the traditional company that does not outsource (Fig. 11.5), thus the latter is not able to survive in the market if it maintains its existing cost structure.

In order to not be forced to close down, traditional companies can also delocalize production or reduce their labor and environmental protections in their home country so they can compete with the new foreign competition. To achieve this goal, some companies will try to save all possible costs in both areas, for example by reducing the number of employees or making their work conditions less stable and more flexible, or even by breaking the law. As we previously mentioned, it seems clear that the gap in social conditions and labor protections between the citizens in the previously closed economy and the country where the company delocalizes is at the root of the problem of the

TABLE 11.1 Effects of some variables on the average wage of workers in cooperative enterprises.

	Net monthly wages (deviations from the average) in %
Male	+7.28
Northeast[a]	+15.05
Northwest[a]	+15.29
Center[a]	+10.08
Intrinsic motivations	From +3.87 to +10[c]
Years of seniority[b]	+1

ICSI Data Bank Number of observations: 4,134. The question used to build the intrinsic motivation indicator. Do you consider that your relationship with the Cooperative is: (i) a purely contractual relationship (strictly an exchange of labor for wages); (ii) a contribution to reach the goals of the cooperative; (iii) a mix of labor and personal growth; (iv) a group of relationships that goes beyond being purely work-related; (v) a common social engagement for you and the cooperative.
[a]Differences with respect to the South.
[b]Effect of the increase of one year of seniority.
[c]Range of effects according to the intrinsic motivation indicator used.

"race to the bottom" effect, and so the latter moving out of poverty becomes a threat to the well-being of the former.

Suppose at this point that a new entrepreneur who is more attentive to social responsibility decides to start a new company in the country where production was delocalized. Unlike the first company that delocalized its production there, the new entrepreneur decides to raise the local social and environmental standards by making a real investment in opportunities to include local workers. The consequences are that its cost curves will not only be higher than that of the local outsourced company, but also higher than the rest who operate on the traditional market (Fig. 11.6). According to traditional economic rules, the new company's fate would be sealed. With the same quality, and with a higher price required to break even compared to the delocalized company or even the companies who decided to continue operations within the country, the new entrepreneur would not find anyone willing to buy its product. This is what happens unless it can use the social and environmental value of its initiative as a means of differentiating itself.

By following this path and advertising the social initiatives taken or obtaining a socio-environmental certification, the entrepreneur can leverage a segment of consumers with social preferences who are willing to pay a higher price — in this case the difference between its and the outsourced company's products — for its product's greater social and environmental responsibility. The sale price of her product will in any case be higher than the traditional

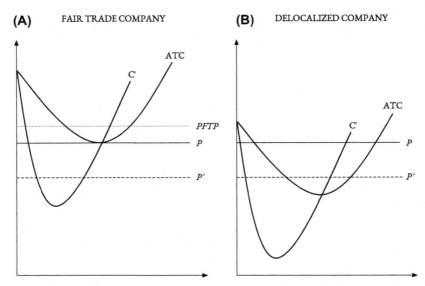

FIG. 11.6 Competition between a fair trade company and an outsourced company. *Note:* A fair trade company (FTC) has higher average and marginal costs than a competitor that has delocalized production to a country with low levels of social and environmental protection. However, the product sold by the fair trade producer has its own specific demand curve (PFTC), which allows it to remain in the market by selling at a price higher than the minimum average cost.

non-delocalized company's, but despite that the company will remain in the market due to the upward shift in demand for its specific socially sustainable product.

A social entrepreneur can thus survive in the market with an apparently paradoxical strategy, which drives its competitors to operate along the same lines. Indeed, to the extent there is a possibility of leveraging this particular demand component, which emerged thanks to the socially responsible entrepreneur's actions, competitors put imitative strategies in place to capture this market by increasing their social responsibility. At the same time, workers in the country where production was delocalized have greater bargaining power in order to improve their working conditions.

Further reading

Acemoglu, D., & Robinson, A. (2012). *Why nations fail: The origins of power, prosperity, and poverty.* New York: Crown Business.

Becchetti, L., & Borzaga, C. (2010). *The economics of social responsibility. The world of social enterprises.* London: Routledge.

Becchetti, L., Castriota, S., & Tortia, E. (2013). Productivity, wages and intrinsic motivation in social enterprises. *Small Business Economics, 41*(2), 379–399 (Springer).

Becchetti, L., Salustri, F., & Pelligra, V. (2018). The impact of redistribution mechanisms in the vote with the wallet game: Experimental results. *Social Choice and Welfare, 51*(4), 595–619 (Springer).

EUROSIF. (2008). *European SRI study*. Eurosif.

Freeman, R. E. (1984). *Strategic management: A stakeholder approach*. Boston: Pitman.

Friedman, M. (1962). *Capitalism and freedom*. Chicago: The University of Chicago Press.

Jensen, M. C. (2001). Value maximization, stakeholder theory, and the corporate objective function. *The Journal of Applied Corporate Finance, 14*(3), 8–21.

Reed, L. R. (2011). *State of the microcredit summit Campaign report*.

SRI. (2007). *Report on socially responsible investing trends in the United States*.

Chapter 12

Happiness, relational goods, and social progress

12.1 The empirical verification of the a priori assumptions of "homo oeconomicus": the economics of happiness

By this point in our discussion the reader will have certainly understood just how important economists think it is to scientifically verify their hypotheses. Knowledge in the discipline of economics progresses primarily by building theoretical models that produce testable hypotheses and by subsequently verifying these hypotheses with data that either do or do not validate the proposed models. In addition to verifications based on historical data, in recent years the addition of experimental economics allows precise testing of theoretical hypotheses by constructing appropriate controlled experiments that allow changing one factor at a time and verifying its effects on the experiment's outcomes. One of the main advantages of experiments is their reproducibility, which allows any other economist to repeat the experiment with a different population sample to verify whether the outcome remains the same. The primary disadvantage is the so-called problem of "external consistency," which is the doubt that the behavior of subjects analyzed in the laboratory faithfully reproduces what the same individuals would do in real life.

Curiously, however, the anthropological assumptions, or the conception of the person that serves as the basis for modeling economic agents and their preference structures, had never been subject to empirical verification prior to the advent of studies on happiness.

Until recently it was not possible to fill in this gap, not for lack of attention to the problem but because the data was not available. It certainly cannot be said that the discipline of economics from its inception thought the problem of happiness, and thus the nature of individual preferences, was unimportant. If we don't want to go back to the 18th century Italian economists, such as Genovesi, Verri, and others who placed "public happiness" at the center of their analysis, we need only consider a comment by the famous economist Thomas Malthus (1798, p. 86). As we noted in the first chapter, when confronting Adam Smith's *Wealth of Nations*, one of the most important works in economic thought, Malthus wrote that:

The Microeconomics of Wellbeing and Sustainability. https://doi.org/10.1016/B978-0-12-816027-5.00012-4

The professed object of Dr. Adam Smith's inquiry is the nature and causes of the wealth of nations. There is another inquiry, however, perhaps still more interesting, which he occasionally mixes with it, I mean an inquiry into the causes which affect the happiness of nations.

Happiness did not become the object of study of economic science for various reasons. One was the difficulty of measuring a vague concept such as happiness, either public or private, which led to substituting utility for happiness at the end of the 19th century. Another was the "bare fact of choice" from Pareto onward in the 20th century, when the theory of the consumer emerged based on preferences, which we studied in the first part of the book.

However, in the last few decades something has changed in the attitude of the social and economic sciences toward the topic of happiness. The availability of many databases from various countries around the world with individuals' stated information on happiness and life satisfaction played an important role in changing this attitude from skepticism to interest. Properly processed, this information can shed a little light on the horizon, allowing us to extend our research and, at least partially, "count the things that count."

12.2 Are the data on happiness trustworthy, and what do they really measure?

Today there are many databases available to scholars to research the determinants of happiness. The **World Value Survey** is among the most important; it collects information on the demographics, economic situations, values, and stated happiness from representative samples of citizens in more than 70 countries around the world. The limit of this source is the impossibility of following the evolution of these variables for each individual over time. There are planned repeats of the survey over the years for each country, but the sample of people interviewed is not the same. *Eurobarometer*, a database similar to the *World Value Survey* that exclusively covers European countries, has the same limitation.

The only databases that have the merit of following the same individuals over time are the *German Socioeconomic Panel* (GSOEP) and the *British Household Survey Panel* (BHSP); however, they have the limitation of collecting information only from citizens of their own countries, so they do not allow comparing between different nations.

The type of question posed to measure the stated degree of happiness is similar to this: "All things considered, are you very happy, somewhat happy, not very happy, or unhappy?".

Alternatively, the person being interviewed might be asked: "All things considered, are you satisfied or unsatisfied with your present life?".

This question can be answered by attributing a value from 0 to 10 for one's level of satisfaction.

So while it is true that empirical scholars of happiness do not impose their own concepts of happiness, but rather ask respondents if they consider themselves happy, it is equally true that the way the questions are posed implies a certain way of revealing happiness that influences how we conceive of it. For example, the above question measures a cognitive dimension of happiness by asking for a considered evaluation about it, while other questions, such as "How many times were you happy or depressed yesterday?" imply an emotive dimension of happiness. Questions such as "How much meaning does your life have?" call a eudaimonistic dimension of happiness into play. Despite these differences, the results on the determinants of happiness are extraordinarily similar. Returning to our question, it is easy to imagine the perplexity of many readers regarding the raw data used in happiness studies investigations. Should we trust what people say? How many possible distortions could prejudice the validity and usability of this subjective information for statistical purposes?

In particular the possibility of interpersonal comparisons on the basis of cardinal values is criticized, or the significance of comparing individuals' stated absolute values. Recalling the topic of cardinality addressed in Chapter 3, Section 1, how can we establish that one person's stated level 5 happiness exactly corresponds to someone else's stated level 5? One response to this question might be that, although such a comparison poses many problems, it is implicitly accepted in other disciplines such as medicine. When doctors press on a sore spot and ask the patient if it hurts, they use the patient's movement when in pain as one element of an evaluation; by implicitly locating the reaction within the range of previously observed reactions, they are making a comparison between absolute values.

Medical research uses a more structured approach with *self-assessed health* (SAH), which is calculated on a scale similar to the happiness scale, as an indicator for verifying the success of therapies and medications.

More generally, scholars studying happiness have formulated several rather robust arguments in defense of the reliability of the data. First, happiness studies have a long tradition in the disciplines of psychology and sociology.

Considering that every methodology in a given discipline must undergo strict scrutiny from researchers, and that, through a system of referees and cross-referential judgments, only the best approaches should survive over time, the resilience of happiness studies in these disciplines gives us a first indication of their trustworthiness.

Second, many medical psychological studies show that there is a significant correlation between respondents' stated happiness and their psychophysical health. Happier people have better cardiovascular health, better hormonal balance, and lower suicidal tendencies. We should thus take stated happiness seriously for the fact alone that it is actually correlated with, and has been shown to influence, our psychophysical conditions.

Third, statements about happiness have proven capable of predicting future behavior. For example, several recent analyses have shown that those who have lower stated levels of happiness at work are more likely to voluntary quit in subsequent years, and couples in which there are higher differences in stated happiness between the husband and wife have a greater probability of separating; that is, the facts corroborate the words. Fourth, respondents' statements about their happiness are strongly correlated with what their closest relatives or friends say about their happiness. Fifth, recent studies in neuroscience show that there seems to be a very close correlation between states of mind or actions that positively influence stated happiness and physiological reactions that are typical of our bodies in moments of happiness. More specifically, significant positive relationships have recently been discovered between alpha wave emission in the left prefrontal cortex in our brains and stated happiness, in parallel with positive correlations of alpha waves with positive feelings associated with an individual's satisfaction stages; in this case our bodies corroborate our statements.

These encouraging confirmations of the reliability of the data on stated happiness do not imply however that the data should not be treated very carefully.

One of the more problematic operations is using them to make comparisons among countries. There are two basic concerns about using the data for this purpose. First, the concept of happiness itself can have different meanings according to the particular meaning of the term used in each language. The Italian word "felicità" derives etymologically from the terms *felix*, *ferax*, or *fecundus*, and it is thus associated with the concept of fecundity and flourishing in one's own life. The English term *happiness* has various shades of meaning, in that it is connected with the verb *to happen* and the concepts of fate and fortune, thus it is less connected to the concept of the self-determination of one's own existence.

A second problem regards the possible cultural biases linked to the particular ways of responding in different cultures. To give a concrete example, if we determine that Italians by their nature tend to complain and exaggerate in describing their own problems, the consequence is that the average happiness stated by citizens of the country would be underestimated with respect to what is stated in other countries. This is only one example, and we could imagine many other distortions of various types. For example, in a culture in which superstition plays an important role, stating that one is happy could be considered a reckless attitude that could invite misfortune. An interesting attempt to overcome these problems is to give people from different countries the same sketch that depicts an individual who is in distress or is particularly well-off. Afterward the respondents are asked to express the individual's happiness by a value from 0 to 10 to observe whether their re-actions are the same or not. The differences in evaluations by different subjects are then used to correct the results for the differences in the happiness scales adopted.

This is why scholars of happiness hold that analyzing the variations in happiness stated by the same individuals over time is much more reliable than interpersonal comparisons between individuals from different cultures. The main results described in the rest of the chapter primarily refer to the first type of analysis.

12.3 Does happiness really coincide with utility? Kahneman's approach

One of the basic objections to using questions that require an overall assess-ment of one's own life was formulated by the psychologist and economist Daniel Kahneman, one of the foremost scholars of happiness who earned the Nobel prize in economics for his studies bridging the two disciplines.

According to Kahneman, individuals' statements about happiness are heavily influenced by the most recent events. To illustrate his concept, Kah-neman talks about the *experiencing self* and the *remembering self*. According to Kahneman, the problem is that the evaluation formulated by the remem-bering self is heavily influenced by the experiencing self. In other words, a life satisfaction statement represents a weighted average of instants of happiness lived at various times in the past, with the weights of the different happiness instants distributed unequally; more specifically, the most recent instants count more heavily. In particular, it has been shown that respondents are particularly sensitive to conditions at that time, but by introducing appropriate questions into the surveys, the distortion can be eliminated. Another curious example of this is the effect tested in an experiment in which all respondents are asked to make a photocopy prior to answering the survey with questions about happiness. Half of them are set up to find a coin in the photocopier. The results of the survey subsequently show that, everything else being equal, those re-spondents state a higher level of utility.

To avoid this problem, Kahneman focuses his attention on the experiencing self by a method that he calls the *Daily Reconstruction Method*. This method consists of asking subjects who participate in the experiment to record at certain moments of the day the events they have just lived and the degree of satisfaction connected with them.

The risk of this approach is that it could end up equating the concept of happiness with pleasure. Furthermore, it is highly likely that the instantaneous reactions to a given event do not necessarily coincide with reactions linked to an evaluation mediated by time, and in particular by the internal resonances lived out in later moments. So between the self that has the experience and the self that remembers it we can hypothesize the presence of a *resounding self*, or the internal resonances that confirm or contradict the immediate judgment. (The evaluation of the effects on one's well-being of taking drugs or excessive alcohol is very different in the immediate and the short run.)

This is why we maintain that studies on stated overall life satisfaction are more interesting, in that we think that the interaction and control of the *resounding self* on the *experiencing self* has already been carried out and that, on average, subjects have the appropriate maturity to be able to give an overall evaluation of their own lives.

A further advantage of the overall life satisfaction approach is that there is less possibility for respondents to understand the reason why the survey is being taken. One of scholars' greatest fears is that respondents to a survey might intuit why the survey is being done and thus respond to the questions in a non-natural manner because they want to send some type of message to the interviewer. In the case of the daily reconstruction method, participants in the experiment understand much more readily that the purpose of the exercise is to relate happiness to various aspects of their lives, so in the simple act of recording their feelings after various events they could add a message, or their conceptual persuasion, they want to communicate to the interviewer.

In the case of studies on declared happiness, the empirical data are taken from surveys with hundreds of questions on various topics and are available for multiple uses that are not defined beforehand. In these cases the particular aspect that future researchers might want to analyze — such as the relationship between happiness and income — could not occur to any of the participants, so the possibility that participants could manipulate their responses is absolutely remote.

Another interesting fact is that, despite the significant differences between this approach and that of an overall evaluation of one's life, there is remarkable agreement between the results obtained regarding the factors that have the greatest impact on happiness. For example, in both methods the importance of sociality and the time spent in relationship emerges as one of the variables with the greatest positive effects on both momentary happiness and overall life satisfaction.

12.4 The stylized facts

12.4.1 Happiness and income

One of the central questions in an introductory economics study that greatly piques students' curiosity is the relationship between happiness and income.

In consumer theory the primary argument is the analysis of the relationship between utility and consumption. Using the traditionally accepted approach to the topic, we built our model of the consumer starting from the assumption of non-satiation and the concavity of the utility function with respect to consumption. This functional form can properly represent the hypothesis of diminishing marginal utility, or the hypothesis that determines how consuming successive units of the same good generates decreasing quantitative satisfaction. Marginal utility can decrease to the point of satiation, and beyond that point additional units of the good do not increase utility (see Chapter 3).

However, since there are countless consumable goods available, and money — whether paper or electronic — serves as a *value reserve* and a *means of exchange*, it is possible to understand why economists think of the relationship between changes in income and changes in utility as always being a positive relationship that is immune from the principle of satiety. In simpler terms, money is not a good we consume directly, but rather a means that can be used to buy all sorts of tradable goods and services. On the assumption that the number of such goods is very high, and that the previously illustrated law of concavity of the utility function applies to each one, we can use our available funds to buy each good and move from good to good as we become satiated with them; in this way we are never satiated with money, or better yet with the things money allows us to buy.

12.4.2 The Easterlin paradox

Does empirical analysis confirm this basic assumption? When verifying this basic hypothesis, the first scholars who had data available on stated happiness found themselves faced with the so-called "Easterlin Paradox," which was apparently in contradiction with the previous assumption. Easterlin's study compared per capita income in real terms with the number of people who stated they were very happy in a representative sample of participants in the United States during the post WWII timeframe from 1946 to 1996. The result, which is immediately evident in graphic form, is that significant per capita income growth was not accompanied by an increase in the number of people who stated they were very happy during that time period (Fig. 12.1).

Similar studies have sought to verify whether the **Easterlin Paradox** applies in different periods and countries. Very similar dynamics were found in many (but not all) cases, such as in the five largest European countries from 1973 to 2004, or among the citizens of the former East Germany from 1991 to 2002. To give an example of this divergence in outcomes, by carrying out the exercise for more limited time intervals we find for example that between 1975 and 2002 (see Figs. 12.2 and 12.3) the Easterlin Paradox seemed to occur in Germany but not in Italy.

It is also significant that in Egypt and Tunisia, the Arab Spring countries the dynamics of per capita GDP and life satisfaction were quite similar to the Easterlin Paradox on the eve of the outbreak of the revolt. One of the shortfalls of political leaders at that time was placing too much trust in the positive dynamics of GDP while ignoring life satisfaction; that is why politicians and

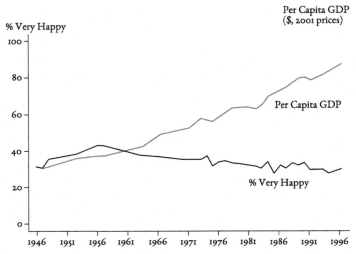

FIG. 12.1 The Easterlin paradox: the relationship between happiness and per capita GDP in the United States in the post-WWII period.

economists are more and more sensitive today to studies of the dynamics of happiness.

The challenge of later studies on the relationship between happiness and income started precisely as an attempt to explain the paradox with more refined statistical and econometric tools in the places where it had been observed.

FIG. 12.2 Happiness and per capita GDP in Italy (1975–2002). *LS*, stated life satisfaction. *Source: Our calculations based on Eurobarometer data.*

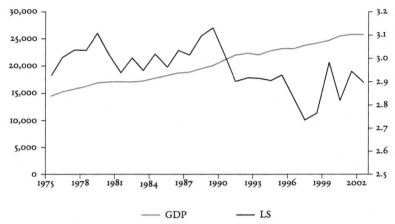

FIG. 12.3 Happiness and per capita GDP in Germany (1975–2002). *LS*, stated life satisfaction. *Source: Our calculations based on Eurobarometer data.*

A simple comparison of the dynamics of the two absolute variables of per capita GDP and the level of stated happiness does not say enough about the real relationship between them, in that many concurring factors could have contributed to determining what was observed. Considering the Easterlin Paradox, Americans may not have shown increases in happiness not because of, but in spite of per capita GDP increases, due rather to other reasons such as a reduction in the quality of relational life, job satisfaction, and so forth.

The task for recent empirical investigations has been to isolate the effect of one of the two variables on the other, net of other factors, with the goal of drawing more precise conclusions.

We can summarize the vast bulk of recent research developing this topic in-depth with the following three empirical regularities:

1. increases in real personal or familial income are significantly correlated *on average* with increases in stated personal happiness, net of all other effects of other variables considered;
2. the wide gap between rich and poor countries in terms of per capita income do not translate into an analogous happiness gap, and in fact in several paradoxical cases, credible investigations on happiness have recorded higher levels of happiness per citizen in poor or emergent countries than in rich countries;
3. there is a significant number of so-called "frustrated achievers," or individuals who, in correspondence with positive changes in real personal or familial income, report lower levels of stated happiness measured on an annual basis.

Instead of resolving, the dilemma seems to only become even more intricate.

How is it possible to reconcile the facts in 1, 2, and 3 among themselves, and how can they explain the Easterlin Paradox?

A preliminary explanation is the confusion between GDP, the variable that Easterlin studied, and economic satisfaction. The latter depends much less on GDP and much more directly on disposable family income, after paying taxes and the essential public goods and services such as education and healthcare. GDP is thus not a good indicator of citizens' economic satisfaction, which is far more directly indicated by disposable family income. Beyond this important introductory clarification, as a partial solution to the dilemma economists have discovered two very interesting phenomena that force us to profoundly rethink our concept of the relationship between utility and income. The two phenomena are the roles of *relative income* and of *hedonic adaptation*.

The concept of **relative income** is very simple, originating from the idea, traditionally developed in sociology, that one of the factors that most influences personal happiness is in comparing oneself with one's peers — with one's "reference group" in sociological terms. In essence we live in continual comparisons, and the "relative income" effect tells us that we draw increases or decreases in happiness from the fact that our income level is greater or less than those whom we consider our peers, those with whom we routinely compare ourselves.

The treadmill effect is a phenomenon associated with the impact of relative income. According to this effect, if relative income is all that counts, it may happen that if an individual "competes" by increasing his own income and quality of life, and his peers do the same, from the standpoint of relative income the reality is as if nothing actually changes.

With the assumption of a proportional effect of the gap between one's income and that of one's reference group, the relative income effect is depicted graphically in Fig. 12.4. The continuous line identifies the relationship between happiness and income without the effect, and the dashed line includes it. As we can see, the negative gap between personal income and the average income of the reference group shifts the happiness curve proportionally downward, while a positive gap shifts it upward. The happiness curve that takes the relative income effect into account thus has a slope that corresponds to the average value of the reference group's income. Just who our peers are is obviously a matter of discussion among scholars. The most generally used approach is to look at the average of the incomes of a subsample of individuals of the same sex, education level, and age group as the subject for whom a reference group income is being constructed. Geographic factors are usually included when comparing individuals who live in regions with significant socioeconomic differences between them.

As a side discussion to the concept of relative income, it is interesting to note how a fruitful integration is taking place in the field of happiness studies among the various social disciplines. To overcome the dichotomy between *homo oeconomicus*, for whom what counts are the results of one's own actions,

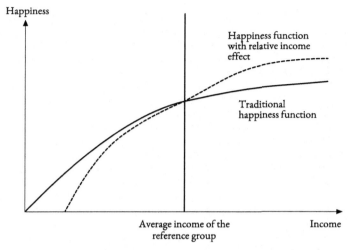

FIG. 12.4 The effect of relative income on a utility function.

and *homo sociologicus*, whose satisfaction depends primarily on one's social context, research on the relationship between happiness and income suggests that the two approaches should necessarily be integrated in factual reality, in which both personal income and relative income, or the relationship between personal income and the average income of the group to whom we compare ourselves, have significant impact on life satisfaction.

Finally, we should note that there are some exceptions to the relative income effect described above. In countries with particularly high social mobility, the growth of the reference group's income can indicate an increase in future earning prospects, and thus it be perceived with satisfaction. As in Hirshmann's well-known tunnel effect, when a driver stopped in traffic sees cars in another lane begin to move, she is happy because she hopes that she too will soon begin to move. Vertical mobility and the dream that "everyone can make it" mitigate the negative consequences of deep income inequality on happiness and social cohesion.

To explain the concept of **hedonic adaptation**, we again start from empirical data. Taken from the *German Socioeconomic Panel*, which represents around 396,000 "person—year" observations over a period from 1984 to 2004, Table 12.1 illustrates the relationship between changes in income, overall life satisfaction, and satisfaction in different areas of people's lives (such as housing conditions, health, domestic life, work, free time, and income) for a vast sample of German citizens. The table lists the number of people who reported decreases or increases in satisfaction indicators in specific areas of their lives for the group of so-called *frustrated achievers* (columns 1 and 2), *frustrated losers* (columns 3 and 4), *satisfied achievers* (columns 5 and 6), and *satisfied losers* (columns 7 and 9).

TABLE 12.1 Reductions and increases in life satisfaction in specific areas for four categories of people defined on the basis of change in income and in overall life satisfaction.

	Frustrated achievers		Frustrated losers		Satisfied achievers		Satisfied losers	
	% of those who reported reductions in the indicated area of satisfaction	% of those who reported increases in the indicated area of satisfaction	% of those who reported reductions in the indicated area of satisfaction	% of those who reported increases in the indicated area of satisfaction	% of those who reported reductions in the indicated area of satisfaction	% of those who reported increases in the indicated area of satisfaction	% of those who reported reductions in the indicated area of satisfaction	% of those who reported increases in the indicated area of satisfaction
Life Satisfaction		0					0	
Living Conditions	40.42	28.48	41.19	27.02	11.09	76.44	10.82	76.54
Health Satisfaction	47.31	24.55	47.70	24.46	11.24	77.13	10.93	77.79
Home Life Satisfaction	22.74	63.79	24.40	60.93	5.97	88.57	6.14	87.99
Job Satisfaction	26.02	59.34	25.31	60.76	5.91	88.07	5.84	88.32

Leisure Time Satisfaction	41.33	34.58	41.05	33.68	11.59	78.85	10.68	79.73
Family Satisfaction								
Income	41.84	31.54	50.25	24.94	9.30	80.64	11.73	77.93

Note: Frustrated Achievers: individuals who reported a simultaneous increase in family income and a reduction in life satisfaction; Frustrated Losers: individuals who reported a simultaneous decrease in family income and a reduction in life satisfaction; Satisfied Achievers: individuals who reported a simultaneous increase in family income and an increase in life satisfaction; Satisfied Losers: individuals who reported a simultaneous decrease in family income and an increase in life satisfaction. All are measured in terms of annual changes.

Source: German Socioeconomic Panel sample, 1984–2004.

As previously explained, frustrated achievers are those who, over the course of a given year, report positive changes in real family income and negative changes in life satisfaction. Frustrated losers report simultaneous negative changes and satisfied achievers report simultaneous positive changes in both indicators. Finally, satisfied losers are those who report negative changes in income and positive changes in life satisfaction in the same year.

A first interesting data point to observe is that at 16% frustrated achievers are a non-negligible portion of the total sample, about a third of all cases of income increases at 32.91%, and just under half of the cases of life satisfaction reduction at 46.23%.

To understand how this may have happened, we illustrate the problem in Fig. 12.5, where we measure utility on the vertical axis and income on the horizontal axis.

From T_0 to T_1 the individual behaves as expected, responding with an increase in happiness corresponding to an income increase. Hedonic adaptation occurs at T_2, where the level of happiness drops even though income has not changed. What probably happened is that the individual raises the bar of his aspirations to T_2, thus automatically reducing the satisfaction level he had previously attributed to any income level. This corresponds on a graph to a downward shift of people's utility functions. Despite a later increase in income from T_2 to T_3 that positively contributes to happiness as expected, when we compare changes in income and satisfaction from T_0 to T_3, due to the downward shift in the utility function from U to U' we obtain the paradoxical result of an income increase on the x-axis associated with a decrease in stated happiness on the y-axis. If we assume that the interval from T_0 to T_3

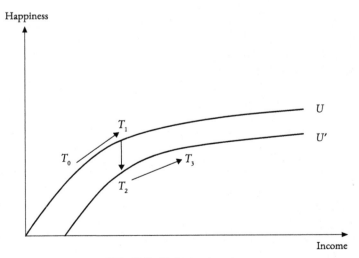

FIG. 12.5 Hedonic adaptation.

corresponds to the previously reported annual survey, the behavior illustrated in the graph exactly corresponds to the case of the frustrated achiever who reported a decline in satisfaction relative to their income.

We should keep in mind that not all the effect measured in the German study can be attributed to the psychological phenomenon of hedonic adaptation described above. There are in fact other possible explanations why individuals can report increases in per capita income from one year to the next that are associated with a decline in the level of satisfaction deriving from their income. One of the simplest is that some participants probably reported a desired increase in income greater than the actual growth in effective income for reasons other than purely psychological hedonic adaptation; for example, the family's expenses may have increased more than the perceived income increase. The difference with the phenomenon of hedonic adaptation is that in this case other factors come into play (other than the change in income itself) that motivate the negative reaction in terms of income satisfaction. In the case of hedonic adaptation, the negative reaction is instead determined without any other concomitant cause and depends solely on the fact that the result achieved suddenly appears less gratifying than it was while struggling to achieve it.

12.4.3 The problem of causality in the relationship between income and happiness

In nearly all cases the problem arises of properly determining a causal nexus between happiness and the factors that contribute to it. As we well know, temporal succession is not sufficient to establish that what happened before was a cause and what happened afterward was an effect; quite frequently the famous Latin saying *post hoc ergo propter hoc* does not apply.

Up to this point we have reasoned with the implicit assumption that causation is unidirectional either from an income level or from changes in income toward stated happiness. In reality it seems equally plausible to argue that causation can go in the opposite direction, from happiness to income. That is, individuals with personality traits that are more inclined toward happiness, such as extroversion, a positive outlook, optimism, and so forth, may also have a greater likelihood of economically establishing themselves in life.

It is interesting to note that, due to the characteristics of their different disciplines in the social sciences, economists tend to prefer the first causal relationship from income to happiness, and psychologists tend to prefer the second from happiness to income. Economists are generally drawn to focus on the effects of life events such as income increases or decreases, losing a job, or rising inflation rates that can affect people's happiness. On the contrary, psychologists primarily study the way our personalities are structured from early childhood and focus attention on the definition of character traits that can only be changed slowly and with difficulty over the course of people's lives.

Clearly, psychologists are more prone to interpret the link between income and happiness in the opposite sense, showing in detail that there are some character types such as optimism about life, self-esteem, extroversion, and sociality that contribute toward a positive outlook on life, which then has positive effects on people's abilities to attain economic success.

Research on the relationship between happiness and income, as with the relationship between happiness and other factors, must solve the causality puzzle. This is done with different approaches, some of which are quite sophisticated from a statistical and econometric viewpoint.

However, the simplest and most interesting approach we will mention here is that of "natural experiments." In order to be sure of the fact that income and changes in income have effects on happiness, it is necessary to start from an exogenous change in income and analyze its subsequent effects on happiness. By "exogenous change" we mean a shock that is not determined by an individual's happiness level or by another variable that may be connected to it. An example of an exogenous shock is winning a lottery. This is a totally random event that cannot be determined by non-random factors, and certainly not by the winner's former level of happiness.

So when analyzing the relationship between changes in income and changes in happiness in the case of winning a lottery, we can be sure that in this situation the discovery of a positive relationship unequivocally indicates a causal link from a change in income to a change in happiness, and not vice versa.

Other interesting cases in exogenous changes that allow us to construct "natural experiments" have been identified in income changes caused by the process of large-scale transitions from communism to a market economy, or from natural disasters such as Hurricane Katrina or a tsunami. Both instances are historical events whose origins can in no way be traced back to individuals' happiness levels. So in this case as well when studying the relationship between income changes generated by such shocks and changes in happiness, we can be sure that causation can be interpreted in light of a causal direction that flows from changes in income to changes in happiness, and not vice versa.

The studies cited show an interesting asymmetry that is consistent with the hypothesis of the concavity of the happiness function (Fig. 12.6). Being unfortunately drawn into a "negative lottery," such as Katrina or a tsunami, has highly negative effects on life satisfaction, as one would expect, even if not all the negative effects on the variable can be explained by the economic shock caused by such disasters. Winning a traditional lottery causes moderate increases in satisfaction that tend to decline over time due to the phenomenon of hedonic adaptation we previously explained. In conclusion, the causal nexus from money to happiness seems much stronger for negative than for positive changes, and when starting from low income rather than when income is already high.

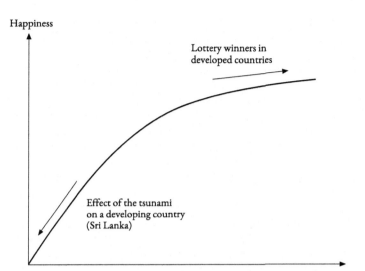

FIG. 12.6 The Effects of Exogenous Shocks on the Happiness—Income Relationship. *Note*: There is evidence of an asymmetry between positive and negative exogenous shocks on happiness in relation to different income levels: negative shocks reduce income and happiness if starting income is low, and positive shocks only weakly increase happiness if starting income is high.

12.4.4 Happiness and relational life

One of the most important contributions of happiness studies is that they have emphasized the fundamental role of people's relational lives on life satisfaction, which economics scholars have decidedly neglected. We find almost no models that directly include social relations among the arguments to individual utility functions among the countless theoretical papers published in international scientific journals, and certainly not in textbook formulations. Studies on happiness seem to indicate that this is an extremely important omission.

Those who support the traditional approach to building preferences can respond to this observation with two types of objections.

The first is that the value of relationships is implicitly incorporated in the goods that go into the utility function. For example, if I choose to buy a spacious house with guest rooms rather than a one bedroom garret in the historic center, by my buying choices I am showing that I place a high value on relationships (at least for those lived out in my home). The response to the objection is that we certainly cannot circumscribe the role and the importance of relational goods within the mere acquisition of consumption items that more or less favor encounters with others. For example, with this approach it is not possible to capture the effect on one's utility function of a stroll with a friend or the breakup of a friendship or an affective relationship.

The second line of defense for traditional economists is that the topic of relationships is included in the choice between work and free time we analyzed when we studied the labor supply (Chapter 9). Here too the response is that the choice of hours in the day dedicated to free time do not exactly coincide with the time spent in relational goods. Part of our free time has no relational connotation, such as driving from home to work and back, time spent alone in front of the television, and so on. Furthermore, it is by no means true that we cannot live in quality relationships in our work environments. On the contrary, in a post-Fordist company productivity depends in large part on carrying out complex tasks that require teamwork, which envisions the quality of relationships among participants as a central and fundamental productivity factor.

A third objection might be to state that economics cannot pay attention to everything, and particularly to topics that are not strictly economic, such as friendship, the time spent in relationships, and so on. The response is that since all economic acts have important non-economic consequences and vice versa, if we do not give attention to all aspects of human life instead of just one part, we cannot understand anything of the reality that surrounds us. Granovetter, a noted sociologist, has even argued that all economic behavior by individuals is mediated by relationships.

So if relationships significantly impact people's utility, and if it is important to pay attention to the basic interaction between relationships and economic choices, then the first thing we must do is define the concept of a relationship. To do that we should begin with what economists have started defining as **relational goods** (Frames 12.1 and 12.2).

12.4.5 Empirical results on the relationship between happiness and relational goods

The results of the relationship between happiness and relational goods seems to unequivocally indicate a tight relationship between the two variables. Investigations carried out on data from the foremost databases that have information on participants' stated happiness highlight that the time spent in relationships has significant positive effects on stated happiness. In the case of the relationship between these two variables, the two approaches of overall life satisfaction and the daily reconstruction method (which looks at participants' immediate reactions to events during the day) seem absolutely in agreement. Kahneman's work stresses that the moments of relational life, such as eating in the company of friends or family, and the time invested in relationships are what determine the highest peaks of satisfaction during the day, and in studies of overall life satisfaction the time invested in relationships is fundamentally important. In the same way, stated life satisfaction studies highlight a positive correlation between satisfaction and the time spent in relationships (Table 12.3).

FRAME 12.1 The relational goods.

According to the economist Benedetto Gui, relational goods can be defined as the "intangible product of a communicative and affective nature generated by interactions between persons." To be clear, the friendly atmosphere that can be created between persons who meet for the first time is a relational good; the encounter is not a relational good in itself, but rather it is its "production function," or the mechanism by which relational goods are produced.

The political scientist Carole Uhlaner defines these goods as "can only be 'possessed' by mutual agreement that they exist after appropriate joint actions have been taken by a person and non-arbitrary others" (1989, p. 254). They are thus dimensions of relationships that can be neither produced nor consumed by one individual, because they depend on the types of interactions with others and can be enjoyed only if they are shared.

The economic approach to relational goods considers them as realities that are *independent* of the relationship itself. Gui explicitly expresses this methodological intention to preserve continuity with economic science, which sees a good as distinct from the effects created in the process of consuming it. This is why he tends to separate the relational good from the people who "prosume" it, (that is, those who produce and consume it together; the term is used today in marketing and social networks). Such a separation is only partially possible, given that the subjective traits of the interacting persons enter into its production.

So in Gui's theory, the relational good is distinct from agents' subjective characteristics and preferences. In particular, he proposes analyzing every form of interaction as a particular production process, which he calls an "encounter". He suggests that other types of intangible outputs of a relational nature are "produced" in an encounter "between a seller and a potential buyer, a doctor and a patient, two work colleagues, or even between two customers of the same store" (Gui, 2005, p. 27), in addition to traditional outputs such as carrying out a transaction, performing a productive task, supplying a service, and so on. These are the changes in human capital in the interacting persons, in their relational assets, which are *relational consumption goods*, or those Gui defines as goods that are relational in nature.

This relational good does not exhaust the set of all of Gui's relational goods, since the ones we just described are only the relational consumption goods. His relational goods also include "relational assets"; these are not single acts of production—consumption (such as a chat with someone unknown on a train whom one will never see again), but "repeatedly fruitful" goods — precisely, a relational asset.

We can try to better understand the characteristics of relational goods by using the taxonomy adopted for understanding the differences between private and public goods (Table 12.2). From this point of view relational goods can be defined as "local public goods," or goods with non-rivalry and non-excludability characteristics that are *local in the sense that they are limited to those who participate in an encounter.*

Actually, the concept of a public good is not adequate to understand relational goods, since non-rivalry does not really grasp the nature of relationships. Non-

Continued

Frame 12.1 The relational goods.—cont'd

rivalry is associated with non-interference in consumption, such as two visitors to a museum who look at a painting at the same time without getting in each other's way (differently from a private good such as a hamburger, fruition of that good from an individual does not prevent fruition of the same good from another individual). Indeed, if we think about it more carefully, the existence of relationships between people are an indispensable element to the quality of the relational good.

This is why relational goods are more appropriately defined as "anti-rivalry" rather than non-rivalry goods. Returning to the example of the museum, we move from a public good (the painting) to a relational good if the two visitors begin to *interact with each other* while looking at the painting; in this case the consumption of a relational good is added to the consumption of a public good.

The simultaneous consumption, production, and in certain cases — such as repeated encounters — investment in relational goods is an additional characteristic. Indeed, if we think about the effect of a meeting between two long-time friends, we can conclude that the meeting is not just the moment when a relational good "friendship between the two" is "produced" and "consumed," but it is also that every time they meet they invest relational good "capital" in an asset; that is, an activity arises that contributes to increasing the value of future relational goods, in that when they meet, they draw greater friendship from the encounter due to the increased value of the relational asset.

Another particular characteristic of relational goods is that they do not generally have diminishing marginal utility. As we saw in consumption theory, while it is reasonable to assume that the principle of gradually lower benefit increments is valid for most goods we consume, the logic of some relational goods seems to follow just the opposite principle, as also happens when consuming creative goods such as classical music or art — a phenomenon that had already been foreseen for music by the British economist Alfred Marshall at the end of the 19th century. That is, the value of a relational good seems to grow as the number of encounters increases (if the friendship works), and on the contrary it can decline if the frequency of encounters decreases. This is similar to what happens with a mountain trail that improves with use and is lost if left unused.

Adam Smith made the astute observation in the *Theory of Moral Sentiments* that some aspects of the quality of an interaction are fundamental for increasing the value of the relational good. The predispositions toward one's interlocutor are quite important. For Smith, moreover, the key factor that gives value to a relationship is *fellow feeling*, or the ability to feel in the same way (common consent), or more poetically, to "vibrate in unison." Smith observed that fellow feeling is decisively nourished by the emotional intensity of time spent together. So not all time has the same qualitative meaning, and sharing deeper aspects contributes more than sharing superficial matters. As Smith acutely observed, one significantly influential factor is the emotional intensity of a shared event rather than its connotation as a happy or unhappy time. From this point of view we observe that participating in a celebration, such as a birthday or a wedding, can be as bonding as attending a sad event, such as a funeral.

Frame 12.1 The relational goods.—cont'd

The theory of relational goods is still fully evolving and developing. The simplified description we developed above does not give a full account of the reasoning regarding their characteristics. In fact, it is useful to think of relational goods as a third *genus* with regard to traditional economic goods classified as "private" and "public", although as we will soon see, there are characteristics of the economic theory of public goods that can shed light on some dimensions of relational goods (without considering them as public goods).

The following are the basic characteristics of a relational good:

a) *Identity:* The identity of the individual persons involved is a fundamental ingredient. This is why Uhlaner (1989) states that relational goods are never anonymous and independent of the other's face. They are goods that are *identity-dependent.* One may not know the other's name or face, but that person is not replaceable in creating the good, such as an equally capable hairdresser who takes over halfway through an appointment when the usual person must abruptly leave; one may chat with the new person, but it is a different reality, a different "good".

b) *Reciprocity:* Because they are goods that are made up of relationships, they can only be enjoyed in reciprocity. "Mutual activity, feeling, and awareness are such a deep part of what love and friendship are that Aristotle is unwilling to say that there is anything worthy of the name of love or friendship left" (Nussbaum, 2001, p. 344). Reciprocity should not be understood here in its strong sense (as for example in an exchange of values, objects, or attitudes that are somewhat symmetrical, although not equivalent), since a relational good may be generated and enjoyed even with someone who is not in a condition to respond symmetrically to someone taking care of her, perhaps because she is very ill. In any case, even an encounter in silence and in partial unawareness by one of the persons can be a matter of reciprocity (the other "says something", even for no other reason than being bodily present).

c) *Simultaneity:* Unlike normal market goods, whether public or private, in which production is technically and logically distinct from consumption, relational goods are produced and consumed simultaneously; the good is co-produced and co-consumed at the same time by those involved. Although the production contribution can be asymmetrical (think of a medical examination or a birthday party[1]), free riding — the total exploitation of the other's commitment — is not possible during the act of consumption, because enjoying the relational good requires that one let oneself become involved in a relationship with the characteristics we are listing. As an example, think of a trip with friends. During that *encounter*, the commitment to create the proper atmosphere can be asymmetric among the various participants, but if one does not somehow enter into the relationships by engaging in reciprocity, and thus deepening one's effort, one may benefit from a standard market good during that day, such as information, knowledge, and so forth, but one will not have enjoyed relational goods.

d) *Emergent Phenomenon:* Relational goods "emerge", as sociologists love to say, within a relationship. Perhaps the category "emergent fact" captures more of

Continued

Frame 12.1 The relational goods.—cont'd

the nature of a relational good than the economic category of "production".[2] Its emergence places the emphasis on the fact that the relational good is a *third* that exceeds the "contributions" made by those involved, and which in many cases was not among their initial intentions. This is why a relational good can "emerge" within a normal market transaction when, at a certain point right in the middle of an ordinary economic relationship, something happens that moves those involved to forget the reason why they met, and the relational good "emerges".

e) *Gratuitousness:* Gratuitousness is a characteristic that concisely sums up relational goods. A relational good is such if the relationship — in particular a relationship that emerges within a normal work encounter — is lived as a good in itself that is not used for anything else. As Nussbaum states, this is why a relational good is a good in which the relationship is the good, a relationship that is not an encounter of self-interests, but rather an encounter in gratuitousness. A relational good requires intrinsic motivations toward that particular relationship.

f) *Good:* Emphasizing it as a noun is a concise way of stating what a relational good is. It is a *good,* but it is not a *commodity*[3]; that is, it has *value* (because it satisfies a need) but it does not have a *price* on the market.

Once these characteristics are listed, however, we must emphasize the difficulty of using economic theory to work with human relationships. Economics looks at the world from the perspective of an *individual who chooses goods*; the relationship escapes his attention by definition, precisely because in this case one begins with two or more, and the other is primarily neither a good nor a constraint. Indeed, if we put all the preceding characteristics together we do not produce a definition that satisfies economists or social scientists, precisely because it is too rich and complete to be useful. This is why the individual disciplines consider only some characteristics when analyzing human relationships, which they define as "relational goods". However, perhaps this partialness is the only way to use the category in actual applications and policies, which are all too important in the social sciences. Every so often it is good to remind ourselves that the story is more complex than what any individual discipline tells, even putting them all together.

---

1 To be precise, in a party or a birthday celebration, there is not just one "presumed" relational good, but the sum of countless encounters that, if placed all together, make up the relational experience of the party.

2 Looking at it closely, "production" and "emergent fact" are only apparently in opposition, or they are if by production we mean an assembly line. But if by production we mean the activity of a research and development group that mostly explores unknown terrain, and in which it is primarily due to the interaction between skills and mental processes that something new may come out of the work, then there is no contradiction: the innovation "emerges" from the interaction among the "producers."

3 In Marx's terms, every commodity is a good, but not all goods are commodities, because a good not produced by the market is not a commodity; it thus has a value but not a price.

FRAME 12.2 **The importance of relationships in economics.**
The quality of relationships can significantly affect economic life. One of the most significant characteristics of the post-modern firm is the transition from standard production models carried out on assembly lines to productive activity based on creating ever new varieties of products that can intercept the diversity of customers' tastes and their changes over time. Creating economic value in this new type of company increasingly depends on the abilities of work teams that bring together people with different and non-overlapping skills to create new processes and new products. Employees' attitudes and the quality of their relationships thus become increasingly important in such a setting. The process of creating value in a team depends on the trust its members have in sharing private information and specific skills with other group members. If that happens "superadditivity" can occur, leading to a result that is greater than the sum of the stand-alone individual contributions. If mistrust prevails, or the fear that some members might abuse the information received or not give credit to its source and use it for themselves, such a virtuous process does not happen, and the company's ability to create value from within is sharply curtailed. When the willingness to share knowledge is praised, it is possible that new paths may open up that are even more extreme than simply sharing in a company work group. The emergence of the open source phenomenon and virtual communities that share knowledge on the Internet (consider Wikipedia) are incredible examples of how it is possible to create knowledge and public goods, as long as the trust and incentives to share overcome the problems of sharing ownership rights and exploitation of the knowledge produced. From a perspective of happiness and in light of this example, we leave a question to the reader: Is it better to be very wealthy but with a low popularity and reputation, or to be a little less wealthy and enjoy the trust and recognition of others? This is why relationships are so important today for economic life.

So it seems that in the case of relational goods there is full correspondence between the evaluations of the experiencing self, the resounding self (the resonance of the conscience that relives lived events from a distance), and the remembering self (the self that remembers and reflects on one's life as a whole).

A serious problem arises regarding the direction of causality even in the relationship between happiness and relationships. Is the quality of relational life what increases happiness, or are people who are more extroverted and have a positive attitude toward life those who inevitably have more relationships and spend more time on them? In this case as well studies seem to show the significance of both causal links. The fact that time spent in relationships increases happiness seems to be confirmed both by studies of overall life satisfaction and by Kahneman's daily reconstruction method (in this case it is clear that the causal link is fairly clear and cannot be interpreted in the opposite direction). At the same time, it seems settled that extroverts who are

TABLE 12.2 Taxonomy of private, public, and relational goods.

	Private goods	Public goods	Relational goods
	Rivalrous	Non-rivalrous	Anti-rivalrous (among participants in an encounter)
	Excludable	Non-excludable	Non-excludable (between participants in the interaction)
Marginal utility	Diminishing		Constant or increasing
Investment, production, and consumption	Separate actions	Separate actions	Coincide

TABLE 12.3 Happiness and time spent in relationships (percentages).

	Relational time index[a]		
	(0–1)	(1–2)	(2–3)
Very happy	18.65	22.27	28.84
Fairly happy	48.72	56.09	53.91
Not Very Happy	24.56	18.20	14.73
Not Happy At All	8.07	3.44	2.52

Number of observations: 84,856

A Index of relational time: the average of the responses given on the frequency of time spent with family, co-workers outside of work hours, religious groups, or friends. There are four possible ways to answer that are assigned increasing values from 0 to 3: never, a few times a year, several times a month, and weekly.

[a]*Relational Time Index: average of the responses given on the frequency of time spent with family, coworkers outside work hours, with religious groups, or with friends. Each question had four possible answers (never, a few times a year, several times a month, every week) assigned an increasing value from 0 to 3.*

Source: Authors' elaboration of data from the World Value Survey (1999–2001).

inclined toward a positive outlook on life have more intense relationships, and transitions from normal times to more depressed times lead to a reduction in relational life. The positive correlation verified in the field can also be the result of a more complex reality in which different types of people choose the lifestyles that fit them best. For example, assume that there are two groups of grumpy and friendly people: the former draw no pleasure from relationships and choose not to have any; the latter draw pleasure from relationships and invest in them. The results of the choices of these two groups yield a positive relationship between time invested in relational goods and happiness, but, given their differences, conclusions about normative policy choices to change their behavior would not be the same. Indeed, forcibly increasing the relational time of the grumps would not have any effect on their stated happiness.

12.4.6 Happiness, income, and relationship: Baumol's disease and trust games

At this point the reader may ask yet again why an economics textbook should give attention to the relationship between happiness and relationships. The reason is quite simple, which has been illustrated several times through this book. In real life, aggregate and personal economic facts have very important non-economic consequences, and at the same time, facts not considered to be strictly economic, such as the quality of relationships, are of fundamental importance for explaining economic facts. Economists who do not pay close attention may snub relational goods, arguing that they are outside the theme of traditional economics, but Internet innovators know quite well that the most successful goods and services they can create are those linked to relational goods. It is no accident that social networks that offer people virtual support for their relational lives, such as Facebook and Twitter, are among the most recent economic successes.

In this section we will give two clear examples of how economic growth can have crowding-out effects on relational life and how relationships are becoming one of the most important production factors in companies.

We can define the first phenomenon as "Baumol's Disease" for relationships. The term "Baumol's Disease" comes from a famous study by an American economist who compared costs and productivity in the performing arts with several mass-produced consumer goods, such as watches. Baumol observed that technological progress had transformed watch production from an artisanal activity to an industrial process, with an enormous increase in productivity and a sharp reduction in costs; the time and quantity of work necessary to produce a watch today is far, far less than 100 years ago. On the contrary, technical progress seems to have had no effect in the performing arts, because the time necessary to put on a live performance, such as an artist playing a musical piece during a concert, is the same today as it was a century ago. This implies that if we consider the relative price of making a watch and putting on a performance as the ratio between their time costs, the relative price of the latter has become quite costly.

We can observe that something similar happens with relational goods. The production of relational goods today requires the same time investment it did 100 years ago, and technological progress does not seem to have modified the situation much. We can agree that mobile phones, Email, and social networks may help cultivate relationships while saving time, but face to face encounters are a different matter, just as the term of a pregnancy and the requirements of caring for young children cannot practically be compressed, and technical progress cannot shorten them.

Following the Baumol's Disease approach, increasing productivity in other sectors of the economy and the "stasis" of productivity in the area of relational goods means that their price becomes astronomical. To give a simple example, maintaining relationships 100 years ago did not have many competitors, while in today's societies they must compete with ever higher income job opportunities, with non-relational free time alone surfing the Internet or watching television, with time "lost" in travel to and from work, and so on. So while the price of investing in relationships has increased considerably due to the opportunity cost of doing so (or the growth of the variety and value of work alternatives to free time), the risk is that investments in relationships will decline (Frame 12.2).

At this point a reader who has studied the labor supply model in depth might pose an important objection. If we admit that the cost of relationships has increased, that does not necessarily entail an increase in unhappiness. Rational choice theory teaches that if I attribute a very high value to relationships in my preferences, and if technical progress has increased my productivity and thus my income per hour, I can learn from the income effect and take advantage of my increased income from an hour worked — which increases the cost of free time — by reducing the number of hours worked and increasing the time dedicated to investing in relationships. Indeed, with a higher salary I can obtain the same income level I previously had while working fewer hours and devote the time gained to relational goods.

The response is that this solution does not take into account the particular nature and the intrinsic fragility of relational goods. Investing in a relationship by its nature exposes one to the risk that one's partner, or the individuals associated with producing a given relational good, will not respond in kind. Recall once again that relational goods must be jointly produced in order to be consumed.

If the substitution effect takes precedence over the income effect for the partners in the relationship — that is, if a higher salary draws them to choose to work more rather than fewer hours — the relational good is not produced, and satisfaction decreases due to the frustration of making an investment when others do not make a corresponding investment. It is impossible to play soccer or tennis alone.

Time will tell whether, despite the opportunity cost increase and the fragility of coordination, the quantity and quality of relational goods in developed economies increase or decrease. Recent work by Stefano Bartolini, an Italian economist, highlights how the available data indicate for the moment a significant decline of time spent on relational life in the United States, with consequent negative reflections in individuals' stated happiness.

What we wanted to demonstrate in developing this argument is that "Baumol's Disease for relationships" is one of the more interesting examples of how economic factors significantly impact non-economic areas of life.

12.4.7 The relationship between happiness and affectionate relationships

We nearly always find participants' marital status among the variables usually considered as factors that can influence life satisfaction. Here again we are on the subject of relational goods, because we can consider marital status as the result of a life choice made when the relational good "affectionate relationship" between two people exceeds a certain quality threshold. There are two status changes connected to this relational good, marrying and separating, that are assumed to have significant effects on life satisfaction. Other related states to assess for impact on happiness are obviously the conditions of being separated, divorced, widowed, or single.

The results of numerous empirical studies seem to identify several significant and quite stable facts on the relationship between happiness and the above-mentioned variables. First, changes in status have a significant and positive impact in the expected direction. Marriage is correlated with a significant increase in happiness, and separation with a significant decrease in happiness. Several particularly detailed studies analyzed the dynamics of life satisfaction around these moments in life and found them to be bell-shaped. That means that the most significant effect happens at the moment of the event, which then tends to slowly diminish as we move farther and farther from it. So here too we can observe the phenomenon of "hedonic adaptation" (which is different from what we studied in the relationship between money and happiness) in which it is possible to verify that the effects of positive or negative life shocks, such as those studied in this section, diminish over time.

Moving from examining changes in status to the impact of life situations themselves on happiness, we observe that, beyond the short-term dynamics, being married contributes positively and significantly to happiness, while being separated or divorced negatively influences happiness.

In this case as well, studies have had to take an in-depth look at the problem of causal direction between the two variables. The question is whether events, such as one's marital status and changes in it, are what impact life satisfaction, or whether some people's personality traits that are more extroverted, optimistic, and positive significantly influence the probability of building successful relationships.

Once again, studies that have researched the problem in depth seem to support the hypothesis that the cause–effect link works in both directions.

12.4.8 Is religion a relational good?

One of the most robust results is the relationship between religion and happiness. In any time interval or sample surveyed, it is possible to verify a positive relationship between stated happiness and religious practice. It is important to point out that the positive relationship only exists when we consider religious practice, and not a religious education received in one's youth that does not translate into religious practice in adult life. Several studies of the data show that religion acts as insurance against the negative shocks that impact people over the course of their lives.

Reflecting on the characteristics of religions and the determinants of happiness, we find that a positive effect can depend on at least four factors. The first is that religion offers a response to questions about the meaning of life and painful events, such as illness and death. The second is that it can also be considered as a factor that leads to higher quality relational goods both horizontally — as Smith taught with the concept of "fellow feeling", in that sharing experiences in greater depth reinforces the bonds of friendship — as well as vertically in one's relationship with God. The third and fourth indicate that religion seems to automatically provide corrections to people's observed tendencies to dampen the effects of positive shocks over time (see our reflection on hedonic adaptation and the effects of events over time, such as marriage) and to not easily forget negative shocks (see the effects of separation and divorce described above). Through practicing gratitude and in giving a meaning to pain, religion seems to be tailor made to counterbalance these two dynamic effects.

12.4.9 Happiness and work

The specific area of happiness studies that works with the relationship between happiness and work seem to contradict another typical simplification of the standard model taught in economics courses, that work-related happiness is linked solely to hourly wages. This is the simplification we considered in Chapter 9 when we discussed the labor supply and individuals' maximization choices that choose between work and free time.

Monetary compensation is not the only benefit that people derive from their working hours. Without ignoring its fatiguing and annoying aspects, in some respects the work itself can be a source of inner satisfaction that can increase life satisfaction. An interesting anecdote confirms this assumption. In Italy a labor judge ordered FIAT (the main Italian car company now merged with Chrysler into FCA) to reinstate several laid off workers in their jobs, and the company decided to pay them their salary but prevent them from returning to the factory. However, the workers were strongly opposed to this solution, showing that the cost of being unemployed went well beyond the loss in monetary compensation. This suggest that the value of work goes beyond its monetary reward and has something to do with its creative or generative nature.

The most definitive proof that work in and of itself does not necessarily have neutral or even negative consequences on individual satisfaction, and that on the contrary it can create non-monetary benefit, is volunteer work. This is in difference with many economic models that assume that the negative effects on an individual's utility are in proportion to the effort required to perform the work. Freeman's expressive definition of volunteer work is "working for nothing" — that is, in light of the model between work and free time presented in Chapter 9, choosing to devote time to uncompensated work. The phenomenon of voluntarism seems to clearly contradict the standard approach of the labor supply model, in which the utility linked to hours worked consists solely in the monetary compensation that allows one to increase consumption.

Several alternate explanations exist that justify voluntarism in utilitarian terms, such as expanding one's circle of acquaintances, increasing one's human capital, or increasing one's future employment opportunities by showing a good attitude toward teamwork in one's CV. However, scholars agree that not all voluntarism can be explained in this way. If voluntarism is about improving one's future job opportunities, why then do so many retired people devote themselves to volunteering?

Volunteering is also an important signal to the market of the social value of the activity carried out by a productive organization, whether a traditional enterprise, a social cooperative, or a social enterprise. If those on the inside who know its operation well decide to offer part of their work as volunteers, without being constrained to do so, that implies that they recognize its values, and they are gratified by participating in the organization's mission. Moreover, the existence of voluntary labor is proof that in work *intrinsic motivations are a substitute — although clearly imperfect — for monetary compensation.* So in activities that are values driven with particularly high intrinsic motivations, they can be sufficient to determine people's choice to work even without a salary. What we are talking about is a fundamental law that business people understand well when they decide to dedicate an important part of their corporate culture to the ethics and values of their companies, or when they allow workers to spend part of their work time in volunteer activities that can indirectly reinforce their intrinsic motivations to work in the company (we partially discussed this in Chapter 11 on corporate social responsibility). Once these basic considerations have been developed, it is possible to explore the aspects of work that can more or less positively influence job satisfaction, and with it individual satisfaction. The results of empirical studies on this emphasize that happiness on the job depends on several fundamental characteristics, without which it would be difficult to understand why many people prefer jobs with lower salaries to others that pay better. These fundamental factors are: flexibility in working hours, stability, decision-making autonomy and independence from hierarchical superiors, the quality of relationships with co-workers, and agreement between their own values and the purpose of the work itself.

We close this discussion on the relationship between work and happiness with a final paradox. Is it a greater source of unhappiness to be unemployed in a region where the unemployment rate is higher, or where it is lower? Economists and sociologists give different answers to this question. For economists, the individual utility function counts more than the situations of one's peers. In a region with lower unemployment, the probability of finding work can be greater, so those who are unemployed should be less unhappy. For sociologists, comparing oneself with one's reference group is more important, and the saying "misery loves company" applies. Thus unemployed people in a region with low unemployment are more unhappy because they feel like they are the exceptions with respect to their peers.

Andrew Clark's recent results from a vast sample of British citizens corroborate the second hypothesis. All this shows that the economics of happiness becomes a meeting ground for different disciplines, requiring that economists supplement their traditional perspective by taking more into account the role that one's peer group has on individual happiness.

12.4.10 Happiness, inflation, and unemployment

One of the more interesting areas of research is analyzing the relationship between happiness, unemployment, and inflation, which can help us understand how happiness studies can provide important considerations when formulating economic policies.

In the past, there was broad consensus among economists about a dilemma that to reduce one of two evils it was necessary to be more lenient toward the other. Thus according to this dilemma, accepting a higher inflation level provided important tools in the fight against unemployment. The idea of the dilemma, depicted graphically in the well-known Phillips curve, has been largely refuted by subsequent developments in macroeconomics. In particular, everyone today agrees that high inflation is an evil to avoid, but the debate continues today whether the optimal inflation level is zero or whether moderate inflation between 2% and 4% can be useful to "grease the gears" of the economy to fight unemployment.

In any case, although macroeconomics today seems to have gone beyond the idea of a direct trade-off between the two variables, politicians still must choose a priority scale for their goals. This priority scale is fundamental, as it impacts choices on how scarce economic resources are allocated. For example, when a country's central bank lowers its benchmark interest rate, it must take into consideration the possibility that giving a stimulus to the economy by easing access to credit can at the same time lead to a higher risk of inflationary pressures due to the increased liquidity in circulation. It is also essential for them to understand the effects of the two evils of inflation and unemployment on their voters.

An implicit way of weighting inflation and unemployment is the *misery index*, which calculates their distance from a socially optimal state as the sum of the rates of inflation and unemployment. In this evaluation there is an implicit one-to-one weighting between the two evils, on the assumption that the social cost of a percentage point of inflation is equal to a percentage point of unemployment.

The assumption of the one-to-one ratio posited by the "misery index" had never been subjected to empirical verification prior to the advent of the new empirical studies on happiness.

With these studies it is finally possible to hazard a response to the following questions: Which makes us unhappier, unemployment or inflation? What is the proportion of the severity of the two evils for the purpose of individual happiness?

Regarding the relationship between unemployment and unhappiness, empirical studies on the topic have succeeded in isolating two negative effects. The first is the personal unhappiness that unemployment creates in those who are unemployed. The second is the negative effect that the aggregate national unemployment level has on the happiness of those who are already employed. In the first case we should emphasize the important difference between an unemployed person and someone who voluntarily decides not to look for work. An unemployed person is someone who is looking for work but does not find it, while the second is someone who does not have a job and is not looking for one. It seems intuitively obvious that looking for something and not finding it causes a reduction in happiness. Studies that have investigated the problem in depth stress that being unemployed usually has, together with the devaluation of his competences, negative psychological consequences, among them a significant loss of self-esteem that easily leads to depression. These undesirable effects are greater the longer a person is in such a condition. Indeed, the risk of being unemployed for a very long time is that people become so discouraged that the likelihood of them finding new jobs becomes extremely difficult.

As mentioned above, the second negative effect unemployment has on happiness is the impact of the unemployment rate on those who are already employed. This is a less obvious but equally important effect. The happiness of those who are employed may become lower as the unemployment rate rises, for two reasons. Some may have unemployed relatives or friends; beyond being unhappy about the situation, if they are part of the family circle they may be called on to contribute some of their own income to support those who are unemployed. Moreover, an unemployment increase can drive governments to increase allocations for active retraining programs for the unemployed, which can end up increasing the tax burden on the employed, and thus reduce the life satisfaction of the latter even when the problem does not affect their close relatives. Even further deterioration of the economic situation implies a greater risk that those who are employed may lose their jobs; a rise in the unemployment rate thus becomes a danger sign for those who are employed. Finally, the presence of many unemployed people creates a "reserve army" that competes with the employed for open jobs, which reduces their bargaining power in salary negotiations with employers.

As for inflation, its negative impact on happiness is clear. Inflation implies a reduction in the purchasing power of wages; in light of the consumer model illustrated in Chapter 3, that implies a shift in the spending possibilities frontier toward the origin of the axes, or a reduction in spending. If buying goods contributes to our happiness, having one's buying possibilities curtailed clearly reduces it. As is well known, even inflation does not affect everyone in the same way, and one's ability to avoid its negative effects depends on the characteristics of one's income and wealth. Those whose salaries are not inflation indexed (that is, those whose salaries are not automatically adjusted for inflation) are more sensitive to the loss of purchasing power. Paradoxically, those who hold nominal debt (debt that is not inflation indexed) see the real value of their debt decline. This is why many states (whose public debt is basically nominal) have been tempted to use inflation to reduce the real cost of their debt.

Using surveys that have information on stated happiness and the employment status of those surveyed, and cross-referencing them with the available data on unemployment and aggregate inflation in the national statistics, it is possible to identify the net effect on happiness of each of the two evils considered separately, and then consider the relationship between them.

The result we obtain in such cases is that the one-to-one hypothesis of the misery index underestimates the effect of unemployment on happiness. The ratio that emerges from the empirical analyses, calculated as the effect of unemployment divided by the effect of inflation, is in fact higher than one and varies according to age groups and countries considered.

An interesting fact is that this ratio tends to coincide with the misery index when we restrict the observation field to those over 60 in countries with the most rigid labor markets (those in which there is greater protection for workers but the possibility for those looking for a job to find one is lower). The ratio becomes much higher — unemployment counts twice as much — for intermediate age groups and in countries with more flexible labor markets (where it is easy for companies to lay people off but it is easier to find a job after being laid off).

The evidence of this is given in Table 12.4. Reading the first line relative to the entire sample, we discover that it indicates that a 1% increase in unemployment reduces the number of the very satisfied by 1.04%.

Moreover, if we compare the economic policies of the two types of countries, we find that the authorities seem quite aware of the problem and adjust their actions accordingly. In the first type of country — Germany prior to

TABLE 12.4 Variations in the number of people who are "very satisfied" with their lives with variations of one percentage point in the unemployment and inflation rates.

	Variations in the share of very satisfied people		
	Increase of one percentage point of unemployment	Increase of one percentage point of inflation	Marginal rate of substitution
Entire sample	−1.04	−0.69	1.51
<29	−0.33	−0.33	1.00
29−42	−0.65	−0.32	2.03
42−64	−0.64	−0.32	2.00
>64	−0.32	−0.32	1.00
Low labor protection	−0.67	−0.27	2.48
High labor protection	−0.28	−0.56	0.50

Note: The numbers shown in the first and second columns represent the percentage change in the number of people who are "very satisfied" with their lives due to a change in the unemployment and inflation rates. The third column shows the marginal rate of substitution between inflation and unemployment, or what increase in the inflation rate would bring people back to the previous level of satisfaction (holding the number of "very satisfied" people constant) after the positive news of a 1% reduction in unemployment. <29, 29−42, 42−64: age groups; low (high) labor protection; countries with a low (high) labor protection level.
Source: Becchetti, L., Castriota, S., Giuntella, C. The effects of age and welfare costs of inflation and unemployment. *European Journal of Political Economy, 26* (1), 137−146.

the EU - the inflation level is relatively lower and unemployment level higher, while in the second group — the United States and the United Kingdom — the opposite happens; the policies to actively counter unemployment are much more developed, and the central banks seem to show a greater concern for the effects of their policies on unemployment and growth.

12.4.11 Happiness, health, and age

One of the most surprising results of studies on happiness is the relationship between life satisfaction and age. Studies of samples from different countries seem to agree that, health being equal, there is a U-shaped relationship between age and stated happiness. Net of all other variables considered, essentially the effect of age seems to be that it is initially negative to a minimum point between 30 and 40 years of age, and subsequently there is a positive relationship between aging and life satisfaction.

For many, this result may seem paradoxical. Western cultures focus greatly on beauty and physical vigor, and one might assume that the gradual loss of these traits would contribute negatively to happiness.

Among possible explanations of the paradox, psychologists have argued that with advancing age people go through a process of reducing their aspirations and learning to manage their emotions better by avoiding negative emotions and concentrating on those with a positive impact.

Another interpretation is that those in middle age suffer from greater time pressure (see Baumol's Disease), are strongly bound to their affective and work choices, and have less possibility of escaping or cultivating the hope of being able to change, as instead happens with younger and older people.

As to the surprising level of happiness of the elderly compared to young people, a possible interpretation is the relationship between age, choices, and opportunity costs. For young people every choice has a significantly higher opportunity cost than an elderly person because the possible options they give up are much greater. Choosing a field of study excludes countless other possible paths, which can pose a dilemma: becoming an economist means never becoming a doctor, a natural scientist, and so on. The literature has very effectively reported this turmoil in youth in many famous works. In short, young people can suffer from a dizzying range of choices, while older people have often already made nearly irreversible choices that put them on a certain track, or that at least restrict the field of possible alternatives for future choices.

There is the possibility, however, that the U-shape of age is a sort of optical illusion. An example may be useful to explain why. Between the late 1960s and the early 1970s there were significant changes in how people dress. Back then it was easy to observe that young people had totally different habits than the adult generation; they drove large, powerful motorcycles, they had a passion for rock music, and so forth. One possible conclusion for observers at the time could have been that as they grew older, young people abandoned their motorcycles and rock music to adopt different lifestyles. While this is partly true, observations over later decades have often suggested just the opposite. The young generation in the 1970s brought along some of their habits, and it is not unusual these days to see those in their 60s riding motorcycles, and especially crowding into rock concerts put on by their idols from their youth.

So when we look at the relationship between age and a certain behavior, there are always two types of explanations: (a) with increasing age behavior changes (after becoming adults they stopped riding motorcycles and going to rock concerts), and (b) every generation has its own habits and consumption independently of their age (the youth of the 1970s continued to ride motorcycles and go to rock concerts when they became adults).

The latter explanation is known as the "cohort effect" (or the age class effect) and can also be applied to the relationship between age and happiness. In fact, theU-shaped relationship could conceal the happiness level of each generation; those in their thirties and forties are the least happy, while those in their twenties and those in their fifties and sixties are the happiest. If this were true, then the passing of the years would not be what changed happiness, in that age alone would determine the characteristics of a generation. In other words, a few years after the age of 40 we should be able to observe a negative relationship between age and happiness.

It is possible to distinguish the cohort effect from one's real age through empirical analyses that follow the same individuals over time. What seems to emerge is that both factors count. The U effect exists, but the characteristics of each generation also play a role in determining individual happiness.

At the beginning of this section we recalled that, beyond a certain threshold, there is a positive relationship between age and happiness, health conditions remaining equal. We should thus certainly consider one of the factors that, according to nearly all research, most impacts personal happiness: health. However, we should not forget the surprising results that indicate that people who have suffered serious health crises are happier over time than outside observers believe. Here too a principle of adaptation and scaling back of expectations is in play, which allows such individuals to attain levels of satisfaction that are surprising to those around them.

12.4.12 Are we really able to explain the Easterlin paradox? Some possible explanations

At this point we can verify how much the results we have discussed to this point can help us explain the starting point of our analysis and modern empirical studies on happiness, or the Easterlin Paradox.

There are at least three possible lines of interpretation of the relationship between happiness and income. Income contributes to individual satisfaction in the form of a contribution to both private and public wealth. Starting from poverty conditions, the impact of income on life satisfaction is quite strong, because people's ability to spend increases significantly with economic well-being. With already high income levels, however, attenuating factors tend to prevail. The marginal utility of income slowly declines to nearly nothing, hedonic adaptation plays a strong role (see Fig. 12.5), and if one's income does not increase along with that of one's reference group, the negative impact can be significant. The section on relationships illustrates further that in wealthy societies the opportunity cost of time explodes, which increases the cost of investing in relational goods and results in an equilibrium with a lower level of relational goods enjoyed. The decline of many relational indicators in Western societies can be an explanation of the paradox.

We add two further explanations to all this. If we shift from relative income to the broader concept of inequality we see when comparing countries that there is a very strong correlation between income inequality and a series of social unrest indicators, such as the number of people in prison, obesity, mental distress, the crime rate, and so on. In the second post-war period — and in the last few decades in particular — income inequality has sharply increased in the Anglo-American countries, and this could contribute to explaining Easterlin's results.

Finally, the paradox can partly depend on the fact that per capita GDP, the variable Easterlin used, is not really a good index of economic well-being. The 2009 financial crisis actually showed how countries such as the United States associate a very high per capita income with a very high cost of some public goods, such as healthcare and education that are free in other countries, and especially that the level of income to family debt and per capita wealth are less than in many countries in continental Europe.

In a nutshell, the message we draw from the interpretation sparked by the paradox is that per capita GDP not only does not necessarily coincide with happiness, but that it is a very partial and non-exhaustive indicator of economic well-being.

12.5 Happiness studies results and Heisenberg's uncertainty principle

Should we consider the results described so far of the effects of different variables on stated happiness as immutable laws, or rather should we properly interpret them with a certain caution? The second attitude is certainly preferable.

Indeed, Heisenberg's **Uncertainty Principle** tells us that even in the physical sciences, the object we are observing changes as a result of our attempts to measure it. (A typical example is attempting to measure the temperature of a cup of tea; inserting a thermometer in the cup slightly lowers the temperature of the water.)

This principle is even more valid in the social sciences and economics, where there is an additional element of uncertainty that we do not find in the natural sciences. The "elementary units" that are the subjects of our observations are in fact flesh and blood people. They not only can have an interest in giving distorted responses to our investigative interviews, they also react to our political economy choices; for example, a tax increase can also increase attempts at tax evasion and have surprising negative effects on revenue expectations.

So if the laws described in the preceding sections accurately describe the relationship between happiness and its determinants over the course of recent decades, we cannot say that they will be able to do so in future years. The evolution of moral and social norms, and of culture in general, can in fact partially modify individual responses to life events, impacting our observations about the relationship between happiness and its possible explanations. The relationship between happiness and its determining factors is mediated by several fundamental components such as culture and virtue. By "virtue" we mean disciplining oneself toward a certain behavior that requires effort at first, but that becomes natural over the course of our lives. An important part of what can make a person happy is represented by the so-called "arduous goods," or goods whose fruition requires a certain effort and fatigue up front to invest the strength and energy required to cultivate a virtuous habit by repeated behavior. Scholastic and professional success, a trek in the mountains, an affective relationship, and so on are arduous goods, so people's individual virtuosity — their greater or lesser discipline in pursuing arduous goods — plays a fundamental role in determining the relationship between happiness and the factors that influence it. To give a very simple example, getting up early in the morning is a pleasure for those who have goals they want to attain in life and who are accustomed to doing so every day, while it is quite a struggle for those who have problems with laziness or dependence.

12.6 Remarks on happiness and economic policies

As we noted in Chapter 1, transitioning from a positive to a normative approach in any area of economics is a delicate matter. This applies even more to studies on happiness.

First, it is necessary to clear the field of the idea that the authorities can pay direct attention to and intrude in citizens' private lives to set the behaviors that determine their life satisfaction. The suspicion of such actions is fueled by the fact that many authoritarian regimes in the past have based their rhetoric on adopting this approach and emphasizing their ability to increase their citizens' happiness. The instinctive reaction to this type of danger is to declare that the State should not become involved in this question, as it remains a fundamentally private matter.

There are two answers to this concern. First, there is no connection between happiness studies and an economic policy that aims to increase the role of the State in the economy. Determining this sort of nexus is an absolutely open problem, and the results of such studies can lead us to think that either more or less presence of the State is needed to increase citizens' happiness.

Second, the hypothesis of a "neutral" State in relation to citizens' happiness is a pure illusion that is belied by the facts. Any decision made by public authorities has immediate relevance to the conditions that can determine our life satisfaction, influencing for example the extent of the tax burden, work conditions and retirement prospects, the compatibility between family life and work life, and so on. In any event, political and economic authorities make decisions that have important effects on factors that influence our life satisfaction, whether they like it or not, and it is better to look into the question in depth rather than neglect it.

Another important criticism of stated happiness as an indicator to measure economic policies is offered by the Nobel laureate Amartya Sen, who stated that the criterion of happiness can be misleading; he explained the problem with the famous example of the "happy slave." Sen observed that there are people who are so completely deprived of rights and whose wills are so subjugated that they do not aspire to improve their condition, so they make up a reason why they are in slavery and end up even feeling happy. Using stated happiness as a reference in such cases could be counterproductive, because that would suggest maintaining the status quo and not committing to their emancipation. This is why Sen proposed the criteria of **capabilities** and **functionalities** to orient policies and serve as the measure of citizens' wellbeing. By aiming to increase people's functionality and their potential to act, which in turn depend on traditionally considered factors such as income, education, political rights, health, and so forth, we use a criterion that is certainly more objective and less opinion-driven for policy actions.

Happiness scholars respond that, from a statistical point of view, happy slaves are the exception, not the rule. Moreover, if we look at the results relative to the most important factors that are able to determine individual happiness, we find many of the variables that decisively determine the level of people's capabilities and functionalities. In a more radical philosophical tone, happiness scholars object that the capabilities approach is affected by the problem of paternalism, just as are indicators of human development or income growth. No one asks the citizens about the most important factors for their happiness; rather, a group of experts decides which factors are important. The only criterion that is free from this paternalistic approach is that of stated happiness.

Once these preliminary misgivings have been avoided, we must be very careful not to automatically draw conclusions from the results obtained when returning to the delicate problem of the relationship between positive and normative moments. The results of the determinants of happiness must be cross-checked against economic, social, and environmental compatibility in order to inspire the correct economic policies.

As an example of the risks we might incur when we move into considering economic policy prescriptions, it is obvious that a proper approach cannot be to propose increasing the current generation's happiness by massive public spending, as that would offload the burden of paying down the debt onto future generations.

The risk is even greater if we use the satisfaction of the experiencing self that Kahneman used in his studies as our criterion. Without the mediation of a posteriori resonance and reflection on one's own life, there is the risk that happiness as a criterion could coincide with pure hedonism and become extremely impoverished. Paradoxically, if a group of lazy citizens were to determine that getting up in the morning is strenuous, a policy seeking to maximize their immediate satisfaction could not oppose them, but rather would have to go along with them.

It is evident that studies on happiness in no way suggest automatically maximizing the criterion of citizens' life satisfaction, for the reasons stated above and which we summarize here as follows: (a) it is necessary to take into account the compatibility of personal life satisfaction with the social, environmental, and economic sustainability of public choices; (b) the greater or lesser degree of citizens' moral and civic sensibilities decisively influences the factors that determine their happiness, particularly when the evaluation of stated happiness is made by the experiencing self without the mediation of reflection and one's conscience.

Having explicitly stated the various precautions in this case, we can now answer the question about the contribution that happiness studies can make to authorities' political and economic choices. One element that certainly emerges from empirical research is the importance of relational life. This result suggests that we should give attention to the crowding-out risks that purely quantitative goals − such as productivity, flexibility, and creating economic value − can bring to bear on the quality of relational life, which in turn is a fundamental pillar that governs how economic relationships work.

People do not live compartmentalized lives in which their productive dimensions are severed from their life satisfaction and the quality of their relational lives. Studying the interactions between these components can be very important, both for creating the conditions that increase citizens' life satisfaction and for supporting their best dispositions to trust in interpersonal relationships, and thus contributing to greater economic value growth (see the trust game in Chapter 6).

Not only economists, but urban planners as well, for example, should take these indications to heart. Building a city fit for people that facilitates people meeting each other and reduces the commute time between home and work can certainly contribute toward increasing collective happiness.

Again, the importance of public goods is a consideration that follows from taking seriously the research on life satisfaction. While health is a basic factor for happiness, as is to be expected, it is also clear that creating economic value counts not only toward increasing per capita income, but also toward the opportunity of increasing the supply of public goods, such as health.

One final note for policy suggestions comes from analyzing the discussion of the cause−effect relationship between happiness and its determinants. If, as we concluded, the reality is halfway between the two extremes of a happiness conditioned entirely by events that happen to us and a happiness that heavily depends on unchanging character traits that themselves cause life events, we realize that policies to improve our social context are only effective for the first type of causal nexus. To give an example, a policy to fight unemployment improves the happiness of those who become unhappy because they lack work, but not of those whose unhappy character, which persists independently of life events, brings about their unemployment problems. We must not forget this so we do not overestimate the role of policy in happiness.

Further reading

Bartolini, S. (2014). *Manifesto for Happiness: Shifting society from money to well-being.* Pennsylvania University Press.

Becchetti, L., Castriota, S., & Giuntella, O. (2010). The effects of age and job protection on the welfare costs of inflation and unemployment. *European Journal of Political Economy, 26*(1), 137–146.

Becchetti, L., & Pelloni, A. (2010). What are we learning from the life satisfaction literature? *Econometrica, 20.*

Bruni, L., & Porta, P. L. (2005). *Economics and happiness: Framings of analysis.* Oxford: Oxford University Press.

Clark, A. E., Frijters, P., & Shields, M. A. (2006). Income and happiness: Evidence, explanations and economic implications. *Paris Jourdan Sciences Economiques*, Pages 64. Working Paper no. 24.

Easterlin, R. A., & Angelescu, L. (2009). Happiness and growth the world over: Time series evidence on the happiness-income paradox. In *IZA discussion paper no. 4060.*

Frey, B., & Stutzer, A. (2018). *Economics of happiness.* Milano: Springer International Publishing.

Gui, B. (2005). From transaction to encounters. The joint generation of relational goods and conventional values. In B. Gui, & R. Sugden (Eds.), *Economics and social interaction: Accounting for interpersonal relations.* Cambridge: Cambridge University Press.

Malthus, T. R. (1798). *An essay on the principle of population.* London: J. Johnson.

Nussbaum, M. (1986–2001). *The fragility of goodness, luck and ethics in Greek tragedy and philosophy* (1st ed.). Cambridge: Cambridge University Press.

Stevenson, B., & Wolfers, J. (2008). *Economic growth and subjective well-being: Reassessing the Easterlin paradox.* NBER Working Paper no. 14282.

Uhlaner, C. J. (1989). Relational goods and participation: Incorporating sociability into a theory of rational action. *Public Choice Journal, 62*(3), 253–285.

Chapter 13

Growth and the environment in the era of globalization

The Question of Growth.

13.1 The importance of the topic of growth

Economic growth is probably the most analyzed and debated topic among economists. Our present economic reality exhibits enormous differences in the levels of well-being between different countries around the world, and the history of the last few decades has charted an incredible variety in per capita income growth performance between different geographical areas and countries. To give just one example, in 1970 Ghana and South Korea had similar per capita income levels ($2590 and $2660 respectively) as well as similar infant mortality rates (183 per 1000 and 135 per 1000 respectively). Since then South Korea has achieved spectacular growth, rising to a per capita income of $15,090 in 2001 and an infant mortality rate of 5 per 1000, while Ghana has declined to the point that today it is one of the poorest countries in the world, with per capita income declining to $2250 and infant mortality at 100 per 1000 in 2001. Similarly, from the second post-war period to today, western European countries — including those that suffered great damage to their production systems and infrastructure during World War II — have reached very high levels of well-being, while during the same time span the extreme poverty of many African countries has remained constant or has declined. The so-called "Asian tigers," the agents of unprecedented growth, have also reached very high levels of economic well-being, and the economic development of China and India has been extraordinary. So much can be done in a single generation! Again referring to the above two indicators, in 1970 Malaysia began from per capita income levels and infant mortality rates similar to those in Indonesia today, and in 2001 it attained the levels of Poland. In the same time horizon, Chile went from the current situation in India to that of Estonia, nearly tripling its per capita income.

More generally, if we consider the time span between 1960 and 2000, the 5 greatest growth successes have been Taiwan, Botswana, South Korea, Hong

The Microeconomics of Wellbeing and Sustainability. https://doi.org/10.1016/B978-0-12-816027-5.00013-6

Kong, and Singapore, while the 5 greatest failures have been Congo, Angola, the Central African Republic, Nicaragua, and Nigeria. The scenario changes radically if we only consider the spectacular growth of China and India over the last decade. The most surprising fact of the last decade has been the resurgence of the African continent. The average GDP growth rate on the continent has exceeded 5% in the last five years, and predictions are that in the next five years it will exceed that of the Asian continent. The list of positive and negative examples could go on. However, while identifying the countries that changed more or less is certainly an interesting study for a good economist, analyzing the causes is much more important; not becoming passionate about the determinants of these development differentials would be like reading a murder mystery without wanting to find out in the end who did it and why.

Studying the determinants of economic growth is fundamental if we want to respond to three crucial questions:

- How is it possible to increase the level of material well-being of a country?
- Why has the growth differential been so great between countries — for example, between Ghana and South Korea — such that it widens incredibly the distance between them?
- What are the formulas and key factors for bringing a nation out of poverty and catching up with respect to more economically developed countries?

From the outset of this chapter we want to emphasize that we will not adopt a unidimensional approach that is focused only on increasing income; on the contrary, we will develop in depth the relationship between economic growth and quality of life. Many affirm, and not without reason, that growth as a goal does not ensure attaining broader and generally more desirable goals, such as sustainable development, well-being, and life flourishing. Recall in particular that these depend not only on individual wealth, but also primarily on non-monetary components.

The problem of the **relationship between economic development and collective happiness** is simply and effectively summarized in a diagram in the World Bank's 2003 Report, in which the traditional channels of production, consumption, and well-being (Fig. 13.1, the center column) are accompanied and complemented by other channels in which the direct enjoyment of human, social, and environmental resources positively contributes to collective well-being, independently of other production considerations.

An interesting way of defining broader well-being indicators was carried out in Italy in 2012—13 with the construction of the "BES" system ("Benessere Equo e Sostenibile", or "Fair and Sustainable Well-Being"). The Italian agency ISTAT convened various social groups and asked them what their areas of well-being were. Once those areas were identified, commissions of experts identified the indicators within each area. The set of areas and indicators

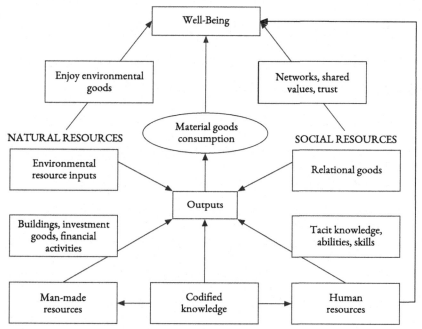

FIG. 13.1   A new conception of well-being. *Source: World Bank, World Development Report 2003: Sustainable Development in a Dynamic World.*

allowed them to design a well-being map of Italy. See Chapter 12 regarding the complex relationship between economic growth and life satisfaction.

A more thorough analysis of the close relationship between economic growth and these dimensions that contribute to individual happiness clearly reveals that the first, or the creation of aggregate economic value, is the source of investable resources for contributing to the development of the second, or investment in education, healthcare, and the maintenance and preservation of environmental goods. Consequently, growth remains a crucial element for developing other non-monetary dimensions of individual well-being (see also Sections 12.4.1–12.4.3 in Chapter 12 on the role of monetary variables on the determinants of life satisfaction).

This is why investigating the determinants of economic development remains one of the more important fields to which economists can contribute in order to achieve the intermediate goal of economic growth, and with it, the additional goals of public happiness and the common good.

From the viewpoint of the history of economic thought, the study of growth can also be seen as economists' response to the failure of Malthusian predictions. As we recalled in Chapter 1, according to Malthus a linear growth in resources combined with a geometric population growth would necessarily lead to increasing poverty by progressively reducing per capita production, and thus wages and personal income as well.

The statistical data suggests exactly the opposite. Over the past century, real wages have risen significantly despite tumultuous population growth. Indirect evidence of what happened comes from analyzing this evolution in the share of the world's population with less than a dollar a day over the last century and a half. In 1820 the share was equal to 83.9%, or a total of around 886 million people. The sustained population growth foreseen by Malthus actually happened, but the predicted catastrophe of an explosion in poverty due to overpopulation is fortunately belied by the facts. The number of people under the threshold of a dollar a day has dramatically fallen in 2018 to 179 million (2.5% of the world population) so that the World Bank has raised the extreme poverty threshold to 1.9 dollars per day (783 million or 10.1% of the global population live below that threshold). The figure implicit in Table 13.1 from beginning to end is the addition of over 7.4 billion people above the poverty threshold to the planet. This outcome would not have been possible without sustained growth in real wages and global per capita income.

What Malthus did not consider was the possibility of highly sustained productivity growth that is able to increase GDP per capita despite the increase in the number of mouths to feed. To reconsider the question posed by Malthus on the basis of students' knowledge acquired in previous chapters, we can use the production function of a company and reason as if the world were in the place of the firm (Fig. 13.2).

In the standard representation we know that, with equal capital, the production function assumes a concave shape when varying the labor input, as measured by the number of workers, or more precisely, by the number of hours worked. If we stop at this level of analysis, Malthus's reasoning would seem convincing. An increase in population at the same level of capital investment progressively decreases the product per capita due to the law of diminishing marginal productivity.

- In reality, this reflection does not take two basic factors into account:
- the possibility of increasing the capital stock and of using it to increase the productivity of the labor factor (consider the Cobb–Douglas production function studied in Chapter 4, in which the two production factors have a multiplicative relationship between themselves, and the marginal productivity of labor is increasing in the capital stock);
- technical progress that, *with the capital stock remaining equal*, is able to shift the production possibility frontier upwards, increasing the product obtained with the same number of hours worked (see Fig. 13.2).

If readers reflect on the history of the last few centuries they will find plenty of examples, beyond innovations in specific sectors, of technological innovations that have had an impact across all sectors and made an enormous contribution to increasing the productivity of labor. Consider the invention of

TABLE 13.1 Evolution in absolute and percentage value of the total world population of those who live on less than one dollar a day (in purchasing power parity).

Year	1820	1929	1950	1960	1970	1980	1987	1992	1998	2010	2018
Share of world population	83.9	56.3	54.8	44	33.6	31.5	28.3	23.7	23.4	22	2.5
Million People	886.8	1150	1176	1231	1343	1431	1183	1176	1175	1200	179

Source: Bourguignon, F., Morrison, C. (2002). Inequality among world citizens: 1820–1992. *American Economic Review*, 92, 727–744 (updates are ours).

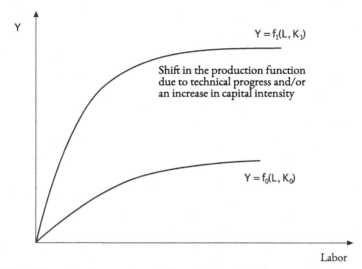

FIG. 13.2 Effect of an increase in capital stock and technical progress on the production function. *Note*: An increase in capital stock (from K_0 to K_1) or the possibility of using a better technology (from f_0 to f_1) to produce a greater output while employing the same labor input.

electricity, the construction of railroads, and more recently, the significant innovation of the Internet and the fourth industrial revolution (industry 4.0) that is creating "smart environments" where "intelligent" machines interact among themselves and with skilled labor. So over time, technological progress has gradually reduced the barriers of space and time along two general lines. Innovations in the transportation sector has reduced the time and cost of moving them to various parts of the world. The electronic and information revolution of the Internet has practically reduced to zero the time to move "weightless" goods, such as voice, data, and images, while simultaneously and drastically reducing the cost of moving them, thanks to the strong competitiveness of the companies operating in those sectors and to their need to attract the greatest number of users necessary to achieve **network economies**. In network economies, the value of a service offered on the network increases as the number of connected users grows. To give a specific example, the value of a videophone placed on the market by a telephony company increases as the number of users who utilize the service grows; the specific value of this communication medium is determined by the possibility of seeing the other party to a call, which only happens if she owns a videophone. As an absurd case, if only one user were to buy the videophone the specific value of the videophone service would be zero.

If we remember that productivity is simply the ability to produce goods and services with given inputs in a given unit of time, we readily understand how innovations in the data transport sector, computer science, and network technologies have markedly increased the ability for everyone to do things in less time. One need only think of what it meant to write a book or carry out a bibliographic search in the era of printed encyclopedias and typewriters, and then compare that with the possibilities we have today when, to consult what has been written on a certain topic (at least in scientific subjects), we need only survey the Internet with a search engine or access specialized sites. In writing a document, the costs of erasing and revising it are dramatically reduced by word processing programs.

After what we have observed, answering a question becomes essential. If the marvels of technological progress have significantly increased productivity, and thus enormously increased real wages and revenue produced globally, why do they not expand uniformly and create benefits for the entire global populace? Why is inequality so very great that, according to calculations of the Oxfam Report, in 2016 8 individuals had the same wealth of the poorest half of the world population (3.6 billion people)?

To answer this question, scientists must yield the floor to economists.

13.2 Several stylized facts on growth and poverty

The study of growth generally begins with several stylized facts as the starting point for analysis; these are statistical regularities relative to the most developed countries that can be readily linked to the production function and its inputs.

These regularities are as follows:

1. Over the past century, the capital stock has grown more than the population, leading to an increase in capital intensity per worker. This is the first variant that Malthus's analysis did not consider. The law of diminishing marginal productivity, which would inevitably lead to poverty in the presence of sustained global population growth, only applies if capital and the level of technological progress remain the same. Even without technological progress, as we saw in Fig. 13.2, simply increasing the supply of capital increases labor productivity.
2. During the same time span there was also a sharp increase in real wages. The explanation is that the combined effect of increasing capital intensity and technological development gradually increased productivity, and thus the economic value of an hour of work. The economic value created was divided between profits and wages, or between savings, which financed the investments necessary to increase the quantity and quality of the capital stock and labor. This consideration on distribution paves the way for the following two stylized facts:
   a. the share of labor in total production has remained substantially stable;
   b. the real interest rate has fluctuated wildly around economic cycles, but it shows no trend toward growth or decline.

3. The average growth rate of the developed economies was 3% a year. This is a growth rate that simple increases in the labor force and the capital stock cannot explain. The growth residual not explained by growth in these two factors must be interpreted as the effect of technological innovation.

4. Growth has translated into a gradual but dramatic reduction in the percentage of global poverty. Returning to the data in Table 13.1, which considers a dollar a day in purchasing power as the poverty threshold, we note that in 1820 there were 886.8 million poor, representing the vast majority of the global populace. As decades passed, we see that while the percentage of the poor population steadily declined until reaching less than one-quarter of the population in 1998, the absolute number of poor fell to 179 million people, but a large share of the world population remains just above that threshold in poor living conditions. We can consider the glass as being half full or half empty. If we derive the global population from the above percentages, we observe that it transitions from around 1 billion in 1820 to around 5 billion in 1998, and more than 7.6 billion as of April 2018. So on the one hand economic development has been able to bring about 7.4 billion more people to the table, allowing them to live above the poverty threshold.[1] On the other hand, a substantial share of indigent people persists, which more distributed growth among the various regions of the world could probably have reduced. Once again we refer to the following pages for the solution to the puzzle about the performance differences between various countries around the world.

5. Underlying the average data on global GDP growth, we observe marked inequalities both between and within countries. In Fig. 13.3 the light gray stripe measures the distance between the incomes of the poorest and the wealthiest people within a given country, excluding the highest and lowest 10% of the poorest and wealthiest. The gray segment in the center indicates the median income distribution at its lowest point and the average income distribution at its highest point. The dark gray segment indicates the inverse, or the average at its lowest point and the median at its highest point. As we can see, even excluding the additional variability at the extremes of the poorest and wealthiest, we find wealthy countries with wide internal differences in income (the United States and Israel), wealthy countries with more contained internal income differences (Denmark), emerging countries with lower average income levels and significant internal variability (Brazil, Argentina, and South Africa), and finally, poor countries with very low average income and low variability (Mali and Cambodia).

6. The final point is that by analyzing the historical data we observe that we can draw the conclusion that significant improvements in the current

---

1. This statement is justified if we define a dollar a day as the poverty threshold. There is actually a sizable share of those five billion that is in the range of two to four dollars a day in purchasing power parities. We should also consider these people as poor or very nearly poor.

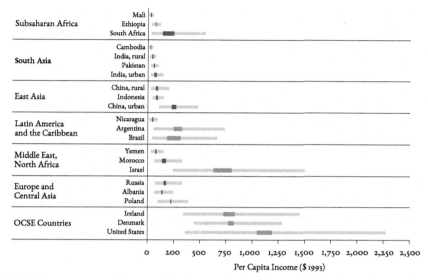

FIG. 13.3   Average, median, and distribution of income from the poorest 10% to the wealthiest 90% of the population. *Note*: the light gray line measures the distance between the poorest and the wealthiest individual incomes within each country, excluding the poorest and the wealthiest 10%. The gray segment in the center indicates the median income distribution at its lowest point and the average income distribution at its highest point. The dark gray segment indicates the inverse, or the average at its lowest point and the median at its highest point. *Source: World Bank, World Development Report 2003: Sustainable Development in a Dynamic World.*

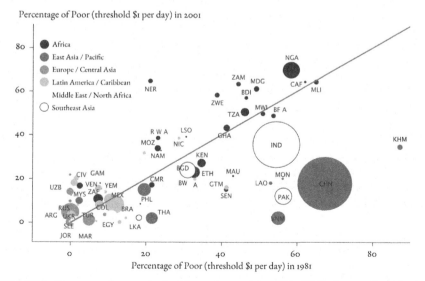

FIG. 13.4   Progress and regress in the fight against poverty (1981–2001). *Source: World Bank, World Development Report 2003: Sustainable Development in a Dynamic World.*

economic situation are possible within just a few decades. In Fig. 13.4, the vertical axis shows the percentage of poor (considered as those below one dollar a day) in 2001, and the horizontal axis shows the same percentages as of 1981. The diagonal in the graph indicates the bisector; below it we find the "virtuous" countries that have been able to reduce their poverty levels over the last 20 years — that is, countries in which the percentage of poor was higher in 1981 than in 2001. Above it are the countries that saw their situations worsen.

For each country considered, the size of the sphere is more or less proportional to its population. The color codes indicate the continent to which each belongs. From the graph it is evident that the greatest progress has been made in Asian countries, in China and India primarily, but also in Vietnam, Thailand, Pakistan, and others. We find the African countries foremost among those that took steps back in the fight against poverty (the darkest spheres).

13.3 Modeling growth

13.3.1 Traditional growth models

What are the causes of such different performance among the world's countries? To answer this question we must study the growth models. The most widely known stylized model in economics textbooks is based on the standard production function (see Chapter 4), which identifies the relationship between production inputs used and the quantities of goods or services obtained. What counts for the purpose of creating value for a given country is the volume of goods and services produced in a given time interval (GDP if geography is the criterion, GNP if using nationality). From this viewpoint, a first critique is the fact that value is created only when the goods and services can be sold on the market, which presupposes synchronicity between when goods are physically produced and when consumers enjoy them on the market. A company may be highly efficient in its technical ability to build things in a given unit of time, but if it cannot sell them it does not contribute to creating economic value.

The first basic input in the production function is the workforce. By workforce we mean a subset of the active populace, conventionally those between 15 and 65 years of age. Only part of the active populace, indicated by the participation rate, decides to take part in the market by seeking employment. The participation rate is highly variable (and well below 100%), especially when considering some particular segments, such as married women. Additionally, since the time each individual devotes to working is highly variable, labor as an input to the production function is more precisely defined not on the basis of active workers, but on the total number of hours worked. So it is evident that a first factor determining growth is the size of the labor force. (GDP is the result of the products and services created in a given number of hours that satisfy consumers' preferences, which can thus be sold on the market.) Only if we take these two basic principles into account is it possible to develop sensible political economy initiatives in order to promote economic growth and well-being while respecting environmental sustainability, which we will consider later.

Solow's model, one of the standard models of economic growth considers, along with the labor factor, physical capital and a *residual component* that captures all the additional factors that move the production frontier ahead, where the latter is also defined as the limit of production possibilities given a certain amount of production factors. This model explains that, in equilibrium, the growth of per capita GDP can only be generated by growth in the residual component. Differences between countries are thus related to persistent structural differences in terms of physical capital accumulation, population growth, and growth rates of the *residual component*.

In the literature on growth that developed after Solow, all the energy was directed to analyzing the "black box" represented by the residual component and the factors that determine it.

Discovering the importance of human capital was a basic contribution toward explaining what is in the black box. Investing in workers' training and education increases not only their skills and productivity, which allows them to shift the production function upwards for a given number of hours worked, but also raises the productivity of coworkers. In this new group of models, education is considered as a sort of capital good in which the stock of knowledge accumulated in a given time period depends on the inbound flow, or individual investments in training, and the outbound flow, or the depreciation of accumulated knowledge due to lack of use. The significant impact of education on GDP growth is supported by abundant empirical microeconomic evidence. In nearly every country in the world, the empirical evidence shows significant wage increases for every additional year of workforce education (the so-called return on schooling), which confirms the hypothesis that education increases productivity, and consequently the contribution of labor as an input to production.

In the case of education, the correspondence is clear between the intermediate goal of economic growth and the broader goal of human development and individual well-being. A more educated workforce stimulates economic growth. At the same time, besides increasing well-being through material production, a higher level of education in and of itself brings about a direct improvement in social well-being — for example, through a better use of cultural goods.

Even from this simple model it is possible to draw out the crucial concept of **conditional convergence**, on which all the modern literature on economic growth is based.

This concept illustrates how developing countries can recover their lag behind more developed countries by growing at a higher rate than the growth in industrialized countries (convergence). However, this process can happen only if these countries satisfy certain conditions (the conditions of convergence) regarding the elimination of the allocation gap in several fundamental factors, such as physical capital, education, and all the factors impacting the residual component that increases the productivity of labor. Put more simply, if a developing country recovers the noted factors compared to high income countries, at that point it is gradually able to make up ground, and thus to converge.

Moav and Galor (2004) provided an important contribution to the role human capital plays in growth and in evaluating its consequences on the relationship between inequality and growth. The two authors stated that the history of economic development can be divided, by way of example, into two stages. The first is the beginning of the Industrial Revolution, in which the accumulation of physical capital was predominant. In this context, inequality ended up having a positive impact on economic growth, in that the high savings rates of the wealthy significantly favored the original capital accumulation necessary to launch the capitalist production system. At the same time, the extreme poverty of the workers and widespread unemployment allowed paying rather low wages, which increased profits and the incentive to invest.

In the second historical phase — the one in which we live — the physical capital and financial assets necessary to finance investments are globally abundant. In a society in which value creation is increasingly based on intangible resources and the economy becomes less and less material, the crucial factor that can incentivize the creation of value is the ability to know how to develop every person's potential by investing in their education. Consequently, a more equitable income distribution has a positive effect on growth in that it ensures equality of opportunity, reduces the financial barriers to investing in human capital, and sustains demand. That guarantees that every person's potential is realized independently of their initial conditions, which increases the population's contribution to economic growth.

Increasing the role of education creates a first important challenge to the standard models of economic growth; the existence of a negative relationship between women's education and fertility, which is by now amply documented empirically, is a clear example of this. More educated women invest a greater portion of their time in their own careers and tend to have fewer children. This creates a methodological problem for the standard model because it highlights that growth in the labor force cannot be considered as exogenous (i.e., independent of other factors), given that human capital, which is one input to the production function, significantly impacts the dynamics of labor, which is another input.

A first important consequence in terms of political economy is that promoting education, particularly for women, has two positive effects on per capita GDP by increasing the numerator on the one hand and by reducing the denominator on the other. This explains the high emphasis that international organizations placed on the **Millennium Development Goals**, or the eight goals that the member states of the United Nations committed in 2000 to implement by 2015: (a) eliminate extreme poverty and hunger; (b) achieve the goal of universal primary education; (c) promote gender equality and women's independence; (d) reduce infant mortality; (e) improve maternal health; (f) combat HIV/AIDS, malaria, and other diseases; (g) ensure environmental sustainability; (h) develop global participation for growth.

However, we must keep in mind the limit to identifying education *tout court* as the panacea and solution for all problems of growth, in that education requires complementary factors in order to fulfill the goal of increasing labor productivity. Two of these factors are adequate job training and the willingness to invest one's human capital in entrepreneurial activity. The contribution by Murphy, Sheifer, and Vishny (1991) is quite interesting in this regard; they argue that gratification and social prestige play a crucial role in determining the field in which the talents acquired through education are used. The authors used this argument to explain why the Industrial Revolution did not happen in China centuries before it did in England, even though nearly all the basic ingredients were present (the presence of an ample market, stable institutions, and the scientific knowledge necessary to develop production technologies). The answer is that the Chinese society of that time was missing a basic component, in that there was scarce social prestige for entrepreneurial activity, or it was less than that of other careers, such as becoming a government official. In such a scenario, it seems understandable that the best talents of Chinese society of that time would not have considered employing their human capital accumulated in education in entrepreneurial activity.

13.3.2 Other determinants of growth and conditional convergence: institutions and cultural and religious foundations

In most recent studies of economic growth, there have been many contributions aiming to identify determinants of additional growth compared to the traditional factors of physical and human capital. In this literature, the quality of institutions has begun to play an increasingly important role.

This increasing interest in the role of institutions is motivated by the evolution of the economic system, and in particular, by the high and ever-increasing integration of the labor, product, and finance markets, which has had the effect of making the production factors of capital and labor increasingly mobile worldwide. In this context, there is less and less of a link between creating domestic value and national production factors. In the final analysis, that means that economic growth depends less and less on the *national* workforce, savings, and human capital. The increasing mobility of factors means that if a country establishes rules and conditions within its own geographic boundaries that make it competitive in attracting other countries' production factors, it is able to obtain greater benefits from globalization, and so it can grow more rapidly.

The increasing importance of creating favorable conditions for attracting inputs from the rest of the world also increases the importance of the prominent role of the quality of institutions in economic development.

Developing this topic further, by "quality of institutions" we mean a broad concept that includes a wide variety of degrees, in which the maximum degree of institutional poverty is represented by civil war, which is immediately followed by corruption and by ethno linguistic fractionalization that create social instability. As we move upwards, we reach the positive indicators of institutional quality, where we find an independent, high quality judicial system that is efficient and able to bring civil disputes to an end in a reasonable time frame (the importance of which cannot be overlooked), an adequate monetary policy that promotes price stability, and an adequate regulation of credit and labor markets and of creating new businesses.

The importance of the role of institutions — and more in detail, of financial institutions — has been widely emphasized in recent literature. The role of government, social and political stability, and corruption are among the various aspects that have been analyzed.

Among the many theoretical and empirical contributions that have aimed to explain the role of the quality of institutions on growth, among the most representative we recall those that affirm that in order for market economies to be successful they especially require good institutions, and more specifically those that protect property rights, support macroeconomic stabilization, and promote social cohesion.

Following a course that constantly seeks to deepen the search for the determinants of economic development, attention focused on the topic of institutions has recently brought to the center of discussion the connected role of various cultural and religious backgrounds as factors constituting the characteristic elements of institutions, which are the fundamentals capable of influencing growth.

Indeed, it is quite clear that culture and religion impact growth not only by directly influencing individual choices, but through a process that shapes and orders a society's set of values; they also influence the formation and quality of institutions and the well-being of nations.

For example, scholars on the subject analyze how religious beliefs can significantly influence a country's financial institutions and judicial system. One of the main results of their analyses shows that creditors' rights are markedly less protected in Catholic countries than in Protestant countries.

The conclusion reached by this extensive literature is that one of the deepest roots of the success or failure of economic growth is represented by:

1. the compatibility of a market system's values with those of a given cultural and religious background;

2. the form and quality of institutions, which are in turn influenced by culture and religion.

Consider that the nexus between religion, culture, institutions, and growth is also confirmed in countries in which religious practice is reduced today, in that the history of the influence of religion on a set of values and its crystallization into a system of rules that shape the current institutional system form the pivotal factor in relationships.

Another foundational strand of studies on the relationship between religion and growth has been to develop in depth Weber's hypothesis of the positive relationship between Protestantism and economic growth. Delacroix (1992) summarizes Weber's arguments, stating that: "The worldview Protestantism spread was a rupture from the traditional orientations of that time due to its (i) emphasis on good behavior, frugality, personal sobriety, and individual responsibility, and (ii) moral approbation of taking on risk and of improving one's own financial condition."

This position has been widely criticized by economic historians, particularly when it translates into a hypothesis of presumed differences between the influence of Protestant and Catholic cultures on economic development. Further research has shown that accumulation and economic prosperity began in the era of the city-states in Italy, long before the Protestant Reformation. The Protestant world assumed the leadership in economic growth only after the Council of Trent's reaction to the Protestant Reformation undermined the balance between "merchants" (primarily income producers and active tax contributors) and "clerics" (primarily beneficiaries of tax collection and social services providers), which increased the burden of supporting the clergy and consequently the tax burden on the merchant classes that had decisively contributed to the economic development of the cities. The disruption of this equilibrium drove a substantial part of the merchant class to move the center of their activities from Florence, the New York of its time, to Flanders, which transformed that region into the new engine of economic development.

13.3.3 Regional integration as an effective means of improving the quality of institutions

If institutions are so important for economic growth, it is essential to understand the best policies to implement to improve their quality.

In some countries fighting corruption and improving institutional quality can be particularly difficult due to the actions of lobbies or powerful groups that try to maintain their privileged status. In such cases, an impetus from outside the country can be particularly useful to help remove the internal obstacles to implementing institutional reforms. One of the strongest drives in this direction can be the desire to become part of the club of the most developed nations, or the desire to create a high level of integration with some of them that is expected to have positive effects on economic growth.

Recent empirical studies strongly support the importance of this hypothesis, showing that the desire to participate in the admission negotiations to the European Union has stimulated many institutional changes, with positive effects on the economic growth of the candidate countries. Furthermore, they show that the convergence process in the direction of the European Monetary Union has significantly improved institutional quality and reduced the volatility of the effective exchange rate in the Eurozone countries, which has had positive effects on economic growth. These studies suggest interesting political economy policy perspectives for many developing countries, emphasizing how EU integration with Turkey and the Mediterranean countries could have decisive effects on the development of the Middle Eastern and North African countries.

13.3.4 Scientific knowledge and technological innovation are important: the new context created by the information revolution and communication technology and by the digital divide

Studies on the determinants of growth could not ignore the major factor that has transformed contemporary society, namely technological innovation and, more specifically, the revolution in information and communication technology (ICT).

Starting with a general observation, when scientific discoveries and technological innovations without patent protection rapidly became public knowledge, these factors were of no relevance in explaining the difference between economic growth rates and GDP between countries, since they could quickly be adopted by anyone in any country in the world. To better explain this with an example, no one recalls the nationality of those who invented the Internet or made a particular discovery that immediately became a common heritage. What makes the difference in development in different countries is not so much the nationality of the inventors as it is their ability to access and use existing, publicly available technologies. Reflecting on the problems of adopting new technologies and of accessing them helps us understand the limits of the first, traditional approach, which denied the relevance of technological progress on growth by summarizing the effects of innovation into a common factor that was common to all countries, or specific to each country but invariant over time (Islam, 1995).

Keeping these reflections in mind, the ICT-induced revolution can be considered both as a change and as an opportunity that can help identify in economic growth terms the effect of changes over time of access to knowledge in a specific country. The difficulties in evaluating the effects of ICT are increased by the complex nature of this component, which on the one hand includes high quality physical capital, and on the other hand, a telecommunications infrastructure that allows easy access to information and knowledge, as well as to new ways of preserving and reproducing this knowledge, such as software and databases. The three components of ICT — hardware, telecommunications, and software — are tightly interconnected, because high quality physical capital is considered the means by which a telecommunications infrastructure can best be used to advantage, thanks to the use of software and databases. These in turn can be used to transfer voice, images, and data, increasing workers' productivity in proportion to their abilities and their human capital.

So with these particular characteristics in mind, what is the channel by which ICT influences economic growth?

Considering the intrinsic characteristics of ICT, such as the expandability and endless reproducibility of software and databases, which are a fundamental part of its innovative content, we can observe how this factor creates economic value by increasing labor productivity and by generating added value to products and services sold.

Summarizing, ICT is a particular type of innovation whose characteristics of expandability and endless reproducibility make it particularly difficult to apply patent protection mechanisms, which makes it much more difficult to privately appropriate its benefits. This is why if an ICT-linked innovation consisted solely of this aspect, it would be immediately available everywhere, without giving particular competitive advantages to the country where it was created. In other words, what impacts the development gaps between countries is not where the Internet and innovations linked to it were designed, but rather the barriers that obstruct access to the Internet and create the so-called **digital divide**.

These barriers are crucially influenced by:

1. the capacity and diffusion of the cellphone and telecommunications network;
2. the possibility of individual access to the network in which intangible innovative products circulate and are exchanged, such as software and databases;
3. the opportunity to deploy the high powered terminals and processors that are able to access and reprocess the information and products available on the Internet.

A unique feature of the ICT revolution has been the difficulty for scholars to identify its significant impacts on productivity and economic growth in the early days of its development. In the 1980s and 1990s, empirical research found no significant increase in production associated with ICT investments.

More recently, however, having new data available and applying new methodologies, empirical research has found that in the second half of the

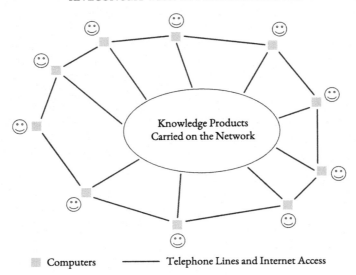

AN ECONOMY WITHOUT A DIGITAL DIVIDE

Knowledge Products
Carried on the Network

▨ Computers ———— Telephone Lines and Internet Access

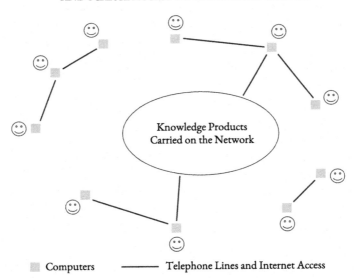

AN ECONOMY WITH A DIGITAL DIVIDE
AND SCARCE ACCESS TO ONLINE KNOWLEDGE

Knowledge Products
Carried on the Network

▨ Computers ———— Telephone Lines and Internet Access

FIG. 13.5 The economy and the digital divide. *Note*: This diagram compares two economies, one with and one without a digital divide. In the former all end users own a computer and are connected with each other on the Internet. In the latter, few users are connected to the Internet, and not all users are connected with each other. Only the first economy fully benefits from the acceleration in the circulation of knowledge and all the factors that can use it to reduce costs and increase productivity.

1990s ICT investment has been correlated with an improvement in productivity and economic growth (Fig. 13.5).

Paul David, an economic historian, has offered an interesting interpretation of the puzzle of the lack of positive correlation in the 1980s and a positive correlation in the 1990s. Recalling the delayed effect on economic growth of another great innovation, electrical energy, he stressed that network innovations in general have a delayed impact on productivity because they require the reorganization of production processes as well as widespread general adoption to deploy their full potential. This also happened for the ICT revolution, which required a complete reorganization of work within companies, along with the emergence of new professional staff to replace others that were now obsolete.

13.3.5 The role of geography, social capital, and natural resources

Although the ancient "climate theories" of the Greek historian Polybius have never been empirically proven, in recent decades there has been a rediscovery of climate as a factor impacting growth. In 1997 Durlauf and Quah, in a list of 87 potential growth determinants, considered *latitude* in addition to the traditional development and convergence factors previously discussed, such as physical and human capital, the quality of institutions, and technological innovation. The geography—growth link does not appear to have been weakened by the ongoing process of world integration, and it turns out that latitude has a significant impact on estimations of economic development in countries.

There is a historical explanation for this phenomenon that at first glance is paradoxical. The colonial powers set up an exchange circuit that conveyed raw materials from less developed countries, typically in a tropical climate, to developed countries in temperate zones, which initiated a progressive impoverishment of the former to the advantage of the latter. Although the developed countries were without raw materials, they held the political and military power, and thus they controlled the international process of value creation and acquired its results.

However, there is also a difference between developing countries in temperate and tropical climates. The impact of latitude has also been traced back to historical causes, such as a greater tendency to settle in countries with a temperate climate (and thus to invest in infrastructure and the general development of the territory) and to use conquered countries with a tropical climate only as a place from which to extract raw materials.

These historical events, and the tendency for countries with important natural resources to attract voracious predators that contributed to creating corruption and institutional weakness if they were not opposed, explain the well-known paradoxical statement by Sachs and Warner of the "curse of natural resources," highlighting the existence of a significant negative relationship between having natural resources and economic growth, net of all other relevant factors. Contrary to what seems reasonable, the historical events we described have meant that countries with more natural resources were not the ones to develop more, but rather those who historically controlled the transformation of those resources; the miracle of South Korea's growth in the last 40 years happened in a country that is entirely poor in natural resources. However, the high growth of two "continents" such as China and India have opened a new era in which the demand for raw materials has increased enormously, and countries rich in raw materials can now have their redress.

13.4 Methodological weaknesses

Typical problems from which all studies on the determinants of growth suffer are endogeneity and the identification of the correct causal nexus between the variables considered. Nearly all the factors we have discussed until now are at once both causes and consequences of economic growth. For example, a more educated labor force is more productive, but higher per capita income allows substantial investments in education and training. Equally, the quality of institutions is foundational for the proper operation of productive activity, protecting property rights, and constructing a system of stable rules that permit economic development. At the same time, however, economic growth itself can bring about reasons and opportunities for developing institutions to become an antidote against the general corruption of public officials, which partly depends on the paucity of their wages. From these two examples it is clear that moving from observing correlations to identifying causal links is difficult, because it is difficult to distinguish the direction of the cause—effect relationship.

The general conclusion researchers have reached on this topic is that for many variables there is a high probability that causality is relevant in both directions. So the impact of growth determinants described above exists and is significant, although it risks being overestimated when directly causal factors are not distinguished from those that are inversely causal.

13.5 The role of globalization in development

The reasoning we have carried out to this point on the determinants of economic development and the tools needed to combat poverty has set aside an analysis of the role of globalization. What has changed with the advent of this important new phase in economic history? The term "globalization" is one of the most used and abused in contemporary debates. The most frequently observed risk is that two sides are forming, one for and one against globalization, rather than a more in-depth development of the meaning of the word itself. The opportunity and duty for economics students who have the privilege of being able to examine in depth these problems, which everyone wants to understand better, is to go beyond the slogans.

There are perhaps three privileged points of view from which to observe this phenomenon: technological, economic, and sociological.

We will begin with the technological aspect because it is definitely what gave rise to globalization. What we are discussing is something different from the progressive integration of markets due to increases in trade between different countries (which is favored by reductions in tariffs and customs protections). From this point of view, we observe no linear evolution. In fact, at the beginning of the 20th century the developed world was already highly integrated from a trade perspective, although the process of integration suffered abrupt setbacks during the two world wars. The resumption of trade liberalization, which has been driven by agreements reached within the large-scale negotiating rounds of multilateral trade organizations such as **GATT** (the General Agreement on Tariffs and Trade) and then the **WTO** (the World Trade Organization), also suffered a slowdown in the last decade due to the rise of protectionism in many countries, as well as the deadlock in negotiations between the most industrialized countries and the group of emerging countries on topics such as agriculture and the liberalization of services. The problem is that, behind the face value of declarations in favor of liberalization, each block defends its own interests by calling for opening markets in the sectors in which it is most competitive, in agriculture for emerging countries and in financial services for more developed countries.

So this is not where we need to look for the origin of the revolution that has profoundly transformed the world from the 1990s onward. Technology was the triggering factor for globalization in recent decades, due to the wave of innovations in the electronics and telecommunications sectors that allowed drastically reducing the cost and time of moving all "weightless goods", such as images, music, data, voice, and so on. We should note that one important element that reflects globalization is the different speed of progress in innovations between "heavy" and "weightless" goods. According to the well-known observation of Dale Jorgenson, a famous productivity scholar, if from the end of the 1970s to today the same increase in speed and cost reduction had happened in the airline industry as happened in microprocessors, we would be able to go from Rome to New York in less than 1 s and pay one cent. This comparison effectively communicates the idea of the incredible progress made in just a few years in one specific sector, which has been of fundamental importance for the economy.

Progress in transporting intangible goods has generated a series of multi-purpose innovations, such as iPods and personal computers, with content such as electronic mail and CAD/CAM for industrial design that can be used horizontally across all other production sectors and sharply reduce their costs. We can easily ascertain the productivity increases (defined, as we recall, as the ability to complete tasks in a given unit of time) made possible by this revolution in a series of common activities ranging from bibliographic research on a topic of interest, to booking a place, train, or hotel reservation, to preparing a written document, and so on.

Having clarified what we mean by the technological aspect of globalization, we can now consider its economic and sociological aspects. From a sociological point of view, the transformations described above have brought about a sense of having eliminated geographic distance and being part of a single global village. The reader may have noticed that the psychological perception of distance between the various regions of a nation that was typical of the previous generation corresponds to the current generation's perception of the distance between various countries around the world. Today we can travel to far distant countries or exotic destinations with the same ease that our parents could travel within their own or immediately adjacent countries. One typical sociological concern about globalization is the disappearance of cultural diversity and the massification and standardization of all cultures. The experience of encountering exotic cultures, at one time the privilege of artists such as Gauguin, missionaries, or adventurers, is within the reach of nearly everyone. This suddenly shifted scenario seems to bring two opposing forces into play. On the one hand, the propagation of the same urban models and lifestyles in all the world's cities is decidedly moving toward a reduction in diversity. On the other hand, the awareness that diversity is cultural wealth, which also translates into originality in commercial products, generates the opposite tendency, which leads to rediscovering and emphasizing diversity for the purpose of satisfying consumers' and tourists' taste for variety, in addition to local communities' desires to preserve their own culture and traditions.

From an economist's perspective, this enormous revolution has the merit of transforming many markets from local to global. As was obviously to be expected, the process has been much more rapid and profound for intangible products or for tangible products with certain characteristics. With regard to the latter type of goods, consider tangible products that have a very high added value, which can offset the cost of shipping from wherever they are produced, in the sense that by moving production they lose part of their value. We are referring to Protected Designation of Origin (PDO) products, such as buffalo milk mozzarella from the Italian region of Campania, for which every kitchen in the world is its reference market. In any case, more than anything else globalization has been about intangible goods, and primarily about financial goods. The financial market is definitely the most globalized market, in which the goods exchanged are financial activities that have a market value but no physical substance. As long as market regulations do not prevent them, it is possible to buy and sell such goods on any market in the world with a click on a computer.

What is globalization's effect on economic growth? To discover this, we must start with its effects on individual people. Electronic and information technology tools are clearly very powerful, but the ability to use them effectively for productive purposes depends on two basic factors. The first is the quality of access to the Internet, including factors such as computer literacy, the availability and speed of a computer or of a cellphone, a fast connection, and so forth. The second is the user's human capital; for example, those who do not know English are cut off from a highly important portion of Internet sites, while an expert in a discipline who knows English can quickly and efficiently find information on a particular research topic. This last point needs to be further explored by inquiring how the global integration of markets acts according to each person's position on the "**talent ladder.**"

The transition of market outlets for goods and services from local to global has greatly increased the earnings of those who are at the top of the ladder, or the leaders in various sectors — the so-called "superstars." The leaders can sell their goods and services on a much broader market, and since their products are the best, they are able to greatly increase their earnings. Those on the opposite end of the talent scale, the unskilled workers, must compete with the great mass of unskilled workers in the various countries in the world due to the global integration of the labor market. The globalization of the labor market makes things difficult, especially for unskilled workers in the wealthiest countries, as they are accustomed to welfare and a good system of protections. Indeed, globalization offers companies the opportunity to choose where each part of their production process is to be carried out. With offshoring and outsourcing, companies tend to transfer the non-strategic phases of production to countries where labor costs are lowest, which brings unskilled but well-protected workers in wealthy countries directly into competition with unskilled workers in poor countries who are willing to work for much lower wages.

We can find traces of this transformation in many cases we probably all know, such as the British railways transferring their call centers to India, several production phases of entire Italian industrial districts being moved to Romania, and so on.

These transformations have profound effects at both the individual and aggregate levels. At the individual level, the first phase of globalization saw growth in the wage differential between workers with different skills and qualifications; the gap between superstars and the unskilled greatly increased, as well as between the least and the most educated. At the country level, the population's quality of access to the Internet made the difference and became one of the basic factors in the process of conditional convergence.

If students have not yet read between the lines the most important point of this transformation for themselves, we will make it explicitly clear: With globalization, ascending the talent ladder becomes fundamental. Attaining excellence in the sector in which one has chosen to work can open the way to significant prospects for development, or in any case to a wider range of possibilities for choices that can have significant effects on one's quality of life. Remaining trapped in the lower part of the ladder means enduring pressure from workers in other countries who start from much worse living conditions, and who are thus far more motivated and willing to work at much lower hourly wages.

Globalization is thus a stimulus to seek excellence in one's own vocation.

13.6 Squaring growth and the environment

As we have emphasized since Chapter 1, one of economists' greatest merits is to be problem solvers, or pragmatic people who accept constraints as a given (without fretting over why they exist) and try to use available resources in the best way possible to achieve established goals. Studying the various chapters we have learned how the theory of rational choices applies in microeconomics to the following choices:

- consumers' choices between various goods (Chapter 3),
- workers' choices between work and leisure (Chapter 9),
- companies' choices between various inputs (Chapter 4).

These choices translate into a constrained maximization in which income, time, and technology are the respective constraints that limit expansion possibilities.

Despite the attention to the objective limits of our possibilities for action, economists have however almost always neglected — at least in the standard model — one of the most important constraints, which is the limited availability of natural and environmental resources. On the contrary, one of natural science scholars' main traits is to focus attention on precisely this problem by emphasizing that uncontrolled economic growth on a planet with more than 6 billion people appears to be unsustainable within the limits of available resources.

After a long tradition of non-communication between the two disciplines, they ended up formulating policy prescriptions that were in stark contrast to each other, such as economists proposed consuming more to grow and defeat poverty, while natural scientists proposed consuming less to stop depleting the planet's natural resources. More recent events linked to global warming seem to have encouraged economists to integrate environmental constraints in their considerations. Consequently, a chapter on the relationship between economics and the environment seems to regularly appear in textbooks now, even though a fully integrated approach of including an environmental constraint when analyzing consumers' and companies' choices has not yet become common practice.

Our purpose in this part of the chapter is to illustrate all the advances made from the perspective of integrating the disciplines of economics and the natural sciences in order to give a few partial answers to the following questions. What are the effects of productive activity on the environment, and vice versa? Is

TABLE 13.2 Environmental resources matrix.

	Renewable	Nonrenewable
Appropriable	Timber	Raw Materials (copper, oil, coal)
Non-appropriable	Fishing, Air Quality	Climate

Note: Environmental resources can be classified according to the renewable/non-renewable and appropriable/non-appropriable matrix, which defines four types of resources.

there a dilemma between growth and environmental sustainability, and what initiatives seem better able to resolve the dilemma?

13.7 The matrix of environmental goods

The first step in analyzing the relationship between the economy and the environment is to define environmental resources. The traditional taxonomy we have shown is based on two coordinates: **renewability** and **appropriability** (see Table 13.2).

The characteristic of renewability concerns a resource's ability to be regenerated by the environment itself once it has been used. This immediately highlights an important difference between environmental goods and traditional goods produced by the market. In the case of non-reproducibility or very slow reproducibility, environmental goods, in difference with traditional goods, cannot be regenerated at will and in reasonably rapid timeframes by either production or natural cycles.

The characteristic of appropriability concerns the public/private nature of an environmental good, or its ability to be privatized. Recalling the classification between private and public goods discussed in Section 8.5.3, an appropriable good must at least potentially have the characteristics of rivalry and excludability, which are typical of private goods.

Analyzing the four possible combinations, we can identify a first category of reproducible and appropriable goods; for example, we find timber in this category. We would do well though to recall that, despite it being reproducible, it requires a long time to do so; consider the damage caused in natural parks by arson. The time necessary to produce extensive damage is very brief, but reproducing the forest requires decades. Despite the problems, reproducibility means that with appropriate policies to invest in reforestation it is possible to increase the overall global area covered by forests. From this perspective, the attention given to the environment in the last few years has allowed reversing the trend, transition from a deficit to a positive balance, and start increasing the global surface area covered by forests.

The situation of appropriable but non-reproducible resources is more complex. In this case we are talking about raw materials such as copper and fossil fuels such as oil and coal. These resources are characterized by extremely slow reproducibility that happens over geological time, thus they should be classified as non-renewable.

So what happens if in this case their use rate is higher than the extraction rate in a dynamic that leads to the depletion of the resource over time? What can help in such a case is the existence of substitutes and markets that can signal the relative scarcity of the resource by its price. A sharply increasing price is an alarm signal, but at the same time it is also an incentive to rebalance resource use, in that it motivates potential buyers of the natural resource to look for substitutes at a lower price. It also motivates producers to implement previously unused but more costly extraction processes with investments that become profitable at the new higher prices. Unfortunately, in the short run the market signal is not always without noise, which can depend on purely financial operations, such as speculative bubbles on the raw materials, or on strategic supply side policies. A paradigm case of the latter was the sharp upturn in crude oil prices in 1974, which was not caused by an unexpectedly higher natural scarcity of oil, but by an artificial scarcity provoked by production caps set by the OPEC cartel countries (see Chapter 2).

While the information content of the signal may be noisy in the short run, the price equilibrium mechanism should still always work. When the price of a resource becomes very high, demand side incentives come into play to identify cheaper alternatives. If alternatives exist, the market can thus move toward equilibrium by reducing demand for the costly raw material, with a subsequent fall of its price. To give just one example, a few decades ago copper was the basic material in telephony, and the risk of its depletion due to overexploitation was considered to be quite real. Technological innovation that lead to the use of fiber optics and satellite radio reduced the use of copper in telecommunications first, which reduced the risk of its depletion and simultaneously led to a reduction in market prices.

What is the current situation? The most recent trend is that the prices of raw materials have risen sharply due to the increasing needs of emerging countries such as India and China. Time will tell whether the challenge of substituting the most expensive natural resources with alternatives, such as the relationship between oil and renewable energy, will again be won, thus avoiding the risk of depleting a basic resource for economic life. According to a famous saying, the Stone Age did not end because we ran out of stone, and the same was true for the Iron Age. The hope is that the same will happen for the oil age.

The third category of goods in the taxonomy shown in Table 13.2 includes renewable but non-appropriable environmental goods. Typical examples are panoramas, fishing, and air quality; even in cases of severe deterioration, renewability is usually possible and does not require geological ages. Given their non-appropriability, these goods have characteristics similar to public goods (or quasi-public, such as common resources). As in the case of common resources, the market in and of itself is unable to solve the problem, since consumption by one person produces a negative externality on the rest of the group. Rules are thus necessary to limit the possibility of excessive exploitation of such goods.

The fourth and final category is that of non-renewable and non-appropriable environmental resources. It is here we find the most difficult problems to resolve. The most obvious problem today is the relationship between carbon dioxide emissions and climate change. The climate is a global public good, and in this case as well it is particularly difficult to limit the negative externalities that individuals and companies create by producing emissions. To give an example, Chinese emissions contribute to pollution in America, but Americans can do little to counteract them. Its non-renewability characteristics, together with being a public good, makes climate deterioration and its consequences for everyone's well-being even more serious. In subsequent sections we will study how it is possible to intervene in such a sensitive contemporary problem.

13.8 Revisiting the income circuit with the creation and destruction of environmental resources

In the introduction we argued that the general perspective of new studies in environmental economics is to integrate economists' and natural scientists' points of view.

After defining the different types of environmental goods with an appropriate taxonomy, a first move toward such an integrated approach requires modifying the basic scheme we used to describe the operation of the economic system. In this section we present an extended version of the income circuit described in Chapter 3.

In that chapter we illustrated how the income circuit can be summarized by the interaction between productive units, or companies, and household units that supply and demand goods and labor on the market (Figure 3.1 in Chapter 3). We can now develop in depth and complete the scheme by taking into account the balance of environmental resources created and destroyed by the production process (Fig. 13.6).

More specifically, businesses transform inputs and natural resources to produce goods or services, but in the process they also produce harmful emissions (e.g., CO_2) and industrial waste (inert material that is not part of the product or service sold). At the same, when consuming goods and services households do not fully use up the material used to produce and package them, resulting in trash and harmful emissions, such as the carbon dioxide produced when driving a car or heating a house.

In this regard and with an eye to environmental sustainability, there is a fundamental distinction between the consumption of rivalrous and non-rivalrous goods. Recalling the taxonomy of public and private goods we

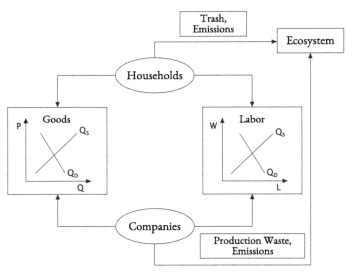

FIG. 13.6 The modified income circuit. *Note*: The consequences of families' and companies' actions on the market for goods and labor create production waste, polluting emissions, and consumption trash that alter the ecosystem we live in.

developed along the lines of rivalry/non-rivalry and excludability/non-excludability, we defined non-rivalry as the characteristic that goods and services do not deteriorate after a consumer makes use of them, thus they remain available for subsequent utilization by another consumer. So when we want to assess the effect of consumption in terms of production or consumer waste, we must distinguish between rivalrous and non-rivalrous goods. Rivalrous goods have a markedly greater environmental impact. A rivalrous good, such as a disposable razor, must be produced anew after each use — or nearly each use — use to allow it to be consumed again. A non-rivalrous good, such as a CD-ROM or an audio file, need not be produced after each use, and so it can create much more economic value at the same level of environmental impact in terms of production waste and trash resulting from its use.

In summary, in our integrated income circuit that includes interactions between the economy and the environment we observe four main effects generated by the production and consumption of goods and services. On the production side, we observe the consumption of natural resources and the production of waste and emissions; on the consumption side, we observe the production of waste and emissions, with the important qualification that the production and consumption of non-rivalrous goods impact the environment much less at the same level of economic value creation.

In light of the matrix of environmental goods we can state that when businesses produce they primarily consume non-renewable and appropriable environmental goods, such as raw materials and oil, as well as non-renewable and non-appropriable environmental goods, through polluting emissions and waste that impact the climate. Moreover, their activity can have effects on renewable and appropriable goods, such as timber for the paper industry, and on non-renewable and non-appropriable goods, such as fishing, air quality, and landscapes. Similarly, consumers primarily consume non-renewable and non-appropriable goods by producing waste and harmful emissions that affect the climate.

The new arrows drawn in the income circuit converge toward the ecosystem. To maintain the balance of the ecosystem it is essential that consumed environmental resources be reproduced, wherever possible, by deliberate human actions. As we have already noted, that is easier for renewable and appropriable goods such as timber because it is possible to anticipate compensatory measures, such as planting new trees to replace those harvested, perhaps even in different areas that are far from where they are harvested. Extensive reforestation programs can compensate for timber harvested for use as inputs to production processes, resulting in a net balance of initiatives launched. Additionally, by planning landscapes, setting fishing limits, and regulating harmful emissions, local and national institutions can limit the degradation of renewable and non-appropriable environmental goods. Regulatory intervention is absolutely necessary in this case, given the public, non-appropriable nature of this asset.

Regarding appropriable but non-renewable goods such as oil and raw materials, the hope is that price signals create the right incentives to find substitutes for resources that become scarce.

In any case, the biggest problem arises once again for non-renewable and non-appropriable goods such as the climate. In this case an international agreement between countries is essential, as the climate is a global public good.

Such agreements have proven to be possible and effective, with limited effects on industry. For example, the hole in the ozone created by chlorofluorocarbon (CFC) emissions has finally begun to shrink after a new international protocol went into effect that banned the production of goods and services that released these gases into the atmosphere. An attempt to define an international agreement on limiting greenhouse gases to slow global warming, which is still in process, is proving more difficult, due in this case to the strongly negative effects on industry because of higher production costs.

One of the primary problems in this instance is the difficulty of measuring the effects of human actions on the environment, which leads sceptics to doubt that there is a clear causal nexus between pollution, greenhouse gases, and climate change. The problem with climate change is that the effects of its degradation are less easily perceived and connectable to human action, even though the constant temperature rise found in recent years, as well as the greater variability of the climate, seem to increasingly attract the attention of the public and of governments. And even if this link were demonstrated with absolute certainty, many could continue to be optimistic about the ability of the environment to adapt to the new situation.

A separate discussion is necessary for waste products. We classified them as non-appropriable and non-renewable goods, but on further analysis this does not appear to be quite correct. Apart from nuclear waste, which has a very long life with serious problems for storage and management, technology is finding new ways to transform waste into appropriable and renewable environmental goods, where by renewability we mean in this case the ability of the environment to get rid of waste because they can be transformed into potential inputs for production. With various techniques and by sorted recycling collection, it is now possible to use waste to produce energy. Unfortunately, this is a production technology that is not entirely without its own noxious environmental effects, and it is still not profitable enough, so it requires public subsidies to be sustained.

In essence, the waste example tells us that the matrix for classifying environmental goods does not have a classification system that is valid once and for all, and that human progress can significantly change the situation and the impact of production on the ecosystem.

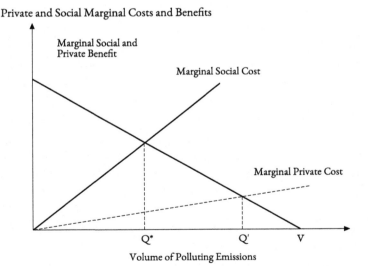

FIG. 13.7 The private and social costs and benefits of pollution. *Note*: The optimal level of polluting emissions for society Q^* (the horizontal axis projection of the point at which the social cost is equal to the social benefit) cannot be reached by the spontaneous initiative of private parties. The reason is that they will choose the volume of emissions that equals the private benefit and private cost, which is higher and equal to Q'.

13.9 The emissions problem and its possible solutions: classical and bottom-up approaches

Economists' traditional approach to the problem of negative environmental repercussions of productive activity is illustrated in Fig. 13.7.

On the vertical axis we find both private and social marginal costs and benefits resulting from polluting emissions. On the horizontal axis we measure the amount of emissions; as we move along the horizontal axis the amount of polluting emissions increases.

In principle, we consider the problem from a social point of view, or from the perspective of the entire community. The marginal social cost of emissions production increases linearly in the graph as the volume of emissions increases. Actually, the emissions problem is more a problem of accumulation than of flow. If the emissions level is already quite high, additional emissions could have far more negative effects on pollution, affecting not only the climate but impacting health as well. If instead we start from a low or zero emissions level, the marginal social cost of an additional unit of emissions is very low. Consequently, even though we have assumed that the line of the marginal social cost of emissions has a constant slope, we should not discard the alternate hypothesis of a non-linear line, since it is not unlikely that additional emissions above a certain accumulation of pollution may have particularly serious effects.

The marginal social benefit of emissions has a negative slope and a high positive intercept on the vertical axis. Emissions are a collateral effect of a firm's production activity, which creates positive social effects by creating economic value. So starting from a zero or low level, the social benefit of a marginal unit of emissions is positive. As the level of emissions grows, the marginal social benefit becomes smaller and smaller. We can hypothesize that when starting from conditions of minimal economic activity in which all companies have low production levels, people will be willing to accept a little pollution as long as it raises their level of development. When production is already quite high, the marginal benefit tends instead to shrink.

The optimal level of emissions from a social perspective is thus determined by the intersection of the social benefit and the social cost, with an equilibrium level in our graph of Q^* tons of emissions.

We will now analyze the private cost and benefit lines, or the cost and benefit of polluting emissions for a single firm. The marginal benefit for the firm is also high at the beginning, and for the sake of simplicity it coincides with the social benefit. A company cannot produce without producing emissions, and so the first units of emissions have a high marginal benefit because they make productive activity possible. As emissions increase, the marginal benefit for the company tends to shrink.

The real difference between the social and private situations is in the marginal cost curves. As can be seen in Fig. 13.7, the company's marginal costs have a positive slope, but they are markedly less than the marginal social costs.

The difference between the marginal social costs and the marginal private costs is determined by the negative externalities, or the indirect negative effects of harmful emissions on others.

This means that when choosing the optimal production level —and consequently the level of harmful emissions — a firm does not take into account the external environmental damage that impacts third parties, because those damages are not a line item in its budget. This substantial difference means that the optimal emissions level (Q') resulting from the intersection of the marginal private cost and benefit is much higher than the socially optimal level.

The two classic approaches to solving this problem are regulation and taxes. According to the first approach, institutions establish an emissions cap for businesses that matches the socially optimal level, which corresponds to $Q*$ in our chart.

The alternative that can attain the same result is a **Pigovian tax**, which is a unit tax on the volume of emissions that can align the marginal cost of emissions with their social cost. A properly calibrated Pigovian tax increases the slope of the private costs line so it coincides with the social cost line, which allows reconciling the private optimum with the social optimum by inducing the company to produce $Q*$ tons of polluting emissions.

Setting aside an analysis of the problem of the costs of implementing these two policies, as well as of monitoring companies' behavior (who checks if companies are complying with the regulations or paying the proper taxes, and how much do such checks cost?), the possibilities of implementing these two solutions is significantly limited in the new context of the global integration of markets.

With globalization, companies can decide to locate their production in other countries, at least when possible and there are no constraints on the mobility of production factors; however, given the technology and the transportation means available, this opportunity seems to be available for most production sectors. So if the environmental regulations and Pigovian taxes are not equally rigorous in all countries, a company can decide to produce where attention to the environment is lower. It is no mystery that many developing countries, where the social costs of pollution are presumably lower because greater attention is given to the problem of economic development, consider this a true competitive factor to attract foreign investments. In this situation the risk is of a race to the bottom, in which the regulatory dynamic within and between countries becomes increasingly lax due to competitive pressure and the desire to attract the highest number of direct foreign investments. These considerations clearly suggest that fighting pollution by a tax on emissions within a single country can bring about productive relocation, with negative effects on employment and production. An increasingly discussed alternative is to transfer the tax to consumers by heavily taxing the consumption of products that have a greater impact on pollution (with a green consumption tax). A consumption tax does not create different burdens on companies based on where their production is located, but rather a common penalty for everyone who sells in a given market.

A possible solution is gaining ground that is complementary to traditional regulations and Pigovian taxes, which is for citizens to exert pressure from the bottom up by voting with their wallets. Suppose that a portion of socially responsible citizens understand, based on the principle of farsighted self-interest, that it is advantageous to reward more environmentally responsible companies in order to prevent the consequences of environmental deterioration from falling on themselves in terms of health problems and the effects of global warming. This portion of responsible consumers may show a willingness to pay for the environmental value of products. At the same price level, this would reduce the demand for companies that pollute more (obviously, this mechanism works if the portion of socially responsible consumers becomes relevant).

At that point, for a company to increase emissions would entail an additional private cost resulting from a reduction in its revenue due to socially responsible consumers voting with their wallets. Similarly, ethical investment funds could sell their shares in companies that are less attentive to the

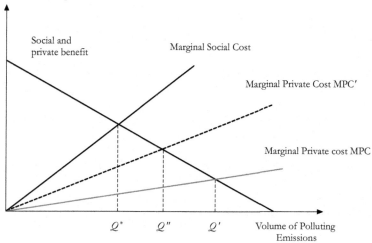

FIG. 13.8 Polluting emissions in the presence of "wallet voting". *Note*: Socially responsible consumers and ethical funds entering the market and deciding to reward with their purchases and savings the companies that are more oriented toward protecting the environment leads to an increase in the marginal private cost of pollution from MPC to MPC'. That means that the quantitative balance of emissions shifts from Q' to Q'', approaching the socially optimal level Q^*.

environment due to their behavior. The hypothesis is not particularly utopian if we consider that in 2007 the total invested in ethical funds (funds that select shares in which to invest on the basis of socially responsible criteria) in the United States amounted to 12 trillion dollars, which corresponds to about one-fourth of the total money placed in investment funds (SIF, 2018) (see also Chapter 11, Section 1).

Suppose also that, due to these effects linked to socially responsible consumers and ethical funds, the slope of the marginal private cost increases —that is, the line MPC is less steep than the line MPC' (Fig. 13.8). This additional cost reduces the volume of emissions corresponding to the private optimum and brings it closer to the social optimum.

This third solution, which is partial and complementary to the others, has the obvious flaw of depending on citizens' good will and sensibility, but it is not subject to the problems of the other two, or production taxes and regulation. We should as well not forget that about 20% of consumption comes from public purchases. With green and social public procurement the government can decide as well to vote with its wallet and thus be consistent with its own social and environmental goals.

The fact that voting with one's wallet can be concentrated more in some countries than others still does not allow companies to escape the consequences of its actions, and it essentially means an increase in costs. Action from the bottom up by consumers can thus be an important complement to the two traditional solutions.

13.10 The economic growth-environment dilemma

One of the central issues to address in this chapter is studying the relationship between the environment and the economy is the dilemma between economic growth and environmental sustainability. The traditional conception is that greater attention to the environment makes measures necessary that implicitly slow down economic development. If we only look to the traditional remedies of Pigovian taxes and controls on the amount of pollution produced, they obviously influence production and consumption and shrink both. Economists are generally averse to this course of action. Such a drastic strategy would end up conflicting with the traditional goals of creating the economic value necessary to finance welfare systems, social protections, and public debt burdens, and to create the basis for reducing poverty (in the case in which the wealth created is well distributed, or in any case in which the economic system is able to reduce the difficulties in access to credit and education for those who are less well off).

This is why it seems difficult to accept de-growth, except as a paradoxical provocation that is perhaps useful to make us think. However, the proponents of this movement have the merit of having directed the debate toward attention to environmental sustainability, opposing the traditional unidimensional perspective that the only purpose to pursue is the growth of material well-being as measured by an expanding GDP, or the sum of goods and services produced in a given country. According to de-growth proponents, the course they indicate would be practicable by reducing the size of the market in favor of non-market transactions such as reciprocity, gift exchange, self-consumption, self-production, and non-monetary exchanges of products, with the awareness that an important part of well-being depends on non-monetary factors (as illustrated in Chapter 12, on happiness). This statement underscores an important element of current economic systems, which is that they have progressively reduced the areas of informality, or the production and exchange of value that is not transacted on the market. Having less than a dollar a day in a developed country in which everything one has must be bought means being truly poor. Having less than a dollar a day in a fertile rural area in a developing country does not necessarily mean not being able to meet one's food needs, in that the widespread presence of informal exchanges and

---

FRAME 13.1 How income and poverty are measured

When seen from afar things always seem clear, but when looking in greater depth we become aware of the problems connected to them, and we nearly come to the Socratic conclusion that "we know we don't know anything."

Measuring wealth and poverty is a problem that is too important for us not to question whether the unit of measure we are using is correct or whether it requires adjustments. The definitions of poverty and wealth that economists use are based on a very precise metric. In the preceding sections we documented the income comparisons among countries with a series of data relative to per capita income "at purchasing power parity." The starting point is thus comparisons of per capita income. If we descend from general comparisons among countries to comparing among individuals, the starting unit is family income. In this case, and particularly for analyzing poverty, we must divide the household income by a quotient that takes into account the number of household members and weight each member in proportion to their economic needs. For example, a standard OCSE criterion weights a spouse at 50% and each child at 30% when considering the wealthiest countries. When investigating poor countries, in general the weights of the other components tend to increase. As well-being decreases, much more income is spent on food, as there are no "economies of scale" in this case; the use of a car can be shared, but each person needs their share of food!

The other basic problem when comparing living standards and poverty between countries is cost of living differences. The salary of a Cuban doctor in 2000 was about $28 a month (thus less than the infamous dollar a day), but the cost of living in Cuba is on average at least 10 times less than that of a wealthy country, because some products, although rationed, are free, and others have very low prices. These differences hold as long as we exclude imported goods in these countries, which cost a fortune compared to the purchasing power of wages. So if we take the factor of 10 as accurate to compare a Cuban doctor's income with that of an Italian doctor in terms of purchasing power, we must multiply the Cuban doctor's salary by 10. But that is not enough.

Continued

Frame 13.1 How income and poverty are measured—cont'd

In poor countries where incomes are very low, the market shrinks in favor of gifts, barter, self-production, and self-consumption. In a wealthy country citizens are totally dependent on goods and services that can be bought on the market, and even more so when some primary public goods, such as healthcare, are paid services. So when we evaluate the income level of people in a poor country, even when correcting for purchasing power parity, we underestimate their ability to provide for themselves. Actually, for an exact comparison between incomes in two countries we should adopt another expedient to calculate their real living standard, that of adding to the "official" income the market value of everything a person in a poor country self-consumes or self-produces (for example, the produce from raising domestic animals or cultivating small gardens) or obtains through gifts, barter, and exchanging used products. This is not to underestimate or minimize the problem of poverty, but to understand why certain poverty indicators must be treated with care; simply comparing per capita income, even if adjusted for purchasing power parity, does not always clarify real living conditions. Very low income thresholds that would mean absolute poverty conditions in highly developed societies do not always correspond to the same standard of living in poor countries.

Reflecting briefly on happiness, we can add another interesting philosophical consideration. People's "wealth" depends on their ability to use or enjoy the material and spiritual goods available. While it is impossible to enjoy a private good one does not have, if we look around we find that there are some freely available public goods whose value is far superior to the most valued private goods; for example, a natural park is generally much larger than a private villa. How much is a waterfront or a boardwalk worth for those who live there and can admire it every day? Paradoxically we could thus conclude that not knowing how to enjoy what one does not own, or not knowing how to benefit from the great abundance of public goods that are available for everyone, contributes greatly to poverty.

In conclusion, we point out that statistical surveys today measure both material and perceived poverty, and they note significant differences between the two. All the elements we have discussed in this frame – differences in purchasing power, differences in the quality of public goods available, and opportunities for self-consumption and self-production – provide key elements to explain this gap.

opportunities for self-consumption and self-production can allow for dignified survival. These two different examples also highlight a statistical problem: per capita income is not able to properly capture differences in quality of life (see Chapter 12). To properly compare them it would be necessary to evaluate at market value the self-production, self-consumption, and informal exchanges used by people who live in rural areas in developing countries in order to have data that is comparable to the most developed economies (see Frame 13.1).

Despite the fact that the above considerations are not insignificant when working with studies on poverty, and despite the fact that advanced countries' economic systems have in some ways forced the centrality of consumption, with negative consequences from an environmental viewpoint (consider how the market economy makes it increasingly less convenient to repair something rather to buy a new one), it is clear that reducing the space of market trans-actions compared to informal transactions certainly cannot compensate for the damages the goal of de-growth would entail, such as reducing the amount available for welfare projects such as healthcare and education, insufficient resources for repaying the public debt, and so forth. In conclusion on this point, we can state that the burden of proof is on the proponents of de-growth. They must demonstrate that there are ways to take such a drastic course of action for environmental sustainability and avoid creating financial crises and abrupt declines in the quality of public services and the collective well-being.

In view of all these considerations, and in order to reconcile the re-quirements of economists and environmentalists, the best course of action remains that of improving the economic system's capacity to produce eco-nomic value in an environmentally sustainable way, for example by increasing the share of non-rivalrous assets in overall production.

13.11 The Kuznets environmental curve

Moving from the extreme pessimism of the proponents of de-growth to the opposite attitude of high optimism on the consequences of growth in terms of

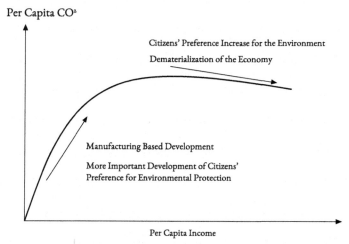

FIG. 13.9   The Kuznets Curve. *Note*: The intensity of pollution increases in the first segment of per capita income growth, reaches a maximum point, and subsequently decreases with further increases in income.

environmental impact, we briefly mention another important thread in the literature that analyzes this dilemma.

The analytic reference of this thread is the so-called Kuznets curve, which is the inverse U relationship that is assumed to exist between per capita income and carbon dioxide emissions per employee (see Fig. 13.9). According to this relationship, economic development per se would contribute to solving the problem, since it is correlated with gradually decreasing environmental impact.

Several empirical studies document the existence of this relationship in several historical eras for several samples of countries considered. As often happens in these types of investigations the **Kuznets curve** mixes "vertical" processes that are intertemporal in nature (the evolution of the intensity of pollution as income increases in a given country) with "horizontal" phenomena that are observable by comparing the situations in countries at different stages of growth at a given moment.

There are basically four explanations for the phenomenon observed and the presumably bell-shaped relationship between per capita income and emissions intensity: (a) from the supply side, the production mix evolves with economic development and the growth of per capita income, with a transition from a prevalence of agricultural and industrial activity, which is more polluting, to a service economy, with more intangible goods and with a higher concentration of non-rivalrous goods; (b) there are economies of scale in lowering the cost of pollution, so when the economy and companies grow, they become more efficient in terms of their energy impact and the amount of emissions is reduced; (c) from the consumption side, emphasis is instead placed on the quality of the environment as a "luxury good," and as citizens become wealthier increasing attention is given to the quality of the environment, and with it the willingness to pay for environmental sustainability and to vote for political coalitions that are more attentive to environmental problems; (d) for the reasons developed in the three preceding points, regulation favoring the environment becomes more rigorous in more developed countries and so contributes to reducing the intensity of emissions as per capita income grows.

So following the Kuznets curve, moving toward the right from lower per capita income levels, the intensity of pollution increases at the beginning. The problem of economic development is in fact the dominant worry for citizens when the economy is predominantly in the agricultural and industrial sectors. Once we pass the maximum point on the curve, when per capita income continues to increase starting from higher levels, citizens who have already reached a moderate level of well-being then demand quality of life, pollution limits, and green spaces when the economy progressively evolves toward the prevalence of the service sector. Regulation tends to become more strict, and the expectation of additional future restrictions also becomes a stimulus for companies to adopt more environmentally friendly processes.

Another interesting fact about studies in this specific field is the identification of the relationship between pollution intensity and control variables other than per capita income. In studies on the "adjusted" Kuznets curve, the role of different energy sources on emissions is emphasized for their contribution to these other factors, for example. A key variable is the share of energy produced by coal, oil, natural gas, or energy from renewable sources. As experts in the natural sciences know, countries whose energy production composition is weighted more toward coal and oil register a significantly greater intensity of pollution, which is consistent with the technical characteristics of energy production from these sources using traditional technologies.

At this point the reader may ask questions like these: Do the results of the literature on the Kuznets curve give us reason to be more optimistic? Is it possible to achieve the goal of environmental sustainability simply by continuing to grow? Unfortunately, the answer is no.

As we have emphasized in previous sections, one of the main problems in the relationship between the economy and the environment regards non-appropriable and non-renewable environmental resources such as the climate (and, more specifically, global warming), which is damaged by CO^2 emissions linked to consumption and economic activity. The impact of emissions on global warming is a problem of the total volume of emissions accumulated over the years rather than flows. In other words, the atmosphere requires many years to dispose of the pollution accumulated due to past choices. So even if the flow of emissions were to fall once a certain accumulation was exceeded, a serious problem would continue to persist for many years. Furthermore, we do not know with certainty whether or not there is a point of no return after a certain level of pollution is exceeded, with consequences for the planet from which it would be difficult to recover. Finally, a tendency toward reducing intensity does not reassure us that the overall volume of pollution produced in a year does not continue to increase; for that it would be enough for the population to increase above a certain threshold, or for the most populous countries to be in the initial growth phase rather than in the final phase of the Kuznets curve.

Again, while the inverted U relationship has been proven for some groups of countries and historical periods regarding CO_2 emissions, the findings on other types of pollutants simply show increasing linear growth, and thus no solution to the growth−environment dilemma regarding the production of these substances.

Finally, it has recently been shown that the bell-shaped relationship between per capita income and carbon dioxide emissions is highly unstable over time. If readers recall the story of the monkeys and the hats (Chapter 11, Frame 11.3), and Heisenberg's Uncertainty Principle applied to the social sciences, they will immediately understand why. What we observe in a given historical period is not the result of scientific determinism, but of choices made by citizens and political authorities who can change their behavior and respond to observed tendencies.

The fact that even the results of the Kuznets curve literature do not give us a reason to be optimistic simply means that, just as in the case of economic growth in which there is no inevitable tendency for divergences to grow or for them to automatically resolve, the question must be resolved by conscious, responsible intervention by people.

Once again the economy presents itself as an area in which there are incredible tools and opportunities, such as the hypothesis of conditional convergence, the rebalancing mechanisms that very slowly correct income differences through movements in workers, companies, and capital (migration, direct investment, remittances, and outsourcing), development opportunities, and technological innovation. These however do not automatically produce the desired results, except through expert and knowledgeable guidance that starts from an awareness of our responsibilities and a sensitivity to the good of others.

Thus the only optimism possible is suggested by the fact that humanity has the potential and the opportunity to effectively respond when faced with emergency situations. The time in which we are living is precisely when the signs of climate deterioration have begun to produce visible consequences, such as an increase in the average temperature of the planet, climatic instability, and an increase in extreme climatic events; these have prompted many initiatives by local, national, and international institutions and by civil society for stricter environmental regulation.

13.12 Toward overcoming the dilemma?

As an overall evaluation, the discussion thread on Kuznets curve studies does not seem to provide reasons to hope that the bell-shaped relationship between per capita emissions intensity and per capita income is the solution to the dilemma between economic growth and the environment that it first seemed.

Rather, the sign of a marked cultural shift on this topic is probably the publication of the Stern Report in 2005, commissioned by the British government, that analyzes the problem of global warming and its consequences for the economic growth of the planet.

The report calculates that with no interventions on greenhouse gas emissions, continuing the current trend of temperature increases would generate economic losses of around 40% of global GDP over the next several years. On the contrary, in the case of decisive political action to reduce emissions, restructuring global production systems would mean the energy sector would become the new driving force for development, with highly important consequences for economic growth. We could conclude from the Stern report that the presumed dilemma between economic development and environmental protection could finally be set aside to open the way for harmony between the two goals.

Paradoxically the question then flips, because the worst situation for economic development would be a scenario without a decisive intervention to reduce greenhouse gases rather than an alternate course. The reason for this is that the environmental reconfiguration of economic systems is one of the most powerful stimuli to growth and research we could imagine. Posing a simple example, if the mayor of a large city were to decide that only the latest generation of cars with the best savings and energy efficiency would be able to drive in the city, such a measure would spur an enormous move to buy new cars, which would be a formidable positive demand shock. The same consequences on an even larger scale could bring about measures requiring the gradual conversion of production processes toward greater energy efficiency and less environmental impact. On an even broader scale, and with even more interesting consequences for employment, would be regulation requiring all dwellings to be reconfigured to reduce their environmental impact in terms of energy use.

This is why some are saying that a true "green revolution" is at hand, with the possibility of creating many "green jobs." It is highly symptomatic that in view of this new scenario, energy efficiency is becoming the most important sector for innovation in Silicon Valley after the information technology era.

13.13 Some microeconomic examples

At the microeconomic level, how is it possible to become more ecological without diminishing the principle of creating economic value at the same time? In this concluding section we will briefly develop three interesting examples by individual companies.

The first is of *energy saving companies*. Suppose each of the 50 residents of a condominium pays 600 dollars a year in energy costs. They live in an old building with limited energy efficiency. The tenants could renovate it at their own expense for around $15,000; when complete this would lead to significant energy savings and lower their energy bills, which they calculate would drop from $600 to $500 per year. However, the tenants are not able to come to agreement on how to split the costs, and they do not want to take on the risk of renovation or pay certain costs today for uncertain future benefits. At this point an energy saving company steps in and proposes to do the renovations at its expense in exchange for the difference between the energy costs before and after renovation over a payback period that allows it to cover its costs and make a small profit. For example, the company explains that by setting a payback period of four years, the tenants would continue to pay the pre-renovation price of $600 each over the four years, and the company would make $100 a year per resident, for a total of $20,000; the company would make a profit of $5000 against the $15,000 invested in the renovation. The profit is actually less if we consider the time span between receipts and payments. For the sake of simplicity in this example, we can abstract from this problem and assume an intertemporal discount rate of 1.

From the economic perspective of those involved, the renovation would create benefits for the residents by reducing their energy bills starting in the fifth year, and for the company because it would earn a profit equal to one-third of its invested capital. From a social well-being perspective, it would create economic value in the amount earned by the company divided between salaries and profit, and it would reduce the environmental impact and increased the energy efficiency of the condominium. Obviously the positive environmental impact must be evaluated net of the environmental effects of the company's business so it does not exceed the positive *permanent* effect of reducing the condominium residents' energy consumption. Finally, if the payback to residents seems too low — recalling that they bear no entrepreneurial risk because they incur no expense for the renovation — it would be possible to propose a mixed solution in which the $100 per resident is immediately divided between the company and the tenants while extending the payback period; for example, tenants could immediately receive a savings of $50 on their energy bills by extending the payback period to 8 years.

A second interesting example of reconciling the creation of economic value and reducing environmental impact is of zero emissions production. There are an increasing number of instances in which the CO_2 emissions of a given productive activity are combined with reforestation projects — trees absorb carbon dioxide — such that the net balance of the operation is zero.

Finally, a third course is a pilot project developed by the United Nations, which proposes to maximize the use of all resources obtained in production.

This approach properly considers that it would be appropriate to reformulate our classic production function by taking into account the fact that production generates not only outputs that can be sold on the market, but waste as well. According to the new production function we would have not only the classic production function of $Y = f(K,L)$, but also a function like this, $W = g(K,L)$ in which W represents the problem of disposing of environmentally harmful substances that are usually considered non-renewable and non-appropriable. The novelty of the approach proposed by this pilot project is in devising a production cycle that is able to give rise to a second production process in which $Y_2 = f(K,L,W)$ — or substituting $Y_2 = f(K,L,g(K,L))$, thus transforming waste into a new production input. In this way it is possible to minimize waste production with the same or a small increase in environmental resource consumption and obtain a greater product quantity.

A specific example is a project developed in Namibia, Sweden, Canada and Japan by "ZERI" (*Zero Emission Research and Initiatives*) organizations that efficiently uses the waste produced by beer production. The beer production process, which uses grain and water, produces beer as an output, but waste products as well in the form of impure water and grain waste. In the ZERI model the wastes are used to grow mushrooms, feed pigs, produce biogas, and grow algae and develop habitats for fish farming. The waste is transformed into a resource for creating income, jobs, and a better environment.

Further reading

Becker, G., Murphy, K. M., & Tamura, R. (1990). Human capital, fertility, and economic growth. *Journal of Political Economy, 98*, S12–S37.

Bouruignon, F., & Morrison, C. (2002). Inequality among world citizens: 1820–1992. *The American Economic Review, 92*, 727–744.

Brynjolfsson, E., & Hitt, L. (2000). Beyond computation: Information technology, organizational transformation, and business performance. *The Journal of Economic Perspectives, 14*(4), 23–48.

Delacroix, J. (1992). *A critical empirical test of the common interpretation of the protestant ethic and the spirit of capitalism.* Leuven, Belgium: International Association Business & Society.

Durlauf, S. N., & Quah, D. T. (1998). *The new empirics of economic growth.* Center for Economic Performance. Discussion Paper no. 384.

Galor, O., & Moav, O. (2004). From physical to human capital accumulation: Inequality in the process of development. *The Review of Economic Studies, 71*(4), 1001–1026.

Islam, N. (1995). Growth empirics: A panel data approach. *Quarterly Journal of Economics, 110*(4), 1127–1169.

Jorgenson, D. W., & Stiroh, K. J. (2000). Raising the speed limit: U.S. Economic growth in the information age. *Brookings Papers on Economic Activity, 1*, 125–211.

Murphy, K., Shleifer, A., & Vishny, R. (1991). The allocation of talent: Implication for growth. *Quarterly Journal of Economics, 106*(2), 503–530.

Sachs, J. D., & Warner, A. M. (2001). Natural resources and economic development, the curse of natural resources. *European Economic Review, 45*, 827–838.

Social Investment Forum. (2018). *Report on social investing trends in the United States.*

Sala-i-Martin, X. (2002). 15 years of new growth economics: What have we learnt? *UPF Economics and Business.* Working Paper no. 620.

Solow, R. M. (1956). A contribution to the theory of economic growth. *Quarterly Journal of Economics, LXX*, 65–94.

Temple, J. (1999). The new growth evidence. *Journal of Economic Literature, 37*, 112–156.

United Nations Conference on Trade and Development. (2005). *The digital divide report, ICT diffusion index.*

Epilogue: from "homo oeconomicus" to "civil animal"

The important message we draw from the discussion developed throughout this book is that the awareness of the existence of both market and government failures should urgently lead us to reconsider the role of civil society, understood as the ensemble of intermediate organizations such as citizens and professional associations, non-governmental organizations, foundations, and independent public groups such as chambers of commerce, universities, and so on. By always and only talking about markets and government, it seems that economic science has ended up forgetting about civil society, which is where the conditions are created for the emergence and proper operation of both the market and the State. We must never forget that these are not primitive or original institutions, because civil society creates both.

We will consider the market first. From previous chapters we have learned that for a market economy to work well and endure over the long run it requires, in addition to *legal norms*, two other categories of rules. *Social rules* can be conceptualized as a form of **reputational human capital**, in which a person knows that there can be a significant personal price to pay for breaking the rules, since an immoral act will put his reputation to the test. The enforcement of *moral rules* depends instead on internal constraints, or on an agent's **moral constitution**.

While moral rules are of great benefit to society, they may not bring direct, immediate advantage to those who put them into practice. These are all rules that help minimize or neutralize various opportunistic behaviors, such as free riding and shirking, that are the source of various cases of market failures. This triple set of rules poses a formidable problem. To produce and enforce the first category of rules, or legal norms, it suffices that an effective institutional structure be coupled with a well-functioning justice system that is able to promptly punish deviant behavior. Equipping society with the other two, the social and moral rules, requires intervening in people's internal motivation structures, that is, in their committed adherence to shared values such as solidarity, reciprocity, and distributive justice. Clearly, civil society is precisely where these values are generated and practiced.

There is an analogous discussion regarding the nexus between the State and civil society. We know that the primary means the State uses to enforce the rules of the economic game is its capacity to punish illegal behavior — a capacity that derives from the fact that the State is the sole institution that holds the power of coercion. However, by now it is well-known that when the number of offenders exceeds a certain threshold, punishment simply does not work. As a trivial but revealing example, consider the punishment for not complying with the law requiring the use of seat belts while driving. Within a few months of its introduction the law was already so widely ignored in some regions and areas as to make attempts to enforce it by fines impractical.

This then is the main point: the possibility of reinforcing people's prosocial economic behavior by legal sanctions is realistically practicable only when such behaviors are already relatively widespread in a populace, otherwise legal enforcement entails such high social costs as to make it impractical. This means that, in the absence of a well-organized civil society that is able to instill in its citizens a sense of responsibility and respect for others, it is completely useless — and indeed counterproductive — to call for a strong, well-functioning State.

Precisely because people's economic behavior is *jointly* motivated by "moral sentiments" (in Adam Smith's sense) and by material incentives, a market society that respects the reasoning underlying liberty cannot establish a system of economic institutions that in practice favor behavior based on incentives to the disadvantage of moral sentiments, thus in fact discouraging the latter's flourishing. Said another way, precisely because there are in reality percentages of antisocial, asocial, and prosocial people (which vary across historical periods and societies), the economic system cannot be designed as if all economic agents were antisocial or asocial. This would be an unacceptable form of moral violence against prosocial agents, of which there are many, fortunately.

From what we have discussed so far it follows that the simultaneous growth of the State and the market over recent decades, which has not been accompanied by adequate development of civil society, explains in large part the problems in the public sector — foremost among which are the public debt and bureaucratic elephantiasis — and numerous market failures. If this is the situation, as it seems to be, the remedy cannot be a radicalization of the State—market alternatives, either by strengthening the State or leaving everything to the market. Rather, we should seek a way to extend all the forms of economic organization that an organized civil society is able to express if left free to do so.

This is why we should put civil society to work in such a way that entities such as social companies, cooperatives, civil enterprises, non-governmental organizations, and foundations can establish a new social economic infrastructure. In a design of this sort, the State would still have an important double role. On the one hand it should recognize — not grant! — the self-organization of collective entities in all the areas in which their fully independent members believe they have legitimate interests to protect. This corresponds to the requirements of the **principle of subsidiarity** in its true sense: a higher organization should not merely delegate or distribute shares of sovereignty to lower organizations, as this would be a deigned or delegated subsidiarity, or simply political and administrative decentralization; rather, it should recognize and foster what lower organizations are capable of doing on their own. On the other hand, the State should ensure the operating rules of this self-organization, such as transparency, rules regarding access to funding sources, and tax systems, while ensuring that fair competition establishes the boundaries between economic agents rather than dirigiste interventions from on high.

This refers back to the notion of a **limited State**, as we like to call it. A limited State is in contrast to both a "minimal State," which should ensure only a few things such as laws, public order, money, and defense, and a "welfare State" that paternalistically and directly decides and provides what is good for its citizens. A limited State is instead one that intervenes, perhaps even strongly, but only in certain areas and not others, while recognizing — not granting — the broadest independence to the free articulation of civil society. This is basically the idea of an *incentivizing State* that promotes and encourages all forms of collective action that have public effects by promoting institutional structures that facilitate the flourishing of intermediate organizations.

In this view, subsidiarity — which, note well, is based on positive liberty, just as the basis of solidarity is an associational covenant that unites citizens — becomes the true principle of social organization, which tends to bring about a virtuous symbiosis between the *invisible hand* of the market, the *visible hand* of the State, and the *fraternal hand* of intermediate organizations. We need all three hands to overcome the obsolete, polemic view of the market economy, and especially to create the governance structures capable of facing the challenges of globalization, first and foremost in access to work, the new welfare model, and the new international economic order.

A second important conclusion that follows from this book is that contemporary economic theory is seeking to go beyond the mainstream precisely in how the ontological premises of the discipline are defined. Today we tend to admit that individuals can be endowed with limited rationality, endogenous preferences, incomplete information, multiple selves, and other-regarding motivations together with self-interest. We also recognize that because of all these traits, it makes no sense to reduce the economy to a pseudo-psychology of optimizing behaviors. There seems to be an awareness now of the fact that, as finite and limited as humanity is, we cannot understand our own behavior if we abstract from the institutions, cultures, values, ethical norms, and particularly from the social relationships that form the societies in which we live.

This reawakening of scientific courage originates from two factors. On the one hand, it is now understood that *utilitarian reductionism* is largely responsible for the inability of the economy to come to grips with the major problems that afflict our society: the increase of economic and social inequality, environmental degradation, the tendency to hollow out democracy, the increase in social exclusion, a loss of meaning in interpersonal relationships, and a decline in public happiness even with increases in per capita income levels. On the other hand, we are becoming aware of the fact that this same reductionism is a major obstacle to new ideas entering the discipline. A growing number of economists now realize the necessity of overcoming the cowardly protectionism with which the academy tries to defend itself from criticisms that arise from facts and innovations coming from other social sciences. We understand today that, underlying everything, the assumption of individualism (rejected by most experimental findings in contemporary behavioral economics) has the nature of an ontological assertion, and as such it must be justified at a philosophical level. But modern orthodox economic thought has not validly justified it on this level.

Finally, we believe that the anthropological reductionism of the dominant theory is viewed with suspicion by a growing number of economists, partly because it entails some degree of responsibility for certain political and economic choices to which it gives more or less implicit justification. By now, it is evident that there really are political and economic choices rather than "nature," much less "human nature," at the origin of many contemporary ills.

Scientific research implies responsibility and risks that are part of the order of ethics and politics, especially in the social sciences. No one today believes anymore in the possibility of *separating* "analysis" from "vision." Indeed, we know that economic theories are not *neutral* tools of pure *knowledge*. They are not neutral because judgments of fact are not separable from judgments of value; rather, they always express particular points of view that conceal — at times quite well — particular interests. They are not pure knowledge, because ideas change people's minds and change the world. Theories of human behavior contribute to building it.

This is why we view developments in contemporary economic science with satisfaction. We do not know where the scientific revolution we are witnessing will lead us, but we know what we are leaving behind. And we believe that the transition from the reductionism of *homo oeconomicus* to an anthropology of the "civil animal" is an obligatory passage in view of reconstructing an economic science that desires to aim for the common good.

As early as 1941 the great economist John Hicks wrote:

> *A man who is a mathematician and nothing but a mathematician ... does not do any harm. An economist who is nothing but an economist is a danger to his neighbors. Economics is not a thing in itself; it is a study of one* aspect *of the life of a man in a society ... The economist of tomorrow (and sometimes of today) will certainly be aware of what to ground his economic advice on; but if [...] his economic knowledge is detached from any background of social philosophy, he runs a real risk of becoming a cheat, capable of implementing enterprising stratagems to find his way out of difficulties, but incapable of staying in contact*

with those fundamental virtues on which a sound society is founded. Modern economics is subject to a real danger of Machiavellism — the treatment of social problems as matters of technique, not as facets of the general search for Good Life.

We would like to close with a thought from the famous Brazilian writer and poet Paulo Coelho, that over the course of our lives every human being can follow two alternate behaviors: building or planting. Sooner or later builders finish what they are doing, and when the construction is finished all that is left is to admire it. Those who plant, however, suffer through storms and seasons; they rarely rest. But unlike the building, the garden never ceases to grow. In this work we have sought to embrace the option to plant.

Index

'Note: Page numbers followed by "f" indicate figures, "t" indicate tables and "b" indicate tables.'

A

Ability to innovate, 119, 334–335
Absence of excludability, 247–248
Absence of rivalry in consumption, 248
Accounting costs, 138
Accounting profit, 141
Administered/politically determined prices, 58–60, 59f, 62f
Affectionate relationships, happiness and, 387
Age, happiness and, 393–395
Agency relationship, 205
Agency theory, 309
Agents' economic decisions, 238
Aggregate demand curve, 52–53, 54f, 86, 151, 248
Aggregate supply curve, 53–55, 79, 86, 151
Airlines, 332b
Akerlof, George, 277–278
American Economic Review (Rabin), 290
American stock exchanges, 324
Appropriability, 425
Arc elasticity, 79–80
Arrow, Kenneth, 232
    impossibility theorem, 240–243
Ars combinatoria, 119
Atkinson's theorem, 252
Attainable utilities frontier, 239–240
Austrian school, 42f, 44–45
Authority, 213–216, 304–305
Average revenue, 142, 162
Average total cost, 130
Average variable cost curve, 131, 132f
Aversion to inequality, 193
Axiological individualism, 231
Axioms, 91, 91b

B

Banca Etica, 344
Baumol's disease and trust games, 385–387
Beccaria, Cesare, 36
Behavioral economics, 291

Benthamism, 229
Bentham's criterion, 229
Bergson, Abraham, 240
Bergson–Samuelson social welfare function, 240
Biodiversity, in civil enterprises, 319–320
Blood donation system, 281b
Bounded rationality, 210–211
Brennan, Geoffrey, 284–285
British blood donation system, 281b
British Household Survey Panel (BHSP), 362–363
British Industrial Revolution, 347
British school, 43–44
Budget constraint, 95–96, 232, 271–272
Business activities, 326
Buyer's reservation price, 54

C

Capabilities, 397–398
Capital dilution, 209–210
Capitalist economies, 295–296
Capitalist enterprise, 303–307
    modern, 308–309
    paradox of, 307–309
Capital stock, 406f
Cardinality, 89–91
Cartel, 173
    instability, 174–175, 175f
Causality, in relationship between income and happiness, 375–376
Century of Smithean economics
    Malthus and population theory, 40–41
    Marx and criticism of the classical economic system, 41–42
    Ricardo's theory of land rent, 37f, 38–40
Certain costs, 330
Certification seals, 340–341
Charism, 304–305
Chicago school, 254
Circular subsidiarity, 256–257
Civil competition, 35–36

Civil economy, 33—34, 195, 302, 309
Civil enterprise, 313, 319
  biodiversity in, 319—320
  difficult innovations of, 317—318
Civil entrepreneurs, 140, 318
Civil firms, 299—303
Civilly responsible enterprise, 302—303
Civil society, 319
  and economies, 320
  role of, 266—268
Civil theory of reciprocity, 289
Clark, Andrew, 390
Classical economic thought, 24
  division of society into well-defined social
    classes, 25
  economic liberalism, 25
  economists, 25—26, 27b
  entrepreneurs/capitalists, 25
  labor theory of value, 25
  "laissez faire" principle, 25
  landowners, 25
  principle of self-interest, 25
  proletariat, 25
  Say's law, 25
Coase theorem, 245—247, 246b
Colonial expansion, 21—22
Colonial policy and protectionism, 21
Colonial products, 76
Coman, Katharine, 259
Commanded labor, 31
Common goods
  economic science and, 258—265
  "Prisoner's Dilemma", 260—261
  tragedy of, 260—263
Company's objective function, 324
Company's social responsibility, 333
Company to market, 309—311
Comparing interpersonal utility, 229
Compartamos, 343
Competitive equilibrium, as pareto optimal,
  235—236
Completeness, 90—91
  and transitivity, 242
Concentration ratio, 161
Conditional convergence, 411
  determinants of, 413—415
Consequentialism, 228
Constrained maximization, 12, 19—20
Consumer surplus, 151, 151f
Consumers, voting with wallets, 330—331
Consumer theory, 108—109, 366—367

Consumption theory, 86, 109
Contract curve, 234—236, 238
Copernicans, 19—20
Corporate civil responsibility, 311
Corporate governance, 326
Corporate social responsibility (CSR),
  300—302, 309, 311, 313f, 320
  competitive factor, 350—355
  criticisms of, 327—328
  debate among economists on, 327—329
  definition of, 324—326
  problem of asymmetric information in,
    340—341
  relationship between CSR and financial
    results, 337—338
  role of, 355—358
  sustainability, 335—340
Cournot point, 163—164
Credit market, informal, 345
Crowding-in phenomenon, 283
Crowding-out models, motivational,
  284—285
Crowding-out theory, 283
CSR. *See* Corporate social responsibility
  (CSR)
Cultural hypothesis, 284—285

D

Daily reconstruction method, 365—366, 378,
  383—385
David, Paul, 419
Debreu, Gerard, 232
Decision-making process, 140
Deductive method, 2
Democracy and Efficiency (Keynes), 256
Dichotomy, 237—238
Digital divide, 417, 418f
Direct reciprocity, 287
Discrete demand curve, 55, 55f
Diseconomies of scale, 129
Dismal science
  Malthus' reasoning, 5—6
  pragmatic idealism, 6
Distributive justice, market and,
  251—252
Diversity, 319—320
  protection, 326
Division of labor, 291
Dynamic competition, 178—180
Dynamic returns to scale, 128

E

Easterlin paradox, 367–375, 368f, 395–396
Economic costs, 138
  and revenues, 141
Economic democracy, 252
Economic growth, 73–74, 401–407,
    413–415
  determinants of, 402–403, 416, 420
  environment dilemma, 434–437
  globalization effect on, 422–423
  protestant and catholic cultures on, 415
  standard models of, 411–412
Economic liberalism, 25, 319–320
Economic model, 2–3, 157, 389
Economic policies, happiness and, 397–399
Economic profit, 141
Economic rules, traditional, 357
Economics
  20th century, 46f, 47–49
  classical economic thought, 24–26
  colonial expansion, 21–22
  Copernicans, 19–20
  disciplines, 16–17
  dismal science, 5–7
  ethical responsibility, 4–5
  France and physiocracy, 22–24
  macroeconomics, 15–16
  mercantilism, 21–22
  microeconomics, 15–16
  model, 2–3
  neoclassical economics, 42–49
  opportunity cost, 7–9
  positive and normative phases
    anti-prohibitionist choice, 9–10
    drug market, 9–10
    presumed objectivity, 9
    "veil of ignorance", 10
  Ptolemaics, 19–20
  schools. See specific schools
  science, 1–2
  social science, 1–2
  theory of rational choices in the presence of
      constraints, 11–15
  three-dimensional approach, 17–19
Economic science, 1, 290–291, 319
  and common goods, 258–265
  investigative method
    deductive method, 2
    inductive method, 2
    reasoning, 2
  social science, 1–2
Economic shock, 376

The Economics of Welfare (Pigou), 227
Economic sustainability, challenges of,
    329–335
Economic theory, 296, 309
  contemporary, 197–198
  economic liberalism, 24–25
  problem, 296
  of public goods, 260
Economist, 25–26, 27b
  constrained maximization, 14
  definition, 11–12
  ethical responsibility, 4–5
  laws abolishing child labor, 6
Economy of Communion, 313
Edgeworth box, 233–235, 234f
Efficiency wage theory, 334
Elements of Pure Economics, 45
Embodied labor, 28
Emergent phenomenon, 381b–382b
Emissions, 430f, 431–434, 433f
  chlorofluorocarbon (CFC) emissions, 429
  marginal social benefit of, 431
  optimal level of, 431
Employment income effect, 273
Engel's law, 102–104, 103f
Engineering efficiency, 117
Enterprise
  capitalist, 303–307
    paradox of, 307–309
  hierarchy, 305–307
Entrepreneur, 25, 321
  civil, 313
  social, 300–301, 358
Entrepreneurship, 117–121
  capitalist company, 121
  characteristics, 119
  companies, 121
  cooperative companies, 121
  distinctive traits, 117–121
  innovativeness, 120b
  interdependence, 120
  public companies, 121
  social companies, 121
Environmental goods, matrix of, 425–429
Environmental innovation, 333–334
Environmental issue, 301
Environmental resources, income circuit with
      creation and destruction of, 427–430,
      428f
Environmental sustainability, 325, 427–428
Ethical banks, 344–345
Ethical risk, 339

European Parliament's Resolution 2008/
  2250, 122b–123b
Excludability, 248
Exogenous change, 376
Exogenous shocks, effects of, 377f
Experience goods, 340–341
Experimental economics, 291
External costs, 137–138
External diseconomies, 244
External economies, 244
Externalities, 243–244
Extrinsic benefits, 139–140
Extrinsic motivations, 121

F

Fair trade, 345–350
Fair trade coffee, 347–348
Fair trade company (FTC), 358f
Fair trade products, 331, 346–348, 349f,
  350–352, 358f
Fair trade vendor (FT), 355f
Family–State model, 297
Filangieri, Gaetano, 34
Financial economies, 136
Firms, new theories
  adverse selection, 202–204
  alternate conceptions, 221–226
    commodity and shareholder value,
      221–223
    connective capital, 225–226
    organizational planning problem,
      223–224
  asymmetric information, 202–206
  behavioral theory, 210–212
  capital markets, 208–209
  competitive markets, 200–202
  complete contracts, 200–202
  contractual incompleteness, 202b
  incentive schemes, 199–200
  incentives constraints, 202
  information imperfection, 204
  limited rationality, 199
  managerial theories, 206–210
    Baumol's model, 206–208, 207f
  moral hazard, 204–206
  neo-institutionalist theory, 212–217
  observable actions, 202
  opportunistic behavior, 201–206
  optimization, 210–212
  organizational dimension, 218–221
    companies and governance structures,
      218–220

  holding company, 220–221
  research, 199–200
  takeovers, 208–209
  verifiable actions, 202
Firm's shareholders, 322
Fixed costs, 130–131
"Food sovereignty", 62
For-profits, 297, 311–314
For-project firms, 311–314
Freeman, Edward, 328
Free-rider problem, 249
Frey, Bruno, 282–283, 314
Friedman, Milton, 327
Friedman's reasoning, 74
Frustrated achievers, 369, 371, 374–375
Functionalities, 397–398

G

Galor, O., 412
Game theory
  action, 182
  axiom of rationality, 183
  backward induction method, 189
  battle of the sexes, 184
  common knowledge, 183
  complete and incomplete information,
    182
  cooperative games, 182
  description, 182
  dynamic games, 182
  equilibrium, 183
  examples, 184–185
  extended form games, 187–190
  historical remarks, 181
  introductory concepts, 180–183
  Nash equilibrium, 185–187
  nature, 182
  non-cooperative games, 182
  normal form games, 183–185
  paradox, 190–193
  payoff, 183
  perfect and imperfect information, 182
  players, 182
  set of actions, 183
  set of strategies, 183
  static games, 182
  strategy, 183
  superadditivity, 191
  trust game, 190–193
    Genovesi version, 193–198
  variable sum games, 185
  zero-sum games, 184

GATT (the General Agreement on Tariffs and Trade), 421
General theory of economic equilibrium, 45
Genovesi, Antonio, 33—34
German Socioeconomic Panel (GSOEP), 362—363
Global economy, competition changes in, 355—358
Globalization, 300, 420—424
 culture, 319
 effect on economic growth, 422—423
Globally integrated market, 322
Global warming, 333—334, 429
Government failure, 253—254, 296
 public intervention and, 253—255
Grameen Bank, 342—343
Gratuitousness, 281—283, 288, 302—303, 315
Green revolution, 441
Gresham's Law, 277, 283
Gross domestic product (GDP) growth, 17, 256, 411
Growth and poverty, facts on, 407—410
Growth convergence, determinants of, 413—415
Growth models, traditional, 410—413
Gui's theory, 379b—382b

H

Happiness
 and affectionate relationships, 387
 and age, 393—395
 coincide with utility, 365—366
 determinants of, 362—365
 and economic policies, 397—399
 economics of, 361—362
 and health, 393—395
 Heisenberg's uncertainty principle, 396—397
 and income, 366—367, 375—376, 377f
 and inflation, 390—393, 393t
 and relational goods, 378—385, 384t
 and relational life, 377—378
 and unemployment, 390—393, 393t
 and work, 388—390
Hardin, Garrett, 259—260
Harrod, Roy, 228—229
Harsanyi, John, 228—229
Hat vendor, 337b
Health, happiness and, 393—395
Hedonic adaptation, 371, 374f, 376
Heisenberg's uncertainty principle, 396—397
Hidden information, 203

Hierarchical contract, 308
Hierarchical principle, 308
Hierarchy, 303—304, 305b
 enterprise, 305—307
Hirschman, Albert O., 310—311
Holding company (H-form), 220
Hollis, M., 229
Homo oeconomicus, 14, 271, 289
 priori assumptions of, 361—362
Homo reciprocans, 286—292
Hotelling's model, 351—352, 352f, 355f
Hourglasses, 274—276
Human rights, 326

I

ICT, 417
 characteristics of, 417
 effects of, 416—417
 revolution, 417
Imitation, 354b
Imitative entrepreneurs, 48
Incentives, monetary, 282—284
Income
 distribution, 408—410, 409f
  pareto optimality, 236—238
 happiness and, 366—367, 375—376, 377f
 and poverty, 435b—436b
 relative, 370, 371f
Income circuit, 83f
 characteristics, 84—85
 consumption and market demand, 84—85
 households, 84
 hypertext
  consumption theory, 86
  labor demand, 86
  labor supply, 86
  production theory, 86
 real one and monetary one, 85
 risk of exhaustion, 85
Income consumption curves, 102—104, 103f
Income effect
 and substitution effect, 104, 105f
 employment, 273
 traditional, 273
Indeterminacy problem, 336
Indifference curves, 46, 91—93, 92f, 93b
Indirect reciprocity, 287—288
Individual demand curves
 income consumption curves and Engel's law, 102—104, 103f
 price-consumption curves, 100—102, 100f—101f

Individualism, 231
Inductive method, 2
Industrial capitalism, 24, 301
Inflation, happiness and, 390−393, 393t
Informal credit market, 345
Information asymmetries, 107−108
Innovations, 178−180
    environmental, 333−334
Innovative entrepreneurs, 48
Innovativeness, 120b
Institutional quality, 414
    improving, 415−416
Institutions, role of, 413−414
Integrated market, 322
Intentional action, unintended consequences
    of, 153
Internal costs, 137
Internalities, 254
Internal organizational dynamics, 287
Intertemporal consumption, 109−112, 110f,
    112f−113f
Intrinsic benefits, 139−140
Intrinsic motivations, 282−284, 335
Intrinsic rewards game, 264−265
Invisible hand, 33, 149
Isomorphism, 319

K

Kahneman's approach, 365−366
Kahneman's daily reconstruction method,
    383−385
Keynes, John Maynard, 256
Knowledge production, 119
Kuznets environmental curve, 437−440, 437f

L

Labor cost per unit of product (LCUP),
    131
Labor-intensive organizations, 274
Labor supply model, 386
    in traditional theory, 271−276
Labor theory of value, 25
"Laissez faire" principle, 25
Lausanne school, 44f, 45
Law of diminishing returns, 125−126, 125f
Leisure time, 273
    consumption and, 272f
Leonardo's workshop, 163
Lerner index, 163−164
Liberal-capitalist tradition, 310
Liberal society, multi-stakeholder, 310

Liberty, democracy and social and economic,
    319−320
Lindahl equilibrium, 249
Local communities, relationships with, 325
Long-run cost curves, 134−136, 135f
Long-run equilibrium, 145, 146f−147f, 147
Long-run production function, 128
Long-run supply curves, 145−147, 146f
Loose holding company, 220

M

Macroeconomics, 15−16
Malthus, Thomas, 361−362
Manual of Political Economy, 46
Marginal cost curves, 131, 132f
Marginal rate of substitution, 93−94, 94b,
    127
Marginal revenue, 143
Marginal utility, 88−89
Market, 296
    abused term, 51−52
    benefits
        beachhouses, 69, 69b
        benevolence of ski resort operators, 71,
            71b
        benevolent planner, 69
        consumer surplus, 70
        exchange, 69−70, 70f
        producer surplus, 70
        quasi-miraculous tool, 69
    curve shifts, 56, 56f
    and distributive justice, 251−252
    dynamic adjustment toward equilibrium
        behavior of markets over time, 66−68,
            66f
        stability, 64−65, 65b
    globally integrated, 322
    limitations, 71−74
    movements along the demand curve, 56
    movements along the supply curve, 57
    non-equilibrium prices
        administered/politically determined
            prices, 58−60, 59f, 62f
        agricultural product, 62
        European price, 63
        "food sovereignty", 62
        rationality of waiting lines, 59−60, 60b
        "virtual lines", 61
    shifts in the supply curve, 57
    slope and elasticity, of demand curve, 79f
        aggregate demand curve, 79
        arc elasticity, 79−80

factor, 81
inelastic, 80
spontaneous evolution/targeted
institutional interventions, 74—76,
77b—78b
stylized characteristics, 53t
aggregate demand curve, 52—53, 54f
aggregate supply curve, 53—55
buyer's reservation price, 54
discrete demand curve, 55, 55f
extensive effect, 54
intensive effect, 54
market equilibrium, 52, 52f
seller's reservation price, 54—55
traditional model of, 347
Market economy, 42
Market enterprises, social, 344
Market equilibrium, 52, 52f, 57—58, 64,
148—150, 148f—149f
Market failure, 204, 253
externalities, 243—244
The Market for Lemons (Akerlof), 277
Market makers, 52
Market to company, 309—311
Mark-up, 163—164
Martin, E., 229
Masochism, 331
Mercantile companies, 21
Mercantilism, 21—22
Mercantilist vice, 154
Merchants' activities, 295
Merit, 250
Merit goods, 250—251
Metaphor, 274, 330
Methodological weaknesses, 420
Micro-credit, 318
Microfinance, 342—344
Microfounded theory of the consumer, 87
Milan school, 34f, 35—38, 36f
Millennium Development Goals, 412—413
Misery index, 391
Mission-driven organizations, 315
Moav, O., 412
Molteni, M., 315
Monetary incentives, 282—284
Monopsony equilibrium, 347
Monopsony market, 348f
Monopsony model, 347
Monotonicity, 90—91
Motivation, 280
Motivational crowding-out models, 284—285
Motivations

intrinsic, 282—284, 335
values-based, 315
Multidivisional form (M-form), 219
Multi-stakeholder liberal society, 310
Musgrave, Richard, 250

N
Nash equilibrium, 263—264
characteristics, 186—187
definition, 185—186
Natural monopoly, 161
Natural resources, 419—420
The Nature of the Firm (Coase), 308
Neapolitan school, 26f, 33—35
Negative externalities, 244
Neoclassical economics
Austrian school, 42f, 44—45
British school, 43—44
elements, 43
Lausanne school, 44f, 45
Pantaleoni and Pareto, 45—47, 45f
Neoclassical revolution, 38, 42
Neo-institutionalist theory, 212—217
authority and property rights, 213—216
Coase's view, 212—213
Grossman theory, 216—217
Hart theory, 216—217
Moore's theory, 216—217
Net benefits, 140—141
Network economies, 404—406
New welfare economics, 230—232
Next generation social companies, 342
Next generation social firms, 341—350
Non-capitalist company, 295—297
Non-competitive markets
cartel, 173
instability, 174—175, 175f
composition of consumption, 159
concentration ratio, 161
contestable markets, 175—177
creative destruction, 178—179
dynamic competition, 178—180
economic activity, 159—161
economic model characteristics, 157
entry barriers, 160b
innovations, 178—180
Leonardo's workshop, 163
market forms, 159—161
market structure endogeneity, 175—177
monopolistic competition, 157—158,
166—168
monopolistic competition, 160—161

Non-competitive markets (*Continued*)
    equilibrium, 166—167, 167f
    perfect competition and monopoly,
        167—168
    monopoly, 157—158, 160—161
        elasticity and marginal revenue, 163b
        equilibrium, 162—164, 162f
        price discrimination, 165—166
        social well-being, 164
    natural monopoly, 161
    nature of profit, 179—180
    oligopolistic collusion, 172—174, 173f
    oligopolistic market
        Bertrand's model, 171—172
        characteristics, 168—169
        Cournot model, 169—171
    prices, 157—159
    Schumpeter's approach, 178—180
    technical progress, 158
    unrecoverable costs, 176
Non-convex indifference curves, 97, 97f
Non-equilibrium prices
    administered/politically determined prices,
        58—60, 59f, 62f
    agricultural product, 62
    European price, 63
    "food sovereignty", 62
    rationality of waiting lines, 59—60, 60b
    "virtual lines", 61
Non-market clearing equilibrium, 58
Non-profits, 257, 297—299
Normal (non-negative) profit, 130,
    147—148
Normative economics, 227
Not Just for the Money (2005) (Frey),
    282—283

O

Occupational "vocation", 284—286
Oil prices, 66, 66f
Old welfare economics, 229
Oligopolistic collusion, 172—174, 173f
Oligopoly, 160—161
Online markets, 51—52
OPEC's strategy, 67—68
Opportunity costs, 7—9, 137—138, 271
Optimum optimorum, 241—242
Ordinality, 89—90
Organizational dynamics, internal, 287
Organizational innovation, 119
Organizational theory, 319
Organization's identity, 316

P

Paradox of water and diamonds, 28, 30b
Pareto criterion, 228—232, 240
Pareto efficiency, 117, 118b—119b
Pareto optimality, 47, 231
    competitive equilibrium as, 235—236
    and income distribution, 236—238
Pareto superior, 231
Payless and get more, 279—282
Perfect competitive markets
    average revenue, 142
    definition, 140—142
    long-run, 144—145
    marginal revenue, 143
    market equilibrium, 148—150, 148f—149f
    problem of supply
        extrinsic benefits, 139—140
        intrinsic benefits, 139—140
        production benefits, 139—140
    revenue function, 142—143, 142f
    short run profit maximization, 143—144,
        143f
    social well-being, 150—152
    supply, 145—148, 146f
    total revenue, 142
Physiocracy, 22, 23f
    agricultural producers, 22
    craftsmen, 22—23
    economic growth, 23
    landowners, 23
Pigovian tax, 432—433
Pioneer social enterprises, 342
Political democracy, 252
Political economy, 4, 17, 412—413
Pollution, 430f, 433f
Population theory, 40—41
Positive economics, 227
Positivism, 42
Post-contractual opportunism, 202—203
"Post-Fordist" society, 276
Poverty
    growth and, facts on, 407—410
    income and, 435b—436b
    progress and regress in against
        (1981—2001), 408—410, 409f
Poverty threshold, 252
Pre-contractual opportunism, 202—203
Price-consumption curves, 100—102,
    100f—101f
Price discrimination, 165—166
    first-degree price discrimination, 165
    second-degree discrimination, 165—166

third-degree discrimination, 166
Primitive society, 28
Principle of self-interest, 25
Prisoner's Dilemma, 187, 289
Private cost, 137, 244
Private—social economy, 298
Problem of "free-riding", 249
Procedural rationality, 210—211
Process innovation, 119
Producer surplus, 151, 151f
Product innovation, 119
Production benefits, 139—140
Production isoquants, 126, 127f
Production process
  costs
    long-run cost curves, 134—136, 135f
    short-run cost curves, 131—132
    two variable inputs, 132—134
    types, 129—131
  economic problem, 115—117
    long run, 116
    outputs, 117
    Pareto efficiency, 117, 118b—119b
    production technology, 117
    short run, 116
    social relationships, 115—116
    substitutability, 117
    technical relationships, 115—116
    value transformation, 115
  economies of scale, 136—137
  entrepreneur, 117—121
    capitalist company, 121
    characteristics, 119
    companies, 121
    cooperative companies, 121
    distinctive traits, 117—121
    innovativeness, 120b
    interdependence, 120
    public companies, 121
    social companies, 121
  external costs, 137—138
  opportunity costs, 137—138
  production function
    diseconomies of scale, 129
    law of diminishing returns, 125—126,
      125f
    long-run production function, 128
    production isoquants, 126, 127f
    short-run production function, 124—125,
      124f
    variability of two inputs, 126—128
Production technology, 117

Production theory, 86
Product quality signaling, 331—332
Profit, 25, 140
Profit maximization principle, 321
Proletariat, 25
Propensity to risk, 119
Proportional effect, 370
Protected Designation of Origin (PDO)
    products, 422
Providence, 33
Ptolemaics, 19—20
Public choice school, 254
Public goods, 247—250, 248f
  economic theory of, 260
Public intervention, and government failure,
    253—255
Publicly traded banks, 328
Publicly traded companies, stock market
    performance of, 338—340
Public warnings, 333b
Pure Economics, 45
Pure public good, 247—248

Q
Quasi-miraculous tool, 69

R
Real economies of scale, 136—137
Reciprocity
  approaches to, 289—292
  civil theory of, 289
  direct, 287
  indirect, 287—288
  principle of, 286—289
Reductionism, 291, 319
  of traditional approach, 321—323
Reductionist approach, 14
Reflexivity, 90—91
Reforestation programs, 429
Relational capital, 224
Relational goods, 378, 379b—382b, 388
  emergent phenomenon, 381b—382b
  good, 382b
  gratuitousness, 382b
  happiness and, 378—385, 384t
  identity, 381b
  reciprocity, 381b
  simultaneity, 381b
  taxonomy of private, public, and, 384t
Relational life, happiness and, 377—378
Relative income, 370, 371f

Renewability, 425
Reputation system, 341
Restitution principle, 255
Returns to scale, 128
Revenue function, 142−143, 142f
Ricardo's theory of land rent, 37f, 38−40
Robert Malthus, Thomas, 40

S

SAH. *See* Self-assessed health (SAH)
Salary policy, 279
Samuelson condition, 248−249
Samuelson, Paul A., 240, 273
Say's law, 25
Schools, 20−21. *See also* specific schools
Schumpeter's approach, 178−180
Scientific asceticism, 4
Scottish school
    commanded labor, 31
    embodied labor, 28
    exchange value, 28
    invisible hand, 33
    market economy, 32
    market price, 30−31
    natural price, 30−31
    paradox of water and diamonds, 28, 30b
    pin factory and division of labor, 28,
        29b−30b
    primitive society, 28
    sympathy, 26
    use value, 28
Self-assessed health (SAH), 363
Self-deception, 33
Seller's reservation price, 54−55
Shareholders, 321, 327, 339
    commodity and, 221−223
    firm, 322
Short-run cost curves, 131−132
Short-run equilibrium, 144
Short-run production function, 124−125,
    124f
Short run profit maximization, 143−144, 143f
Short-run supply curve, 144, 146, 146f
Slutsky's equation
    Giffen inferior goods, 106
    graphic properties, 104−105
    income effect, 104, 105f
    inferior goods, 106
    normal goods, 106
    substitution effect, 104
Smith, Adam, 258

Soccer policy, 302
Social capital, 419−420
Social companies, next generation, 342
Social contract, 263−264
Social cooperation, 318
Social-cooperative economy, 310
Social-cooperative tradition, 310
Social cost, 137, 244
Social economy, 298
Social enterprises, 299b, 300
    pioneer, 342
Social entrepreneur, 358
Social firms, 299−303
    next generation, 341−350
Sociality, non-instrumental forms of,
    290−291
Social liberty, 319−320
Socially responsible company, 139, 325,
    329−335, 341−350
Social market enterprises, 344
Social market firms, 350−355
Social responsibility, 298−300, 311−312,
    314, 323, 338−340
    corporate, 300−301, 311, 320
    costs and benefits of, 329, 335
Social welfare function (SWF), 240−243,
    240f−241f
Social well-being, 150−152, 164
Socioeconomic system, 322−323
Socio-environmental certification, 357−358
Solidarity trade, 345−350
Solow's model, 411
Squaring growth, and environment, 424−425
Stakeholders, 312, 322−324
    transaction costs, minimizing, 333
Standard labor supply theory, 276
Static returns to scale, 128
Stigler, 254
Stock market, 52
    performance of publicly traded companies,
        338−340
Strategic altruism, 193
Strategic interdependence, 120−121
Street markets, 51
Strong reciprocity theory, 288−289
Strong sustainability, 335
Stuart Mill, JohnSubsidies, 41, 245−247,
    306b
Substitution effect, traditional, 273
Sum-ranking, 46, 228
SWF. *See* Social welfare function (SWF)

T

Takeover theory, 208–209
  costs to predators, 209–210
  perverse effects, 209–210
Talent ladder, 422–423
Taxes, 245–247
Technical indivisibility, 128
Technological interdependence, 120
Tendential law, 1
Theory of consumption, 86–87
  anthropological models, 108–109
  consumer rationality and constrained
      maximization, 98–100
  consumer theory, 108–109
  income circuit, 83–85
    hypertext, 85–86
  individual demand curves, 100–104
  intertemporal consumption, 109–112,
      110f, 112f–113f
  maximizing consumer utility
    axioms, 91, 91b
    cardinality, 89–90
    completeness, 90–91
    diminishing marginal utility, 87–89, 88f
    indifference curves, 91–93
    law of increasing marginal utility, 89,
      90b
    marginal rate of substitution, 93–94
    marginal utility, 88–89
    monotonicity, 90–91
    optimal combination of goods, 94–98
    ordinality, 89–90
    point of satiation, 89, 89f
    reflexivity, 90–91
    transitivity, 90–91
  prices and information, 107–108
  Slutsky's equation, 104–107
Theory of decreasing rents, 39
Theory of Moral Sentiments (Smith),
    379b–382b
Theory of rational choices in the presence of
    constraints
  constrained maximization, 12
  criticisms, 13
  homooeconomicus, 14
  reductionist approach, 14
  "virtual" loss, 13–14
  weak-hearted traders, 13–14
Theory of relative costs, 39
Third sector, 297–299
Three-dimensional approach
  environment, 18

global warming and balancing ecosystems,
    18
  gross domestic product (GDP) growth, 17
  social sustainability, 18–19
  unidimensional approach, 19
Tight holding company, 221
Tirole, Jacques, 329
Tirole, Jean, 344
Trade
  fair, 345–350
  solidarity, 345–350
Trade protectionism, 21
Traditional economic rules, 357
Traditional growth models, 410–413
Traditional income effect, 273
Traditional manufacturer (TM), 355f
Traditional market, 51
Traditional substitution effect, 273
Traditional welfare economics, 228
The Tragedy of the Commons (Hardin), 259
Transaction costs
  stakeholder, minimizing, 333
Transcendent motivations, 139–140
Transitivity, 90–91
Treadmill effect, 370

U

Uncertainty principle, 396–397
Unemployment, 275
  happiness and, 390–393, 393t
Unidimensional model (U-form), 218–219
Unsustainability, 335
Utilitarian ethics, 227–229
Utilitarianism, 228
Utility-possibility frontiers
  and invisible hand, 238–240, 238f–239f

V

Value judgment, 228
Values-based motivations, 315
Values-based organizations (VBOs),
    279–280, 285–286, 315–317
Variable costs, 130
VBOs. *See* Values-based organizations
    (VBOs)
"Veil of ignorance", 10
Verri, Pietro, 36
Vocation
  occupational, 284–286
  workers selection with, 276–279
Voluntarism, 298

Volunteering, 389—390
Voting with wallets, consumers, 330—331

W

Wallets
  consumers voting with, 330—331
  vote with their wallets, 76
Walrasian general equilibrium, 232—233
Walrasian theory, 232—233
Weak sustainability, 335
Wealth of Nations (Smith), 361—362
Weber's hypothesis, 415
Welfare capitalism, 257
Welfare economics, 227—232, 251
  new welfare economics, 230—232
  old welfare economics, 229
  theorems, 232—238
    edgeworth box, 233—235, 234f
    first welfare theorem, 235—236
    second welfare theorem, 236—238, 236f
    Walrasian general equilibrium, 232—233
  traditional, 228
Welfare state to welfare society, 255—257

Welfare theorem
  first, 235—236
  second, 236—238, 236f
Welfarism, 228
Western economic system, 295—296
Workers
  productivity increase, 334—335
  relationships with, 325
  selection with vocation, 276—279
Work, happiness and, 388—390
World Value Survey, 362
WTO (World Trade Organization), 421

Y

Yunus, M., 313—314

Z

ZERI (Zero Emission Research and
    Initiatives) model, 442—443
Zero-sum games, 22, 184
Zingales, Luigi, 307

Printed in the United States
By Bookmasters